Multicultural Education

Fifteenth Edition

EDITOR

Nancy P. Gallavan, PhD
University of Central Arkansas

Nancy P. Gallavan, PhD, professor of teacher education at the University of Central Arkansas, earned a BS in Elementary Education from Southwest Missouri State University in 1976; an MA in curriculum and instruction from the University of Colorado, Boulder, in 1983; an elementary school administrator's certificate from the University of Colorado, Denver, in 1988; and a PhD from the University of Denver in 1994. She taught elementary school and middle level classroom in the St. Vrain Valley and Cherry Creek School Districts in Colorado for 20 years before entering higher education at the University of Nevada, Las Vegas. She joined the University of Central Arkansas in 2006, serving first as Associate Dean and now in a faculty position. Nancy is active in the American Educational Research Association (AERA), the Association of Teacher Educators (ATE), the National Association for Multicultural Education (NAME), and the National Council for the Social Studies (NCSS). Her research focuses on the sociocultural context of teaching and learning with an emphasis on self-assessment.

ANNUAL EDITIONS: MULTICULTURAL EDUCATION, FIFTEENTH EDITION

Published by McGraw-Hill, a business unit of The McGraw-Hill Companies, Inc., 1221 Avenue of the Americas, New York, NY 10020. Copyright © 2010 by The McGraw-Hill Companies, Inc. All rights reserved. Previous edition(s) 1994–2009. No part of this publication may be reproduced or distributed in any form or by any means, or stored in a database or retrieval system, without the prior written consent of The McGraw-Hill Companies, Inc., including, but not limited to, in any network or other electronic storage or transmission, or broadcast for distance learning.

Some ancillaries, including electronic and print components, may not be available to customers outside the United States.

Annual Editions® is a registered trademark of the McGraw-Hill Companies, Inc.

Annual Editions is published by the **Contemporary Learning Series** group within the McGraw-Hill Higher Education division.

1 2 3 4 5 6 7 8 9 0 QPD/QPD 0 9

ISBN 978–0–07–339780–1
MHID 0–07–339780–6
ISSN 1092–924X

Managing Editor: *Larry Loeppke*
Senior Managing Editor: *Faye Schilling*
Developmental Editor: *Dave Welsh*
Editorial Coordinator: *Mary Foust*
Editorial Assistant: *Cindy Hedley*
Production Service Assistant: *Rita Hingtgen*
Permissions Coordinator: *DeAnna Dausener*
Senior Marketing Manager: *Julie Keck*
Marketing Communications Specialist: *Mary Klein*
Marketing Coordinator: *Alice Link*
Project Manager: *Joyce Watters*
Design Specialist: *Tara McDermott*
Production Supervisor: *Sue Culbertson*
Cover Graphics: *Kristine Jubeck*

Compositor: Laserwords Private Limited
Cover Image: © Greatstock Photographic Library/Alamy/RF (inset); © Corbis/PictureQuest/RF (background)

Library in Congress Cataloging-in-Publication Data
Main entry under title: Annual Editions: Multicultural Education. 2010/2011.
  1. Multicultural Education—Periodicals. I. Gallavan, Nancy P., *comp*. II. Title: Multicultural Education.
658'.05

www.mhhe.com

Editors/Academic Advisory Board

Members of the Academic Advisory Board are instrumental in the final selection of articles for each edition of ANNUAL EDITIONS. Their review of articles for content, level, and appropriateness provides critical direction to the editors and staff. We think that you will find their careful consideration well reflected in this volume.

ANNUAL EDITIONS: Multicultural Education 10/11
15th Edition

EDITOR

Nancy P. Gallavan
University of Central Arkansas

ACADEMIC ADVISORY BOARD MEMBERS

Preface

In publishing ANNUAL EDITIONS we recognize the enormous role played by the magazines, newspapers, and journals of the public press in providing current, first-rate educational information in a broad spectrum of interest areas. Many of these articles are appropriate for students, researchers, and professionals seeking accurate, current material to help bridge the gap between principles and theories and the real world. These articles, however, become more useful for study when those of lasting value are carefully collected, organized, indexed, and reproduced in a low-cost format, which provides easy and permanent access when the material is needed. That is the role played by ANNUAL EDITIONS.

Beginning with this edition, the fifteenth edition of *Annual Editions: Multicultural Education,* we introduce our new editor, who brings a fresh passion coupled with invigorating practices that inform and support the extensive purposes for teaching, learning, and schooling in a multicultural context. The study of cultures has been an integral part of education in the United States since the country began. However, enveloped in literature, history, geography, and later sociology, the study of cultures initially was limited to examining groups of people as specimens in isolation identified with token contributions to the country's establishment and well being. Through the years, few individuals expressed the courage to voice the need for the studies of all cultures to be conducted with honesty, respect, and acceptance, and, most important, about equity and social justice. That was a time when people adhered to the notion that particular cultural characteristics, qualities, and beliefs were deemed superior, and, therefore, individuals possessing such identities were dominant.

Many years in United States history would pass before the ideals of equality and social justice would start moving from the obscure written documents upon which the country was founded to the visible daily interactions found among the citizenry. Throughout the second half of the twentieth century, the breadth and depth of social change became the realities as the social context and communal fabric of the country transformed. Through the concerted efforts of many different and dedicated citizens across the country, issues related to ensuring democratic principles and social justice for everyone began to arise. The civil unrest of the 1950s and 1960s opened the doors, and the classrooms became increasingly accessible and equitable.

The formal conversation called multicultural education began based on theory, research, and practice. Although great resistance could be found in schools and classrooms, multicultural education evolved from learning about nondominant groups within the U.S. society to increasing awareness of oneself, one another, and society, locally and globally, by focusing on everyone's cultures, characteristics, and contributions; multicultural education examined both similarities and differences. Concepts and practices of multicultural education were incorporated into primarily social studies courses within the middle level/junior high schools and high schools as well as higher education, and especially teacher education. Some schools held multicultural festivals and fairs highlighted with foods, costumes, games, etc., from various countries around the world. If students and their families indicated that they were recent immigrants or familiar with a particular country, frequently they would be asked to share their foods or teach their customs. It would have been more appropriate to label these approaches to multicultural education as international education.

During the mid 1990s, multicultural education slowly changed into a more natural, authentic, and holistic approach of valuing diversity. Unlike the past when multicultural education had a tendency to teach about various aspects of nondominant cultures in isolation, valuing diversity emphasized the processes of learning. This dynamic transformation involved everyone becoming part of the story and part of the experience. Instead of learning about other people unlike oneself and encouraging assimilation into the dominant culture, valuing diversity delved into examining one's own characteristics, qualities, and beliefs and their impact on one's thoughts, words, and actions. Everyone needed to reflect on themselves and take more responsibility. Classroom teachers were encouraged to integrate their curriculum, instruction, and assessments so all students could learn about all students, and all students could achieve excellence. Emphasis on equity and excellence for everyone required teachers and administrators to rethink their academic standards, their course content, their instructional strategies, the assessment techniques, their classroom management, and their consequences systems (both rewards and punishments). This movement changed the emphasis on what is multicultural education to how to value diversity.

Now another generation in the conversation has begun. The movement has evolved from the questions of *what* and *how* to the question of *why.* The current term focuses on cultural competence, and it means simply this: doing the right thing because it is the right thing to do. Educators know what to teach and they are prepared for teaching it effectively. The need is for educators to take their responsibilities seriously and to ensure that all students are taught with equality and excellence. No students are expendable; no one and no group in society dominates other individuals and groups. Cultural competence expects all educators to be aware of their thoughts, words, and actions at all times and with all students and their families. The future is depending upon all educators to do the right thing and right now for the future of humankind and the planet Earth.

The author of the articles included in the fifteenth edition of *Annual Editions: Multicultural Education* will impress you with their experiences and insights. Unit 1 establishes a sense of place with a selection of articles related to the world's citizens and the importance of intercultural socialization. Unit 2 discusses who is coming to school and who is learning in today's classrooms. Unit 3 narrows the classroom focus to issues and trends related to curricular development and instructional strategies. Unit 4 emphasizes the importance of and efforts for educating all students. Unit 5 delves into multiple forms of literacy and language to honor each student's story and culture. Unit 6 shares approaches for motivating students' involvement in social action outcomes related to classroom assignments and community efforts. Unit 7 provides an overview of professional development suggestions for classroom teachers to enrich their knowledge, expand their skills, and enhance their dispositions for becoming culturally competent while ensuring equity and excellence in their classroom and among their students.

Once again we are including important *Internet References*, which sites can be used to further explore article topics. These sites are cross-referenced by number in the topic guide.

Thank you for welcoming me as the new editor of *Annual Editions: Multicultural Education.* I also want to thank David Welsh who has provided me the necessary guidance and support to maintain the outstanding quality we have come to expect from this outstanding publication. I have used *Annual Editions: Multicultural Education* for many years with my undergraduate and graduate teacher candidates as well as my master and doctorate candidates. Each year, the volume of articles surpasses my expectations for a well-organized and meaningful collection of research and practice that I can use with my students and to teach to my students. I am pleased with the submitted articles and encourage readers to submit more articles for future volumes. Please complete and return the form at the back of the book. We look forward to hearing from you.

Nancy P. Gallavan

Nancy P. Gallavan, PhD
Editor

Contents

UNIT 1
Understanding Today's World

The concepts in bold italics are developed in the article. For further expansion, please refer to the Topic Guide.

UNIT 2
Examining Schools and Classrooms

The concepts in bold italics are developed in the article. For further expansion, please refer to the Topic Guide.

UNIT 3
Developing Curriculum and Instruction

The concepts in bold italics are developed in the article. For further expansion, please refer to the Topic Guide.

UNIT 4
Educating All Students

The concepts in bold italics are developed in the article. For further expansion, please refer to the Topic Guide.

The concepts in bold italics are developed in the article. For further expansion, please refer to the Topic Guide.

UNIT 5
Expanding Learning with Language and Literacy

The concepts in bold italics are developed in the article. For further expansion, please refer to the Topic Guide.

UNIT 6
Motivating Involvement and Social Action

UNIT 7
Providing Professional Development for Teachers

The concepts in bold italics are developed in the article. For further expansion, please refer to the Topic Guide.

The concepts in bold italics are developed in the article. For further expansion, please refer to the Topic Guide.

Correlation Guide

The *Annual Editions* series provides students with convenient, inexpensive access to current, carefully selected articles from the public press. **Annual Editions: Multicultural Education, 15/e** is an easy-to-use reader that presents articles on important topics such as *diversity, religion, poverty,* and many more. For more information on *Annual Editions* and other *McGraw-Hill Contemporary Learning Series* titles, visit www.mhhe.com/cls.

This convenient guide matches the units in **Annual Editions: Multicultural Education, 15/e** with the corresponding chapters in our two best-selling McGraw-Hill Multicultural Education textbooks by Cushner et al. and Florence.

Annual Editions: Multicultural Education, 15/e	Human Diversity in Education: An Integrative Approach by Cushner et al.	Multiculturalism 101 by Florence
Unit 1: Understanding Today's World	**Chapter 1:** Education in a Changing Society **Chapter 3:** Culture and the Culture-Learning Process **Chapter 9:** Religious Pluralism in Secular Classrooms	**Chapter 1:** Democracy and Cultural Inclusion
Unit 2: Examining Schools and Classrooms	**Chapter 4:** Classrooms and Schools as Cultural Crossroads **Chapter 6:** Creating Classrooms That Address Race and Ethnicity	**Chapter 3:** Class: The Neighborhood in Classrooms **Chapter 6:** A Multicultural Community: Beyond Political Correctness
Unit 3: Developing Curriculum and Instruction	**Chapter 6:** Creating Classrooms That Address Race and Ethnicity **Chapter 13:** Improving Schools for All Children: The Role of Social Class and Social Status in Teaching and Learning	**Chapter 3:** Class: The Neighborhood in Classrooms **Chapter 5:** Race/Ethnicity in Curriculum **Chapter 6:** A Multicultural Community: Beyond Political Correctness
Unit 4: Educating All Students	**Chapter 3:** Culture and the Culture-Learning Process **Chapter 6:** Creating Classrooms That Address Race and Ethnicity **Chapter 8:** Developing Learning Communities: Language and Learning Style	**Chapter 1:** Democracy and Cultural Inclusion **Chapter 5:** Race/Ethnicity in Curriculum **Chapter 6:** A Multicultural Community: Beyond Political Correctness
Unit 5: Expanding Learning with Language and Literacy	**Chapter 8:** Developing Learning Communities: Language and Learning Style	
Unit 6: Motivating Involvement and Social Action	**Chapter 1:** Education in a Changing Society **Chapter 6:** Creating Classrooms That Address Race and Ethnicity	**Chapter 5:** Race/Ethnicity in Curriculum **Chapter 6:** A Multicultural Community: Beyond Political Correctness
Unit 7: Providing Professional Development for Teachers	**Chapter 4:** Classrooms and Schools as Cultural Crossroads	**Chapter 7:** Reflective Practice: There is Still More to Do

Topic Guide

This topic guide suggests how the selections in this book relate to the subjects covered in your course. You may want to use the topics listed on these pages to search the Web more easily.

On the following pages a number of websites have been gathered specifically for this book. They are arranged to reflect the units of this Annual Editions reader. You can link to these sites by going to *http://www.mhcls.com*.

All the articles that relate to each topic are listed below the bold-faced term.

Accountability
22. The Need to Reestablish Schools as Dynamic Positive Human Energy Systems That Are Non-Linear and Self-Organizing

African American students
34. The Promise of Black Teachers' Success with Black Students

African American teachers
34. The Promise of Black Teachers' Success with Black Students

Arab children's literature
28. Celebrating Diversity through Explorations of Arab Children's Literature

Alternative education
13. Mother Goose Teaches on the Wild Side: Motivating At-Risk Mexican and Chicano Youngsters via a Multicultural Curriculum

Biracial identity
8. "What Are You?" Biracial Children in the Classroom

Black colleges and universities
31. Framing the Effect of Multiculturalism on Diversity Outcomes among Students at Historically Black Colleges and Universities

Chica lit
29. Chica Lit: Multicultural Literature Blurs Borders

Children in poverty
32. Building the Movement to End Educational Inequity

Civil rights groups
23. Moment of Truth

Critical voices
20. A Critically Compassionate Intellectualism for Latina/o Students: Raising Voices above the Silencing in Our Schools

Cultural competence
18. The Trail to Progress

Curriculum and instruction
13. Mother Goose Teaches on the Wild Side: Motivating At-Risk Mexican and Chicano Youngsters via a Multicultural Curriculum
17. Arts in the Classroom
19. An Investigation of How Culture Shapes Curriculum in Early Care and Education Programs on a Native American Indian Reservation

Deficit model
16. Discarding the Deficit Model

Discrimination
6. Because I Had a Turban

Educational inequity
32. Building the Movement to End Educational Inequity

Educational reform
22. The Need to Reestablish Schools as Dynamic Positive Human Energy Systems That Are Non-Linear and Self-Organizing

English language learners (ELLs)
21. Educating Vietnamese American Students
26. Output Strategies for English-Language Learners: Theory to Practice

Gay and lesbian themes in literature
27. Controversial Books in the Middle School: Can They Make a Difference?

Global competence
1. Becoming Citizens of the World

High performing schools
22. The Need to Reestablish Schools as Dynamic Positive Human Energy Systems That Are Non-Linear and Self-Organizing

Hispanic Americans
13. Mother Goose Teaches on the Wild Side: Motivating At-Risk Mexican and Chicano Youngsters via a Multicultural Curriculum
20. A Critically Compassionate Intellectualism for Latina/o Students: Raising Voices above the Silencing in Our Schools

Human rights
11. The Human Right to Education: Freedom and Empowerment

Identity development
4. Beyond "Culture Clash": Understandings of Immigrant Experiences

Indian Americans
6. Because I Had a Turban

Integrated multicultural education
13. Mother Goose Teaches on the Wild Side: Motivating At-Risk Mexican and Chicano Youngsters via a Multicultural Curriculum

Intellectual capacities
20. A Critically Compassionate Intellectualism for Latina/o Students: Raising Voices above the Silencing in Our Schools

Internal cultures
22. The Need to Reestablish Schools as Dynamic Positive Human Energy Systems That Are Non-Linear and Self-Organizing

International migration patterns
1. Becoming Citizens of the World
4. Beyond "Culture Clash": Understandings of Immigrant Experiences

Internet References

The following Internet sites have been selected to support the articles found in this reader. These sites were available at the time of publication. However, because websites often change their structure and content, the information listed may no longer be available. We invite you to visit *http://www.mhcls.com* for easy access to these sites.

Annual Editions: Multicultural Education 15e

General Sources

Center for Multicultural Education
http://education.washington.edu/cme/

From the University of Washington, College of Education, this site provides programs, projects, and publications addressing all areas of cultural diversity.

Electronic Magazine of Multicultural Education
http://www.eastern.edu/publications/emme/

Now succeeded by the *International Journal of Multicultural Education* (IJME) at http://ijme-journal.org/index.php/ijme, these websites provide research and practices appropriate for all classrooms and educators.

Multicultural Education
http://www.emtech.net/multicultural_education.html

Here you will find links to information about international cultures and guidance for effective multicultural education.

Multicultural Pavilion
http://www.edchange.org/multicultural/

Featuring resources, research, opportunities, quotations, and activities including an awareness quiz, this website provides an extensive amount of information related to all areas of multicultural education.

Multicultural Education Internet Resource Guide
http://jan.ucc.nau.edu/~jar/Multi.html

More than 50 Internet resources are linked to this website providing an extraordinary collection of information, guidance, and support for students, teachers, administrators, professors, and families.

National Association for Multicultural Education (NAME)
http://www.nameorg.org/

A non-profit association founded in 1990, NAME provides guidance and support for all educators with links to information, research, conferences, and publications.

UNIT 1: Understanding Today's World

The Big Religion Chart
http://www.religionfacts.com/big_religion_chart.htm

At this site you will find an incredible collection of facts about the world's 42 religions from which you can easily compare and contrast religions with one another.

Census Data
http://www.census.gov/

To understand the population within the United States, look at the information included in this site that describes people and households, business and industry, geography and many different special topics.

Census Bureau; International Data Base (IDB)
http://www.census.gov/ipc/www/idb/

Here you will find population information describing the 227 countries in today's world so you can better understand a particular country in relationship to other countries.

Centers for Disease Control/National Center for Health Statistics
http://www.cdc.gov/nchswww/

This site provides an extensive examination of the health of the U.S. population, noting changes over time and the impact their knowledge, practices, and attitudes make on the world.

Demographic and Healthy Surveys
http://www.measuredhs.com

Here you will find quality information about the world's population and health situations with data reported from residents in more than 75 countries.

Major Religions of the World
http://www.adherents.com/Religions_By_Adherents.html

Data at this site is organized into 22 religions categorized by a variety of topics allowing the reader to compare, contrast, and comprehend the complexity of each religion.

State of the World's Children
http://www.unicef.org/apublic/

Well-known to many educators, UNICEF is an organization that provides goods and services for less fortunate children around the world. From this site, the reader can review past endeavors as well as view current enterprises and future efforts.

The World Bank
http://web.worldbank.org/

Look here to find insightful data describing the wealth indices from more than 186 countries with financial and technical assistance for third world countries. This organization is made up of two groups: the International Bank for Reconstruction and Development (IBRD) and the International Development Association (IDA) collaborating to advance the vision of inclusive and sustainable globalization.

UNIT 2: Examining Schools and Classrooms

Awesome Library for Teachers
http://www.awesomelibrary.org/teacher.html

Open this page for many links and access to information on many topics of interest and concern to all educators.

National Black Child Development Institute
http://www.nbcdi.org

Resources for improving the quality of life for African American children through public education programs are provided at this site.

National Economics and Social Rights Initiative
http://www.nesri.org/?gclid=CIPVtYyWxJoCFRufnAodY1Q8sg

On the National Economic and Social Rights Initiative (NESRI) website, you will find information about promoting a human rights vision for the United States that ensures dignity and access to the basic resources needed for human development and civic participation.

Scholastic News-Immigration
http://teacher.scholastic.com/activities/immigration/index.htm

Internet References

Stories about immigration from yesterday and today are featured on this student-centered website with many resources for curriculum and instruction, especially literature reading lists.

Social Statistics Briefing Room
http://www.whitehouse.gov/briefing_room/

The purpose of this website is to provide easy access to current United States statistics including demographic, safety, economic, education, and health statistics that teachers can incorporate into their curriculum and instruction.

Statistical Abstract of the United States
http://www.census.gov/compendia/statab/

This link provides statistics on the social, political, and economic organization of the United States gathered from the Census Bureau, the Bureau of Labor Statistics, the Bureau of Economic Analysis, and many other federal agencies, and provider organizations.

Tribal Government Information
http://www.usa.gov/Government/Tribal.shtml

An extensive collection of information and resources, this website offers background and guidance on many different topics related to tribal organization, cultural resources, and governmental services.

United States Historical Census Data Browser
http://fisher.lib.virginia.edu/census/

Data and terminology from the historical census data browser are organized and presented in this website to examine the U.S. census of population and housing.

UNIT 3: Developing Curriculum and Instruction

Library of Congress
http://www.loc.gov/index.html?gclid=CLTW28rd2JkCFRINDQodpgGqVA

Filled with an abundance of collections from the past and present, this informative website provides resources for students and teachers on many different topics and issues.

United Nations
http://www.un.org/en/documents/udhr/

Here you will find information and links to resources and publications related to the United Nations with emphases on human rights, peace and security, development, humanitarian affairs, and international law.

United States Census Bureau and Poverty
http://www.census.gov/hhes/www/poverty/poverty.html

This website provides an overview, news, publications, definitions, descriptions, resources, and access to information related to poverty, issues associated with poverty, and the measurement of poverty in the United States.

United States Citizenship and Immigration Services
http://www.uscis.gov/portal/site/uscis

Information and links related to citizenship and immigration are provided at this website, including a general overview, services and benefits, immigration forms, laws and regulations, along with education and resources.

United States Department of Health and Human Services
http://www.hhs.gov/specificpopulations/

Here you will find information and resources related to protecting the health of all Americans, offering insights for families and teachers related to prevention of diseases, and regulations with connections to grants, funding, and jobs.

United States Department of Justice
http://www.usdoj.gov/

Information and resources related to the DOJ are found here with information, archives, policies, and accessibility featured.

United States Equal Employment Opportunity Commission
http://www.eeoc.gov/types/race.html

An extensive collection of information related to race and race relations in the United States is located at this website including the law, areas of discrimination, concerns with compliance, and recorded statistics.

United States Immigration and Customs
http://www.ice.gov/

The immigration and customs enforcement website contains information and links to resources related to protective services, intelligence, international affairs, and border enforcement including news, programs, and careers.

UNIT 4: Educating All Students

Association for Moral Education
http://www.amenetwork.org/

This website provides an interdisciplinary forum for professionals interested in the moral dimensions of educational theory and practice with links for education, grants, publications, and conferences.

International Programs Center (IPC)
http://www.census.gov/ipc/www/

Census data about the countries of the world (beginning in 1945) with additional resources are provided at this site. Demographic and sociological studies can be accessed.

Native American Facts for Kids
http://www.native-languages.org/kids.htm

This non-profit organization works to preserve and promote American Indian languages with information and resources readily available for students and teachers about all American Indian tribes.

PBS: Biracial American Portraits
http://www.pbs.org/wgbh/pages/frontline/shows/secret/portraits/

A subsection of the PBS website, here you will find descriptions and discussions related to biracial populations and cultural interactions appropriate for students and teachers. A link for searching one's family tree is featured.

Urban Education Institute
http://uei.uchicago.edu/

A resource related to urban education, this website offers information and links to research and practices to reach and teach all children.

UNIT 5: Expanding Learning with Language and Literacy

American Psychological Association
http://www.apa.org/topics/homepage.html

Organizational information, writing guidelines, psychology topics, and research publications can be accessed at this website to inform students, teachers, administrators, parents, and professors.

Center for Global Development
http://www.cgdev.org/section/initiatives/_active/globalizationandinequality?gclid=CKTYxrGWxJoCFRufnAodY1Q8sg

Internet References

This website offers independent research and practical ideas for global prosperity with links to initials, research topics, publications, opinions, events, experts, and blogs.

North American Reggio Emilia Alliance
http://www.reggioalliance.org/

Here you will find information and resources dedicated to the education and well-being of young children (up to age six) with links to professional development and international networks.

United States Department of Education, Office of English Language Acquisition
http://www.ed.gov/about/offices/list/oela/index.html

This website is created to fulfill two missions: to provide national leadership (1) to help ensure that English language learners and immigrant students attain English proficiency and achieve academically, and (2) to assist in building the nation's capacity in critical foreign languages with resources for students, parents, teachers, and school administrators.

UNESCO
http://unescostat.unesco.org/

Themes, highlights, surveys, and statistics are featured on this website from the United Nations Organization for Education, Science, and Culture equipping educators with facts and policies.

United States Government
www.firstgov.gov

This government sponsored website provides news, resources, and services for all aspects of the United States government appropriate for all teachers, learners, businesses, employees, and visitors.

UNIT 6: Motivating Involvement and Social Action

Center for Social Justice
http://csj.georgetown.edu/

Located at Georgetown University in Washington, DC, this site offers information and support related to infusing social justice in all research, teaching, and service.

Human Rights Watch
http://www.hrw.org/

Focused on international events, this website provides news, publications, and multimedia related to ensuring human rights around the world.

Hunger and World Poverty
http://www.poverty.com

This site connects poverty and hunger as global challenge by linking the concerns with diseases that impact everyone internationally.

UNIT 7: Providing Professional Development for Teachers

Education World
http://www.education-world.com

This website connects the reader to seemingly endless resources related to teaching, learning, and schooling more effectively and efficiently.

Infonation
http://www.un.org/Pubs/CyberSchoolBus/infonation/e_infonation.htm

Here you will find information related to developing curriculum and building community in the classroom with respect for multicultural education.

National Association of Social Workers
http://www.socialworkers.org/pressroom/features/issue/peace.asp

To promote social justice in schools and classrooms, this website extends the knowledge, skills, and dispositions from the field of social work into education to guide teachers, administrators, families, and professors.

UNIT 1

Understanding Today's World

Unit Selections

Key Points to Consider

- Who are today's world citizens, and what are their cultural backgrounds?
- What are the global trends that impact all of the world's citizens?
- What does global competence look like, and why it is essential for everyone?
- How can teachers prepare themselves and today's youth for adulthood in an interdependent global society?
- How can U.S. teachers help immigrant students to construct their new cultural identities?
- Why is it important to teach about religions in schools?
- How should religions be taught?
- How does westernization affect people in the United States as well as people around the world?

Student Website
www.mhcls.com

Internet References

The Big Religion Chart
http://www.religionfacts.com/big_religion_chart.htm

Census Data
http://www.census.gov/

Census Bureau; International Data Base (IDB)
http://www.census.gov/ipc/www/idb/

Center for Disease Control/National Center for Health Statistics
http://www.cdc.gov/nchswww/

Demographic and Health Surveys
http://www.measuredhs.com

Human Rights Watch
http://www.hrw.org

Infonation
http://www.un.org/Pubs/CyberSchoolBus/infonation/e_infonation.htm

International Health Statistics
http://www.spri.se/english/i_engli_eng.htm

Major Religions of the World
http://www.adherents.com/Religions_By_Adherents.html

Religious Tolerance
http://www.religioustolerance.org/var_rel.htm

Scholastic News-Immigration
http://teacher.scholastic.com/activities/immigration/index.htm

Social Statistics Briefing Room
http://www.whitehouse.gov/fsbr/ssbr.html

State of the World's Children
http://www.unicef.org/apublic/

Statistical Abstract of the United States
http://www.census.gov/prod/www/statistical-abstract-us.html

Study of World Religions
http://www.mnsu.edu/emuseum/cultural/religion

The World Bank
http://web.worldbank.org/

UNESCO
http://unescostat.unesco.org/en/stats/stats.htm

United Nations
http://www.un.org/en/documents/udhr

United States Citizenship and Immigration Services
http://www.uscis.gov/portal/site/uscis

United States Government
www.firstgov.gov

United States Historical Census Data Browser
http://fisher.lib.virginia.edu/census

World Population Trends and Social Issues
http://www.undp.org/popin/wdtrends/wdtrends.htm

World Religions
http://www.mnsu.edu/emuseum/cultural/religion

Many years ago, similar types of people could be described as a particular group of individuals living in an isolated geographic location, speaking their own language, maintaining a unique way of life, and sharing a specific collection of characteristics, qualities, and beliefs. Long before modern inventions impacting transportation and communication were developed and distributed, people were known primarily for their geography, both physical and cultural. Groups created their own language and lifestyles that became their culture and how they were identified. However, far too often, groups of people did not interact cooperatively with one another; frequently, their clashes were based more on their perceptions and fears rather than on the realities and facts. People's perceptions were founded on actual or perceived barriers associated with control, power, and privilege. People around the world would focus more on their differences and dominance rather than their similarities and support.

Over time, many of the people of the world have changed. Today's world has become much more interconnected through technological advancements and cultural concern. All kinds of people live, work, and play in all kinds of places, and people frequently move in search of new and better opportunities for themselves and their families. Individuals often travel near and far for business and pleasure. Through film and television, we see people, places, and events from the past, the present, and projected into the future at our fingertips and from multiple perspectives. Thanks to the Internet, people communicate instantly with one another all around the world. Some people say that the world is a smaller place due to technological advances. Perhaps the world seems like a smaller place because there are more people sharing the space and we are quickly realizing the importance of cooperating with one another for the future of people and the perils of the planet.

The paradox becomes evident that while most people want to maintain their special characteristics, qualities, and beliefs that allow them to bond with other people with similar characteristics, qualities, and beliefs, most people also want to live in harmony with and show respect for people who they consider being different from themselves. However, given the prevalent historical influences associated with our (mis)perceptions for not trusting or honoring one another based on our perceptions of our differences rather than the realities of our similarities, relationships within and among classrooms, schools, neighborhoods, regions, and countries continue to challenge the citizens of the world.

This societal dilemma is complicated by two vital factors: (1) Groups of people no longer share all aspects of their once common historical identities and (2) many people no longer want to be identified solely by their perceived historical identifications. As people have migrated, the world has become a multiracial, multiethnic, multilingual, multireligious, multi-interest . . . multicultural society. Many people are comfortable wherever they are, and they want to help everyone to understand and appreciate one another for the sake of all humans and the Earth. Coexistence has become more than a philosophy; it has become a pathway through life and all aspects of life.

Today's world involves a vibrant society seeking information about everyone, everywhere, and everything. People around the world want equal access and unlimited opportunities to fulfill their lives. Classroom teachers and school administrators serve as the gatekeepers who can open (limit or close) the gates of information, access, and opportunity to the young people and students of today in their journeys in their preparation to be the adults and leaders of tomorrow. Through their messages and modeling, teachers guide and empower their students to ask meaningful questions, search for assorted answers, and try various approaches for expressing learning and experiencing living. When teachers introduce their students to a range of possibilities, they equip their students with tools for life. Their students experience multiple views and multicultural education for themselves; and students' new perceptions become the realities that transform their sense of cultural competence and coexistence.

The articles in Unit 1 introduce the reader to the context of today's world from the vantage of the United States. The articles present a view of the world's populations, the changes associated with diversity for knowing ourselves, the view of Native Americans, the experiences of immigrants entering the United States, the existence of many religions in one country, and the benefits of intercultural socialization for adults and young people. All people need chances to better understand themselves individually. From individual discoveries, one grows to understand, respect, and appreciate other people. Comfort with oneself and other individuals develops into living harmoniously with other cultures throughout society.

Becoming Citizens of the World

The future is here. It's multiethnic, multicultural, and multilingual. But are students ready for it?

VIVIEN STEWART

The world into which today's high school students will graduate is fundamentally different from the one in which many of us grew up. We're increasingly living in a globalized society that has a whole new set of challenges. Four trends have brought us here.

The first trend is economic. The globalization of economies and the rise of Asia are central facts of the early 21st century. Since 1990, 3 billion people in China, India, and the former Soviet Union have moved from closed economies into a global one. The economies of China, India, and Japan, which represented 18 percent of the world's gross domestic product (GDP) in 2004, are expected to represent 50 percent of the world's GDP within 30 years (Wilson, 2005). One in five U.S. jobs is now tied to international trade, a proportion that will continue to increase (U.S. Census Bureau, 2004). Moreover, most U.S. companies expect the majority of their growth to be in overseas markets, which means they will increasingly require a workforce with international competence. According to the Committee for Economic Development (2006),

> To compete successfully in the global marketplace, both U.S.-based multinational corporations as well as small businesses increasingly need employees with knowledge of foreign languages and cultures to market products to customers around the globe and to work effectively with foreign employees and partners in other countries.

Science and technology are changing the world and represent a second trend. In *The World Is Flat,* Thomas Friedman (2005) describes how the "wiring of the world" and the digitization of production since 1998 are making it possible for people to do increasing amounts of work anywhere and anytime. Global production teams are becoming commonplace in business. In addition, scientific research, a key driver of innovation, will increasingly be conducted by international teams as other countries ramp-up their scientific capacity.

The third trend involves health and security matters. Every major issue that people face—from environmental degradation and global warming, to pandemic diseases, to energy and water shortages, to terrorism and weapons proliferation—has

an international dimension. Solving these problems will require international cooperation among governments, professional organizations, and corporations. Also, as the line between domestic and international affairs blurs, U.S. citizens will increasingly vote and act on issues—such as alternative energy sources or security measures linked to terrorism—that require a greater knowledge of the world. In response to this need, a 2006 report from the National Association of State Boards of Education recommends infusing classroom instruction with a strong global perspective and incorporating discussions of current local, national, and international issues and events.

The fourth trend is changing demographics. Globalization has accelerated international migration. New immigrants from such regions as Asia and Central and South America are generating a diversity in U.S. communities that mirrors the diversity of the world. Knowledge of other cultures will help students understand and respect classmates from different countries and will promote effective leadership abroad.

In short, U.S. high school graduates will

- Sell to the world.
- Buy from the world.
- Work for international companies.
- Manage employees from other cultures and countries.
- Collaborate with people all over the world in joint ventures.
- Compete with people on the other side of the world for jobs and markets.
- Tackle global problems, such as AIDS, avian flu, pollution, and disaster recovery (Center for International Understanding, 2005).

However, U.S. schools are not adequately preparing students for these challenges. Surveys conducted by the Asia Society (2002) and National Geographic-Roper (2002) indicated that, compared with students in nine other industrialized countries, U.S. students lack knowledge of world geography, history, and current events. And shockingly few U.S. students learn languages that large numbers of people speak, such as Chinese (1.3 billion speakers) and Arabic (246 million speakers).

Many countries in Europe and Asia are preparing their students for the global age by raising their levels of education attainment; emphasizing international knowledge, skills, and language acquisition; and fostering respect for other cultures. The United States must create its own education response to globalization, which should include raising standards, increasing high school and college graduation rates, and modernizing and internationalizing the curriculum.

What Global Competence Looks Like

The new skill set that students will need goes well beyond the United States' current focus on the basics and on math, science, and technology. These skills are necessary, of course, but to be successful global citizens, workers, and leaders, students will need to be knowledgeable about the world, be able to communicate in languages other than English, and be informed and active citizens.

World Knowledge

Teaching about the rest of the world in U.S. schools has often focused on the superficial: food, fun, and festivals. Today, we need deeper knowledge, such as understanding significant global trends in science and technology, how regions and cultures have developed and how they interconnect, and how international trade and the global economy work. For example, students might consider how increasing the supply of fresh water or changing forms of energy use in one country could have major effects on another country.

In a world in which knowledge is changing rapidly and technology is providing access to vast amounts of information, our challenge is not merely to give students more facts about geography, customs, or particular conflicts. Rather, our challenge is to hone students' critical-thinking skills and to familiarize students with key concepts that they can apply to new situations. In this way, they can make sense of the explosion of information from different sources around the world and put factual information into perspective and context. Only then can this information become meaningful.

Teaching students about the world is not a subject in itself, separate from other content areas, but should be an integral part of *all* subjects taught. We need to open global gateways and inspire students to explore beyond their national borders. Programs like iLEARN and Global Learning and Observations to Benefit the Environment (GLOBE) make it possible for students to work collaboratively with peers in other countries. School-to-school partnerships enable both real and virtual exchanges.

U.S. students are global teenagers, similar in many ways to their technology-enabled peers around the world. Adding an international dimension to subjects and encouraging students to reach out to peers in other countries are powerful ways to make the curriculum relevant and engaging to today's youth.

Language Skills

Only about one-half of U.S. high school students study a foreign language. The majority never go beyond the introductory level, and 70 percent study Spanish (Draper & Hicks, 2002). This results in a serious lack of capacity in such languages as Arabic and Chinese, both of which are crucial to the prosperity and security of the United States.

The United States should do as other industrialized countries in Europe and Asia do—start offering foreign languages in the elementary grades, where research has shown that language learning is most effective (Pufahl, Rhodes, & Christian, 2001), and continue the emphasis in secondary school to create pipelines of proficient language speakers. U.S. students need opportunities to learn a broader range of languages, as in Australia, where 25 percent of students now learn an Asian language (Asia Society, 2002). Heritage communities in the United States—communities in which a non-English language is spoken at home, such as Spanish or Navajo—provide rich sources of teachers, students, and cultural experiences (National Language Conference, 2005). Specific practices, such as immersion experiences, can greatly enhance language proficiency.

As the line between domestic and international affairs blurs, U.S. citizens will increasingly vote and act on issues that require a greater knowledge of the world.

The growing interest in learning Chinese, as shown by the fact that 2,400 U.S. high schools expressed interest in offering the new advanced placement course in Mandarin, suggests that parents and teachers are realizing the importance of communication skills in a multilingual, multicultural world (see www.AskAsia.org/Chinese). Even if graduates don't use a second language at work, quite possibly they will work in cross-cultural teams and environments.

Civic Values

U.S. students need to extend traditional American values into the global arena. These include a concern for human rights and respect for cultures that differ from the United States. By learning to understand other perspectives, students can develop critical-thinking skills and enhance their creativity.

Students should focus on becoming active and engaged citizens in both their local and global environments. Schools can promote civic engagement by weaving discussions of current events throughout the school day and through participatory forms of education, such as Model UN or the Capitol Forum on America's Future, in which high school students voice their opinions on current international issues. Schools should use technology to connect students directly to peers in other parts of the world and promote service learning projects on issues that students can address at both the local and international levels, such as alleviating hunger, providing education support to students in poverty, and improving the environment.

What Schools Can Do

Across the United States, many schools already define their mission as producing students who are prepared for work, citizenship, and leadership in the global era. These schools have found that internationalizing the curriculum creates a more exciting environment for students and teachers alike (Bell-Rose & Desai, 2005). Several approaches have proven successful.

Have a large vision of what you want to achieve, but start slowly, one course or grade level at a time.

Introducing an international studies requirement for graduation. More than a decade ago, the school board of Evanston Township, Illinois, introduced an international studies requirement for graduation and asked the high school's teachers to develop the necessary courses. Now, every sophomore in this diverse Chicago suburb must complete the one-year international studies requirement. Students choose from a series of in-depth humanities courses on the history, literature, and art of Asia, Africa, Latin America, and the Middle East. Simulations and participatory projects are central to instruction, and partnerships with local universities ensure that teachers have ongoing professional development in international affairs.

Creating an elementary school immersion program. After surveying parents and local businesses about the future needs of the community—they cited skills in English, Spanish, and Japanese as important—Seattle public schools created the John Stanford International School, a public elementary bilingual immersion school. Students spend half the day studying math, science, culture, and literacy in either Japanese or Spanish; they spend the other half of the day learning reading, writing, and social studies in English. The school also offers English as a second language courses for immigrant students and after-school courses for their parents. As a result of the school's success, the city of Seattle has recently decided to open 10 more internationally oriented schools.

Developing international schools-within-schools. The Eugene International High School is a school-within-a-school on four high school campuses in Eugene, Oregon. The school is open to all interested students. The four-year sequence of courses centers thematically on culture, history, and the political, economic, and belief systems of different world regions, such as Asia, Africa, the Middle East, and Latin America. The school also emphasizes independent research courses to give students the tools to address global issues. An extended essay and a community-service requirement in 11th and 12th grade both have an international focus. For example, one student wrote a 4,000-word research essay on hydrogen cars and their place in the world economy. Students volunteer at such places as Centro

Latino Americano, University of Oregon International Education and Exchange, and Holt International Children's Services. Finally, students have the option of pursuing the International Baccalaureate.

Teaching crucial language skills to prepare for the global economy. With strong support from Mayor Richard M. Daley, whose goal is to make Chicago a hub for international trade, the city has created the largest Chinese-language program in the United States. Twenty public schools teach Mandarin, from an all-black school on the West Side to a nearly all-Hispanic school on the South Side to more diverse schools throughout the city. For many of these students, Chinese is their third language after English and Spanish. The program resulted from partnerships among political, business, school, and community leaders and the Chinese Ministry of Education, which provides Chinese teachers and organizes a summer cultural program for Chicago educators in China.

Redesigning urban secondary schools with an international focus. Using the International High School of the Americas in San Antonio, Texas, and the Metropolitan Learning Center in Hartford, Connecticut, as anchor schools, the Asia Society has created a network of small, internationally themed secondary schools across the United States (see www.international studiesschools.org/). The mission of each school is to prepare low-income students for college and to promote their knowledge of world regions and international issues. Each public or charter school incorporates international content across the curriculum, offers both Asian and European languages, provides international exchange opportunities, and provides links to international organizations and community-service opportunities. To date, 10 schools have opened in New York City; Los Angeles; Charlotte, North Carolina; Denver, Colorado; and Houston, Texas. Additional schools are slated to open in other locations, such as Mathis and Austin, Texas, and Philadelphia, Pennsylvania.

Using student-faculty exchanges to promote curriculum change. Two public high schools in Newton, Massachusetts—Newton North and Newton South—run an exchange program with the Jingshan School in Beijing, China. Created by two teachers in 1979, the exchange enables U.S. and Chinese teachers and students to spend time in one another's schools every year. The program has served as a catalyst for districtwide curriculum change, bringing the study of Asian cultures into various academic disciplines, from social studies to science, and adding Chinese to the district's broad array of language options. The leaders of this exchange now help schools around the United States develop exchange programs with China as a way to internationalize their curriculums.

Using a K–12 foreign language sequence to promote excellence. The Glastonbury School District in Connecticut has long promoted language study, beginning with a K–8 language requirement. Ninety-three percent of students study at least one foreign language, and 30 percent study more than one. The foreign language curriculum is thematic and interdisciplinary, integrating both foreign language and world history standards. All high school students take a one-semester history course on a non-Western geographic/cultural region and a civics/current issues course that includes international content. The school district's reputation for languages and international studies is a major draw for families moving to the area.

These and other pioneering schools offer models that all schools can replicate. What are the lessons learned? Have a large vision of what you want to achieve, but start slowly, one course or grade level at a time. Involve parents as well as business and community leaders in planning and supporting international education and world languages. Focus on professional development for teachers, including partnerships with local colleges, so teachers can broaden and deepen their international knowledge. Include a focus on mastery of languages, including nontraditional languages, and start at the lowest grade levels possible. Use international exchanges, both real and virtual, to enable students to gain firsthand knowledge of the culture they are studying. If it is unfeasible for students to travel, try technology-based alternatives, such as classroom-to-classroom linkages, global science projects, and videoconferences (Sachar, 2004).

What Policymakers Can Do

Recognizing that future economic development and jobs in their states will be linked to success in the global economy, many states are developing innovations to promote international knowledge and skills. Nineteen states have been working together through the Asia Society's States Network on International Education in the Schools. States have developed commissions (North Carolina, Vermont); statewide summits (Delaware, Indiana, Massachusetts, Washington); and reports to assess the status of international education in their state (North Carolina, New Jersey, Wisconsin, West Virginia). They have created mechanisms, such as International or Global Education Councils (Ohio, Indiana, Wisconsin), and appointed International Education Coordinators to develop new policies and action plans (Delaware, Indiana, Ohio, New Jersey, Wisconsin). They are revising standards (Delaware, Idaho) or high school graduation requirements (New Mexico, Virginia) to incorporate international content. Some states are offering professional development (Oklahoma); initiating new language programs (Connecticut, Delaware, Illinois, Minnesota, Wisconsin, Wyoming); engaging in school exchanges with China (Connecticut, Massachusetts); adding crucial foreign language courses to their virtual high schools (Kentucky); and adding an international dimension to science, technology, engineering, and math (STEM) schools (Ohio, Texas). Finally, some (Arizona, Massachusetts, North Carolina, Washington) have introduced state legislation to provide additional funds to incorporate a global dimension into their schools (see http://Internationaled.org/states).

Many states recognize that future economic development and jobs in their states will be linked to success in the global economy.

In 2006, the National Governors Association held a session on International Education at its annual meeting. In addition,

the Council of Chief State School Officers recently adopted a new policy statement on global education (2007). These state efforts are a good start, but the United States has yet to make international knowledge and skills a policy priority on the federal level and develop the systems and supports necessary to get high-quality international content into U.S. classrooms.

States need to pursue four policy goals to make this happen. They should

- Redesign high schools and create new graduation requirements to motivate higher achievement and promote important international knowledge and key skills.
- Expand teacher training to deliver rigorous study in world history and cultures, economics, world regions, and global challenges.
- Develop world language pipelines from primary school to college that focus on crucial languages, such as Chinese, and that address the acute shortage of language teachers.
- Use technology in innovative ways to expand the availability of international courses and ensure that every school in the United States has an ongoing virtual link to schools in other countries.

For almost 50 years, the U.S. government has played a crucial role in fostering foreign languages and international education in *higher* education. We need to extend this commitment to K–12 education and make it an urgent priority. By doing so, we can improve students' international knowledge and skills and increase both the competitive edge and security of the United States.

In his 2006 report, *The Economics of Knowledge: Why Education Is Key for Europe's Success*, Andreas Schleicher from the Organisation for Economic Cooperation and Development wrote,

The world is indifferent to tradition and past reputations, unforgiving of frailty and ignorant of custom or practice. Success will go to those individuals and countries which are swift to adapt, slow to complain, and open to change.

Part of the great strength of the United States is its adaptability. U.S. schools adapted to the agrarian age, then to the industrial age. It's time to open to change once more and adapt to the global age.

References

Asia Society. (2002). *States institute on international education in the schools: Institute report, November* 20–22, 2002. New York: Author.

Bell-Rose, S., & Desai, V. N. (2005). *Educating leaders for a global society.* New York: Goldman Sachs Foundation.

Center for International Understanding. (2005). *North Carolina in the world: A plan to increase student knowledge and skills about the world.* Raleigh, NC: Author.

Committee for Economic Development. (2006). *Education for global leadership: The importance of international studies and foreign language education for U.S. economic and national security.* Washington, DC: Author. Available: www.ced.org/docs/report/report_foreignlanguages.pdf

Council of Chief State School Officers. (2007). *Global education policy statement.* Washington, DC: Author. Available: www.ccsso.org/projects/International_Education/Global_Education_Policy_Statement/

Draper, J. B., & Hicks, J. H. (2002). *Foreign language enrollments in secondary schools, fall 2000.* Washington, DC: American Council on the Teaching of Foreign Languages. Available: http://actfl.org/files/public/Enroll2000.pdf

Friedman, T. L. (2005). *The world is flat: A brief history of the twenty-first century.* New York: Farrar, Straus, and Giroux.

National Association of State Boards of Education. (2006). *Citizens for the 21st century: Revitalizing the civic mission of schools.* Alexandria, VA: Author. Available: www.nasbe.org/publications/Civic_Ed/civic_ed.html

National Geographic-Roper. (2002). *2002 global geographic literacy survey.* Washington, DC: Author.

National Language Conference. (2005). *A call to action for national foreign language capabilities.* Washington, DC: Author. Available: www.nlconference.org/docs/White_Paper.pdf

Pufahl, I., Rhodes, N. C., & Christian, N. (2001). *What we can learn from foreign language teaching in other countries.* Washington, DC: Center for Applied Linguistics.

Sachar, E. (2004). *Schools for the global age: Promising practices in international education.* New York: Asia Society.

Schleicher, A. (2006). *The economics of knowledge: Why education is key for Europe's success.* Brussels: Lisbon Council. Available: www.oecd.org/dataoecd/43/11/36278531.pdf

U.S. Census Bureau. (2004). Table 2. In *Exports from manufacturing establishments: 2001* (p. 8). Washington, DC: U.S. Department of Commerce.

Wilson, W. T. (2005). *The dawn of the India century: Why India is poised to challenge China and the United States for global economic hegemony in the 21st century.* Chicago: Keystone India. Available: www.keystone-india.com/pdfs/The%20India%20Century.pdf

VIVIEN STEWART is Vice President, Education, at the Asia Society, 725 Park Ave., New York, New York, 10021; vstewart@asiasoc.org.

As Diversity Grows, So Must We

Schools that experience rapid demographic shifts can meet the challenge by implementing five phases of professional development.

GARY R. HOWARD

Many school districts nationwide are experiencing rapid growth in the number of students of color, culturally and linguistically diverse students, and students from low-income families. From my work with education leaders in some of these diversity-enhanced school districts, I know they are places of vibrant opportunity—places that call us to meaningful and exciting work. In these "welcome-to-America" schools, the global community shows up in our classrooms every day, inviting us—even requiring us—to grow as we learn from and with our students and their families.

The Need for Growth

All is not well, however, in these rapidly transitioning schools. Some teachers, administrators, and parents view their schools' increasing diversity as a problem rather than an opportunity. For example, in a school district on the West Coast where the number of Latino students has quadrupled in the past 10 years, a teacher recently asked me, "Why are they sending these kids to our school?" In another district outside New York City—where the student population was once predominantly rich, white, and Jewish but is now about 90 percent low-income kids of color, mostly from the Caribbean and Latin America—a principal remarked in one workshop, "These kids don't value education, and their parents aren't helping either. They don't seem to care about their children's future." In a school district near Minneapolis with a rapidly increasing black population, a white parent remarked, "Students who are coming here now don't have much respect for authority. That's why we have so many discipline problems."

> **Diversity-enhanced schools are places of vibrant opportunity—places that call us as educators to meaningful and exciting work.**

Other educators and parents, although less negative, still feel uneasy about their schools' new demographics. In a high school outside Washington, D.C., where the Latino immigrant population is increasing rapidly, a teacher told me that he was disappointed in himself for not feeling comfortable engaging his students in a discussion of immigration issues, a hot topic in the community in spring 2006. "I knew the kids needed to talk, but I just couldn't go there." And a black teacher who taught French successfully for many years in predominantly white suburban schools told me recently, "When I first found myself teaching classes of mostly black kids, I went home frustrated every night because I knew I wasn't getting through to them, and they were giving me a hard time. It only started getting better when I finally figured out that I had to reexamine everything I was doing."

This teacher has it right. As educators in rapidly transitioning schools, we need to reexamine everything we're doing. Continuing with business as usual will mean failure or mediocrity for too many of our students, as the data related to racial, cultural, linguistic, and economic achievement gaps demonstrate (National Center for Education Statistics, 2005). Rapidly changing demographics demand that we engage in a vigorous, ongoing, and systemic process of professional development to prepare all educators in the school to function effectively in a highly diverse environment.

Many education leaders in diversity-enhanced schools are moving beyond blame and befuddlement and working to transform themselves and their schools to serve all their students well. From observing and collaborating with them, I have learned that this transformative work proceeds best in five phases: (1) building trust, (2) engaging personal culture, (3) confronting issues of social dominance and social justice, (4) transforming instructional practices, and (5) engaging the entire school community

Phase 1: Building Trust

Ninety percent of U.S. public school teachers are white; most grew up and attended school in middle-class, English-speaking, predominantly white communities and received their teacher preparation in predominantly white colleges and universities (Gay, Dingus, Jackson, 2003). Thus, many white educators simply have not acquired the experiential and education

8

background that would prepare them for the growing diversity of their students (Ladson-Billings, 2002; Vavrus, 2002).

The first priority in the trust phase is to acknowledge this challenge in a positive, inclusive, and honest way. School leaders should base initial discussions on the following assumptions:

- Inequities in diverse schools are not, for the most part, a function of intentional discrimination.
- Educators of *all* racial and cultural groups need to develop new competencies and pedagogies to successfully engage our changing populations.
- White teachers have their own cultural connections and unique personal narratives that are legitimate aspects of the overall mix of school diversity

School leaders should also model for their colleagues inclusive and nonjudgmental discussion, reflection, and engagement strategies that teachers can use to establish positive learning communities in their classrooms.

For example, school leaders in the Apple Valley Unified School District in Southern California, where racial, cultural, and linguistic diversity is rapidly increasing, have invested considerable time and resources in creating a climate of openness and trust. They recently implemented four days of intensive work with teams from each school, including principals, teacher leaders, union representatives, parents, clergy, business leaders, and community activists from the NAACP and other organizations.

One essential outcome in this initial phase of the conversation is to establish that racial, cultural, and economic differences are real—and that they make a difference in education outcomes. Said one Apple Valley participant, "I have become aware that the issue of race needs to be dealt with, not minimized." Said another, "I need to move beyond being color-blind." A second key outcome is to establish the need for a personal and professional journey toward greater awareness. As an Apple Valley educator noted, "There were a lot of different stories and viewpoints shared at this inservice, but the one thing we can agree on is that everyone needs to improve in certain areas." A third key outcome in the trust phase is to demonstrate that difficult topics can be discussed in an environment that is honest, safe, and productive. One Apple Valley teacher commented, "We were able to talk about all of the issues and not worry about being politically correct."

Through this work, Apple Valley educators and community leaders established a climate of constructive collaboration that can be directed toward addressing the district's new challenges. From the perspective of the school superintendent, "This is a conversation our community is not used to having, so we had to build a positive climate before moving to the harder questions of action."

Phase 2: Engaging Personal Culture

Change has to start with educators before it can realistically begin to take place with students. The central aim of the second phase of the work is building educators' *cultural competence*—their ability to form authentic and effective relationships across differences.

Young people, particularly those from historically marginalized groups, have sensitive antennae for authenticity. I recently asked a group of racially and culturally diverse high school students to name the teachers in their school who really cared about them, respected them, and enjoyed getting to know them as people. Forty students pooling their answers could name only 10 teachers from a faculty of 120, which may be one reason this high school has a 50 percent dropout rate for students of color.

Aronson and Steele's (2005) work on stereotype threat demonstrates that intellectual performance, rather than being a fixed and constant quality, is quite fragile and can vary greatly depending on the social and interpersonal context of learning. In repeated studies, these researchers found that three factors have a major effect on students' motivation and performance: their feelings of belonging, their trust in the people around them, and their belief that teachers value their intellectual competence. This research suggests that the capacity of adults in the school to form trusting relationships with and supportive learning environments for their students can greatly influence achievement outcomes.

Leaders in the Metropolitan School District of Lawrence Township, outside Indianapolis, have taken this perspective seriously. Clear data showed gaps among ethnic groups in achievement, participation in higher-level courses, discipline referrals, and dropout rates. In response, district teachers and administrators engaged in a vigorous and ongoing process of self-examination and personal growth related to cultural competence.

Central-office and building administrators started with themselves. Along with selected teachers from each school, they engaged in a multiyear program of shared reading, reflective conversations, professional development activities, and joint planning to increase their own and their colleagues' levels of cultural competence. They studied and practiced Margaret Wheatley's (2002) principles of conversation, with particular emphasis on her admonitions to expect things to be messy and to be willing to be disturbed. They designed their own Socratic seminars using chapters from *We Can't Teach What We Don't Know* (Howard, 2006) and used the stages of personal identity development model from that book as a foundation for ongoing reflective conversations about their own journeys toward cultural competence.

As this work among leaders began to be applied in various school buildings, one principal observed, "We are talking about things that we were afraid to talk about before—like our own prejudices and the biases in some of our curriculum materials." In another school, educators' discussions led to a decision to move parent-teacher conferences out of the school building and into the apartment complexes where their black and Latino students live.

Phase 3: Confronting Social Dominance and Social Justice

When we look at school outcome data, the history of racism, classism, and exclusion in the United States stares us in the face. Systems of privilege and preference often create enclaves of exclusivity in schools, in which certain demographic groups are served well while others languish in failure or mediocrity. As diversity grows in rapidly transitioning school districts, demographic gaps become increasingly apparent.

Educators of *all* racial and cultural groups need to develop new competencies and pedagogies to successfully engage our changing populations.

In phase three, educators directly confront the current and historical inequities that affect education. The central purpose of this phase is to construct a compelling narrative of social justice that will inform, inspire, and sustain educators in their work, without falling into the rhetoric of shame and blame. School leaders and teachers engage in a lively conversation about race, class, gender, sexual orientation, immigration, and other dimensions of diversity and social dominance. David Koyama, principal of a diversity-enhanced elementary school outside Seattle, said, "One of my most important functions as a school leader is to transform political jargon like 'no child left behind' into a moral imperative that inspires teachers to work toward justice, not mere compliance."

Unraveling social dominance takes courage—the kind of courage shown by the central office and school leadership team in the Roseville Area School District outside the twin cities of Minneapolis and St. Paul. Roseville is in the midst of a rapid demographic shift. As we approached this phase of the work, I asked Roseville leaders to examine how issues of privilege, power, and dominance might be functioning in their schools to shape educators' assumptions and beliefs about students and create inequitable outcomes.

One of the workshop activities engaged participants in a forced-choice simulation requiring them to choose which aspects of their identity they would give up or deny for the sake of personal survival in a hostile environment. Choosing from such identities as race, ethnicity, language, religion, values, and vocation, many white educators were quick to give up race. Among the Roseville administrative team, which is 95 percent white, the one white principal who chose to keep his racial identity during the simulation said during the debriefing discussion, "I seriously challenge my white colleagues who so easily gave up their race. I think if we are honest with ourselves, few would choose to lose the privilege and power that come with being white in the United States."

As an outgrowth of the authentic and sometimes contentious conversations that emerged from this and other activities, several core leaders and the superintendent identified a need to craft a strong Equity Vision statement for the district. The Equity Vision now headlines all opening-of-school events each year and is publicly displayed in district offices and schools. It reads,

> Roseville Area Schools is committed to ensuring an equitable and respectful educational experience for every student, family, and staff member, regardless of race,

gender, sexual orientation, socioeconomic status, ability, home or first language, religion, national origin, or age.

As a result of the increased consciousness about issues of dominance and social justice, several schools have formed Equity Teams of teachers and students, and an Equity Parent Group has begun to meet. The district is looking seriously at how many students from dominant and subordinate groups are in its gifted and AP classes and is conscientiously working for more balance.

Like Roseville, other diversity-enhanced districts must establish clear public markers that unambiguously state, "This is who we are, this is what we believe, and this is what we will do." Any approach to school reform that does not honestly engage issues of power, privilege, and social dominance is naive, ungrounded in history, and unlikely to yield the deep changes needed to make schools more inclusive and equitable.

Phase 4: Transforming Instructional Practices

In this phase, schools assess and, where necessary, transform the way they carry out instruction to become more responsive to diversity. For teachers, this means examining pedagogy and curriculum, as well as expectations and interaction patterns with students. It means looking honestly at outcome data and creating new strategies designed to serve the students whom current instruction is not reaching. For school leaders, this often means facing the limits of their own knowledge and skills and becoming colearners with teachers to find ways to transform classroom practices.

In Loudoun County Public Schools, outside Washington, D.C., teachers and school leaders are taking this work seriously. One of the fastest-growing school systems in the United States, Loudoun County is experiencing rapid increases in racial, cultural, linguistic, and economic diversity on its eastern edge, closer to the city, while remaining more monocultural to the west. Six of Loudoun's most diverse schools have formed leadership teams to promote the following essential elements of culturally responsive teaching (CRT):

- Forming authentic and caring relationships with students.
- Using curriculum that honors each student's culture and life experience.
- Shifting instructional strategies to meet the diverse learning needs of students.
- Communicating respect for each student's intelligence.
- Holding consistent and high expectations for all learners. (Gay, 2000; Ladson-Billings, 1994; McKinley, 2005; Shade, Kelly, & Oberg, 1997)

CRT teams vary in size and membership but usually include principals, assistant principals, counselors, lead teachers, specialists, and, in some cases, parents. In addition to engaging deeply in the phases outlined above, these teams have begun to work with their broader school faculties to transform instruction. At Loudoun County's Sugarland Elementary, teacher members of the CRT team have designed student-based action research projects. They selected individual students from their most academically challenged demographic groups and then used the principles of CRT to plan new interventions to engage these students and track their progress.

As educators in rapidly transitioning schools, we need to reexamine everything we're doing.

In one action research project, a 5th grade teacher focused on a Latino student, an English language learner who "couldn't put two sentences together, let alone write the five-paragraph essay that is required to pass our 5th grade assessment." The teacher's first reaction was to ask, "How was this student allowed to slip by all these years without learning anything beyond 2nd grade writing skills?" When the teacher launched her CRT project, however, her perspective became more proactive. She realized that she couldn't just deliver the 5th grade curriculum—she had to meet this student where he was. She built a personal connection with the student, learned about his family culture and interests (a fascination with monkeys was a major access point), and used this relationship to reinforce his academic development. The student responded to her high expectations and passed his 5th grade writing assessment. And after missing its No Child Left Behind compliance goals in past years, Sugarland recently achieved adequate yearly progress for all subgroups in its highly diverse student population.

This phase requires a crucial paradigm shift, in which teachers and other school professionals stop blaming students and their families for gaps in academic achievement. Instead of pointing fingers, educators in Loudoun schools are placing their energies where they will have the most impact—in changing their *own* attitudes, beliefs, expectations, and practices. I frequently ask teachers and school leaders, "Of all the many factors that determine school success for our students, where can we as educators have the most influence?" After educators participate in the work outlined here, the answer is always, "Changing ourselves."

Phase 5: Engaging the Entire School Community

Changing demographics have profound implications for all levels and functions of the school system. To create welcoming and equitable learning environments for diverse students and their families, school leaders must engage the entire school community.

Leaders in the East Ramapo Central School District in New York State have committed themselves to just such a system-wide initiative. The school district, which lies across the Tappan Zee Bridge from New York City, has experienced a dramatic shift in student population in the past 15 years as low-income Haitian, Jamaican, Dominican, Latino, and black families from

the city have moved into the community and middle-class white families have, unfortunately but predictably, fled to private schools or other less diverse districts.

In the midst of this demographic revolution, East Ramapo's broad-based diversity initiative has engaged all groups and constituencies in the school district community, not just teachers and administrators. For example, the district has provided workshops to help classified employees acknowledge their powerful role in setting a welcoming tone and creating an inclusive climate for students, parents, and colleagues in school offices, lunchrooms, hallways, and on the playground. For bus drivers, this work has meant gaining cultural competence skills for managing their immense safety responsibilities while communicating clearly and compassionately across many languages and cultures on their buses.

In one session that I led with school secretaries, we worked through their confusion and frustration related to all the diverse languages being spoken in the school offices and, in some cases, their feelings of anger and resentment about the demographic changes that had taken place in "their" schools. Asked what they learned from the session, participants commented, "I saw the frustration people can have, especially if they are from another country." "We all basically have the same feelings about family, pride in our culture, and the importance of getting along." "I learned from white people that they can also sometimes feel like a minority." In addition to these sessions, East Ramapo has created learning opportunities for school board members, parents, students, counselors, and special education classroom assistants. The district has convened regular community forums focusing on student achievement and creating conversations across many diverse cultures. White parents who have kept their children in the public schools because they see the value of diversity in their education have been significant participants in these conversations.

As a result of East Ramapo's efforts, the achievement gaps in test scores along ethnic and economic lines have significantly narrowed. In the six years since the district consciously began implementing the professional development model discussed here, the pass rate for black and Hispanic students combined on the New York State elementary language arts test increased from 43 percent in 2000 to 54 percent in 2006; on the math test, the pass rate increased from 40 percent to 61 percent. During that same period, the gap between black and Hispanic students (combined) and white and Asian students (combined) decreased by 6 percentage points in language arts and 23 percentage points in math. The achievement gap between low-income elementary students and the general population decreased by 10 points in language arts and 6 points in math—results that are particularly impressive, given that the proportion of economically disadvantaged students grew from 51 percent in 2000 to 72 percent in 2006.

A Journey toward Awareness

Professional development for creating inclusive, equitable, and excellent schools is a long-term process. The school districts described here are at various stages in the process. Everyone involved would agree that the work is messier and more complex than can be communicated in this brief overview. However, one central leadership commitment is clear in all of these rapidly transitioning districts: When diversity comes to town, we are all challenged to grow.

References

Aronson, J., & Steele, C. M. (2005). Stereotypes and the fragility of human competence, motivation, and self-concept. In C. Dweck & E. Elliot (Eds.), *Handbook of competence and motivation* (pp. 436–456). New York: Guilford.

Gay, G. (2000). *Culturally responsive teaching: Theory, research, and practice.* New York: Teachers College Press.

Gay, G., Dingus, J. E., & Jackson, C. W. (2003, July). *The presence and performance of teachers of color in the profession.* Unpublished report prepared for the National Collaborative on Diversity in the Teaching Force, Washington, DC.

Howard, G. (2006). *We can't teach what we don't know: White teachers in multiracial schools* (2nd ed.). New York: Teachers College Press.

Ladson-Billings, G. (1994). *The dreamkeepers: Successful teachers of African American students.* San Francisco: Jossey-Bass.

Ladson-Billings, G. (2002). *Crossing over to Canaan: The journey of new teachers in diverse classrooms.* San Francisco: Jossey-Bass.

McKinley, J. H. (2005, March). *Culturally responsive teaching and learning.* Paper presented at the Annual State Conference of the Washington Alliance of Black School Educators, Bellevue, WA.

National Center for Education Statistics. (2005). *The nation's report card.* Washington, DC: Author.

Shade, B. J., Kelly, C., & Oberg, M. (1997). *Creating culturally responsive classrooms.* Washington, DC: American Psychological Association.

Vavrus, M. (2002). *Transforming the multiculrural education of teachers: Theory, research and practice.* New York: Teachers College Press.

Wheatley, M. (2002). *Turning to one another: Simple conversations to restore hope to the future.* San Francisco: Barrett-Koehler.

GARY R. HOWARD is Founder and President of the REACH Center for Multicultural Education in Seattle (www.reachctr.org); 206-634-2073; garyhoward@earthlink.net. He is the author of *We Can't Teach What We Don't Know: White Teachers, Multiracial Schools* (Teachers College Press, 2nd ed., 2006).

From *Educational Leadership,* March 2007, pp. 16–22. Copyright © 2007 by ASCD. Reprinted by permission. The Association for Supervision and Curriculum Development is a worldwide community of educators advocating sound policies and sharing best practices to achieve the success of each learner. To learn more, visit ASCD at www.ascd.org

Colorblind to the Reality of Race in America

IAN F. HANEY LÓPEZ

How will race as a social practice evolve in the United States over the next few decades? The American public, and indeed many scholars, increasingly believe that the country is leaving race and racism behind. Some credit Brown v. Board of Education, the revered 1954 U.S. Supreme Court decision pronouncing segregated schools unequal, and the broad civil-rights movement of which the decision was a part, with turning the nation away from segregation and toward equality. Others point to changing demographics, emphasizing the rising number of mixed-race marriages and the increasing Asian and Hispanic populations that are blurring the historic black-white divide.

My sense of our racial future differs. Not only do I fear that race will continue to fundamentally skew American society over the coming decades, but I worry that the belief in the diminished salience of race makes that more likely rather than less. I suspect that the laws supposedly protecting against racial discrimination are partly to blame, for they no longer contribute to racial justice but instead legitimate continued inequality. We find ourselves now in the midst of a racial era marked by what I term "colorblind white dominance," in which a public consensus committed to formal antiracism deters effective remediation of racial inequality, protecting the racial status quo while insulating new forms of racism and xenophobia.

The Jefferson County school district, in Kentucky, covers Louisville and surrounding suburbs. A target of decades of litigation to eradicate Jim Crow school segregation and its vestiges, the district has since 2001 voluntarily pursued efforts to maintain what is now one of the most integrated school systems in the country. But not everyone supports those efforts, especially when they involve taking race into consideration in pupil assignments. In 2004 a white lawyer named Teddy B. Gordon ran for a seat on the Jefferson County School Board, promising to end endeavors to maintain integrated schools. He finished dead last, behind three other candidates. Indifferent to public repudiation, he is back—this time in the courtroom. Gordon's argument is seductively simple: Brown forbids all governmental uses of race, even if designed to achieve or maintain an integrated society.

He has already lost at the trial level and before an appellate court, as have two other sets of plaintiffs challenging similar integration-preserving efforts by school districts in Seattle and in Lynn, Mass. But Gordon and the conservative think tanks and advocacy groups that back him, including the self-styled Center for Equal Opportunity, are not without hope. To begin with, over the past three decades the courts have come ever closer to fully embracing a colorblind Constitution—colorblind in the sense of disfavoring all uses of race, irrespective of whether they are intended to perpetuate or ameliorate racial oppression. More immediately, last June the Supreme Court voted to review the Louisville and Seattle cases—Meredith v. Jefferson County Board of Education and Parents Involved in Community Schools v. Seattle School District.

Roger Clegg, president and general counsel of the Center for Equal Opportunity, is thrilled. As he gleefully noted in The National Review, there's an old saw that the court does not hear cases it plans to affirm. The Bush administration, too, supports Gordon and his efforts. The U.S. solicitor general recently submitted a friend-of-the-court brief urging the justices to prevent school districts across the country from paying attention to race.

At issue is a legally backed ideology of colorblindness that could have implications beyond schools—for higher education and the wider society. Yes, in a narrowly tailored decision three years ago, the Supreme Court allowed the University of Michigan to consider race as one factor in law-school admissions. But since then, conservative advocacy groups have used the threat of lawsuits to intimidate many institutions into halting race-based college financial-aid and orientation programs, as well as graduate stipends and fellowships, and those groups are now taking aim at faculty hiring procedures. This month Michigan voters will decide whether to amend the state constitution to ban racial and gender preferences wherever practiced. And looming on the horizon are renewed efforts to enact legislation forbidding the federal and state governments from collecting statistics that track racial disparities, efforts that are themselves part of a broader campaign to expunge race from the national vocabulary.

Gordon predicts that if he prevails, Louisville schools will rapidly resegregate. He is sanguine about the prospect. "We're a diverse society, a multiethnic society, a colorblind society," he told The New York Times. "Race is history."

But the past is never really past, especially not when one talks about race and the law in the United States. We remain a racially stratified country, though for some that constitutes an argument for rather than against colorblindness. Given the long and sorry history of racial subordination, there is tremendous rhetorical appeal to Justice John Marshall Harlan's famous dissent in Plessy v. Ferguson, the 1896 case upholding segregated railway cars: "Our Constitution is color-blind, and neither knows nor tolerates classes among citizens."

Contemporary proponents of colorblindness almost invariably draw a straight line from that dissent to their own impassioned advocacy for being blind to race today. But in doing so, partisans excise Harlan's acknowledgment of white superiority in the very paragraph in which he extolled colorblindness: "The white race deems itself to be the dominant race in this country. And so it is, in prestige, in achievements, in education, in wealth and in power. So, I doubt not, it will continue to be for all time." That omission obscures a more significant elision: Harlan objected not to all governmental uses of race, but to those he thought would unduly oppress black people.

As viewed by Harlan and the court, the central question was where to place limits on government support for the separation of racial groups that were understood to be unequal by nature (hence Harlan's comfortable endorsement of white superiority). He and the majority agreed that the state could enforce racial separation in the "social" but not in the "civil" arenas; they differed on the contours of the spheres. Harlan believed that segregated train cars limited the capacity of black people to participate as full citizens in civic life, while the majority saw such segregation only as a regulation of social relations sanctioned by custom. The scope of the civil arena mattered so greatly precisely because state exclusions from public life threatened to once again reduce the recently emancipated to an inferior caste defined by law.

For the first half of the 20th century, colorblindness represented the radical and wholly unrealized aspiration of dismantling de jure racial subordination. Thus Thurgood Marshall, as counsel to the National Association for the Advancement of Colored People in the late 1940s and early 1950s, cited Harlan's celebration of colorblindness to argue that racial distinctions are "contrary to our Constitution and laws." But neither society nor the courts embraced colorblindness when doing so might have sped the demise of white supremacy. Even during the civil-rights era, colorblindness as a strategy for racial emancipation did not take hold. Congress and the courts dismantled Jim Crow segregation and proscribed egregious forms of private discrimination in a piecemeal manner, banning only the most noxious misuses of race, not any reference to race whatsoever.

In the wake of the civil-rights movement's limited but significant triumphs, the relationship between colorblindness and racial reform changed markedly. The greatest potency of colorblindness came to lie in preserving, rather than challenging, the racial status quo. When the end of explicit race-based subordination did not eradicate stubborn racial inequalities, progressives increasingly recognized the need for state and private actors to intervene along racial lines. Rather than call for colorblindness, they began to insist on the need for affirmative race-conscious remedies. In that new context, colorblindness appealed to those opposing racial integration. Enshrouded with the moral raiment of the civil-rights movement, colorblindness provided cover for opposition to racial reform.

Within a year of Brown, Southern school districts and courts had recognized that they could forestall integration by insisting that the Constitution allowed them to use only "race neutral" means to end segregation—school-choice plans that predictably produced virtually no integration whatsoever. In 1965 a federal court in South Carolina put it squarely: "The Constitution is color-blind; it should no more be violated to attempt integration than to preserve segregation."

Wielding the ideal of colorblindness as a sword, in the past three decades racial conservatives on the Supreme Court have increasingly refought the battles lost during the civil-rights era, cutting back on protections against racial discrimination as well as severely limiting race-conscious remedies. In several cases in the 1970s—including North Carolina State Board of Education v. Swann, upholding school-assignment plans, and Regents of the University of California v. Bakke—the court ruled that the need to redress the legacy of segregation made strict colorblindness impossible. But as the 1980s went on, in other cases—McCleskey v. Kemp, which upheld Georgia's death penalty despite uncontroverted statistical evidence that African-Americans convicted of murder were 22 times as likely to be sentenced to death if their victims were white rather than black, and City of Richmond v. Croson, which rejected a city affirmative-action program steering some construction dollars to minority-owned companies despite the fact that otherwise only two-thirds of 1 percent of city contracts went to minority companies in a city 50 percent African-American—the court presented race as a phenomenon called into existence just when someone employed a racial term. Discrimination existed only but every time someone used racial language. Thus the court found no harm in Georgia's penal system, because no evidence surfaced of a specific bad actor muttering racial epithets, while it espied racism in Richmond's affirmative-action program because it set aside contracts for "minorities."

That approach ignores the continuing power of race as a society-altering category. The civil-rights movement changed the racial zeitgeist of the nation by rendering illegitimate all explicit invocations of white supremacy, a shift that surely marked an important step toward a more egalitarian society. But it did not bring into actual existence that ideal, as white people remain dominant across virtually every social, political, and economic domain. In 2003 the poverty rate was 24 percent among African-Americans, 23 percent among Latinos, and 8 percent among white people. That same year, an estimated 20 percent of African-Americans and 33 percent of Latinos had no health insurance, while 11 percent of white people were uninsured. Discrepancies in incarceration rates are particularly staggering, with African-American men vastly more likely to spend time in prison than white men are.

Or forget the numbers and recall for a moment the graphic parade of images from Hurricane Katrina. Or consider access to country clubs and gated communities, in-group preferences for jobs and housing, the moral certainty shared by many white folks regarding their civic belonging and fundamental goodness. Or, to tie back to Louisville, reflect on what you already know about the vast, racially correlated disparities in resources available to public (and still more to private) schools across the country. Racial dominance by white people continues as a central element of our society.

What may be changing, however, is how membership in the white group is defined. The term "white" has a far more complicated—and fluid—history in the United States than people commonly recognize. For most of our history, whiteness stood in contrast to the nonwhite identities imposed upon Africans, American Indians, Mexican peoples of the Southwest, and Asian immigrants, marking one pole in the racial hierarchy. Simultaneously, however, putative "racial" divisions separated Europeans, so that in the United States presumptions of gross racial inferiority were removed from Germans only in the 1840s through 1860s, the Irish in the 1850s through 1880s, and Eastern and Southern Europeans in the 1900s to 1920s. The melding of various European groups into the monolithic, undifferentiated "white" category we recognize today is a recent innovation, only fully consolidated in the mid-20th century. Now white identity may be expanding to include persons and groups with ancestors far beyond Europe.

Perhaps we should distinguish here among three sorts of white identity. Consider first persons who are "fully white," in the sense that, with all of the racially relevant facts about them widely known, they would generally be considered white by the community at large. (Obviously, racial identity is a matter not of biology but of social understandings, although those may give great weight to purportedly salient differences in morphology and ancestry.) In contrast to that group, there have long been those "passing as white"—people whose physical appearance allowed them to claim a white identity when social custom would have assigned them to a nonwhite group had their ancestry been widely known. Of people of Irish and Jewish descent in the United States, for example, one might say that while initially some were able to pass as white, now all are fully white.

Today a new group is emerging, perhaps best described as "honorary whites." Apartheid South Africa first formally crafted this identity: Seeking to engage in trade and commerce with nations cast as inferior by apartheid logic, particularly Japan, South Africa extended to individuals from such countries the status of honorary white people, allowing them to travel, reside, relax, and conduct business in South African venues that were otherwise strictly "whites only." Persons who pass as white hide racially relevant parts of their identity; honorary whites are extended the status of whiteness despite the public recognition that, from a bioracial perspective, they are not fully white.

In the United States, honorary-white status seems increasingly to exist for certain people and groups. The quintessential example is certain Asian-Americans, particularly East Asians.

Although Asians have long been racialized as nonwhite as a matter of law and social practice, the model-minority myth and professional success have combined to free some Asian-Americans from the most pernicious negative beliefs regarding their racial character. In part this trend represents a shift toward a socially based, as opposed to biologically based, definition of race. Individuals and communities with the highest levels of acculturation, achievement, and wealth increasingly find themselves functioning as white, at least as measured by professional integration, residential patterns, and intermarriage rates.

Latinos also have access to honorary-white identity, although their situation differs from that of Asian-Americans. Unlike the latter, and also unlike African-Americans, Latinos in the United States have long been on the cusp between white and nonwhite. Despite pervasive and often violent racial prejudice against Mexicans in the Southwest and Puerto Ricans and other Hispanic groups elsewhere, the most elite Latin Americans in the United States have historically been accepted as fully white. With no clear identity under the continental theory of race (which at its most basic identifies blacks as from Africa, whites from Europe, reds from the Americas, and yellows from Asia), and with a tremendous range of somatic features marking this heterogeneous population, there has long been relatively more room for the use of social rather than strictly biological factors in the imputation of race to particular Hispanic individuals and groups.

It seems likely that an increasing number of Latinos—those who have fair features, material wealth, and high social status, aided also by Anglo surnames—will both claim and be accorded a position in U.S. society as fully white. Simultaneously, many more—similarly situated in terms of material and status position, but perhaps with slightly darker features or a surname or accent suggesting Latin-American origins—will become honorary whites. Meanwhile, the majority of Latinos will continue to be relegated to nonwhite categories.

The continuing evolution in who counts as white is neither particularly startling nor especially felicitous. Not only have racial categories and ideologies always mutated, but race has long turned on questions of wealth, professional attainment, and social position. A developing scholarship now impressively demonstrates that even during and immediately after slavery, at a time when racial identity in the United States was presumably most rigidly fixed in terms of biological difference and descent, and even in the hyperformal legal setting of the courtroom, determinations of racial identity often took place on the basis of social indicia like the nature of one's employment or one's choice of sexual partners.

Nor will categories like black, brown, white, yellow, and red soon disappear. Buttressed by the continued belief in continental racial divisions, physical features those divisions supposedly connote will remain foundational to racial classification. The stain of African ancestry—so central to the elaboration of race in the United States—ensures a persistent special stigma for black people. Honorary-white status will be available only to the most exceptional—and the most light-skinned—African-Americans, and on terms far more restrictive than those on which whiteness will be extended to many Latinos and Asian-Americans.

Those many in our society who are darker, poorer, more identifiably foreign will continue to suffer the poverty, marginalization, immiseration, incarceration, and exclusion historically accorded to those whose skin and other features socially mark them as nonwhite. Even under a redefined white category, racial hierarchy will continue as the links are strengthened between nonwhite identity and social disadvantage on the one hand, and whiteness and privilege on the other. Under antebellum racial logic, those black people with the fairest features were sometimes described as "light, bright, and damn near white." If today we switch out "damn near" for "honorary" and fold in a few other minorities, how much has really changed?

In the face of continued racial hierarchy, it is crucial that we understand the colorblind ideology at issue in the school cases before the Supreme Court. "In the eyes of government, we are just one race here," Justice Antonin Scalia intoned in 1995. "It is American." That sentiment is stirring as an aspiration, but disheartening as a description of reality, and even more so as a prescription for racial policies. All persons of good will aspire to a society free from racial hierarchy. We should embrace colorblindness—in the sense of holding it up as an ideal. But however far the civil-rights struggle has moved us, we remain far from a racially egalitarian utopia.

In this context, the value of repudiating all governmental uses of race must depend on a demonstrated ability to remedy racial hierarchy. Colorblindness as a policy prescription merits neither fealty nor moral stature by virtue of the attractiveness of colorblindness as an ideal. In the hands of a Thurgood Marshall, who sought to end Jim Crow segregation and to foster an integrated society, colorblindness was a transformative, progressive practice. But when Teddy Gordon, Roger Clegg, the Bush administration, and the conservative justices on the Supreme Court call for banning governmental uses of race, they aim to end the efforts of local majorities to respond constructively to racial inequality. In so doing, they are making their version of colorblindness a reactionary doctrine.

Contemporary colorblindness is a set of understandings—buttressed by law and the courts, and reinforcing racial patterns of white dominance—that define how people comprehend, rationalize, and act on race. As applied, however much some people genuinely believe that the best way to get beyond racism is to get beyond race, colorblindness continues to retard racial progress. It does so for a simple reason: It focuses on the surface, on the bare fact of racial classification, rather than looking down into the nature of social practices. It gets racism and racial remediation exactly backward, and insulates new forms of race baiting.

White dominance continues with few open appeals to race. Consider the harms wrought by segregated schools today. Schools in predominantly white suburbs are far more likely to have adequate buildings, teachers, and books, while the schools serving mainly minority children are more commonly underfinanced, unsafe, and in a state of disrepair. Such harms

acccumulate, encouraging white flight to avoid the expected deterioration in schools and the violence that is supposedly second nature to "them," only to precipitate the collapse in the tax base that in fact ensures a decline not only in schools but also in a range of social services. Such material differences in turn buttress seemingly common-sense ideas about disparate groups, so that we tend to see pristine schools and suburbs as a testament to white accomplishment and values. When violence does erupt, it is laid at the feet of alienated and troubled teenagers, not a dysfunctional culture. Yet we see the metal detectors guarding entrances to minority schoolhouses (harbingers of the prison bars to come) as evidence not of the social dynamics of exclusion and privilege, but of innate pathologies. No one need talk about the dynamics of privilege and exclusion. No one need cite white-supremacist arguments nor openly refer to race—race exists in the concrete of our gated communities and barrios, in government policies and programs, in cultural norms and beliefs, and in the way Americans lead their lives.

Colorblindness badly errs when it excuses racially correlated inequality in our society as unproblematic so long as no one uses a racial epithet. It also egregiously fails when it tars every explicit reference to race. To break the interlocking patterns of racial hierarchy, there is no other way but to focus on, talk about, and put into effect constructive policies explicitly engaged with race. To be sure, inequality in wealth is a major and increasing challenge for our society, but class is not a substitute for a racial analysis—though, likewise, racial oppression cannot be lessened without sustained attention to poverty. It's no accident that the poorest schools in the country warehouse minorities, while the richest serve whites; the national education crisis reflects deeply intertwined racial and class politics. One does not deny the imbrication of race and class by insisting on the importance of race-conscious remedies: The best strategies for social repair will give explicit attention to race as well as to other sources of inequality, and to their complex interrelationship.

The claim that race and racism exist only when specifically mentioned allows colorblindness to protect a new racial politics from criticism. The mobilization of public fears along racial lines has continued over the past several decades under the guise of interlinked panics about criminals, welfare cheats, terrorists, and—most immediately in this political season—illegal immigrants. Attacks ostensibly targeting "culture" or "behavior" rather than "race" now define the diatribes of today's racial reactionaries. Samuel P. Huntington's jeremiad against Latino immigration in his book *Who Are We?: The Challenges to America's National Identity* rejects older forms of white supremacy, but it promotes the idea of a superior Anglo-Protestant culture. Patrick J. Buchanan defends his latest screed attacking "illegal immigrants," *State of Emergency: The Third World Invasion and Conquest of America*, against the charge of racism by insisting that he's indifferent to race but outraged by those with different cultures who violate our laws. My point is not simply that culture and behavior provide coded language for old prejudices, but that colorblindness excuses and insulates this recrudescence of xenophobia by insisting that only the explicit use of racial nomenclature counts as racism.

Contemporary colorblindness loudly proclaims its antiracist pretensions. To actually move toward a racially egalitarian society, however, requires that we forthrightly respond to racial inequality today. The alternative is the continuation of colorblind white dominance. As Justice Harry Blackmun enjoined in defending affirmative action in Bakke: "In order to get beyond racism, we must first take account of race. There is no other way."

Ian F. Haney López is a professor at the Boalt Hall School of Law at the University of California at Berkeley. New York University Press has just issued a 10th-anniversary edition of his White by Law: The Legal Construction of Race, with a new chapter on colorblind white dominance.

To actually move toward a racially egalitarian society requires that we forthrightly respond to racial inequality today. The alternative is the continuation of colorblind white dominance.

Beyond "Culture Clash": Understandings of Immigrant Experiences

This article addresses the ways in which the experiences of immigrant youth and families in U.S. schools and society have been conceptualized primarily as conflicts between immigrant cultures and dominant U.S. culture. Exemplified by the discourse of culture clash or of immigrants being torn between two worlds, this prevalent understanding structures the experiences, cultures, and identities of immigrants as unchanging and fixed in time. This article illustrates the ways that culture and identity are constructed within the double movement of discourse and representation. It offers examples of how dominant representations create simplistic understandings of the identities of immigrant youth, as well as the ways youth are constructing new identities.

BIC NGO

As a researcher interested in the experiences of immigrant families in the United States, I try to pay attention to news stories about immigrants. More often than not, these stories highlight the *clash of cultures,* or the ways that immigrant youth are torn or caught between two worlds with ubiquitous headlines such as "Generation 1.5: Young immigrants in two worlds" (Feagans, 2006), "Taking on two worlds" (Do, 2002), and "Mother's Fray: Culture clash puts special strain on immigrant moms and daughters" (Wax, 1998). One dimension of this focus on cultural conflict emphasizes the differences between immigrant cultures (East) and U.S. culture (West). In the practices of the popular press, we see dualisms of traditional/modern or rural/urban in explanations of immigrant culture and U.S. culture. For example, in a series highlighting the ways that Hmong girls have been *Shamed into Silence* by Hmong culture, Louwagie and Browning (2005a, 2005b) pointed out that "culture clash can stymie help" (2005b, p. 11A) for Hmong girls who have been raped by Hmong gang members. In their explication of the culture clash, the journalists highlighted the contrast, "Adapting any non-Western culture to the United States is a formidable task. For the Hmong community, which hails from isolated mountain villages in Laos and refugee camps in Thailand, settling in urban areas such as St. Paul has meant a bigger change" (Louwagie & Browning, 2005b, p. 11A). Here, the identity and culture—beliefs, behaviors, and values—of immigrants such as the Hmong are characterized as traditional, patriarchal, and rural, in contrast to a highly modern and civilized U.S. society.

Another dimension of the culture clash discourse emphasizes the differences between the first-generation (parents) and second-generation (youth). This dichotomy results in a preoccupation with intergenerational conflict where arguments that immigrant youth and adults have over clothes or dating restrictions are construed to be clashes between the traditional values of immigrant parents versus modern values of youth who are influenced by contemporary U.S. practices. Again, the *Shamed into Silence* series is illustrative: "The problem comes in mixing Hmong traditions with American culture, many agree. While Hmong refugees are struggling to survive in a culture foreign to them, their children are adapting more quickly and disobeying what they see as their parents' antiquated rules" (Louwagie & Browning, 2005b, p. 11A). Implicitly and explicitly, the values and practices of Hmong immigrants are depicted as backward or stuck in time.

In education, the cultural difference model for explaining immigrant student achievement problematically positions educational outcomes as a product of the cultural practices of immigrants. At one extreme, explanations of low achievement point to bad cultural practices for the under-achievement of immigrant students (S. J. Lee, 1997; Ngo, 2002). Hmong students' decisions to drop out of school to marry, for instance, are viewed as choices that are tied to traditional values—rather than as a response to oppressive social structures (Ngo, 2002). At the other extreme, cultural values based on Buddhist and Confucian beliefs are used to account for educational progress and attainment. Vietnamese students' high success is attributed to a strong work ethic and family support (Zhou & Bankston, 2001).

As a result of this either–or framework, immigrant students are viewed as gangsters and delinquents or as academic superstars and model minorities. Immigrant families are viewed as supportive and functional or as unsupportive and dysfunctional.

Even though I want to recognize the importance of the cultural difference research in drawing attention to the struggles of immigrants, I also want to point out the insidious effects of a singular focus on cultural conflict. The cultural difference model for understanding immigrant experiences sets up binary oppositions between tradition and modernity, East and West, and First World and Third World, among others. This oppositional framework is problematic for at least two reasons. First, the emphasis on traditional cultural values reifies the notion of culture, positioning it as some thing that is fixed or a given, rather than as a social process that finds meaning within social relationships and practices. Second, binary oppositions inscribe judgment and a pecking order (i.e., good/bad, ours/theirs) into cultural practices and values. Moreover, as Lowe (1996) convincingly argued, "the reduction of the cultural politics of racialized ethnic groups, like Asian Americans, to first-generation/second-generation struggles displaces social differences into a privatized familial opposition" (p. 63). The challenges faced by immigrant youth and adults are relegated to the private sphere of the home. This focus on intergenerational conflict problematically absolves institutions of education, labor, and government of responsibility, and deflects attention from exclusionary historical practices as well as discrimination immigrants continue to face (Jaret, 1999; Olneck, 2003).

In order to account for the complexity of immigrant students' and families' experiences, and the ever-changing nature of culture and identity, we need to move beyond discrete understandings of culture and identity as good/bad, traditional/modern, us/them. In this article, I suggest that we move toward seeing the changes or the *in-between* (Bhabha, 1994) of culture and identity. To do so, I illustrate the ways that culture and identity are constructed within discourse and representation. In the following section, I explicate an understanding of identity that accounts for its dynamic, contested, and messy nature that moves beyond the fixity of binary categories. I then offer examples from my work with Lao American immigrant students to illustrate how this plays out in students' lives.

Understanding Culture and Identity as Dynamic

The work of cultural studies theorists such as Hall (1989, 1990) and Bhabha (1994) provides a foundation for understanding culture and identity that takes into account the continuous process of change and negotiation. These theorists reject the definition of cultural identity based on an understanding of a singular, shared culture of a collective *one true self* shared by people of a common history and ancestry (Hall, 1990). Drawing on this work, I understand *identity* as constructed through discourse and representation and involving the play of power (Hall, 1996). Rather than whole, seamless, or naturally-occurring, culture and identity are the result of differentiation in social relations

precisely because identities are constructed within, not outside discourse, we need to understand them as produced in specific historical and institutional sites within specific discursive formations and practices, by specific enunciative strategies. Moreover, they emerge within the play of specific modalities of power, and thus are more the product of the marking of difference and exclusion, than they are the sign of an identical, naturally-constituted unity. (Hall, 1996, p. 4)

Because identity is constructed through the "play of specific modalities of power, and thus are more the product of the marking of difference and exclusion," (Hall, 1996, p. 4) identity is a *positioning*—political and negotiated.

I understand *discourse* to mean the spoken and written language and images used in popular and academic arenas. Discourse is more than simply a collection of statements or images, but is a set of historically grounded (yet evolving) statements and images that function to create a certain reality (Gee, 1996).[1] For example, the dominant discourse about Asian Americans highlights their status as a model minority. This image of success emphasizes the role of hard work, family support, and cultural values in the high educational attainment of Asian Americans (S. J. Lee, 1996). This dominant discourse of the Asian American model minority positions Asian Americans as the poster-child of American meritocracy, as it simultaneously blames other groups (e.g., African Americans, Latino Americans) for their underachievement (Osajima, 1987).

An important assumption of this understanding of discourse is that some discourses have been so ingrained through repetition that they seem to be natural and have become dominant. The repetition and naturalization of dominant discourses have masked their social and continuous construction. These dominant discourses conceal the existence of competing discourses. From the above example, the dominant discourse of Asian American success masks discourses that account for the struggles of Southeast Asians such as the Lao and Hmong (Ngo, 2006). Because identity is reflective of power and takes place within discursive relations, characterizations of immigrants as traditional, patriarchal, and resistant to assimilationist demands are neither neutral nor harmless. They reflect political positions, values, and social practices (Hall, 1990; Kumashiro, 2002).

From this understanding of *identity* and *discourse,* identity construction involves a double movement, where we are identified by a history of discourses—ideas and images of who we are—and identify ourselves by responding to the representations that have already identified us (Hall, 1996). The ways we respond may repeat, resist, or contradict how we have been identified. As we draw on discourses to make meaning for ourselves, others also use discourses that are available to understand or identify us. For instance, as a person of Vietnamese heritage who has lived in the United States for most of my life, I might identify myself as an Asian American. However, others may identify me as Chinese because my physical appearance matches with what they know about people of Chinese descent. This double movement creates an identity that is "fragmented and fractured; never singular but multiply constructed across different, often intersecting and antagonistic, discourses, practices and positions" (Hall, 1996, p. 4). This understanding of identity as shaped through discourse and representation allows for sites to continuously open for reexpression (Bhabha, 1994; Hall, 1990). Bhabha called the space that opens up for negotiation and change the third space, ambivalent space, or *in-between*. He maintained that "we should remember that it is the 'inter'—the cutting edge of translation and negotiation, the *in-between* space—that carries the burden of the meaning of culture" (Bhabha, 1994, p. 38).

By looking in the *in-between,* we may see how immigrant students work with or rework discourses that have already identified them. Next I draw on data from an ethnographic study[2] with Lao American students at an urban public high school, to illustrate the double movement of identity and the *in-between* of Lao immigrant students' identity.

The Double Movement of Identity
Dominant Discourses at Work: Lumping Lao Students as "Chinese"

One way to think about dominant discourses is to think about the stereotypes or myths that exist and are circulated about different immigrant groups. For immigrants in general, these dominant discourses or stereotypes include the perception that immigrants are a burden on the U.S. economy or take jobs from so-called real Americans. For Asian immigrants in particular, some stereotypes include the perception that Asian immigrants are all computer geniuses, good at math, passive and quiet, or martial arts experts.[3] An important characteristic of stereotypes or dominant discourses is that they lump individuals into one-dimensional, generalizing categories that ignore the complexity of their lives and experiences.

This was the case in my research with Lao immigrant students at Dynamic High School.[4] Dynamic was an urban public high school that enrolled approximately 1,482 students from across the city. The majority of the students were either African American (43%), Asian American (mostly Hmong American) (38%), and White (16%). According to the school brochure, its richness in cultural and ethnic diversity was notable in the 41 languages and dialects spoken by students and staff. Of the large number of Asian American students, the majority were Hmong. Even though the non-Asian students and teachers at Dynamic knew that most of the Asian American students were Hmong, many still referred to all Asian students as Chinese.

The lack of understanding and acknowledgment of the differences within Asian ethnic groups at Dynamic High reflects the dominant ways in which Asian immigrants are represented and understood within the popular imagination, as a homogeneous group who are all the same (S. J. Lee, 1996).[5] Problematically, this obscures the diversity of Asian groups and the variation in immigration experiences, educational attainment, and economic status (Ngo, 2006). Although Asian Americans are comprised of numerous groups, including those of Cambodian, Chinese, East Indian, Filipino, Guamanian, Hawaiian, Hmong, Indonesian, Japanese, Korean, Laotian, Samoan, Taiwanese, and Vietnamese

heritages[6] (Pang, 1990), dominant discourses mask this enormous variety. Individuals of Asian descent are all lumped into simplistic categories such as *Chinese* or *Japanese.*

For example, at Dynamic High, despite the fact that school records revealed that although none of the students were Chinese, all Asian students were labeled as Chinese. Consider what Chintana, one of my Lao student participants, said when I asked her if students and staff knew the difference between Hmong and Lao students:

Chintana: A lot of people like call Asian people like just Chinese or something. I hear it all the time . . . I've heard it like they'll say "That Chinese boy." And I'm sitting here thinking, "He's not Chinese." 'Cause I can tell the difference almost all the time.

Researcher: They don't say he's Hmong or they're all Hmong?

Chintana: No. Some of them say it, because then most of them think that everybody here is Hmong. But most of them think it's like Chinese or something (laughs).

Two discourses about the culture and identity of Asian students dominated at Dynamic High. The first racialized and identified all Asian ethnic groups (e.g., Lao, Hmong, Cambodian) as Asian; and the second identified all Asian students as Chinese. This occurred even though most of the students knew that the majority of the students at the school were Hmong. The remarks of Ms. Anderson, an ESL teacher, highlight the role of the media in framing the identities of Asian immigrant students:

Okay, students who are Hmong obviously know that the Lao kids are Lao. And other Asian kids know. But I think that as far as, if you look at the African kids, they have no idea. No idea who's Hmong and who's Lao and who's Chinese. I mean I've had a lot of the kids in my 6th hour who refer to all Hmong as Chinese. And like Jackie Chan is like their sort of national hero.

In these remarks, Ms. Anderson reiterated the identification of all Asian students as Chinese. Her reference to how non-Asian students perceived Jackie Chan as the national hero for the Asian American students also alludes to the role of popular culture in defining Asian identity and heritage. Informed by popular representation, this understanding exemplifies two stereotypes about individuals of Asian heritage: all Asians look the same and all Asians know martial arts or kung fu (R. Lee, 1999). Such understandings about Asian American students and families do little to capture the change and complexities of their lives in the United States.

Conflicting Discourses: Redefining Identity in the In-Between

In the double movement of identity, our identities are not exclusively determined by dominant discourses of other people. Because culture and identity are shaped within social relationships (Hall, 1996), the work of identity construction is fraught with tensions and disagreements that are belied by notions of identity construction and negotiation that allude to a trouble-free process (West, 2002). At the same time that others use discourses to identify us, we also draw on discourses to make meaning for ourselves. In the *in-between* (Bhabha, 1994) of culture and identity, expectations from others of who we are or should be may collide and conflict with how we want to identify ourselves. Although discourses of the experiences of immigrant families frame the choices and struggles of culture and identity within East/West or immigrant/nonimmigrant binaries, my work with Lao students revealed the salience of "different, often intersecting and antagonistic, discourses, practices and positions" (Hall, 1996, p. 4).

I found that the tensions that arose in students' identity work came from expectations by non-Lao students, as well as family members and Lao peers. For example, in Mindy's case, her association with the Hmong students at the school was problematic to her identity as Lao. As she shared: "I think my friends are getting mad at me 'cause I'm hanging out with too many Hmong people. . . . I think that they think I'm becoming one of them." Friends as well as family accused her of wanting to be Hmong. According to Mindy, her parents asked "Why you trying to be like Hmong people, dying your hair and stuff like that?" Her parents particularly worried that she would "turn out bad":

Mindy: It's like they think if I hang out with Hmong people I'm going to be bad, right? But to me, I hang out with different kind of people, you know and I don't turn out bad. I know what's right and what's wrong sometime.
Researcher: What are your parents afraid of? Like when you say they're afraid you're going to turn out bad—what are they afraid of?
Mindy: Like becoming a slut, like kind of forgetting your own race kind of.
Researcher: What does that mean?
Mindy: Like I would talk American, English at home a lot. They be like "Don't talk American, you're going to forget your own race, you're going to be American" and stuff like that.

In Mindy's experience, her identity work was problematic for her parents and Lao friends in at least two ways. First, speaking English or "American" was an activity that would lead to her forgetting her identity as a Lao person. Second, having Hmong American friends meant that she was choosing a Hmong identity over her Lao identity. This emphasis on her Lao identity is remarkable because she is half Lao and half Vietnamese.

In addition, the presence of multiple discourses at play in Mindy's experiences with her parents is especially notable. From Mindy's account, her parents associated being Hmong with conceptions of Americanization that included putting red or blonde streaks in her long black hair and "turn[ing] out bad." Turning out bad included "forgetting your own race" and being sexually promiscuous or "becoming a slut." This understanding of Hmong culture and identity is also noteworthy because in some ways it echoes popular discourses of Hmong immigrants that emphasize the role of Hmong traditional practices in contributing to the high rate of pregnancy and marriage among

Hmong teenage girls (S. J. Lee, 1997; Ngo, 2002). In other ways, it contradicts the dominant discourse that frames Hmong culture and identity as rooted in tradition. From the perspective of Mindy's Lao parents, what it means to be Hmong links Hmong culture and identity to the harmful influences of Americanization and practices of Western society rather than notions of tradition.

Conclusion

In the social construction of identity, a Lao student may consider herself Asian American, her parents may consider her Lao, and non-Lao students may consider her as Chinese or Asian. The double movement of identity opens up a space of change and negotiation. Here, the identity that individuals such as Lao American students may want to claim is not recognized or misrecognized by others because it disrupts ingrained discourses of who they should be. In Mindy's case, who she thinks she is and the way she wants to represent herself are at odds with perceptions and expectations of friends and family. The culture and identity of immigrant students and families thus cannot be conceptualized simply as something that is static, passed from one generation to the next. Notions of immigrant experiences must move beyond an either–or paradigm (i.e., either one is traditional or modern), toward an understanding of the *in-between* (Bhabha, 1994). In the *in-between* of culture and identity, students such as Mindy are changing what it means to look and behave as a Lao American. Accordingly, perceptions about immigrants must move beyond a culture clash understanding in order to account for the work of immigrants to redefine and reexpress what it means to be parents and youth in U.S. schools and society.

As educators, community members, and policymakers, this means attending to the dominant discourses that we invoke to understand immigrant families. Paying attention to these discourses will allow us to question the assumptions and representations underlying them. For example, we might ask ourselves:

1. What are the binary discourses that we use to understand the educational experiences of immigrant students and families?
2. What are alternative discourses or explanations for understanding the experiences and actions of immigrant students and parents?
3. How might we look at the *in-between* to account for changes as it relates to issues such as gender roles, family authority, identity, and economic survival?

For educators interested in moving beyond a culture clash understanding of immigrant experiences and toward a notion of *in-between,* there are a few practical recommendations to keep in mind. First, it is important to learn about and address the dominant representations or stereotypes of immigrants in general and specific immigrant groups in particular. For example, class lessons might examine the various stereotypes of immigrants, such as the ever-present myth that immigrants are a burden on the U.S. economy.[7] Second, because identity and representation have political underpinnings, it is important to learn and teach about the motivations and contexts for the representations. For instance, stereotypes of Asian Americans as the *yellow peril* and model minority have historical roots in U.S. labor and civil rights movements respectively (R. Lee, 1999). Finally, because culture and identity are in a continuous process of change, it is important to address how this is occurring in the everyday practices, interests, and experiences of immigrant youth and families. Class lessons that delve into the outside school interests of students might reveal, for example, that immigrant adolescents are identifying as hip-hop spoken-word artists.

Additionally, it is important to remember that all discourses are political. All discourses position individuals within specific power relations, and prompt us to attend to certain issues but ignore others. Understanding immigrants as *traditional* positions immigrant youth and families as backward, failing to assimilate, and thwarting assistance (Louwagie & Browning, 2005a, 2005b). This has implications for how we view immigrant students and families, and the types of services and assistance we provide as educators. Consequently, we need to ask: What kinds of educational initiatives are possible by our discourses or understandings? What kinds of initiatives are possible when we position Muslim immigrants as patriarchal and sexist? What kinds of initiatives are possible when we position Vietnamese parents as deeply committed to their children's education? These questions are critical for recognizing the political and educational implications of what we choose to emphasize as educators and researchers—because different discourses make possible different ways of teaching individual students and organizing schools.

Notes

1. See Fairclough (1992), Gee (1996), Mills (1997), Popkewitz and Brennan (1998), and Wodak (1996) for more extensive discussions of discourse.

2. See Ngo (2003) for more information about the study and methods.

3. For a thorough explanation of the dominant stereotypes of Asian Americans, see R. Lee's (1999) *Orientals: Asian Americans in Popular Culture.*

4. All names of people and places are pseudonyms.

5. A resource that examines this stereotype is Soe's film (1986), *All Orientals Look the Same.*

6. Additionally, the U.S. Bureau of the Census included smaller Asian American groups within the category of "All Other Asians" in the 1980 Census: Bangladeshi, Bhutanese, Bornean, Burmese, Celbesian, Cernan, Indochinese, Iwo-Jiman, Javanese, Malayan, Maldivian, Nepali, Okinawan, Sikkimese, Singaporean, and Sri Lankan (Pang, 1990).

7. For resources, see websites such as http://immigrationforum.org/ and http://www.mnadvocates.org.

References

Bhabha, H. (1994). *The location of culture.* New York: Routledge.

Do, A. (2002, January 11). Taking on two worlds. *Orange County Register.* Retrieved November 15, 2006, from http://www.proquest.umi.com.

Fairclough, N. (1992). *Discourse and social change.* Cambridge, England: Polity Press.

Feagans, B. (2006, September 3). Generation 1.5: Young immigrants in two worlds. *The Atlanta Journal—Constitution.* Retrieved November 15, 2006, from http://www.proquest.umi.com

Gee, J. (1996). *Social linguistics and literacies: Ideology and discourses* (2nd ed.). Philadelphia: Falmer Press.

Hall, S. (1989). New ethnicities. In D. Morley & K. H. Chen (Eds.), *Stuart Hall: Critical dialogues in cultural studies* (pp. 441–449). London: Routledge.

Hall, S. (1990). Cultural identity and diaspora. In J. Rutherford (Ed.), *Identity: Community, culture, difference* (pp. 222–239). London: Lawrence and Wishart.

Hall, S. (1996). Introduction: Who needs 'identity'? In S. Hall & P. du Gay (Eds.), *Questions of cultural identity* (pp. 1–17). Thousand Oaks, CA: Sage.

Jaret, C. (1999). Troubled by newcomers: Anti-immigrant attitudes and action during two eras of mass immigration to the United States. *Journal of American Ethnic History, 18,* 9–39.

Kumashiro, K. (2002). Against repetition: Addressing resistance to anti-oppressive change in the practices of learning, teaching, supervising and researching. *Harvard Educational Review, 72,* 67–92.

Lee, R. (1999). *Orientals: Asian Americans in popular culture.* Philadelphia, PA: Temple University Press.

Lee, S. J. (1996). *Unraveling the "model minority" stereotype: Listening to Asian American youth.* New York: Teachers College Press.

Lee, S. J. (1997). The road to college: Hmong American women's pursuit of higher education. *Harvard Educational Review, 67,* 803–827.

Louwagie, P., & Browning, D. (2005a, October 9). Shamed into silence. *Star Tribune.* Retrieved November 15, 2006, from http://www.proquest.umi.com

Louwagie, P., & Browning, D. (2005b, October 10). Shamed into silence: Culture clash can stymie help. *Star Tribune.* Retrieved November 15, 2006, from http://www.proquest.umi.com

Lowe, L. (1996). *Immigrant acts: On Asian American cultural politics.* Durham, NC: Duke University Press.

Mills, S. (1997). *Discourse.* New York: Routledge.

Ngo, B. (2002). Contesting "culture": The perspectives of Hmong American female students on early marriage. *Anthropology and Education Quarterly, 33,* 163–188.

Ngo, B. (2003). Citing discourses: Making sense of homophobia and heteronormativity at Dynamic High School. *Equity and Excellence in Education, 36,* 115–124.

Ngo, B. (2006). Learning from the margins: Southeast and South Asian education in context. *Race, Ethnicity and Education, 9,* 51–65.

Olneck, M. (2003). Immigrants and education in the United States. In J. A. Banks & C. M. Banks (Eds.), *Handbook of research on multicultural education* (pp. 381–403). New York: Macmillan.

Osajima, K. (1987). Asian Americans as the model minority: An analysis of the popular press image in the 1960s and 1980s. In G. Y. Okihiro, S. Hune, A. A. Hansen, & J. M. Lie (Eds.), *Reflections on shattered windows: Promises and prospects for Asian Americans studies* (pp. 166–174). Pullman: Washington State University Press.

Pang, V. (1990). Asian American children: A diverse population. In T. Nakanishi & T. Nishida (Eds.), *The Asian American educational experience* (pp. 167–179). New York: Routledge.

Popkewitz, T., & Brennan, M. (1998). Restructuring of social and political theory in education: Foucault and a social epistemology of school practices. In T. Popkewitz & M. Brennan (Eds.), *Foucault's challenge: Discourse, knowledge and power in education* (pp. 3–35). New York: Teachers College.

Soe, V. (Producer/Director). (1986). *All orientals look the same* [Experimental/Documentary]. Available from the Center for Asian American Media: http://www.asianamericanmedia.org

Wax, E. (1998, May 10). Mother's fray: Culture clash puts special strain on immigrant moms and daughters. *Newsday.* Retrieved November 15, 2006, from http://www.proquest.umi.com

West, T. R. (2002). *Signs of struggle: The rhetorical politics of cultural difference.* New York: SUNY Press.

Wodak, R. (1996). *Disorders of discourse.* New York: Longman Press.

Zhou, M., & Bankston, C. L. (1998). *Growing up American: How Vietnamese children adapt to life in the United States.* New York: Russell Sage Foundation.

Bic Ngo is an assistant professor of immigrant education at the University of Minnesota.

Correspondence should be sent to Bic Ngo, Assistant Professor, Immigrant Education, University of Minnesota, Department of Curriculum and Instruction, 152C Peik Hall, 159 Pillsbury Drive SE, Minneapolis, MN 55455. E-mail: bcngo@umn.edu.

From *Theory Into Practice,* 2008, pp. 4–11. Copyright © 2008 by Taylor & Francis—Philadelphia. Reprinted by permission via Copyright Clearance Center.

One Nation, Many Gods

Seven years ago, Modesto, Calif., became the only school district in the country to require a world religions course for graduation. Now, research shows the course helps reduce religious intolerance among students without undermining students' religious beliefs. The lessons learned in Modesto may provide a helpful roadmap for schools across the nation.

CARRIE KILMAN

In West Virginia, a public high school refuses to remove a painting of Jesus that hangs outside the principal's office. In Georgia, legislators vote to include the Bible in a statewide public school curriculum. And in New York, officials prohibit the scheduling of standardized tests on religious holidays, after protest over a statewide exam held on a Muslim holy day.

For decades, educators have wrestled with how to handle the increasingly diverse religions of an increasingly diverse student body. Sometimes, the line between church and state—what schools can and cannot do under the Constitution—can feel confusing and slippery.

Today, religion has become a subject one high school teacher calls even more controversial than teaching sex-ed. Teachers feel ill-equipped to talk about it. In a post-9-11 world, students increasingly face harassment for what they believe.

And yet, today's students will interact with a far more pluralistic society than their parents or grandparents did. Some educators see in this a call for urgency. If faith-based intolerance is ever to be confronted, they say schools are exactly the place religion should be addressed.

"Schools are the one place where all of these different religions meet," said one educator. "It follows that religious diversity must be dealt with in school curriculum if we're going to learn to live together."

For the past seven years, the school district in Modesto, Calif., has done just that.

After a divisive, public battle over the role of tolerance in the city's schools, a small group of teachers developed a world religions curriculum for every 9th-grade class in the district. Now, Modesto stands out as the only school district in the country that mandates a world religions course for high school graduation.

New research shows the course has increased students' respect for religious diversity. And teachers here hope their efforts will encourage other districts across the country to follow their lead.

California's "Bible Belt"

Modesto was a surprising birthplace for such a risky venture.

The city of about 200,000 sprawls across Northern California's Central Valley, about 90 miles east of San Francisco. Residents call the area the "Bible Belt of California," for its conservative roots and vocal evangelical community. But a growing immigrant population has infused Modesto with a jolt of religious diversity, adding to the mix growing numbers of Buddhists, Hindus, Muslims and Sikhs.

Several years ago, a move to add gay and lesbian students to the school district's safe-schools policy, titled "Principles of Tolerance, Respect and Dignity," caused an uproar among local religious leaders. The conflict lasted for months. Finally, district officials turned to Charles Haynes, director of the Arlington, Va.-based First Amendment Center, for help.

"I thought I was meeting with the committee appointed to deal with this issue," Haynes said. "I went into the school cafeteria, and there was a 'committee' of about 115 people. Everyone wanted a voice in this issue–gay and lesbian students, local pastors, teachers, administrators—but people were speaking past one another."

He suggested they abandon the word "tolerance"—many religious conservatives thought it meant the school district was "taking a stand on homosexuality." Instead, Haynes asked the group whether all students, regardless of their beliefs or lifestyle, had the right to be safe at school and free from bullying.

Everyone agreed.

"The pastor who was in charge of the opposition stood up and said, 'If this is what the district means, we're fully for that. We're Christians—we don't want anyone beat up or hurt'," Haynes recalled. "A gay student stood up and said, 'Well, that's all we want, too.'"

Together, they crafted a new safe-schools policy grounded in the First Amendment right of free expression, and the responsibility to safeguard that right for others.

The school board unanimously adopted it.

From the policy stemmed many new initiatives, such as a character education course and human rights clubs. Among them was a new focus on teaching about religious diversity.

"When you don't know about something, you fear it—and when you fear something, you become more likely to strike out against it," said Modesto teacher Yvonne Taylor. "We wanted students to understand that even if we disagree with a group of people, they still have the right to be here."

"You Can't Teach Religion"

Modesto requires that every 9th-grader in the district enroll in a semester-long world religions course. Ninth grade made sense—students were old enough to handle the subject material, and the emphasis on religious diversity happened to coincide with the district's desire to enhance the 9th-grade history and social studies curriculum. Since then, state standards have changed—the world religions course no longer fulfills specific state curricular requirements, but it's been so successful in changing attitudes that school officials decided to keep the course in place.

"(At the beginning of) every semester, the kids say, 'You can't teach about religion!'" said Jennie Sweeney, the curriculum coordinator who organized the course's development. "And we say, 'Yes, we can—we're going to teach *about* religion, we're not going to *teach* religion.' There's a big difference."

By law, public schools cannot show preference to one religion [although, in implicit ways, many do—see "Because I Had a Turban,"]. Yet they can legally address religion in ways that are both fair and neutral.

Modesto's world religions course is modeled after the same First Amendment principles that guided the safe-schools policy. "You can be staunch in your own personal beliefs, yet also staunch in respecting and protecting the religious liberties of other people," said Sherry Sheppard, who teaches the course at Modesto's Johansen High.

The class begins with an overview of First Amendment rights and responsibilities. Teachers emphasize the importance of respectful inquiry, and students learn catch-phrases for keeping each other in check to minimize disrespectful remarks.

Next, students delve into six religious units, covering Buddhism, Christianity, Hinduism, Islam, Judaism and Sikhism. The class spends equal time on each unit, studying the history of each faith, the basic tenets, and examples of each religion's societal significance (i.e., Hinduism's influence on Gandhi and the concept of nonviolence).

For the sake of neutrality, teachers aren't allowed to share their own faith backgrounds during the semester, nor are outside speakers welcome. Every class in the district reads the same textbook, watches the same videos and follows the same scripted lesson plans. "It can almost feel prescribed," Sheppard said, "but it prevents teachers from sliding in their own biases."

Students, though, are encouraged to share their own beliefs and ask questions.

As a result, the course provides a safe space to talk about sensitive issues in ways that otherwise might be inappropriate or impolite. It's not unusual, for example, for students to come to class with questions about the man wearing a turban in the grocery store, or a person sporting some other form of religious garb.

"They get excited as the course goes on, because they realize it's something they've never learned about before," said Taylor, who also teaches the course at Johansen.

During the course's inaugural semester, a student who was Buddhist left school on a Friday afternoon with a full head of hair and, to everyone's surprise, returned Monday with a shaved head. His uncle had died, and, in his honor, the student became a Buddhist monk over the weekend, committing to six weeks of service to the temple.

The world religions course became a forum where the student could speak openly about his experience. Because the class had spent weeks exploring different aspects of multiple faiths, classmates viewed the student's decision with interest and respectful curiosity instead of derision.

"For a lot of non-Christian kids, they feel validated at school for the first time," Taylor said. "They say, 'I have a voice now, I'm proud of who I am, and now I can share that and talk about it in a safe environment.'"

The district provides an opt-out policy for parents uncomfortable with the curriculum. Since the program's launch seven years ago, fewer than ten parents have taken advantage of the policy.

"My parents thought it was really interesting," said Lakhbir Kaur, now a senior. "They asked a lot of questions and talked about it at dinner. There was some stuff I learned (during the class) about my own religion that I didn't know, and I went home and asked my mom about it. It was eye-opening."

"Not Different after All"

In May 2006, researchers from the First Amendment Center released the results of a comprehensive study of Modesto's world religions course. They wanted to know if teaching

25

Toolbox
10 Tips for Starting a World Religions Curriculum

1. **Involve the community.** Teachers in Modesto invited community members to review the curriculum, hosted a meeting with local faith leaders during the curriculum's development, and toured several local houses of worship. "It gave people a voice in the process, which helped create community buy-in," says one teacher.

2. **Engage diverse voices.** Make sure every religion represented in your area has a place at the table. Be sure to make space for atheism, too.

3. **Build trust.** "People can be suspicious of schools," says one Modesto teacher. "You need to build trust with different key constituencies before you attempt something like this."

4. **Be sensitive.** Religion is a touchy subject. For many people, it's directly connected to culture, language and ethnicity. Recognize and respect the multiple layers of identity at play.

5. **Get district buy-in.** "This cannot be done by one teacher at one school," says another Modesto teacher. Support from the district—in time, money and resources—is key.

6. **Training, training, training.** Recognize that you can never have enough training. Provide it before the semester starts and throughout the year.

7. **Opt-in for teachers.** Some teachers might not feel comfortable teaching about religion, and classes should by taught by teachers who volunteer to teach them.

8. **Communicate with parents.** "At the open house every year, I give parents a briefing," says teacher Sherry Sheppard, at Modesto's Johansen High. "I assure them that my job is to teach and not preach. It has been such an easy thing."

9. **Lay the groundwork for respect.** "I am adamant (in the beginning of the semester) that if students have a comment that may come across as hurtful, they think about it first," says another Johansen teacher. "I get a lot of 'wow, that's interesting.' What they might be thinking is, 'wow, that's weird,' but they don't dare say it."

10. **Maintain neutrality.** "It made a big difference that teachers didn't take sides," says Edward Zeiden, now a senior at Johansen High. Added classmate Amy Boudsady: "It made me feel safe to share my own beliefs. I didn't feel like someone was judging me."

---

about diverse religions had any impact on students' religious tolerance.

"We've never really known what effect it would have if we taught more about different religions in public schools," Haynes said. "We've always said it was a good idea—but in terms of empirical evidence, what it does for our kids, this study is the first indication of what it might do."

Researchers interviewed students before, during and immediately after the semester, and again six months after the course ended. Over and over, they found that students had become more tolerant of other religions and more willing to protect the rights of people of other faiths.

In their own words, students say the course broadened their views and empowered them to fight back against faith-based bullying.

"I didn't know anything about any religion other than mine," said Kristin Busby, now a senior. "By the end [of the semester], we were all much more accepting toward one another. You realize that we're all not that different after all. We all have these necessities, and these religions provide for those necessities, just in different ways."

By the end [of the semester], we were all much more accepting toward one another.

Added Ishmael Athneil, a freshman: "If some of my friends are talking about someone and saying, 'Wow that's weird,' now I can jump in and say, 'Well, actually, this is why he does that.'"

However, this increase in religious tolerance was not accompanied by a change in students' personal religious beliefs, a finding of huge interest to researchers. "This is important," Haynes said. "It means that learning about different religions will not undermine the faith of the family."

Students who began the semester with strong religious convictions ended the semester with the same beliefs.

"My mom and dad were biased against this course," said 9th-grader Richard Dysart. "They were afraid I'd convert and get confused about what my family believes. But if you're part of a culture, you won't switch just by learning about how other people live."

The course's ability to offset religious intolerance was put to the test at the beginning of its second year.

"We had just made it through the first year without a single complaint from a parent," Sheppard said. "We walked into that September feeling kind of cocky. Then 9-11 happened."

The training for the world religions course prepared teachers to handle the issues and questions that arose that year.

"We realized we'd have to be very delicate with this, making sure the difference was explicit between Islam as a religion and the people who committed that act," Sheppard recalled. "We still emphasize that point when we get to Islam."

Across the country, reports of schoolyard harassment against Muslim students escalated in the months immediately following 9–11. In Modesto, not a single act of harassment was reported against a Muslim student during the 2001–2002 school year.

Not in This Alone

These results, teachers said, didn't happen by accident.

The teacher-led committee that created Modesto's curriculum worked closely with the local community during the course's development. First, teachers identified each religion that would comprise the curriculum; next, they worked in teams to research the different faiths.

Part of that research involved field trips. Teachers toured several houses of worship and invited religious leaders from multiple faith backgrounds to attend a meeting at the school, to explain the purpose of the curriculum and ask for input.

Before the course launched, teachers asked local religious representatives to review the textbook. "There are an equal number of pages given to each religion," Sweeney said. "We knew they would count."

In addition, the book contains a section on nonbelievers; whether teachers delve into atheism (some do, some don't) seems to be one of the few ways that different classes deviate from the curriculum.

For all of its successes, researchers did identify some curricular shortcomings. They faulted the Modesto course for failing to address the negative aspects of religions, to give students a more accurate picture. Researchers questioned the policy of forbidding guest speakers, and they suggested that Modesto's teachers would benefit from more robust training.

Teachers, for their part, questioned these criticisms. "They weren't sensitive to what we were trying to do and the limitations we faced," Sweeney said.

Currently, teachers who volunteer to instruct the course must first attend a 30-hour workshop on how to teach about religion. In addition, the district tries to provide time and space throughout the year for the world religions teachers from each campus to meet, share ideas and discuss concerns.

While this in-service training isn't as frequent as the researchers would like, it does add value to teachers' experiences. "We know we're not in this alone," explained Taylor. "I think this is one of the best things I've done in 35 years of teaching."

If Here, Anywhere

The moral of Modesto's success isn't that every district should rush to create its own world religions requirement. "Not all districts can, because there simply isn't room in the curriculum," Haynes said.

But schools *can* reconsider how and what they teach when it comes to religion. More schools could offer world religion electives, improve the religion sections of their social studies curricula, or implement school policies that are more inclusive of diverse faiths (i.e. not scheduling tests on religious holidays).

Specifically, Modesto's success suggests more schools should do the following:

- **Improve teacher training.** "The biggest barriers (to teaching about religion) are not parents or the community or the law," said Haynes. "The biggest barriers are that teachers do not feel prepared to teach about religion."

   Researchers at the First Amendment Center suggest a world religions requirement for every pre-service social studies teacher in the country, religious studies courses incorporated into teacher training programs, and improved in-service training for teachers already on the job.

- **Understand the law.** Many school districts still think it's constitutionally problematic to discuss religion in schools. Some districts think neutrality means silence. Others address some religions but exclude others (i.e. an elective on the Christian Bible, but no equivalent for other religions).

   "Neutrality, in a word, means 'fairness,'" said Haynes. "School officials are supposed to be the fair, honest, neutral brokers who allow various voices to be heard."

- **Work with communities, not against them.** Parents and religious leaders can be seen as the enemies of efforts to address religious pluralism in schools. But teachers in Modesto attribute their success, in part, to how well they worked with the community.

   As a result, Sweeney said, parental complaints have been minimal: "Because we have support from the religious community, I think they've told their members not to worry about this."

- **Consider it a core mission.** "Students *need* to learn these things," said Modesto student Edward Zeiden, of his school's world religions course. "It should be required, just like history."

Resources

The First Amendment Center works to preserve and protect First Amendment freedoms through information and education. The Center serves as a forum for the study and exploration of free-expression issues, including freedom of speech and religion. www.firstamendmentcenter.org

Sponsored by the First Amendment Center, **First Amendment Schools** represent a national initiative designed to transform how schools teach and practice the rights and responsibilities of citizenship that frame civic life in our democracy. www.firstamendmentschools.org

A collaboration of NPR's "Justice Talking" and The New York Times Learning Network, **Justice Learning** uses multimedia, including audio and news articles, to engage high school students in informed political discourse. The website also offers curricular materials and other age-appropriate classroom resources. The "Religion in Schools" section offers an interactive timeline and student quiz.
www.justicelearning.org

The Pew Forum offers a variety of resources that explores the relationship between religion and public schools, including reports, event transcripts, polling data and the latest news.
www.pewforum.org/religion-schools

"Because I Had a Turban"

In almost every public school in the United States, attitudes and behaviors in the classroom presume an unacknowledged, yet pervasive, Christian norm. How does this affect students who are not Christian?

KHYATI Y. JOSHI

In American society, as in many others, religion shapes and informs everything from our language to our social habits. For us, one particular religion plays the hegemonic role: Christianity.

It is celebrated both in our calendars—where school breaks often coincide with Christmas and Easter, but rarely with the major holidays of other religions—and in our curricula, through "seasonal" art projects and activities like Easter egg drawings and "holiday" pageants.

Christianity is present in the turns of phrase from "turning the other cheek" and being a "good Samaritan," to being a "sacrificial lamb."

Taken together, these activities and experiences cause students who identify with Christianity to find their identity affirmed in school. Yet today, our classrooms include students from many religious backgrounds, and this "Christian normalcy" causes those who are not Christian to feel just the opposite.

My research into the life experiences of Hindu, Muslim, and Sikh students of Indian American backgrounds uncovered the hidden cost of this "normalcy" in public schools.

Many students reported school experiences in which their religious identity was ignored, marginalized, or actively discriminated against in a host of ways. The intense turmoil caused by these experiences threatened their ethnic identity development, their relationships with peers and family members, and their academic outcomes.

Their experiences offer insight and guidance for schools and educators.

Family Ties and Feelings of Exclusion

Classroom conversations about going to church, celebrating holidays, or participating in Christian youth group activities produced extreme anxiety for students interviewed during my study.

For many Hindu, Muslim, and Sikh students, religion is intrinsically tied to ethnic identity. Frequently their immigrant parents use religious activities and organizations as a way to gather with people like themselves and transmit culture to their children.

And yet, faced with Christian normalcy and feeling the normal childhood yearning to fit in with peers, many students were embarrassed to be associated with their own families and ethnic communities. Some avoided learning about their home religions.

"I remember at Christmastime having to lie about what my parents got me," said Priti, a Hindu student. Her parents "wouldn't get me too much, because they really didn't have the concept of" Christmas. Priti felt that describing the small gifts she received would emphasize her differentness from her Christian peers.

Priti also described how "on many occasions, when we would celebrate Christian holidays [in class], I definitely get the feeling that I was not a part of that celebration. . . . There wasn't one solitary event, but a string of events for many years that made me feel that I was not part of this group."

Over time, this exclusion caused many students to feel self-conscious and even ashamed of coming from a faith tradition that was not perceived as "normal" by their teachers and classmates.

These feelings often had long-term ramifications—not only in diminished self-esteem, but also in the loss of knowledge about rituals and traditions, of aptitude with the home language, and even of connections with family.

Targets for Discrimination

But Christian normalcy, like religious dominance in many countries, is only one facet of religious oppression, which is not about theology so much as power. A religion becomes oppressive when its followers use it to subordinate the beliefs of others, to marginalize, exclude and deny privileges and access to people of other faiths.

The Indian Americans in my study shared stories of being targeted for discrimination and mockery because of their religions. One young Muslim reported that his homeroom teacher would often duck when he entered the classroom, saying, "You don't have a bomb in that backpack, do you?" The rest of the class had a good laugh, and this student felt compelled to laugh along throughout the school year.

Harpreet, a male Sikh who wears a turban, recalled his high school's annual tradition of hosting a Christmas Dinner for the homeless, where students dressed up as different characters.

His teacher asked Harpreet to dress up as Jafar, the villain from the Disney film *Aladdin,* he said, "because I had a turban." The teacher treated Harpreet's turban as something cartoonish, ignoring its religious significance to Sikhs and conflating it with an Arab cultural emblem.

Other students were told they were "going to hell" or that they and their families needed to "be saved." When teachers overheard comments like these and did not intervene, many students took their silence as an endorsement of religious discrimination.

It's Academic

While many school districts make accommodations for students who are not Christian—for example, by excusing students for certain religious holidays—these accommodations can result in educational experiences that are unequal.

Consider the voice of a 13-year-old Hindu girl from Ohio:

I hate skipping school to celebrate Diwali. After we celebrate, I still have to do all the in-class assignments and the homework for the next day. Now I tell my parents I'd rather just go to school.

"Making up" for religious observances is a burden Christian students do not carry. This reality can make it difficult for some non-Christian students to stay on equal footing with Christian peers, socially and academically.

Another Hindu student, Nikhil, faced a different kind of academic challenge.

Since elementary school, Nikhil had experienced being teased for "praying to cows" and being "reincarnated from a dog." Like many Indian Americans, he developed the habit of keeping his home life separate from his school life.

When his public school's National Honor Society chapter decided to visit different churches to learn about religious diversity, Nikhil offered to share his religious life with his NHS peers.

"I told them that we should go to one of the Hindu services," Nikhil said, "and the NHS faculty sponsor said, 'No, we're not going to do that." When his offer was rejected, Nikhil decided he would stop attending Christian services with the honor society. As a result, he was dismissed from the NHS for "inadequate participation."

Nikhil feared academic retribution if he did anything about the expulsion. "[The NHS advisor] was also my English teacher," he said, "and I was afraid . . . it would reflect on my grade, so I never said anything."

When I interviewed him more than a decade later, Nikhil's voice still quivered with emotion as he recalled feeling "very, very mad. I was graduating in the top five of my class. Everybody around me had the honor stole on except for me—and the only reason was because I refused to go to church."

Making Religion Matter

As practitioners of multicultural education, we must recognize and respond to religion's importance as a cultural marker for many students, Christians and non-Christians alike. We must acknowledge and correct Christian normalcy in our classrooms and curricula. The answer is not to ignore or exclude Christianity; in fact, the opposite is true.

Consider these suggestions:

1. **Know our own students.** There are a lot of religions in the world. Start with the ones present in your classroom.
2. **Learn our ABCDs.** We don't need to be theologians, but we can at least learn the:

   - **A**rchitecture: Know what the house of worship is called, like *mandir* (Hindu), *masjid* or *mosque* (Muslim), and *gurdwara* (Sikh).
   - **B**ooks: Know the name(s) of the religion's holy text(s).
   - **C**ities: Know the names and locations of the religion's holiest cities, like Amritsar (Sikhism), Mecca and Medina (Islam), and Varanasi/Benares (Hinduism).
   - **D**ays: Know the names and meanings of the religion's major holidays, like Diwali and Holi (Hinduism), Ramadan and Eid ul' Fitr (Islam), and Vaisaki (Sikhism).

3. **Recognize religion as part of students' social identities.** Religion and religious institutions are one of the major ways ethnic communities—particularly immigrant communities—organize and gather. Understand how this makes religion especially salient for some students, and how the family's religion may be important even to students who don't see themselves as "religious."
4. **Avoid the urge to "Christianize" religions and holidays.** Observe religious holidays in their own context and their own time, instead of lumping them all together in December. Don't assume holidays that fall close to a Christian holiday on the calendar share the same social or theological meaning. Likewise, don't diminish other religions by drawing analogies to Christian holidays–*e.g.,* saying "Ramadan is like Lent" or "Janmastami is like Christmas."
5. **Include religion in our curricula whenever it's appropriate.** Knowledge about religions is important for students living in our religiously pluralistic democracy, and in our global community. Religions influence the behavior of individuals and nations and have inspired some of the world's most beautiful art, architecture, literature, music, and forms of government. When discussing these subjects, it's okay

to acknowledge religion and its impact. Discuss how different religions deal with the concept at hand.

Understanding religious differences and the role of religion in the contemporary world—and in our students' lives—can alleviate prejudice and help all students grow into the thoughtful global citizens our world requires.

KHYATI Y. JOSHI is an assistant professor in the Peter Sammartino School of Education at Fairleigh Dickinson University in Teaneck, New Jersey. The interviews quoted in this article are also the subject matter of her first book, *New Roots in America's Sacred Ground: Religion, Race and Ethnicity in Indian America* (Rutgers University Press, 2006).

Metaphors of Hope

Refusing to be disheartened by all the negative press surrounding education today, Ms. Chenfeld travels the country and encounters one inspiring educator after another. She tells four of their stories here.

MIMI BRODSKY CHENFELD

On the Big Island of Hawaii, there's a forest of lava-crusted hills and bare corpses of trees called Devastation Trail. Old volcanic eruptions burnt the Ohia trees and left this once-lush terrain barren and ashen.

Walking on the wooden paths through the devastation, one could easily miss the tiny flowers remarkably pushing through the charred earth. The markers that identify these flowers read: Thimbleberry, Swordfern, Creeping Dayflower, and Nutgrass. While others aimed their cameras at the stark, mysterious lava hills, I focused on the flowers. In the midst of such a desolate scene, these perky "signs of life" seemed to be symbols of courage and persistence.

Reading daily the bleak headlines and articles that stress the stress by focusing on bullying, violence, gangs and cliques, and numerous random acts of unkindness and hostility in our seemingly devastated educational landscape, one could easily sink into despair. However, as a stubborn optimist, I always search for markers of thimbleberry, swordfern, creeping dayflower, and nutgrass—metaphors of hope!

When Mr. T (also known as Tom Tenerovich) was moved upstairs after years of teaching kindergarten classes, he observed that second-graders were more vocal, more argumentative, more opinionated! A voracious reader of books about education, he was familiar with many theories and programs. *But reading about ideas is different from doing.*

One idea that intrigued Mr. T was that of Town Meeting. He and his students discussed building a structure that would enable all voices to be heard, problems to be solved, and good listening habits to be formed.[1]

The class added mayor and assistant mayor to the list of jobs on their classroom helpers board. During the year, every student would be assigned to these jobs for a one-week term of office.

The Town Meeting works this way: each week, the mayor and assistant mayor, along with Tom, write an agenda for two, 30- to 40-minute Town Meetings. Any student can submit a proposal for discussion, but it has to be written and include name, date, and the issue to be discussed. Some of the issues concerning the students have included changing seats, playground rules,

classmates being hurtful, picking team members, and activities for "Fun Fridays."

At the Town Meeting, the class discusses the topic and votes to resolve the issue. "Even if they disagree, it's so sweet to hear how they disagree," Tom reports. "They're really beginning to listen to each other." He continues,

> It's amazing the way it works out. None of the kids are bossy when they become mayor. Even our most timid children became good mayors. Believe it or not, one of my most high-maintenance tough kids was the best mayor! He took charge in a fair way—he knew what to do—he behaved appropriately.
>
> Even I became an agenda issue! One of the kids reminded me that I hadn't done something I promised. That was important to the children, and I had to remedy it.

Committees formed from discussions: academic committees, playground committees (to see that no students were left out of games or weren't chosen for teams), and classroom improvement committees. Tom was thrilled to see how the twice-weekly Town Meetings honoring the feelings and agendas of the students carried over into the everyday life of the group. "This really is democracy in action! Points of view are freely expressed. All opinions are valued and respected. You can see and feel the increase of courtesy and kindness."

The school mascot is a bobcat. Tom and his second-graders added the idea of Bobcat Purrs to their Town Meeting. Like "warm fuzzies," pats on the back, recognition of positive acts, observations of improvements, Bobcat Purrs were "built into our meetings," Tom explains, "and became part of our culture. Children wrote up a 'purr,' decorated it, and handed it to the mayor, who read it and presented it. No one was ever left out. We promised *not* to just recognize our best friends. Children looked for what their classmates were doing well. They were very specific."

One student, who had experienced alienation, low self-image, and loneliness in earlier years and whose posture defined his feelings, received a Bobcat Purr during a Town Meeting that stated how proudly he was standing. He was standing up straight! The boy beamed!

Another student who had difficulty finishing her work received a Bobcat Purr from a classmate honoring her for finishing *all* of her work. Everyone rejoiced.

When children live in a climate that accentuates the positive, their eagle eyes catch the flickering light of flames that are almost burnt out.

The picture I want to snap for my Album of Hope is of a proud second-grader standing up straight with the mayor, assistant mayor, his teacher, and all of his classmates honoring him with a Bobcat Purr during the Town Meeting.[2]

Swordfern: Cathy

Cathy Arment and her first-graders are not involved in the building of structures like Town Meetings. With their teacher, this group of students from diverse cultures, races, and religions works hard and plays hard together. Cathy described a memorable scene in a telephone message: "I was reading the children Jonathan London's *Froggy's First Kiss*—you know, for Valentine week. Mim, I looked up from the story to see the children sitting in clusters, their arms around each other, their eyes wide as I turned the pages, so totally involved. I almost began to weep at the sight of their beauty."

Here we have students with Ethiopian, Mexican, Appalachian, Southeast Asian, and African American backgrounds. How did such a diverse group of children learn to love one another?

Here we have students with Ethiopian, Mexican, Appalachian, Southeast Asian, and African American backgrounds—children who are newcomers, some from dysfunctional homes, some from foster homes, some with hardship home lives, some at risk. How did such a diverse group of children learn to love one another?

Cathy and I talked at length. With all the realities of alienation, anxiety, insecurity, and mean-spiritedness that these students face, *how is such a warm and loving environment created?* What is the strategy? What are the techniques? Cathy thought long and hard about these questions. She realized that she did not have a preconceived plan for helping her students build positive classroom relationships. She hadn't adopted a program specifically aimed at such outcomes. Nowhere in her plan book were consciously chosen activities based on proven behavior management theories. *She just did what she did because of who she was and what she believed.* Reviewing her ideas, she said:

> All I can think of is that from day one, we are together. We verbalize feelings—good and bad. We're not afraid to share. From our first moment together, we talked about respecting everyone. Some of my children have heavy accents. They are "different." Many of them have been

made fun of. We talk about how hurtful it is to be teased, to put people down and to be put down. We begin to listen to each other. To care about each other. *My children never, ever tease!* And—I'm a human being, too—I share with them. They'll ask me, "Teacher, what did YOU read? What did YOU do over the weekend? Did YOU have a fun holiday?" When a child has a low day, we all try to cheer that child. Sometimes I have a gray day. The kids will go out of their way to brighten me. They know we stick together, that I care for them very deeply. They know that we are all safe in our room.

When the children wrote and illustrated their "I Have A Dream" papers inspired by Dr. Martin Luther King, Jr.'s famous speech, many of them expressed the warm feelings they experienced in the classroom and wrote dreams like these: "I have a dream to be with my family and to give love to everybody and to care about everybody" (Abigail). "I have a dream that people would be nice to other people and, if people are hurt, other people could help them just like other people help me" (Carissa).

The Israeli-Yemenite dancer Margolith Ovid once said, "The greatest technique in the universe is the technique in the human heart."

The picture I would snap for my Album of Hope is of Cathy's kids, arms around each other, sitting in clusters, listening to Froggy's First Kiss.[3]

Creeping Dayflower: Ms. Gibson

Before the new school year even begins, Dee Gibson sends warm *Welcome to the Family* cards to her future students! These fortunate first-graders know—from everything said and done, from words and actions, activities and discussions, planning and projects—that their class is a second family in which each and every family member is important and connected to everyone else. This is not a theme or a curriculum item or a subject area—*it's the way it is* in Ms. Gibson's class. Because she is passionate, articulate, and committed to creating, with her children and families, a safe, encouraging, caring community that really is a second family (and for some children over the years, a first family!), the experiences of her students are very special. They help one another. They cooperate. They plan and talk together. They are totally involved in the life they share together in this home away from home.

We can't take the environment for granted. We are the architects of the culture of the school, of the program.

When the children were asked such questions as "What is it like being in this kind of class family? What do you do? How do you feel?" the responses were honest and forthcoming:

> We're all together. We get in pods. We work together. If two kids are having an argument, the whole class stops till

we work it out. We really feel like everyone cares about each other.—*Jay*

***

We're like teamwork. We help each other with work and to pick up. Everyone here sticks together —*Lauri*

***

All the kids are friends. Arguing doesn't really happen much—everyone cooperates.—*Ryan*

***

Our teacher treats people fair. The other kids act very kind together. She teaches us how to work together.—*Barrett*

***

We don't really get in fights!—*Nikki*

***

Everybody is nice to each other, and they act like a family. Ms. Gibson is like one of the family.—*Danielle*

The language in this class is the language of respect, acceptance, courtesy, responsibility, and cooperation. It's not limited to a week's celebration of a theme! It's the vocabulary of a close-knit family. That's an everyday reality.

The picture I want to take for my Album of Hope is of the children holding up their summer "Welcome to the Family" cards. A sequel to that picture is of children discovering that the welcome cards were not a gimmick! They were the real thing.[4]

Nutgrass: Anne and Claudette

Partners in Educating All Children Equally (PEACE), Anne Price and Claudette Cole travel to schools, programs, and conferences, spreading very simple messages—especially to administrators who too often don't attend workshops that are aimed directly at the heart. Anne and Claudette remind those directors, managers, principals, and superintendents that their influence in the creation of positive, life-affirming school climates is immeasurable. They *really can* make the difference between the life and death of an entire program or school.

Claudette and Anne discuss ways of helping teachers to develop positive relationships with their students and to motivate the students to develop caring and respectful relationships with one another. What are some suggestions for doing so? Usually, without hesitation, most of the administrators offer such actions as recognizing students, paying attention to them, appreciating their talents and efforts, encouraging them to cooperate with and be considerate of one another, and inviting students to share ideas and input so that they are directly involved in the success of the school.

Claudette and Anne gently turn these ideas around, directing them to the administrators. "Just as we advocate developmentally appropriate practices for teaching children, so we have to apply those ideas to our staff." Anne explains their simple, direct approach: "It's our responsibility to pay attention to the needs of staff so they can meet the children's needs."

What are some of the greatest trouble spots in the dynamics of any school or program? Absenteeism, turnover, bullying, discipline problems, low morale, lack of trust, miscommunication—to name just a few. It's so obvious to Anne and Claudette that these problems, often reflecting a disconnected and resentful staff, carry over to the students and poison the atmosphere. (Think lava!)

Think of ways to inspire and create a healthy workplace for all who spend time there. Claudette asks, "Does the staff feel appreciated? Respected? Do they feel they have ownership of and an investment in the success of the program? Are their efforts and contributions valued? Do we keep all avenues of communication open? Do we trust enough to be honest with each other without fear of reprisal?"

Anne reminds participants in her workshops that we can't take the environment for granted. *We are the architects of the culture of the school, of the program.* "You'll see the difference in an environment where children, staff, families, and communities are nurtured and respected. Ideas flow freely, teamwork flourishes, staff feels open and trusting with each other and with the administration—now, will the turnover be as great? The absenteeism? The low morale?" She challenges her groups to talk honestly about these vital components that make for a healthy, positive school culture.

"And," she warns, "you can't give it if it's not in you to give. That's why we constantly have to think about our commitments, beliefs, and goals. How we feel about those deeper questions will generate our behavior."

Claudette and Anne inspire those who lead to look deeply into their own hearts and souls and honestly find whether their beliefs, actions, and words are in harmony. Their decisions will shape the culture of their schools, affecting children, staff, families, and neighbors.

The image for my Album of Hope is a group of administrators exchanging ideas and experiences, sharing feelings, and being energized by the process and promise of making a real difference in the lives of those they guide.[5]

These are just four examples of courageous, confident, hopeful educators who, like our four brave little flowers, insist on growing through hardened and lava-crusted times! I must tell you, I have gathered hundreds and hundreds of examples of educators throughout the land who inspire and nurture caring, compassionate communities of learners.

All of them give themselves wholly to this "holy" process. Their words aren't slogans. Their promises are not bulletin-board displays or mottos. Their commitments are demonstrated every day by how they meet and greet, listen and talk, share and care in their numerous interactions with children and adults.

They know that nothing is to be taken for granted. Tom's Town Meeting is not guaranteed to succeed. A teacher who does not teach in the "key of life," who doesn't listen to or respect the students, who is rigid and devoid of joy and humor, can follow the recipe for a Town Meeting to the last syllable, but it will yield nothing that will teach the children, *through doing,* the art of building positive classroom relationships.

I have gathered hundreds and hundreds of examples of educators throughout the land who inspire and nurture caring, compassionate communities of learners.

Cathy didn't adopt a specific program. She and her children *are* the program, and their mutuality, kindness, and concern for one another are expressed in everything they do. There is no place for bullying in the safe place of Cathy's classroom. She teaches by heart!

Unless one believes it deeply and demonstrates that belief in everything he or she does (from the smallest acts to the largest), even a stellar concept like *family* will be another act of betrayal. Dee Gibson truly believes in establishing a second family with her children. This is not a once-a-month, set-aside time slot; it's the air they breathe and everything they do. Children are acutely alert to hypocrisy. They know when their teachers speak empty words. Lip service is disservice! They learn those lessons well.

Anne and Claudette, in their workshops, invite administrators to examine their own beliefs, motivations, and actions. Joanne Rooney, in her excellent article "Principals Who Care: A Personal Reflection," wrote:

> Good principals model care. Their words and behavior explicitly show that caring is not optional. Nothing can substitute for this leadership. Phoniness doesn't cut it. No principal can ask any teacher, student, or parent to travel down the uncertain path of caring if the principal will not lead the way.[6]

The way through these often grim times is through dedication and commitment, courage, persistence and fierce optimism. Just as Swordfern, Nutgrass, Creeping Dayflower, and Thimbleberry push their bright colors through seemingly solid lava, countless teachers and administrators shine their lights—brightening the sacred spaces they influence, dotting the charred landscape with blossoms of hope.

Notes

1. Tom was inspired by A. S. Neill, *Summerhill School* (New York: St. Martin's Griffin, 1992).

2. Tom Tenerovich and his second-graders enjoyed their Town Meetings at the Royal Palm Beach Elementary School, Royal Palm Beach, Fla. Tom currently teaches second grade at Equestrian Trails Elementary school in Wellington, Fla.

3. Cathy Arment and her loving first-graders listened to *Froggy's First Kiss* at the Etna Road School, Whitehall-Yearling Public Schools, Whitehall, Ohio, where she was voted Teacher of the Year 2004.

4. Dee Gibson and her family of first-graders thrive in the Walden School, Deerfield Public Schools, Deerfield, Ill. Dee was featured in my guest editorial, "Welcome to the Family," *Early Childhood Education Journal,* Summer 2003, pp. 201–2.

5. Anne Price and Claudette Cole are PEACEmakers in Cleveland, Ohio. You can contact Anne and Claudette at www.peaceeducation.com.

6. Joanne Rooney, "Principals Who Care: A Personal Reflection," *Educational Leadership,* March 2003, p. 77.

MIMI BRODSKY CHENFIELD began teaching in 1956. She works and plays with people of all ages and grade levels throughout the country. Among her books are *Teaching in the Key of Life* (National Association for the Education of Young Children, 1993), *Teaching by Heart* (Redleaf Press, 2001), and *Creative Experiences for Young Children,* 3rd ed. (Heinemann, 2002). She lives in Columbus, Ohio. She dedicates this article to the memory of Pauline Gough, whose life's work, brightening the way for educators and children, is a stellar example of metaphors of hope.

From *Phi Delta Kappan,* by Mimi Brodsky Chenfield, December 2004, pp. 271–275. Copyright © 2004 by Phi Delta Kappan. Reprinted by permission of the publisher and author. Mimi Brodsky Chenfield, teacher/author, has also published TEACHING IN THE KEY OF LIFE (NAEYC), TEACHER BY HEART (Redleaf), and CREATIVE EXPERIENCES FOR YOUNG CHILDREN (Heinemann).

UNIT 2

Examining Schools and Classrooms

Unit Selections

Key Points to Consider

- What is the history for reporting one's heritage in the United States?

- Why is it important for the U.S. census to allow individuals to report their biracial heritage?

- How can schools ensure that all students receive educations that are equitable and excellent?

- What is the concept of social justice in multicultural urban schools?

- What are the classroom implications for teaching social justice in multicultural urban schools?

- Describe productive classrooms as cultures and learning communities.

Student Website
www.mhcls.com

Internet References

Center for Social Justice
   http://csj.georgetown.edu/
Center for Global Development
   http://www.cgdev.org/section/initiatives/_active/globalizationandinequality?gclid=CKTYxrGWxJoCFRufnAodY1Q8sg
PBS: Biracial American Portraits
   http://www.pbs.org/wgbh/pages/frontline/shows/secret/portraits/
Genealogy Organization
   http://www.genealogy.org/
National Association of Social Workers
   http://www.socialworkers.org/pressroom/features/issue/peace.asp
National Economics and Social Rights Initiative
   http://www.nesri.org/?gclid=CIPVtYyWxJoCFRufnAodY1Q8sg
United States Census Bureau Genealogy Data
   http://www.census.gov/genealogy/www/
Urban Education Institute
   http://uei.uchicago.edu/

Classrooms and schools encapsulate hope and promise for the future. Young people come to school everyday wanting to understand themselves, one another, and the greater society. They are eager to interact with their friends, investigate the world around them, and try new experiences. It may seem like students are preoccupied, distracted, and resistant to learning; remember they are attempting to balance acceptance by their peers, compliance with their parents, and respect for their teachers. Fortunately, multicultural education provides the ways, means, and purposes for achieving the balance.

Every school and classroom is a microcosm of the world. People may talk in terms of degrees of diversity, but the references are unsound and unclear. Every group of learners includes individuals who share similarities and offer differences. No two learners are identical in every way, even identical twins. Our cultural characteristics, qualities, and beliefs consist of one's race, ethnicity, gender, social class, religion, nationality, geography, language, size, sexual orientation, abilities, education, interests, and so forth. The list is endless and we customize the categories and descriptors to accommodate our individual situation and need.

Some aspects of our cultural identities remain the same throughout our lives either by chance or by choice. Some aspects of our cultural identities change throughout our lives, again by chance and by choice. Some aspects of our cultural identities are selected for us; some aspects we select ourselves. And, sometimes we make new or different choices as we grow older, move, and experience changes through our lives.

The blend of static and dynamic qualities combined with choice and chance creates our individual being. Choice is the key element. No one is born with bias, prejudice, or stereotyping. These are learned behaviors, and, sadly, they are learned from the people most of us hold near and dear to us: our parents, grandparents, teachers, religious leaders, and community members. Children as young as kindergarten students arrive at school with a predetermined set of beliefs about themselves, one another, and the world. Every kindergarten teacher is fully aware of the conversations and experiences that have taken place in each student's life. Reflect on your own elementary school days and you, too, can recall understanding your peers' cultural characteristics, qualities, and beliefs.

Classrooms and schools may offer the only places where young people can go to safely and comfortably learn about multicultural education in ways that value cultural diversity to enhance their cultural competence. To achieve these outcomes, classroom teachers and school administrators must understand multicultural education in ways that value cultural diversity to ensure cultural competence for everyone, everywhere, and all of the time. This charge is neither quick nor easy. Educators are people who bring their own set of biases, prejudices, and stereotypes learned from an early age and people they love and honor. Educators may or may not have experienced an effective course during their university preparation

© Greatstock Photographic Library/Alamy

programs to equip them with the tools and techniques necessary to ensure democratic principles and social justice in various educational contexts.

And, unfortunately, educators may be expected to follow an agenda imposed on them by their immediate communities, or they may bring their own agendas that usurp cultural competence. These agendas may be overt, meaning that everyone is fully aware of the expectations, or these agendas may be covert meaning that the agendas are not public, they are covered or hidden to fulfill expectations for selected individuals with public awareness. For many years in the United States, classrooms and schools operated with overt agendas that segregated students, teachers, and families. Frequently, information, access, and opportunities were limited to the cultural dominant members of society.

Today, covert agendas can be detected in classrooms and schools. Educators may or may not even realize that they are promoting inequities. Although educators are expected to fulfill state academic standards, classroom teachers and school administrators are the ones who develop their own content curricula, select their instructional strategies, align their assessment techniques, and establish their learning communities. Too often, all school services are not provided to all students. Questions arise related to the students who are placed in special services and detention. Perhaps classrooms and schools need to examine their practices so all students feel safe, welcomed, and wanted.

U.S. schools are a long way from achieving a teaching force that replicates the country's demographics in the P-12th grade classrooms as well as in higher education. This means that every teacher in every educational setting must ensure equity and excellence for all students. Teacher education programs must focus on providing specific courses that examine cultural competence accompanied with pedagogy for valuing cultural diversity effectively. Multicultural education must be present in the curriculum, taught directly to all students at all ages and stages, infused into all courses, and modeled by all educators.

Extensive, not selective, cultural competence must be present in all formal and informal, direct and indirect exchanges in all educational settings. Teacher educators must accept their responsibilities for preparing teacher candidates for today's world; school administrators must ensure that the cultural competence is demonstrated in all communities of learning and systems of classroom management and school disciplinary programs.

The articles in Unit 2 offer theory, research, and practices that prepare teacher candidates, classroom teachers, school administrators, teacher educators, and educational researchers for investigating schools and classrooms. The examination processes must be organized and methodical in order to collect useful data to be analyzed productively. Schools and classrooms offer laboratories of human interactions that educators and policy makers need to know and understand completely so sound decisions can be formulated that not only guide and fund each institution's future, but produce educated individuals ready for life and strengthen society.

"What Are You?" Biracial Children in the Classroom

TRACI P. BAXLEY

Over the last 30 years, biracial individuals have become one of the fastest growing populations in the United States. Despite this rapid growth, these citizens are only slowly beginning to be acknowledged among monoracial groups and in academia ("New Way," 2001; Root, 1996; Wardle, 2007). Because biracial identities "potentially disrupt the white/'of color' dichotomy, and thus call into question the assumptions on which racial inequality is based," society has a difficult time acknowledging this section of the population (Dutro, Kazemi, & Balf 2005, p. 98).

Biracial heritage can mean mixed parentage of any kind. This can include, but is not limited to, African American, white, Latino, Asian, and Native American. "Biracial," "interracial," "multiracial," and "mixed-race" are used interchangeably and are often self-prescribed by individuals and their families (McClain, 2004; Root, 1996; Wardle, 1992). As this group increases in the general population, teachers are beginning to see more of these children in their classrooms. How are biracial children different from monoracial children? How do biracial children challenge us to think differently about racial identity and curricular issues in our classrooms?

Historical Glance at Biracial Children

Biracial children and their families are often marginalized by members of monoracial heritage, and specifically by leaders of minority communities (Root, 1996; Wardle, 2006). According to Brunsma (2005), biracial people have always been an issue for U.S. society, because they go against the structure of American's racial order and white privilege preservation. Many white slave owners and enslaved black women produced light-skinned offspring, known as "mulattoes," who sometimes looked more like the fathers than their mothers. Having a biracial heritage was not a choice at the time and these children were categorized not by their appearance, but rather by the "one drop rule," meaning if one had *any* known African ancestry, one was considered black both legally and socially (Tatum, 1997). The "one drop rule" was established by the U.S. Census Bureau. Before the 1920s, the Census count categorized "mulatto" and "pure Negro." Between the 1920s and 1960s, the previous categories were dropped and replaced with "black," as defined by the "one drop rule."

In 1967, a Supreme Court ruling in the case of *Loving v. Virginia* overturned the remaining laws prohibiting interracial marriages (FindLaw, 2007). The ruling not only helped remove the legal taboo, it may have increased acceptance of, and therefore the number of, interracial marriages in the United States.

Not until the 2000 Census, however, were Americans given the opportunity to identify themselves as multiracial (CensusScope, n.d.; "New Way," 2001). About 2.4 percent of Americans (equal to about 6.8 million people) were able to validate all of their heritages. The four most commonly reported interracial categories were white and some other race—white and American Indian, white and Asian, and white and black. From the multiracial community's perspective, this was a giant step in the right direction. However, many minority groups, including the National Association for the Advancement of Colored People and the National Asian Pacific American Legal Consortium, were not in favor of this new Census category because of the possibility of jeopardizing federal funds, civil rights laws, and voting rights issues ("New Way," 2001). Selecting more than one race can affect the number of people who previously checked one of the single minority boxes.

Biracial Identity

Experts recognize that biracial identity development is different from that of white and minority children (Tatum, 1997; Wardle, 1992). Multiple factors should be considered when racial identity is developing, including individual personalities and phenotype, familial relationships and racial identities, and geographical locations and local communities (Root, 1996; Tatum, 1997). Root (1996) recognizes five possible options for biracial identity: 1) accept the racial identity given by society; 2) identify with the minority race; 3) identify as white, if the individual physical features allow; 4) identify as "biracial" (no individual race identified); and 5) identify with more than one race. Root (1996) states that any of these choices can be positive if the individual makes that choice and if that individual doesn't feel compromised or marginalized by his/her choice.

Earlier studies concluded that biracial children were confused about their identity due to their lack of ability to connect completely to either of their heritages (Brandell, 1988; Gibbs, 1987; Herring, 1992). More recently, researchers believe that unresolved identity issues remain for biracial children because their unique heritages are not acknowledged by schools or society in general (Tatum, 1997; Wardle, 1992). In spite of this resistance from society, biracial citizens have demonstrated a sense of achievement, positive self-awareness, and emotional well-being (Tatum, 1997; Tizard & Phoenix, 1995).

Wardle (2007), when analyzing current child development textbooks, found that only two of 12 books addressed multiracial children at all. Wardle also addressed the absence of biracial people in many multicultural education books that focus solely on monoracial and monoethnic groups of people. Wardle suggests that biracial children are not included within the diversity construct of academia because multicultural and diversity experts view America as a "salad bowl" with separate racial/ethnic contributions, view diversity from a narrow-minded American viewpoint, and rely on one critical theory—the ownership of power—that requires each race/ethnic group to be completely separate in a hierarchically oppressed system.

Classroom Practices to Support Biracial Children

The 2000 Census revealed that approximately 4 percent of all children under 18 in the United States are multiracial, and that there are 1.6 million interracial married couples (CensusScope, n.d.). This cannot be ignored when it comes to classroom practices. Teachers who say they treat everyone in the class "the same" need to re-evaluate the idea of equity, ensuring that *every* student is afforded opportunities for academic excellence, and begin to acknowledge their own misconceptions and discomforts when addressing racial issues and identity in their classrooms. This includes investigating their personal stance regarding biracial children (Wardle, 1992). When conducting a self-analysis, a teacher might ask such questions as: How do I feel about interracial marriages? What preconceived notions do I have about biracial people? What have my experiences been with biracial people? Do these experiences impact my perceptions about biracial people? If so, what can I do about it? (Harris, 2002; Tatum, 1997). Biracial parents often feel as if "at best, teachers do not know how to support their children's healthy identity development in the classroom and, at worst, force them to identify with their parent of color, or parent of lowest status" (Wardle & Cruz-Janzen, 2004, p. 13).

In 2002, Harris found that school personnel who were actively engaged in cultural diversity and awareness programs held more accurate perceptions of biracial children. Ignoring students' racial identities and being "color blind" is actually a disservice, not only to biracial students, but also to all students. Biracial individuals may begin their schooling having embraced their double heritage and possessing positive self-images; however, their monoracial classmates may not understand them, and, even worse, may have preconceived notions regarding race. Biracial

children who appear to "look black" may be taunted by monoracial black students for being light-skinned and having curly hair. Similarly, a biracial child who appears to be more "white" may receive negative comments from peers when her black parent enters the classroom. Living in a racially and culturally conscious society dictates that the classroom climate should deal fairly with racially charged issues and enable students to work toward positive solutions.

The parents of biracial children hold various views regarding their children's identity. Therefore, it is imperative that teachers communicate with these parents and ask them what racial designation they feel most appropriately conveys their child's heritage. More and more parents are teaching their children to embrace the term "biracial" in order to identify with both heritages (Tatum, 1997). Teachers can develop appropriate activities for their curriculum by listening to parents' suggestions regarding ways to increase awareness of biracial children.

The growth in the number of biracial students in classrooms requires educators to examine their instructional practices and evaluate any adjustments in order to acknowledge and accommodate this population. According to Wardle and Cruz-Janzen (2004), biracial students are "totally invisible in the schools' curriculum: no stories, pictures, articles and reports, books or textbook items that reflect their unique family experiences" (p. 13). Biracial students present a distinctive challenge to educators partly because of prevailing stereotypes that surround their identity. One stereotype is that biracial children must *choose* to identify with one racial heritage only, usually that of a minority heritage (Harris, 2002; Wardle, 2006). Although this practice may have held sway in the past, thereby causing feelings of guilt over the rejection of the other parent, the last 30 years have given biracial children more choices. Biracial youth are proud of their heritages and are becoming more proactive in speaking out against the racism and opposition around them. Organizations, such as the Association of Multi-Ethnic Americans (AMEA), have sprung up as resources to support multiracial families while educating people from monoracial backgrounds. Teachers who want to address issues regarding biracial students can find a wealth of information from these organizations.

Another stereotype is that biracial students do not want to talk about their racial identity or that they have racial identity issues (Harris, 2002; Tatum, 1997; Wardle, 2006). While some may find it difficult to discuss these issues, educators need to make certain that their questions are sincere and nonjudgmental (Harris, 2002). Many families of biracial children are proactive in communicating to their children who they are and teaching them to have pride in their background (Wardle & Cruz-Janzen, 2004). Teachers need to include an extensive array of approaches and practices in their instruction in order to encourage peers to acknowledge and accept biracial children, as well as to support biracial children in developing positive identities. In addition, teachers should model appropriate ways to engage in discussions focused on people's similarities and differences.

We must move beyond what Banks (2003) calls the "heroes and holidays" approach to teaching multicultural education, in which only surface level concepts are being taught but the mainstream curriculum remains the same. According to Wardle and Cruz-Janzen

(2004), this approach "marginalizes and trivializes" non-mainstream white cultures (p. 40). Instead, teachers need to encourage students to shift to Banks' (2003) social action approach. This approach is more comprehensive and means that students must engage in problem-solving and critical thinking activities that require them to *evaluate* and *take action* on social issues.

Balf's 4th-and 5th-grade class was assigned a critical literacy culture project in which three biracial students were able to reveal both parts of their heritage and discuss it with their peers (Dutro, Kazemi, & Balf 2005). Most classmates were not aware of the students' backgrounds. From this assignment, subsequent whole-group discussions became necessary in order for the biracial students to articulate how they felt, both positively and negatively, about being biracial. Ultimately, these discussions became insightful for the researchers, the teacher, and the other students. More important, it changed the way the monoracial students viewed the biracial students in the class.

Biracial students should see themselves in the curriculum through famous biracial or multiracial historical individuals, such as George Washington Carver, Frederick Douglass, W. E. B. DuBois, as well as more contemporary ones, such as Bob Marley, Tiger Woods, Colin Powell, Halle Berry, Derek Jeter, Alicia Keys, and Barack Obama. Also, inviting members from the local community into schools to reinforce the presence of biracial role models not only validates racial identity for biracial students, but also helps white and other minority children recognize the growing number of biracial and multiracial people around them. Having real role models is crucial to students' overall success and positive racial identity (Wardle & Cruz-Janzen, 2004).

Finally, teachers should supply their classroom libraries with picture books, adolescent novels, and reference books that focus on biracial children. This requires effort on the teachers' part, due to many schools' and libraries' lack of resources about biracial children. The following list of resources may be helpful in supporting teachers as they incorporate culturally responsive practices in their classrooms.

Reference Books

Dalmage, H. M. (2000). *Tripping on the color line: Black-white multiracial families in a racially divided world.* New Brunswick, NJ: Rutgers University Press.

Gaskins, P. F. (1999). *What are you?: Voices of mixed-race young people.* New York: Henry Holt & Company.

Nissel, A. (2006). *Mixed: My life in black & white.* New York: Random House Publishing Group.

Rockquemore, K. (2005). *Raising biracial children.* New York: AltaMira Press.

Wright, M. A. (1998). *I'm chocolate, you're vanilla: Raising healthy black and biracial children in a race-conscious world.* San Francisco: Jossey-Bass.

Picture Books

Ada, A. F. *I love Saturdays y Domingos.* New York: Atheneum.

Adoff, A. (1973). *Black is brown is tan.* New York: Harper.

Adoff, A. (1991). *Hard to be six.* New York: Lothrop.

Cheng, A. (2000). *Grandfather counts.* New York: Lee & Low.

Cisneros, S. (1994). *Hairs/Pelitos.* New York: Knopf.

Cole, H., & Vogl, N. (2005). *Am I a color too?* Bellevue, WA: Illumination Arts Publishing Company.

Davol, M. W. (1993). *Black, white, just right.* Morton Grove, IL: Albert Whitman & Company.

Edmonds, L. (2004). *An African princess.* Cambridge, MA: Candlewick Press.

Friedman, I. (1984). *How my parents learned to eat.* New York: Houghton.

Hoffman, M. (1990). *Nancy no-size.* New York: Mammoth.

Igus, T., & Sisnett, A. (1996). *Two Mrs. Gibsons.* New York: Little Book Press.

Johnson, A. (1996). *The aunt in our house.* New York: Orchard Books.

Katz, K. (1999). *The color of us.* New York: Henry Holt & Company.

Lamperti, N. (2000). *Brown like me.* Norwich, VT: New Victoria Publisher.

Little, O. M. (1996). *Yoshiko and the foreigner.* New York: Farrar Straus & Giroux.

Mills, C. (1992). *A visit to Amy-Claire.* New York: Macmillan.

Monk, I. (1998). *Hope.* New York: Carolrhoda Books.

Rattigan, J. K. (1993). *Dumpling soup.* New York: Little, Brown Books.

Ringgold, F. (1996). *Bonjour, Lonnie.* New York: Hyperion.

Spohn, D. (1991). *Winter wood.* New York: Lothrop.

Straight, S. (1995). *Bear E. Bear.* New York: Hyperion.

Wing, N. (1999). *Jalapeno bagels.* New York: Atheneum.

Wyeth, D. S. (1996). *Ginger brown: Too many houses.* New York: Random House.

Adolescent Books

Curry, J. (2005). *Black canary.* New York: Simon & Schuster Children's Publishing Division.

Forrester, S. (1999). *Dust from old bones.* New York: HarperCollins.

Meyer, C. (2007). *Jubilee journey.* New York: Harcourt.

Nash, R. D. (1995). *Coping as a biracial/ biethnic teen.* New York: The Rosen Publishing Group.

Viglucci, C. P. (1996). *Sun dance at turtle rock.* Rochester, NY: Stone Pine Books.

Woodson, J. (2003). *The house you pass on the way.* New York: Puffin Books.

Wyeth, D. S. (1995). *The world of daughter McGuire.* New York: Yearling Books.

Websites

Association of Multi-Ethnic Americans (AMEA): www.ameasite.org

Center for the Study of Biracial Children: www.csbc.cncfamily.com/

Interracial Voices: www.interracialvoice.com

The Multiracial Activist: www.multiracial.com

New People E-Magazine: www.newpeoplemagazine.com

Representation of Mixed Race People: www.mixedfolks.com

References

Banks, J. A. (2003). *Teaching strategies for ethnic studies* (7th ed.). New York: Pearson Education Group.

Brandell, J. R. (1988). Treatment of the biracial child: Theoretical and clinical issues. *Journal of Multicultural Counseling and Development, 16,* 176–187.

Brunsma, D. L. (2005). Interracial families and the racial identification of mixed-raced children: Evidence from the early childhood longitudinal study. *Social Forces, 84*(2), 1131–1157.

CensusScope. (n.d.). Retrieved September 29, 2007, from www.censusscope.org/us/chart_multi.html

Dutro, E., Kazemi, E., & Balf, R. (2005). The aftermath of "you're only half": Multiracial identities in the literacy classroom. *Language Arts, 83*(2), 96–106.

FindLaw. (2007). *The fortieth anniversary of Loving v. Virginia: The personal and cultural legacy of the case that ended legal prohibitions on interracial marriage.* Retrieved September 27, 2007, from http://communities.justicetalking.org/blogs/findlaw/archive/2007/05/29/the-fortieth-anniversary-of-loving-v-virginia-the-personal-and-cultural-legacy-of-the-case-that-ended-legal-prohibitions-on-interracial-marriage-part-one-in-a-two-part-series.aspx

Gibbs, J. T. (1987). Identity and marginality: Issues in the treatment of biracial adolescents. *American Journal of Orthopsychiatry, 57,* 265–278.

Harris, H. (2002). School counselors' perceptions of biracial children: Pilot study. *Professional School Counseling Online.* Retrieved October 6, 2007, from http://findarticles.com/p/articles/mi_m0KOC/is_2_6/ai_96194762

Herring, P. D. (1992). Biracial children: An increasing concern for elementary and middle school counselors. *Elementary School Guidance and Counseling, 27,* 123–130.

Lanier, S. (2000). *Jefferson's children: The story of one American family.* New York: Random House Books for Young Readers.

McClain, C. S. (2004). Black by choice: Identity preferences of Americans of black/white parentage. *The Black Scholar, 34*(2), 43–54.

New way to measure America. (2001). Retrieved September 8, 2007, from www.tolerance.org/news/article_print.jsp?id=140

Root, M. (1996). A bill of rights for racially mixed people. In M. Root (Ed.), *The multiracial experience: Racial boarders as the new frontier.* Thousand Oaks, CA: Sage.

Tatum, B. D. (1997). *"Why are all the black kids sitting together in the cafeteria?" And other conversations about race.* New York: Basic Books.

Tizard, B., & Phoenix, A. (1995). The identity of mixed parentage adolescents. *Journal of Child Psychology and Psychiatry, 36,* 1399–1410.

Wardle, F. (1992). Supporting the biracial children in the school setting. *Education & Treatment of Children, 15*(2), 163.

Wardle, F. (2006). *Myths and realities.* Retrieved September 13, 2007, from http://csbchome.org/

Wardle, F. (2007). *Why diversity experts hate the multiracial movement.* Retrieved September 13, 2007, from http://csbchome.org/

Wardle, F., & Cruz-Janzen, M. I. (2004). *Meeting the needs of multiethnic and multiracial children in schools.* New York: Pearson Education.

TRACI P. BAXLEY is Assistant Professor of Literacy, Department of Teaching and Learning, Florida Atlantic University, Boca Raton.

Author Note—Traci P. Baxley is the mother of four biracial children.

Dare to Be Different

Can a school choose its own path despite the pressures of accountability? In the end, Ms. Wassermann says, it is possible to act on our beliefs within the constraints that bind us.

Selma Wassermann

Charles Dickens Elementary School, with its scarlet brick exterior, is a hundred-year-old relic from a time when schools were built as no-nonsense fortresses to contain and socialize a swelling immigrant population. In spite of its down-at-the-heels condition, it manages to retain its grandeur, wearing its red coat as a banner of bravado: Dare to Be Different. For Charles Dickens Elementary is as distinct in its ethos as in its appearance from most other public schools in the city of Vancouver—and perhaps throughout the entire province of British Columbia.

The Vietnamese pho shops and other low-rent cafés that hawk sushi, samosas, pizza, and dim sum on the Kingsway, just up the block, manifest the diversity of the area and signal the ethnic mix of the children in the school. Many of them are new Canadians; some speak English as yet haltingly; others, not quite yet. In Annie O'Donaghue's class of third- through fifth-graders, a children-drawn world map on the bulletin board shows the students' countries of origin: El Salvador, Honduras, India, Canada, Portugal, China, Vietnam, Philippines, Ireland. Many of the children who are identified as coming from Canada are of First Nations heritage.

Dickens is not the school one would have picked as most likely to defy every new curriculum du jour handed down by school boards and ministries of education over the last 30 years. It is certainly not the school one would have picked to remain true to its child-centered roots, facing off against such educational tsunamis as the back-to-basics movement, Madeline Hunter's direct instruction, and now the high-stakes testing madness that is passing for educational quality. And this is certainly not the school, given the challenges of the student population, that one would have picked to demonstrate such high performance levels, showing us once again what many educators know: that given the "right stuff"—the right teachers, the right administration, the right conditions—all children can be successful learners.

I came to visit Charles Dickens and left humbled at what I saw, for surely this is the kind of school and the quality of education that we all say we want for our children. I wanted to know what made it "work" and how, in the past 20 years, it has held onto its autonomy and endured as a beacon of what a school can and should be.

Scenes from the School

I walk up the steep stone steps and enter a large hallway, looking for the general office. The floor is patterned linoleum worn by the footsteps of hundreds and thousands of winter boots, but the visitor's eye is immediately drawn to the colors—children's art on every wall, including large-scale murals painted directly on the hallway lockers. Even the tops of the lockers are used to display children's dioramas. The colorful exhibits speak of the value put on children's creative work, and it is obvious that the students themselves, not the teachers, have put this art on display. In the rear area of the hallway, under the staircase, an old couch, some easy chairs, and a small bookcase containing paperback books and magazines make an informal reading corner. No one is on guard here; all the doors are unlocked, and the school can be entered from any side. There is a sense of "non-orderliness" here—not sloppy or unclean, but put together by children. The informality of it all is striking, and it is immediately clear that children own this environment and that order and control are not key issues in this school.

John Perpich, principal of Charles Dickens Elementary School for the last six years, escorts me upstairs to Annie O'Donaghue's classroom. Like every other class in the school, this is a multi-age grouping: grades 3, 4, and 5 combined. The rationale for multi-age grouping, Perpich says, is that the numbers of same-age children in the school population of 455 children do not allow for even distribution into grade-level classes. He smiles when he says this, suggesting a hidden agenda, which he immediately reveals. This school believes in multi-age grouping. It is a mainstay of the program. Insofar as logistics permit, teachers work with the same group of children over a three-year period, getting to know them well enough to understand individual learning needs and provide appropriate instruction that addresses those needs. Perpich says that in single-year transitions, it often takes teachers about six weeks to "learn" the learning styles of each new student. In the multi-age arrangement, teachers and students simply pick up in September where they left off in June—a seamless continuum rather than a brand-new experience. It is the kind of organization that allows for and facilitates continuous student learning.

Another advantage of multi-age grouping is that it implants in students the notion that their classroom is a family, in which the older children look out for the younger ones, caring for them, helping them out socially and educationally, and taking responsibility for being the "older brothers and sisters." This outlook filters down through the ages, so that when the "littles" move up the chronological ladder and become the "olders," they too take on the mantle of helpers and caretakers. It becomes natural for children to work with those of their own age, with some who are younger, and with some who are older. Age demarcations that contribute to unhealthy social attitudes simply do not exist here.

My eyes scan the classroom. Bulletin boards "owned" by the children display poems, stories, artwork, and newspaper clippings with headlines such as "Don Baker, 41, Pleads Guilty to Raping Prostitutes, Sex with Kids," and "Huge Crowds Throng St. Peter's Square," and "Canada's Leading Architect Arthur Erikson Puts His Touch on New Tower." I am immediately reminded of Sylvia Ashton-Warner's advice to teachers: "Let life come in the door."[1] If these are the headlines that children see on newsstands and on the kitchen tables in their homes, why should they not be put under thoughtful scrutiny in the classroom?

> After each reading, the children offer feedback, and I hear critiques that go to the heart of what makes a poem good—descriptor words, imagery, cadence, the ability to evoke pictures in the mind.

The informality I observed in the corridor carries over into the classroom. Annie sits on a low chair, and the children gather around her. They are having "writer's workshop," in which they share their poetry with one another and solicit informed feedback. Their poems reflect a previous lesson on alliteration and imagery, and it appears that even children new to English can use language in spectacular and powerful ways. After each reading, the children call on their classmates who raise their hands to offer feedback, and I

hear critiques that go to the heart of what makes a poem good—descriptor words, imagery, cadence, the ability to evoke pictures in the mind. These poems are first drafts, and the children, after reading and feedback, will have an opportunity to redraft until the poems reach their final, polished stage. In this group of 24 mixed-age children, there is no sign of restlessness or inattention. In fact, there is a calmness here and an interest in the work that is palpable. Critical feedback is focused on what's good and what might be added to strengthen the poem. It is always respectful, a learned skill, and a key aspect of "writer's workshop." After the readings, the children leave the whole group to work individually to redraft their poems. When Annie has to leave the room, the children seem unaware that she has gone; they simply continue with their work, interacting with one another, talking quietly, and some coming over to visit with me, swarming like butterflies.

"So how old are you, anyway?" Rahul asks, looking me over as if I were last week's hamburger.

"Hmm," I look him in the eye. "What would you think?"

The children appraise me and I wonder if I haven't given them license to stretch the truth.

"I think you're 49," Christina says in all seriousness.

"Forty-nine!" I gasp, astonished at this gift.

"But don't worry," she quickly replies. "You only look 45."

They are as close to Ashton-Warner's "natural child" as I have seen in many, many school visits.[2]

Back at the office, Perpich hands me the recent evaluations of students' progress in "meeting writing goals." The table for spring 2005 presents data on writing development in grades 5, 6, and 7. At the grade-7 level, a total of four children have been recorded as "not meeting expectations." Seventeen children are "minimally meeting expectations." Fifty-three children are "meeting expectations." And 26 children are "exceeding expectations," making a total of 96% of seventh-graders who are "meeting or exceeding the standards for that grade level." Perpich says that "we are still working on the total of 36% from combined grades 5, 6, and 7 who are not yet, or minimally, meeting expectations, which is largely due to the numbers of ESL children in that group." In the last year, there was a 40% increase in the number of children meeting or exceeding expectations in literacy, and the expectation is that the coming year will show similar if not better results.

Keys to the School Operation

When parents enroll their children at Charles Dickens, they are handed a brochure with the mission statement of the school, developed by the previous principal, Corine Clark, her staff, and a group of parents. On the front of the brochure, a photo of the school caps the statement: "Together we bring alive our commitment to develop each child's potential in all domains through a long-established philosophy built on mutual respect, continuous learning, and opportunities for leadership within a child-centered, multi-aged framework." This statement is expanded in the list of beliefs that underlie the operating practices of the school:

- Learning requires the active participation of the learner.
- People learn in different ways and at different rates.
- Learning is built on individual and social processes.
- The learner is the focus of education, not the curriculum.
- The integration of subjects is necessary.
- Curiosity, creativity, and cooperation should be nurtured.
- Creative and critical problem-solving skills should be taught.
- Play is a condition of learning.
- Questions should be valued.
- A sense of responsibility in decision making should be fostered.
- A sense of self as an individual and as part of the group is important.

The brochure introduces parents to the specific features of the school that are based on these beliefs: an orientation toward continuous progress; appropriate evaluation of progress; schoolwide team-teaching; anecdotal reporting to parents, instead of letter grades; a collegial and collaborative working relationship between teachers and administrators, with consensus decision making in staff meetings; mentoring for student teachers who come from the two major universities' teacher training programs; advocacy teams to recommend school policy directions and school improvement plans; an active student council; and a parent involvement advocacy team and parent advisory council. Reading the brochure, I am reminded of the quote "What a wise and good parent will desire for his own child, a nation must desire for all children"[3] and think sadly how far so many schools have strayed from that standard.

While any child from the school catchment area may attend Charles Dickens Elementary School, out-of-district parents who are interested in having their children attend Dickens can apply for admission. There is currently a waiting list of applicants; many parents willingly drive their children across the city to attend the school.

A Little History

John Wormsbecker, former assistant superintendent of schools in Vancouver, talked to me about early days, when "open education" was being looked to as an antidote to the "crisis in the classroom" arising from too much emphasis on silence, obedience, and workbook and textbook exercises that numbed the mind and depleted the soul.[4] In the early seventies, groups of educators from North America undertook educational pilgrimages to the U.K. to see first-hand the child-centered programs that were part of the British Primary School movement. (After more than 20 successful years of operation, open education in Great Britain was swept away by the broom of the "iron lady," Prime Minister Margaret Thatcher, who gleefully presided over its demise. This was not a matter of what was good for children; it was purely a matter of economics and budget cutting.)

During the 1970s, Wormsbecker and others from the Vancouver District Office went to England to see for themselves what the British primary classroom looked like and had to offer teachers and students in Vancouver. When they returned, they brought over specialists to give workshops and provide support to teachers and schools in Vancouver that tilted in favor of more child-centered programs. The child-centered philosophy then spread throughout British Columbia (as it did in places in the U.S.), and more child-centered programs appeared in provincial public school classrooms. While many Vancouver schools were initially involved, the programs began to falter during the reactive "back-to-basics" thrust of the 1980s. Although one can still find classrooms throughout the province where teachers remain wedded to their child-centered practices, it is rare today to find an entire school that is wholly consistent in its dedication to such principles.

When the honeymoon with open education was over, Dickens found itself, like other schools, with a few teachers outside the mainstream whose practice was guided by their open education philosophy. The arrival in 1988 of George Rooney, the new principal, changed all of that. Rooney, credited with the resurrection of open education at Charles Dickens, stood by his child-centered beliefs and, slowly but surely, took the steps that would ensure that Dickens became a lighthouse school for child-centered education. Rooney, who retired in 1995, was succeeded by Tom Robb and then Corine Clark, both of whom committed themselves to carrying on the child-centered programs. When John Perpich took over the administrative reins, he willingly accepted the responsibility of keeping it all alive.

What Makes Dickens Run?

Dickens has officially been granted "alternative school" status by the ministry of education and the Vancouver school board. This designation gives them more degrees of freedom and allows them to depart, in giant steps, from mainstream practices seen throughout the district. For example, standardized tests, such as the CAT (Canadian Achievement Tests), the CTSB (Canadian Tests of Basic Skills), and the Stanford Achievement Test, used in Vancouver and other provincial schools as means of assessing performance, are rejected in favor of the professional judgments of teams of teachers, based on their day-to-day observations and evaluations of students' work. (The Foundation Skills Assessments [FSA], a provincewide test, is mandated for all schools, and Dickens is not exempt from this requirement.) When I asked about how this approach was possible in such a climate of high-stakes testing, Perpich told me, "Of course, we are required to document a student's levels of achievement. And as long as I can document the children's progress and successful performance, 'downtown' is happy. Of course, there are many ways to do this." I was astonished to learn that each school in the district has many options with respect to providing high-quality education for all students and evaluating student performance. Perpich and his staff have chosen "continuous progress." Other schools have chosen differently. I wonder what it takes to dare to march to the drummer of one's educational beliefs.

Because there is no "grade-level curriculum," each child's learning needs are met along a continuum of progress.

Most of the school's 30 teachers teach in teams of two and sometimes three. Team-teaching creates opportunities for teachers to examine and discuss instructional strategies, the assessment of learning needs, appropriate interventions, teacher/student interactions, and "whether the plans are working." Every classroom is a learning laboratory, every teacher a professional.

As noted earlier, teachers remain with the same group of children for three years. Thus they get to know the students better and to become familiar with their individual learning needs and styles. Because there is no "grade-level curriculum," each child's learning needs are met along a continuum of progress. The teachers use a "theme" approach to curriculum, so that each child may work at his or her own level. In the continuous progress system, no child is a failure who would be subject to the ridicule of his or her classmates. Perpich says, "Our school does not use a 'deficit' model; here, we emphasize efficacy and success."

Perpich tells the story of "Mike," a boy who transferred from another school. Mike had been branded as a "five-er"—that is, a child with letter grades of "E" based on gradewide tests given three times a year, which he consistently failed. After transferring to Dickens, where the pressure to achieve on standardized tests was removed, Mike began to succeed. This is not miraculous or anomalous but is simply an example of learning that builds on success rather than failure.

As explained in the parents' brochure, there are no grades given at Dickens Elementary School. Parents receive anecdotal reports written by the teachers. Attached to these reports are the students' self-evaluations of their performance. Both the principal and the teachers have observed that in such a climate of openness and respect, children evaluate themselves with great honesty and perception—and are often less generous in their assessments than are their teachers.

And the parents' response to narrative reporting? Parents claim that the narratives tell them much more than letter grades about how and what their children are learning. Some parents still ask for letter grades, and the school does provide them if requested. However, such requests are rare.

There are observable effects on children's behavior in this school. I'm told, "There's no attitude problem here; what's more, as the kids go on into secondary school, there's no attitude problem there, either." Perpich tells me that, as principal in his previous school, he would return from lunch to face a long line of children waiting outside his office to be "disciplined" for biting, kicking, punching, hair pulling, and on and on. At Dickens, there is no line of children, and his disciplinary work is virtually nonexistent.

The Teachers Hold the Keys

It is not difficult to see that the critical force in initiating and maintaining a child-centered philosophy in a school is the teaching staff. Without like-minded teachers who perform at the highest levels and are respected as professionals, no educational program, let alone a child-centered one, can endure. Teachers must see the school as a place where all children can satisfy their curiosity, develop their abilities and talents, pursue their interests, and, through their interactions with their teachers and the older children around them, get a glimpse of the great variety and richness of life.[5]

When Rooney stepped in as principal of Dickens Elementary, he actively searched for and recruited teachers with such a perspective. Rather than rely on résumés and interviews, he actually visited classrooms and watched teachers in action. Based on his observations, he hired his initial Dickens staff. Teachers who "came with the school" and did not share the child-centered philosophy were invited to transfer to other, more congenial schools in Vancouver, and 11 teachers left when Rooney established the operating principles for the school.

Rooney was able to gather a critical mass of teachers who could be counted on to be strong advocates of open education and whose classroom practices matched those principles. Once those teachers were in place, the school began to attract attention for its students' academic success, its high regard in the parent community, and its status in the academy, with both universities in the area vying for student teacher placements. Dickens eventually became a magnet for other like-minded teachers, and recruitment and sustainability were no longer problems.

The staff at Dickens is exceptional in many ways. Teachers share decision making with respect to policy and practice in the school, and their professional autonomy is unquestioned. They function on an extremely high level in virtually every area of teacher expertise. In deciding class makeup for the next school year, for example, teachers are more than willing to accept their share of the "more difficult" children. Children who present the greatest challenges are not "dumped" on teachers who are new to the school; decisions about placement are based on which teacher is best qualified to meet a particular child's needs.

Perpich tells me that in the staff room, when teachers talk about students, they never complain or make negative comments. These teachers, Perpich says, love what they do, and it shows. When there is an opening for a new teacher, several members of the staff join the principal in the interview process. This practice goes to the edge of the envelope of what the union allows, but Perpich is willing to take the risk to get the teachers he wants. The school's job postings these days are worded in a way that will very nearly ensure that only those teachers sharing a like-minded philosophy will even apply.

It Takes Two to Tango

If the staff holds the keys to the successes of Charles Dickens, it is the principal who supports, encourages, facilitates, and explicitly appreciates what the teachers do. The teachers could not function at such a high level without strong administrative support, and Rooney, Robb, Clark, and Perpich have all been exemplary in providing it.

A successful alternative school requires an educational leader who is willing to take a stand on what he or she believes and stay the course. As Joanna McClelland Glass writes in her brilliant play, *Trying,* "You just lace up your skates and hit the ice."[6] Of course, the principal must be clear about his or her beliefs and be able and willing to act on them. As noted earlier, Dickens had to obtain special permission from the school board for some of its practices, such as anecdotal reporting instead of letter grades, and this was granted. Much of what is done at Dickens, however, is done without special permission. "We are quiet about it; my strategy is to do it first and then beg forgiveness after," Perpich tells me. The school is left largely to its own devices because of two essential conditions: there is no flak from parents or kids because they are well satisfied, and the kids are clearly cared about and performing at high levels of achievement.

Perpich is in his last year as principal before he retires, but he already has plans in the works for recruiting and hiring the principal who will replace him. He and his staff will decide on who will next carry the ball to keep the spirit and practice of Charles Dickens Elementary School alive and well.

But What Happens in Secondary School?

Because Charles Dickens has been in operation for nearly 20 years, there is now a history of reports about students who graduate from grade 7 and go on to junior and senior secondary schools in the district. In June 2004, for example, more than 50% of those who graduated from Dickens and applied to the secondary "mini schools" (schools-within-schools that offer special programs and enroll a small cadre of talented and high-functioning students) were accepted. The feedback from teachers at the mini schools and other high schools accepting Dickens students is that these young people are well-rounded, can carry on good discussions focused on the "big ideas," are good leaders, are good team players, are autonomous, are flexible and make good adjustments to high school, and are personally responsible. These reports remind me of the descriptions of the high school graduates from the Eight-Year Study program, which emphasized a richer and learner-centered curriculum and a healthy respect for student autonomy.[7]

Good News and Bad News

My observations at Dickens and interviews with the principal, teachers, and former district officials have provided a richly textured view of how a school with a highly challenging student population has not only survived but flourished. In the face of the prevailing educational ethos, which celebrates the trivial and downplays much of what we know is right and good for kids, Dickens has maintained its dedication to a child-centered program that actively reveres children and treats them with the respect that they deserve while ensuring that each one learns to his or her greatest ability. It's not a big mystery. All that is needed is the will, the instructional talent, the treatment of teachers as the high-functioning professionals they are, the administrative leadership, and the expertise to pull it all together to make it work. But none of this is news; this is what we, as educators, have known all along—from the early days of the Eight-Year Study to studies of the open classroom in the 1970s to more recent studies of single schools' alternative programs.[8]

So what is the bad news? From the safe haven of my office and desk, where I can look out at the cruise ships making their way up the inland waterway to Alaska, I feel sadness in recognizing that there is no magic formula that others can use to replicate what happens in this school. Dickens exists because a group of educators made tough decisions about what they thought was right and good for children. They stood by their decisions and played clean (and a little dirty) to get what they wanted. They never backed down.

In the end, it all comes down to choices—and educators have more choices than they might realize. It's one thing to knuckle under and accept what we hate and put that into practice, knowing all the while that we don't believe in it and wish it would go away. It's another thing to find out what options we do have and see how best we can maneuver to maintain and act on our beliefs within the constraints that bind us.

What can we do? And how far can we go? It may be possible to go much farther than we at first thought, if we can stand up and say, "This is what we believe. This is what's right." Having the toughness to do that is perhaps easy for me to advocate but hard in the field. For what it takes is "stand-up" leadership from principals, who must buffer the school from district and provincial demands. It takes school boards and provincial and state authorities who aren't afraid to give the professionals in the field the autonomy to follow a different pathway in meeting rigorous standards. Without such mettle, we will continue to bend and sway with the winds of change, and children will be the losers.

Notes

1. Sylvia Ashton-Warner, *Teacher* (New York: Simon & Schuster, 1962).

2. Sylvia Ashton-Warner, *Spearpoint: Teacher in America* (New York: Knopf, 1972).

3. Mary Brown and Norman Precious, *The Integrated Day in the Primary School* (London: Ward Lock, 1970), p. 36.

4. Charles Silberman, *Crisis in the Classroom* (New York: Random House, 1970).

5. Brown and Precious, p. 42.

6. Joanna McClelland Glass, *Trying* (Toronto: Playwrights Canada Press, 2005).

7. Wilford M. Aiken, *The Story of the Eight-Year Study* (New York Harper & Brothers, 1948).

8. See, among others, Deborah Meier, *The Power of Their Ideas: Lessons for America from a Small School in Harlem* (Boston: Beacon Press, 2003); Mary Ann Raywid, "Central Park East Secondary School: The Anatomy of Success," *Journal of Education for Students Placed at Risk,* vol. 4, 1999, pp. 131–51; and Charles Silberman, *The Open Classroom Reader* (New York: Random House, 1970).

SELMA WASSERMANN is a professor emerita, Simon Fraser University, Vancouver, B.C. She wishes to thank Larry Cuban, John Persich, Linda McLean, and Anne Luckhart for their feedback on earlier drafts of this article.

Teaching for Social Justice in Multicultural Urban Schools: Conceptualization and Classroom Implication

JOSE LALAS

Presumably, everyone shares the understanding that teaching for social justice means providing students with a supportive learning environment that is just, fair, democratic, and even compassionate. In reality, people are probably using this term to mean many things without actually embracing it as a perspective for educating students in urban school settings.

Is teaching for social justice a process of conveying a set of radical beliefs related to equity, diversity, and racial differences? Does it mean taking a political stand and becoming a change agent in diminishing the inequities in schools? Is it a virtue? Is it possessing certain abilities and knowing certain kinds of knowledge to do certain things in the classroom that reflect equality?

In this article, I examine the different definitions and conceptualizations offered by a number of educator-researchers on teaching and learning for social justice and identify the common principles that are applicable, relevant, and translatable into classroom practice. I then offer a personal perspective on how the notion of teaching for social justice can develop, evolve, and become part of an ideological and political commitment for educational advocacy and activism.

A Glimpse of Urban School Reality

One has to be aware of the demographic situation in urban areas and the social reality of isolation and poverty faced by its residents to make the connection how these conditions affect urban schools and why there is a need to teach for social justice in an attempt to raise the students' identity, provide equitable access to appropriate curriculum and instruction, and remedy any existing harmful inequities.

Jean Anyon (1997) documented that most residents of large urban areas across the United States are African American or Latino. They can be found in New York (57%), Chicago (62%), Los Angeles (63%), Atlanta (70%), Detroit (79%), and Miami (88%). More than half African American, Latino, and Asian reside in the cities of Baltimore, Cleveland, El Paso, Memphis, San Antonio, San Francisco, San Jose, and Washington, D.C. The relatively poorer urban residents who mostly belong to minority populations are isolated from the economic mainstream of middle class jobs and not provided adequate social services because of the impoverished situations of many city governments.

Urban schools are directly affected by the overall political and economic conditions in urban areas and provide what Anyon termed "ghetto schooling" to its diverse student population (Anyon, 1997). Kozol (2005) described the "savage inequities" in inner-city schools further by reporting that nowadays scripted rote-and-drill drill curricula, prepackaged lessons, standard-naming and numbering rituals, display of standards in bulletin boards, rewards and sanctions, and other forms of control on every intellectual activity are prevalent. He also observed that "the more experienced instructors teach the children of the privileged and the least experienced are sent to teach the children of minorities" (p. 275).

Kozol cited Gary Orfield and his colleagues at the Civil Rights Project at Harvard University who reported that "almost three-fourths of Black and Latino students attend schools that are predominantly minority . . . attend schools which we call apartheid schools (in which 99% to 100% of students are nonwhite). Kozol (2005) concluded that "these are confections of apartheid, and no matter by what arguments of urgency or practicality they have been justified, they cannot fail to further deepen the divisions of society" (p. 275).

Kincheloe (2004) asserted that "urban education is always in crisis—yesterday, today, and certainly in the near future" and that we need to develop a powerful urban pedagogy and a rigorous urban education. In an essay "What Is Urban Education in an Age of Standardization and Scripted Learning?" Hill (2004) writes:

> Urban, we know, is the environment of a city: a complex hub of human endeavor, a place of dense population of diverse peoples, an important location for financial and governmental affairs, and a rich center of cultural imagination and artistic creation. Urban environments are some of the most contradictory areas of our world, where the extremes of our civilization coexist—the richest of the rich and the poorest of the poor, the most privileged and the most disenfranchised, live and work here in large concentrations. (p. 119)

In summary, urban schools serve a big, complex, and diverse group of students in areas marked by profound socioeconomic disparity, ethnic diversity, and higher immigrant populations. Inner-city schools are also more susceptible to educational mandates and sanctions, usually called "reforms," that are monitored carefully for their strict adherence to regulated curricula, technical standards, standardized evaluations, and high-stakes testing preparation and performance.

Educational Inequities in Urban Schools

Clearly, "teaching for social justice" at this point sounds essential for all children in the increasingly diverse urban schools in the United States, where inequities seem to abound and where the majority are refugee students, English language learners, and students of color attend (Goldenberg, 2004; McBrien, 2005).

Rumberger and Gandara (2004) explained with thorough documentation the "seven inequitable conditions" existing in California schools that affect the opportunities of the English learners (ELs) to learn and contribute to the academic gap between them and their English-only counterparts: (1) inequitable access to appropriately trained teachers—25 percent of teachers of ELs were not fully certified and thus ELs are significantly less likely to have a fully credentialed teacher than other low-income non-EL peers; (2) inadequate professional development opportunities for teachers—very little support with only 7% to 10% of reported professional development time focused on the instruction of ELs; (3) inequitable access to appropriate assessment—the only measures of achievement for ELs are tests administered in English with an exclusive reliance on an English-language norm-referenced achievement test for ELs; (4) inadequate instructional time—a great deal of instructional time is lost while ELs are in the structured English immersion program and waiting for their permanent classroom to be assigned, and classrooms with large numbers of ELs have fewer assistants in them to help; (5) inequitable access to instructional materials and curriculum—75% of the teachers surveyed said that they use the same textbooks for their ELs and English-only students with no materials adapted to their linguistic needs, and teachers with high percentages of ELs are less likely than teachers with low percentages of ELs to have access to appropriate textbooks and instructional materials; (6) inequitable access to adequate facilities—schools with a high concentration of ELs have overcrowded classrooms, poorer working conditions for teachers, less parental involvement, and more neighborhood crime; and (7) intense segregation into schools and classrooms that place them at high risk for educational failure—55% of all elementary-aged ELs in California are enrolled in schools with large concentrations of ELs, two-thirds of ELs attended classrooms in which more than 50% of their classmates were ELs, thus denying them the opportunity to interact with peers who could be English language models and who are achieving at high or even moderate levels.

As you can see from the reported educational inequities in California, that are consciously or unconsciously created and perpetuated, the English language learners are very far from receiving a just, equitable, and fair education in urban schools.

Similarly, McBrien (2005) explained that as children of refugees from usually war-torn countries settle in and attend high-poverty urban areas, they often end up in "a negative, subtractive assimilation pattern, rejecting their family and cultural ties in hopes of being accepted by American peers" (p. 355). Her research warned that "misunderstanding the dire situations of parents, the role of trauma in refugees' behaviors, cultural differences, and best practices in language acquisition has caused many school personnel to hold prejudiced attitudes that lead to discrimination" (p. 356).

In a related study, Lalas and Valle (2005) in a narrative inquiry described the set of inequities perceived by students of color in their school experiences in inner-city schools. Their perceived inequities included interracial differences, racial segregation, racial violence, stereotyping, bullying, religious intolerance, gender segregation, unfair treatment, language barriers, cultural clash, drug and alcohol abuse, gangs, and low income. Lalas and Valle concluded that students' voices need to be heard so teachers can understand their students and "create a caring environment to pave the path for social justice."

While many more recent studies have supported the assertion that students in urban schools, indeed, face many challenges associated with race, ethnicity, and poverty (Haycock, Jerald, & Huang, 2001; Singham, 2003), many educational reforms have also been primarily initiated to improve the academic performance and achievement of inner-city students. Some of these reforms included joint-decision making among teachers and administrators, flexible scheduling, core planning in individual schools, teaming of teachers, integration of curriculum, class size reduction, parental involvement, new forms of assessment, corporate models, and many other research-based approaches.

However, Rothstein (2004) explained that school reforms alone including higher standards, better teachers, more accountability, better discipline, and other effective practices are not enough to overcome the effect of the "social-class characteristics" in widening the academic gap between White, middle class students and their minority and lower-class counterparts. I therefore suggest in this article that teachers and teacher educators must play key roles in the reform effort because reforms are, in the final analysis, classroom reforms that are directly in their hands and the inner-city students they interact with. But can teachers do it alone?

Teachers for Social Justice: Key to Classroom Reforms

It has been well-documented and well-argued that educational reforms are mitigated by urban poverty and cannot transform inequities in schools without thinking about restructuring the "city environment itself, which produces these students and the failing schools" (Anyon, 1997, p. 13). In fact, Anyon (2005) showed that "job, wage, housing, tax, and transportation policies maintain minority poverty in urban neighborhoods, and thereby create environments that overwhelm the potential of educational policy to create systemic, sustained improvements in the schools" (p. 66).

However, classroom teachers are the most essential element because they have the ultimate responsibility to navigate the curriculum and instruction with their students in the classroom. They can examine the impact of race, ethnicity, class, gender, sexual orientation, disability, and poverty itself on the educational outcomes of students in urban schools. They have the intellectual and critical capacity to analyze the purposes, practices, and policies of schools and the impact on students' life opportunities. They may not be able to transform the society's fundamental inequities, but they can contribute in many practical ways by raising the level of social awareness of their students and guiding the curriculum for social justice instruction.

It is imperative that both pre-service and in-service teachers be assisted and guided in developing their content knowledge, pedagogical skills, and advocacy for social justice to improve the overall education of their students in urban schools. However, Cochran-Smith (2004) asserted that there are multiple paths for pursuing the social justice agenda and she called for a broad participation of school- and university-based educators, including classroom teachers, teacher educators, and community advocates who are willing to "rethink beliefs and attitudes about difference, privilege, diversity, and culture" and work "together as teachers but also learners, and as educators but also activists" (p. 156).

What Does It Really Mean to Teach for Social Justice?

Generally, educators may view teaching for social justice as a way of recognizing, respecting, and valuing differences in race, cultural beliefs, social norms, intellectual flexibility, and personal perspectives and dispositions among students in a typically multicultural classroom in urban schools. Many classroom teachers may believe that social justice can be cultivated in the classroom by appreciating diversity, promoting equity, advancing broad-mindedness, and encouraging voice and expression (Brooks & Thompson, 2005). Recently, urban school counselors relate an emphasis in social justice as an essential skill in assuming an advocacy role as part of their work and paying attention to social, political, and economic realities of students and families (Bemak & Chung, 2005).

According to Brown (2004), being administrators and leaders for social justice requires grounding in learning theories, transformative pedagogy, and critical discourse and reflection, and aims "to perceive social, political, and economic contradictions, and to take action against the oppressive elements of reality."

Whatever lens is used in explaining the term, a compelling argument needs to be made for "the necessity of a social justice agenda in a democratic and increasingly diverse society" (Cochran-Smith, 2004, p. 168). Some experts believe that it is quite ironic and a sad statement on the moral responsibility of our schools that one has to even advocate for teaching for social justice (Kohl, 2001; Shamsher & Decker, 2004).

Teaching for social justice can be also defined as a set of beliefs that emphasizes equity, ethical values, justice, care, and respect (Marshall & Oliva, 2006). Practically, it can also translate to making the necessary instructional adaptations for diverse and special needs students to remedy any problem in securing equitable access to instruction and assessment for them (Solomon, Lalas, & Franklin, 2006).

Others frame learning to teach for social justice as a lifelong undertaking that involves:

> coming to understand oneself in relation to others; examining how society constructs privilege and inequality and how this affects one's own opportunities as well as those of different people; exploring the experiences of others and appreciating how those inform their worldviews, perspectives, and opportunities; and evaluating how schools and classrooms operate and can be structured to value diverse human experiences and to enable learning for all students. (Darling-Hammond, 2005, p. 201)

As you can surmise from the definition she uses in working with her teacher candidates, Darling-Hammond (2005) suggests that teachers for social justice need to understand one's identity, other people's background and their worldviews, and the sources of inequities and privileges. Sensitivity to these issues will be helpful in facilitating the learning of students authentically and making a difference in the their lives.

Bell (1997) explains in an even more global and philosophical sense that teaching for social justice means providing all groups in a society full and equal participation in meeting their needs:

Social justice includes a vision of society in which the distribution of resources is equitable and all members are physically and psychologically safe and secure . . . Social justice involves social actors who have a sense of their own agency as well as a sense of social responsibility toward and with others and the society as a whole. (p.1)

It is clear from Bell's conceptualization that teachers, both pre-service and in-service, who would like to practice social justice, need to understand that all individuals in the society must be responsible to each other and deserve to enjoy equity, security, safety, and involvement in their interaction and dealing with others and the society.

Cochran-Smith (2004) frames teaching for social justice as connected to teacher preparation when she asserts in her book that:

the conception of teaching and learning to teach that underlie the social justice agenda include learning to represent complex knowledge in accessible and culturally responsive ways, learning to ask good questions, use diversified forms of assessment to shape curriculum and instruction, develop relationships with students that support and sustain learning, work with—not against—parents and community members, collaborate with other professionals, interpret multiple data sources in support of pupils' learning, maintain high academic standards for students of all abilities and backgrounds, engage in classroom inquiry in the service of pupil and teacher learning, and join with others in larger movements for educational and social equity. (p. 159)

In this description of the "social justice agenda," Cochran-Smith outlines the knowledge, skills, abilities, and disposition that teachers need to develop to move this agenda forward, which include culturally responsive teaching, making content comprehensible and accessible, effective and purposeful questioning, use of different forms assessment to inform instruction, support for students, collaboration with parents, community members, and other professionals, knowing how to interpret data, maintaining high academic standards, being a teacher-researcher, and strong advocacy for equity.

Cochran-Smith (2000) also explains emphatically that teachers and teacher educators, to be effective, need "to struggle to unlearn racism itself" and understand that teaching does not require content knowledge and verbal ability alone in raising pupils' test scores and academic achievement. Teaching, from a social justice perspective, is not a matter simply of transmitting knowledge and equating pupil learning to higher scores on high-stakes tests, but rather engaging pupils in "developing critical habits of mind, understanding and sorting out multiple perspectives, and learning to participate in and contribute to a democratic society by developing both the skill and the inclination for civic engagement" (Cochran-Smith, 2004, p. 159).

Aside from democratic citizenship and a focus on democracy, others suggest that teaching for social justice also includes "anti-oppression education" which highlights diversity in schools and

proposes different ways of confronting the inequities faced by students in urban multicultural environments (Brandes & Kelly, 2004).

Many classroom practitioners have also begun designing and implementing instruction that reflects social justice instruction and critical teaching through students' personal stories, use of literature, critical literacy as comprehension (McLaughlin & DeVoogd, 2004), "acting for justice" lessons (Christensen, 2001), thematic units (Beale, 2004), service learning (Lucas, 2005), cooperative learning (Sapon-Shevin, 2004), and other learning strategies across differences (Shor & Pari, 1999).

Classroom Implications

In summary, the conceptualizations of teaching for social justice by several educator-researchers described in this article reveal some common principles that are relevant, appropriate, and translatable to classroom teaching. At this point, it is essential to understand that the teaching and learning processes that occur are facilitated by the on-going dynamic interaction of three major components—namely, the learner, teacher, and the classroom context, as clearly described in the sociocognitive interaction model of meaning construction in reading formulated by Ruddell and Unrau (2004). In this meaning-construction process, both the learner and the teacher use their life experiences, personal values and beliefs, personal and world knowledge, abilities to construct, monitor, and represent knowledge, and personal meaning construction and decision-making disposition in the instructional context of the classroom.

The classroom context where the interaction, generation, and negotiation of meaningful experiences happen is broadly defined here to include the physical classroom arrangement, classroom discipline, key sources of authority where meanings reside, textbooks, assessment instruments, assignments, and many other visual and supplementary materials. Thus, it is through the dynamic interchange of the learner, teacher, and classroom context that the following teaching and learning principles drawn from the teaching for social justice conceptualizations can be applied:

1. Understanding oneself in relation to other individual or group of individuals.
2. Appreciating diversity and promoting equity.
3. Recognizing inequities and how to diminish them.
4. Equitable participation and allocation of resources.
5. Creating a caring and culturally responsive learning environment.
6. Working together as a learning community.
7. Engagement in classroom inquiry.
8. Critical thinking and reflection.
9. Using varied forms of assessment for equitable and fair monitoring of student progress.

This list of common principles implies the significant roles that a classroom teacher and learner must play as he or she interacts, shares, negotiates, and generates knowledge in the classroom context. The infusion of these principles in the classroom occurs only when the teacher, the learner, and the classroom context are joined together as significant variables and consciously relied upon as meaningful and influential sources in the construction and acquisition of knowledge. The student and the teacher not only bring their own personal, social, cultural, economic, and political values from prior beliefs and experiences into the classroom, they also interpret the classroom culture and social life they find there.

As such, providing teaching and learning contexts to students in urban schools and preparing teachers to work in diverse classroom will continue to challenge pre-service and in-service teachers and teacher educators because, as Cochran-Smith (2004) declares with authority, teacher education for social justice is a "learning problem" and a "political problem."

As she suggests, it is not just knowing a content area or body of knowledge, and possessing the pedagogical skills to deliver it, but it is also being reflective and critical as "part of community where the participants deliberately claim the role of educator as well as activist, based on ideological commitment to diminishing the inequities of American life" (p. 19).

References

Adams, M., Bell, L., & Griffin, P. (Eds.) (1997). *Teaching for diversity and social justice.* New York: Routledge.

Anyon, J. (1997). *Ghetto schooling: A political economy of urban educational reform.* New York: Teachers College Press.

Anyon, J. (2005). What "counts" as educational policy? Notes toward a new paradigm. *Harvard Educational Review, 75*(1), 65–88.

Beale, U. (2004). Family is someone to tuck you into bed: Teaching a unit on family diversity. In M. Shamnsher, E. Decker, G. Brandes & D. Kelly (Eds.), *Teaching for social justice.* Vancouver, BC: British Columbia Teachers' Federation.

Bell, L. (1997). Theoretical foundations for social justice education. In M. Adams., L. Bell & P. Griffin (Eds.), *Teaching for diversity and social justice.* New York: Routledge.

Brandes, G. & Kelly, D. (2004). Teaching for social justice: Teachers inquire into their practice. In M. Shamnsher, E. Decker, G. Brandes & D. Kelly (Eds.), *Teaching for social justice.* Vancouver, BC: British Columbia Teachers' Federation.

Bemak, F. & Chung, R. (2005). Advocacy as a critical role for urban school counselors: Working toward equity and social justice. *ASCA Professional School Counseling,* February 2005, 196–202.

Brooks, J., & Thompson, E. (2005). Social justice in the classroom. *Educational Leadership,* September 2005, 48–52.

Brown, K. (2004). Leadership for social justice and equity: Weaving a transformative framework and pedagogy. *Educational Administration Quarterly, 40*(1), 77–108.

Christensen, L. (2001). Acting for justice. *Rethinking Schools Online, 15*(2), Winter.

Cochran-Smith, M. (2000). Blind vision: Unlearning racism in teacher education. *Harvard Educational Review, 70*(2), 157–190.

Cochran-Smith, M. (2004). *Walking the road: Race, diversity, and social justice.* New York: Teachers College Press.

Darling-Hammond, L., French, J., & Garcia-Lopez, S. (Eds.). (2002). *Learning to teach for social justice.* New York: Teachers College Press.

Genesee, F., Lindholm-Leary, K., Saunders, W., & Christian, D. English language learners in U.S. schools: An overview of research findings. *Journal of Education for Students Placed at Risk, 10*(4), 363–385.

Goldenberg, C. (2004). Literacy for all children in the increasingly diverse schools of the United States. In R. Ruddell & N. Unrau (Eds.), *Theoretical models and processes of reading, fifth edition.* Newark, DE: International Reading Association.

Haycock, K., Jerald, C., & Huang, S. (2001). Closing the gap: Done in a decade. *Thinking K-16,* Spring 2001. Washington, DC: Education Trust.

Hill, J. (2004). What is urban education in an age of standardization and scripted learning? In S. Steinberg & K. Kincheloe (Eds.), *19 Urban questions: Teaching in the city.* New York: Peter Lang.

Kincheloe, J. (2004). Why a book on urban education? In S. Steinberg & K. Kincheloe (Eds.), *19 Urban questions: Teaching in the city.* New York: Peter Lang.

Kohl, H. (2001). Teaching for social justice. *Rethinking Schools Online, 15*(2), Winter.

Kozol, J. (2005). Confections of apartheid: A stick-and-carrot pedagogy for the children of our inner-city poor. *Phi Delta Kappan, 87*(4), 265–275.

Lalas, J. & Valle, M.E., (2005). Paving the path for social justice in teacher education: Responding to urban student voices. Unpublished manuscript, presented at the Educational Leadership for Social Justice Institute: University of Redlands.

Lucas, T. (2005). Fostering a commitment to social justice through service learning in a teacher education course. In N. Michelli & D. Keiser (Eds.), *Teacher education for democracy and social justice.* New York and London: Routledge.

Marshall, C., & Oliva, M. (2006). *Leadership for social justice: Making revolutions in education.* Boston: Pearson Allyn & Bacon.

McBrien, J. (2005). Educational needs and barriers for refugee students in the United States: A review of the literature. *Review of Educational Research, 75*(3), 329–364.

McLaughlin, M. & Devoogd, G. (2004). Critical literacy as comprehension: Expanding reader response. *The Reading Teacher, 48,* 52–62.

Michelli, N., & Keiser, D. (Eds.). (2005). *Teacher education for democracy and social justice.* New York and London: Routledge.

Rothstein, R. (2004). A wider lens on the Black-White achievement gap. *Phi Delta Kappan, 86*(2), 104–113.

Ruddell, R. & Unrau, N. (2004). Reading as a meaning-construction process: The reader, the text, and the teacher. In R. Ruddell & N. Unrau (Eds.), *Theoretical models and processes of reading.* Newark, DE: International Reading Association.

Rumberger, R., & Gandara, P. (2004). Seeking equity in the education of California's English learners. *Teachers College Record, 106*(10), 2032–2056.

Rusch, E. (2004). Gender and race in leadership preparation: A constrained discourse. *Educational Administration Quarterly, 40*(1), 14–46.

Shamsher, M., & Decker E. (2004). Editors' foreword. In M. Shamnsher, E. Decker, G. Brandes & D. Kelly (Eds.), *Teaching for social justice.* Vancouver, BC: British Columbia Teachers' Federation.

Shamsher M., Decker, E., Brandes, G., & Kelly, D. (Eds.). (2004). *Teaching for social justice.* Vancouver, BC: British Columbia Teachers' Federation.

Shields, C. (2004). Dialogic leadership for social justice: Overcoming pathologies of silence. *Educational Administration Quarterly, 40*(1), 109–132.

Shor, I., & Pari, C. (1999). *Education is politics: Critical teaching across differences.* Portsmouth, NH: Heinemann.

Singham, M. (2003). The achievement gap: Myths and reality. *Phi Delta Kappan, 84,* 586–591.

Solomon, M., Lalas, J., & Franklin, C. (2006). Making instructional adaptations for English learners in the mainstream classroom: is it good enough? *Multicultural Education, 13*(3), 42–45.

JOSE LALAS is associate dean, professor of literacy, and director of teacher education with the School of Education at the University of Redlands, Redlands, California.

The Human Right to Education
Freedom and Empowerment

Caetano Pimentel

Introduction

Education is widely understood as the gradual process of acquiring knowledge or the process of training through which one teaches or learns specific skills; furthermore, it can be understood as disciplining the character. It is undoubtedly the spread of knowledge and information but, more than this, the imparting of experience, knowledge, and wisdom. One of the fundamental goals of education is the transmission of culture between generations.

In a broader sense, education begins with life itself[1] and goes beyond formal or informal schooling, encompassing the struggles and triumphs of daily life. It is essential both for children and adults—in the case of the latter, to replace or prolong initial education in schools, colleges, and universities as well as in apprenticeship.[2]

Religious values, political needs, and the system of production have always determined the standards of education. Indeed, education has always been subordinated to the expectations concerning the roles individuals would perform in their social group.

But the importance of education has been acknowledged in a much broader sense:

Dakar Framework for Action:

6. (. . .)[Education] is the key to sustainable development and peace and stability within and among countries, and thus an indispensable means for effective participation in the societies and economies of the twenty-first century, which are affected by rapid globalization.(. . .)

Indeed, as a human right, education is the acknowledgement of the individual's rights rather than his or her role in the capitalist goals of the economic growth; the human right to education is the way through which one can conquer freedom and become a genuine individuated[3] being, self-aware and yet deeply and truly connected to others.

The Brazilian educator Paulo Freire formulated ideas concerning literacy (and the learning process as a whole) which became influential internationally. According to Freire, the process of learning necessarily goes along with the learner's ever-increasing awareness of his/her existential condition and of the possibility of acting independently to change it—with individuals reflecting on their values, their concern for a more equitable society, and their willingness to support others in the community. Learning process is what Freire called 'conscientization,' an empowerment of the individual.

Freire expanded education's technical-pedagogic dimension to a political one, which demands a major shift of the education paradigm into 'praxis': reflection plus action, which highlights the importance of learners becoming active subjects in the learning process, taking a position of agents.

Education throughout History[4]

Education has taken as many forms as cultural, political, and religious values have been created by human kind. In Egypt and Mesopotamia (3000 B.C.), the first formal group education appeared as Scribal schools. In primitive societies of hunters and gatherers, learning process was based on watching and imitating. Jewish religious education was a way to glorify God. In Greece, a man-centered approach to education was available to a privileged male few, both at home and in State schools—but, still, the whole purpose of education was to subordinate the individual to the needs of the State.

Medieval education was an evolution of Catholic catechetical schools of the second century—Monasteries were both for those preparing for a monastic vocation (oblati) and those whose aims were secular (extend); the later Middle Ages witnessed the rise of the great cathedral schools followed by the ascendancy of the universities and the complexities of scholasticism.

During the Renaissance, there was a turn back to humanistic cultural values of Classical Greece and Rome. Based mainly on parish church provisions and also found in some monasteries and palaces, primary schools were mostly limited to elites. Changes in economical relations arising at the time led to the education of some new skills, such as computation and bookkeeping.

In the following centuries, complex changes on economic, political, technological, religious, scientific, and aesthetic levels demanded a substantial increase in provisions for schooling and the access to schools. The fullest expression of the need to broaden formal educational opportunity came in calls for universal schooling. Convictions and trends moved in the direction of enlarged access despite the persistence of some conservative medieval opposition. These convictions and trends meant increasing the number of schools and putting them near potential student populations in towns and villages—and a big challenge was to find a sufficient number of competent schoolmasters.

The 18th century gave way to the emergence of the idea that schools should be instruments of social reform (Samuel Hartlib, John Dury, John Comenius), and access to them should be increased. Social and religious reforms, nationalism, commerce and industry, colonization, and scientific methods of inquiry and technological innovations were responsible for the development of a number of theories concerning education and school access, amongst them the ideas of secular universal elementary schooling and the development of critical rational thinking.

The North American colonies along the Atlantic coast (17th–18th centuries) transplanted the ideas of Renaissance (South), Reformation (North), and Enlightenment (Franklin and Jefferson), whereas earlier settlements established by Spain and France maintained a parish organization of schools. Private schools (Franklin), free public school for all (Jefferson), language teaching, and the diffusion of knowledge were some of the trends concerning education for white boys and girls.

In Brazil, Asia, and Africa, Jesuit Priests were in charge of the catechisation of natives and the children of the first colonisers. Particularly in Brazil, their mission was to teach them to read, perform labor, and organize themselves in order to protect the land occupied, which led the native culture to be nearly extinguished. The Jesuits remained in Brazil until 1759, when they were sent away from the country by Marques de Pombal, whose goals were to create an administrative elite and increase the production of raw materials and commodities (e.g., sugar) to be traded by Portugal.

Major social, political, cultural, and economical changes arose after the French and American revolutions, when four major trends to modern western democracies were established: the rise of nation states, urbanization and industrialization, secularization, and popular participation.

Nation states, with their enormous power to gather and focus both human and material resources, have come to interfere increasingly in the definition of educational policy and schooling. Industrialization and urbanization resulted in a concentration of human populations more and more diverse. Secularization has meant an augmenting emphasis on rational/empirical modes of explanation. Popular participation refers to an enlarging access to involvement in the governance of public life.

These trends have not and do not come about in a linear way, nor are they alike everywhere, either in timing or scope. Changes are still operating in many western and eastern countries today, and as a result we can find four major issues that modern states are yet to sort out: social stratification and class interests, religion and ideology, race and ethnicity, and geography (i.e., localism, regionalism).

The Right to Education—A Historical Background

Educational process implies a number of actors: those who receive education, those who provide education, and those who are responsible for the ones who receive education.[5] The first legislation on educational issues were an attempt to balance the complex relations between these actors. The social, cultural, political, and economical changes brought about in the modern age by the emancipation of the individual have had a great impact on the relationship between the individual and the state. The recognition of rights of individuals and duties of state are both a reflection and a consequence of these changes.

Although we may find today the right to education enshrined in many provisions of human rights law, none of the classical civil instruments such as the British Bill of Rights of 1689, the Virginia Declaration of Rights of 1776, the American Declaration of Independence of 1776, and the French Declaration of Rights of Man contained any language specifically related to the right to education, although some recognised the freedom of teaching from state interference. Indeed,

> Public education was perceived as a means to realising the egalitarian ideals upon which these revolutions were based (. . .).[6]

Child labor in England had been subject to legal regulation since the first Factory Act in 1802 (Health and Morals of Apprentices Act), but it was not until the Factory Act of 1833 that legal provisions imposed restrictions on child labor and created the obligation of school attendance—first in textile establishments, and then the Mines Act came later in 1842.

The Constitution of the State of Indiana (1816), in its article IX, recognized the importance of education to the preservation of free government (sect. 1) and also stated goals to provide for a general system of education, free and equally open to all (sect. 2).[7]

The socialist ideas of a paternal state, drafted by Marx and Engels, and the liberal anti-clerical concepts of freedom (of science, research and teaching, among others) also influenced the definition of the educational rights by means of compulsory school attendance and similar measures. In the latter half of the 19th century the Constitution of the German Empire contained a section entitled "Basic Rights of German People," and the German Weimar Constitution of 1919 included a section on "Education and Schooling."[8]

The first provision on the human right to education with a corresponding duty of the state to provide education was in Stalin's Soviet Constitution of 1936. As a matter of fact, the right to education has been a major fundamental right in all constitutions of socialist states.[9]

As a major interest of the state and society, education turned out to be a right of the individual, rather than solely a duty of state or parents. And in the 20th century, many international and regional instruments and a number of national constitutions have recognized the right to education, which thus has become a fundamental human right.

At the international level, peaceful resolution of conflicts has always been a major concern: the International Peace Conference (The Hague, 1899), the League of Nations (Versailles, 1919), and the Declaration by United Nations (1942) to support the fight against the Axis Powers were the expression of nations' concern about peace and security.

When the Second World War was over, representatives of 50 countries met in San Francisco, in 1945, to draft the United Nations Charter. The purpose of the United Nations, set forth by the charter, comprehends not only peace and security goals, but a broader scope of actions and international cooperation efforts concerning economic, social, cultural, and humanitarian problems and, above all,

> to reaffirm faith in fundamental human rights, in the dignity and worth of the human person, in the equal rights of men and women end of nations large and small (. . .).[10]

UNESCO, the United Nations Educational, Scientific, and Cultural Organization, was born in the same year. Peace and security, justice, the rule of law and the human rights, and fundamental freedoms are clearly expressed in its declaration of purpose.

The United Nations' Universal Declaration of Human Rights (UDHR) (1948) enshrines, in its Article 26, the right of everyone to free and compulsory education and recognizes the role of education in the development of the human personality and the respect for human rights and fundamental freedoms.

The process of positivization of the rights contained in the UDHR at the international level started with the two covenants adopted in 1966. Concerning education, the International Covenant on Economic, Social, and Cultural Rights spells out in more detail the right to education, in its articles 13 and 14, including the right to free compulsory primary education, adult education, freedom to choose education, and recognition of the role of education in enabling all persons to participate effectively in a free society.

Education as a Human Right

Emphasising education as a basic human right shifts the focus from simply concentrating on the contribution that education can make to economic development. The focus on education as a fundamental human right is that the internationally agreed Human Right treaties form a common platform for enshrining equal rights to education for all citizens. In this perspective the individual in society is viewed as a stakeholder with rights and not an object of charity or investment.[11]

The international community has embraced education as a basic human right, as major international and regional instruments disclose a number of important State obligations.

The right to education is recognized as the one which empowers individuals to cope with basic needs, such as health and dignity, and which enables the full and free development of his or her personality. Also, education is required for the implementation of the collective right to development—which means that any society depends on the education of its members to enjoy satisfactory conditions of life and fully achieve its goals, to assure that they will be able to fulfill personal needs such as housing, health, and food.

Education is now recognized as the pathway to freedom, and free democratic society depends on its members' abilities to freely choose, think, and express themselves, and to actively contribute to the political and social processes in pursuit of their interests.

Education is assigned to the "second generation" of human rights, those related to equality. The nature of second generation rights is fundamentally social, economic, and cultural. In social terms, they ensure different members of the community equal conditions and treatment, securing the ability of the individual to lead a self-directed life and to pursue the development of his or her personality.[12]

Second generation Human Rights are mostly positive rights, "rights (or guarantees) to," as opposed to negative rights which are "rights from," usually freedom from abuse or oppression by others. Hence, education must be provided by a series of positive actions by others: school systems, teachers, and materials must be actively provided in order for such a right to be fulfilled, representing things that the State is required to provide to the people under its jurisdiction.

But the Right to Education can also be linked to first generation (freedom) rights, for it entitles individuals to a certain degree of liberty and autonomy before states and their institutions (the right to choose education), and to third generation (solidarity) rights: the right to self-determination, to economic and social development, and to participate in the common heritage of mankind,[13] aspiring ultimately to the full respect for and protection of all human rights. The article 8(1) of the Declaration on the Right to Development reads as follows:

> States should undertake, at the national level, all necessary measures for the realization of the right to development and shall ensure, *inter alia*, equality of opportunity for all in their access to basic resources, education, health services, food, housing, employment and the fair distribution of income. Effective measures should be undertaken to ensure that women have an active role in the development process. Appropriate economic and social reforms should be carried out with a view to eradicating all social injustices.[14] (emphasis added)

The right to education is complex and demands strong commitments at many levels to be implemented. As a result, many different aspects of the right to education have been emphasized by the international community since the Universal Declaration of Human Rights, perhaps due to a lack of full commitment to the principles related to this multifaceted right.[15]

In the subjective dimension of the right to education, we can take the definition given by Canotilho[16] to social rights:

> Social rights are subjective rights inherent to the portion of space where the citizen lives, independently of immediate justitiability or exequibility. (. . .) Neither the state nor third parties can damage re-entrant juridical positions in the ambit of protection of these rights.

In the objective dimension, the right to education, as any other social right, according to Canotilho, can be put into practice through lawmaking processes, in order to create material and institutional conditions for these rights to be granted to individuals. In addition, it must be provided as a materialization of the subjective dimension of these rights and a duty of the state to comply with its institutional obligations. These obligations range from minimum guarantees inspired by neoliberal principles to the full wide-ranging welfare model adopted by social-democracies in northern Europe, for instance.

Education Today

Albeit the repeated affirmation and recognition of education as a human right, one hundred and thirteen million children around the world are not enrolled in school and many more than that drop out before being able to read or do simple mathematics. These figures will add to the ranks of 880 million illiterate adults in the world[17] and to escalating unemployment, poverty, and income disparities. A lot has changed since the rise of nation-states, but educational policies are still ruled by economical and political interests.

Since 1950, the estimated illiteracy rates have significantly declined,[18] but as a complex right which consists of quantitative and qualitative aspects, these numbers fall short on describing how well all the purposes comprised by the Article 26 of the Universal Declaration have been fulfilled. On this matter, Joel Samoff has stated:

> The most important measures of success of an education programme are the learning that has taken place and the attitudes and values that have been developed. There is little point in reducing the cost of 'delivering education services' without attention to whether or not learning is taking place. Assessing learning and socialization is both complex and difficult. That it is difficult makes it all the more important that it be addressed systematically and critically.[19]

Although in most countries primary education is compulsory by law, it is rarely enforced. From the Proclamation of Teheran, in 1968, to the World Declaration on Education for All adopted by the World Conference on Education for All in Jomtien, Thailand in 1990, and the Dakar Framework for Action of 2000, many changes took place, especially with regard to the focus of education.[20]

Basic principles, such as "free education" and "primary education," have been distorted to exempt governments from the duty of implementing education as set by international and national law. In contrast, statements concerning the international community's agreement on the education's purpose have been considerably broadened:

> Taking into account all of the above, the vision of education's aims and purposes that has emerged over the past several decades is essentially focused on two inter-related themes. The first, which can be broadly labelled as 'Education for peace, human rights and democracy', is directly linked to—indeed, has largely been inspired by—the aims and purposes proclaimed in Article 26 of the Universal Declaration. The second, which can be broadly labelled as 'Education for development,' is linked to Article 26 in a more complex way.[21]

Right to Education v. Access to Education

According to the Annual Report 2004 by the UN Special Rapporteur on the Right to Education, Professor Katarina Tomasevski, there are many obstacles to the full realization of the right to education: the commercial approach to education (rather than a human-right approach), gender discrimination, and school drop-out are the ones which deserve special attention.

The liberalization of education, under the World Trade Organization GATS (General Agreement on Trade in Services), is within the concept of free market and competitiveness, raising a conflict between trade law and human rights law.[22] Deregulation, privatization, and reduction of public spending leads to the elimination of public funding or subsidy to public services—and that includes education. The underlying philosophy of this process leads to a change of perception from public and community good to individualism and individual responsibility.[23]

In this context, education is not regarded as a right which must be made freely available, accessible, acceptable, and adaptable. It is reflected in an altered vocabulary, as pointed out by Prof. Tomasevski, in which "access" to education does not grant free education funded by the government.[24] Education is no longer provided by the entitlement to rights; it is determined by purchasing power and the rules of self-regulation of the market, as a part of a creeping privatization of education that causes the transference of education costs to poor families. An astonishing array of education charges, from direct school fees to indirect costs for books, pencils, uniforms, and transportation, are supposed to be afforded by family units worldwide.[25]

We must take into account that the expansion of private education is creating a two-tiered system that creates inequities rooted in social class, caste, and gender—where public education, in very poor condition due to lack of resources, is only used by those who cannot afford to pay for better quality schooling provided by private institutions. This dual education system creates and perpetuates a divided society, and this division goes beyond purchasing power, for this inequality also reflects discrimination on the basis of religion, language, race, and gender.

Moreover, not every family can afford having one or more of their children going to school instead of helping the family earn more income. Very often, costs are cited by parents as the major factor in deciding to keep children out of school.[26]

Education is the way to break out of the poverty cycle: through education children, particularly girls, can ultimately help increase the family income, and stay healthier. Education is definitely the foundation for equitable human and economic development.

In developing countries, the education crisis is also a crisis of education quality. Those children who do attend school in the world's poor countries face enormous obstacles to their learning. A chronic teacher shortage most of the time results in large-sized classes, multi-graded or divided by shifts. Another problem is the inadequate supply of basic materials, such as books, desks, and benches, not to mention the lack of transportation for students and the too-often empty stomach.

Gender Inequalities

Gender issues concerning education are also a major concern,[27] for very large gender inequalities still exist in the majority of developing countries. Education not only provides basic knowledge and skills to improve health and income, but it empowers women to take their rightful place in society and the development process. It gives them status and confidence to influence household decisions—women who have been to school tend to marry later and have smaller families. Their children are better nourished and are far more likely to do well at school. Educated women can overcome cultural and social factors, such as lack of family planning and the spread of disease, which contribute to the cycle of poverty.[28]

But girls are needed at home and they contribute largely to the family income: they look after siblings, nurse sick relatives (e.g., in the context of HIV/AIDS in Africa), and do domestic tasks. Besides that, the low number of government schools and the limited public transport make distance a barrier for both boys and girls, but for reasons of safety and security, most parents are reluctant to let their daughters walk long distances to school. In some African countries, sexual abuse of girl pupils—at school and on the way to school—is one of the main reasons parents withdraw their daughters from school.[29]

Girls and women have been victimized by economic factors not only in the realm of education, as it has been pointed out by Prof. Tomasevski.[30] A major shift on many other factors is equally necessary to ensure employment and political representation opportunities—but equal access to education is a significant start to achieve gender equality.[31]

Inclusive Education

Another step in universal education goals is inclusive education: a strategy contributing towards the ultimate goal of promoting an inclusive society, one which enables all children/adults, whatever their gender, age, ability, ethnicity, refugee status, impairment or HIV status, to participate in and contribute to that society. Difference is respected and valued. Discrimination and prejudice must be actively combated in policies, institutions and behavior.[32]

Within schools inclusive education is an approach which aims to develop a child-focus by acknowledging that all children/adults are individuals with different learning needs and speeds. It leads people to learn about themselves and understand their strengths and limitations, which makes them better able to recognize and understand not only individual health and physical conditions, but also the political, economic, and social conditions that surround them. One must view oneself positively in order to move from passive to active participation.

School Drop-Out

Providing schools is only part of the problem—a huge one for sure, but still only a part of it; the drop-out phenomenon poses another challenge to schools, families, and governments, as well as to the quality of education provided in many countries.[33]

According to Paulo Freire,[34] society itself prevents students from having access to and remaining at school; indeed, dropout is nothing but "school push-out," i.e., children/adults are expelled from school for a number of social, economic, and cultural factors.

The causes that give rise to the dropout/push-out of students are many, such as to help their families, course failure, pregnancy, lack of interest, addiction to drug/alcohol, financial reasons, gender and ethnic discrimination, not getting along with teachers and/or other students, or criminality. School drop-out/push-out is an issue which concerns both developed and underdeveloped countries—and it does not refer only to minority groups such as immigrants and indigenous populations.

Effective and relevant education is important to combat school dropout/push-out. It helps the promotion of the personal development of the individual, ensuring that educational content, method, and scheduling are appropriate to the different needs and circumstances of each person—as in the case of rural areas, where harvest season can make children and adults prioritize work rather than school,[35] or school-dropout caused by the student's mere lack of interest.

Indeed, concerning this problem in China and Colombia, Prof. Tomasevski stated in her Annual Report 2004:

> (. . .) an important reason for children's dropping out of school was their dislike of the education provided them. That many children, when asked whether they liked school—rarely as this happens—answered in the negative is a sobering lesson for education authorities.

From sub-Saharan Africa to Canada, from rich to poor, from eastern to western culture countries, the world cannot refrain from dealing with education issues—such as exclusion and poor quality education—raised by many cultural, religious, ethnic, social, or economic factors, and their impact on the educational process.

The Dakar Framework for Action affirms:

> 43. Evidence over the past decade has shown that efforts to expand enrollment must be accompanied by attempts to enhance educational quality if children are to be attracted to school, stay there, and achieve meaningful learning outcomes.

To address these problems, it is necessary to promote a shift in the education paradigm. Students are not supposed to be coadjuvants to education process and schools should not be an instrument of dominant economic and political purposes.

All students in school is inclusive education in the broadest sense—regardless of their strengths or weaknesses in any area, they become part of the school community. They are included in the feeling of belonging among other students, teachers, and support staff.[36]

A New Approach to Education

The strategic objectives of UNESCO's Medium-Term Strategy for 2002–2007 provide a new vision and a new profile for education, as follows:

- Promoting education as a fundamental right in accordance with the Universal Declaration of Human Rights;
- Improving the quality of education through the diversification of contents and methods and the promotion of universally shared values;
- Promoting experimentation, innovation and the diffusion and sharing of information and best practices as well as policy dialogue in education.

It is important to highlight the concern towards the methods and contents of education, an important issue which has been raised in recent years in order to achieve the higher purpose of education, that is to say, the learner's achievement and development.

In addition, there must be developed a deeper understanding of literacy, a core educational issue, which is widely seen as essential for enabling a person to function fully in his/her society and is often reduced to the ability to read and write in the official language.

This narrow understanding of literacy, developed in the last two centuries with the formation of the nation state, industrialization, and mass schooling, does not recognize the role it plays as a key to developing a critical mind—which does not rely merely on the development of such skills, but on the liberation and full development of the individual.

Human Rights Education

Human rights education has been proclaimed in various global and regional legal instruments, such as The Charter of the United Nations, which reads:

> To achieve international co-operation in solving international problems of an economic, social, cultural, or humanitarian character, and in *promoting and encouraging respect for human rights and for fundamental freedoms* for all without distinction as to race, sex, language, or religion; (. . .)[37] (emphasis added)

Moreover, the Universal Declaration of Human Rights proclaimed

> as a common standard of achievement for all peoples and all nations, to the end that every individual and every organ of society, keeping this Declaration constantly in mind, shall strive by *teaching and education to promote respect for these rights and freedoms* (. . .)[38] (emphasis added)

At the regional level, the African Charter on Human and Peoples' Rights, in its article 25, explicitly calls on African states to

> promote and ensure *through teaching, education and publication, the respect for the rights and freedoms contained in the present Charter* and to see to it that these freedoms and rights as well as corresponding obligations and duties are understood, (emphasis added)

In 1994, the General Assembly of the United Nations proclaimed the United Nations Decade for Human Rights Education (1996–2004), on recommendation of the World Conference on Human Rights (Vienna, June 1994).

The recognition of education as a major instrument to promote and enforce human rights is based on the conviction that we all have the right to know our rights—and it can only be enforced when we learn and understand about the human rights enshrined in national constitutions and in all international human rights instruments.

People are empowered to act when they learn about their human rights and can actively defend themselves from abuses, overcoming their lack of concern towards politics. In addition, imparting of knowledge and skills regarding human rights promotes

a. The strengthening of respect for human rights and fundamental freedoms;
b. The full development of the human personality and the sense of its dignity;
c. The promotion of understanding, tolerance, gender equality and friendship among all nations, indigenous peoples and racial, national, ethnic, religious, and linguistic groups;
d. The enabling of all persons to participate effectively in a free society;
e. The furtherance of the activities of the United Nations for the maintenance of peace.[39]

Empowerment through human rights education develops the individual's awareness of rights and obligations regarding his/her human condition and includes everyone in the citizenry; it charges people with the responsibility of claiming rights for themselves and others, as well as respecting those rights. People become aware of the difference individuals can make and the importance of joining efforts to do so. Additionally, human rights can become more tangible when related to people's own life experiences, which strengthens the power of these rights in the process of building a more equitable, just, and peaceful world.

The implementation of human rights education goes beyond inclusion in the schools' curricula, for it involves a whole commitment to human rights, from the training of teachers to a safe and healthy learning environment. Human rights education is not only a set of contents to be transmitted to learners, but also understandings of how and where it will be done. Schools' staff must be fully aware of human rights, which should be incorporated in all strategies, procedures, and activities developed and performed by them.

Finally, human rights education should be an integral part of the right to education,[40] both in formal and non-formal schooling.

Sex Education

Education on sexuality, relationships, and reproductive health is deeply connected with women's and girls' rights. The Convention on the Elimination of All Forms of Discrimination against Women (CEDAW) and the recommendations of the General Comments of the related Committee are clear on the importance of sex education.[41] Nevertheless, sexuality is inherent to human beings and men and women, boys and girls, every person should have the right to be educated on sexual health, and the Committee of the Rights of the Child states that

> Adequate measures to address HIV/AIDS can be undertaken only if the rights of children and adolescents are fully respected. The most relevant rights in this regard, in addition to those enumerated in paragraph 5 above, are the following: (. . .) the right to preventive health care, sex education and family planning education and services(. . .).[42]

Sex education is the process of acquiring knowledge and skills concerning sexual behaviour (which comprises sexual orientation, relationships, birth control, and disease prevention), empowering individuals to make decisions, assert their choices, and protect their physical, emotional, and moral integrity. As a result, individuals learn when and how to seek help and become better able to engage in healthier relationships, exert control over their own lives, and recognize other people's rights, cultural differences, and attitudes towards sexuality—mainly regarding sensitive issues such as sexual orientation, contraception methods, abortion, and gender roles.[43]

One could never emphasise enough the core importance of sex education to children—especially girls—with regards to HIV/AIDS prevention, family planning, and elimination of gender discrimination. The right to sex education should be realized with the inclusion of sex education in the curricula worldwide, despite large obstacles such as cultural, religious, and political factors which might tend to prevent schools and educational authorities from enforcing such education.

Education Paradigm Shift

Independently of the reasons, be they economic, social, or cultural, a major change in the pedagogical approach is necessary to deal with the current education crisis. Curriculum adaptation, special programs, acknowledgement of cultural peculiarities, and flexible school schedules are many of the potential solutions for such educational problems as large classes, uncaring and untrained teachers, passive teaching methods, inappropriate curriculum, inappropriate testing/student retention, and lack of parent involvement.

A *Manual on Rights-Based Education* has been developed as a result of collaboration between UNESCO Bangkok and the UN Special Rapporteur. Such an approach recognizes that human rights are interdependent and inter-related and seeks to protect and put them into effect. Human rights are the means, the ends, the mechanisms of evaluation, and the focal point of Rights-Based Education. The manual is based on international human rights law, aiming to bring human rights standards into educational practice, encompassing health, nutrition, safety, and protection from abuse and violence.

One of the issues addressed in the manual is the quality of education, which should be learner-centred and relevant to learners, as well as respectful to human rights, such as privacy, gender equality, freedom of expression, and the participation of learners in the education process.[44] This means that both content and pedagogical approach are crucial to quality of education.

Furthermore, the content should be related to real-life experiences and learners' cultural and social context, encouraging full participation of all parties involved, enforcing their fundamental rights of freedom of expression, access to information, privacy, and health, among others. The importance of education content has also been recognised by the Committee of the Rights of the Child.[45]

A propos, Freire had always stressed the need to change the traditional schooling system, which treats students as objects and contributes to the marginalization of minorities, as opposed to "liberatory" pedagogy, one that uses the dialogical method to facilitate the growth of humanization and empowerment[46] and enforces the principle of equality while respecting differences. The focus must be on education for equity, transformation, and inclusion of all individuals through the development of consciousness and critical thinking.

Freire has based his work on the belief in the power of education to change the world for the better, supporting freedom from oppression and inclusion of all individuals. In his book *Pedagogia da Autonomia* (Pedagogy for Autonomy), he enunciates the three pillar concepts of teaching:

1. there is no teaching without learning;
2. to teach is not to transmit knowledge; and
3. the process of education is a human peculiarity.[47]

Freire's pedagogy requires a whole new approach to the exercise of power over education; responsibility is to be shared between all parties involved (teachers, learners, those responsible for learners, and the community at large) from the curriculum planning to the process of learning. The dialogical process resulting herein comes about from the recognition of and respect for each individual's personal knowledge and skills, which enables all to participate equally in the organization and development of education.

Teachers and learners share equally the experience of learning through questioning, reflecting, and participating; as a result, this process contributes to the enforcement of infinitely diverse human potentials, instead of refuting, weakening, distorting, or repressing them.

Such a pedagogical approach builds up to the formation of critical consciousness and allows people to question the nature of their historical and social situation—to "read their world"—becoming more than a mere passive object to the information disseminated by others.[48]

The schooling system is not supposed to be limited to reproducing a dominant ideology, to teach a truth that is not true for all, fostering impossible dreams and hopes in the learners; but at the same time it must allow them to dream. It requires an affectionate—yet scientific—posture by the teacher.[49]

The role of the teacher is crucial, but s/he cannot be just an individual in the world, rather than an individual with the world and with other people, sharing the experience of being in "quest"—in a permanent process of questioning, changing, growing, learning, improving, and finding new directions.[50]

Teachers become educators when they get fully aware of the surrounding world's influence on every individual. And, most of all, they must be open to the reality of learners, get acquainted with their way of being, adhere to their right to be. Educators choose to change the world with learners.[51]

Being actively aware of the world, the teacher becomes better able to do more than just disciplining the process through which the world gets into the students, imitating the world, filling their empty vessels with chunks of knowledge.[52]

In an ever-increasing globalized world, learning processes must recognize and value differences; teachers must be prepared to deal with diversity in every level (cultural, social, economic, religious, ethnic, and linguistic) and schools must be prepared to cultivate a joyful environment to foster this get-together. Learning is to celebrate the communication and interaction between people.

Conclusion

The future of humankind relies on the fulfillment of the right to education: equality, freedom, dignity, equitable social and economic development, sustainable development, and peace are highly dependent on successful universal education policies.

Nevertheless, just providing universal formal schooling is not a guarantee of an educational system that prepares the individuals to be free. Although it is clear that a lot of work needs to be done until every individual is provided education worldwide, the process of learning can always be improved to achieve its goals of preparing people to participate actively and consciously in the society of which they are part. And education must be respectful of every individual's cultural background so that each person can make the most of it in their personal journey and in their interaction with others.

A rights-based approach to education requires respect for the human rights of all individuals involved in the learning process; it offers education as an entitlement, rather than as a privilege, and does not exempt any actor of the learning process from his/her responsibility for the full protection and fulfilment of any other fundamental right.

Such an approach to education takes place when learners are respected for their autonomy and dignity; moreover, they must be provided all things necessary for them to take part actively in the learning process and to develop their awareness of reality. They learn about their past, understand their present, and acknowledge their power to fight for their future.

Education requires dialogue and affection between teachers and learners. The learning process involves joy, beauty, affection, ethics, equality, mutual respect, and faith in a better world.

Notes

1. World Declaration on Education For All, Jomtien, 1990, article 6. Learning begins at birth. This calls for early childhood care and initial education. These can be provided through arrangements involving families, communities, or institutional programmes, as appropriate.
2. CRC General Comments General Comment no. 1: The Aims of Education, Article 29 (1).
3. According to Jung, individuation is "a process by which individual beings are being formed and differentiated . . . having as its goal the development of the individual personality" (Jung, C.W. 6: par. 767), bearing in mind that "As the individual is not just a single, separate being, but by his very existence presupposes a collective relationship, it follows that the process of individuation must lead to more intense and broader collective relationships and not to isolation." (CW 6, par. 768) "Individuation does not shut one out from the world, but gathers the world to itself." (CW 8, par. 432) quoted in Sharp, 1991.
4. Bowen, 2003.
5. Nowak, 2001:190.
6. Hodgson, 1998:8.
7. "Article 9: sect. 1st. Knowledge and learning generally diffused, through a community, being essential to the preservation of a free Government, and spreading the opportunities, and advantages of education through the various parts of the Country, (. . .) shall be and remain a fund for the exclusive purpose of promoting the interest of Literature, and the sciences, and for the support of seminaries and public schools.(. . .); sect. 2. It shall be the duty of the General assembly, as soon as circumstances will permit, to provide, by law, for a general system of education, ascending in a regular gradation, from township schools to a state university, wherein tuition shall be gratis, and equally open to all." As in http://www.in.gov/icpr/archives/constitution/1816.html#art9
8. Hodgson, 1998:8.
9. Nowak, 2001:192.
10. United Nations Charter, Preamble.
11. Education, Democracy and Human Rights in Swedish development co-operation, Swedish International Development Cooperation Agency, 2004: p. 17.
12. Nowak, 2001:196.
13. As in http://www.fact-index.com/t/th/three_generations_of_human_right8.html
14. Declaration on the Right to Development, adopted by the General Assembly in 1986.
15. World Education Report 2000:23.
16. Gomes Canotilho, 1998:434.
17. Dakar Framework for Action-Education For All: Meeting Our Collective Commitments Text adopted by the World Education Forum-Dakar, Senegal, 26–28 April 2000: 6. (. . .) it is unacceptable in the year 2000 that more than 113 million children have no access to primary education, 880 million adults are illiterate, gender discrimination continues to permeate education systems, and the quality of learning and the acquisition of human values and skills fall far short of the aspirations and needs of individuals and societies.(. . .)
18. World Education Report 2000:17.
19. J. Samofi; Education for What? Education for Whom? Guidelines for National Policy Reports in Education, UNESCO, Paris, 1994, p. 28. quoted in Special Raporteur's Annual Report 2004.
20. "Every person—child, youth, and adult—shall be able to benefit from educational opportunities designed to meet their basic learning needs. These needs comprise both essential learning tools (such as literacy, oral expression, numeracy, and problem

solving) and the basic learning content (such as knowledge, skills, values, and attitudes) required by human beings to be able to survive, to develop their full capacities, to live and work in dignity, to participate fully in development, to improve the quality of their lives, to make informed decisions, and to continue learning. . . ." (Jomtien Declaration, 1990: article 1)

21. World Education Report 2000:76.

22. Special Rapporteur Annual Report 2004, par. 15.

23. As seen in http://campus.northpark.edu/history/Koeller/ ModWorld/Development/neoliberalism.htm; website on longer on line.

24. Special Rapporteur Annual Report 2004, par. 8.

25. OXFAM Briefing Paper 3, "A Tax on Human Development", 2001:2.

26. Not surprisingly, social protection is one of the prevention measures of International Programme on the Elimination of Child Labour of the ILO, so that families do not have to rely on their children's workforce to pay for their living.

27. World Declaration on Education For All, Jomtien, 1990: Article 3 (3) The most urgent priority is to ensure access to, and improve the quality of, education for girls and women, and to remove every obstacle that hampers their active participation. All gender stereotyping in education should be eliminated.

28. A Fair Chance, Global Campaign for Education, April 2003:2.

29. Ibid, p. 25.

30. Special Rapporteur Annual Report 2004, par. 32.

31. As seen in http://www.unesco.org/education/educnews/20_12_ 12/gender.htm; website on longer on line.

32. As seen in http://www.eenet.org.uk/theory_ practice/whatisit .shtml; website no longer on line.

33. World Declaration on Education For AU, Jomtien, 1990, Preamble: "More than 100 million children and countless adults fail to complete basic education programmes; millions more satisfy the attendance requirements but do not acquire essential knowledge and skills; (. . .)"

34. Freire, 2000:50–51.

35. A Fair Chance, Global Campaign for Education, April 2003: 24.

36. Dakar Framework for Action, par. 67: There is an urgent need to adopt effective strategies to identify and include the socially, culturally and economically excluded. This requires participatory analysis of exclusion at household, community and school levels, and the development of diverse, flexible, and innovative approaches to learning and an environment that fosters mutual respect and trust."

37. Charter of the United Nations, article 1(3).

38. Universal Declaration of Human Rights, proclamation.

39. Report of the United Nations High Commissioner for Human Rights on the implementation of the Plan of Action for the United Nations Decade for Human Rights Education, Appendix, par. 2.

40. UNESCO Executive Board 165th Session-Elements for an Overall Unesco Strategy on Human Rights, par. 31.

41. CEDAW, Article 10(h): "Access to specific educational information to help to ensure the health and well-being of families, including information and advice on family planning." General Recommendations of the Committee, 21: "In order to make an informed decision about safe and reliable contraceptive measures, women must have information about contraceptive measures and their use, and guaranteed access to sex education and family planning services, as provided in article 10 (h) of the Convention." Recommendations for government action, par. 31: "States parties should also, in particular: (c) Prioritize the prevention of unwanted pregnancy through family planning and sex education."

42. Committee of the Rights of the Child, General Comments 3, par. 6.

43. As in http://www.avert.org/sexedu.htm

44. *Manual on Rights-Based Education.* Collaborative project between Katarina Tomasevski (UN. Special Rapporteur on the Right to Education) and UNESCO Asia and Pacific Regional Bureau for Education, Bangkok, Thailand.

45. General Comment no. 1 (on the article 29 [I]) "The Aims of Education", par. 3: "The child's right to education is not only a matter of access (CRC—art. 28) but also of content. (. . .)"

46. Freire, 1970: 43.

47. Freire, 1998.

48. Freire, 1970: 68.

49. Freire, 1998.

50. Freire, ibid.

51. Freire, ibid.

52. Freire, 1970: 36.

References

Bowen, James (2003), *A History of Western Education,* Vol. I–III, Routledge.

Canotilho, J.J. Gomes (1998), *Direito Constitucional e Teoria da Constituição,* Almedina.

Freire, Paulo (1970), *Pedagogia do Oprimido,* Paz e Terra, versão.

Freire, Paulo (1997) *Pedagogia da Autonomia: Saberes necessaries à pratica educativa,* Paz e Terra, versão e-book.

Freire, Paulo (2000), *A Educaçao na Cidade.*Cortez, versao e-book.

Hodgson, Douglas (1998), *The Human Right to Education.* Ashgate.

Nowak, Manfred (2001). The Right to Education. In Asbjorn Eide, Catarina Krause, & Allan Rosas, *Economic, Social and Cultural Rights—A Textbook,* Martinus Nifhoff Publishers, pp. 189–211.

CAETANO PIMENTEL resides in Rio de Janeiro, Brazil. This article is based on a monograph he wrote for a post-graduation course on Human Rights and Democracy at the University of Coimbra, Coimbra, Portugal.

Asian American Teachers

Do they impact the curriculum? Are there support systems for them?

HEMA RAMANATHAN

Introduction

The significance and importance of global education and a culturally relevant curriculum have been thrown into relief by the events of Sept. 11, 2001, emphasizing the urgency to understand and be accepting of diverse cultures. This has a strong bearing on the "enculturation" role of schools, as agents of cultural reproduction.

The traditional curriculum transmits Euro-American norms that are seen as the primary American culture. The possible positive effects of a culturally responsive and diverse curriculum (CDC) have been detailed, including affirming the value of cooperation, helping students and teachers build an identity by comparing what they have learned in the classroom with their own experiences, and the importance of a caring community (Gay, 2000; Ladson-Billings, 1992b; Sleeter & Grant, 1991; Zimpher & Ashburn, 1984).

There is little doubt that schools should be more inclusive and that school-based personnel should appreciate and affirm what minority teachers bring to facilitate the development of a culturally relevant curriculum that is academically rigorous (Quiocho & Rios, 2000) but there is no systemic effort to genuinely shift from a Western perspective to include other perspectives and materials (Foster, 1994, cited in Quiocho & Rios, 2000; Gay, 2000).

However, adopting CDC or culturally congruent approaches to teaching has its own pitfalls. They can render teachers suspect by the broader school community since such approaches do not conform to the mainstream (Conner, 2002; Foster, 1994; Lipka, 1994, cited in Quiocho & Rios, 2000). Further, race and race-related pedagogy are not considered appropriate topics for discussion among faculty members, and issues regarding them are not raised in faculty forums (Foster, 1994, cited in Quiocho & Rios, 2000).

Where there is no self-examination, there is unlikely to be an expectation of overt support. The result is that the voices of minority teachers have been silenced and many of them do not have a role as decision-makers beyond the everyday decisions that teachers make in the classroom (Goodwin, Genishi, Asher, & Woo, 1997; Irvine, 2002; Quiocho & Rios, 2000).

These issues as they relate to Asian Americans have other features that complicate the matter. The term "Asian American,"

classed as one group for purposes of census and political policy, embraces sub-groups that differ widely in matters of language, religion, and cultural practices and beliefs. This multicultural, multi-ethnic, multi-literate profile engenders a lack of coherent cultural identity so that only a narrow slice is represented in the broad spectrum of the curriculum (Gay, 2000).

In the past three decades, the Asian-American population has been overlooked in terms of the demographic profile in spite of a dramatic increase of about 63%. Of Asian Americans, nearly a fourth is under 17 and of school-going age, accounting for about 3% of the total K–12 student population (Smith, Rogers, Alsalam, Perie, Mahoney, & Martin, 1994) while accounting for only 1.2% of the nation's teaching force (Snyder & Hoffman, 1994). Their low visibility is compounded by the fact that they are not evenly represented across the country in all regions; clustered along the East and West coasts, they are largely "missing in action" in the Midwest and South (U.S. Census Bureau, 2000).

Unlike other minority communities, there is no scarcity of qualified persons in this community in which 37% aged 25 or older is college educated. Yet, specifically among Asian-American women who hold degrees, only 1% goes into teaching, a profession still dominated by women. Many of the rest opt for jobs in technical and scientific fields which are higher-paying and where discrimination is perceived to be less of a barrier to advancement (Rong & Preissle, 1997; Su, Goldstein, Suzuki & Kim, 1997).

Emerging literature on Asian Americans shows that perceptions about the community are often at odds with reality. Asian Americans desire to be 'normal,' to fit in (Gordon, 2000). Whether it is to be accepted as "honorary Whites" so as not to remain "forever foreigners," or to get by in a racist society by staying quiet and behaving so that nobody would bother them (Tuan, 1998), Asian Americans indicate a desire to assimilate and to nullify their Asian roots. Their integration seems to depend on how mainstream they are, which argues for assimilation not accommodation.

Viewed as a "model minority," self-esteem issues that are cited in support of African-American and Hispanic profiles in the curriculum may not appear to be applicable to Asian-American students. While it is true that Asian-American students by and large are academic achievers and the Asian-American community appears to be successful economically, second- and third-generation Asian-American students in schools have to contend with cultural, social, and emotional issues like any other minority group (Siu, 1996).

Among all ethnic groups, the extremely limited research that is available on Asian-American teachers is a matter of deep concern (Quiocho & Rios, 2000). The available data focus on issues of motivation, explaining why Asian Americans are drawn to teaching and what may keep them in the profession (Goodwin, Genishi, Asher, & Woo, 1997; Gordon, 2000; Rong & Preissle, 1997; Su, Goldstein, Suzuki, & Kim, 1997). There are few studies that address the effect Asian-American teachers could have on the curriculum or the issues they may have to deal with in their work environment (Gay, 2000; Goodwin, Genishi, Asher, & Woo, 1997; Quiocho & Rios, 2000).

The purpose of this descriptive study was: (1) to understand problems Asian Americans may face as minority teachers; (2) to examine any impact they may have on curricula and academic experiences at the building level; and (3) to identify support systems available to them to implement desired changes.

Methodology

A survey of 23 items based on the research questions was designed. Of the 15 of these items that dealt with issues of identity of the Asian-American teachers and other professionals in the building, five explored the respondents' perceptions of the effect of their ethnicity on the curriculum and related activities in school. Seven items focused on how peers, administrators, students, and their parents related to issues of acceptance of their identity, and support that was or could be offered. Three items questioned the respondents about their awareness of and membership in professional ethnic support groups. Since the sampling frame of Asian-American teachers available was small, the survey was piloted with African-American teachers to test for a minority perspective.

The Midwestern state chosen for study mirrored the changing national demographics with regard to the Asian-American population (U.S. Bureau of Census, 1997). A list of all Asian-American teachers, obtained from the state Department of Education, provided an initial sampling frame of 106. Deletion of those no longer teaching and additions of names suggested by respondents defined a final sample of 96.

The final survey, with a cover letter and a stamped envelope for returning the completed survey, was mailed to all participants. Reminders over a period of two months included postcards, phone calls, and duplicate surveys. Forty participants responded to the survey for a return rate of 41.7%. Four of them declined to participate; they felt their ethnic identity as Asian Americans was not relevant to their identity as teachers. Another respondent stated that since he was mistaken for a Caucasian, his responses were not relevant. A sixth respondent chose not to complete the survey since the questions dealt with "delicate issues." Eventually 34 surveys were deemed useable. The data were coded and categorized by the researcher using open coding techniques (Strauss & Corbin, 1990).

Findings and Discussion
Curricular Issues

The presence of Asian-American teachers appears to have little effect on the curriculum or the academic experiences of students, and core content courses are not affected by the presence of Asian-American teachers in schools. Given that five of the respondents stated that they did not see themselves as Asian American, it is likely that their curriculum is not affected by ethnic perspectives.

Of the 34 usable responses, only three related their ethnicity to the content formally. Two taught Japanese and Chinese languages in their schools, supporting Ladson-Billings' (1992a) statement that there is a distinct ethnic-specific cultural preference for language that teachers bring into the classroom. The Japanese language teacher was also in charge of an after-school Japanese club. A music teacher incorporated a few Japanese songs into the repertoire.

Three other respondents brought their experience and knowledge of "otherness" into the curriculum informally, reflecting the findings of Goodwin, Genishi, Asher, and Woo (1997). They referred to world literature and global issues while discussing their content; this was not a requirement of the curriculum but was made possible by their wide experience. For example, a teacher from India compared Third World conditions to the U.S. to illustrate differences in life styles and to inculcate sensitivity to environmental issues.

Any other references to the ethnicity of the Asian-American teachers were sporadic and "add-ons." Four respondents said they incorporated activities related to their culture in their classroom but were not specific about the purpose or the learning expected from the students. Eight of the 34 responded that they had been used as resource persons by other teachers in the building.

In a scenario that is easily recognized, they were invited to talk to other classes about their culture, ethnicity, and country of origin or affiliation. The topics most often included the "visible" features of culture such as food, festivals, customs, and rituals, especially of marriage. On a more personal and serious note, a Japanese American was invited to talk about the experiences of Japanese Americans interned in concentration camps in the U.S. during World War II.

Decision-Making

Asian-American teachers are curriculum deliverers (Twisleton, 2004), not involved in defining the curriculum and with no opportunity to influence either the structures or the people in their working environment.

The Japanese language teacher stated that he wished that he were included in decisions regarding establishing or abolishing a foreign language department or offering Japanese but seemed to have no belief that his wish would be granted. A second respondent was both skeptical and cautious about her presence on any decision-making body. She believed that there was a danger of "being tokenized or less than appreciated because the teachers may have little understanding of non-mainstream experiences."

With the exception of one school building which had three Asian-American teachers, all the other respondents were the only Asian Americans in their schools. This lack of critical numbers may preclude their having an impact on decision-making at the building level.

The teachers were cautious about establishing an alternative culturally-responsive pedagogy and curriculum, unlike those studied by Su (1997). Except for two respondents, none of the others expressed a desire to be involved in re-designing the curriculum with a view to incorporating Asian-American elements. Rather than see schools as sites for diversity, anti-racism, social justice, and transformation (Feuerverger, 1997; Foster, 1994; Klassen & Carr, 1997, cited in Quiocho & Rios, 2000), most of these Asian-American teachers appear to want to maintain the status quo.

Issues of Support
Administrators and Peers
Asian-American teachers appreciated the support they receive from both administrators and their peers and detailed generic teacher needs in the areas of teaching, curriculum, and discipline.

Of the 34 usable responses to this set of questions, 15 respondents stated that they were supported by their peers in two areas—professional and personal—while 12 felt that they were not. Like all teachers, they looked to the administration for help with planning and implementing their teaching responsibilities and with student discipline.

Peripheral experiences of sharing information related to their ethnicity were seen as acknowledgement by peers and administrators of their uniqueness. Thus, most of the support they asked for was not curricular re-alignment, representation in the curriculum, or cultural mores of expectation and behavior that might distinguish them from their 'mainstream' peers.

Students
Asian Americans are proud of their ethnicity and yet wish to blend in with the dominant group (Gordon, 2000b). This dichotomy of appearance and perception was clearly noticeable in their interpretation of student appreciation. Asian-American teachers were pleased both when students noticed their ethnicity and when they did not. They welcomed being treated like all other teachers regardless of their ethnicity. On the other hand, they enjoyed the attention students paid to their different cultural background.

Fully a third of the respondents indicated that their ethnic identity did not impinge itself on the students. They believed that they were successful teachers because they were like any other teachers and exhibited the same characteristics of concern and caring. As one respondent colorfully phrased it, "I could be purple and still (the students) would enjoy my class, hopefully because I teach with caring and love." Another respondent commented,

> More than 80% of my students and parents like and appreciate the things I'm doing to help my students learn. I use my lunch hour to help the slow students. I always find time to help my students.

Yet students were not entirely blind to their teachers' differences. Their curiosity was piqued by their teachers' ethnicity and the respondents saw this as an indication of a positive attitude. Students questioned their teachers about their personal background and culture. The respondents felt that sometimes students "look(ed) to me as a source of information about Asia." Students are also curious about the country of origin of the Asian-American teachers. "They love to see some real samples from China/Taiwan and hear about the Chinese zodiac."

Some respondents were also subliminally conscious that students' perceptions of race and ability are influenced by the teacher's ethnicity. Beyond seeing the teachers as sources of trivia, two clear statements made by the respondents point to their belief that minority students are conscious and appreciative of the teachers modeling a minority status. They "appreciate the fact that (the teacher) can connect with them in different ways . . . can talk about skin color and speaking languages other than English with a certain depth of understanding."

As another respondent said, "My students realize that teachers don't just come in Black and White background. Anyone with the right qualifications (education) can become a teacher."

Professional Support Groups
Eighteen of the respondents indicated that they would join a group that addressed Asian-American issues related to teaching and teachers while nine did not wish to be part of any group. There are two professional organizations already in existence that are based on Asian-American ethnicity: the Chinese Language Teachers Association and an organization for music teachers founded by one of the respondents.

Yet, except for two respondents who each identified one organization, the others were unaware of the existence of these organizations. However, respondents felt the need for such support systems that would help them in their professional life, which are not available to them at present.

Role as Interlocutors
Falling outside the "color lines" of traditional racial discourse provides Asian-American teachers a role not obviously available to African-American or European-American teachers in a school building: interlocutors in a racially-charged incident. Being neither Black nor White, they are seen either as neutral, "colorless," or as either color, as may suit the students. "I can be seen as White by White students and as Black by Black students," a participant stated.

At the very least, Asian-American teachers see themselves as a "bridge between worlds and between people." This seems to be a great advantage with parents who are not hostile or wary of their 'allegiance.' As one respondent said,

> I'm in a high-minority population school and being non-White is an advantage with African Americans, Hispanic, and Asian parents. I don't sense the immediate mistrust that I see directed towards White educators. I've been asked to sit in on conferences where the educators were all White and the parents were non-White, for that very reason.

Their strength is derived from their being perceived as impartial. As mediators, they have been able to explain grading issues to minority students, defusing potential problems. Since they do not "belong" to the "other side," their words have veracity and carry weight with all stakeholders in a school building. As two respondents said,

> (Being an Asian American helps) with my students simply because it aids me in discussing fairness of rules, policies, treatment of minorities, or any related issues from a minority perspective.

> Some of my African-American students have accused other White teachers of giving out low grades to Black students because they are prejudiced. Since I'm not White, I was able to play neutral ground and explain to them how mistaken the students were, since grades are *earned* and not *given* by the teachers.

Non-Responses

Four respondents declined to participate; they felt that their ethnic identity as Asian Americans was not relevant to their identity as teachers. Another respondent stated that since he was often mistaken for a Caucasian, his responses would not be relevant. A significant third of them are either not conscious of their ethnicity or choose not to bring them into play. Their claim to be Caucasian or mainstream distinguishes them from those who would like to see their ethnicity as a strength and would like to have active support from their peers to explore it.

A sixth respondent chose not to complete the survey though she was repeatedly assured that her anonymity and that of the school would be maintained. As she explained in a telephone conversation, the questions dealt with "delicate issues" that she did not want to talk about.

Discussion

Asian-American teachers in this study appear to be well-integrated into the school system with regard to a teacher's life, role, and responsibilities, unlike the teachers in Goodwin, Genishi, Asher, and Woo (1997). They feel accepted and supported by peers and students and believe that their concerns are heard. Their problems relating to issues of curriculum, student discipline, and professional support are no different from other teachers in U.S. schools in most respects. Thus, the Asian part of their identity does not seem to count with them at all or to be an issue, and they do not seem to be overly concerned about being underrepresented in their schools or in the curriculum.

For change to be effected a critical mass has to be achieved. The desire on the part of Asian-American teachers to maintain the status quo may be prompted by a lack on numbers in their school buildings. In most cases, as the sole representative of their community, the desire to make a change in the curriculum may not seem feasible to them and therefore may not be entertained.

Calls for a wider, more multicultural curricula have not gone unheard. It is clear that students of today will need to know more about Asia than was required of the previous generation.

The economic growth of India and China make it apparent that in the future students will have to be more familiar with the present histories and cultures of such countries.

With this in mind, schools should be more deliberate about diversifying the curriculum. It should be apparent that teaching Asia in two weeks in a high school Social Studies class will not meet these needs, and that a more equitable distribution of time, addressing various cultures, is necessary (Conner, 2002).

Content teachers should become more knowledgeable about Asian cultures and a growing body of Asian literature in English. It seems natural that Asian-American teachers would be more intentionally involved in such curricular decisions about internationalizing the curriculum and making it more globally focused.

Recent world events have shown the need for foreign language expertise in this country and that promoting a functionally monolingual education is totally inadequate. Schools could offer an Asian language as part of its curriculum. Apart from the need for students to become well-rounded adults with knowledge of the world, the growth of India and China as global economic forces make it important for them to learn about Asia. It then would seem to follow that Asian-American teachers would be a rich resource.

With minority teachers a rarity in the teaching force and growing scarcer, attracting Asian Americans into the teaching profession will require that certain features such as salaries be amended (Su, 1997). Perhaps they could be offered inducements and bonuses and differentiated contracts as is offered to math and science teachers in some school districts. Calls for increasing teacher pay have come from a wide spectrum of society (Blair, 2001; Bond, 2001; Johnson, 2000). Whether this will come to pass is a question but until the monetary benefits are appreciably increased, Asian Americans are unlikely to enter the teaching profession in any substantial numbers.

The variety of roles that teachers play in a school in providing support for each other could be limited if they are not aware of their own strengths. The ability to offer differing viewpoints and perspectives on issues so that they can act as interlocutors in race-related matters could be significant to the well-being and growth of school and society. For example, Asian-American teachers could mediate in racially-charged situations where trust is challenged and communication lines are broken. They could explicate to minority students the nuanced perspectives of the educational system and, on appropriate occasions, advocate for the perceptions of beleaguered minority students.

The larger question is about teacher professional identity in which ethnicity is assimilated or absorbed. The most common way minority groups address conflicts in identity is either by adopting the dominant mode of identification and ignoring or relegating to the background their own ethnic features.

Ethnic organizations may exist in part because of the desire of the community to maintain its identity (Barth, 1969; Gordon, 1964). The case in point of a teacher being unwilling to respond to an anonymous survey is deeply disturbing and is a telling comment on the insecurity that some Asian-American teachers deal with in their work environment. The reluctance to address what is probably an unpleasant situation may indicate a peer group or administration that could be deliberately vindictive at being portrayed in unflattering terms.

Professional support groups could help Asian-American teachers identify and retain their cultural and ethnic features without jeopardizing their career or professional persona. Exploring and affirming their identity, and in turn finding ways of understanding and valuing it, will mitigate the marginalization of Asian-American teachers. However, the practically nonexistent research on the formation of an ethnic professional identity precludes a detailed discussion in an empirical study.

Conclusion

It is increasingly apparent that the conversations about race in the U.S. cannot continue to be a Black-White issue but must include Asian Americans and Hispanic Americans. The violence inflicted on Asian Americans in the aftermath of Sept. 11 was only one in a long line of attacks on them. The incidents by the "dot-busters" in Jersey City dating from the 1980s to the ransacking of Korean shops in 1992 were unfortunately not isolated occurrences (Zia, 2000).

Asian-American teachers appear to be an untapped resource; they should recognize that they are a "salient marker" (Tuan, 1998) to their students and other stakeholders, making it essential for them not to make their ethnic identity a private affair.

The U.S. perceives itself as a unique multiracial and multiethnic society. Schools claim to help their students value and celebrate diversity. Raising the profile of the largely invisible Asian-American teachers in schools is a viable starting point in achieving these objectives. It remains to be seen what the map of a school would look like if Asian-American teachers were to emphasize their ethnicity and not conform to the generic role that a teacher is expected to play in a school.

References

American Association of Colleges of Teacher Education. (1994). *Teacher education pipeline III: Schools, Colleges and Departments of Education enrollments by race, ethnicity, and gender.* Washington, DC: Author.

Banks, J. A. (1994), Transforming the mainstream curriculum. *Educational Leadership, 51*(8), 4–8.

Banks, J. A. (Ed.) (1996). *Multicultural education, transformative knowledge, and action: Historical and contemporary perspectives.* New York: Teachers College Press.

Barth, F. (1969). *Ethnic groups and boundaries: The social organization of cultural differences.* London, UK: Allen & Unwin.

Blair, J., (2001, February 21), Lawmakers plunge into teacher pay. *Education Week.* Retrieved September 2005, from http://www.edweek.org

Bond, C. K. (2001). Do teacher salaries matter? Unpublished doctoral dissertation, Teachers College, Columbia University, New York.

Gay, G. (2000). *Culturally responsive teaching: Theory, research and practice.* New York: Teachers College Press.

Goodwin, A. L., Genishi, C., Asher, N., & Woo, K. A. (1997). Voices from the margins: Asian American teachers' experiences in the profession. In D. M. Byrd & D. J. McIntyre (Eds.) *Research*

on the education of our nation's teachers. Teacher education Yearbook V. Thousand Oaks, CA: Corwin Press.

Gordon, J. (2000a). Asian-American resistance to selecting teaching as a career: The power of community and tradition. *Teachers College Record, 102*(1), 173–96.

Gordon, J. (2000b). *The color of teaching.* New York: Routledge Falmer

Gordon, M. (1964). *Assimilation in American life.* New York: Oxford University Press.

Irvine, J. J. (Ed.) *In search of wholeness: African-American teachers and their culturally specific classroom practices.* New York: New York University, Institute for Education and Social Policy.

Johnson, S. M. (2000, June 7). Teaching's next generation. *Education Week.* Retrieved September 2005, from http://www.edweek.org

Kincheloe, J. L & Steinberg, S. R. (1997). *Changing multiculturalism.* Philadelphia: Open University Press.

Ladson-Billings, G. (1992a). Culturally relevant teaching: The key to making multicultural education work. In C. Grant (Ed.), *Research and multicultural education.* London, UK: Falmer Press.

Ladson-Billings, G. (1992b). Reading between the lines and beyond the pages: A culturally relevant approach to literacy teaching. *Theory into Practice, 31,* 312–320.

Ladson-Billings, G. (1994). *The dreamkeepers: Successful teachers of African American children.* San Francisco: Jossey-Bass.

Morishima, J. K., & Mizokawa, D. T. (1980). *Education for, by, and of Asian/Pacific Americans, II.* ERIC Documents. ED199356.

Phinney, J. (2000). Ethnic identity. In A. Kazdin (Ed.), *Encyclopedia of psychology. 3.* Washington, DC: American Psychological Association.

Quiocho, A., & Rios, F. (2000). The power of their presence: Minority group teachers and schooling. *Review of Educational Research, 70*(4), 485–528.

Rong, X. L., & Priessle, J. (1997). The continuing decline in Asian-American teachers. *American Educational Research Journal, 34*(2), 267–93.

Shain F. (2003). *The schooling and identity of Asian girls.* Sterling, VA: Trentham Books.

Siu, S-F. (1996). *Asian-American students at risk: A literature review. Report No. 8.* ERIC Reproduction Services ED404406.

Sleeter, C. E., & Grant, C.A. (1991). Mapping terrains of power: Student cultural knowledge versus classroom knowledge. In C. E. Sleeter (Ed.), *Empowerment through multicultural education.* Albany, NY: State University of New York Press.

Smith, T. M., Rogers, G. T., Alsalam, N., Perie, M., Mahoney, R. P., & Martin, V. (1994). *The Condition of education, 1994.* Washington, DC National Center for Education Statistics, Department of Education. ED371491.

Snyder, T. D., & Hoffman, C. M. (1994). *Digest of education statistics, 1994.* Washington, DC National Center for Education Statistics, Department of Education. ED377253.

Strauss, A. L., & Corbin, J. M. (1998). *Basics of qualitative research: Techniques and procedures for developing grounded theory.* Thousand Oaks, CA: Sage.

Su, Z. (1997). Teaching as a profession and as a career: Minority candidates' perspectives. *Teaching and Teacher Education, 13*(3), 325–40.

Su, Z., Goldstein, S., Suzuki, G., & Kim, J. (1997). Socialization of Asian Americans in human services professional schools: A comparative study *Urban Education, 32*(3), 279–303.

Tuan, M. (1998). *Forever foreigners or honorary whites: The Asian American experience today.* New Brunswick, NJ: Rutgers University Press.

Twisleton, S. (2004). The role of teacher identities in learning to teach primary literacy. *Educational Review, 56*(2), 157–164.

U.S. Census Bureau. (2000). *Statistical abstract of the United States: 2000* (120th Edition). Washington DC: United States Department of Commerce.

Ware, F. (2002) Black teachers' perceptions of their roles and practices. In J. J. Irvine (Ed)., *In search of wholeness: African-American teachers and their culturally specific classroom practices.* New York: New York University, Institute for Education and Social Policy.

Waters, M. C. (1990). *Ethnic options: Choosing ethnic identities in America.* Berkeley, CA: University of California Press.

Yon, D. (1996). Identity and differences in the Canadian diaspora: Case study from Metropolitan Toronto. In A. Ruprecht & C. Tiana (Eds.), *The re-ordering of cultures: Caribbean, Latin America, and Canada in the hood.* Ottawa, ON: Carleton Press.

Zia, H. (2000). *Asian American dream: The emergence of an American people.* New York: Farrar, Strauss & Giroux.

Hema Ramanathan is an associate professor in the Department of Curriculum and Instruction of the College of Education at the University of West Georgia, Carrollton, Georgia.

UNIT 3

Developing Curriculum and Instruction

Unit Selections

Key Points to Consider

- How can teachers negotiate the requirement to meet all students' needs and avoid the deficit model?

- What are ethnic affiliation and ethnic identity?

- How does a person become the recipient of ethnic miseducation and how does it impact one's teaching?

- How can teachers overcome the silencing of Latina/o students?

- Describe various approaches for educating children of poverty for a social justice-based education.

Student Website

www.mhcls.com

Internet References

Hunger and World Poverty
   http://www.poverty.com/
North American Reggio Emilia Alliance
   http://www.reggioalliance.org/
United States Census Bureau and Poverty
   http://www.census.gov/hhes/www/poverty/poverty.html
The World Bank
   http://web.worldbank.org/

Most teachers are responsible for developing curriculum that is standards based and content intense. Members of every academic discipline have dedicated much time, money, and energy crafting the minimal expectations that all students should know, do, and believe related to a particular subject area. The outcomes have been prioritized and ordered so curriculum offers both a comprehensive scope within each grade level or course of study coordinated with a smooth sequence so all students are exposed to all expectations during one's academic career.

Ideally, curriculum developers collaborate with instructional strategies so the academic content and pedagogical practices fit together seamlessly equipping teachers to facilitate student-centered learning that engages each student in developmentally appropriate activities and assignments. The curriculum and instruction should align with the classroom assessments that are established clearly in advance of the teaching and learning so teachers, students, and students' families know what is suppose to occur, how it is going to occur, why it is going to occur, who is responsible, and when events will occur or are due. By starting with the end product, the teacher can work backwards to design instruction to effectively guide the process and support each learner to achieve the learner's potential. When teaching and learning are assessed frequently and properly, teachers' decisions and student growth are both data-driven and purposeful.

However, in order for learning to be student-centered, the teacher needs to become fully acquainted with each individual student. Understanding each student via the cognitive, physical, affective, and social domains of learning for every subject area presents an overwhelming task for even the most seasoned accomplished educator. Yet teachers must attempt to achieve this goal so they can choreograph the most effective and efficient teaching and learning environments multiple times per day.

Too often, the phrase that today's classrooms are more challenging, particularly with the increase in diverse student populations, is repeated. Some teachers defer to this unsound analysis to account for their success and satisfaction. Yet many more teachers enter the classroom every day fully aware that every classroom is filled with diverse student populations and that all classrooms have always been filled with diverse student populations.

Becoming acquainted with each student in all four domains of learning means recognizing and accepting all forms of diversity; it is the student's cultural characteristics that frame the student's world and, thus, the student's learning. Each student's cultural characteristics are a combination of nature and nurture: the characteristics with which one is born and the influences one receives from interactions with families, communities, and opportunities that happen by chance and by choice through life. Students mature at individual rates into a range of unique individuals, all of whom comprise our multicultural world. Thus, classrooms are filled with diverse student populations even if the teacher believes that everyone in the classroom seems to be the same.

© Lars Niki

The concept of multiculturalism is essential for educators to develop curriculum and design instruction that is culturally competent. Teachers must organize and prepare their course content and pedagogical strategies so all students are motivated to learn, are fully engaged in the learning, connect the learning to their own backgrounds, collaborate with their peers, express the learning through their individual learning styles and strengths, exchange discoveries with peers, and assess their own progress and assess the progress of their peers. These guidelines apply to all students; teachers cannot decide who will receive the more effective and efficient educations and who will not.

To achieve cultural competence, teachers must infuse multicultural education across the curriculum and instruction too. All students need to learn about all people. The curricular content must infuse information related to all cultures; the content cannot be limited to the dominant culture represented of selected cultural characteristics. The pedagogical strategies must offer students learning experiences to build upon their strengths and fortify their weaker areas so learning is balanced. Teachers cannot decide in advance the curriculum and instruction that are appropriate for particular students; all students are entitled to the same opportunities to learn and grow.

The articles in Unit 3 provide an array of practices based on research for educators to ensure that all students are receiving a well-balanced education. The articles promote the concepts of creativity and play, key elements of motivation and engagement; the goals of equity and excellence for all students, significant aspects of effective classrooms; and the strategies of integration and infusion, imperative practices for teaching all students about all students and preparing everyone for the future. Teaching and learning that are culturally competent offer all students the same information about themselves, one another, and the world; the same access to new learning and forms of expression; and the same opportunities to engage in learning and experience every event offered to all other students. With equal information, access, and opportunity, today's students learn to accept themselves and one another without bias, stereotyping, and prejudice—traits that are learned in life, not acquired at birth. Culturally competent teachers strive to teach all students in ways that are conscientious, compassionate, and constructive.

Mother Goose Teaches on the Wild Side

Motivating At-Risk Mexican and Chicano Youngsters via a Multicultural Curriculum

MARTHA CASAS

When students believe that their culture is of no value or interest to their teachers, school principals, and others responsible for determining and structuring the academic milieu, their attitude toward learning is affected adversely (Tobin, Tary, Sprague, & Jeffrey, 2002). Therefore, establishing and maintaining cultural diversity in school curricula is important. Moreover, research has demonstrated that young teens who have been adjudicated have higher dropout rates and higher probabilities of being incarcerated in prisons later on as adults (Hagedorn, 1998). Therefore, today's educators must find ways to keep these youngsters in school. With this goal in mind, I designed a curriculum that I believed could serve as a catalyst for learning because it validated the cultural heritage of Mexican and Chicano students. The objectives of the study were to determine: (1) if a multicultural curriculum could motivate these alternative education students to learn; and (2) whether, if the students became reengaged in learning, their reading abilities would improve.[1]

Reading was the subject selected to be assessed, because this content area is measured via the Texas Assessment of knowledge and Skills Test in the sixth, seventh, and eighth grades, so it is possible to determine if there has been academic growth from one year to the next (Texas Education Agency, 2004). Unfortunately, at the middle school level, writing and social studies are not assessed yearly. Writing is assessed in the seventh grade only and social studies content in the eighth grade only, making it difficult for a yearly assessment of both content areas.

Background

"Mother Goose" is a name that students enrolled in an alternative education program at a local middle school gave me seven years ago. At the time, I was teaching in the eighth grade gifted and talented science program. However, during my conference period I would sometimes tutor the boys and girls in the alternative education program, because I wanted to learn why these students could not succeed in a regular education classroom. Some of the boys had been adjudicated youths who belonged to neighborhood gangs and had committed criminal activities including drug dealing, stealing, and assault.

Although I could work with these youngsters for only a short time each day, the students and I began to bond. One morning, a boy named Juan asked me if the students could call me "Mother Goose." When I asked him why they had chosen the name Mother Goose, Juan explained that Mother Goose is a childhood symbol, and they all believed that I was trying to give them a childhood despite the fact that they were living in a rough neighborhood where children grow up too quickly. Although the director of the alternative education program instructed the students to not call me by that name, I often heard the students whisper "Mother Goose is coming" when they saw me approaching their classroom. I never felt insulted by the name but was happy that the boys and girls had come to trust me and felt comfortable with me. After the academic year was over, I received my doctorate and left middle school teaching.

Currently, I am a professor in a teacher education program. My primary duty is to prepare people to enter the teaching profession. Two years ago, one of my students asked me for advice on how to teach and motivate students who are enrolled in alternative education programs for antisocial behavior. Although I could offer some suggestions, I found that my knowledge on the subject was limited. I decided to conduct research in a public middle school alternative education program. I believed that I could gain better insight into how teachers can help these students learn through personal experience.

I conducted this study in the same middle school where I had been a classroom teacher years earlier. The student population of the campus consists of approximately 98 percent Mexican immigrants or Chicanos, and two percent African Americans.[2] The school is located in an area of the city called Segundo Barrio. The children who grow up in this neighborhood, for the most part, live and breathe the Mexican culture. Small businesses in this community consist of family-owned grocery stores, bakeries, and restaurants. Spanish is the dominant language used for communication.

The alternative education program at the school consists of one classroom in which the most behaviorally challenging students are sent from the sixth, seventh, and eighth grades.

Truancy and fighting at school are common infractions. However, some students are in the program because of a court order. After being released from the juvenile detention center for committing crimes such as selling, or taking drugs, vandalizing, stealing, and committing assaults, the students must enroll in an alternative education facility or classroom before being allowed to return to a regular academic program. On any given day, the numbers of students enrolled in the alternative education program at this campus averages between 16 and 24. The period of time that they must remain in the program is generally six weeks. Afterward, they are sent back to the regular classroom. For those students who have committed severe offenses, the period of time spent in the program is longer.

Two points regarding this study must be noted. First, this alternative education program, in general, embraces a more traditional approach to teaching and learning. The teachers implement some group work, direct instruction, and traditional assessments. Teaching via textbook assignments and worksheets are the principal modes of instruction. The program is "alternative" only in that the teachers come to the classroom to instruct the students. Each content area is taught by a different teacher.

Second, there was no connection between the multicultural curriculum that I designed and the rest of the alternative education program. When I worked with the children, I did not follow a traditional teaching approach. I employed the best practices, such as cooperative learning, authentic instruction, and authentic assessment—the use of rubrics for assessing student work. The principal and the director of the alternative education program allowed me to teach according to my own teaching philosophy. Doing my curriculum was voluntary. Parents had to sign permission slips to allow me to work with their children. Also, I asked the students to sign permission slips. I did not want any student to feel obligated to participate in my study. Fortunately, all parents and students signed and returned the permission slips.

On Mondays, Wednesdays, and Fridays the students were taught by their teachers, and I taught them via my multicultural curriculum on Tuesdays and Thursdays. I asked the director what content the students were learning that week in their subject areas, and I designed my lessons and activities to address those same instructional objectives. In short, the students were taught the content via two different curricula and instructional strategies. Since this was an initial study, I believed that I needed to determine how a multicultural curriculum could benefit these students before I took my study to the next level—working with classroom teachers who instruct children at risk of dropping out of school due to antisocial behavior.

On the days I was not teaching, the director gave the students additional work that I left for them to do if there was sufficient time. The students did my lessons, and I evaluated their work afterward. Student work was assessed primarily through rubrics. On occasion students were given opportunities to grade each other and themselves through the use of rubrics.

This study involved 52 students—40 males and 12 females. Throughout the study, the class consisted of more male than female students. On any given day, the ratio of males to females was ten to one. All students were Mexican or Chicano.

Designing and Teaching a Multicultural Curriculum

Writing a curriculum was challenging, because the alternative education program at the school draws students from all three grades. To address this problem, I selected the seventh grade as my focal point. I reasoned that it would be easier for me to downgrade the content to a sixth-grade level, or upgrade it to the eighth grade if necessary. The Texas Essential Knowledge and Skills (the state mandated goals and objectives) served as the cornerstone of my culturally based curriculum (Texas Education Agency, 2004). Social studies, language arts, music, and art were the content areas woven into the curriculum.

It was possible to work within the state's curricular framework in designing a multicultural curriculum that focused primarily on Mexican culture. In addition to learning about their own heritage, however, the children were exposed to African-American, American Indian, Anglo, and Asian cultures.

After receiving a grant to design my curriculum, I began reading and purchasing sets of books appropriate for middle school youngsters that had Latino children as the principal characters in the stories. Books that were written by Latino authors were also selected. However, the students read books by non-Latino authors and stories in which the major characters were non-Latino as well. Within the first week of the study, I encountered a problem. Some of the children were not reading at a middle school grade level. As a result, I purchased books that were written for lower grade students.

The cornerstone of the multicultural curriculum was social studies. Literature sets of books, videotapes, and movies that complemented the content found in their social studies textbooks were purchased. In the seventh grade social studies curriculum, for example, students learn about the Alamo. After the students read about this major event, I had them view the movie *The Alamo*. The students were encouraged to think critically about the film. They responded to questions such as, "Do you believe this movie depicted an accurate interpretation of the events surrounding the siege of the Alamo?" and "How were the Mexicans portrayed in the movie?" In keeping with the study of this state's history, notably the Civil War and Reconstruction in Texas, I had the students view the movie *Glory* to set the stage for learning about the Civil War. They learned of the bravery of many Black soldiers who fought to end slavery. Before seeing this film, the students had not known that Black soldiers fought in the Civil War.

Over 80 percent of the curriculum involved reading and writing activities. I designed activities for each paperback book assigned. For example, after reading two or three chapters in the book, students were required to answer a series of questions to determine their level of comprehension. The questions were designed to follow Bloom's Taxonomy (Bloom et al., 1956). Simple recall questions requiring students to provide the names of the characters and the settings of the stories were included, as well as questions reflecting levels of higher order thinking (Figure 1).

After the students and I discussed chapters in the books, they were given opportunities to read aloud. Some of the

```
Name_____
Assignment: #3


"Blackmail" from Gary Soto's book Local News.


TEKS:
Language Arts (7.8) The student reads widely for different
purposes in varied sources.
Language Arts (7.10) The student uses a variety of
strategies to comprehend a wide range of texts of
increasing levels of difficulty.


1. What did Weasel do to his brother Angel that made him
   so angry?


2. What did Angel do to blackmail his brother?


3. How would you feel if you had been Angel?


4. Which character do you identify with more, Weasel or
   Angel, and why?
```

Figure 1   Book 1.

youngsters chose to read orally by themselves, while others preferred choral reading in which they could recite with others. For the students who had difficulty with reading, choral reading was the preferred method of oral reading. Students were never forced to read aloud. At the beginning, few students volunteered to read orally. However, as time went on, all of the children had taken turns reading aloud as individuals or with their peers.

In addition to using the paperback books and movies as instructional materials to accompany the textbooks, these media were used to introduce students to the issues of racial and ethnic diversity and also provided glimpses as to how other ethnic groups live or have lived in the past. Reading stories, for example, about African-American children, such as the main character in *Sounder,* helped them to see that regardless of color, boys experience many of the same feelings growing up, such as a close relationship with a pet. *Hoops,* by Walter Dean Myers, helped them to realize that other children living in poor neighborhoods face similar struggles. Reading about Kino's loss of his family in Pearl S. Buck's *The Big Wave* helped the children to realize that in addition to Latinos, other ethnic groups value and maintain close family ties. Prior to reading this book, many of the students believed that Latinos were the only ethnic group that cherished familial bonds.

Moreover, these stories served as wonderful gateways to learning about other cultures. After reading *The Big Wave,* the students wanted to learn more about Japan. They went to the

library and searched the Internet, books, and reference materials to learn about Japan and Japanese culture.

The books opened the way for discussions of racism and prejudice. Fortunately, the school library had an excellent collection of books that described and addressed these topics. Whole group discussions were very productive in encouraging the children to speak about their views on prejudice and discrimination. They wanted to talk about what it means to be a Mexican or a Chicano living in the United States. Soon discussions regarding ethnic slurs such as "beaner," "greaser," and "wetback" ensued. The students shared their views concerning discrimination against Latinos. Seizing on their interest in racial slurs against Mexicans and Chicanos, I broadened our discussions to include the derogatory insults aimed at other ethnic groups. We discussed how African Americans, Asians, and American Indians have also suffered discrimination and oppression. The students read about slavery, the Japanese incarceration during World War II, and the Indian Removal Act of 1830.

In addition to making my curriculum multicultural, I wanted to link it to the real-life experiences of the children.

In addition to making my curriculum multicultural, I wanted to link it to the real-life experiences of the children. The reading materials purchased for the curriculum included books in which the characters were troubled teens facing some of the problems and challenges that my youngsters were also experiencing, such as problems in school and at home, gang involvement, drugs, and fighting.

Besides requiring students to read and write, the curriculum encouraged them to express themselves through other mediums such as painting, clay sculpturing, and computer technology. The students enjoyed working together at tables doing art projects. Music sometimes played softly in the background while everyone worked together. The students stated that the music was calming and helped them to concentrate better. They were asked to bring the music that they wanted to hear. Moreover, the lessons implemented the best practices, including cooperative learning and the use of rubrics and portfolios to assess student learning.

Students followed the writer's workshop process. They brainstormed ideas, designed graphic organizers, wrote drafts, and edited their drafts and those of their classmates before submitting a polished product. As a culminating activity, students were encouraged to read their narratives aloud to the class. They were happy that I posted their good work on a bulletin board and did not require them to take their work home. The students explained to me that being seen taking home A or B work by one's homeboys or homegirls could get them beaten up. Being a "nerd" by carrying home books and good schoolwork did not fit the image of a gang member.

Solving mazes and puzzles was a big hit with the children. I purchased a commercial package of mazes and puzzle worksheets that were very challenging (Phillips, 1983). When I told

Name				Date	Points
Skills	**Criteria**				
	1	2	3	4	
Helping The teacher observed you offering assistance to others.	**None** of the time	**Some** of the time	**Most** of the time	**All** of the time	
Listening The teacher observed you listening to others in the group.	**None** of the time	**Some** of the time	**Most** of the time	**All** of the time	
Participating The teacher observed you contributing to the group activity.	**None** of the time	**Some** of the time	**Most** of the time	**All** of the time	
Persuading The teacher observed you exchange, defend, and rethink ideas within the group.	**None** of the time	**Some** of the time	**Most** of the time	**All** of the time	
Questioning The teacher observed you interacting, discussing, and asking questions to every group member.	**None** of the time	**Some** of the time	**Most** of the time	**All** of the time	
Respecting The teacher observed you encouraging and supporting the ideas and efforts of others in the group.	**None** of the time	**Some** of the time	**Most** of the time	**All** of the time	
Sharing The teacher observed you offering ideas to other members of the group.	**None** of the time	**Some** of the time	**Most** of the time	**All** of the time	

Figure 2   Rubric for debate assessment.

the students that these puzzles were meant for adults because of their level of complexity, they immediately wanted to do the exercises. Enrique stated, "I can do it; watch me." I was amazed at how quickly the children completed the puzzles and mazes. I must admit that I was stumped on several occasions and the students had to help me complete them.

Students went on field trips as part of the curriculum. On one occasion we visited the local university. My colleagues in the university helped to make the trip a smashing success. They met with the students, and afterward many students expressed a desire to go to college.

Assessing student work was done via rubrics. Rubrics in which 4 was considered the highest score and 1 the lowest were used to evaluate student work (Figure 2). The students found this mode of assessment appealing because the criteria used for evaluation was specified. On occasion they were asked to assess their performance and that of their peers on the completion of group projects such as drawings, debates, and short stories written by two or three students collectively.[3]

After four months working with the students, I overhead Adrian telling another student, "I still haven't finished my work for Mother Goose." Years had passed since I had been called

by that name. Immediately, I asked the boy why he called me Mother Goose and he replied, "The older guys in the barrio told me that was the name he and the other kids called you when you worked here a long time ago." I was pleasantly surprised. Now a younger group of children was calling me by that name. The students never addressed me directly as Mother Goose, but when they thought I was out of hearing range, they would sometimes refer to me by that nickname when speaking with their peers. One day I overheard Leticia say, "Mother Goose teaches on the wild side." When I asked her what "teaches on the wild side" meant, she stated that I teach differently from other teachers. When I asked her to explain, she stated, "You're cool. You make the work interesting and not boring. You take chances with us because you're not afraid of us, and you like kids like us who get in trouble all the time."

Evaluation of the Curriculum

The two principal evaluators of the curriculum were the director of the alternative education program, Carlos Reyes, and the students themselves. Once a week, the director and I would sit

1. Do you think curriculum has been successful with the students? If so, how?
2. Do you think the students' reading, writing, and social studies skills have improved as a result of the curriculum, and if so, how?
3. Did the students complete all assignments?
4. Do you think a multicultural curriculum is beneficial to the students? If so, how?
5. Did integrating the content areas make learning easier for the students?
6. How do you think the fourteen-month study went as a whole? Were you able to work with the investigator? Was the investigator always there when she said she would be there? Was there a constant open line of communication between you and the professor?
7. Did the students enjoy doing the assignments and activities?
8. Did the investigator get along with the students?
9. Describe how she worked with the students.
10. Is the curriculum doable in a classroom? If so, why? If not, please explain.
11. Are the instructional strategies doable in an alternative education classroom? If so, why? If not, please explain.
12. Now that fourteen months have passed, how do you feel about university professors and teachers working together to do research? Do you think more of this kind of resreach should be done?
13. How can university teacher education programs help school districts with regard to alternative education?

Figure 3 Director of alternative education questionnaire.

1. Did you enjoy doing the lessons and activities that were part of the investigator's curriculum?
2. Did you enjoy reading stories and books about Mexican and Chicano youngsters? If so, tell me why.
3. Did you enjoy watching movies that had Mexicans or Chicanos as the leading characters? Please explain.
4. Did you think that teachers should include more stories about Mexican and Chicanos? If yes, please explain.
5. What suggestions can you give your teachers working in the alternative education program to help you?
6. Did you enjoy working in groups? If you did, tell me why. If not, please explain.
7. Did you like being graded by rubrics? If so, tell me why. If not, please explain.
8. What do you think teachers can do in the regular education classroom to prevent students from misbehaving and being sent to alternative education?
9. Name three things that you learned about each of these cultures: African-Americans, American Indians, Anglos, and Asians.

Figure 4 Student Questionnaire.

down and discuss how the curriculum was progressing. Notes were taken at each meeting. The notes became a good source of data.

The director's primary role was to determine if the lessons were successful in getting the children to do the work and if they enjoyed doing the assignments. We had agreed at the onset of the study that he would ask the children when I was not present. He would also observe me working with the students and operate the video camera during some of the sessions. We viewed these tapes together afterward to study the children's body language and their comments. In addition, the director kept me informed as to which students would be absent, at the juvenile detention center, or attending court hearings. Our working relationship was a positive and productive one because we had the children's best interests at heart. In short, we worked as a team. Whenever I wanted to test an instructional strategy, the director was always accommodating. I can truly say that we never had a single disagreement throughout the 14-month study. Mr. Reyes and I now give presentations at conferences regarding this investigation.

I must also acknowledge Rosa Lovelace, the school principal, for allowing me access into her school and the alternative education program. She truly embraces the concept of university and public school faculty working together to improve education for all children.

At the end of the study, the director completed a questionnaire (Figure 3) to determine if the curriculum was successful and if so, how. He made a videotape of his critique of the curriculum at the completion of the project. The students evaluated the curriculum on an ongoing basis. They were asked what books, movies, and activities they had enjoyed the most and why. Their views were tape-recorded or written down. In essence, the students told me what worked and what did not and why. The students were also given an anonymous questionnaire at the end of the study to ascertain their views toward the curriculum (Figure 4). In summary the data used to ascertain the effectiveness of the curriculum included questionnaires, videotaped and nonvideotaped interviews of the director and the students, student work, and notes taken from meetings with the director. In addition, the Texas Assessment of Academic Skills (TAKS) test was used as an instrument to determine if there had been improvement in reading.

Results

After examining their standardized test scores in reading on the TAKS, the data reveal that 85 percent of the students showed improvement in reading. The students who showed the most gain, however, were enrolled in the program for 6 months or longer. They scored a minimum of 56 to 252+ points or higher in 2003–2004 than in the previous year, 2002–2003.

The two students whose scores improved 200+ points were in the program the entire academic year due to a continuous pattern of offenses.[4] Although the sample of students is small, the data suggest that the multicultural curriculum did contribute to their growth in reading.[5] In a videotaped interview with the school principal, she acknowledges the success of the curriculum, stating, "I looked at the data and I was very impressed with the gains the children made. . . . I have 875 students on this campus who have been labeled at risk." So any gains in student achievement are important. In this same interview, I asked her how she felt about teachers implementing a multicultural curriculum in the classroom, and she responded, "If you use books that address our culture and talk about people such as Cesar

Students Enrolled for Six Months or Longer

Student	2002–2003	2003–2004	Variance
28278x	1695	1947	252
33692x	2084	*2309	225
32823x	1994	*2110	116
29360x	1759	1839	80
34951x	2023	2074	51
32466x	2223	*2245	12

Passing Score: 2100
For School to Be Recognized: 2400 *Passed TAKS Test

Chavez, that's going to make the children feel proud and they will have a greater interest in reading" (Rosa Lovelace interview, 2005).

The curriculum was deemed successful by the director of the alternative education program. He stated that the "curriculum is effective because the children enjoyed what they were doing, which made them want to complete the assignments." He said that there are major benefits to be gained from the implementation of a multicultural curriculum. First, reading stories about characters that come from the same cultural backgrounds as the students encourages them to realize that their culture is being validated in the schools. Second, the students are "motivated to want to read and do the work. They can buy into the curriculum." Regarding the use of best practices, including cooperative learning, oral presentation, and writing across the curriculum, the director stated that these modes of instruction were successful.[6]

One hundred percent of the children who participated in the study for six weeks or more found the lessons enjoyable and meaningful. They expressed a desire for their teachers in the regular education program to use the same instructional strategies that I implemented throughout the study. Some of the children stated that they would misbehave less in their regular education classes if their teachers were more creative, made learning fun, and showed them more respect.

Moreover, the children stated that they identified with the Latino characters that they read about or viewed through movies such as Stand and Deliver. They felt that their culture was being validated. As Brian stated, "I like reading about our people. I'm proud of being a Chicano, and when I read about guys like me, I enjoy it. We don't have to read about us all the time—but now and then. Why do we always have too [sic] read about white kids? There [sic] world isn't my world, you know."

The books that the students enjoyed reading the most were On My Honor by Marion Dane Bauer, Seedfolks by Paul Fleischman, Shark Beneath the Reef by Jean Craighead George, Julie of the Wolves by Jean Craighead George, Parrot in the Oven by Victor Martinez, The Black Pearl by Scott O'Dell, The Cay by Theodore Taylor, and The Maldonado Miracle, also by Theodore Taylor. Interestingly, not all of these books feature Latino characters. S. E. Hinton's That Was Then, This

Is Now was the book that generated the most lively discussion regarding teen behavior. This was one of the stories that all the students read and discussed as a class. However, most chose to reread the book during silent reading. The book describes youngsters involved in gang activities, drugs, and encounters with law enforcement—three issues that some of the children in this study were familiar with.

Moreover, the students' reading and writing skills improved. The director of the alternative education program wrote:

> The curriculum was successful. I believe that their reading and writing skills have improved because they were always reading and writing and with all that practice they improved. It shows in their work (i.e., their spelling has improved). Also, the curriculum was set at the students' level so it was very doable. Plus the students understood what they had to do. They enjoyed doing her work. . . . There was a huge amount of group work.

The children stated that what they enjoyed most about the curriculum was how the majority of the lessons involved group work. They liked working together because at times when they did not understand the content matter, they asked their peers for help. They also expressed that working in groups made them feel relaxed and not pressured to have to come up with the right answers all the time. In addition, they felt that working with others helped to take each student out of the spotlight every time a question was asked. As one student wrote, "When you asked us questions about the assignment we were working on, we felt that we could respond as a group—we could help each other to answer your questions."

More importantly, however, was the improvement in behavior when the students worked in groups. In the beginning, there was bickering and complaining about who would be working with whom. The desire to work with friends was a problem at first. However, as time passed the children complained less and were willing to work with every student in the classroom.

Limitations of the Study

One limitation was that students were entering and exiting the alternative education program throughout the 14-month period. After six weeks, some would leave while others remained, and new students were being admitted into the program on a regular basis. The director and I decided that I would continue on with the curriculum because there were students who had been in the program since the beginning. We were afraid that the content would be boring to them if I continually stopped and reviewed the material for the benefit of the newer students. However, I made sure to allow for some time to work with the newer students individually until they caught up with the rest of the class. The director also worked with the newer students to help them catch up.

Fifty-two students were enrolled in the alternative education program during the 14 months. Fifty of them left the program to return to the regular classroom, leaving two students who remained in the program throughout the entire study. Of the 50 children who left the program, data for only 20 were recorded, because those 20 were in the program at least six weeks. The other students who left were in the program for only a few weeks or days, not long enough for serious data to be collected, Therefore, the total of number of students whose data was recorded was 20.

A second limitation surrounding this study is the fact that I was unable to ascertain if the students in this alternative education class were able to transfer their motivation to learn to their regular education classes. My research objectives did not include monitoring the behavior of the students once they exited the alternative education program.

Conclusion

The youngsters in this study enjoyed learning via a multicultural curriculum. Reading books in which Latinos were the primary characters helped them to relate more readily to the content. For example, they could identify easily with the gastronomic delight of a Mexican boy who was eating a burrito of carne asada and chile verde in a story. What was most amazing to observe was how much more willing the children were to read and write by the end of their stay in the alternative education program. There were fewer groans when they were given such assignments.

The results of the study have encouraged the director of the alternative education program, Mr. Reyes, to continue the instructional strategies that I used throughout the study. For example, he is currently using the same books that I purchased. He is allowing for a longer period of silent reading and using some of the classroom management practices that discouraged disruptive behavior. Mr. Reyes has shared my instructional strategies with the teachers in the alternative education program. As I was working with the children, he would observe me and write down ideas to share with the teachers. In a videotaped interview, he stated, "The research project was a success. The students really enjoyed working with the professor. The curriculum itself was a great success. She included Chicano studies—topics and issues that the students could relate to. They read about people like Cesar Chavez. This made their levels of self-esteem higher." (Carlos Reyes interview, May 2004).

In addition to demonstrating that multicultural curricula benefit children's learning, this study validates the claim that authentic instruction encourages students to become more engaged in what they are learning (Carlin & Ciaccio, 1997; Raywid, 2001; Eggen & Kauchak, 2001). If a child can see value in completing an assignment and view it as intrinsically worthwhile, he or she will become involved in the learning exercise. Unfortunately, the numbers of children enrolled in alternative education programs due to antisocial behavior are on the rise (Tobin, Tary, Sprague, & Jeffrey, 2002). As of 2000–2001, 39 percent of U.S. public school districts have maintained alternative education programs for students who cannot learn in a regular classroom (Steptoe, 2001). We need to halt this growth. Teachers and school administrators need as much information as possible on ways to motivate adjudicated youngsters and students who misbehave regularly in schools. Studies have shown that motivation is the key to learning at all ages (National Research Council, 2004; Jacobsen, Eggen, & Kauchak, 2002; Jessor, Turbin,

& Costa, 1998; Stipek, 1998; Finn & Rock, 1997). We cannot allow these children to fall through the cracks. There are no "bad children"—only children who make "unwise choices."

> **Teachers and school administrators need as much information as possible on ways to motivate adjudicated youngsters and students who misbehave regularly in schools.**

Furthermore, this investigation supports the conclusions of researchers who argue that having students complete assignments in small groups will help them to develop social skills, such as sharing with others, learning how to compromise, learning how to accept other students' opinions, and above all how to work together to complete a task (Emmer & Gerwels, 2002; Vaughan, 2002). It is imperative, therefore, that children who exhibit antisocial behavior be given opportunities to learn in groups.

While the students in this case study were Mexican and Chicano, much of the research findings can apply to young teenagers of other racial and ethnic groups as well. For example, the children in this study enjoyed working on projects and assignments in groups; cooperative learning was a great success. Young teens enjoy working with their peers regardless of color.

Moreover, it is important to remember that all children need to make connections across cultures, including white children. Implementing a multicultural curriculum in schools affords children of all racial and ethnic groups the opportunity to learn about different cultures and enables them to realize that although the color of their skin may be darker or lighter, they do have many things in common. The youngsters in this study were all Mexican or Chicano.[7] They live in a community in which there are no other ethnic groups besides their own. However, reading literature reflecting various ethnic and racial groups gave them a glimpse of how other children from different cultural backgrounds live. In neighborhoods where the population is predominantly white, school districts must make every attempt to ensure that the children they are serving learn about cultural diversity.

Working with these young people has strengthened my desire to continue helping preservice teachers and veteran teachers to work with students who exhibit antisocial behavior. It was a pleasure and a privilege to work with these youngsters. My research on this particular student population will continue. However, whether they choose to continue calling me Mother Goose will be up to them.

References

The Alamo. (2004). Walt Disney Video.
Armstrong, W. (1969). *Sounder.* New York: New York. Harper Trophy.
Bauer, M. D. (1986). *On my honor.* New York: Dell.

Bloom, B., et al. (1956). *Taxonomy of educational objectives: Cognitive domain.* New York: Longman.

Buck, P. (1947). *The big wave.* New York: Curtis Publishing.

Carlin, M. B., & Ciaccio, L. (1997). Improving high school students' performance via discovery learning, collaboration, and technology. *THE Journal* 24, 10: 62–66.

De Anda, R. M. (1996). *Chicanas and Chicanos in contemporary society.* Boston: Allyn and Bacon.

Delpit, L. (1995). *Other people's children: Cultural conflict in the classroom.* New York: New Press.

Eggen, P., & Kauchak, D. (2001). *Strategies for teachers: Teaching content and thinking skills.* Needham Heights, Mass.: Allyn and Bacon.

Emmer, E. & Gerwels, M. C. (2002). Cooperative learning in elementary classrooms: Teaching practices and lesson characteristics. *The Elementary School Journal,* 103: 75–91.

Finn, J., and Rock, D. (1997). Academic success among students at risk for school failure. *Journal of Applied Psychology,* 82: 221–234.

Fleischman, P. (1997). *Seedfolks.* New York: Harper Trophy.

George, J. C. (1972). *Julie of the wolves.* New York: Harper Trophy.

George, J. C. (1989). *Shark beneath the reef.* New York: Harper Trophy.

Glory. (1989). TriStar Pictures.

Goldenberg, C., and Gallimore, R. (1995). Immigrant Latino parents' values and beliefs about their children's education. In P. R. Pintrich and M. Maehr (Eds.), *Advances in motivation and achievement* (pp. 183–228). Greenwich, Conn.: JAI Press.

Hagedorn. J. M. (1998). Gang violence in the postindustrial era. *Crime and Justice,* 24: 365–419.

Hinton, S. E. (1971). *That was then, this is now.* New York: Penguin.

Howard, G. (1999). *We can't teach what we don't know: White teachers, multiracial schools.* New York Teachers College Press.

Jacobsen, D., Eggen, P., and Kauchak, D. (2002). *Methods for teaching: Promoting student learning.* Columbus, Ohio: Merrill.

Jessor, R., Turbin, M. S., and Costa, F. M. (1998). Protection in successful outcomes among disadvantaged adolescents. *Applied Developmental Science,* 2: 198–208.

Martinez, V. (1996). *Parrot in the Oven: Mi vida.* New York: Harper Trophy.

Myers, W. D. (1983). *Hoops.* New York: New York: Dell.

National Research Council. (2004). *Engaging schools: Fostering high school students' motivation to learn.* Washington, D.C.: The National Academies Press.

Nieto, S. (1999). *The light in their eyes: Creating multicultural learning communities.* New York: Teachers College Press.

O'Dell, S. (1967). *The black pearl.* New York: Dell.

Phillips, D. (1983). *Hidden treasure: Maze book.* New York: Dover Publications.

Powell, R., McLaughlin, H., Savage, T., and Zehm, S. (2001). *Classroom management: Perspectives on the social curriculum.* Columbus, Ohio: Merrill.

Raywid, M. A. (2001). What to do with students who are not succeeding. *Phi Delta Kappan,* 82(8): 582–585.

Sleeter, C. and Grant, C. (2003). *Making choices for multicultural education: Five approaches to race, class, and gender.* (4th ed). New York: Wiley.

Stand and deliver. (1988). Warner Home Video.

Steptoe, S. (2001). Taking the alternative route. *Time,* 167(2): 3.

Stipek, D. (1998). *Motivation to learn: From theory to practice.* Boston: Allyn and Bacon.

Tatum, B. D. (1997). *Why are the Black kids sitting together in the cafeteria?* New York: Basic Books.

Taylor, T. (1969). *The Cay.* New York: Dell.

Taylor, T. (1973). *The Maldonado miracle.* San Diego: Harcourt.

Texas Education Agency. (2004). The Texas Essential Knowledge and Skills (TEKS), 19. Texas Administrative Code Chapter 74, 1998.

Tobin, T., Tary, R., Sprague, J.R., and Jeffrey, L. (2002). Alternative education strategies: Reducing violence in school and the community. *Journal of Emotional & Behavioral Disorders,* 8: 1–16.

Valencia, R. R. (1991). *Chicano school failure and success: Research and policy agendas for the 1990s.* Philadelphia: Falmer Press.

Valenzuela, A. (1999). *Subtractive schooling.* Albany: State Univ. of New York Press.

Vaughan, W. (2002). Effects of cooperative learning on achievement and attitude among students of color. *The Journal of Educational Research,* 95: 359–364.

Vigil, J. (1988). *Barrio gangs: Street life and identity in Southern California.* Austin: Univ. of Texas Press.

Notes

1. I would like to thank the El Paso Independent School District in El Paso, Texas; Mrs. Rosa Lovelace, school principal of Guillen Middle School; Mr. Carlos Reyes, director of the alternative education program; the teachers and staff; the wonderful children enrolled in the alternative class; and their parents for giving me permission to conduct this 14-month study. Their support was instrumental in helping me to complete it. Also, I would like to extend a special note of gratitude to the Hervey Foundation for granting me the funding necessary to purchase the books and materials for my multicultural curriculum.

2. The word "Mexican" refers to individuals who were born in Mexico. Mexican Americans are people of Mexican descent who were born in the United States. Chicanos, like Mexican Americans, are people of Mexican descent who were born in the United States but have an awareness of a historically oppressive relationship. The children in this study who were of Mexican descent and who were born in the United States preferred to be called Chicanos instead of Mexican Americans.

3. Although student work was graded, these marks were not included into the calculation of grades assigned by their regular classroom teachers. The grades they received on their report cards reflected only the work that they had done with their teachers. The students were aware of this fact, but they chose to do all the assignments.

4. What was most surprising to me regarding the test data is that José, who made the highest gains on the test (252 points), was the student who had the most behavioral problems. He had to attend several court hearings throughout the year. As the assistant principal reviewed the results with me, he pointed to this test score and the student identification number and told me the name of the student. I was very happy that despite his behavioral problems, he had made such good progress in reading.

5. One of the most challenging aspects of working with children in alternative education programs is that they can remain in the

program for only a short period of time, unless they continue to commit acts reflecting negative behavior, which increases their stay in the program.

6. The director of the alternative education program made notes of all of the instructional strategies that I was using with the children to share with the teachers who might be interested. As stated in the article, I did not want to work directly with the children's teachers because this study was simply to determine if a multicultural curriculum could help these youngsters become engaged in learning before I worked with classroom teachers. I reasoned that if my study revealed some success, then I would take it to the next level and work with a few teachers.

7. I selected this area of the city to conduct my study because I have close familial ties. My mother, uncles, and aunts were born and grew up in Segundo Barrio. Although our family now lives in various sections across the city, some of us remain active in the barrio. Segundo Barrio will always be my "true" home. Also, I taught elementary and middle school children in this area. As an educator, I have developed a deep bond with the children who live in the community.

MARTHA CASAS is a professor of teacher eduation at the University of Texas-El Paso.

From *Multicultural Review*, Winter 2006, pp. 24–31. Copyright © 2006 by Multicultural Review. Reprinted by permission of The Goldman Group, Inc.

Promoting School Achievement among American Indian Students throughout the School Years

As American Indian children develop, they gain social awareness and their cultural identity becomes stronger; thus, they become more cognizant of the cultural disconnect between their non-Indian school and their Indian culture.

KRISTIN POWERS

American Indian students as a population are not achieving high academic standards. For example, only 57 percent of American Indians who took the 8th-grade National Assessment of Educational Progress reading test in 2003 scored at or above the basic level, and only 16 percent scored at or above the proficient reading level (versus 83 percent and 41 percent, respectively, of white students) (National Center for Education Statistics, 2004). Yet school failure appears to be acquired rather than inherent at the onset of schooling. Many researchers have reported that American Indian children function at an average range academically until the 4th grade; by 10th grade, however, they are, on average, three years behind their non-Native peers (Hornett, 1990; Rampaul, Singh, & Didyk, 1984; Safran, Safran, & Pirozak, 1994). The reasons for this "crossover" effect are not clear, although a combination of school, family, and student characteristics most likely is at work.

Underachievement among Native students often is attributed to culturally incongruent school settings. At school, many American Indian students must negotiate unfamiliar discipline, instruction and evaluation methods, rules for forming interpersonal relationships, and curricula that diverge from those promoted by their family, tribe, and community (Chrisjohn, Towson, & Peters, 1988; Lomawaima, 1995; Snipp, 1995). If cultural differences between home and school are the source of academic failure among American Indian students, the decline in achievement would suggest that these differences widen as youth age. Elementary curricula and instructional methods may be more aligned to Native cultural values (e.g., cooperation, thematic or holistic learning, oral recital) than those in the later grades. Hornett (1990) suggests that developmental changes within the child contribute to the cultural gap. He argued that as

American Indian children develop, they gain social awareness and their cultural identity becomes stronger; thus, they become more cognizant of the cultural disconnect between their non-Indian school and their Indian culture. The challenge, therefore, is determining how to bridge the cultural gap while maintaining high standards and promoting a positive climate for school learning.

The Research Project

Extant survey data collected from 240 urban American Indian youth (primarily Ojibwa, Lakota, and Dakota) from two large urban Midwestern cities, ages 9 to 18, were examined to identify educational variables that were negatively correlated with students' age (Geenen, 1998). Fifty-eight survey items were combined into 11 scales that measured 10 educational variables (e.g., student achievement, home-school collaboration, and achievement motivation) and the respondents' affiliation with their Native culture.

A negative correlation between age and student achievement ($r = -.379$; $p \leq .001$), as measured by self-reported grades and overall achievement, was found, which supports the "crossover" effect. Similarly, American Indian students' school attendance and participation were negatively correlated with age ($r = -.248$; $p \leq .001$). Thus, older American Indian students were less likely than younger American Indian students to report passing grades, consistent attendance, and high levels of engagement with school activities—all important indicators of educational attainment and success.

The hypothesis that declining student achievement is associated with increasing discontinuity between the culture of the school and home was not supported by these data. Neither the respondents' affiliation with their Native culture (e.g., how important Indian values are, speaking a tribal language in the home, participation in traditional activities and rituals) nor the extent to which their school embraced Native culture (e.g., teaching Indian cultural values, history, stories, and tribal languages at school; attending school with other Native youth) was correlated with age. While this study is very preliminary and based only on cross-sectional survey data, it does suggest that the crossover effect is not simply a result of cultural discontinuity. Some of the educational factors that were negatively correlated to age may deserve greater attention as school personnel attempt to combat underachievement among older American Indian students. These efforts are described next.

Student Achievement Motivation

Like non-Native students, American Indian students' achievement motivation is central to their academic achievement and persistence in school (McInerney & Swisher, 1995). McInerney and Swisher hypothesized that the presence of achievement motivation may indicate that American Indian students have successfully negotiated the cultural discontinuity of the school by adopting some of the mainstream strategies for school success without feeling that they have abandoned their cultural heritage. Conversely, the absence of a desire to achieve, attend, and participate in school may be symptomatic of what Ogbu (1981) described as the demand to develop alternative competencies. Faced with a long history of racial discrimination, some American Indian adolescents may discredit the importance of school and develop alternative competencies and motivations that are in opposition to school values.

In the present study, student achievement motivation, as measured by such items as "I try to do my best at school" and "It is important to me to be proud of my school work," was negatively correlated with student age ($r = -.169$; $p = .009$). This suggests that American Indian students may become less motivated to do well in school as they age. Therefore, primary, elementary, and secondary teachers should strive to provide engaging instruction for their American Indian students by adhering to universal principles of effective instruction while incorporating native culture and content into the curriculum (Powers, in press). Culture-based educational programs, such as the Kamehameha Early Education Program (KEEP) (Goldenberg & Gallimore, 1989) or the inquiry-based Rough Rock program (McCarthy, Wallace, Lynch, & Benally, 1991), which incorporate Native themes, languages, and Elders in the content and delivery of instruction, may serve as viable models for keeping American Indian students academically motivated. Efforts to increase student achievement motivation also should be directed at decreasing remediation. Repeated exposure to remedial activities that lack a cognitive and a cultural emphasis is likely to deplete students' desire to commit to academic tasks.

Teacher Expectations

Some evidence suggests that teacher expectations for American Indian students' success declines as the students progress through the grades (Rampaul, Singh, & Didyk, 1984). In the present study, students were asked whether they thought their school work was too easy, too hard, or just right; whether people at their school expect them to do well; and whether the adults at their school encourage them to do the best that they can. The American Indian students' responses to this teacher expectation scale were not correlated with age, suggesting that youth of all ages in this sample reported similarly about teacher expectations. Ideally, this finding would indicate that teachers maintain high and attainable expectations for their American Indian students across the various grades. Yet, failure to find a statistically significant correlation between teachers' expectations and age may also be due to either insufficient sample size or indicate low teacher expectations across the age groups. Teachers of American Indian students should constantly ask themselves: "Am I holding my American Indian students to the same rigorous standards that I expect from my other students?" Again, an overreliance on remediation rather than in-depth, inquiry-based instructional activities should be a signal to teachers to reconsider their expectations for American Indian students.

Teacher Supportiveness

American Indian students' ability to access the social capital of school personnel also may be compromised by their divergent cultural competencies. Plank's (1994) in-depth study of Navajo reservation school teachers illustrates how intercultural communication differences impede social bonding between teachers and students. For example, an experienced teacher of Navajo students stated:

> If I'm walking with . . . a Navajo, we may not say anything, and they are comfortable with that. Me, on the one (sic) hand, I feel like I should be saying something (Plank, 1994, p. 8).

Teachers may misread American Indian students as being uninterested in developing a relationship with them, or as overly shy, rude, or immature; this misperception is likely to impede the formation of interpersonal relationships between school staff and Indian students (Hornett, 1990; Kasten, 1992; Plank, 1994). A lack of interpersonal relationships with school personnel puts American Indian students at a disadvantage because those social bonds are critical to fostering a sense of belonging to school that leads to students' confidence in their own academic abilities and the availability of educators to provide academic support (Finn, 1989; Goodenow, 1993). Corner (1984) has observed that "when the school staff fail to permit positive attachment and identification, attachment and identification take place in a negative way" (p. 327). Interviews conducted with American Indian dropouts suggest that de-identification with school personnel and the norms of the school is a part of the drop-out process (Dehyle, 1992). The cross-over effect in American Indian student achievement may be the result of declines in school staff accessibility and supportiveness as American Indian students develop.

In the present study, teacher supportiveness was negatively correlated with student age ($r = -.183$, $p = .004$), which suggests that older youth found their teachers to be less available and supportive than younger youth. Items on this scale include: "Do you get along with your teachers?" "Has a teacher gotten to know you really well?" "Would you turn to a teacher for help if you were depressed?" These results raise the possibility that improved interpersonal relationships with teachers may help middle childhood and adolescent students remain committed to school. Teachers' and students' relationships will be strengthened through meaningful mentoring, extracurricular, and community-based programs, such as the American Indian Reservation Project, in which student teachers provide "academic tutoring, companionship and role modeling" while boarding with their Navajo students (Stachowski, 1998).

Family Involvement

Parents' presence and participation at school may buffer American Indian students from declining teacher expectations, supportiveness, and accessibility by promoting greater cultural consistency within academic programs and by offering additional academic assistance. Parental involvement is critical to assisting American Indian students in negotiating the mainstream culture of public school (Friedel, 1999). Surprisingly, older American Indian students did not report lower rates of parental involvement in school than younger students in the present study. It is possible that the attempts made by the districts in this study to incorporate Native culture into the curricula and instruction fostered greater parental involvement. For example, most of the respondents indicated that they had learned about Indian culture (86 percent) and Indian legends (75 percent) at school.

> A lack of interpersonal relationships with school personnel puts American Indian students at a disadvantage, because those social bonds are critical to fostering a sense of belonging to school that leads to students' confidence in their own academic abilities.

Including Native American culture in the curriculum design and instruction may entice American Indian parents to remain involved in home-school collaborations as their children develop; yet, some American Indian parents may need assistance in helping their older youth meet academic demands. Historically low rates of educational attainment among American Indians make it more likely that American Indian parents lack the content skills necessary to assist their children as the curriculum becomes more advanced. For example, a study of over a thousand 5th- and 6th-grade students found American Indians to be twice as likely as African American or Anglo students to report that they had no one to ask for help on their mathematics homework (Mather, 1997).

Safe and Drug-Free Schools

Older students in this study reported the occurrence of much more fighting and alcohol and drug use than did younger students. Urban American Indian youth may experience even greater risks associated with violence and alcohol and drug use than their rural or reservation dwelling peers because they have lost the support of extended kin who often assist in mentoring and disciplining adolescents (Machamer & Gruber, 1998). Parental involvement and a sense of belonging to the culture and norms of the school protect adolescents from deviant and potentially harmful behaviors such as alcohol, tobacco, and other drug (ATOD) use (Hawkins, Guo, Hill, Battin-Pearson, & Abbott, 2001). Rather than embracing "zero tolerance" policies, which Watts and Erevelles (2004) argue give "schools new ways to justify the expulsion, exclusion, shaming and labeling of students who need professional help rather than punishment" (p. 281), schools should improve parental involvement and students' sense of belonging to the culture and norms of the school in order to protect American Indian adolescents from school violence and ATOD use (Hawkins et al., 2001).

Implications for School Personnel

Teachers should consider, first and foremost, strengthening their interpersonal connections with their American Indian students. Strong relationships between students and teachers promote a sense of belonging, freedom to take academic risks, and investment in academic learning (i.e., academic motivation), and may help American Indian students negotiate cultural discontinuities between school and home. Teacher training on Native cultural competencies is a positive step toward increasing teachers' understanding and commitment to forming positive relationships with their students. School-wide anti-bullying, anger management, and substance abuse programs also may curb declines in student achievement. Finally, school-wide screenings may be effective in identifying American Indian students before underachievement becomes entrenched. An individualized intervention plan for American Indian students when they begin to fall behind in achievement or attendance should be implemented, monitored, and revised until the desired outcomes are achieved. This plan should be based on ecological assessments that consider developmental imperatives and individual assets (e.g., native cultural affiliation, parent support for learning) and vulnerabilities (e.g., insufficient teacher support, violence, and ATOD use at school) in selecting from among various intervention options.

Achievement data on sub-populations of students, such as American Indian students, should be examined regularly for signs of underperformance at each grade level. However, school personnel should understand that not all American Indian students identify with their Native culture in the same way. Cultural differences exist within and among the different tribes; thus, some students, particularly urban students who are three or four generations removed from their tribal homeland, may identify more with the mainstream culture of their school than with their Native culture. Accordingly, addressing cultural discontinuity may or may not improve achievement among older American Indian students. However, sufficient access to meaningful learning opportunities, supportive teachers, and safe schools is likely to propagate school success.

References

Chrisjohn, R., Towson, S., & Peters, M. (1988). Indian achievement in school: Adaptation to hostile environments. In J. W. Berry, S. H. Irvine, & E. B. Hunt (Eds.), *Indigenous cognition: Functioning in cultural context* (pp. 257–283). Dordrecht, The Netherlands: Marinus Nijhoff.

Comer, J. P. (1984). Home-school relationships as they affect the academic success of children. *Education and Urban Society, 16*(3), 323–337.

Dehyle, D. (1992). Constructing failure and maintaining cultural identity: Navajo and Ute school leavers. *Journal of American Indian Education, 31*(2), 24–47.

Finn, J. D. (1989). Withdrawing from school. *Review of Educational Research, 59*(2), 117–142.

Friedel, T. L. (1999). The role of Aboriginal parents in public education: Barriers to change in an urban setting. *Canadian Journal of Native Education, 23*(2), 139–157.

Geenen, K. (1998). *A model of school learning for American Indian Youth* (Doctoral dissertation, University of Minnesota, Minneapolis, 1998). Retrieved August 30, 2004, from Digital Dissertation at www.lib.umi.com/dissertations/.

Goldenberg, C., & Gallimore, R. (1989). Teaching California's diverse student population: The common ground between educational and cultural research. *California Public Schools Forum, 3*, 41–56.

Goodenow, C. (1993). The psychological sense of school membership among adolescents: Scale development and educational correlates. *Psychology in the Schools, 30*(1), 79–90.

Hawkins, J. D., Guo, J., Hill, K. G., Battin-Pearson, S., & Abbott, R. D. (2001). Long-term effects of the Seattle Social Development intervention on school bonding trajectories. *Applied Developmental Science, 5*(4), 225–236.

Hornett, D. M. (1990). Elementary-age tasks, cultural identity, and the academic performance of young American Indian children. *Action in Teacher Education, 12*(3), 43–49.

Kasten, W. C. (1992). Bridging the horizon: American Indian beliefs and whole language learning. *Anthropology, and Education Quarterly, 23*, 108–119.

Lomawaima, K. T. (1995). Educating Native Americans. In J. A. Banks & C. A. M. Banks (Eds.), *The handbook of research on multicultural education* (pp. 331–345). New York: Macmillan.

Machamer, A. M., & Gruber, E. (1998). Secondary school, family and educational risk: Comparing American Indian adolescents and their peers. *Journal of Educational Research, 91*(6), 357–370.

Mather, J. R. C. (1997). How do American Indian fifth and sixth graders perceive mathematics and the mathematics classroom? *Journal of American Indian Education, 36*(2), 39–48.

McCarthy, T. L., Wallace, S., Lynch, R. H., & Benally, A. (1991). Classroom inquiry and Navajo learning styles: A call for reassessment. *Anthropology and Education Quarterly, 22*(1), 42–59.

McInerney, D. M., & Swisher, K. G. (1995). Exploring Navajo motivation in school settings. *Journal of American Indian Education, 36*(3), 28–51.

National Center for Education Statistics. (2003). *Percentage of students, by reading achievement level and race/ethnicity, grade 4: 1992–2003*. Retrieved August 25, 2004, from http://nces.ed.gov/nationsreportcard/reading/results2003/natachieve-re-g4.asp

Ogbu, J. (1981). Origins of human competence: A cultural-ecological perspective. *Child Development, 52*, 413–429.

Plank, G. A. (1994). What silence means for educators of American Indian children. *Journal of American Indian Education, 34*(1), 3–19.

Powers, K. (in press). An exploratory study of cultural identify and culture-based educational programs for urban American Indian students. *Urban Education.*

Rampaul, W. E., Singh, M., & Didyk, J. (1984). The relationship between academic achievement, self-concept, creativity, and teacher expectations among Native children in a northern Manitoba school. *The Alberta Journal of Educational Research, 30*(3), 213–225.

Safran, S. P., Safran, J. S., & Pirozak, E. (1994). Native American youth: Meeting their needs in a multicultural society. *Journal of Humanistic Education and Development, 33*(2), 50–57.

Snipp, C. M. (1995). American Indian Studies. In J. A. Banks & C. A. McGee Banks (Eds.), *Handbook of research on multicultural education* (pp. 245–258). New York: Macmillan.

Stachowski, L. L. (1998). Student teachers' efforts to promote self-esteem in Navajo pupils. *The Educational Forum, 62*, 341–346.

Watts, I. E., & Erevelles, N. (2004). These deadly times: Reconceptualizing school violence by using critical race theory and disability studies. *American Educational Research Journal, 41*(2), 271–299.

KRISTIN POWERS is Assistant Professor, College of Education, California State University Long Beach.

From *Childhood Education*, International Focus Issue, 2005, pp. 338–342. Copyright © 2005 by the Association for Childhood Education International. Reprinted by permission of Kristin Powers and the Association for Childhood Education International.

Family and Consumer Sciences Delivers Middle School Multicultural Education

This We Believe *Characteristics*

- Multiple learning and teaching approaches that respond to their diversity
- Curriculum that is relevant, challenging, integrative, and exploratory
- Students and teachers engaged in active learning
- An inviting, supportive, and safe environment
- School-wide efforts and policies that foster health, wellness, and safety

BARBARA A. CLAUSS

Vive la difference! This expression is often used to suggest that the differences between males and females are to be appreciated, yet it means so much more! Human diversity, in *all* its forms, deserves to be acknowledged and respected. Indeed, the multiplicity of the population of the United States calls for all people to demonstrate respect for differences through appropriate interpersonal skills. However, we are not born valuing individual and group differences or knowing how to interact effectively with a variety of people in school, in the workplace, and in the community. Fortunately, we can *learn* it through multicultural education, and an excellent setting is middle school family and consumer sciences.

Why Multicultural Education?

The goal of multicultural education is to teach the knowledge, skills, and attitudes *all* students will need to survive and function effectively in the future (Banks, 2002). It is based on the core values of acknowledging and prizing cultural diversity, respecting universal human rights, supporting human dignity, taking responsibility for a world community, and revering the earth.

Student outcomes of multicultural education include multicultural competence, which is comprised of the development of knowledge, perception, critical thinking, and behavior from multiple perspectives. It emphasizes understanding diversity and effective functioning in a diverse, global society (Bennett, 2003). The core values relate to all people, regardless of culture, ethnicity, social class, religion, gender, age, or abilities.

Effective communication is key to multicultural competence. Through interaction, we gain insight beyond our personal experiences and become more aware of the influence of our own cultures on our perspectives (Banks, 2002; Bennett, 2003).

The development of multicultural competence is essential for effective functioning in a global society. Nevertheless, the standards movement in education, with its focus on achievement of competencies in language arts, math, science, and social studies, has made it less likely that multicultural competence is promoted in school curricula. Consequently, multicultural education has been limited to superficial applications in which a culture's music, art, literature, food, dress, and housing are noted in social studies, language arts, or fine arts.

Sadly, such cursory acknowledgment of cultures distorts and degrades their complex, dynamic nature. As a result, students fail to grasp the essence of cultural diversity and the associated competencies. Few of them leave school with the knowledge, skills, and attitudes to function effectively in work, community, and personal realms (Carnegie Council on Adolescent Development, 1989).

Given the increasing diversity of the population of the United States, future adults must have greater skill at interacting with a variety of people in family, school, work, and community settings. It is imperative that students gain multicultural competence before they leave school, and the most appropriate level to embark on this process is middle school.

Why Middle School?

Since young adolescents' attitudes and beliefs are very malleable, the prime setting for multicultural education is middle school (Manning, 1999/2000). During the age span from 10 to 15 years, youth tend to focus on developing a sense of self, forming cultural identities, enlarging their social sphere beyond the family, establishing close friendships with others, forming opinions about others, and developing a sense of fairness and justness. This transitional phase is a critical period during which information and positive experiences with others can leave lasting impressions. Family and consumer sciences (FACS) is well prepared to be that favorable influence.

Why Family and Consumer Sciences?

FACS teachers are in a particularly appropriate position to foster in their students a greater understanding of cultures, respect for individual and group differences, and ability to develop essential interpersonal skills (Clausell, 1998; Greenwood, Darling, & Hansen-Gandy, 1997). A closer look reveals that FACS teachers impart the knowledge, facilitate the skills, and encourage the attitudes that *all* students will need to survive and function effectively in the future. In other words, they teach multicultural education.

Corresponding Philosophies

Philosophically, FACS and multicultural education share many ideals. The Vision Statement of the Family and Consumer Sciences Education Division (FACSED) of the Association for Career and Technical Education (ACTE) (1994) affirmed that "Family and Consumer Sciences Education empowers individuals and families across the life span to manage the challenges of living and working in a diverse global society. Our unique focus is on families, work, and their interrelationships" (ACTE, 1994). With a firm belief in cultivating well-being, citizenship, effective functioning, and appreciation of human worth, FACS is an inherently appropriate context for multicultural education.

For example, while studying a unit on family relationships, students may focus on strategies to manage the challenges of living and working in the 21st century. In addition to outlining the practices of families in dominant American culture (i.e., white, middle-class, professional), students can examine family forms and the function of family members in other cultures, within and outside the U.S. In doing so, they learn that there are adaptive functions to various family forms, such as three-generation or communal households. One measurable student outcome of this learning experience is ability to analyze family management strategies in response to demands of employment, with an emphasis on the flexibility of various cultural responses.

FACS Curriculum: Standards

The National Standards for Family and Consumer Sciences Education (FACSE) (National Association of State Administrators of Family and Consumer Sciences Education [NASAFACS], 1998) outlined comprehensive content standards and recommended FACS core concepts and student competencies to guide planning, implementation, and assessment. Of particular relevance are the standards pertaining to family, interpersonal relationships, and human development. They share a focus on respecting diversity and examining factors that influence self-concept, perceptions of others, values, and interpersonal relationships.

For example, a concept found in the standards is "global influences on today's families." To gain a historical perspective, middle school students can research management strategies developed by families during World War II, when many men were in the military and many women joined the workforce. Students can compare and contrast those experiences to the family management strategies employed by contemporary military families. While students would find differences based on the economic, social, and political climates and technological development, they would also find similarities in some resources families use, such as tangible social support. A measurable student outcome of this learning experience is ability to compare and contrast military family management during wartime.

Applied Nature of FACS Education

FACS is a multidisciplinary field, drawing on physical and social sciences, mathematics, art, humanities, and philosophy (East, 1980). The applied nature of FACS in middle school brings abstract concepts from its root disciplines into daily life and makes them meaningful and useful in the here and now.

> **The applied nature of FACS in the middle school brings abstract concepts from its root disciplines into daily life and makes them meaningful.**

For example, the concept "stereotype" may be addressed in social studies, but it is in a FACS class where the concept assumes personal relevance in a lesson on barriers to effective interpersonal relationships. Perhaps middle school students participate in a perspective-taking activity in which they are assigned to a cultural group with which they do not identify. Group members discuss the stereotypes of their assigned culture that they have heard or themselves believe. Next, they assume the position of a member of the cultural group and prepare a list of things they wish people would stop saying about them and doing to them. Then, they list the things they wish people would say and do instead. After sharing their ideas with the class, students reflect on the impact of their belief in stereotypes on their relationships with classmates. One measurable student outcome for this learning experience is ability to analyze and evaluate stereotypes. Students' attitudes may also be affected; one student outcome reflecting affective development is ability to become aware of the negative impact stereotypes can have on relationships. Not only can students explain the concept and give examples of it, they can feel its impact personally, by "walking in another's shoes."

FACS Curriculum: Processes

The applied nature of FACS relates not only to the immediate relevance of the factual information, but the use of specific actions. The explosion of information and innovation in the 21st century combined with diversity of lived experience makes teaching all pertinent content impossible (Costa & Liebmann, 1997). That is why the National Standards for FACSE include process questions that pertain to thinking, communication, leadership, and management (NASAFACS, 1998). The emphasis is not on a single, correct answer (Fox, 1997), but on processes, or the "how" of learning (Costa & Liebmann, 1997). Four primary processes undergird FACS education and are apparent in every facet of the curriculum.

Thinking. The National Standards for FACSE emphasize intentional and goal-directed thinking that is both critical and creative.

Critical thinking involves methodical examination of perspectives to determine assumptions and values, opinions and facts. While critical thinking is systematic and analytical, creative thinking is novel—a departure from a critique of what is known to valuing unusual, original perspectives (NASAFACS, 1998). Problems of daily life may be analyzed and evaluated systematically; creative thinking is useful for understanding others and carrying out social action.

For example, students read a critical incident—a situation requiring a decision to be made. Incidents are considered critical if the wrong decision were to be made there would be serious consequences; yet there is no obvious, correct decision (Pederson, 2004). Perhaps an African American high school student has been invited to speak at an assembly of primarily white, middle class elementary school students, most of whom have never known an African American child or adult. She was asked to address racism, the progress made in combating it, and steps that have yet to be taken. She has been asked to speak on behalf of African Americans across the United States. She must decide what to do.

FACS students can analyze the critical incident to determine the issues involved and possible courses of action to be followed by the high school student. An essential piece of this learning experience is predicting consequences of behavior; hence a measurable student outcome is ability to choose a course of action based on careful consideration of the issues and consequences.

Communication. Communication is critical to multicultural education, as it is the mechanism through which individuals and groups exchange views and mediate conflict (NASAFACS, 1998). "Communication is the transmission or interchange of thoughts, feelings, opinions, and information between a sender and a receiver" (NASAFACS, p. 18). It involves not only speaking and listening, but nonverbal interchanges, as well. Reading and writing are also important forms of communication in personal, academic, and workforce contexts.

FACS students learn how to listen actively, paraphrase senders' messages, and express their own beliefs, feelings, and experiences effectively through "I" messages. These skills are developed through practice and role-playing. Yet, there are other facets of communication that are key to multicultural education.

For example, not only are there differences in communication styles and dialects from one country to another, there are differences from one state to another and from one region to another within a state. Since not many middle school students have had the opportunity to travel extensively within the United States, a good activity for expanding their perceptions of communication styles involves viewing and listening to a video in which age-mates from different locations in the U.S. engage in casual conversation about the same topic. Each segment of the video isolates a single location.

During the video, students paraphrase the message they perceive and note unique, unfamiliar, or indistinguishable words or sounds, as well as novel nonverbal communication. At the end of each segment, students summarize the conversation. Referring to a script of each segment, the teacher can clarify or correct students' perceptions, while explaining origins of unfamiliar words. Students describe the impact of each group's communication style on their own understanding of the conversation and their overall perception of the group. Finally, students discuss the impact of their own communication styles on people from other geographic locations or cultural groups. One measurable student outcome of this learning experience is ability to project the impact of regional and cultural differences in communication on accuracy of message transmission. Students will also become aware of subtle and obvious features of communication style by regional or cultural group.

Leadership. Leadership processes include managing, facilitating, negotiating, encouraging, and participating, as well as directing. "Leaders tell, sell, participate, and delegate, using different strategies at different times and with different group members in order to involve and encourage everyone toward achieving the shared vision" (NASAFACS, 1998, p. 19). Effective leadership empowers all group members to make decisions, act, and contribute to group cohesiveness. It is fundamental to social action in the workplace, community, and personal domains. Working in groups with assigned roles and responsibilities, students realize that every classmate contributes to learning.

For example, a group of five middle school students choose to create a wildflower garden on the school campus as their service-learning project. Each one is assigned a role—project manager, secretary/treasurer, fund raiser, landscape architect, or planting/maintenance manager. Each student is responsible for performing specialized tasks and engaging the other group members in supporting roles to complete the work (e.g., the landscape architect is responsible for designing the garden plot, but will rely on other group members for suggestions and feedback).

As the project is being completed, the group members assess progress according to such criteria as adherence to the time line, adherence to the budget, perceptions of each other's ability to fulfill responsibilities, and so on. When the project is complete, students assess the product according to criteria, such as relationship of actual product to planned product, or more specific criteria, such as consistency of the finished product with the architect's plan. Two of the many possible measurable student outcomes of this experience are ability to delegate responsibility effectively and ability to evaluate process and product.

Management. Management is a broad, often complex concept involving many specific processes such as goal-setting, planning, decision-making/problem solving, implementing, and evaluating. These processes are used by individuals and families to meet their needs and satisfy their wants (NASAFACS, 1998). Management entails three types of action that are essential to the practical problems approach (NASAFACS, 1998).

While technical action is based on objective information, interpretive action relies on interaction with others to share ideas and understand others' perspectives.

Technical action pertains to knowledge, facts, and manipulative skills. It can be seen as a response to the question "What?" For example, students take technical action to contrast characteristics of high-context cultures to characteristics of low-context cultures, relying on "what is known," that is, research on characteristics of high- and low-context cultures (Figure 1). The measurable student outcome of this learning experience is ability to analyze information on high- and low-context cultures.

Figure 1
Definition and Characteristics of High- and Low-Context Cultures

- A *high-context culture* is a culture in which the individual has internalized meaning and information so that little is explicitly stated in written or spoken messages. In conversation, the listener knows what is meant. Because the speaker and listener share the same knowledge and assumptions, the listener can piece together the speaker's meaning. China is an example of a high-context culture.

- A low-context culture is one in which information and meaning are explicitly stated in the message or communication. Individuals in a low-context culture expect explanations when statements or situations are unclear, as they often are. Information and meaning are not internalized by the individual but are derived from context, e.g., from the situation or an event. The United States is an example of a low-context culture.

High-Context Culture

1. Implicitly embeds meanings at different levels of the sociocultural context.
2. Values group sense.
3. Tends to take time to cultivate and establish a permanent personal relationship.
4. Emphasizes spiral logic.
5. Values indirect verbal interaction and is more able to read nonverbal expressions.
6. Tends to use more "feeling" in expression.
7. Tends to give simple, ambiguous, noncontexting messages.

Low-Context Culture

1. Overtly displays meanings through direct communication forms.
2. Values individualism.
3. Tends to develop transitory personal relationships.
4. Emphasizes linear logic.
5. Values direct verbal interaction and is less able to read nonverbal expressions.
6. Tends to use "logic" to present ideas.
7. Tends to emphasize highly structured messages, give details, and place great stress on words and technical signs.

Sources: Retrieved January 16, 2006, from http://academic.brooklyn.cuny.edu/english/melani/cs6/tan.html

While technical action is based on objective information, *interpretive action* relies on interaction with others to share ideas and understand others' perspectives. It can be seen as a response to the question "So what?" For example, students take interpretive action when they role-play the part of an English-speaking student in a monolingual (Spanish) classroom. Students can ask themselves "how are my relationships with others affected by my inability to communicate with my peers and the teacher?" A measurable student outcome of this learning experience is ability to demonstrate language barriers to effective communication.

Reflective action goes beyond interpretive action to involve evaluation of alternatives. It is a response to the question "Now what?" Choices are made based on what is considered most appropriate for the situation. For example, students take reflective action when they observe the discrimination of some students on a school bus and devise a plan of action to end the discrimination. Measurable student outcomes of this learning experience include ability to formulate a plan and ability to advocate for others' rights. Indeed, students will encounter decisions and problems in all areas of their lives; process skills will be essential.

FACS Teaching Strategies

For decades, FACS teachers have been educated to employ teaching strategies that are consistent with multicultural education. Key strategies include small- and large-group discussions, cooperative learning, and simulated experiences (see Blankenship & Moerchen, 1979; Chamberlain, 1992; Chamberlain & Cummings, 2003;

Chamberlain & Kelly, 1975, 1981; Hatcher & Halchin, 1973). In addition, service learning is considered a specific component of FACS (see Chamberlain & Cummings, 2003).

Discussion. Discussions are planned experiences in which members of a group respond to lead questions and interact to express their experiences and opinions and listen to others (Chamberlain & Cummings, 2003). Group members "practice tackling an issue, rather than attacking the person discussing the issue" (p. 125). Discussion is key to understanding many FACS concepts, as there is often no single, answer (Fox, 1997). The answer to the questions "What?" and "How?" is often "It depends."

For example, students may discuss media portrayals of men, women, teens, and the elderly, then discuss the impact of the portrayals on identity formation and perceptions of others. Since students bring different views to the discussion based on their unique life experiences and family values, structures, and functions, they can learn how others are affected. A measurable student outcome of this learning experience is ability to compare and contrast personal perceptions of media portrayals with those of classmates. In addition, students can develop sensitivity to the impact of media portrayals on others.

Cooperative learning. Cooperative learning usually occurs in groups of three to five students formed according to criteria established for the project as well as goals for the functioning of the group (Chamberlain & Cummings, 2003). Cooperative learning encourages interdependence through the assignment of roles, group process, and accomplishment of a group goal or product, while students take responsibility for their own learning and tasks. Social skills, such as active listening, turn taking, and conflict management are required.

For example, Manning (1999/2000) proposed that implementation of cooperative groups can facilitate multicultural competence when teachers form heterogeneous groups. When assigned to examine textbooks for stereotypes and discrimination, group members can assist each other in perceiving blatant and subtle instances.

Through interaction, students help each other understand the concepts, (Banks, 2002) while facilitating students' socialization needs (NASSP's Council on Middle Level Education, 1989). Not only are students gaining understanding of others' perspectives, they are working to empower those who are marginalized by the dominant culture of the school or community. One measurable student outcome of this learning experience is ability to analyze literature for stereotypes while assuming responsibility for another student's learning.

Simulated experiences. Simulated experiences include a variety of strategies that bring subject matter to life by replicating situations in daily life. Skits, role-plays, sociodramas, case studies, visual situations, and computer simulations (Chamberlain & Cummings, 2003) are types of simulations in which students assume roles to grapple with practical problems in a safe environment (Blankenship & Moerchen, 1979). These situations may pertain to social issues that Beane (1993) considers relevant in the middle level curriculum, such as interdependence among peoples in near as well as global environments, cultural diversity in those environments, problems experienced by some in the physical, political, and economic environments, and the impact of technology on human relationships.

Simulated experiences have the potential to yield many benefits to students, including the abilities to gain intrapersonal and interpersonal insight, express feelings, improve communication skills, adopt a different perspective, and gain confidence. Moreover, students will be able to think critically, increase objectivity, make decisions, and solve problems (Chamberlain & Cummings, 2003).

For example, students may read a case study about residents of a run-down, poorly funded institution for the aging and disabled in their hometown. Students analyze and evaluate the case for the impact of the living conditions on the physical, cognitive, social, and emotional health of the residents. They investigate community resources and decide what can be done to improve the living conditions and present their plan at a mock city council meeting. A measurable student outcome of this learning experience is ability to propose changes to improve the health and well-being of individuals who cannot do it for themselves. In this example, students are not only gaining understanding of others' perspectives, they are practicing to advocate for those who are marginalized and lacking power to care for themselves.

Service Learning. Service learning is the application of knowledge and skills in the curriculum to community needs and goals (Chamberlain & Cummings, 2003). Learning occurs as students take part in the experience and later, as they reflect on the experience and its consequences (Wither & Anderson, 1994). The democratic process is essential to service learning where all students work together with the teacher to plan the project (Wither & Anderson, 1994).

Students benefit from participation in service learning in various ways. Academically, students are actively involved and con-

tribute to a solution, so learning tends to last longer. They gain skills in authentic situations; this has value in future educational and employment opportunities. Socially, students hone their interpersonal skills and learn how to work on a team. Personally, they feel a sense of accomplishment and self-worth. In addition, students experience emotions reflecting commitment to a cause and to particular people. As citizens, students may learn more about their community and increase their awareness of strategies for improving it (Chamberlain & Cummings, 2003).

For example, a popular service-learning activity in middle level schools is a recycling project (see "Reduce, reuse, recycle," 1996). Students may work with the municipal solid waste management agency to determine waste disposal problems in the community. Based on concepts and processes pertaining to waste management learned in class, students devise and carry out a project in which they collect waste to recycle. In addition, they plan and implement an educational program in elementary schools to prevent littering in the future. One measurable student outcome of this learning experience is ability to construct a recycling collection program. Another student outcome is ability to assume responsibility for the physical environment.

Students are actively involved and contribute to a solution, so learning tends to last longer.

This example illustrates service learning as well as cooperative learning. Moreover, it pertains to two of the values of multicultural education proposed by Bennett (2003)—"responsibility to a world community" and "reverence for the earth" (p. 16). FACS is concerned with individual, family, community, and global well-being in general and resource management in particular. Conserving and sharing resources such as energy, water, and soil punctuates the interdependence of humanity and its reliance on the physical environment for its survival.

Summary and Implications

The middle school years are optimal for multicultural education (Manning, 1999/2000). Students are in the throes of working through issues they face now (Beane, 1993) and anticipating issues they will encounter in the future (Chamberlain & Cummings, 2003). A successful middle school curriculum supports its students in these processes (Beane, 1993). In this, FACS can play a primary role.

FACS classes must no longer be viewed as useful for other subject areas' multicultural lessons in predictable and limited ways, such as cooking food or sewing costumes. These approaches limit students to recognizing superficial features or commercialized characteristics of other countries. Such token acknowledgment of cultures distorts and undermines their complex, dynamic nature and ignores the call for interpersonal knowledge and skills needed for effective daily functioning. Moreover, they ignore the unique, valuable contribution FACS can make to students' development of multicultural competence.

Multicultural education and family and consumer sciences are both concerned with interpersonal relationships. FACS teachers do not need to step outside their curriculum to make it multicultural. By the very nature of the discipline and its scholarship, they teach core concepts and skills in the context of a diverse society.

Furthermore, when FACS teachers are numbered among the colleagues of an advisory team, they are in a position to contribute to the themes and learning goals established for a group of students. Prepared for action with an appropriate philosophy, an essential body of core concepts, standards, and competencies, and a repertoire of appropriate teaching strategies, FACS teachers can do more than embellish others' multicultural education efforts; they can bring to front and center the very knowledge and skills students need for effective participation in a global society. From its philosophical foundation, through its national curriculum standards and curriculum processes, to its key teaching strategies, FACS makes a significant contribution to our children's competency to thrive in a multicultural world.

References

Association for Career and Technical Education. (1994). Family and consumer sciences vision and mission statement. Alexandria, VA: Author.

Banks, J. A. (2002). *An introduction to multicultural education* (3rd ed.). Boston: Allyn & Bacon.

Beane, J. A. (1993). *A middle school curriculum: From rhetoric to reality* (2nd ed.). Columbus, OH: National Middle School Association.

Bennett, C. I. (2003). *Comprehensive multicultural education theory and practice* (5th ed.). Boston: Allyn & Bacon.

Blankenship, M. L., & Moerchen, B. D. (1979). *Home economics education.* Boston: Houghton Mifflin.

Carnegie Council on Adolescent Development. (1989). *Turning points: Preparing American youth for the 21st century.* New York: Carnegie Corporation.

Chamberlain, V. M. (1992). *Creative home economics instruction* (3rd ed.). Peoria, IL: Glencoe MacMillan/McGraw-Hill.

Chamberlain, V. M., & Cummings, M. N. (2003). *Creative instructional methods for family and consumer sciences, nutrition & wellness.* Peoria, IL: Glencoe McGraw-Hill.

Chamberlain, V. M., & Kelly, J. (1975). *Creative home economics instruction.* New York: McGraw-Hill.

Chamberlain, V. M., & Kelly, J. (1981). *Creative home economics instruction* (2nd ed.). New York: McGraw-Hill.

Clausell, M. (1998). Challenges and opportunities for family and consumer sciences professionals in the new America. *Journal of Family and Consumer Sciences, 90*(1), 3–7.

Costa, A. L., & Liebmann, R. M. (1997). Difficulties with disciplines. In A. L. Costa & R. M. Liebmann (Eds.), *Envisioning process as content: Toward a Renaissance curriculum* (pp. 21–31). Thousand Oaks, CA: Corwin Press.

East, M. (1980). *Home economics: Past, present, and future.* Boston: Allyn & Bacon.

Fox, C. K. (1997). Incorporating the practical problem-solving approach in the classroom. *Journal of Family and Consumer Sciences, 89*(2), 37–40.

Greenwood, B. B., Darling, C. A., & Hansen-Gandy, S. (1997). A call to the profession: Serving culturally diverse individuals and families. *Journal of Family and Consumer Sciences, 89*(1), 36–41.

Hatcher, H. M., & Halchin, L. C. (1973). *The teaching of home economics* (3rd ed.). Boston: Houghton Mifflin.

Manning, L. (1999/2000). Developmentally responsive multicultural education for young adolescents. *Childhood Education, 76*(2), 82–87.

NASSP's Council on Middle Level Education. (1989). *Middle level education's responsibility for intellectual development.* Reston, VA: National Association of Secondary School Principals.

National Association of State Administrators of Family and Consumer Sciences Education. (1998). *National standards for family and consumer sciences education.* Decatur, GA: Vocational-Technical Education Consortium of States.

Pederson, P. (2004). *110 experiences for multicultural learning.* Washington, DC: American Psychological Association.

Reduce, reuse, recycle: A thematic module from the Indiana middle school curriculum framework for family and consumer sciences. (1996). Indianapolis: Indiana Department of Education.

Wither, J. T., & Anderson, C. S. (1994). *How to establish a high school service learning program.* Alexandria, VA: Association for Supervision and Curriculum Development.

BARBARA A. CLAUSS is an assistant professor of family and consumer sciences at Indiana State University, Terre Haute. E-mail: b-clauss@indstate.edu.

Discarding the Deficit Model

Ambiguity and subjectivity contribute to the disproportionate placement of minorities in special education.

BETH HARRY AND JANETTE KLINGNER

Many authors in this issue of *Educational Leadership* describe students as having "learning needs" and "learning challenges." How we wish this language truly reflected the common approach to students who have difficulty mastering the information and skills that schools value! Many students have special learning needs, and many experience challenges learning school material. But does this mean they have *disabilities?* Can we help students without undermining their self-confidence and stigmatizing them with a label? Does it matter whether we use the word *disability* instead of *need* and *challenge?*

Language in itself is not the problem. What *is* problematic is the belief system that this language represents. The provision of special education services under U.S. law—the Education for All Handicapped Children Act in 1975 and the Individuals with Disabilities Education Improvement Act in 2004—ensured that schools could no longer turn away students on the basis of perceived developmental, sensory, physical, or cognitive limitations. However, the downside of the law is that it has historically relied on identifying a disability thought to exist within a child. The main criterion for eligibility for special education services, then, has been *proof of intrinsic deficit*. There are two problems with this focus: First, defining and identifying high-incidence disabilities are ambiguous and subjective processes. Second, the focus on disability has become so intertwined with the historical devaluing of minorities in the United States that these two deficit lenses now deeply influence the special education placement process.

We recently completed a three-year study that throws some light on the issue (Harry & Klingner, 2006). We looked at the special education placement process for black and Hispanic students in a large urban school district in a southeastern U.S. state. The 12 elementary schools involved represented a range of ethnicities, socioeconomic statuses, and rates of special education placement. On the basis of data we gathered from classroom observations, school-based conferences, interviews with school personnel and family members, and examination of student documents (such as individualized education programs, behavioral referrals, and evaluation reports), we found that several conditions seriously marred the placement process. These included lack of adequate classroom instruction prior to the student's referral, inconsistencies in policy implementation, and arbitrary referrals and assessment decisions. It was also clear that students in poor neighborhoods were at risk of receiving poor schooling, which increased their risk of failing and of being placed in special education.

Minorities in Special Ed

The disproportionate placement of some minority groups in special education continues to be a central problem in the field. As noted in a report by the National Research Council (2002), the categories with the highest incidence of disproportionate minority-group placement are also those categories whose criteria are based on clinical judgment: Educable Mental Retardation, Emotional/Behavioral Disorders, and Learning Disability. The categories whose criteria are based on biologically verifiable conditions—such as deafness or visual impairment—do not show disproportionality by ethnicity.

Across the United States, African American students are represented in the category of Educable Mental Retardation at twice the rate of their white peers; in the category of Emotional/Behavioral Disorders, they are represented at one and one-half times the rate of their white peers. In some states, Native American and Hispanic students are overrepresented in the Learning Disability category (National Research Council, 2002).

The roots of this problem lie deep in U.S. history. Looking at how the mandate for school integration intertwined with special education, Ferri and Connor (2006) analyzed public documents and newspaper articles dating from *Brown v. Board of Education* in 1954 to the inception of the Education for All Handicapped Children Act in 1975. The authors show how African American students entering public schools through forced integration were subject to low expectations and intense efforts to keep them separate from the white mainstream. As the provision of services for students with disabilities became a legal mandate, clear patterns of overrepresentation of Mexican American and African American students in special education programs emerged. Plagued by ambiguous definitions and subjectivity in clinical judgments, these categories often have more to do with administrative, curricular, and instructional decisions than with students' inherent abilities.

Dilemmas of LD and EMR

The label of Learning Disability (LD) used to be assigned mainly to white and middle-class students. African American students—and in some states, Hispanic and Native American students—were more likely to be disproportionately assigned to the more severe category of Educable Mental Retardation (EMR). More than two decades ago, various scholars offered thoughtful analyses of these patterns. Sleeter (1986) argued that the Learning Disability category came into being to create a space for students from predominantly white and middle-class homes who were not living up to family and community expectations. She noted that the other side of this coin was that students with learning difficulties who were from low-income homes were more likely to end up in the Educable Mental Retardation category.

In a careful examination of how the construction of the Learning Disability category affected African American students, Collins and Camblin (1983) argued that the definition of *learning disability* and the means of identifying it guaranteed this pattern. First, the requirement for a discrepancy between IQ score and academic achievement was designed to indicate that the student was unexpectedly achieving below his or her measured potential. This requirement was intended to ensure that the learning difficulty was the result of a specific, not generalized, learning disability. In other words, the student was capable of higher achievement, as evidenced by his or her IQ score, but some specific disability seemed to be holding him or her back.

But how do we measure cognitive potential? Through IQ tests. It is widely acknowledged that IQ tests are really "tests of general achievement, reflecting broad, culturally rooted ways of thinking and problem solving" (Donovan & Cross, 2002, p. 284). It is not surprising, therefore, that if we measure intelligence this way, then groups with inadequate exposure to the skills and knowledge required to do well on these tests will score lower than their mainstream counterparts. Thus, as Collins and Camblin pointed out, African American students' lower scores on IQ tests make it more unlikely that their scores will reflect the "discrepancy" required for admittance into the Learning Disability category.

Collins and Camblin's second argument focused on the "exclusionary clause" of the Learning Disability definition. In addition to ensuring that the student does not have some other intrinsic limitation, such as mental retardation or sensory impairments, the exclusionary clause requires that school personnel establish that the source of the problem inheres in the student, not in his or her environment or experience. Consequently, African American students living in poor socioeconomic circumstances were less likely to receive the Learning Disability label because their environments tended to exclude them from this category.

This brings us to the paradoxical impact of the Learning Disability category on minority students. On the one hand, the underrepresentation of poor and minority students in this category—also known as a pattern of false negatives—is a problem if it means that students fall between the cracks and do not receive appropriate instruction. Further, there are benefits associated with the Learning Disability label. For example, students in this category can receive accommodations on secondary and college-level testing, which many middle-class white families continue to take advantage of.

On the other hand, the number of minorities represented in this category has begun to increase. We might now face the possibility of overrepresentation of minorities—or false positives—in the Learning Disability group. Some researchers have argued that many students currently in the category should actually qualify for Educable Mental Retardation (MacMillan, Gresham, & Bocian, 1998). Moreover, our research showed that some psychologists use the Learning Disability label to protect a student from the more stigmatizing and isolating label of Emotional/Behavioral Disorders (Harry & Klingner, 2006).

The real problem is the arbitrariness and stigmatizing effects of the entire process. Students shouldn't need a false disability label to receive appropriate support. They also shouldn't acquire that label because they had inappropriate or inadequate opportunities to learn. And they shouldn't end up in programs that don't offer the truly specialized instruction they need.

Students shouldn't need a false disability label to receive appropriate support.

Dilemmas of EBD

The use of the Emotional/Behavioral Disorders (EBD) label grew by 500 percent between 1974 and 1998, from just over 1 percent in 1974 to just over 5 percent in 1998 (National Research Council, 2002). This category is plagued by as much ambiguity as the Learning Disability category is. To qualify for the EBD label, a student must display inappropriate behaviors to a "marked degree" and for a "length of time." These criteria depend on subjective judgment.

Also, decisions about what evaluation instruments to use vary widely across states (Hosp & Reschly, 2002). Some states use projective tests, which are well known for their inherent subjectivity. Students respond to stimuli, such as pictures or sentences, and then a psychologist interprets their responses as a projection of their feelings. Other states rely on checklists, which are equally subjective. Our research revealed that different teachers using the same instrument rated the same student very differently. For example, using a behavioral checklist to rate a 2nd grade African American boy, one teacher checked four items relating to poor self-concept as occurring "excessively" (more than 50 percent of the time), whereas another teacher checked those same items as occurring "seldom" (1–10 percent of the time).

One teacher in the study commented, "They're not disturbed. They're just a pain in the neck!" As many scholars have observed, it's often difficult to tell whether the behavior is mostly troubling to school personnel or whether it reflects a troubled child.

Two Distorting Lenses

The intertwining of race and perceptions of disability are so deeply embedded in our way of thinking that many people are not even aware of how one concept influences the other. Let's consider how this works in light of the study we conducted.

The Disability Deficit Lens

Many teachers in the study saw disability as a simple fact. One teacher noted, "These children have disabilities, just like some children have blue eyes." When a student experiences continued difficulty mastering academic skills, all too often the first question someone asks is, "Does this student have a disability?" The Learning Disability label requires that we exclude potential environmental reasons for the student's difficulties. But barring obvious developmental limitations, how can we separate a student from his or her social and cultural experience?

Let's consider some environmental experiences that could interfere with a student's learning. Most often, the experiences cited as exclusionary include poverty, detrimental home and community environments, or lack of opportunity to learn. In and of itself, poverty does not cause learning difficulties. Most children from poor homes have effectively mastered the usual developmental childhood tasks of motor and language skills, and they have learned the values and social practices of their homes and neighborhoods. But they often haven't learned particular forms of the language or the ways in which schools use that language to the extent that their middle-income peers have.

For example, in a study of African American preschoolers' language development, Brice-Heath (1983) demonstrated how their social environments prepared students for an imaginative form of storytelling but not for answering the testlike, factual questions prevalent in schools. Moreover, the students' vocabularies may not be as extensive or as sophisticated as those of children growing up in middle-class homes. Students may also not have had extensive experience handling printed materials or listening to stories told in the linear fashion so common to many children's books. Their lack of experience in some of these areas can make children seem unprepared for academic learning.

Absence from school as well as poor instruction in the early years can also be sources of a student's low achievement. Our research found that school personnel were always ready to blame the students' home contexts but seldom examined the school context. Even when students were referred for special education evaluation, members of the placement teams seldom asked whether poor classroom climate or instruction contributed to the students' difficulties or whether peer pressures could be the source of their withdrawal or acting out.

School personnel were always ready to blame the students' home contexts but seldom examined the school context.

The Social/Cultural Deficit Lens

When a habit of looking for intrinsic deficit intertwines with a habit of interpreting cultural and racial difference as a deficit, the deck is powerfully loaded against poor students of color. Speaking about her African American 1st graders, one teacher in the study pointed out that "they don't know how to walk, talk, or sit in a chair. It's cultural!" Comments like this really don't refer to whether the students can or cannot do these things. Instead, they show that the manner in which the students do these things is unacceptable to the teacher. The teacher's focus on deficiencies predisposed her to see the students as limited by their culture and, ultimately, to refer almost one-half of her class of normally developing children for evaluation for special education.

If it is evident that students' early home and community experiences have not prepared them well for schooling, what do schools do? Do the schools then provide the students with adequate and appropriate opportunities to learn? Does instruction begin where the students are? Does it move at a pace that enables them to become accustomed to the new norms and expectations? Are the students made to feel that the school values the knowledge they bring from their homes and communities? Do teachers build on these "funds of knowledge" (Moll, 1990), or do they see only deficits in the students?

Variation, Not Pathology

Beyond the fact that these processes affect minorities unduly, the steady and dramatic increase in the use of disability labels in our schools is a cause for serious concern. The figures are startling. According to the National Research Council (2002), the risk of *any* student (averaged across ethnic groups) being identified as having Specific Learning Disabilities has increased from 1.21 percent in 1974 to 6.02 percent in 1998.

The truth is that the law's provision of disability categories for students who have learning and behavioral difficulties has become a way for schools to dodge their responsibility to provide high-quality general education. The deficit model is based on the normative development of students whose homes and communities have prepared them for schooling long before they enter school. Children who come to school without that preparation, and without the continuing home support of family members who can reinforce the goals of schooling, face expectations that they have not had the opportunity to fulfill. All too quickly the students become candidates for suspected "disability." Further, the special education programs into which they are placed are disproportionately of low quality in terms of curriculum, instruction, and ratio of students to teachers.

So why can't we see students' difficulties as "human variation rather than pathology" (Reid & Valle, 2004, p. 473)? Some encouraging trends are under way. The recent reauthorization of the Individuals with Disabilities Education Act allows for a change in the discrepancy model. The law now recommends tiered interventions by which schools can screen students early for signs of difficulty and provide more intensive and individualized instruction in needed areas without applying a special education label. The recent reauthorization enables schools to spend 15 percent of their special education funds on early intervention services.

The three-tiered Response to Intervention (RTI) model is currently receiving great attention in the field (Klingner & Edwards, 2006). The first tier involves quality instruction and ongoing monitoring within the general education classroom. In the second tier, schools provide intensive intervention support for students who have not met expected benchmarks. In the final tier, students who do not respond to second-tier interventions are evaluated for possible placement in special education.

The RTI model holds promise for preventing academic failure. It also provides support for culturally and linguistically diverse students before they underachieve. Educators are becoming increasingly aware that they need to apply the model in culturally responsive ways (see Klingner & Edwards, 2006). This might mean considering whether suggested instructional interventions have proven effective with *all* students, including English language learners. Also, educators should avoid a one-size-fits-all approach because culturally diverse students or English language learners may require different tier-one or tier-two interventions.

The law also calls for increased and specific efforts to include parents in all phases of the placement process. Schools must ensure that parents understand the proceedings of individualized education program (IEP) meetings and provide an interpreter if necessary. They also must notify parents early on about meetings to help ensure attendance and provide parents with a copy of the IEP.

These changes in the law signal a need for revising the concept of "disability" as the single criterion for eligibility for specialized and intensive services. We need a new vision of special education—one that reserves the notion of disability for students with clear-cut diagnoses of biological or psychological limitations and uses the categorization only for the purpose of delivering intensive, specialized services in the least restrictive education environment possible. Students who have no clear-cut diagnoses but who struggle to master school-based tasks should be eligible for specialized services according to explicit criteria based on level of achievement. The Response to Intervention model monitors the progress of all students so that teachers can provide extra support—within the general education context—to those students who are not making adequate progress.

Rather than devoting extensive resources to finding out whether students "have" disabilities, we should devote those resources to assessing students' exact instructional needs using models like Response to Intervention. Schools will need to provide this instruction through collaboration between general and special education personnel to ensure that all students continue to have full access to the general curriculum. As Lisa Delpit (2006) noted, let's stop looking for disabilities and just "teach the children what they need to know" (p. 3).

References

Brice-Heath, S. (1983). *Ways with words: Language, life, and work in communities and classrooms.* Cambridge, UK: Cambridge University Press.

Collins, R., & Camblin, L. D. (1983). The politics and science of learning disability classification: Implications for black children. *Contemporary Education, 54*(2), 113–118.

Delpit, L. (2006). Foreword. In B. Harry & J. K. Klingner, *Why are so many minority students in special education? Understanding race and disability in schools.* New York: Teachers College Press.

Donovan, S., & Cross, C. (2002). *Minority students in special and gifted education.* Washington, DC: National Academies Press.

Ferri, B. A., & Connor, D. J. (2006). *Reading resistance: Discourses of exclusion in desegregation and inclusion debates.* New York: Peter Lang.

Harry, B., & Klingner, J. K. (2006). *Why are so many minority students in special education? Understanding race and disability in schools.* New York: Teachers College Press.

Hosp, J. L., & Reschly, D. J. (2002). Regional differences in school psychology practice. *School Psychology Review, 31,* 11–29.

Klingner, J. K., & Edwards, P. (2006). Cultural considerations with response-to-intervention models. *Reading Research Quarterly, 41,* 108–117.

MacMillan, D. L., Gresham, F. M., & Bocian, K. M. (1998). Discrepancy between definitions of learning disabilities and school practices: An empirical investigation. *Journal of Learning Disabilities, 31,* 314–326.

Moll, L. C. (Ed.). (1990). *Vygotsky and education: Instructional implications and applications of socio-historical psychology.* Cambridge, UK: Cambridge University Press.

National Research Council. (2002). *Minority students in special and gifted education.* Washington, DC: National Academies Press.

Reid, K., & Valle, J. W. (2004). The discursive practice of learning disability: Implications for instruction and parent-school relations. *Journal of Learning Disabilities, 37*(6), 466–481.

Sleeter, C. (1986). Learning disabilities: The social construction of a special education category. *Exceptional Children, 53,* 46–54.

BETH HARRY is Professor in the Department of Teaching and Learning at the University of Miami, Florida; 305–284–5363; bebeharry@aol.com. **JANETTE KLINGNER** is Associate Professor in Bilingual Special Education in the Division for Educational Equity and Cultural Diversity at the University of Colorado, Boulder; 303–492–0773; jkklingner@aol.com.

Arts in the Classroom

"La Llave" (The Key) to Awareness, Community Relations, and Parental Involvement

MARGARITA MACHADO-CASAS
University of North Carolina at Chapel Hill

As a teacher and a person of color, I am committed to social justice, equity, and meaningful teaching that takes students' cultural heritage into consideration in the workplace. Yet this is not easy in American schools. When entering the classroom we are expected to act as if we are blind to the social-economic issues our students struggle with daily. We are expected to teach only academic subjects and not deal with what school really is about—an extension of home and preparation for real life situations that are more complex than just dealing with character education. When in the classroom we are trained to be authoritative beings that control through "regimentation," "depositing," and "manipulation." As teachers we become our students' oppressors (Freire, 1970, p. 107). Being and acting as teacher the oppressor is harmful for all students but particularly for immigrants who on top of having to learn a new language, and a new educational system, have to suppress their cultural being,—all they have known in order to fit into American schools.

I was born in Nicaragua, from which seven in my family and I fled to Panama escaping from war and an oppressive government. We lived in Panama for five and a half years before political instability caused turmoil in that country as well. Having experienced this oppression before, my father courageously opted to bring the family to the United States. I arrived in California at the age of 14. Knowing less than basic English I was enrolled in a middle school in Fullerton, California, where I was placed in an ESL (Sheltered English class). My initial school experience was devastating. I not only did not know the language enough to communicate my thoughts and feelings in an understandable manner, but I was also having to re-learn school and the behaviors one is to display when in school. For example, back in both Nicaragua and Panama, students were expected to have an opinion and to express it without raising their hands.

As a child in the U.S., I was often the translator, the bridge between my parents and schools, the one person who in the process of translating became responsible for getting the message across properly. My parents were never invited to school events and were too busy working to get involved. Schools did nothing to encourage parental involvement of immigrant parents. As a student my experience, life, language, and family were ignored. I was being told in school that "Yo" (me) was not good enough for this society, and I had to change. This sudden alienation became an everyday event; one that persisted throughout my school years. I felt culturally and cognitively abused, "Whether urbane or harsh, cultural invasion is thus always an act of violence against the persons of the invaded culture, who lose their originality or face the threat of losing it" (Freire, p. 133).

Being successful in our current educational system means being able to acculturate to the dominant culture (Credit Nieto, 1999, pg. 75), and, now with accountability, demands it means being able to successfully pass a test. When I came into the country as an immigrant child, I remember the struggles I went through, I was invisible, my "real" life experiences were ignored. In my case, I came to see "real" life experiences as those we live daily, e.g., encounters with strangers, family members, friends, and community members that make us happy and/or sad. I also saw real life in our homes and school, where we saw, touched, smelled, and used our other senses. Reality, to me, included reactions with and from others; looks we are given and names we are called; pains, struggles, faces that make sad; actions, mannerism that make us who we are; love, interactions with others; what we eat; what we dance to; the languages we speak; and the way we act and think in the world. I would have been better prepared to deal with these struggles if I had had a school environment where school was an extension of home, real life, a place where acculturation was not the goal, but rather self-exploration, critical thinking, and exposure to real life situations to bring about "concientization" (Freire, 1970, p. 140) to promote action. Creating this kind of environment would have allowed me to break the current mold of thinking and begin to create new ways of thinking. As a teacher, I wanted my students to have what I did not. In my own classroom I wanted to create new ways of thinking that addressed students' different life situations. I began thinking about what I had that I could use. I realized the starting points were the classroom and myself.

I wanted the classroom to be an open-safe-respectful environment where all cultures, races, and ethnic differences were celebrated and promoted and where the home culture and school experience came together in significant ways. I learned this was revolutionary, "Revolution is achieved with neither verbalism or activism, but rather with praxis, that is, with reflection and action directed at the structures to be transformed" (Freire, p. 107). I began to organize my classroom into a community that was very much connected with home and real life situations. I wanted to make real life social justice issues accessible, visible, and practiced. Yet, I was in need of the "La llave" [the key] that would enable all this, and arts integration became "mi llave" [my key].

What constitutes arts? I define arts by not just a drawing, song, dance, but rather by those everyday experiences that lead us to thinking, questioning, talking, communicating with others, communicating our feelings, doing, hurting, loving, but most importantly feeling and voice/expression. Why the arts? We are surrounded by arts. We breathe them, live them, touch them, and experience the arts daily, both consciously and unconsciously. From the time we are born we are invaded with artistic gestures that portray love, affection, beauty, pain, suffering, and everyday life: "Experiences in the arts richly augment our ordinary life experiences and by doing so, often lead us to tactical understanding of the deeper meaning of our existence, our culture, and our world" (Fisher & McDonald, 2002, p. 1). Through the "arts," students and parents in my classroom began cooperating with their children. This, in turn, created reflection and action in both the classroom and community. Arts created a praxis that allowed students and parents to engage in dialogue and to get involved in school and acting.

Thinking about Being the Teacher

The teacher is a sociocultural mediator when she or he "becomes the link between the child's sociocultural experiences at home and school. That is the teacher becomes the sociocultural, sociohistorical mediator of important formal and informal knowledge

about the culture and society in which children develop" (Diaz & Flores, 2000). Therefore, taking the role of a teacher as a sociocultural mediator involves making connections with students and those who impact student's lives. Teachers have the power to bring students and parents into a three-way relationship I call *sociocultural triangulation* (See Figure 1).

Sociocultural triangulation assumes all three are equal and equally responsible to promote a child's progress. The role of the teacher in this triangulation process is to start the communication between student, parent or guardian and teacher that will promote sociocultural acceptance and inclusion in the classroom. The role of the teacher in this case is redefined and restructured to give up control in order to allow dialogue, thinking, and reflection to occur, "If the true commitment to the people, involving transformation of the reality by which they are oppressed, required a theory of transforming action, this theory cannot fail to assign the people a fundamental role in the transformation process" (Freire, p. 108).

In this article I describe how arts integration enabled me to develop such triangulation that resulted in shifting of the roles of the parties involved. Further, I will explain the ways in which organized art activities helped create a classroom environment where relationships between student and parents or guardians evolved in order to promote individuality, cultural inclusion, "conscientization," and equity. By utilizing arts as the "llave" [key] we began to create a cultural platform between a diverse classroom and an equally diverse community. In order to illuminate this, I will explore three areas I organized to achieve these goals: my classroom, my teachings, and community connections. Along with arts integration these three connections (which also lead to sociocultural triangulation) were essential to the creation of a new platform that connected the community and school in a new way of thinking about learning through the arts.

The Classroom

My classroom was a 4th grade two-way immersion classroom in which instruction in the fourth grade was provided in both English and Spanish. Fifty percent of the time instruction was provided in English and fifty percent of the time in Spanish. Half of the students were minorities, mostly Latino/a and Chicano/a, and the other half of the class was White or other ethnicities. The class was considerably from a low socioeconomic background as well as considerably diverse. Class diversity was represented

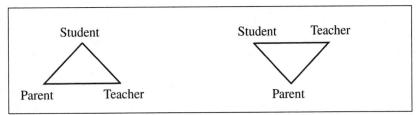

Figure 1 Sociocultural triangulation*

*This triangulation can be initiated by anyone and no one is the head or controller of this process.

both economically and socially. Parents' occupations ranged from housewives, "campesinos" [farm workers], factory workers, teachers, and professionals working for the government.

When walking into the classroom one would immediately notice how the classroom was divided into different sections or walls. Looking south was the children's international diversity wall, which included pictures of children from around the world. Each picture was enlarged and it included a narrative written by the child or an adult about that child's experience. This wall was of great success in the classroom. Both students and parents enjoyed looking at the pictures and reading the narratives. Still on the south side of the wall, immediately after that wall was a calendar wall, which was in both English and Spanish and more pictures and narratives of children from all over the world. North of the international diversity wall was the social studies wall that presented issues related to subjects being studied in class. The wall contained writing samples of all children. East of the room was the creative wall, this wall was initially designed to give children the opportunity to post drawings, but after I began the sociocultural triangulation process through arts it became the most important wall in the classroom—one both students and parents helped design and maintain.

The classroom was not solely mine, but instead a more collective community space where students, parents, guardians, and I were responsible to make sure the classroom was running smoothly. Before the school year started I contacted all parents via telephone or correspondence. I introduced myself and told them a little bit about my life; this gave parents the opportunity to get to know my life experiences and me. I then proceeded to tell parents that there was an "open door" policy, and that they were welcomed and encouraged to come to volunteer in the classroom. I invited them over to the classroom prior to school starting. Many came and we talked about what they saw as the struggles their children have had, frustrations they have had, and ways in which I could help them both. At this time I informed parents that I was going to be calling them every Friday to give them updates and reports of how the classroom was going. They seemed both shocked, and doubtful; I later found out that the majority of them did not think I was going to be actually calling them every Friday.

As I came from a working class family, I am aware of parents' busy schedules as well as the necessity to sometimes carry more than one job to sustain a family. To that end, I explained to parents that *how* they are involved with their child's schooling is more important than the *amount* of involvement. I wanted parents to be able to express their experiences with their children and me (optional). I wanted parents to begin dialogue, to talk to their children about their struggles when they bring an issue home, to ask their children about school, to share their qualities (those things they are good at), whatever they might be, and most importantly to talk and reflect with them. Some parents expressed concerns that they "Did not have anything they were good at, many of us are just housewives or factory workers, 'campesinos' (farm workers)." I reiterated that everyone has something they are good at and that I was sure that if I asked their children what their parents or guardians were good

at they could tell me in a second. I reinforced the concept that children appreciate any interaction with parents; and the most important interaction was one that started dialogue and reflection. I explained to parents that I was committed to doing all that was in my power to inform parents and guardians of what we were doing in class, that I saw them as colleagues, so input given to me was appreciated and encouraged. By being including and welcoming, parents and guardians and students began to feel comfortable around the classroom, with me, and with other students. They began to trust me and the classroom environment.

As I wanted my classroom to be an extension of home, of real life experiences, I needed a way for parents to participate. Moreover, I wanted this participation to be something that was special and not something that would merely help the teacher with her tasks. It seemed to me that one way to accomplish this was to build a partnership with parents through arts. I began to do this by assigning creative projects to students that involved math, social studies, language arts, and arts. The assignments consisted of students going home and finding things around the classroom and/or neighborhood that had to do with school activities. The goal was for students and parents to look around their world, their reality and find beauty and art within it. For example, when we discussed geometric shapes in the classroom I asked students to go home and with parental or guardian help they were to find an object that would match the shapes we were studying. If they could not find one like it, they had to select objects that when connected to others, created that shape. It was a project that everyone seemed to enjoy. One student could not find the shape of a trapezoid, so his father helped him create one with old car parts. Along with the parent, the student sketched each part of the car where it was taken from and explained the process of figuring out what parts would fit together to create a trapezoid. The student also talked about the process of how the metal was bent, welded, and put together. The student brought it to class to share his invention along with an explanation of how he did it. I used that moment to explain to students that arts does not only involve drawing and coloring but also creating new things out of old ones; arts involves everyday experiences and objects that surround us.

My Teaching

Arts have been one of my favorite tools in the classroom. It was a great source of release when I was a child, as it was through the arts I that was able to express many emotions, feelings, and thoughts. For this reason, I felt that including arts in the classroom and in my lessons was imperative. Initially, arts were used in the classroom as a way to express or retell what students were writing or working on. As in the trapezoid example mentioned above, this was very superficial, and it did not require much critical thinking. I began thinking about my intentions and what art expression meant to me while growing up as an immigrant. With that in mind, I began to think about my goal and about changing my role as a teacher. My goal was to promote critical thinking, a sense of commonality, transcendence of time, connection with real life situations, and recognition of power structures that affected characters in the past and that are still affecting many today. After I had a vision of what could be achieved and my role as the sociocultural mediator, I began to think about ways in which I could utilize the arts to raise awareness, promote critical thinking, equity, and social justice. I had my work cut out for me!

Children are always really excited to read about others' experiences, lives, and struggles. Therefore, I chose several biographies and gave students a summary of the biographies that included some of the accomplishments of the characters. I asked the class to choose one biography and write why they wanted to read that particular biography. Students then took the biographies home and shared with their parents the choices they had. Many children returned to class with their favorites and their parents' favorites. Students were also instructed to draw a picture that predicted events which they thought were going to take place in the story; they were to do this with only the information I provided for them. Some parents wrote their favorites on a piece a paper along with the reasons why they liked that particular biography. Some parents wrote it in Spanish and others in English. This allowed them to be included regardless of the language they spoke. I explained to students that I asked them to come up with reasons as to why we should read these biographies in order for them to begin to think about social-political and cultural issues they and their parents are interested in. I then asked for volunteers to discuss their prediction drawings. They were to explain what it was and why they chose those colors, background, and the meaning behind the scene. This became a wonderful artistic activity and experience given that every student had a different interpretation of each of the stories, and therefore colors, background, and scene were and had different meaning. The three biographies they chose were Frida Kahlo, Anne Frank, and Biddy Mason. Frida Kahlo was read in English, Anne Frank in Spanish, and Biddy Mason in Spanish. We began by reading Anne Frank. To save space here, I will only discuss Anne Frank.

The story of Anne Frank is a book that is filled with socio-political issues. First, we began the unit by reading the book and talking about Germany during that time. I provided the class with historical information about Hitler, the Jewish community, and Germany. None of these historical facts included pictures of Hitler. They were then asked to create a portrait of Germany during those times. The portrait was to include the feeling, struggles, and emotions students thought were being felt by either Germans, Jews, or Hitler. Many drew either a picture of Hitler or included Hitler in their portraits; surprisingly enough almost all but two students drew Hitler with blond hair and blue eyes. When asked to share their portraits with the class many expressed that Hitler was blond with blue eyes because he liked people who were "like him, blond with blue eyes." Here students began to make a connection to their own life experiences, their feeling comfortable or liking people who were like them. So, if Hitler liked people who were blond with blue eyes, then he must be blond and have blue eyes. When they all finished presenting their portraits, I showed them several pictures of Hitler. They were all shocked

to find out that Hitler was not blond, nor did he have blue eyes. I also told them that Hitler's mother was Jewish. And they suddenly began to think. Their eyes were wide open; they were in deep thought. We talked about why it was more acceptable for Hitler to be blond with blue eyes than for him to have dark hair and brown eyes. I got responses such as, "If he was just like the Jews, brown hair, and dark eyes, then why did he dislike them?" "He must not like himself." "I know some people who are mean to many who are like them; like Latinos hurting Latinos."

We talked about what life was about during that time, and what it was to be a young woman without the opportunity to experience "la vida" (life). This conversation about Anne Frank was happening in the classroom and at home. I asked parents to begin a portrait of the Anne Frank story at home. I explained to them that as the story proceeded they were to add something to the portrait. I felt this was a great opportunity to get parents involved and share their experiences their "vida" (life). I asked parents to share how their experiences were similar to those of Anne Frank. Hence, together with their children, many parents worked on the Anne Frank portrait. As the story proceeded they were to add whatever from Anne's life or their life they thought was important to the portrait.

Although this story was one that touched them, they were still responding superficially to the story. I wanted them to feel like the key person in the story, to put their feet in Anne Frank's shoes. Therefore, I asked them to literally take their shoes off and to share them with the person next to them and to put each other's shoes on. I too had to exchange shoes with a student. They were all really excited about doing this. I moved the desks, dimmed the lights, and had students close their eyes. I began playing German classical music and we all began to "walk in someone else's shoes." I asked the class to think about their feelings, emotions, to imagine being a teenager during the holocaust and not being able to enjoy life fully, to imagine being imprisoned, trapped, and scared because of persecution. After the exercise was completed, they were quiet, and some raised their hands. They shared how it felt to imagine being someone else. Many talked about being powerless or "sin poder," frightened, trapped, and caged "como un animal." This activity provided students with a more creative way of looking at the arts. It was the arts that involved movement, sense of one's place, and thinking about others while being here. For fourth graders this was a unique way of feeling the arts—seeing beauty, pain, and otherness.

I asked them to think about the way they felt and to portray their feelings in any way they wanted to. They could do this by singing, acting, drawing, or creating a mini-book. Two created sketches, one sang, and the rest created portraits of what they experienced while being in someone else's shoes. One child drew a portrait of Anne as a girl crying, in one corner was the Star of David and on the other side were armed forces. The side of the face that had armed forces was white with blue eyes and blond hair and the side with the Star of David was brown with black eyes and dark hair. Bars imprisoned the girl, and a tear was coming out of her eye. In the writing description, it said, "The

Hitler army wants her to be white, blond with blue eyes, but she has black hair and dark eyes, and that is why she is in a prison; the attic of that home. Anne was an amazing girl who was proud of who she was and who wrote those letters to let us know what not to do and to take people like they are." One child performed a sketch that connected her own personal experiences with those of Anne Frank. The sketch was a moving and sad story of her grandmother and her family running away from Mexico, away from the threat of being killed. This skit created an interesting conversation between the entire class. Children began to talk about oppression, ethnicity, race, power, powerlessness, discrimination, racism, genocide, social political implications, survival, and what it means to us now. Since many of them did not know the terminology, they only expressed themselves through experiences and examples. As they were giving me examples I began to provide them with the terms that described that particular situation. For example, Hitler killed thousands of people and this is called genocide. We talked about color and preconceived notions many have about a particular race because of the color of their skin. Another student began to sing about class differences, which lead us to talk about privilege and poverty. Many students could relate to this given that many had felt mistreatment because of their social class.

They all had wonderful examples of artistic expressions; their feelings and reactions showed they understood how struggle is painful regardless of when it happens. With this activity, it did not matter if you could draw, sing, or dance. Any form of artistic expression was accepted; it became the universal language of acceptance. Arts became a universal voice that was open and accessible to all.

Community

As parents began to get involved and informed about what was going on in the classroom, other family members became involved as well. Many parents were immigrants and their migration experiences as well as their struggles with a life in a new country had valuable lessons for their children. Being an immigrant whose experiences were ignored, I reiterated to parents that their experiences were valuable and appreciated. Parents became involved in helping to create portraits, giving children ideas, and sharing their own stories. They were dialoguing, communicating, and reflecting on their experiences together. Students began sharing their family stories with the class to find out that many of our stories were similar.

I noticed that children were really interested in other children's stories, in their own family stories, and the way each child expressed their stories through the use the art. Because I was aware that "men and women . . . [are] beings who cannot be truly human apart from communication, for they are essentially communicative creatures" and that "to impede communication is to reduce men to the status of 'things'" (Freire, p. 109), I decided to invite parents, grandparents, guardians, uncles, friends and anyone who wanted to share their struggles, motivations, purpose, moments of feeling powerless, and the

sources of their strengths to participate. Parents were encouraged to create or do something artistic with their children to bring them to class and also present with their son or daughter. I announced this activity a month or two in advance just as I began to make home visits. During home visits we began to share life experiences, anecdotes, and stories. I asked parents, guardians, grandparents, and other family members if they would be willing to share their stories and argued it was important for them to tell children their "whys." Most importantly, I wanted them to share the "whys" for their being in this country and what their motivations and hopes were. In addition, they were asked to share what the lack of opportunities and struggles were that motivated them to flee their own countries. Visiting with them at home and calling parents every Friday worked well and helped me schedule the first couple of presentations. Prior to parents presenting, I sent a bulletin home that included some of the portraits students had created along with a brief description of what we were doing in class. In the bulletin I invited parents to come in and observe other parents' presentations, and I told them I was going to provide snacks and drinks for students and parents.

More than half of the parents showed up that afternoon to hear the presentations. They brought multi-ethnic foods and drinks. One even brought "taquitos" for the entire class. Since it was my idea to do this, I decided to begin the presentations. I talked to the class about coming to the United States, learning the language, and the struggles my parents overcame in this country. I told them about my going to college and trying to be a good teacher who promotes social justice. I showed pictures of my country, my family, and sang for the class. An immigrant mother who had only been in the United States for three years gave the second presentation. She had been a teacher in Mexico and was a factory worker here. She had two jobs and the father of the family had three jobs. The mother and son had created a collage of pictures and portraits that illustrated their story. The son introduced his mother. "This is 'mi Jefa' (my boss or mother), and she is going to share our story with you. Please listen to her; she does not know English, but I will tell you what she is telling and our teacher will help me if need help." The mother began to share that they were a middle class family in Mexico; they owned a house, two cows, and at least three-dozen chickens. The animals enabled them to survive while growing up. She got up every morning to work on the farm, went to school, and then came back after school to work some more. She loved books and really wanted to be a teacher; so she begged her parents to let her go to school. They agreed but only if she continued helping with the animals on the farm. When she started attending university, she took a bus for two hours to get to classes everyday. After graduation, her father became ill. Since she could not support the farm with her salary, and they lost everything. She and her husband were the only two working. She was making less than fifty dollars a month, and her husband made even less. They were really struggling. She said that she wanted her children to go to college and have a better life.

So, they came to this country hoping to be able to do better here. Indeed she had hoped she could teach here. She was shocked when she found out that her degree was worth nothing here and her skills were not appreciated. She decided to place her children in the dual immersion program my class was part of because she wanted to be able to communicate with the teacher. But most importantly she wanted her children to maintain their language. They shared the collage they had created and the portraits of "el ranchito" they had in Mexico. The mother shared that she was not a very artistic person, but creating a collage gave her a new way to look at art. She called it "el arte de mis recuerdos" [the art of my memories]. The son then proceeded to talk about why it was so important for him to go to school. He said, "I need to go to school so that I can buy 'mi jefa un ranchito.'"

Third, an Anglo family of three (mother, father, and son) presented. They spoke only English so their son translated into Spanish. They brought a song to share with the class. Both parents were professionals who lived in an upper middle class neighborhood. They wanted their children to be in the two-way immersion program because they wanted their children to be culturally well rounded, not racist, and to speak a second language. They shared with the class that in their neighborhood there are not any minorities, and they thought it was important for their children to experience being with other children. They also mentioned that three generations before their parents came from Germany not knowing the language and struggling like many of the parents and guardians who are in the class. They also brought black and white pictures of their family in Germany and talked about how excited they were to have children who are bilingual when they are not. They then began to sing a song they sang at home, as a family. This family song had become the way to connect past with present, to maintain their history and to keep their ancestors alive.

These community meetings became the high points of the school year. They became events where the parents and guardians shared their culinary arts and a time for us to learn about foods and experiences from different parts of the world. The classroom became a larger community that consisted of students, teacher, and family members. It was a community in which everyday diversity, differences, struggles, achievements, and pains were shared and respected. Many of the students and parents had known each other only briefly and did not even know that they had so much in common. Some became good friends and started talking on the phone. Others just began to understand many of the struggles others parents had gone through. Others collaborated in creating arts projects with other families who had similar experiences or who were neighbors. Some parents united to bring issues pertaining to them and their children to school officials and school board meetings. They began to have voice. These meetings continued throughout the year as a way to share what is so natural if explored: artistic expression.

Conclusion

Being a teacher of color means being a political being (Apple, 1990). Yet, "la llave," a key, is needed to invite parents and guardians into the education of their students. The arts became a means to begin dialogue where students and parents and guardians could communicate, express themselves, and connect their personal experiences. Arts became an expression of their lives, a way to see the world, and a way to understand different points of view. Through the arts they expressed their desires and needs. They also came to see school differently. Their children were engaged in their real lives as actors and critics.

Students were not just making pictures. Rather they began to experience differences of opinions through arts. They began to explore their own beliefs and those beliefs of their parents and guardians. They began to think critically about the sociopolitical implications mentioned in Anne Frank and other biographies, and how these implications apply to them today. Students began to recognize the difficulties of walking in other people's shoes and found the arts as a way to accomplish this. Art also was used to make writing more interesting, fun, and to make it theirs: to own it.

Arts also became the way for parents to communicate with their children, to talk, to share, to work together, to get to know each other. Parents also learned about each other's families and the reasons why they were in a two-way immersion program and, for some, in this country. It gave students the opportunity to feel proud of their cultural heritage, their family, and their classmates. It provided all of us with a community where social justice, critical thinking, respect, and consciousness were valued. It provided parents, students and me, the teacher, with a process of critical pedagogy. This process was discovery oriented and used the arts as a way of looking at differences. An arts pedagogy was used as a platform to provide a safe method and space for different groups to express traditions and perspectives, to articulate social injustices, to ultimately dialogue, think, reflect and act. Parents and students empowered themselves through their artistic expression. The arts are "La llave" [the key] that teachers can use to create a classroom where all children and their parents and guardians are accepted, respected, and seen as powerful political beings.

References

Diaz, E., & Flores, B. (2000). Teacher as sociocultural mediator: Teaching to the potential. In M. de la cruz Reyes & J. Halcon (Eds.), *Best for Latino children: Critical literacy perspectives.* New York: Teachers College Press.

Fisher, D. & McDonald, N. (2002). *Developing arts-loving readers: Top 10 questions teachers are asking about integrated arts education.* Maryland: Scarecrow Press.

Freire, P. (1970). *Pedagogy of the oppressed.* New York: Seabury.

Nieto, S. (1999). *The light in their eyes: Creating multicultural learning communities.* New York: Teachers College Press.

From *Multicultural Education,* Winter 2004, pp. 89–102. Copyright © 2004 by Caddo Gap Press. Reprinted by permission.

UNIT 4

Educating All Students

Unit Selections

Key Points to Consider

- How do dropout rates compare and contrast for Native American students? What do these rates reveal?

- What is the relationship between most Native American tribes and the federal government?

- How does the presence of family and community culture in curriculum and instruction aid in teaching and learning?

- How have Latina/o students been silenced in schools and classrooms?

- What is meant by a critically compassionate intellectualism?

- Describe the number of teacher and student populations of California.

- How can cognitive academic language proficiency be addressed effectively and efficiently especially for Vietnamese American students?

- Describe the Learning Partnership Model.

- Why might nonlinear schools be more successful?

- How can school district boundaries be drawn to meet the needs of most people?

Student Website
www.mhcls.com

Internet References

United States Department of Health and Human Services
   http://www.hhs.gov/specificpopulations/
United States Department of Justice
   http://www.usdoj.gov/
United States Equal Employment Opportunity Commission
   http://www.eeoc.gov/types/race.html

Education in the United States is not only a right, it is a responsibility of each state's government to guarantee that the people living in each state are offered an education and become educated. The majority of each state's revenue is dedicated to education costs. Yet, over time the federal government has become more involved legally and financially for education. Policies and regulations have changed many times and in many ways since the United States and each state were established.

Educating all students presents myriad challenges for everyone. Issues impacting education are not relegated to students currently enrolled in the P–12th grades and the students' families. Every person living in the state and across the United States is a stakeholder in education. The social, political, and economic well-being of each state and the United States relies upon the continuation of an educated population.

That means that everyone is responsible for educating all students; we are all in this endeavor together. And we need for all students to be educated to their maximum potential with clear evidence of cognitive, physical, affective, and social growth and development. Educators and most of society acknowledge that there are multiple ways of learning and expressing one's learning. We all know that people acquire knowledge, skills, and dispositions about many different topics and issues. The term, "multiple intelligences," is an established part of the popular contemporary culture. Thanks to our recognition of multiple intelligences, educators are equipped with avenues to reach each student so the citizenry is prepared with people possessing all kinds of strengths to contribute to society.

However, when individuals study both the history and the current operations within their states and the country, their investigations reveal that education has not been offered to all people throughout time in ways that would be considered equal or excellent. Not all schools and classrooms are equipped with the best materials, resources, tools, and technologies. Not all teachers are prepared the same; not all teachers facilitate teaching and learning the same; and not all teachers are rewarded the same. So all students are not taught the same.

One might retort that schools are funded primarily by local tax dollars, so, therefore, if the local region is less wealthy, the school will have fewer resources and cannot hire the best or the brightest teachers. This summation raises many questions: Why do state governments continue to function this way? Is this design useful in any way? Why would a population purposely deny the right of education to children because their parents and families live in geographic regions where there is less wealth? Are we not continuing to restrict the opportunity to people to advance their economic situation to better not only themselves but to improve the region?

Let's say you are injured through no fault of your own and severely enough that you should seek medical attention. The wound needs to be treated and you need to fill a prescription so you return to your former fully functioning self. However, instead of treating the wound, you buy items to pamper other parts of your body. Rather than attending to the area needing help, you focus on areas that do not need help. Your injury does not heal; soon it becomes infected and much worse. The infection spreads, and the whole body becomes quite ill, requiring major intervention.

© Dream Pictures/VStock/Getty Images

This analogy reflects what happens in education. The classrooms, schools, and districts who need attention are not always assisted or with enough treatment for them to heal. Other classrooms, schools, and districts who appear to be quite healthy receive attention and thrive. Many states need major intervention to help their education systems. Too many students are not becoming educated; the chances are strong that these students will not become contributing members of society. The citizenry will experience the "generational perpetuation of practice" as young adults continue the low expectations of their children repeating the low expectations asked of them as children and students at school.

The lowering of expectations lies with many educators too. For years, educators claimed that they were not raised with people generally unlike themselves physically, intellectually, socially, economically, and so forth. These educators ascribed to the belief that they did not know students and families unlike themselves or how to teach students unlike their own children. Therefore, teacher education programs created courses in multicultural education and infused multicultural education curriculum and instruction throughout their program courses. These changes were initiated during the 1990s and teacher education programs have been held accountable for their progress.

Yet, educators still purport that they do not understand how to reach all students. And too often, educators infer that it is "those students" who are not learning. Results from studies conducted by many different educational researchers reveal that some educators not only tend to resist learning about culturally competence, some educators resist changing their practices and becoming culturally competent. Evidence of bias, and stereotyping, and prejudice can be found in every state across the United States in classrooms, schools, school districts, and government agencies.

Think again about your injury. If you are not healing, then you change the medication. Therefore, if students are not learning, then the teaching needs to change. In Unit 4, the articles offer findings from research to ensure that all students are educated. All students have the right to be educated, and all citizens should guarantee that all schools, classrooms, and teachers are fulfilling their responsibilities.

The Trail to Progress

For Native American students to succeed, strong partnerships between schools and communities are vital. Just ask officials in Tahlequah, Okla.

NAOMI DILLON

On most days of the year, traffic in Tahlequah, Okla., is a five-minute wait at the town's busiest intersection. But once a year, over the Labor Day weekend, this small, rural town on the easternmost edge of the state is a mob scene, as thousands of visitors stream into the area to celebrate one of the largest American Indian festivals: the Cherokee National Holiday.

This year was no different, except for the fact that the Cherokee Nation gave equal billing to Oklahoma, which is celebrating its centennial as a state. It was a notable acknowledgment, considering the history between the two.

Thriving and culturally rich, Tahlequah today shows no outward signs that it marked the end of the Trail of Tears, a sordid and shameful piece of American history where the federal government forced the relocation of 17,000 Cherokees from present-day Georgia into the territory, which later became part of Oklahoma.

"There hasn't been a lot to brag about in the last 100 years," says Cherokee Principal Chief Chad Smith, listing a series of efforts by the state to disperse the Cherokee population, sell off their lands, and withhold rightfully earned revenues from the tribe.

In fact, it hasn't been until the last 15 years that the state and the Cherokee Nation have found some common ground, mostly in education. In 2006, Tahlequah Public Schools—where 60 percent of the district's 3,500 students are American Indian—either beat or closely matched the state average in every grade and subject tested. And as a state, Oklahoma's Native American students, which represent about 20 percent of the student population, outperformed all other American Indian students in the United States.

Certain realities contribute to those numbers, including the absence of reservation trust land, where many Native Americans live in impoverished conditions. But the recent work in Tahlequah and the state cannot be ignored. In fact, it can be looked at as a model for other communities.

Cultural Imperialism

The lessons of Tahlequah and Oklahoma are pertinent for every district that educates a low-income and minority population. In many ways, the problems of Native American students echo those of other disadvantaged students.

Dropout rates for Native American children are higher for every other subgroup except Latinos. In 2003, two-thirds of American Indian eighth-graders reported being absent at least once in the previous month, compared to 58 percent of Hispanic and 56 percent of black students. Also in 2003, more American Indian students reported being threatened or injured with a weapon on school grounds than any other demographic; they were also twice as likely to report carrying a weapon.

Yet in many ways, American Indians, who comprise about 1.5 percent of the U.S. population and 1 percent of public school students, are distinct from other ethnic minorities.

Most significantly, Native Americans are the only ethnic group that has a direct relationship with the federal government, which, in theory, means the 561 federally recognized tribes enjoy the same power and autonomy as the U.S. government and can levy their own taxes, write their own laws, and establish their own judicial system.

These are not privileges or benefits, but rights afforded and promised to them through treaties the federal government entered into with tribes in exchange for land. Many of these treaties or promises contained provisions specifically for education that still exist today.

"People don't understand the relationship that Indian tribes have with the federal government, why that relationship exists, and what it means," says John Tippeconnic, an education professor and director of the American Indian Leadership program at Pennsylvania State University. "It's there. It's real."

And for most Native Americans, it's been a letdown. Under the federal government, education for American Indians was merely a crash course in cultural imperialism until the 1960s. Often sent to boarding schools far from home, Native American children were prohibited from speaking their own language, wearing their native clothes, or even using their own names.

Federal policy now officially encourages American Indian communities to make their children's education reflect their culture and beliefs. Psychologically, however, many American Indian communities still are influenced by centuries of being treated as inferior.

Native American Education: A Timeline

1771–1870

The federal government signs nearly 400 treaties with Indian nations and tribes, creating trust agreements and promising that the government will provide technical, agricultural, medical, and education services.

1870s

The government begins building its Indian boarding school system, often using deserted Army bases. The most infamous one, the Carlisle Indian Industrial School, in Carlisle, Pa., was based on the belief that it was necessary "to kill the Indian and save the man."

1887

The General Allotment Act, or Dawes Act, allows the government to survey American Indian land and divvy up sections to individual tribe members, with the surplus going to non-Indians.

1928

The Institute for Government Research (now the Brookings Institution) releases the Meriam Report, a comprehensive look at the condition of American Indian life, and determines the federal government is providing inadequate services.

1934

The Indian Reorganization Act stops the allotment process and provides American Indians with more power to govern and determine their futures. The Johnson O'Malley Act, also passed in 1934, allowed the government to contract with states to provide education services.

1950

Impact Aid legislation compensates public school districts with nontaxable federal land, particularly reservation land, within their school boundaries. American Indian parents were supposed to have a say in how these monies were used.

1950–1965

The Elementary and Secondary Education Act encourages more tribal and parental involvement and, overall, offers more aid for disadvantaged children.

1968

President Johnson calls for the establishment of American Indian school boards at federally managed and Bureau of Indian Affairs (BIA) schools.

1972

The Indian Education Act establishes the Office of Indian Education, now under the Department of Education, and provides funds for education from pre-K to college.

1975

The Indian Self-Determination and Education Assistance Act authorizes the government to contract with tribes for the operation of BIA and Indian Health Service programs.

1978

Education amendments state "it shall be the policy of the BIA in carrying out the functions of the Bureau, to facilitate Indian control of Indian affairs in all matters relating to education."

1990

The Native American Languages Act protects the "status of the cultures and languages of Native Americans," and makes it federal policy to "promote the rights and freedom of Native Americans to use, practice, and develop [their] language."

"There is something inherent in a population where the federal policy toward them was to extract the 'Indianess,'" says Elona Street-Stewart, president of the National School Boards Association's American Indian/Alaska Native caucus and a school board member in St. Paul, Minn. "We should not be surprised that for most Indian families, schools aren't a very comfortable place to be."

Schools remain an uncomfortable and foreign place for those families because public education—which serves more than 90 percent of all Native American children—has not done a good job of making American Indians feel like they belong.

The power of Inclusion

The orientation lunch at Tahlequah High School is meant to acquaint the school's American Indian students—who make up more than half of the student body—with the wide range of services and programs available to them.

But it also offers a glimpse of how diverse this population is. The teens that show up are a cross-section of high school stereotypes: jocks and cheerleaders, brainiacs and loners. Some wear their culture proudly, reflecting it through a T-shirt, a piece of jewelry, or long braids. Others are indistinguishable from mainstream society, sporting purple hair and the fairest of skin and blue eyes.

For more on Naomi Dillon's reporting in Oklahoma, visit *ASBJ*'s blog—The Leading Source—http://leadingsource.asbj.com

The luncheon provides insight into another matter: Leroy Qualls, the district's Indian education director, is a jokester. "This is a meeting for Indian students, but we've still got to be worldly," begins Qualls. Then, after a beat, "So we've got pizza."

School Opens Doors, Provides Opportunities for Native American Students

Dorm life at Sequoyah High School begins at 6:30 sharp every weekday morning, with a series of chores, a shower, and a quick breakfast before classes begin 90 minutes later. Discipline is still a part of this Indian boarding school on the edge of Tahlequah, Okla. But instead of narrowing the opportunities of its American Indian students, the school is there to open as many doors and fuel as many dreams for its young pupils as possible.

It's a far cry from the school's previous roles: as an orphan asylum in 1871, and, later, as a vocational school.

By and large, American Indian students today are served by the public education system, with 92 percent attending public schools. But less than a century earlier, most Native American children were funneled into boarding schools operated by the federal Bureau of Indian Affairs (BIA), as part of an overall government policy to "civilize" the population.

The easiest way to retrain the American Indian, the federal government believed, was to begin at the beginning. Hence the children of many tribes were taken, often against their will, and placed in boarding schools. Many of these schools were abandoned Army posts and barracks that extended the rigidity and regimentation of military life to their new inhabitants.

By the beginning of World War II, many of these schools were shuttered as the government sought to assimilate the Native American population by sending them to public schools. A few boarding schools still remained open.

In 1985, Sequoyah High School was facing the threat of closure, when the Cherokee Nation decided to take over the reins. Currently, about 120 of the 184 BIA schools are run under contract by tribes.

"In theory, what [tribally controlled] schools do is more community based and relevant to students," says John Tippeconnic, an education professor at Pennsylvania State University and a former director of Indian education programs at both the BIA and the U.S. Department of Education. "But today, they have to adhere to the provisions of NCLB just like public education, even though there are difficulties with the law."

Sequoyah would not undergo substantial changes until 1991, when Chad Smith became principal chief and focused his attention on education. "Sequoyah has evolved from a school of last resort to a school of first choice," Smith says.

Indeed, Superintendent Gina Stanley says she joined the staff in the early 1990s reluctantly. "It was almost like a reform school; it looked like an institution," she says. "Any good student was run off by the bad ones. I wouldn't have sent my kids here at one time."

Policy changes and initiatives, including raising admissions standards and graduation requirements that are now even more stringent than the state's, has changed Sequoyah's reality and reputation. Today, 415 students representing 31 different tribes attend Sequoyah, with about 150 living in the dorms. Just last year, the Cherokee Nation added seventh and eighth grades and has more expansion plans.

"Sequoyah is not only a historic school but a laboratory in which to experiment with things like Cherokee language and history courses and export them to public schools," Smith says. "We're not in a position to run public schools, but we are in a position to advance education in them."

A sense of humor is mandatory in education, and Qualls holds on to his through the parts of his job that aren't funny. He recently counseled a girl caught between staying in school and working to support herself. He helped another find a foster home. Qualls describes his role as a student advocate, though much of his job is also about finding and developing resources wherever he can.

Before he took his post four years ago, Qualls says, Johnson O'Malley grants—federal funds for states to supplement cultural-based programs for American Indians—impacted about 900 students. With a more proactive approach and better coordination, the grants now yield enough money to support 13,300 students in Tahlequah.

That money can help pay for school supplies, SAT tests, caps and gowns, and a host of other things. About 70 percent of Qualls' students qualify for free or reduced-price lunches.

Having a designated person oversee Indian education can make a difference in a school district. It has in Tahlequah, especially under Qualls, who brought with him years of personal and professional dealings with the Cherokee Nation and other local tribes.

"I'm here to help ensure student success," he tells the students during the orientation. "But there doesn't need to be a problem for that to happen. Any time you see me in the hall and want to talk, come and talk to me."

Collaboration Is Critical

What really sets Tahlequah and Oklahoma apart, however, is the deliberate and focused collaboration among tribes, the state, and school districts. That sentiment was reinforced during this year's Cherokee National Holiday, which had the theme "Common Ground, Common Values."

"We need to think about, 'What can we do as a community together,' so we can define the future to be better," Smith says.

Both the Cherokee Nation and the United Keetowah Band of Cherokee Indians are headquartered in Tahlequah—39 tribes call Oklahoma home—and each has played a large hand in education. The tribes have spent millions of dollars on public schools and on their own education endeavors, which include the Cherokee-run Sequoyah High School.

The state also has made a concerted and renewed effort to live up to legislation passed in 1992, which called for a greater sensitivity and acknowledgment of Native Americans in Oklahoma.

"They feel it's time for students to learn about the tribes' influence in the development of the state, and the current contributions they make," says Valeria Littlecreek, director of tribal affairs for the Oklahoma Department of Education. For example, students do parallel Native American units when they learn about topics such as the 1800s' government-sanctioned land run. "It helps both sides understand there were some positive and negative things that happened," she says.

Indeed, the importance of presenting a balanced and diverse curriculum was noted as far back as 1928, in one of the first comprehensive looks at the federal policy toward American Indians. "The most fundamental need in Indian education," the Meriam Report stated, "is a change in point of view."

A Different Perspective

All students, not just American Indians, benefit from learning about tribal contributions and their role in American history. It also helps when school leaders are aware of Native American concerns.

Street-Stewart is the first American Indian to be elected to Minnesota's St. Paul Public Schools board, a distinction she was keenly aware of during her campaign six years ago. "When I was first running, they had these candidate forums and I was asked, 'Would I only be serving the needs of American Indian students?'" she recalls. "Nobody asked the African American candidate that question."

Street-Stewart acknowledges she brings a higher consciousness of Native American issues to the board. It's been useful in many areas, like setting school calendars, identifying students, and purchasing textbooks.

"The companies that create the textbooks aren't friends to the Indians," Street-Stewart says. "The reality of American Indian history should be interwoven into every state history, not separate. Instead, we are typically reduced to a couple of paragraphs, always in the past tense, and after we learn how other people from other countries got here."

In 2003, roughly 10 percent of American Indian students were classified as English Language Learners, with more than double that amount reporting another language besides English was spoken more than half of the time at home.

A lower than average vocabulary and weaker grasp of English—a function of living in isolated areas—set the stage for a continual struggle in school for many Native American students, says Sandra J. Fox, an Albuquerque-based education consultant and curriculum specialist who began her education career as a high school English teacher in both public and BIA schools.

"It was a time, very much like now, when the focus was on the deficit approach," she says. "Indian children could not learn, so we needed to drill and kill."

Direct learning was as ineffective then as it is now, Fox says, because it doesn't let students think for themselves. The injection of culture brings a reference point, a familiar foundation. But too many educators don't know how to utilize this approach.

"One of the mistakes people make when they incorporate culture is they think it's something separate from the regular curriculum," she says. "It's not. It's giving Indian kids examples from their own life. It makes it more relevant."

Creating a Better Understanding

As a high school social studies teacher at Rapid City (S.D.) Area Schools, Robert Cook employed those very methods with students who were transitioning into ninth grade and considered at

risk. In 2003, 104 Native American ninth-graders should have graduated from the district four years later, but only 11 did.

"As an American Indian male, I wanted to show my students you could take whatever subject you were learning and integrate culture," Cook says.

In studying Greek mythology, for example, Cook shared and contrasted the creationist stories of Native American tribes. Another time, he took his pupils on a field trip near the Black Hills, where they made pottery and talked to local artists.

His efforts yielded great results; he doubled the retention rate after leading the program for only two years. He was recognized as the state's 2005 Milken Educator and later as the National Indian Education Association teacher of the year.

But, as Cook discovered, it's not only about creating understanding in the classroom but also understanding throughout the school and the community. His approach wasn't always appreciated by his peers and the greater community, who wondered why he was integrating so much culture into his teaching.

Many of his colleagues didn't understand how much culture influences Native American life, even in things as basic as the family structure, which is an extended model where aunts are considered mothers and uncles are called fathers. "'How many grandpas do you have? Every time I turn around, you are losing a grandpa.' I've heard a teacher say that," Cook says.

Currently serving as the cultural affairs specialist at the Crazy Horse Memorial, Cook is contemplating his next move into school administration. "You can have tremendous impact within the four walls of your class, but it's limited," he says. "As an administrator, your vision can go schoolwide with the support of your staff and community."

A Time to Rejoice

Inequalities are still painfully present in many American Indian communities.

The U.S. Commission on Civil Rights wrote a scathing report in 2003, after reviewing the budgets of the six main federal agencies responsible for the welfare of American Indians. Among other things, the commission found that roughly 40 percent of reservation homes were inadequate, with one in five lacking complete plumbing. It also determined that the federal government spends less on Indian health care than for any other party they are responsible for, including prisoners.

Many American Indian students come to school with these realities. But considering where they came from, they also bring hope and anticipation for the future. Just look at Tahlequah.

"When you've lost a quarter of your population and had an internal war, yeah, we basically had to start over," says Principal Chief Smith, who has become known as the education leader because of his conviction that it is the way to a prosperous future. "We want to remove the possibility of a third Trail of Tears because the second was the Great Depression."

NAOMI DILLON (ndillon@nsba.org) is a senior editor of *American School Board Journal.*

An Investigation of How Culture Shapes Curriculum in Early Care and Education Programs on a Native American Indian Reservation

The drum is considered the heartbeat of the community.

JENNIFER L. GILLIARD AND RITA A. MOORE

Introduction

Instruction informed by children's home and community culture is critical to supporting a sense of belongingness that ultimately impacts academic achievement (Banks, 2002; Osterman, 2000). American school populations are increasingly diversified with immigrants and English language learners; but American teachers are over 90% European American (Nieto, 2000). Educators who are from different cultural perspectives than those present in the families and communities of the children they teach, "may render it difficult to "see" the cultural identities shaping the behaviors and achievement of their students" (Moore, 2004a). How then do we prepare the predominantly European American teaching force to strengthen the connection between home and school cultures for children of diverse backgrounds?

Many researchers have examined schooling or education in culture, affording opportunities for educators to broaden their knowledge base and learn about delivering curriculum from multiple cultural perspectives (Bullock, 2005; Lee & Walsh, 2005; Luo & Gilliard, 2006; Nagayama & Gilliard, 2005; Walsh, 2002). For example, Nagayama and Gilliard (2005) investigated similarities and differences in curriculum in early childhood programs in Japan and in the United States. The present study extends these efforts to understand education and culture in early learning programs on a Native American Indian Reservation.

The purpose of this study was to explore the presence of family and community culture in curriculum at three tribal early care and education programs. Classroom observations and open-ended interview questions with eight early childhood teachers were conducted at three early learning programs, two infant and toddler programs and one toddler and preschool program on the Flathead Indian Reservation. Data were collected by four preservice early childhood

teachers as a culminating field experience for a special topic university course called Cultures and Communities, in which the preservice teachers were enrolled. Two university professors served as investigators for this study, one of whom taught the course and accompanied the preservice teachers on the field experience that resulted in data collection.

Culture and education in the three tribal early learning programs were explored in this study through teacher responses to interview questions, field notes taken during classroom observations, and journals written by the preservice teachers who collected the data. The research question that guided the study was: How does the culture of the family and community shape curriculum?

Rationale and Conceptual Framework

In an essay exploring the dynamics between the school and home culture in addition to a transformative approach to bringing family and community culture into the schools, Moore (2004a) suggested two issues emerged: the treatment of a child's personal, social, and cultural literacies within school cultures affects the child's sense of belonging as well as achievement (Osterman, 2000), and the fact that most educators are unprepared to work with cultural values different from their own (Banks, 2002; Nieto, 2002).

Children experience a sense of belongingness when their home culture is not alienated from the school culture (Osterman, 2000). When the school culture that reflects the culture of a teaching force that is 90% European American (Nieto, 2000) is the dominant culture, there is potential for the marginalization of children from cultural and linguistic minorities (Moll, 1992). To provide maximum learning opportunities for all children, "School and home connections should work toward establishing a network of interactions and authentic learning situations that draw immediately from student background, language, and culture" (Moore, 2004a, p. 23). Skilled educators motivate students to learn by inviting participation of multiple cultures and perspectives, providing students with opportunities to connect curriculum with their own funds of knowledge (Allen & Labbo, 2001; Moll, 1992; Moore with Seeger, 2005).

The notion of children having a sense of belongingness within school cultures is clearly demonstrated in many Native American communities, especially in tribal K-12 schools on reservations, where the majority of teachers are of European American descent. For example, according to the Department Head of Tribal Education on the Flathead Reservation, the vast majority of teachers in the public tribal schools are women, middle class, and Anglo. She suggested that the educators have little or no training in dealing with a culture different from their own which has a negative effect on the social belongingness and academic achievement of Native children (J. Silverstone, personal communication, January 23, 2003). It is interesting to note that this fact did not hold true for the early childhood teacher participants in this study; all but one of the teachers were registered tribal members and all seemed motivated to provide early learning curriculum within the context of family and community culture.

It is often difficult for educators who do not share their students' culture to provide curriculum within the context of their students' family and community cultures (McIntosh, 1989; Moore with Seeger, 2005). The education literature suggests that a successful strategy for teaching children from diverse cultures and languages is teachers exploring who their students are in order to understand their students' family and community contexts (Jones & Derman-Sparks, 1992; Luo & Gilliard, 2006; Moore, 2004a; Van Horn & Segal, 2000; Yang & McMullen, 2003) as well as educators examining their cultural identities and how their cultural lens affects their teaching (Allen & Labbo, 2001; Grossman, 1999; McIntosh, 1989; Moore, 2004a; Van Horn & Segal, 2000).

The purpose of this study was to explore the presence of family and community culture in curriculum at three tribal early care and education programs on the Flathead Indian Reservation. The present study extends the literature that focuses on examining education in culture providing opportunities for educators to expand their knowledge base through learning about delivering curriculum from multiple cultural perspectives (Bullock, 2005; Lee & Walsh, 2005; Luo & Gilliard, 2006; Nagayama & Gilliard, 2005; Walsh, 2002).

Overview of the Study and Method
The Participants and Setting
The participants of the study were eight female early childhood educators with at least three years of experience. Three of the teachers earned Associate's degrees in Early Childhood Education, three earned Bachelor's degrees in Education or a related field,

and two earned Child Development Associate Certificates (CDAs). Seven out of eight were registered members of the Salish or Kootenai tribes, or were descendants of another American Indian tribe. Four female preservice teachers enrolled in an early childhood education Associate's degree program in a small university in Montana collected the data. Data were collected as a culminating research project for a special topic course: Cultures and Communities. Two university professors, both teacher educators, served as investigators for the study. One of the investigators, L. Jennifer, was also the instructor for the course in which the preservice teachers were enrolled and for which the data for the present study were collected.

The study took place on the Flathead Indian Reservation. Two infant-toddler centers and one toddler-preschool center located on the Flathead Reservation were sites for the study. One of the programs was located on the campus of a small four-year degree granting tribal college, and two of the programs were located in nearby tribal early learning facilities. Many of the families enrolled in the programs were members or descendants of the Salish and Kootenai tribes or members or descendants of other American Indian tribes; and they were defined as being of low socioeconomic status.

The Flathead Indian Reservation located in Montana is home to the Confederated Salish and Kootenai tribes. The tribes are a combination of the Salish, Pend d'Oreille, and Kootenai and have lived in this region for thousands of years (Travel Montana, 2006). As of July 2003, the 1.2 million acre reservation had 4,457 enrolled tribal members living on the reservation, accounting for 17% of the population on the reservation, and 2,481 enrolled members living off the reservation (First Class News, 2003).

Additionally, Montana is ranked 48th in the United States in terms of unemployment: in some Montana counties the unemployment rate is between 5–10% and on the Flathead Reservation the unemployment rate is 41%. Of those who are employed on the Flathead Indian Reservation, 38–48% access poverty-based services on a seasonal basis (First Class News, 2003). In 2001, Montana had the fifth lowest per capita income among all 50 states and the average personal income was $22,532. The Montana reservations' per capita income in 2000 was estimated at a low of $7,100 and a high of $22,754, with the average per capita income $14,738 (First Class News, 2003).

Research Questions and Data Sources
The research was guided by the following question: How does the culture of the family and community shape curriculum in the investigated tribal early childhood programs?

Prior to the study, the preservice teachers were instructed by their professor on a phenomenological approach to qualitative research (Valle & King, 1978) along with interview and observation procedures and qualitative research design (Creswell, 1998; Moore, 2004b). In addition, the preservice teachers engaged in multiple class activities and read from multiple sources that explored background information and knowledge on how cultures influence communities and schooling.

Data were collected at the end of two full days of observation and interviews. Data sources for the study included the following:

Table 1 Interview Questions

What is your work title and the name of the school/institution for which you work?

Please describe any training or education you have had to prepare you for your job as an early childhood educator. Have you taken some college courses or hold a degree or CDA? If so, in what area is your degree?

Would you please describe your culture and ethnicity?

Please describe the children you teach. How old are they? Do they have special learning needs? Describe their culture and ethnicity. Would you describe your teaching philosophy or beliefs? How are aspects of culture or multiple cultures included in your curriculum?

Please describe a typical day in your classroom.

How are parents included in your program/classroom?

Do you believe that your culture has influenced your teaching or instruction? If so, how?

Do you believe that the culture of the children you teach has influenced your teaching? If so, how?

How do you individualize instruction around the culture of the children you teach?

What are some cultural issues that might impact learning in your classroom?

What do you believe is important for teachers to know about instructing children from diverse cultures or backgrounds?

Is there anything else you would like to tell me that might be helpful to me as an early childhood teacher who is interested in adapting instruction to cultural differences of learners?

(1) the reflective journals in which the preservice teachers wrote responses to what they were learning about home and school culture in the tribal early childhood programs; (2) interview responses from the early childhood teachers; and (3) field notes of the principal investigator and the preservice teachers. A copy of the interview questions is provided in Table 1.

Procedures

Classroom observations and open-ended questions with eight early childhood teachers were conducted by preservice teachers at three tribal early learning programs, two infant-toddler centers and one toddler-preschool center on the Flathead Indian Reservation. Interview sessions were tape recorded and transcribed by interviewers. The study occurred near the end of the university's May interim session, 2006, as a culminating field experience for a course about cultures and communities.

Prior to the study, the preservice teachers were asked to respond to a survey prompting them to think about how their culture and their perceptions of diverse cultures might influence their teaching beliefs and actions. During the two-day study, preservice teachers were instructed to write reflective journals in which they wrote responses to what they were learning about home and school culture in the tribal early childhood programs and to keep detailed field notes of their classroom observations. At the end of the observation and interview period, preservice teachers submitted transcribed interviews, field notes of observations, and reflective journals to

the course instructor. Jennifer, the investigator who also taught the communities and cultures course, regularly visited the classrooms to which the preservice teachers were assigned, writing field notes during each visit.

Data Analysis

At the end of the course, the investigators, Jennifer and Rita, sorted the data by color coding pertinent responses to the research question. Separately, we each color coded the responses from the three data sources: preservice teachers and Jennifer's field notes; preservice teachers' reflective journals; and transcribed interview responses of the early childhood teachers.

Next, we compared our coded data for accuracy, discussing any variations. We then read the data another time for the purpose of developing clarifying themes within the research question. Themes were determined by noting whether at least eight responses from the three data sources alluded to the main concept of the theme (Lincoln & Guba, 1985).

After that, we re-read the data, marking categorization changes as needed. After discussion of meaning, minimal modifications were made involving interpretation of responses. Trustworthiness was established through careful triangulation of data in which at least three data sources cross checked the findings for the research question. To be considered relevant to the question, a similar response from each data source had to be sorted to a question at least five times (Lincoln & Guba, 1985).

Results of the Study

The results of the study are grouped below according to the research question. They are examined through themes that consistently emerged under the question.

Question

How does the culture of the family and the community shape curriculum in the early learning programs we investigated on the Flathead Indian Reservation? The theme focusing this question was: different ways of understanding and defining culture. Three distinct categories emerged within this theme: respect of children, families, and community, building a sense of belongingness and community through ritual, and the importance of family values and beliefs.

Data sources used to support this theme were preservice teachers' journals, Jennifer and the preservice teachers' field notes, and the early educators' responses to interview questions.

Different Ways of Understanding and Defining Culture

The early educators interviewed in this study did not define their interactions with the children and families with whom they worked as necessarily influenced by culture but rather by respect and understanding. They described their part in honoring and perpetuating the day-to-day rituals, routines, and beliefs of the place in which they lived.

Three categories within this theme consistently emerged. Categories were: respect of children, families, and community, building a sense of belongingness and community through ritual, and the importance of family values and beliefs.

Respect of Children, Families, and Community

The data suggested that respect was central to the early learning curriculum in these programs. Stated beliefs and observed interactions revealed that the early educators approached their interactions with children, families, and community in a reflective and respectful fashion. For example, one preservice teacher wrote in her journal:

> The parents' personal wishes, beliefs, and ideas about child care are honored and respected in the classroom. . . . The providers are doing an excellent job researching parents' values and keeping so much of it at the heart of learning for the children in these environments.

Another topic that emerged regarding respect was the early childhood teachers' acceptance of the tribal tradition of honoring life in death. Death is considered a celebration of life on the reservation and the entire family, including children, and community comes together for a week to support each other and remember and honor the one who died. The educators' acceptance of family and community practices around death is illustrated in the following statement made by one of the teachers during her interview:

> Another thing I've noticed in the classroom, and it also involves death, is that if there is a death in the family or community everybody goes and so they will miss about a week of school. I am very accepting of that.

Another example of respect that consistently surfaced in the data was awareness of what curricular activities may offend certain tribes. For example, telling of the "Coyote Stories" (Confederated Salish & Kootenai Tribes, 1999), children's tribal stories passed down by elders, came up repeatedly as an activity that some tribes believe should only occur during the winter. Thus the early educators in these tribal programs ask parents before they proceed with many curricular activities such as the telling of the "Coyote Stories" so they do not offend any of the families by going against their beliefs. As one teacher indicated in her interview:

> Because we do have so many different tribal cultures represented in the classroom, one of the things you have to be aware of is doing something that one tribe thinks is okay and another does not. The "Coyote Story" is an example of that. Around here they are only told during the winter so it would be totally inappropriate for us to read one during late spring. And, you need to check before you do something like that.

Last, all of the reflective journals contained descriptions of how soft, quiet and gentle the interactions were between educators and children. One preservice teacher wrote, "The words spoken were kind and tender, the touches and sounds were reassuring and encouraging."

Building a Sense of Belongingness and Community through Ritual

The data revealed a number of rituals that served to bring together the children, parents and teachers as well as the community. The ritual that was common to all three data sources was the powwow. Powwows, common to most American Indian tribal customs, bring together the tribal community both in preparation for the event and for the actual powwow; they are festive, cultural celebrations of life. (Schultz, 2001).

Interviews and observations for this study were conducted one week after an annual powwow celebration on the Flathead Reservation so teachers were rich with stories about the event. Preparation for the powwow consisted of teachers, children and parents working together to make the children Native outfits including moccasins, ribbon shirts and dresses, as well as shawls. At the center and in their homes, the older children were encouraged to dance, sing and drum together in preparation for the event. Some parents showed the older children dances they knew at the centers; dances vary depending on a person's tribe so children were exposed to different ways of celebrating through dance. During her interview one teacher described the powwow:

> We had a powwow. We do this every year. It is usually the first Friday of May. Each child is given a pair of moccasins for the powwow. This year, our center and parents decided to make their own outfits, so we had someone (from the community) come in and help with ribbon dresses and the parents helped with that, too. And, some of them decided to do their own moccasins. So, the parents are really involved.

The ritual of drumming and music was clearly associated with daily classroom curriculum. Drums were found in all programs and children were encouraged to play the drums, dance and sing to drumming plus come together for group activities when teachers drummed. As a non-native teacher at one program stated:

> One of the things I do notice is that every tribe has the drum as the center of their music and dancing and I didn't realize when I first started teaching how much it draws people into the circle and it does. The drum is the heartbeat and it does draw the children in.

Similarly, one of the preservice teachers wrote in her daily journal, "The drum is considered the heartbeat of the community."

Other rituals described in the data were as follows: community work days; the tribal celebration of life in death; the practice of swaddling infants and teaching swaddling of infants; families bringing or wearing different patterns marked on their clothing or as decoration; and regularly planned feasts such as the Bitterroot Feast. For this feast the community comes together to commemorate the beginning of spring through digging the bitterroot for medicinal purposes and through sharing in a celebratory feast.

Importance of Family Values and Beliefs

The data in this category showed that the early educators valued parent involvement in their program curricula. All of the educators gave examples of including parents, and even extended family, in program activities and events. For example, all three programs requested that parents participate in social gatherings that provided meals so families could get to know each other and so teachers and families could spend time conversing. Parents were invited to participate in: regularly scheduled center meals including breakfast and lunch; special holiday meals or celebrations; the day-to-day classroom activities; for example, some teen parents spend 40 minutes a day in the classroom, feeding and playing with their infants and toddlers; field trips; special cooking and dancing demonstrations; and preparation for powwows.

Data reflecting the day-to-day interactions between parents and teachers revealed that although educators included families in the curriculum through a more traditional additive fashion as defined by the parent involvement activities above, they also worked to connect home and school culture through a more transformative approach (Moore with Seeger, 2005) where understanding of parents' beliefs and values was sought and this understanding was used to transform curriculum. That is, daily respectful interactions provided families with voice to shape and extend curriculum in their children's programs. As one educator suggested:

I think you just need to be aware . . . there are many different cultures and many different ways to do different things . . . and just don't learn about the culture, a little bit. You could talk with the family and learn about what their beliefs are. You know, the way they do things.

The data provide several examples of parent voice in the early learning programs. For example, an interview with one teacher revealed that parents in her program had day-to-day decision-making power through voting on and planning curriculum activities. Parents decided what types of special activities the children would do around holiday and cultural celebrations. For example, in one program, parents decided that the children would make their own moccasins for the annual powwow.

Another instance of parent voice was the fact that parents could bring their family's tribal language into the center through word labels, music, and modeling of their language. Most of the programs taught the Salish language but many of the children were members of or descendants of other tribes and spoke a variety of tribal languages. Educators were very respectful and asked parents clarifying questions about each child's home language or languages. Although challenging, educators tried to reinforce for children the importance of speaking in their various tribal languages.

An additional case of respectfully discussing parent values while taking into account the caretaking needs of the educators was as follows: a mother brought her child to the center secured to a cradle board to help the child grow and maintain strength. This was a family tradition for this mother and the elders in her family believed strongly that this was a necessary custom when raising an infant. The educators were respectful of the mother's values, allowing the infant to be secured to a cradle board while at the center, but presented her with their concerns of not being able to burp or hold the infant, or help him quickly enough if he choked. After a few days of these respectful discussions, the mother elected to leave the cradle board at home.

Limitations of the Investigation

The authors acknowledge that the participants were able to observe and conduct interviews for only two days; however, funding for the field experience was limited. Consequently, the number of participants was limited to eight and the number of programs studied was limited to three.

Discussion

The literature suggests that the largely European American teaching force is unprepared to work with an increasing population of ethnically diverse children (Banks, 2002; Nieto, 2002). Thus educators fail to link home and community culture to school culture, failing to foster a sense of belongingness in children that promotes academic achievement (Moore, 2004a; Osterman, 2000). However, the early educators in this study seemed sensitive to the need to link home and community culture to school curriculum and worked on a daily basis through respectful and thoughtful planning and interactions to learn about as well as to honor parent beliefs and values.

Interestingly, seven of the eight early childhood teacher participants were members of the Salish or Kootenai tribes or descendants of the tribes. The majority of K-12 teachers on the Flathead Indian Reservation are Anglo according to the Department Head of Tribal Education (J. Silverstone, personal communication, January 23, 2003). It is also noteworthy that these Native early educators did not define their teaching or actions within the context of culture but rather as acts of respect and knowing. One teacher stated in response to a question regarding whether or not the culture of the children and families affected her teaching, "No, because I'm pretty much the same . . . I don't think what I do is cultural." Another educator described herself as being more sensitive to cultural issues because she, too, is Native.

The early childhood teachers were able to clearly describe how they thought children learned as well as what defined their teaching practices such as valuing children's knowledge, learning by listening or by watching someone who wants to pass down knowledge, and learning through hands-on experience; however, they did not associate their beliefs as cultural or unique to a Native American classroom. Lee and Walsh (2005) defined folk pedagogy as "the taken-for-granted practices that emerge from deeply embedded cultural beliefs about how children learn and how teachers should teach" (p. 60). Perhaps the Native teachers were steered by a folk pedagogy that was in synch with the home and community culture of the children they taught. However, the educators did make several references to diverse tribal beliefs and practices as "something to watch out for," or "something to be aware of" indicating their awareness of variations between their culture and the home and community culture of the children they taught.

The data clearly revealed the relevance of ritual in building a sense of belongingness and community within the early childhood programs we studied. Ritual and customs are integral to the perpetuation of culture (Banks, 2002) and we saw, in this study, the richness of educators, children, families and community participating in unison in various tribal traditions such as preparation for and partaking in a powwow. The powwow brought family and community members into the children's school environment to craft outfits along with practice singing and dancing. Mutual involvement in cultural rituals provided for a seamless connection between school culture and the community and home cultures of the children in these early learning programs.

Perhaps the most consistent finding in the data was the strong evidence of the teachers' commitment to honoring family beliefs and practices. All of the teachers emphasized the importance of involving parents and even extended family in curriculum development and instruction. The teachers not only suggested that they believed that the children's parents are their most important teachers, their practice of consistently seeking information and understanding about home cultures through day-to-day interactions with parents demonstrated congruence between their beliefs and their actions. The teachers did not describe parents' wishes as frustrating or inconvenient as is often the case with educators who offer a fixed or static curriculum (Goldstein, 2003; Moore with Seeger, 2005); but rather, they welcomed family input and saw the care and education of the children in their programs as a partnership between themselves and the parents.

Fostering a child's sense of belonging and ultimately his or her academic achievement requires congruence between the school culture with the home and community culture of the children we teach (Nieto, 2002; Osterman, 2000). Given the lack of preparedness of a largely European American teaching force to educate children from diverse cultural backgrounds (Nieto, 2002), English language learners and ethnically diverse children are at risk of being marginalized in our American classrooms (Moll, 1992). Studying ethnically diverse classrooms and educators such as the classrooms and educators in this research may offer early educators lessons that will enable them to bridge the gap between the culture of their classrooms and the home and community culture of the ethnically diverse children they teach.

The findings from this study suggest the following implications for early educators for connecting the culture of their school or classroom with the home and community culture of the children they teach: the value of respecting and honoring parents' beliefs and wishes in a way that transforms curriculum, and the significance of building belongingness through authentic school participation in family and community cultural rituals.

References

Allen, J., & Labbo, L. (2001). Giving it a second thought: Making culturally engaged teaching culturally engaging. *Language Arts, 79*(1), 40–52.

Banks, J. (2002). *Teaching strategies for ethnic studies* (7th ed.). Boston: Allyn & Bacon.

Bullock, J. (2005). Early care, education, and family life in rural Fiji: Experiences and reflections. *Early Childhood Education Journal, 33*(1), 47–52.

Confederated Salish & Kootenai Tribes. (1999). *Coyote stories of the Montana Salish Indians.* Helena, MT: Montana Historical Press.

Creswell, J. W. (1998). *Qualitative inquiry and research design: Choosing among five traditions.* Thousand Oaks, CA: Sage Publications.

First Class News. (2003). Retrieved September 3, 2006, from http://72.14.203.104/search?q=cache:StkQ_jRYYeIJ:firstclass.skc.edu/news/0000D3A8–80000002/S004061D3-004061DF.2/Carol%2520Juneau%2520-%2520information.doc+Flathead+Indian+Reservation+average+Income+2002&hl=en&gl=us&ct=clnk&cd=2.

Goldstein, L. S. (2003). Preservice teachers, caring communities, and parent partnerships: challenges and possibilities for early childhood teacher education. *Journal of Early Childhood Teacher Education, 24,* 61–71.

Grossman, S. (1999). Examining the origins of our beliefs about parents. *Childhood Education, 76*(1), 24–27.

Jones, E., & Derman-Sparks, D. (1992). Meeting the challenge of diversity. *Young Children, 47*(2), 12–18.

Lee, K., & Walsh, D. J. (2005). Independence and community: Teaching Midwestern. *Journal of Early Childhood Teacher Education, 26,* 59–77.

Lincoln, Y., & Guba, E. (1985). *Naturalistic inquiry.* London: Sage.

Luo, N., & Gilliard, J. L. (2006). Crossing the cultural divide in early childhood teacher education programs: A study of Chinese graduate students' perceptions of American early care and education. *Journal of Early Childhood Teacher Education, 27:* 171–183.

McIntosh, P. (1989). White privilege: Unpacking the invisible knapsack. *Peace and Freedom, 49*(4), 10–12.

Moll, L. (1992). Bilingual classroom studies and community analysis: Some recent trends. *Educational Researcher, 2*(2), 20–24.

Moore, R. A. (2004a). The impact of community and culture on literacy teaching and learning: We know the problems but we don't understand them. *Journal of Reading Education, 29(30),* 19–27.

Moore, R. A. (2004b). Classroom research for teachers: A practical guide. Norwood, MA: Christopher Gordon.

Moore, R. A., with Seger, V. (2005). Rich or poor? Examining the image of family literacy in the K-6 curriculum. *Language and Literacy Spectrum, 15*(3), 53–61.

Nagayama, M., & Gilliard, J. L. (2005). An investigation of Japanese and American early care and education. *Early Childhood Education Journal, 33*(3), 137–143.

Nieto, S. (2000). Placing equity front and center: Some thoughts on transforming teacher education for a new century. *Journal of Teacher Education, 51*(3), 180–187.

Nieto, S. (2002). *Language, culture, and teaching: critical perspectives for a new century.* Mahwah, NJ: Erlbaum.

Osterman, K. (2000). Students' need for belongingness in the school community. *Review of Educational Research, 70,* 323–367.

Schultz, B. A. (2001) Powwow power. Retrieved July 29, 2006, from http://www.powwoww-power.com/powwow history.html.

Travel Montana. (2006). Retrieved September 3, 2006, from http://montanakids.com/db_engine/presentations/presentation.asp?pid=170&sub=Tribal+Histories. Retrieved September 3, 2006.

VanHorn, J., & Segal, P. (2000). Talk to your baby: Honoring diversity while practicing from an evidence base. *Zero to Three, 23*(5), 33–35.

Valle, R. S., & King, M. (1978). *Existential phenomenological alternatives for psychology.* New York: Oxford University Press.

Walsh, D. J. (2002). The development of self in Japanese preschools: Negotiating space. In L. Bresler & A. Ardichvili (Eds.), *Research in international education, Experience, theory, and practice* (pp. 213–245). New York: Peter Lang.

Yang, H., & McMullen, M. B. (2003). Understanding the relationships among American primary-grade teachers and Korean mothers: The role of communication and cultural sensitivity in the linguistically diverse classroom. *Early Childhood Research and Practice, 5*(1), 1–19.

JENNIFER L. GILLIARD is in Department of Education, Early Childhood Division, The University of Montana—Western, 710 S. Atlantic Street, Dillon, MT 59725, USA. RITA A. MOORE is in Department of Education, The University of Montana—Western, 710 S. Atlantic Street, Dillon, MT 59725, USA.

Correspondence should be directed to Jennifer L. Gilliard, Department of Education, Early Childhood Division, The University of Montana—Western, 710 S. Atlantic Street, Dillon, MT 59725, USA., e-mail: j_gilliard@umwestern.edu.

A Critically Compassionate Intellectualism for Latina/o Students

Raising Voices above the Silencing in Our Schools

Julio Cammarota and Augustine Romero

Latina/o students often experience coursework that is remedial and unchallenging—benign at best, a dumbing-down at worst (Solórzano & Yosso, 2001). This potential limiting curriculum is not only failing to provide Latinas/os with the credentials necessary to advance economically, but their education denies them the opportunity to develop the critical voices and intellectual capacities necessary to do something about it. To borrow the words of Carter G. Woodson (1977), there is a "mis-education of Latinas/os," in which their voices and potentialities to challenge an unjust world is suppressed by the consistent battery of standardized tests, rote learning, and curricular content that has little bearing on their everyday struggles as young people of color.

Thus, the standard educational experience for young Latinas/os tends to submerge them into silence, where they are taught to be quiet and avoid independent and critical thinking. This is a dangerous lesson for them to learn, and it is dangerous for everyone. Young Latinas/os are the next generation that will significantly change the composition of our society. And if they are encouraged to become silent adults, this new burgeoning majority will not have the capacity to effect social change that moves toward an egalitarian reality for all people.

In this article, we present an educational model based on a critically compassionate intellectualism that can foster the liberation of Latinas/os as well as other students of color from the oppression of silencing they currently experience in school. A teacher following critically compassionate intellectualism implements the educational trilogy of critical pedagogy (Freire, 1993), authentic caring (Valenzuela, 1999), and a social justice centered curriculum (Ginwright & Cammarota, 2002). For students of color, critical pedagogy affords them the opportunity to become critical agents of social and structural transformation. Authentic caring promotes student-teacher relationships characterized by respect, admiration, and love and inspires young Latinas/os to better themselves and their communities. A social justice curriculum dispels ideological notions of racial inferiority while cultivating the intellectual capacities of students of color.

We argue that the trilogy's elements—critical pedagogy, authentic caring, and social justice curriculum—must be implemented simultaneously in the classroom to present the most effective preparation for Latina/o students to participate in the development of a truly democratic society. Each element becomes stronger and more effective with the integration and reinforcement of the additional constituent elements. In critically compassionate intellectualism, the sum is much greater than its separate educational parts, and the individual parts become greater when they are combined in a collective, tripartite approach.

The Silencing of Latina/o Students

Studying a cohort of Latino students at different grade levels, Quiroz (1997, 2001) compares their autobiographical narratives written in the 8th grade and then again in the 11th grade, noticing that silencing was a common theme throughout the texts. She discovers that the students' reactions to silencing change over time, with the effects becoming more profound toward the end of their grade school tenure. In the 8th grade, students respond by engaging "in self-denigration, internalizing failure in school and directing anger at themselves instead of at those responsible for their failure" (2001, p. 340). By the 11th grade, they are more familiar with the institutional factors behind their marginalization and adhere to "perceptions of apathy, injustice, and racism, as students recognize how profoundly these conditions affect their educational lives, and many are convinced of teachers' general lack of interest in their educational progress" (2001, p. 339).

The eventual outcome of the "schoolsponsored silencing" (2001, p. 328) is the students' widely held belief that academic success is unattainable for them. Quiroz argues that such beliefs explain "why the majority of these students disengage from schooling or only perform intermittently" (1997, p. 14). The irony, as Quiroz (2001, p. 328) points out, is that these Latina/o students could communicate in more than one language, yet "had no voice, at least in matters related to their schooling. They spoke through their narratives but no one listened."

The Uses of Power in School-Sponsored Silencing

The urban, low-track curriculum emphasizes order and discipline, and as Michelle Fine (1991) argues, it also actively silences young people by treating them and their intellectual capacities as insignificant. Principally, it is through "power" that educational institutions "nurture, sustain, and legitimate silencing" (Weiss, Fine, & Lareau, 1992, p. 1). The power in school-sponsored silencing is exercised and experienced through the curriculum, teacher and student relationships, and racist discourse.

Regarding power in the curriculum, Bourdieu (1977a, 1977b) argues that educational content based on the achievements of the dominant group actively silences the cultural capital[1] and thus intellectual contributions of subordinate groups. Schools accomplish silencing by rendering certain curricular processes, such as the acquisition and exposition of "valid" school knowledge, appear universally available and possible for every student. However, Bourdieu argues that educational institutions, which are invested in maintaining certain power relations, elide the fact that "valid" school knowledge is culturally specific and thus not universally available. Bourdieu (1977a, p. 494) states:

> By doing away with giving explicitly to everyone what it implicitly demands of everyone, the educational system demands of everyone alike that they have what it does not give. This consists mainly of . . . cultural competence and that relationship of familiarity with culture which can only be produced by family upbringing when it transmits the dominant culture.

Knowledge acquisition is easier, in most societies, for one social group—the group that has the power to control educational institutions. In reality, access to "valid" school knowledge is an arbitrary process related to one's social and cultural location. If a student is a member of the dominant group, he or she will display all the mannerisms, codes, and communication patterns that symbolize, according to the dominant group's criteria, someone who is knowledgeable. The opposite is true for students from subordinate groups. Educational institutions silence—through curricula highlighting the contributions of the dominant group—the subordinate group's knowledge and intellectual capacities.

Freire (1993, 1998) writes extensively about the traditional teacher and student relationship, and how it might contribute to the silencing of students. In the traditional educational format, which he categorizes as "banking education," the teacher is perceived as the only true authority of knowledge while the student is perceived as an unknowing subject that should passively accept, without questioning, the knowledge disseminated by the "legitimate" authority within the pedagogical process. Freire (1998, p. 71) illustrates the practice and effects of banking education:

The teacher's task is to . . . "fill" the student by making deposits of information which he or she considers to constitute true knowledge. And since people "receive" the world as passive entities, education should make them more passive still . . . Translated into practice, this concept is well suited to the purposes of the oppressors, whose tranquility rests on how well people fit the world the oppressors have created, and how little they question it.

Although Freire wrote about banking education some 30 years ago, the practice is still prevalent in our schools today. The primary assumption holds true; teachers supposedly possess all the knowledge, and their job is to fill students' supposedly blank minds with the state's official perception and understanding of the world. The result of such direct, one-way depositing of information is the cultivation of students who are taught to accept the conditions of their existence "as is" and forced into a marginal space where racial discourse maintains a silence about their potential to rectify problems of injustice. They are left thinking that their world will never change, or more importantly, that they can never change it. Thus, their realities become nihilistic states of suffering and distress whereby they believe that nothing can be done but accept the way things are—including the inequities that cause the suffering of many, and in some situations, themselves.

Although acts of power experienced through the curriculum and pedagogy may impede the academic progress of Latina/o students, everyday racism in society and schools has enough impact, in and of itself, to present serious impediments to success. For example, teachers who believe that Latina/o students are hopelessly and helplessly uneducable could countermand the positive effects of a democratic pedagogy and culturally competent curriculum. Thus, the effects of racism upon teachers who then transmit racist ideas to their students can stand alone and have a destructive impact on academic outcomes (Reyes & Rios, 2003).

The historical backdrop, according to Pollock (2001, p. 9), of "American racism" consists of "naturalizing a racial hierarchy of academic and intellectual potential ever since racial categories were created and solidified with pseudo-science." This nefarious racial dynamic of the American past is still active today in the consistent and widespread expectation and acceptance that racial differences in achievement are part of the normal outcomes of education (Pollock, 2001; Spring, 2001). Thus, racism in schools reinforces a racialization process that constructs a hierarchical order of social groups. This stratified racial order corresponds to capitalist imperatives for subordinate classes that are in turn exploited economically by a dominant ruling class (Darder & Torres, 2004). A certain economic utility underpins the schools' production of racial differences in academic outcomes.

Governments, districts, officials, administrators, teachers, parents, and even students often internalize the belief that people who are phenotypically light tend to be smarter than their darker-skinned counterparts. Although biological explanations for racial differences in achievement are somewhat passé, current theories harboring assumptions about deficiencies in the culture, normative structures, and environments of non-White communities not only have a similar ring but have attained significant currency in many educational settings (Valencia & Black, 2002).

For example, in Pollock's (2001) study of racial achievement patterns in a California high school, she discusses how teachers and administrators often cite "culture" and "parents" as explanations for the failure of students of color. These culturally based explanations contribute to racist ideology because they do nothing more than point to the putative "foibles" in certain races while avoiding the real systemic problems of racism, White supremacy, and White privilege.

In short, power is enacted through the curriculum, through pedagogy, as well as racist ideologies. Power issued through these particular forms foments a practice of silencing that can permeate attitudes, policies, and actions and thus instigate the treatment of students of color as intellectually inferior and ultimately uneducable. These abuses of power in education invariably impel students to withdraw, either permanently by dropping out or partially by "checking out" mentally and becoming silent.

The Social Justice Class in Tucson

We have the opportunity to implement and develop an alternative, social justice pedagogy in a high school located in Tucson, Arizona. The school principal allowed us to work with a cohort of 20 Latina/o students during their junior and senior years, teaching them the state's social studies requirements but adjusting the content and pedagogy in ways that facilitated the students' critical consciousness around racial inequalities affecting their educational and general life experiences. The students participated in this social justice curriculum for two years and received credit for all high school graduation requirements in U.S. History and U.S. Government.

More importantly, these students were afforded the opportunity to cultivate the skills and knowledge to address everyday injustices that limit their own future opportunities, and those of other Latina/o youth. Our goal was to help students' raise their own voices above the silencing of traditional schooling. In addition, we hoped that they would become active citizens armed with a critical consciousness that could lead them toward the transformation of educational and social structures presently failing to meet their specific needs.

The location for the social justice education course is Cerro High School.[2] The socioeconomic status of many Latino families served by Cerro is among the lowest in the Tucson metropolitan area. Consequently, two-thirds of all Cerro students receive free lunch, a rate that is more than 25% higher than the Tucson district-wide average of 39%. Student Achievement Accountability for Results (STAAR)—a set of standardized tests measuring academic performance—reports that Cerro has the lowest ranking in standardized test scores of any public high school in Tucson. Furthermore, in 2004–05, Cerro offered only seven Advanced Placement (AP) courses, while the most predominately White (64% White to 20% Latina/o) school in the district, Ultimate High School, offered 62 advanced placement courses.

The history of racial inequality at Cerro makes for interesting dynamics in implementing social justice education. Latinas/os represent 62% of the Cerro student population, and they are more likely to fill the lower ranks of the school's academic hierarchy. Sixty percent of the Latina/o students at Cerro write below a level denoted as "standard" by the state, while White students are the highest performing group on campus. Whites represent 51% of the students enrolled in AP courses while comprising only 18% of the student population. A counselor at Cerro mentioned that the special magnet program at Cerro, which offers many of the advance placements courses, has only 20 Latinas/os enrolled out of 400 students. The overwhelming majority consists of White students.

In addition, White students receive most college scholarships given to Cerro graduates. Although Latinas/os are more than 60% of the student population, they received only 31.3% of the college scholarship money given to graduates in 2002. Some 60% of this scholarship money goes to White students. Cerro High School has been more efficient at guiding these students into academic tracks and on to college.

A Critically Compassionate Intellectualism

Drawing from our experiences in the social justice class and from the voices of the social justice students, we have developed an approach to educating Latina/o students that can help them to deflect the institutional power maintaining their silence. This approach follows a trilogy of educational practice, combining the essential characteristics of critical pedagogy, compassionate student/teacher relationships, and social justice content. We call this pedagogical trilogy *critically compassionate intellectualism,* and it is our belief that educators who implement this learning process will provide their students with the opportunity to counter the institutional silencing that prevents their full and active participation in shaping their futures.

The following sections will delineate the parameters for a critically compassionate intellectualism while showing how each part of the trilogy is inextricably related to the others and necessary in combination for breaking through the silence and promoting critically engaged citizenship among students of color.

Critical Consciousness in Education

In the social justice education course, our experiences with the students have been both encouraging and troubling. On the one hand, the curriculum has been effective in raising the students' consciousness with regards to racial inequalities. On the other hand, the innovative instruction has also revealed the failure of the standard public school curriculum to help young people evolve into critically minded citizens who actively work toward improving conditions in their communities and society at large.

This failure became evident during a student photo presentation on the challenges for Chicano/Latino students. The students chose to take photos and develop attendant slide presentations on topics related to a critical study of their educational experiences. For two weeks, students roamed around their high school campus with disposable cameras and took pictures related to racial stereotypes, cultural oppression, misrepresentation of students of color, and critical thinking vs. passivity in education. It was during the slide presentation on critical thinking vs. passivity and comments made by a specific student that we realized the standard education for many Latinas/os at this school was practically barren of any content encouraging critical thinking.

High school student Kati Diaz showed a slide of students in the auto-shop class, who were primarily Latino males. At first we didn't know what this slide had to do with critical thinking, but Kati made these comments.

> In advanced placement [AP] classes, students are always being challenged . . . always using your brain, you are always moving a step ahead. And how critical can auto shop be? And I don't see any difference between the people here and the people in AP classes except race.

Kati's comments parallel the analysis that education scholar Jeannie Oakes (1985) reported in her book, *Keeping Track.* Oakes states that Latinas/os as well as African Americans tend to fill the ranks of the lower academic tracks, which focus more on remedial or vocational education. In contrast, White students are more apt to be placed in the advanced placement classes, preparing them for the best universities in the country. One of the most interesting findings in Oakes' study was that:

> . . . teachers of high-track classes were more likely to emphasize such behaviors as critical thinking, independent work, active participation, self-direction, and creativity. At the same time, teachers of low-track classes were more likely than others to emphasize student conformity, students getting along with one another, working quietly . . . being punctual, and conforming to classroom rules and expectations. (1985, p. 85)

These habits of conformity and complacence encouraged in lower tracks stifle students' expression and thinking, and lead to the passive silence evident in the education of Latino/a students at Cerro.

Another student in our social justice course, Sandra Sanchez, is concerned about her classmates' perceptions of their own muteness and concomitant inefficacy. Similar to the juniors in Quiroz' study (2001), Sandra started to comprehend the impact of racism and injustice on her education, as well as that of other students of color. She spoke about racial bias evident in news reports on Tucson schools. In her low-income community, reports tend to focus on negative traits, such as poor performance on standardized tests, whereas the media represents schools located in whiter and wealthier areas in the most positive light. She adds, "We are good students and we are very respectful compared to other schools, but I don't think we show them how great we are by test scores. We could show them in many other ways. But the difference is, will they listen?" Sandra

recognizes the injustices around her, but feels her words on these matters would fall on deaf ears.

A Pedagogy of Critical Literacy

In the social justice education course, our pedagogical approach is greatly influenced by the work of education scholar Paulo Freire. We design lessons from the framework of critical pedagogy and related non-banking education approaches to teaching. This framework is based on the key premise that the high school students should be equal partners in the construction of knowledge, identification of problems of social injustice, and implementation of solutions to these problems.

Therefore, we offer the students a curriculum that closely follows Freire's concept of critical literacy, which encourages students to adopt "an attitude of creation and re-creation, a self-transformation producing a stance of intervention in one's context" (Freire, 1998, p. 86). Critical literacy renders both students and educators as subjects of knowledge, collaborative creators of knowledge that can be used to transform the oppressive conditions of reality.

To establish this type of a learning partnership—knowledge production through collaboration—between high school students and classroom coordinators (high school teacher of record and university researchers), we structure lessons so that we (students and coordinators) are consistently engaged in dialogue. Our first dialogical exercise involved having students and coordinators write poems about their identities. The poems, or what we call *I Am Poems,* gave us the opportunity to understand the students' realities, to see where they were coming from and how they comprehend the issues and problems most relevant to their lives.

As Freire states, "the starting point for a political-pedagogical project must be precisely at the level of the people's aspirations and dreams, their understanding of reality and their forms of action and struggle" (Freire, 1998, p. 214). The coordinators and students shared their own dreams and realities by writing poems that they presented to the entire class. See Figure 1 for an example of an "I Am" poem.

The coordinators used generative themes and issues discovered in the poems to create questionnaires for the students to fill out. We studied their responses and created a list of potential topics that could function in many ways as particular lenses for the students to conduct a class research project on inequalities in education. The students and coordinators dialogued and came up with the four research topics: *cultural assimilation, critical thinking vs. passivity in education, racial and gender stereotypes of students, media representations of students of color.* These topics became the basis for student research and subsequent presentations to the school, district officials, academics, educators and community members, with the intent of making recommendations to improve education for students of color in their district.

The back-and-forth dialogue between students and coordinators lasted for over two months; this lengthy process was necessary to empower students to become equal partners in the research project. Otherwise we would be guilty of establishing a learning process that would amount to no more than another

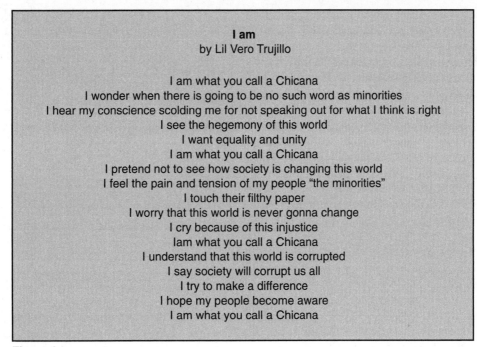

I am
by Lil Vero Trujillo

I am what you call a Chicana
I wonder when there is going to be no such word as minorities
I hear my conscience scolding me for not speaking out for what I think is right
I see the hegemony of this world
I want equality and unity
I am what you call a Chicana
I pretend not to see how society is changing this world
I feel the pain and tension of my people "the minorities"
I touch their filthy paper
I worry that this world is never gonna change
I cry because of this injustice
Iam what you call a Chicana
I understand that this world is corrupted
I say society will corrupt us all
I try to make a difference
I hope my people become aware
I am what you call a Chicana

Figure 1

form of oppression. According to Freire, "coordinators must be converted to dialogue in order to carry out education rather than domestication. Dialogue is an I-Thou relationship, and thus necessarily a relationship between two Subjects. Each time the 'thou' is changed into an object, an 'it,' dialogue is subverted and education is changed to deformation" (1998, p. 89). We wanted to avoid providing the students yet another experience of being the static objects of learning, stuffing information into them without having them criticize, discuss, or question what is being taught. Such educational experiences represent the norm for these students and force them to be uncritical and tolerant of a life of subordination.

Because students are more familiar with banking education, encouraging them to think critically, to voice their opinions, and to contribute to the construction of knowledge are challenging tasks. Most of their educational experiences have revolved around the banking mode of learning. Many students recount how they have experienced years and years of banking education: teachers constantly telling them what to do, what they should learn, and never asking them about their opinions or asking them for their input, suggestions, comments, feedback, or thoughts about their education. The students said they are conditioned to learn within that type of education.

So now, in the social justice class, when we ask them to speak up, give their opinions and think critically, they really have a hard time. In fact, Sandra Sanchez said that if we don't tell them what to do, "crack the whip," and get on them to make sure things are done, they will just sit there and not do anything. She added that they do not know how to take the initiative to become responsible for their own education, have input on what they learn, or participate in the construction of their own knowledge.

We are amazed how Freire (1993) was right in terms of the oppressive and stifling effects of colonization. According to Freire, liberation from the silencing force of oppression is extremely difficult for the colonized, because they tend to gravitate toward the model of living imposed by the dominant class. The model emphasizes the tacit acceptance of the established hierarchical order of domination and subordination. Because this model is so pervasive—so entrenched in the psyche of the oppressed—they have difficulty acting differently or deviating from it. The students first needed to *unlearn* the myriad lessons of banking education to feel confident and capable voicing their opinions and engaging in dialogue.

Although the challenges of establishing a critical pedagogy seem overwhelming at times, educators must stay on task to avoid failure and the continued subordination of their students. The stakes are too high to loosen the commitment to critical pedagogy. Latino students can no longer remain silent; becoming vocal is imperative for them to attain some faith in their intellectual abilities. It is important to note that the silencing they experience in school does more than keep them quiet.

We stated earlier that school silencing encompasses enactments of power through the curriculum, traditional pedagogy, and racist ideology, with the intended effect of erasing the intellectual potential of students of color. Therefore, learning to speak one's voice is vital for advancement to the higher levels of education and society. The converse leads us towards the depths of oppression wherein Latinas/os are abysmally exploited for capitalistic gains (Delgado, 1999).

Compassionate Relationships between Students and Teachers

After struggling with the numerous days of silent students, we realized compassion was necessary to establish a strong and trusting relationship between students and coordinators, which in turn would lay the foundation for free-flowing dialogue. The need for compassion in education became apparent when a student, Kati Diaz, told us after class that perhaps we (classroom coordinators) would have an easier time getting the students to talk if we would open up and let them know us personally.

She suggested that we start talking about ourselves as people. In essence, the students wanted to know something about our lives and family experiences. According to Kati, students wanted to trust us first before talking and communicating with us. We, in positions of institutional power, had to take the first step before we could expect the students to open up.

We took the first step by sharing our feelings and concerns. Students needed to see us as complete human beings and interact with us on an emotional level before engaging with us intellectually.

Our response to this student's request was to create and read our own "I Am" poems. The poem in Figure 2 reflects one of the author's experiences as a Puerto Rican male, and the personal and social struggles that have captivated his attention and energy throughout his life.

We realized that a critical yet humanizing pedagogy was crucial for generating dialogue and a sense of ownership among the students. The following is an excerpt from an exit interview conducted with two students who graduated from the social justice class. Their words demonstrate how a humanizing pedagogy can help students to feel they are knowledgeable Subjects that guide the educational process.

Vanessa Acosta: The social justice class was interesting because we had a part in it. And usually we don't have a voice in nothing. So that's why it interested us and plus what it was about. And plus all our subjects. And plus our teachers were cool too.

Julio Cammarota: Was it interesting for you because you were looking at some of the problems in society and trying to find out solutions for the problems?

VA: We got to explain to other people. To teachers what was going on. We got to tell them.

Maria Perez: We got to teach them.

VA: Yeah. And they loved it. And they loved us. And that was bad [meaning 'good'] too.

MP: And some of them said they didn't even realize that we were teenagers.

VA: They loved us.

MP: We are loved.

JC: Did you have any other opportunities like this in other classes?

MP: No.

VA: In other classes its like open your book. "Do this." "That's it." "Write this."

JC: Tell you what to do?

VA: Yeah. You couldn't be like, "well could I do this?" "No." I think that if we had more classes like the social justice class then a lot more kids would be interested in school. They would want to learn.

I hear, sometimes, voices of family and friends who have passed away. My Titi Elsa, Abuelo julio, Cunado Renzo, and mi Chavalo Fabricio, who died from broken hearts and gunshots. But appear to me when I need strength and, guidance to overcome obstacles of self-doubt arising from that imposed inferiority.

I see faces of people who I don't know... but I will know, maybe not now, but in the future or in the past that is still unknown to me. I want peace, justice, equality for all people who suffer from oppression, from poverty, from the pain of having one's heart, mind, and soul be invisible to those willing to sacrifice their hearts, minds, and souls for the power to dominate and control.

Figure 2

When they presented their social justice research to educators, administrators, and other members of their community, the students' sense of empowerment extended beyond the classroom. The presentations in the community and at academic and youth conferences offered them the rare opportunity to see themselves as knowledgeable Subjects. In contrast, the standard educational system treats them as empty slates ready to be carved and etched on by teachers. In the presentations, they were carving and etching out knowledge. Our deepest hope was that the students would gain a 'voice' in the class and carry their confidence and sense of efficacy to the world outside the classroom walls.

Thus, dialogue—real discussion for generating ideas that construct knowledge—occurs through a humanizing as well as critical pedagogy, in which genuine and compassionate relationships form between students and educators. Freire states:

Love is at the same time the foundation of dialogue and dialogue itself. . . . Dialogue cannot exist, however, in the absence of a profound love for the world and for people. The naming of the world, which is an act of creation and re-creation, is not possible if it is not infused with love . . . because love is an act of courage, not of fear, love is commitment to others. (1993, p. 70)

A humanizing pedagogy is accomplished by educators interacting with students on an emotional level and sharing their deepest concerns and feelings about life. What must be avoided at all costs is treating students solely as empty receptacles that must be filled with academic skills. An educator should not only reveal what he or she cares about personally but also show the students that he or she loves them in the caring sense and shares similar concerns about the world. Compassion is another crucial step for enacting a critical pedagogy and ultimately a critically compassionate intellectualism.

The idea of a critical yet humanizing pedagogy correlates with the caring literature in education (Noddings, 1984, 1992; Valenzuela, 1999). Valenzuela (1999) claims that the lack of care and respect in teacher/student relationships may be a key factor behind the failure of Latina/o students. Her study is based on research conducted at a high school in Texas with primarily Mexican American and Mexican immigrant student populations.

At this school, she noticed two types of teaching methods: authentic caring and aesthetic caring. Valenzuela (1999, p. 61) states that authentic caring is a "form of caring that emphasizes relations of reciprocity between teachers and students." That is, the teacher establishes that emotional, human connection with his or her students and demonstrates a real interest with the students' overall wellbeing. Aesthetic caring is tantamount to treating students like objects, seeing them only as blank slates that need to be inscribed with academic skills, and not as complete people with real-life problems.

Lalo Garcia, a classroom teacher from our social justice course, engages in authentic caring. We observed this while he was consulting with a student about his future academic plans. Nestor wants so badly to drop out of Cerro, because school is not engaging him. He is failing in his classes, and wants and needs to move on in life. His mother is leaving Tucson and moving in with her boyfriend who lives in California. Nestor has the option of moving with her, but he has so many ties in Tucson that he is preparing to stay. He states, "I need a full-time job to support myself, because I will be on my own."

There is an opportunity cost for Nestor: stay in school where he is failing or drop out to find a job to support himself. He understands that life will be harder for him without a high school education, so he says that when he drops out he will obtain a GED. Lalo spoke with him earnestly. He said that he understood Nestor's situation. He gave Nestor several options to stay in Tucson—making up credits at charter schools or staying at Cerro to graduate. Nestor said that's a possibility but he preferred getting a GED and to start working full-time.

We noticed how Lalo was talking with Nestor. He listened to Nestor and his words and actions were filled with love and respect. Lalo figuratively had become a father figure. Nestor's body language indicated that he was taking Lalo's words seriously. He seemed relaxed in the chair, although a bit pensive about his situation. His posture indicated that perhaps a positive outcome would result from the conversation, because he was conversing with someone who genuinely cares about his fate. We liked how Lalo didn't refute or put down Nestor's ideas. He said that they were good ideas and possibilities, but also mentioned others, such as charter or weekend school, that Nestor might consider.

Lalo's interaction with Nestor is a good example of authentic caring in action. He was able to give Nestor authentic advice, because he developed a caring relationship with him. Lalo acknowledged the social and economic conditions impacting Nestor's life. Therefore, Lalo could provide advice formulated from a viewpoint that emerges from Nestor's reality. Listening to the students' problems and showing some compassion for their situation may be necessary actions for educators to improve relationships with their students.

Unfortunately, at Cerro High School, most teachers or teaching styles fall under the category of aesthetic caring, being concerned with only the technical (i.e., skill level) side of their students' experiences. With the current climate in education, resulting from high-stakes testing policies such as No Child Left Behind (NCLB), aesthetic caring is becoming more prevalent in schools such as Cerro High. Because of the fear of being labeled "under-performing" as a result of standardized tests, Cerro High and the school district pressure teachers to barrage students with test content. The students in our social justice course consistently speak of how they are inundated with a curriculum that prepares them solely for standardized tests.

These test-based lessons, called "focus lessons," review test content in multiple subjects (math, English, etc.), and usually it is the same exact focus lesson reviewed repeatedly in every class throughout the school day. Furthermore, the increased focus or state-mandated testing forces an aesthetic pedagogy upon the teachers. Cerro student Validia Tejerina says,

> Focus lesson usually takes the whole period. It's the same thing over and over and over. With the focus lesson you go from one period to another learning the same thing: It's usually like . . . before the AIMS [Arizona Instrument for Measuring Standards] test [is administered] here . . . the whole week is just focused on focus lessons, you know, they are just reading it over and over and over. Each period. So that when the test comes along you can remember. You don't learn anything.

Validia asserts that the boredom of the focus lesson has the tendency to disengage students from their education.

Social Justice Content in Education

Social justice educational content is the basis for promoting authentic caring. Teaching to the test—course work that drills students on academic skills—will create a chasm that places teachers and students miles apart from each other. On the other hand, teachers will make strong connections with students when the educational content is based on matters most significant and meaningful to the students' lives. And what matters a great deal to many of the students in our social justice course is determining how to challenge social forms of oppression that limit opportunities for themselves, their families, and communities.

At Cerro High School, students are familiar with oppression produced by racist ideology. Suggestions of racial inferiority besiege students of color on a regular basis. Conversations with Cerro students reveal this consistent burden of injustice. Validia Tejerina mentions how teachers regularly tell Latina/o students that they are incapable of academic success and should drop out. She talks about a specific event in which she was supposed to turn in a report to her teacher but forgot to bring it to school on the due date. When the teacher asked for the report, she said she forgot. The teacher then said, "You should just drop out of school and work in a restaurant and wash dishes."

Validia interprets these comments as racist. First, by telling her that she should drop out, the teacher indicates that she has no belief in Validia's intellectual capacity. Second, because she suggests Validia should work as a dishwasher, the teacher implies that is all Validia is capable of accomplishing in life. Validia adds that when she was a freshman, a science teacher told her the same thing—that she should drop out of school. Arturo Reyes said that he had the same teacher who told Validia to become a dishwasher, and this teacher told Arturo that he shouldn't even bother trying to pass this class and he should drop out of school.

We must recognize how racist ideology engenders conflict between students and teachers and prevents them from forming strong meaningful relationships. Indeed, Freire emphasizes that oppression prevents us from realizing our full humanity, and oppression must be challenged to reach the point of seeing the full humanity in others and in ourselves. It is at this point of mutual recognition and respect for each other's humanity that strong human connections are established.

Teachers cannot become authentic caregivers to students of color unless they merge their caring with counter-hegemonic content that dispels notions of racial inferiority and recognizes the wealth of knowledge, culture, and understanding of every student who walks into the classroom. This is the moment when caring evolves into compassion for the student's social and economic situation that may render him or her less than human and thus deny him or her any possibility for self-determination.

The Practice of Critically Compassionate Intellectualism

Educators can attain a liberating education for Latina/o students by combining three approaches to learning into one educational framework—critically compassionate intellectualism. The following represents the three components of critically compassionate intellectualism:

1. *Critical Pedagogy*—elevating students to the status of Subjects in the creation of knowledge.
2. *Authentic Caring*—treating students as full and complete human beings.
3. *Social Justice Content*—teaching content that directly counters racism and racist stereotypes through epistemological contextualization of the students' social, economic, and cultural realities.

To facilitate critically compassionate intellectualism, we recommend that a social justice perspective feed into and guide all educational practices. That is, we suggest progressing beyond the ordinary multicultural approach that at best validates the cultural capital of marginalized groups (Banks, 2002; Nieto, 2000; Sleeter, 1996). Although elevating the cultural capital of such groups is essential, students should focus on the injustices that engender marginalization in the first place, and then develop remedies for palliating them. This has been our approach in the social justice course.

For instance, this course provided Latina/o students with the opportunity to discuss their experiences with the state's oppressive language policies that have essentially banned bilingual education. In effect, the state of Arizona's Proposition 203 has followed in the footsteps of California's Proposition 227 by rendering English the only instructional language in the school system. Our students have spent numerous hours discussing the direct and subtle effects of this proposition.

Students contend that Spanish speakers are now more likely to drop out, because teachers cannot by law speak to them in any language except English. Since these Spanish-speaking students do not understand what's happening in the classroom, they simply disengage, biding time until they leave school altogether. The students of our social justice course have decided to bring this problem to the Tucson school board, and recommend the development of a waiver program that expands outreach to Latina/o communities and supports administrators and teachers who wish to adequately serve their Spanish-speaking students by implementing bilingual education.

The study of language and cultural politics via Proposition 203 served as a vehicle for critically compassionate intellectualism. By positioning the students' experiences with anti-bilingual language policy as the centerpiece for knowledge acquisition, students share the status of co-investigators—equal with the project coordinators. Students and coordinators both become Subjects and equal partners in the construction of knowledge. In addition, focusing on language and cultural oppression meant that the students' education related to something that mattered to them. It matters to them, their families, and their younger brothers and sisters, because they perceive Proposition 203 as an attempt at eradicating a language essential for the development and advancement of Latina/o communities—their communities.

By examining ways to preserve the vitality of the Spanish language, students recognize our intentions as sincerely demonstrating compassion for them and their families' futures. Finally, the students engage in social justice work by taking their concerns to policymakers (i.e., the school board) with the hope of rectifying a problem that threatens the academic success as well as the intellectual development of many Latina/o students. Critically compassionate intellectualism involves more than discussing problems of inequality; it requires students to engage in activities that promote social justice in their own context.

Concluding Remarks

We will end our discussion on critically compassionate intellectualism with Bell Hooks' description of teachers she had while attending segregated schools in the South. Her description highlights the importance of a pedagogy of liberation, and suggests that other factors—beyond lack of resources—may impede the progress of students of color. In particular, schools often fail to prepare these students to deal with a society that treats them as racially inferior. Our sense is that the teachers from Bell Hooks' childhood engaged in critically compassionate intellectualism, because they achieved authentic caring through a critical yet humanizing pedagogy that promoted a social justice perspective. Adopting this perspective counters notions of inferiority that result from the institutional dehumanization of children of color. hooks describes how:

> The work of all our progressive teachers, was not to teach us solely the knowledge in books, but to teach us an oppositional world view—different from that of our exploiters and oppressors, a world view that would enable us to see ourselves not through the lens of racism or racist stereotypes but one that would enable us to focus clearly and succinctly . . . to see ourselves first and foremost as striving for wholeness, for unity of heart, mind, body, and spirit. (1989, p. 49)

Despite a lack of resources, these teachers instilled in their students a critical perspective on the hegemony they experienced, as well as a belief in their own humanity.

It is essential that we implement an education for Latina/o students that follows critically compassionate intellectualism by drawing on critical pedagogy, authentic caring, and social justice content. This educational trilogy may elevate the voices of Latina/o students and expand their rights in this society. We live in precarious times in which apartheid is looming on the horizon. Latinas/os are one of the fastest growing racial groups in the country, yet Whites still hold onto the key positions of power in state institutions. The net effect of such an unfair distribution of power is that Whites will continue to fill the classroom seats of the most privileged universities, while Latinas/os will more likely fill the service jobs (janitors, cooks, etc.) at these same privileged universities.

Educational disparities have other frightening consequences. As the U.S. government and corporate leaders wage their wars for global dominance, it is young Brown and Black blood they trade for brown and black oil. It is in our best interest to transform the education of our people so that our blood is no longer used to grease the wheels of global capitalist greed.

Notes

1. Cultural capital refers to the mannerisms, style, dispositions, customs, and cultural knowledge that symbolize and confer a certain degree of social currency or value. That is, cultural capital has social values or "symbolic value" that distinguishes a person's different and higher social standing in relation to others (Bourdieu, 1977b.).

2. The names of schools have been changed for reasons of confidentiality.

References

Banks, J. A. (2002). *An introduction to multicultural education.* Boston: Allyn & Bacon.

Bourdieu, P. (1977a). Cultural reproduction and social reproduction. In J. Karabel & A. H. Halsey (Eds.), *Power and ideology in education.* Oxford, UK: Oxford University Press.

Bourdieu, P. (1977b). *Outline of a theory of practice.* Cambridge, UK: Cambridge University Press.

Darder, A. & Torres, R. (2004). *After race: Racism after multiculturalism.* New York: New York University Press.

Delgado, R. (1999). *When equality ends: Stories about race and resistance.* Boulder: CO. Westview Press.

Fine, M. (1991). *Framing dropouts: Notes on the politics of an urban public high school.* Albany, NY: State University of New York Press.

Freire, P. (1993). *Pedagogy of the oppressed.* New York: Continuum.

Freire, P. (1998). *The Paulo Freire reader.* A. M. Freire & D. Macedo (Eds.). New York: The Continuum Press.

Ginwright, S., & Cammarota, J. (2002). New terrain in youth development: The promise of a social justice approach. *Social Justice, 29*(4), 82.

hooks, b. (1989). *Talking back: Thinking feminist, thinking Black.* Boston: South End Press.

Nieto, S. (2000). *Affirming diversity: The sociopolitical context of multicultural education.* New York: Longman.

Noddings, N. (1984). *Caring: A feminine approach to ethics and moral education.* Berkeley, CA: University of California Press.

Noddings, N. (1992). *The challenge to care in schools: An alternative approach to education.* New York: Teachers College Press.

Oakes, J. (1985). *Keeping track: How schools structure inequality.* New Haven, CT: Yale University Press.

Pollock, M. (2001). How the question we ask most about race in education is the very question we most suppress. *Educational Researcher, 30*(9), 2–11.

Quiroz, P. A. (1997). The "silencing" of the lambs: How Latino students lose their "voice" in school. ISRI Working Paper No. 31. East Lansing, MI: Michigan State University, Julian Samora Research Institute.

Quiroz, P. A. (2001). The silencing of the Latino student "voice": Puerto Rican and Mexican narratives in eighth grade and high school. *Anthropology & Education Quarterly, 32*(3): 326–349.

Reyes, X. A., & Rios, D. I. (2003). Imaging teachers: In fact and in the mass media. *Journal of Latinos and Education, 2*(1), 3–11.

Sleeter, C. E. (1996). *Multicultural education as social activism.* Albany, NY: State University of New York Press.

Solórzano, D. G., & Yosso, T. J. (2001). From racial stereotyping and deficit discourse toward a critical race theory in teacher education. *Multicultural Education, 9*(1), 2–8.

Steele, C. M. (1992). Race and the schooling of Black Americans. *The Atlantic Monthly, 269*(4), 68–78.

Spring, J. H. (2001). *Deculturalization and the struggle for equality: A brief history of the education of dominated cultures in the United States.* Boston: McGraw-Hill.

Valencia, & Black. (2002). Mexican Americans don't value education. *Journal of Latinos and Education, 1*(2), 81–103.

Valenzuela, A. (1999). *Subtractive schooling: U.S.-Mexican youth and the politics of caring.* Albany, NY: State University of New York Press.

Weis, L., Fine, M., & Lareau, A. (1992). *Schooling and the silenced "others": Race and class in schools.* Special studies in teaching and teacher education, Number Seven. Buffalo: State University of New York, Buffalo, Graduate School of Education, 1–81.

Woodson, C. G. (1977). *The mis-education of the Negro.* New York: AMS Press.

Related Articles

Julio Cammarota and Augustine Romeo. (2004). Reflexiones Pedagogicas: A Critically Compassionate Pedagogy for Latino Youth. *Latino Studies, 4,* 305–312.

Julio Cammarota. (2006). Disappearing in the Houdini Tradition: The Experience of Race and Invisibility among Latina/o Students. *Multicultural Education, 14*(1), 2–10.

JULIO CAMMAROTA is an assistant professor and **AUGUSTINE ROMERO,** is a graduate student in the Bureau of Applied Research in Anthropology and the Mexican-American Studies and Research Center at the University of Arizona, Tucson, Arizona.

Educating Vietnamese American Students

HUONG TRAN NGUYEN

Promotion of English proficiency for students from disadvantaged backgrounds was one of the major provisions of the *No Child Left Behind* federal act of 2001. This act mandated that limited English proficient (LEP) students or English language learners (ELL) "learn English as quickly and effectively as possible," and receive instruction "through scientifically based teaching methods" delivered by "high quality" teachers in every core content classroom (U.S. Department of Education, Major Provisions of the Conference Report to H.R. 1, the NCLB Act, August 23, 2003).

In California the teacher population is 74.2% Caucasian and 25.8% ethnic minority, but the students they teach are 32% Caucasian and 68% ethnic minority. Over 1.5 million of those students are ELL (California State Department of Education, 2001–2002).

Many ELL students struggle to function in English-only classes and to compete with their native English-speaking peers, and tend not to fare well on high-stakes testing (Cummins, 2000). Regardless of student demographics, locales, staffing, and available resources, schools must, by law, provide necessary means for all students to achieve.

City Middle School

At City Middle School (a pseudonym) we identified 14 Vietnamese American students whose reading levels ranged from an alarming 1.5 to 4 (mid-year first grade to fourth grade), and English language development (ELD) from level 1 (beginning) to level 3 (Intermediate). Although there were far more ELL middle schoolers in need, there were only three pre-service teachers available to help, so we had to identify the most needy, which amounted to 14. What support would these middle school students (MSS) need in order to function in their English-only classes?

Although their *basic interpersonal communicative skills* (BICS) in English were passable, their *cognitive academic language proficiency* (CALP) severely lagged behind that of their native English-speaking peers (Cummins, 2000). The school administration, some of the teachers, and the MSS themselves recognized that they had been experiencing difficulty in their English-only core subject classes.

In order for these ELL students to become proficient in English (L2) and in content area knowledge, it would be logical and theoretically sound that instruction be delivered in their heritage language (L1), a language with which they would be more familiar. Reading and writing skills acquired through L1 provide a foundation for L2 development, being that academic skills and knowledge transfer across languages (Cummins, 2000).

Standardized tests have placed undue pressure on school administrators and teachers to push their ELL students to gain speedy English acquisition, overlooking the fact that it takes three to five years to develop oral proficiency and four to seven years for academic proficiency (Cummins, 2000).

Under Proposition 227 in California, ELL students would receive English-only *structured immersion* or *sheltered English immersion* (SEI) instruction for just one year. Rossell (2004–2005) reported that most immigrant children in mainstream classrooms ". . . seem to swim, not sink" (p. 36) after one year of SEI instruction. However, Hakuta, Butler, and Witt (2000) argued that the one-year time period of "sheltered English immersion" (SEI) was "wildly unrealistic" (p. 13). This arbitrary one-year period was a broad-brush determination, but it does not paint an accurate English acquisition picture for many ELL students, including the fourteen middle school students described below.

Context for My Involvement at City Middle School

In addition to teaching required core courses at a local university for CLAD (Crosscultural, Language, and Academic Development) certification in the Single Subject Credential Program, I have also been supervising the practicum of Multiple Subject Credential Program pre-service teachers (PST)—also known as student teachers—for CLAD and BCLAD (Bilingual Crosscultural, Language, and Academic Development) certification at various schools in different school districts.

The administration and school achievement teacher (SAT) at City Middle School sought my guidance regarding fourteen "at risk" students from grades 6 to 8 in need of support (I had worked with this administration in the past). Three out of five of the PSTs under my supervision were placed at City Middle School to fulfill their CLAD certification practicum; thus, it made sense for these three PSTs to work with the fourteen MSS and fulfill their BCLAD certification practicum hours at the same site as well.

Based on the school's needs and schedule, I recommended an after-school program with class sessions meeting twice a week, totaling to four hours, to which the administration agreed. The administration, the teachers in charge, the PSTs, and I realized that it would be unrealistic to expect formidable growth results from the MSS after a brief semester in terms of their CALP, but the MSS could use some assistance.

With data provided by the ELD teacher (in charge of all of the school's ELL population) and in consultation with me, the PSTs developed lessons and activities collaboratively based on the English language arts content standards. Each PST was responsible for the instruction of her own group of MSS in English and in Vietnamese, but a few sessions were conducted with all fourteen MSS together. Each PST took turns in teaching those lessons and activities during said sessions, which gave the MSS an opportunity to work with their peers and the PSTs to become acquainted with all fourteen MSS, both in a small group and a large group setting.

Twelve of the MMS were born in Vietnam, one in Oslo (Norway), and one in Malaysia. All arrived in the United States with their families from various destinations, one in 2001, one in 2002, three in 2003, one in 2004, and eight in 2005. Similar to the background of their MSS, all three PSTs were born in Vietnam and arrived in the U.S. with their families as refugees in 1975. Two of the PSTs started pre-school in the U.S.; the third was French-schooled in Vietnam and resumed her education in the U.S. in 11th grade. She made a career move in her mid-forties.

In addition to informal conversations, a writing sample, student interactions, and class discussions, the PSTs and I hoped to learn more about the MSS, so we designed a 20-item survey (in English and in Vietnamese) and administered it to the MSS at the end of the after-school program.

Survey

The survey (see Table 1) consisted of three parts. The first set of three items (1-3) consisted of fill-in-the-blank statements or questions regarding personal information about the participants' initial U.S. arrival and schooling experience both in the U.S. and the country of origin. In the second set of ten items (4-13), participants responded to statements of a quantitative nature based on a rating scale (*agree, strongly agree, disagree, to strongly disagree*), culminating in Table 2. The last set of six items (14-19) consisted of open-ended questions asking participants to elaborate on specific questions, and the last item (20) was reserved for any additional comments. Although there were 14 MSS enrolled in this after-school program, three were absent on the day this survey was administered. Respondents had the option to write their answers in English, Vietnamese or both; seven did so in English, the other four in Vietnamese, and all remained anonymous.

Discussion of Survey Results

Items 4-7 aimed at finding out how MSS felt about Vietnamese and English. Respondents unanimously agreed that Vietnamese was their predominant language of oral communication in their respective families (items 4 and 5). However, since items 6 and 7 included speaking *and* writing skills, the responses varied from those in the previous items.

For example, seven MSS agreed or strongly agreed that they were more comfortable speaking and writing in English, but four disagreed. The latter four were more truthful in their self-assessment in indicating that their oral proficiency (BICS) in English was functional, but their academic proficiency (CALP) was another matter altogether. (Judging by the written responses on the survey by the other seven respondents, it was clear that their CALP needed much refinement).

This is consistent with Cummins' (2000) finding that it takes three to five years to develop oral proficiency and four to seven years for academic proficiency, and that the one-year time period of sheltered English immersion (SEI) as proposed by Proposition 227 was inadequate for ELL to acquire academic proficiency (Hakuta, Butler, & Witt, 2000).

In terms of the importance of English and Vietnamese, ten out of eleven students were in agreement that these languages were equal in that regard (item 8). As far as being taught by the PST, all MSS unanimously agreed or strongly agreed that they liked the additional assistance they received (item 9), which they felt have helped them to improve in their regular English-only classes (item 10).

Insofar as items 11-13 were concerned, the notion of respect (in the students' cultural frame of understanding) often came up in informal discussions with the MSS or among themselves. All of them agreed or strongly agreed that students should demonstrate respect toward their teachers but believed that the reverse should hold true as well.

Interestingly, the group observed that "American" teachers did not have the same level of respect as their teachers did in Vietnam (item 13). The MSS shed light on the meaning of respect, elaborating on how important it was to them and to their parents who insisted that they respected their teachers (and elders) and looked to them for directions and sage advice (items 14-19).

Hence, they were surprised to find that respect was not as valued in U.S. classrooms and that "American" teachers tolerated disrespectful behavior from students far more often than they should have. According to the MSS, such student behavior would not have been tolerated in Vietnam and would result in severe punishment.

In terms of L1 support from the PSTs, the MSS benefited from having abstract concepts and ideas explicated in Vietnamese and supported with relevant examples deriving from familiar cultural practices which made learning refreshing, less intimidating, and more comprehensible. For example, in a story some of the MSS had read in their regular class, the author described a family's harvesting and preparation of an authentic dish with potatoes, unique to a U.S. region. The MSS were unfamiliar with that American dish, potatoes, and the region where this story took place.

Table 1 The Survey

Survey Items 1–3: Personal Information

1. I arrived in the U.S. on _____ (date/month), in _____ (year) with _____ (family members or others).
2. I was born in _____ (city & country) in _____ (year).
3. The first school I attended in the U.S. was _____ (name) in the city of _____ and the sate of _____ .

Survey Items 4–14: Quantitative Section

(Based on a rating scale of: Agree, Strongly Agree, Disagree, Strongly Disagree)

4. I speak more <u>Vietnamese</u> than English with my parents, brothers, and sisters at home.
5. I speak more <u>English</u> than Vietnamese with my parents, brothers, and sisters at home.
6. I am more comfortable speaking and writing in <u>Vietnamese</u> than in English.
7. I am more comfortable speaking and writing in <u>English</u> than in Vietnamese.
8. In my opinion, English <u>and</u> Vietnamese are <u>equally</u> important.
9. I like to be taught by the three Vietnamese American student teachers.
10. Having a Vietnamese teacher helps me to learn my subject matter and do better in my regular classes.
11. Students must always show respect to their teachers.
12. Teachers must also demonstrate respect toward their students.
13. Respect for teachers in Vietnam means the same as respect for teachers in the U.S.

Survey Items 14–19: Qualitative Section

14. What did you learn from your parents about respect for others?
15. In what ways have the Vietnamese American student teachers helped you with learning your subject matter?
16. Of the lessons and/or activities that the Vietnamese American student teachers taught you, which one(s) did you like the most and why? the least and why?
17. What do you think about the style of teaching of the Vietnamese American student teachers?

Survey Item 20

You are invited to write any additional comments. Thank you for your input and participation.

Table 2 Results of the Quantitative Section Questions

Question	Agree	Strongly Agree	Disagree	Strongly Disagree
4. I speak more Vietnamese than English with my parents, brothers, and sisters at home.	5	6	0	0
5. I speak more English than Vietnamese with my parents, brothers, and sisters at home.	1	1	9	0
6. I am more comfortable speaking and writing in Vietnamese than in English.	4	2	5	0
7. I am more comfortable speaking and writing in English than in Vietnamese.	5	2	4	0
8. In my opinion, English and Vietnamese are equally important.	7	3	1	0
9. I like to be taught by the three Vietnamese American pre-service teachers.	6	5	0	0
10. Having a Vietnamese teacher helps me to learn my subject matter and do better in my regular class.	1	10	0	0
11. Students must always show respect to their teachers.	2	9	0	0
12. Teachers must also demonstrate respect toward their students.	7	4	0	0
13. Respect for teachers in Vietnam means the same as respect for teachers in the U.S.	0	0	1	10

The PSTs contextualized the story by referring to a U.S. map, pointing to the region in question, and explaining that it the farming community relied on its own harvest to sustain its families. When translating "potato" to "khoai," (a term in Vietnamese), the PST brought realia (real objects) such as a potato and other roots (e.g., yam, sweet potato, taro), and paralleled this American dish to other Vietnamese stew-like recipes that used a couple of these roots, but that potatoes could have be substituted.

The MSS were excited about this lesson because it tapped into their prior knowledge. They each wanted to share a mouth-watering dish that their mother used to prepare with these ingredients. This is an example of making learning relevant to students' lives by connecting the story to the students' experience made possible because the PSTs and MSS shared a similar background and cultural practice.

Through L1 support, the MSS were able to ask the PSTs for clarification or elaboration without the anxiety of formulating questions in English instantaneously while monitoring their pronunciation, proper vocabulary and syntactical usage (items 15-16). Moreover, the MS discussed how the hands-on approach to teaching (e.g., visuals, manipulatives, Total Physical Response or TPR, and so on) helped them tremendously, particularly when it came to figurative language (e.g., idioms, metaphors, analogies, inference) often found in literature. Through the analogy below, a PST described how she viewed Specially Designed Academic Instruction in English (SDAIE) strategies:

> As an umbrella shelters a pedestrian in a rain storm, the SDAIE techniques or sheltered classes offer these ELL students some protection from the storms of concepts and language, thus giving them an opportunity to progress academically, as they are still acquiring the language and U.S. cultural ways. [JT_5-17-06]

Although one could not claim that this brief after-school program will have a long-term impact on the learning outcomes of these middle school students, it would be difficult to disregard the apparent joy with which these students bonded and related to one another and the PST in charge and pride in using their L1. It appeared that the MSS were comfortable with disclosing their struggle with balancing between being an American teenager and adopting U.S. values and being a Vietnamese son/daughter bound by traditional familial values.

Seven Key Factors

What factors should teachers take into account when working with students of a similar language and culture as these Vietnamese Americans?

Develop Students' Background Knowledge and Foundation of Subject Matter

It would be dangerous for teachers to assume that ELL students entering their classrooms would have had a literacy base in their heritage language (L1) and/or in English (L2) as well as adequate exposure to using L2 in conversational and academic settings. Therefore, teachers would need to provide ELL students with basic knowledge and foundation of the subject matter being taught, including the usage of SDAIE (e.g., slower speech, clear enunciation, quality visuals, gestures, facial expressions, and contextualized vocabulary, and so on).

If the classroom teacher was bilingual or had a bilingual aide, the use of L1 to support student comprehension of subject matter would be ideal. In this case, concepts would be previewed in L1, followed by the teacher's direct instruction in L2, then reviewed in L1 to make certain that the ELL students understood key concepts and ideas and asked related questions.

Recognize and Build upon Students' Dual Identity

Being a bilingual individual (including U.S. born) means to be part of both cultures. Many ELL students struggled with being perceived as less intelligent and less capable because they had not adequately demonstrated strong command of English, familiarity with cultural ways of the U.S., and difficulty with fitting into the total school population. Build on what they know. Validate who they are and the familial resources they bring. Never insist on their shedding their L1 in order to acquire their L2.

Allow for Think Time and Wait Time

Though many ELL students have been considered as conscientious and hard working by some of their teachers, they often felt shy and uncomfortable about classroom participation. Slow in raising their hands, they had to process the question and the answer in English as well as the terminology in that subject matter, and tended to become frustrated when their classmates' hands went up immediately after the teacher had posed a question.

If longer think and wait time had been allowed, these ELL students would have stood a better chance of formulating their answers before making their responses public and risking "losing face" in front of others. How about signaling to ELL students that they would be called on and giving them appropriate time to get ready? What about broadening the definition of "participation" to include other ways of responding to questions to include writing assignments, small group discussion, pair-share, use of post-it notes, thumbs up/thumbs down, or individual erasable white boards as part of participation? Lack of verbal participation may not necessarily equate to lack of understanding.

Deliver Instruction at a Slower Pace

For ELL students, instruction and class discussion in English-only classes seemed to occur at a-mile-a-minute pace, leaving them inundated with information and overwhelmed with English "noise." How about verbally communicating key concepts and terminology and write these ideas on the board (supported by relevant examples)? Guide students in taking notes of important ideas and in making sense of essential concepts in order for them to demonstrate their understanding of the material in course assignments, discussions, and examinations.

For instance, content standards are written in such a way that even teachers can find them confounding and ambiguous. Therefore, break content standards into smaller chunks and help students to read between the lines in terms of what teachers are expected to teach and students are to learn and be able to do.

Emphasize Note Taking and Organization

Teachers often assumed that by the time students, including ELL students, arrived in middle school, they would already have learned how to take proper notes from class lectures and organize them into folders/binders from one class period to the next. However, some may not have mastered these skills. If a teacher taught her students how to take notes from a reading assignment, students would be able to focus attention on key concepts and ideas in order to study for exams.

Furthermore, it is important for teachers to make a habit of reminding students when and what to take notes of so that it becomes a pattern for them. For ELL students, this process may take some time. How about assigning a percentage of the total course grade to note taking and organization?

Maximize Multiple Learning Modalities

To minimize teacher talk and to increase student understanding of material taught, teachers might employ visual, tactile, and kinesthetic modalities (Kellough & Roberts, 2002) in order to tap upon the multiple intelligences of learners (Gardner, 1983) and to allow more than one way for students to demonstrate knowledge. Strategies such as TPR and SDAIE should be used as much as possible to make input comprehensible and concepts less abstract (Asher, 1965; Krashen, 1995), thus benefiting not only ELL students but other students as well.

Establish a Support System

Besides the teacher, an older student, an English-proficient classmate, a teacher/college aide, a parent or a community volunteer could also assist the ELL students with class work by supplementing, not supplanting, the teacher's role. Hence, the *zone of proximal development* (ZPD) of the ELL students would be "stretched" from their current level of understanding to their potential state of development (Vygotsky, 1962).

One of the reasons ELL students hesitated to raise their hands was because they preferred not to call attention to themselves for fear of being labeled as "braggers" or "know it alls" by their classmates. Furthermore, ELL students rarely asked questions even if they did not understand. Why show others what they did not know?

Teachers should make time to talk to and connect with ELL students personally as much as possible. For many ELL students, group success is far more important than individual success. Teachers do affect the lives of students who cross their paths and to ensure that giving up should not be an option for teachers or students. No child should be left behind.

References

Asher, J. (1966). The strategy of the total physical response: A review. *Modern Language Journal, 50,* 79–84.

Bielenberg, B., & Fillmore, L. W. (December 2004-January 2005). The English they need for the test. *Association for Supervision and Curriculum Development, 62*(4), 45–49.

Cummins, J. (2000). *Language, power and pedagogy: Bilingual children in the crossfire.* Clevedon, UK: Multilingual Matters.

Gardner, J. (1983). *Frames of mind.* New York: Basic Books.

Hakuta, K., Butler, Y. G., & Witt, D. (2000). *How long does it take English learners to attain proficiency?* Santa Barbara, CA: University of California Linguistic Minority Research Institute.

Krashen, S (1995). *Principles and practice in second language acquisition.* New York: Phoenix ELT.

Kellough, R. D., & Roberts, P. (2002). *A resource guide for elementary school teaching: Planning for competence* (5th Ed.). Upper Saddle River, NJ: Merrill Prentice Hall.

Rossell, C. (December 2004-January 2005). Teaching English through English. *Association for Supervision and Curriculum Development, 62*(4), 32–36.

Vygotsky, L. S. (1962). *Thought and language.* Cambridge, MA: MIT Press.

HUONG TRAN NGUYEN is an assistant professor in the Department of Teacher Education, College of Education, California State University, Long Beach, Long Beach, California.

From *Multicultural Education,* Fall, 2007, pp. 23–26. Copyright © 2007 by Caddo Gap Press. Reprinted by permission.

The Need to Reestablish Schools as Dynamic Positive Human Energy Systems That Are Non-Linear and Self-Organizing

The Learning Partnership Tree

MICHELE ACKER-HOCEVAR ET AL.

Introduction

With the *No Child Left Behind Act of 2001* (NCLB) all states are required to implement some iteration of standards-based, accountability-driven reform. In the United States NCLB is the primary federal policy tool to deliver educational services to children of low socioeconomic (low-SES) status and limited English proficiency (LEP), otherwise called English Language Learners (ELL). Florida has embarked upon this mandated, educational reform movement with high-stakes testing at its center. Although each state has the prerogative of creating its own accountability system, Florida has chosen a punitive system based on the Sunshine State Standards. Known as the *A + Plan,* and primarily based on the Florida Comprehensive Achievement Test (FCAT), this plan determines how schools are assigned letter grades on an "A" through "F" scale.

This scale is a fundamental tenet of *Florida's System of School Improvement and Accountability,* which reports annually schools' accomplishments. Low performing schools, designated "D" or "F," typically have disproportionately high numbers of low-SES students, racial and ethnic minority student (students of color and LEP/ELL) (Yan, 1999) and rarely attain "C" or above (Acker-Hocevar & Touchton, 2002). The dearth of research on schools attaining high performance with students who typically underperform their more affluent and native English-speaking peers (Valdés, 1996) led to this study. As such, this study is of great interest to policymakers and educators. Given the politics of high-stakes testing, and the fact that few other educators (Carter, 2000; Charles A. Dana Center, 1999; Scheurich, 1998 for exceptions) have been able to accomplish what these high-performing schools have (Education Commission of the States, 1998), the study provides glimpses into internal practices which have sustained these schools' reform efforts and, offers a description of how these practices work synergistically in a model. This article is the second of two reporting the findings; the first laid out the initial framework for the study (Schoon, Wilson, Walker, Cruz-Janzen, Acker-Hocevar, & Brown, 2003).

Method
Selection of Schools

Nine schools met the following criteria: 1) sustained achievement in reading and math for three consecutive FCAT years; 2) competence in these disciplines for three years at grades 3, 4, and 5; 3) 50% or greater low-SES students as defined by Title I; and 4) 10% or greater LEP students as defined by Title VII and the Multicultural Education Training Advocacy (META). LEP/ELL students receiving English for Speakers of Other Languages (ESOL) services for two years or less were not part of the reported scores.

Sustained achievement is depicted in Table 1. Although the State criteria have changed every year, making comparisons impractical, trends can be noted.

Design

The Interview Protocol was developed to elicit information regarding best practices at the school and classroom levels and about the schools' perceptions of best practices at the district level in relation to the schools. Questions were grouped according to 10 constructs linked to student achievement and grounded on school effectiveness literature (Edmonds, 1979; Purkey & Smith, 1993; Spillane & Seashore Louis, 2002; Teddlie & Reynolds, 2000; Wiggins & McTighe, 1998). Constructs were organized as a two-dimensional model with outer and inner cores (Schoon et al., 2003). The outer core represented constructs deemed pivotal to standards-based school effectiveness: Information Management, Accountability, Personnel, Instruction, and Resources (Carter, 1997; Siegel, 2003). The inner core represented constructs deemed integral, yet not viewed as the driving force behind

Table 1 Summary of High-Performing School Grades by Year and School

School[1]	1998–99	1999–00	2000–01	2001–02	2002–03
X 1	A	C	A	B	A
X 2	C	B	A	A	A
X 3	C	A	B	A	A
X 4	C	A	A	A	A
X 5	C	B	A	A	A
X 6	B	A	A	A	B
X 7	C	C	A	A	A
X 8	D	C	C	A	A
X 9	D	C	C	B	A

[1]Note. State of Florida (2003).

standards-based school reform: Leadership, Decision Making, Culture and Climate, Communication, and Parent and Community Involvement (Elmore, 2000; Scheurich & Skrla, 2003; Scribner, Young, & Pedroza, 1999; Sergiovanni, 1994; Snyder, Acker-Hocevar, & Snyder, 2000; Spillane, Halverson, & Diamond, 2001). According to this model, the inner core provides the impetus for changes but the outer core is the most direct link to school effectiveness and improvement. This was called the Systems Alignment Model (SAM) (Schoon et al., 2003).

Ron Edmonds (1979) demonstrated that schools can attain high academic achievement with low-SES students and students of color, laying a foundation for other scholars to further identify practices affecting student achievement positively. As researchers, we sought to answer three questions:

What theories-in-use seem to sustain school progress over time?

What practices lend credibility to the initial conceptual lenses for this study?

Do practices in high-performing schools confirm or reject the Systems Alignment Model?

Site visits were conducted in fall of 2002 and spring of 2003. During the two-day site visits interviews were held with individual principals, assistant principals, in several instances with both, and separately with groups of teachers and parents. The interviews were recorded, transcribed, and coded by two independent researchers. Once agreement was reached the codes served to examine practices across schools (Merriam, 2001).

Theories-In-Use

Three theories-in-use emerged from the findings and provide a backdrop for interpretation and discussion of results. First, systems theory frames how these schools worked in collaborative partnerships to shape and improve their "work systems and services and to assess the quality of effects on those being served" (Snyder, Acker-Hocevar, & Snyder, 2000, p. 211). Next, power theories clarify how educators constructed "partnership power beliefs" within their unique settings. Last, "additive schooling" explains how these schools were able to sustain high achievement over time with diverse populations.

The schools used information systems to respond to changes in their environment in natural ways. Organizational theorists (Senge, 1990; Wheatley, 1992) suggest that healthy systems can promote disequilibria in natural ways through the sharing of information and ongoing dialogue. Information can be used to respond to subtle environmental changes, stimulating variable and adaptive growth. This ability is more likely to happen when power is disbursed and shared broadly throughout the organization.

Drawing on a metaphor of power, "The Power River" illustrates power relationships along four places: Power over, Power to, Power with and Power through (Snyder et al., 2000). *Power over* and *Power to* are set within a bureaucratic and dominator framework, while *Power with* and *Power through* are set within a contrasting framework of partnership and community power socially constructed between educators and communities.

The first place on the river is Power over, the most limited use of power, with restricted access to resources and opportunities within a hierarchical, top-down, controlling, and bureaucratic perspective. Power over is increasingly exercised through federal and state threats of punishment for districts' and schools' failure to produce changes within acceptable levels and timelines.

Power to represents the dominator bureaucratic power framework that begins to unleash its hold over resources and opportunities to develop the skills of others and share some access to resources; power appears more widely shared than it is. Only when the Power River shifts its energy and direction beyond the bureaucratic and dominator paradigm does power give way to *Power with*. This changes dramatically the way people work together to solve problems and extends access to the broader community. There is an underlying belief in the expertise of the internal community that builds a collective sense of purpose.

Finally, *Power through* is enacted when power is loosely coupled with everyone, including parents and the community, working as partners to build learning communities through shared expertise and vision. There is an ethic of care and concern for each person connected to this broader community vision.

Partnership practices seem to underpin additive schooling, the third theory-in-use within the schools. The focus of the nine schools was on the community's culture(s) and language(s). This was termed additive schooling by the researchers. Drawing on the work of Valenzuela (1999), the assumptions underpinning subtractive schooling, and its converse: additive schooling, were examined. Subtractive schooling posits that today's schools work to fracture communities' cultural and social capital.

Several well-established notions drive additive schooling. First, it has been demonstrated that schoolwork cultures do make a difference in "the lives of children and also in a school's ability to meet accountability requirements" (Cummins, 1996; Espinoza-Herold, 2003; Snyder et al., 2000, p. 202). Further, cultural and language minority students perform better in nurturing environments that embrace and affirm their heritages (Beck, 1994). The goal must be to narrow the gap between teachers' and students' social and cultural differences (Banks, 2001; Nieto, 2001; Sleeter, 1992). As long as those in charge are uneducated on the needs of either ELL or culturally marginalized students, schooling has the potential to continue to subtract resources from them (Valenzuela, 1999).

Embracing students' and communities' cultural and social capital as integral components of the schools' network leads to a joint and reciprocal effort to educate everyone in the organization; children, community members, and school personnel (Valenzuela, 1999). Mutual trust is guided by the belief that both schools and parents have genuine interest and agency in children's educational and social competency. Parents must trust schools as places where their children are safe and educated as wholesome individuals who value themselves and their communities, and others in the world beyond (Espinoza-Herold, 2003; Valenzuela, 1999).

A New Model Emerges

This study found support for schools as non-linear, less bureaucratic, living systems capable of self-organization (Meier, 1995). Learning organizations are enabling, capacity building, human energy systems empowered to mediate external controls. Although the schools existed within a *Power Over* paradigm, they were organized around partnership and constructivist relationships. The original Systems Alignment Model had to be reconceptualized to account for the theories-in-use. The new model depicts both sets of constructs as interconnected, interactive, and interdependent parts of a dynamic living system.

The Outer Core was reclassified as Organizing Variables. The Inner Core was renamed Sustaining Variables when it was found that while these variables often function in less observable and quantifiable ways, they are essential for the healthy life of the entire learning organization and were, in fact, the synergy driving the entire system. In the words of Deborah Meier (1995), it would take a "strong storm" to "uproot or break" strong learning organizations. The Sustaining Variables, then, are the fuel driving the Organizing Variables. They create the synergy to transform the Organizing Variables into practices that better meet the needs of students. The Organizing and Sustaining Variables became the lenses through which beliefs and practices were examined.

Organizing Variables: School Practices

Accountability in these schools is driven by the internal core values and vision of the organization. In one school, this is expressed as, "You never settle for what you have, but always strive to be better." The school works together to analyze the needs of students and look broadly at what is required to help them achieve. Most of the information gathered internally assists to evaluate student achievement. Monitoring techniques include pretests, progress checks, performance assessments, portfolios, weekly progress report, and pacing charts for long range planning. In several of the schools, survey feedback keeps the pulse on the academic climate to see what resources are needed in classrooms, including professional development, and/or planning time. Sharing high expectations built a culture where learning was central to how teachers, principals, and parents talked about the school, particularly student learning. Accountability for excellence was one of the internal norms bonding everyone. Teachers considered their commitment and dedication to collegiality as contributing to their success. The schools educated parents on what standards meant for their child's learning.

At school #X8 "There is one teacher assigned to make sure that they are working on the standards and that they have the techniques and materials to do so." Most of the schools relied heavily on the knowledge and expertise of teachers within the building. In all the schools standards were aligned across grade levels, along with the grades above and below. Notably, when principals were asked how they held teachers accountable, they stated that they ensured teachers had the necessary resources and professional development to be successful. The focus was not on surveillance, or monitoring, but direct instructional assistance when students were not achieving. It was clear that all educators shared a common sense of accountability and responsibility for successfully educating all children, including working with the child and the child's family. Principals kept books in their offices and freely gave them to parents. School media centers were open into the evenings for parents and students. "The priority is that students are going to succeed regardless of what it takes for the administration, faculty and parents" (School #X2).

Resources. Although districts provide a so-called "operating budget," all the schools agreed that, the district, state, or federal government did not generally fund "A or D," schools adequately. After paying for staff, supplies, materials, and operational expenses, very little is left. As funds dwindle each passing year schools have a harder time purchasing basic instructional materials. All schools reported budget cuts forcing program and instructional personnel reductions with increased class sizes. Although all the schools received "FCAT Merit" funds, as reward for high marks according to the A+ Plan, most reported using these funds to purchase basic instructional materials and support tutorial programs, especially with 3rd graders, who risk mandatory retention if they fail the FCAT.

All schools reported that their allocated budgets were insufficient to maintain and upgrade technology. Although expected to integrate technology in instruction, most stated that districts generally did not fund technology sufficiently to stay current. Schools varied widely on their technology programs and ability to obtain outside funding for technology. School #X9 had few computers and even lacked Internet. Moreover, some of the principals reported funding teacher, student, and parent recognition awards from personal income. The principal at School #X2 personally conducted her school's Saturday tutorial because they had no funds to pay teachers. The role of principals and leadership teams has expanded to include, in the words of a respondent, "begging"—"I never thought that being a principal meant begging."

Criteria for school effectiveness have grown to include individual schools' ability to aggressively secure external funding. For many schools this really means balancing the negative equation created by deficit funding; not to enhance, but survive. This assault on schools' financial viability escalates as higher SES communities add significantly to their school's budgets, even doubling it through monetary and in-kind contributions.

All the schools depended on volunteers to supplement insufficient staffing, assist classrooms, and tutor. The ability to secure volunteers is tied to the community's resources as well as parents' work and family demands. Schools in communities that cannot contribute significantly, financially or in-kind, were forced to secure resources through grants and/or partnerships. Although many districts have partnerships with local businesses, contributions tend to be limited (food, school supplies, etc.) and are chased by far too many needy schools. Add to this the reality that external funding is closely related to the skills and connections of leadership team members, and a truly disproportionate picture unfolds. Some educational leaders, be they teachers, parents, or principals, become adept at grant writing and/or hold personal connections to external funding sources (Brown & Cornwall, 2000).

Some schools attracted funding by establishing reputations as effective spenders. School #X7, which had already secured an excess of $1.3 million dollars in grants over a three-year period, received an additional $10,000 when a district agency discovered unspent money. This school leader received an unanticipated phone call and asked to spend the money before weeks' end. In his words: "I was called because people knew I could spend money well. Many other schools cannot put together a spending plan that quickly." Although all the schools agreed that what really matters in school effectiveness and student achievement was teacher quality, many openly expressed that schools perceived as having the most resources and community support, tended to attract and retain the best teachers.

Instruction. Each of the nine schools stated vehemently that they "don't teach to the FCAT," but rather teach students to think. To quote a principal, "Schools that teach to the FCAT are not going to be really successful." While all the schools agreed that the FCAT provided them with information, they overwhelmingly disagreed with how it was used to penalize students and schools. Schools aligned their curriculum and assessments with the district's standards, which in turn aligned their standards to the State's. These schools, however, consistently developed curriculum beyond the core academics and agreed: "Students need

the arts, the fitness; the intra-personal and the inter-personal." Schools offered before, during, and after school programs that included tutorials, fine arts, dance, chorus, chess, videography, cheerleading, etc. An important observation was that the schools consistently related the curriculum to students' lives and needs, and their future as productive, socially conscientious citizens. This made the curriculum relevant to empower students as problem-solvers within their own communities and beyond. Instruction included environmental concerns, as well as local, national, and geopolitical and economic issues (Meier, 1995).

Schools employed many assessment strategies and tools, including teacher-developed tests and, in fact, indicated that they were already utilizing a variety of assessments, particularly authentic assessments, to monitor student progress and self-reflect about their own organizational effectiveness, before the FCAT. Some of the externally mandated assessments were described as content-based or specific strategy-based and not accurate measures of students' critical thinking. Schools geared much of their in-house assessments at higher order thinking, and targeted various forms of intelligences. Schools focused on literacy across all the content areas. Although districts heavily controlled instructional programs and materials, these schools selected strategies that supported the unique needs of their students. ELL students were supported through numerous research-based strategies and assessments that, while effective with most students, have been demonstrated as uniquely valuable with second language learners. Most of the schools indicated that their teachers had much instructional flexibility: "If you want to teach in a tree and that works, you can teach in a tree."

These schools promoted infused multiculturalism on a daily basis throughout the school year to affirm students' cultural assets and validate other cultures (Banks, 2001; Sleeter, 1992). Many had multicultural committees to implement special programs as assemblies and festivals. Teachers purchased culturally authentic materials and libraries held a wide variety of books by authors of diverse backgrounds. The schools hired sufficient teachers proficient in students' native languages to provide self-contained bilingual and/or content area education, especially in math, science, and social studies along with English literacy. Two-Way bilingual education was found in the majority of the schools. They also mainstreamed LEP/ELL students with additional English instruction. The least effective model was not employed in any of the schools. This model, used widely in the State, is the traditional ESOL pullout program with no support in the student's native language. Team-teaching and articulation within and between grades ensured that Bilingual/ESOL and regular students were instructed in the same content and with the same grade-level materials and expectations—the curriculum was not "watered down."

Because of mandatory 3rd grade retention, disproportionately impacting ELL students, whose FCAT scores count after only one year of Bilingual/ESOL education, retention is often used district-wide to coerce a focus on English language skills, even at the expense of other content areas. Yet, in this study's schools, retention was neither used to coerce nor punish; once the teacher ensured that the student is ready to move on, the school promotes the child without forcing for the child to spend an entire school year in that grade. Thus, while adhering to the state's 3rd grade retention law, learning is recognized for ELL students.

Information management. The ability to have a good information management system was directly related schools' ability to be accountable and responsive. This fostered autonomy and flexibility for success beyond the status quo and compliance requirements. Schools demonstrated valuing information/data as part of their ongoing self-assessment and improvement. Accountability was driven by the internal core values and vision linked to information management. One principal states, "So in addition to whatever the district has identified we also decided what tools we were going to use and how we were going to use them. But we have done it for us." Schools employed numerous methods and formats, including quantitative and qualitative, to obtain a broad range of credible, relevant, and timely information/data from within and outside. Members became their own internal evaluators. Self-assessment included School Climate Surveys for teachers and parents. Although assessment data drove instruction, decisions on students were made on an individual basis. All the schools had already established information management processes before the FCAT was mandated. Data provided through the State and district was viewed as additional information to support organizational growth.

Personnel. Across most districts, principals are assigned and can be re-assigned or removed at any time. Although schools are given some flexibility in the selection of instructional staff, it is not uncommon for excessed teachers to be assigned to schools, regardless. Principals expressed looking for teachers wanting to be part of a community, and for "someone that had a real need to see children succeed. I don't think that I can mention anyone on the staff that wouldn't give their all" (School #X8). Most schools experienced very low teacher turnover. Teachers described schools as families supportive of them and their work. In school #X3, teachers left only when promoted. Then, the staff commiserated on how much the person was missed. These schools made a conscious effort to blur the boundaries of seniority between faculty with newly hired faculty immersed into the school culture at once.

Teachers saw themselves as life-long learners, involved in providing in-house professional development, and attending state and national conferences. Repeatedly, teachers stated that their professional development was linked to student learning and needs. They were encouraged to try new things as team teaching, looping, and observing peers. The school cultures encouraged inclusiveness, consensus building, openness, and sharing. Teachers talked about feeling motivated to seek creative and alternative ways of reaching students, and to assume greater personal responsibility for the school's well being. A teacher in school #X2 said, "The principal just fosters that; she gives you the encouragement to just succeed at anything for your students and at a personal and professional level."

Sustaining Variables: School Practices

Culture and climate. The core culture of learning organizations is reciprocally shaped by the sustaining variables, and particularly the organizational leadership style. All schools demonstrated a culture unified by common family/team spirit where each member is a valuable and essential asset and leader, whether openly designated or not. Teachers addressed themselves and were addressed as professional by the school's designated leaders and parents. A strong sense of collegiality permeated the school culture. Teachers expressed high levels of ethical and professional expectations, standards, and motivation. This was matched with high expectations for everyone in the learning organization, especially students. They openly affirmed each other's expertise in numerous areas and willingness to work collaboratively. Teachers mentored new faculty and each other and were not inhibited and/or threatened by visiting each other's classrooms to provide support. While everyone recognized that their job was "very tough" and "even harder than most other schools," they defined it within a positive challenge paradigm, seeing the numerous obstacles as challenges they could overcome through teamwork. All of this led to productive synergy sustained through incentives and celebrations of achievement, even approximations. Continually, teachers, students, and parents were recognized.

A significant finding in all schools was a strong sense that the students and communities were an asset, including their culture(s) and language(s) (Cummins, 1996; Nieto, 2000; Valenzuela, 1999). Relationships with students and communities were premised on authentic caring. Our findings demonstrated that to the extent the schools embraced and validated students' cultural and linguistic background, respect and trust were reciprocally established between schools and communities.

Leadership. The formal leadership in schools was affirming, nurturing, inclusive, and willing to share power with teachers and/or parents. In all but one of the schools, teachers described leaders as democratic, consensus builders, and participatory. Principals were attuned to moving their schools forward, rather than resting on their laurels. Instead, they sustained the energy for ongoing improvement through professional dialogue and collaboration. Teachers were given common planning times within and cross grade levels, and with feeder schools. Repeatedly, parents commented on the schools' access to them and willingness to respond quickly to their needs. One parent talked about how in a previous school, it took weeks for the teacher or principal to get back to her. In these schools, however, teachers and principal were in daily contact with parents and responded to concerns immediately.

Principals recognized teachers were key to successful learning cultures in all of the schools. There was an expressed view of teachers as capable. "I like to find the strengths in the teachers and build on that. . . ." School leadership was not vested in the principal. The administrators at school #X2 described the leadership like this:

We have a leadership team. Everyone basically in the school is a leader . . . I think that, very quickly when you come into this

Table 2 School Ratings and Power Relations between the Administration with Teachers and Parents

School[1]	98–99	99–00	00–01	01–02	02–03	Power Relations	
						Teachers	Parents
X1	A	C	A	B	A	Through	With
X2	C	B	A	A	A	To	Over
X3	C	A	B	A	A	Through	Through
X4	C	A	A	A	A	Through	With
X5	C	B	A	A	A	Through	With
X6	B	A	A	A	B	Through	With
X7	C	C	A	A	A	Through	With
X8	D	C	C	A	A	With	To
X9	D	C	C	B	A	With	To

[1]Note. School grade data are from The Florida School Report (State of Florida, 2003).

building you realize that this is a building where, everyone is expected to bring something to the table, and they are allowed to share what they feel would be the best course. And so it's very expected and very welcomed when people bring ideas to the table . . . .

Leaders encouraged teachers to talk about the school, not just their individual classrooms. This collective vision evoked language such as "we are all in this together" and "we work hard on school improvement here." Teachers were willing to share resources, prioritize them based on school needs, and dispense with the idea that everyone getting whatever resources they needed was equitable. Leadership was seen as collective accountability for student learning.

Decision making. Staff perceptions were valued over external judgments. Table 2 reflects how power was enacted within schools and communities.

It was not surprising that schools #X8 and #X9 had the least developed Cultures/Climates and Core Values, as well as the most fragile levels of achievement. Both had the least finely honed practices of shared power with parents. School #X2, had a second year principal who moved the school's relationship with parents from *power with* to *power over*. The school culture acquiesced to the principal's dominating power and relationships with teachers also shifted from *power with* to *power to*. These parents were the most ignorant of school leadership processes, decisions, and the school mission and improvement plan. They expressed that their involvement in decision-making was minimal and limited to a small group of parents. Teachers expressed a shift from the previous administrator's practices of more involvement. School #X3 had the most developed partnership culture. The principal envisioned a "break-the-mold" school of empowered staff, minimal bureaucracy, and achievement focused on integrating multiple intelligences into all aspects of the curriculum. The vision focused on democratic processes and consensus. The leadership team was comprised of administration, a secretary, a paraprofessional, a cafeteria worker, a custodian, two teachers, two parents, and a member-at-large.

Communication. Communication with parents was strong in all schools. Information was sent home in student's native language and English. Parents often attributed few discipline problems to the robust communication. "Most of the parents agree with the teachers. They want their kids to come to school; they want their kids to learn. If their child is misbehaving, they want to know and they put an end to that" (School #X8). Teachers communicated to parents that they cared about their students. Frequently, parents commented on the accessibility of the teachers and administrators: "They are always at school." Teachers displayed student work prominently, communicated weekly student progress, held frequent parent-teacher conferences, and generally created openness for parents. Parents could verbalize the missions and knew how decisions were made in all schools but one. Parents and teachers shared how their input was always welcomed, if not sought, except in school #X2.

Parent and community involvement. Research supports that students whose parents are consistently involved in their education attain higher academic achievement levels. Programs with high parent involvement are more successful than those with less involvement. The effects of parental involvement linger through the middle school level (Decker & Decker, 2000). Learning organizations ensure significant parent and community involvement. All the schools supported bilingual communication with parents, including translations during meetings. Parent and community involvement specialists, which included school counselors, made home visits, arranged workshops for parents, and secured speakers from the community. Parents were provided opportunities to enhance their native language literacy, English literacy through ESOL, computer skills, parenting, and behavior management. Parents in all schools were provided instructional materials and strategies to support their children at home. All the schools indicated willingness to teach parents how to get involved in an equitable manner to the maximum extent possible according to their work and family responsibilities. With one exception, all schools continually worked to augment parents' abilities to participate in decision-making.

Training included information about how the school and district works, and where information is located about their child.

All schools encouraged parents to continue speaking and reading to their children in their native languages. They believed that parents were essential partners in developing foundational concepts in the native language that could transfer later into English. Support for the home language sent a strong message to students that they were valued and respected.

Establishing Schools as Learning Partnerships
The Learning Partnership Tree

The emergent framework, termed the Learning Partnership Tree, describes how the Organizing and Sustaining Variables were found to work in concert in the nine schools (see Figure 1). There was little, if any, vertical alignment between districts and schools on the Organizing Variables except for Information Management and Accountability. Schools perceived that the Sustaining Variables were not considered as significant within the state-mandated framework that sought to focus on the quantifiable constructs and centered on Accountability and Information Management.

Contrary to the state focus, the framework that emerged from the findings is grounded on strong vertical and horizontal alignments between internal accountability measures reflecting how beliefs were constructed and power shared within these systems. Externally mandated accountability measures were integrated within the core beliefs and selectively negotiated by each school to serve its unique needs and objectives.

Represented as a tree, above the ground is the trunk (Organizational Core Values) supporting the branches (Organizing Variables) and canopy. The trunk (Core Values) must be structurally strong to support the branches and entire system upright. The Organizing Variables, while essential to the system, fluctuate at different times, depending on the system's interaction with its surroundings. All the Organizing Variables are interrelated, interdependent, and aligned at the juncture with the Core Values, signifying the system's internal determination of when and how to access the Organizing Variables according to priorities mediated through its Core Values. The Organizing Variables are the parts of the system most visible, concrete, and quantifiable, and thus, most focused on today.

Below the ground is the taproot (Culture/Climate) with its branching secondary root system (Sustaining Variables). The Sustaining Variables, while also essential to the system, exist in fluctuating proportions at different times and act in response to numerous factors found in the underground environment. Often, these components are less focused on, as they tend to be less visible, more abstract, and less quantifiable. All the Sustaining Variables are interrelated and interdependent and aligned at the juncture with the grounding organizational Culture/Climate. This juncture signifies the point where incoming nutrients merge to sustain the taproot (Culture/Climate) and develop into the Core Values that contributed to additive schooling.

While all the variables are essential to the whole system's health, the system is critically dependent on the Sustaining Variables, which provide the nutrients essential for a strong Culture/Climate. As the taproot grows, so does the trunk and vice versa. As the Core Values evolve through interaction with the outside environment, the organizational Culture/Climate responds in tandem. The upper part of the system reaches out to the surrounding environment and it too receives sustaining nutrients. Healthy systems use information and resources to move flexibly; failure to do so could destroy them.

What must not be ignored is that the overall health of the upper tree cannot be sustained without a strong root system. Often, what surprises unaware observers is that the root system (i.e., an organization's Culture/Climate and other Sustaining Variables) must be equally as large (or even larger) and equally as strong (or even stronger) as the parts above the ground. Another surprising aspect of this interrelationship is that as long as the root system remains healthy and strong, it can often re-sprout to re-create the tree. An extension of this to the upper tree is not always the case; for a trunk and branches cannot often re-sprout roots.

There exists an interrelated and interdependent connection between Organizing and Sustaining Variables. The trunk and canopy cannot continue growing indefinitely without the growth of the roots. And so, schools' Organizing Variables cannot be sustained without strong structural and supportive Core Values grounded by a strong Culture/Climate. Additionally, the Organizing Variables cannot be imposed on the system without the existence of this strong structuring and grounding.

Discussion and Conclusions

This study supports the view of schools as living, natural systems that cannot be dissected into isolated parts (Snyder et al., 2000). When we engage in educational reform, we must look at the entire system and not simply those parts that are most apparent and quantifiable.

A principal's knowledge is no longer "sufficient to actuate change" (Snyder et al., 2000). Effective change is created and sustained through team effort and shared leadership. Leadership requires principals working through democratic processes and consensus. Power must be distributed; accountability shared, and work equitable and collaborative.

Evidence of collegial norms encompassing attitudes and beliefs of support, trust, and openness to learning, with dedication to collective responsibility and accountability, seemed to assist these schools in adapting their work context to high stakes testing and standards based instruction. Yet, the traditional role of principals remains entrenched in a bureaucratic, managerial, model that most districts reinforce by not accepting a more distributed leadership model. By holding principals accountable for "running" the building and answering for all the decisions made in the school, the power of synergy among parents, teachers, and leaders is ignored.

Furthermore, the view of schools as natural human systems requires relationship building, self-reflection, mutual respect, and core values grounded on "inquiry as well as responsibility"

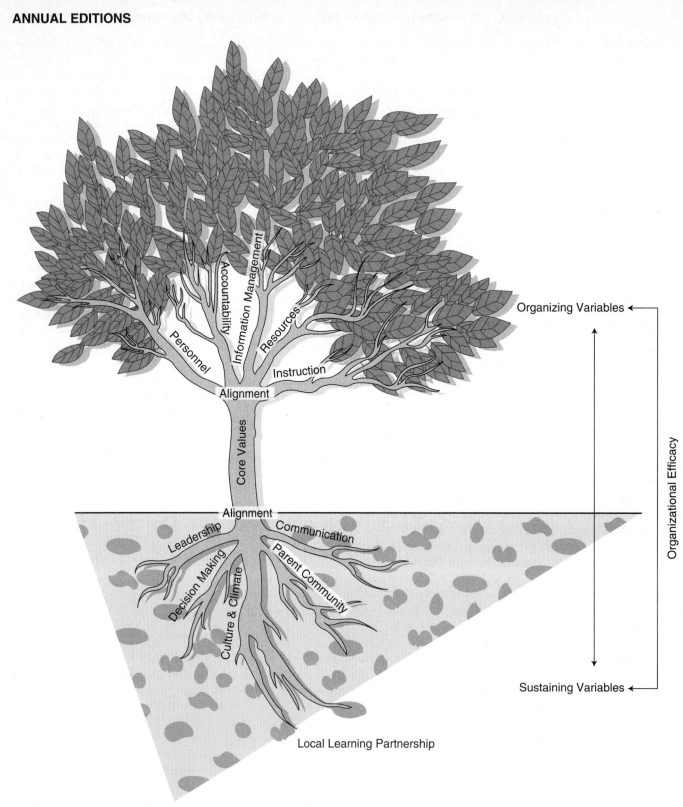

Figure 1 Learning partnership tree.

(Meier, 1995). It is evident that this is crucial for low performing schools where principal turnover occurs with abnormal frequency. With each new principal, there is also staff turnover and
the anticipation, with the remaining staff, of surviving yet another
principal. Such schools are not able to establish supportive organizational core values and stable shared leadership.

Two major, albeit misguided, assumptions undergird the
current state-mandated framework. First, that school improvement must be driven by top-down and external vertical alignment of the Organizing Variables between districts and schools.
Specifically, this means that the District superimposes, for
example, an information management system, and so forth, for

each of the Organizing Variables. Significantly, this hierarchical approach also assumes that while both sets of variables are necessary for school effectiveness and improvement, the Organizing Variables take the front seat in educational reform and school effectiveness, particularly Information Management and Accountability.

A second major assumption is that school improvement is then driven by increased external domination and supervision over schools and classrooms through the Organizing Variables, particularly Accountability and Information Management Systems, perceived as being responsible for "tightening the screws" on educators. This ignores all the other variables that make schools successful and is conceived narrowly within a highly technical and rational "power over" system of control. This contributes to the dysfunctional fragmentation of today's educational systems. A hidden, highly detrimental, assumption of the statemandated model is that schools lack the know-how and/or motivation to effectuate improvement on their own. This perception reinforces negative perceptions of those at the bottom of the education pyramid: teachers, students, and parents.

The classroom is left straddled with the most direct, massive, and cumulative effects of external demands. Systems alignment has meant "teaching to the test," forcing schools and teachers to work in isolation, and competing rather than collaborating. Teacher isolation hinders problem solving, creation of supportive networks, and collective self-reflection (Sleeter, 1992).

This study supports the notion that what appears to be most important is what happens at the school level and how the district can support the school site. Sleeter (1992), among other educational researchers, sees the school rather than individual teachers, as the center of reform and recommends shifting the focus to the organizational arrangements, conditions, and processes at each building. She suggests turning the lens at the collective, people who work in schools, and the culture/climate they create, within the broader external context in which schools exist.

Further, this study reaffirms that educational reform must be grounded within individual schools and classrooms that need increased autonomy from external domination (Meier, 1995; Snyder et al., 2000), particularly domination based on fear. In the words of Meier (1995), it may be possible to have "schools that work" but that requires abandonment of the "stance of outsiders."

The state and districts appear primarily concerned with supervision of FCAT scores, rather than the Instruction, Resources, and Personnel required for effective school improvement. It was clearly perceived by the schools that the Sustaining Variables were not deemed as significant within the statemandated framework. The emergent framework is grounded on high vertical and horizontal alignment of internal accountability measures within each school. These schools had begun establishing these internal alignments and accountability networks before the statemandates, meaning that strong structural and supportive Core Values, grounded by a strong Culture/Climate, orchestrated the Organizing and Sustaining Variables. Rather than focusing initial and immediate attention on the upper parts of the tree, the findings of this study suggest priority development of strong and supportive root systems.

Further, since little vertical alignment was found between these high-performing schools and districts in the area of Instruction, one might presume that districts do not want to intervene in a system of instruction that worked well. In fact, it was found that in these high-performing schools educators had more autonomy, which empowered them to negotiate external intrusion and even "massage" instructional plans to fit their unique needs and reduce massive, regimented, student testing. While local autonomy is a requirement for school effectiveness, schools that do not meet externally imposed standards of achievement are indeed the ones most straddled with external domination and little ability to self-organize. Districts tend to reduce the demands placed on high-performing schools, allowing them more freedom to grow internally. Ironically, most high-performing schools tend to represent more affluent and mainstream White/Caucasian student populations that continue to enjoy greater self-determination and autonomy.

This study supports a holistic approach to school effectiveness and educational reform focusing deeply below the surface, on those not-so-apparent structures and processes, which hold the sustaining nutrients to keep the entire system moving in responsive directions. Those rushing to control and punish schools, teachers, and children simply do not understand the nature of schools as human energy systems, the significance of power relations in establishing healthy and strong core values, or the notion of schools as learning partnerships. They fail to understand that the nutrients of sustainable school progress are found in positive relationships, sharing of power and information, the valuing of others, and the building of strong, stable, and trusting relationships. They do not understand that there are no fixed recipes for success, only a philosophy that promotes additive schooling, includes professional respect and dedication, supports shared leadership, and the building of collective expertise (Neumann, King, & Rigdon, 1997).

References

Acker-Hocevar, M., & Touchton, D. (2002). How principals level the playing field of accountability in Florida's high poverty/low-performing schools: Part I: The intersection of high-stakes testing and effects of poverty on teaching and learning. *International Journal of Educational Reform, 11*(2), 106–24.

Banks, J. A. (2001). *Cultural diversity and education: Foundations, curriculum, and teaching.* Boston, MA: Allyn and Bacon.

Beck, L. (1994). *Reclaiming educational administration as a caring profession.* New York: Teachers College Press.

Brown, R. J., & Cornwall, J. R. (2000). *The entrepreneurial educator.* Lanham, MD: Scarecrow Press.

Carter, D. (1997). Information management for site based decision making in school improvement and change. *International Journal of Education Reform, 6,* 174–188.

Carter, S. C. (2000). *No excuses: Lessons from 21 high-performing, high poverty schools.* Washington, DC: Heritage Foundation.

Charles A. Dana Center, University of Texas at Austin. (1999). *Hope for urban education: A study of nine high-performing, high-poverty, urban elementary schools.* Washington, DC: U.S. Department of Education, Planning, and Evaluation Service.

Cummins, J. (1996). *Negotiating identities: Education for empowerment in a diverse society.* Ontario, CA: California Association for Bilingual Education.

Decker, L. & Decker, V. A. (2000). *Engaging families and communities: Pathways to educational success.* Fairfax, VA: National Community Education Association.

Edmonds, R. R. (1979). Some schools work and more can. *Social Policy, 9*(2), 28–32.

Education Commission of the States. (1998). *Turning around low-performing schools: A guide for state and local leaders:* Denver, CO: Author.

Elmore, R. F. (2000). *Building a new structure for school leadership.* Washington, DC: Albert Schanker Institute.

Espinoza-Herold, M. (2003). *Issues in Latino education: Race, school culture and the politics of academic success.* Boston, MA: Allyn and Bacon.

Meier, D. (1995). *The power of their ideas: A fiery manifesto for the salvation of public education.* Boston, MA: Beacon Press.

Merriam, S. B. (2001). *Qualitative research and case study applications in education.* San Francisco: Jossey-Bass.

Neumann, F. M., King, M. B., & Rigdon, M. (1997). Accountability and school performance: Implications from restructuring schools. *Harvard Educational Review, 67*(1), 41–74.

Nieto, S. (2001). *Affirming diversity* (3rd ed.). New York: Longman.

No Child Left Behind. Retrieved April 13, 2003 from www.NoChildLeftBehind.gov

Purkey, S. C., & Smith, M. S. (1993). Effective schools: A review. *Elementary School Journal, 83,* 427–452.

Scheurich, J. J. (1998). Highly successful and loving public elementary schools populated mainly by low-SES children of color. Core beliefs and cultural characteristics. *Urban Education, 33*(4), 451–491.

Scheurich, J. J. & Skrla, L. (2003). *Leadership for equity and excellence: Creating high-achievement classrooms, schools, and districts.*

Schoon, P., Wilson, C. L., Walker, D., Cruz-Janzen, M. I., & Acker-Hocevar, M. (2003). A systems alignment model for examining school practices that sustain standards based reforms in high poverty and English language learner schools. Paper presented at annual international conference of the American Educational Research Association (AERA), Chicago, Illinois.

Scribner, J. D., Young, M. D., & Pedroza, A. (1999). Building collaborative relationships with parents. In P. Reyes, J. D. Scribner, & A. Paredes Scribner (Eds.), *Lessons from high-performing Hispanic schools: Creating learning communities* (pp. 36–60). New York: Teachers College Press.

Senge, P. M. (1990). The fifth discipline: The art and practice of the learning organizations. New York: Doubleday.

Sergiovanni, T. J. (1994). *Building community in schools.* San Francisco: Jossey-Bass.

Siegel, D. (2003). *Performance-driven budgeting: The example of New York City's schools* (Report No. EDO-EA-03-05). East Lansing, MI: National Center for Research on Teacher Learning. (ERIC Document Reproduction Service No. ED474305).

Sleeter, C. (1992). *Keepers of the American dream: A study of staff development and multicultural education.* Washington, DC: The Falmer Press.

Snyder, K. J., Acker-Hocevar, M., & Snyder, K. M. (2000). *Living on the edge of chaos: Leading schools into the global age.* Milwaukee, WI: ASQ.

Spillane, J. P., Halverson, R., & Diamond, J. B. (2001). Investigating school leadership practice: A distributed perspective. *Educational Researcher, 30*(3), 23–38.

Spillane, J. P., & Seashore Louis, K. (2002). School improvement processes and practices: Professional learning for building instructional capacity. In J. Murphy (Ed.), *The Educational Leadership Challenge: Redefining Leadership for the 21st Century* (pp. 83–104). Chicago, IL: The University of Chicago Press.

State of Florida. (2003). *Florida school report.* Retrieved August 6, 2003, from http://www.firm.edu/doe/evaluation/home0018.htm

Teddlie, C., & Reynolds, D. (2000). *The international handbook of school effectiveness research.* New York: Falmer.

Valdés, G. (1996). *Con respeto: Bridging the distance between culturally diverse families and schools.* New York: Teachers College Press.

Valenzuela, A. (1999). *Subtractive schooling: U.S.-Mexican youth and the politics of caring.* Albany: State University of New York.

Wheatly, M. (1992). Leadership and the new science: Learning about organization from an orderly universe. San Francisco, CA: Berrett-Koelhler.

Wiggins, G. P., & McTighe, J. (1998). *Understanding by design.* Alexandria, VA: ASCD.

Yan, J. (1999). *What affects test scores?* Miami: Applied Sciences and Technology.

DR MICHELE ACKER-HOCEVAR Research focus on school organizations, school development, instructional leadership, and altering power relations, most especially for disadvantaged schools and communities. **DR. MARTA CRUZ-JANZEN** Research focus on impact of P/K-12 curricula on self-concept and academic achievement of students of color, reform of teacher preparation, and Latino racial identity development. **DR. CYNTHIA L. WILSON** Research interests include preparation for pre-service teachers and professional development for in-service teachers. Primary focus is literacy achievement of at risk-students and students with mild disabilities. **DR. PERRY SCHOON** Research interests in the area of mental modeling and expert systems. Co-author of "Instructional Technology, Process and Product." **DR. DAVID WALKER** Research interests in areas of research methodology, statistics, and K-12 teaching and learning reform.

From *International Journal of Learning,* Vol. 12, No. 10, 2005/2006, pp. 255–266. Copyright © 2006 by Common Ground Publishing, Melbourne Australia. Reprinted by permission.

Moment of Truth

A generation after white flight, districts continue to face awkward discussions and painful choices in an attempt to achieve diversity.

DEL STOVER

On a sunny morning at Omaha South High School, Principal Nancy Faber enters the performing arts wing to find a handful of students gathered around a piano. After a cheerful greeting and some lighthearted banter, the students cajole Faber into joining them in a rendition of country singer George Strait's "I Cross My Heart."

It's an idyllic scene. And as the group—white, black, and Hispanic—raises its collective voice in song, this inner-city magnet school achieves the highest aspirations of public education: children from all walks of life learning together in a safe, caring environment.

Such a school should be celebrated by its community. But for the better part of two years, the Omaha Public Schools and its surrounding suburban districts—indeed, much of Nebraska—have been engaged in a difficult and contentious debate over how much they value such racially integrated schools as Omaha South High, and what price they are willing to pay to achieve such integration.

For most Americans, the only part of the debate that's garnered attention was the state legislature's passage of a bill dividing Omaha into three distinct school districts. And that made headlines last spring because the statute implied the new districts might be organized along racial lines, a prospect that civil rights groups condemned as a return to state-sponsored racial segregation.

> **Omaha's real issue is the same one that confronts small metropolitan regions across the nation: What can policymakers do about the slow but steady migration of white and affluent families to outlying suburbs?**

There is much, much more to the story. Omaha's real issue is the same one that confronts small metropolitan regions across

the nation: What can policymakers do about the slow but steady migration of white and affluent families to outlying suburbs, a disturbing encore to the white flight that plagued larger cities in the 1970s and 1980s? It's a trend that's exacerbating racial and economic isolation in these small cities and making it harder for districts to promote diversity within the schools. What's more, it threatens to undermine the districts' academic success, for a host of reasons known all too well by educators.

"If there was such a thing as separate but equal, there wouldn't be these problems," says Myron Orfield, executive director of the University of Minnesota's Institute on Race and Poverty. But "that kind of segregation is wicked . . . absolutely devastating for children."

School officials are, of course, attempting to stem the tide. Most districts have instituted voluntary integration plans that rely on magnet schools or carefully drawn attendance boundaries to promote diversity. Yet, these efforts do not go unchallenged: Sometime in the coming months, the U.S. Supreme Court will rule on the constitutionality of race-based admissions policies in Seattle and Louisville, Ky., and, some fear, will narrow the options available to policymakers.

None of this bodes well for the future. If not schools, then what institution will prepare today's children to live and work successfully in a nation that's increasingly diverse racially? A generation after white flight ravaged many of the nation's largest urban school districts, both racially and economically, a number of small metropolitan areas are now facing, in the words of one education analyst, "their moment of truth."

The Perspective of Hindsight

If that moment hasn't yet arrived in Omaha, it's not far off. White enrollment in the 47,000-student district has fallen from 59.6 percent in 1997 to 42.7 percent today. Ten years ago, 22 schools had a minority-majority enrollment; today, there are 48. The Latino population has nearly tripled, and the number of English language learners now tops 6,000.

These demographics are far better than many small-city districts, and Omaha officials are making the most of them. Since the district ended mandatory busing for integration in 1999, Superintendent John Mackiel and the school board have put together an impressive network of academically themed magnet schools to encourage students and parents to make the cross-town trip to neighborhoods unlike their own.

Omaha South is one example. Housing information technology and visual/performing arts magnet programs, the older building on the city's poor, eastern side has been extensively remodeled. It now features modern computer labs, a small aquarium, an auditorium and stage, and even a practice room for ballet dancers. The neighborhood may be poor, but its hallways are filled with children of all races and income levels. "People are blown away when they visit," Faber says. "They don't expect an inner-city school to have such facilities."

Still, officials can do little about the changes taking place outside the school doors. Although redevelopment is under way on the city's riverfront, much of the region's growth is centered to the west of Omaha's boundaries. While surrounding school districts are seeing shopping malls and residential subdivisions build up their tax bases, the inner city must rely on older downtown neighborhoods, some dominated by dilapidated storefronts, liquor stores, and abandoned car lots.

Part of the problem stems from mistakes made decades ago. In the 1970s, as court-ordered desegregation loomed, distracted Omaha school officials failed to invoke an 1891 law that allowed the school system to grow with the city. So, as the city annexed new territory and expanded its tax base, the surrounding school districts not only stayed in business, but also flourished. Now the Omaha school district is hemmed in, with potentially dire financial consequences.

Although Omaha's growth constraints are self-inflicted, its dilemma is common, Orfield says. In the Northeast and Midwest, state legislatures decades ago limited the annexation powers of cities, allowing them to be hemmed in by incorporated suburbs. "Particularly in predominately black cities, it was one of the factors that contributed to their financial woes."

It may take another decade or two, but Mackiel foresees a dangerous convergence of trends. Although the district's finances today do not significantly trail those of its suburban counterparts, rising poverty levels could impact the tax base and threaten future revenues. And that would come at a time when Omaha will be asked to educate even greater numbers of disadvantaged students.

"The bottom line is this school district has all the ingredients to go the way of many large-city school systems," Mackiel says. "The fact is that we'll be unable to integrate our schools in five years, 10 years, 15 years. . . . Ought we not be planning and engaging in a comprehensive conversation of what we expect?"

Perceptions and Politics

The answer, of course, is rhetorical, for Omaha officials already see signs that public confidence in the city schools is not what it should be. Although the city boasts many excellent schools, and its overall performance is better than that of most metropolitan school systems, the lackluster performance of its low-income students undermines its attractiveness to new families. School officials report stories of real estate agents who steer families to neighborhoods outside the district. Under the state's generous school choice program, the number of students living inside Omaha's boundaries who commute to suburban districts increased almost five-fold—from 744 to 3,529—in the past eight years.

That figure underscores another danger facing smaller urban centers: Perceptions are as damaging as reality. Long ago, the Little Rock, Ark., school district lost many white students to private and suburban schools because of concerns about the quality of the predominately black city schools. It's a phenomenon that many argue can become a self-fulfilling prophecy: Once enough middle-class families move out, the schools' test scores drop and academic expectations fall.

None of this surprises Glenn Singleton, executive director of the Pacific Educational Group, a San Francisco-based consulting firm that helps school policymakers meet the needs of minority students. His experience is that white parents in many metropolitan areas never seriously consider enrolling their children in the city school system.

"When a white family," he says, "looks at that high-performing school of color . . . that urban magnet that's an amazing school, there is still the question: 'Do I want to send my child here?'"

For years, Mackiel says, school officials sought to engage suburban and state policymakers in a dialogue about what could be done to ensure Omaha didn't go the way of many big city districts. But, he says, they made no headway. In the short term, Omaha had enough money to get the job done. The suburbs saw no problems ahead. The district concerns fell on deaf ears—until, frustrated, the school board filed suit in 2003 challenging the state's funding formula.

The lawsuit did nothing to win friends in the state legislature. But, in June 2005, the district escalated matters when it shocked the region with a "one city, one school district" proposal, dusting off the long-ignored annexation law to take control of large parts of neighboring districts with valuable real estate within Omaha city limits.

If school officials seriously thought they could win that annexation fight—or at least pressure policymakers into concessions—they badly miscalculated. Initially blindsided, suburban officials soon expressed outrage and defiance at what they saw as a heavy-handed attempt to solve Omaha's problems at the expense of their communities. "The cordial nature and willingness to talk on any level deteriorated significantly," recalls Brian Hale, communications director of the Nebraska Association of School Boards. "Last year, everybody was giving everybody the silent treatment."

But it was the state legislature that ultimately dropped the biggest bombshell on the region. As Omaha and its neighbors bickered and threatened litigation, Ron Raikes, chair of the Senate Education Committee, joined forces with Sen. Ernie Chambers, the state's only black lawmaker and a long-time Omaha Public Schools critic, to champion LB 1024. The bill

Providing a "Social Context" for Diversity

For all the talk about preparing young people for a racially diverse society—as well as a competitive global economy—the nation still struggles to provide students with more learning opportunities alongside those of different races, cultures, and life experiences.

A half century after *Brown v. Board of Education* broke down state-sanctioned segregation, and with the rolls of minority students expanding, more children than ever attend "multiracial" schools—those with at least three minority groups of 10 percent or more. That's the good news.

But alarmingly, the numbers of students segregated along racial or economic lines also is growing. Nearly 40 percent of black and Latino minorities attend schools that are 90 percent or more minority, according to *Looking to the Future,* a 2005 report by the NAACP Legal Defense and Educational Fund, the Civil Rights Project at Harvard University, and the Center for the Study of Race and Law at the University of Virginia Law School. Meanwhile, it reports, whites are among the most segregated of students.

Forces outside the control of local school boards—segregated housing, white flight, and growing poverty in metropolitan areas, to name just a few—are largely to blame. But, if school officials cannot directly influence policies in this area, they can speak up about the value of promoting student diversity—and the dangers to this nation in allowing segregation to take hold.

Some education observers suggest the future of the nation and its democratic system may depend in part on integrated schools. Edwin C. Darden, director of education policy for Appleseed, a Washington, D.C., public interest group, says children who grow up in racial isolation will be ill equipped to deal with the diversity of tomorrow—either in the workplace or in the political arena.

"If public education doesn't provide a social context, then we're going to have massive misunderstandings down the road," says Darden, who also writes the "School Law" column for *ASBJ.* "If children have no direct experience with people who are different from them, then it's going to be very, very easy for them 10 to 20 years hence, when they've got power and decision-making authority, to be callous and to deal with stereotypes rather than seeing folks as real, sensitive human beings."

National polls show that most citizens recognize the value of school integration. Yet, ironically, parental calls for school districts to create "neighborhood schools" work against efforts to use carefully crafted school boundaries and magnet programs to encourage diversity.

Such calls also overlook some of the lessons of *Brown.* Part of the legal reasoning of that landmark court case had nothing to do with the historically inferior resources devoted to minority children, notes *Looking to the Future,* Racial isolation also diminishes access to peers and parents with high educational expectations, community resources, and a network of contacts with the resources to help students get post-secondary opportunities.

"After the influence of family income, the support and success of [your] peers is your most powerful predictor of whether you go on to college and beyond," adds Myron Orfield, executive director of the University of Minnesota's Institute on Race and Poverty. "It's a tremendously important thing. It's a system that is moving the city in the right direction. It doesn't pull everyone along equally. It's not a panacea. But it increases the odds of kids being pulled through the system and getting a good job."

In its *amicus* brief to the U.S. Supreme Court, which is reviewing race-based school admissions policies in Seattle and Louisville, Ky., the National School Boards Association argued that school boards and their local communities should be left to make the decisions regarding this important educational role of diversity.

But whatever the court ruling, school officials will always continue to face their biggest challenge: convincing parents to overcome racial stereotypes and support voluntary integration plans. In Omaha, as in so many school districts around the nation, high-quality magnet programs have made a difference in integrating the schools—and have changed some attitudes.

Eight years ago, when Principal Cara Churchich-Riggs was first given the task of converting Omaha's Beveridge Middle School into an arts and global studies magnet, she encountered community unease at the idea. Today, she gets calls from parents looking to enroll their students because of the diverse learning environment.

"After that initial reaction, everyone learned it worked fine or they just refused to accept it and jumped over to the districts that look like what their children look like."

sought to resolve many of the issues in the debate by forcing Omaha and 10 adjacent school districts into a regional "learning community" that would share tax money and coordinate a metropolitan-area school integration initiative.

A late-breaking amendment to the bill ultimately threw a monkey wrench into its chances of acceptance. The amendment called for the breakup of Omaha into three new districts, but language concerning how new district lines would be drawn, along with comments by lawmakers during debate, suggested the city schools could be divided along white, black, and Hispanic lines.

Issues Not Discussed

Opponents to the amended bill seized upon that interpretation to draw national attention to Omaha, which ultimately led to lawsuits that have prevented the plan's implementation. As a result, state lawmakers started this year's legislative session with an assortment of bills revisiting the issues. Some would repeal LB 1024; others would tweak it. At the beginning of the session, Chambers was pushing forward with his efforts to break up the Omaha school district.

A 37-year veteran of the Senate, Chambers has views that could hold sway in the final outcome of this debate. And, unlike many lawmakers, he's doesn't sugarcoat his opinions. For instance, he dismisses outright the arguments of the NAACP and other civil rights groups that condemn LB 1024 as segregationist. He says he's not interested in talk of segregation—or integration.

"I'm interested in quality education," he says.

That message strikes a chord with more people than education policymakers sometimes like to admit. Despite polls showing strong support for school diversity efforts, the decisions parents make about where to enroll their children suggest otherwise. Many white and affluent minority families aren't interested in integration, Orfield says. Their interest is simply in the best educational opportunities for their children. That opinion also holds sway in minority communities, where black parents remember that their peers were usually the ones bused across town in the name of integration. Today's rallying cry is neighborhood schools.

Another way to describe the phenomenon is what Joe White, chairman of the school board in Charlotte, N.C., calls "me-ism." Rather than consider the greater good of the community, White says parents take a myopic view. He points to the 1999 court ruling that forced Charlotte to stop using a race-based admissions policy and led to a return to neighborhood schools. The result: growing segregation.

The same dynamic has been seen in countless communities across the nation and led to the Supreme Court's consideration of voluntary integration plans in Seattle and Louisville. The court's decision, expected by June, could have a dramatic effect on how schools assign students to achieve diversity.

In Omaha, Chambers argues that policymakers are just playing at the edges of the issue. The metropolitan area is clearly divided along racial lines, with one school district that is practically surrounded by Omaha Public Schools, yet specifically protected from annexation by special legislation. No one, he says, complained when white policymakers took control of the education of their children.

"When black people aspire to the same thing," he says, "it's called segregation."

Indeed, examine the debate in Omaha and what stands out are the issues of race that go undiscussed. While policymakers would be quick to denounce an overt act of racism, more subtle forms get little more than a nod of acknowledgment. There's plenty of talk about the need to close the racial achievement gap, but little is said about tackling the social and economic forces that perpetuate that gap. Much is argued about whether a racially segregated school district needs more money to succeed, but no serious effort is made to redress funding differences between rich and poor districts. And where is the talk about dealing with segregated housing or encouraging reinvestment in the city's older neighborhoods?

"We are just so ill-equipped to have a conversation on race," Singleton adds. "We tend to be a country that goes into this conversation only when we're on fire—literally."

For all the mishaps and controversy, school officials in the Omaha area have come to some agreement about the future. Alarm about LB 1024's usurpation of local control has outweighed feelings of betrayal and anger, and after tempers cooled, 10 of the 11 metropolitan area superintendents got together and hammered out a legislative package they hope state lawmakers will endorse as an alternative approach to future integration issues. The package keeps Omaha's boundaries intact.

For Superintendent Keith Lutz of the Millard School District, the past two years have taken their toll. "Anyone who says there's no emotion in policymaking would be in error," says Lutz, whose district borders Omaha on the western side. "There are always emotions. To say the trust level is fully restored would be a mistake, too. But we all know this is a fragile situation. We've tried to eliminate all the noise and, as superintendents, sit down and try to work for the betterment of kids in our area."

Sandra Jensen, chair of the Omaha school board, says there's a lesson to be learned about how to address tough issues. "Sometimes you have to put on the table topics that are not popular but need to be discussed. You need to put things down that make people uncomfortable," she says. "But I do think that, once good people are given the opportunity and the time to get through a bit of consternation, they will sit down and have a dialogue."

It's not clear how the superintendents' plan will fare. Senators Raikes and Chambers have their own ideas. But, at least, the challenges facing the metropolitan area are on the bargaining table. With luck, a sensible plan will give Omaha a chance to beat the odds and perhaps provide the nation with a model for the future.

DEL STOVER (dstover@nsba.org) is a senior editor of *American School Board Journal.*

In Urban America, Many Students Fail to Finish High School

Faced with a deteriorating pipeline of students, colleges in cities like Compton, Calif., struggle to serve their local neighborhoods.

KARIN FISCHER

Edith J. Negrete's big dreams defy her modest means. In those dreams, Ms. Negrete is an anesthesiologist, earning a comfortable salary that pays for a fancy car and a nice home for her 8-year-old son, Joshua.

Her reality is more complicated. Ms. Negrete, who dropped out of high school at age 15 to get married, recently lost her job as a clerk at a moving company here and has moved in with her father to make ends meet. Now 27, she is raising Joshua on her own and getting a divorce from her husband, who is in prison.

But Ms. Negrete says she has hope for the future, in the form of the local community college, El Camino College Compton Center. Inspired by a former co-worker, who studied for a psychology degree during lunch breaks, Ms. Negrete enrolled at the college three years ago. Eventually, she wants to transfer to the University of California at Los Angeles.

"As you get older, you really know what you want," says Ms. Negrete, who is the first in her family to attend college. "Once you have an education, have a paper in your hand, then a lot of doors open."

The situation Ms. Negrete faced mirrors what is happening in low-income urban centers across America. Hindered by poor-performing public schools, many residents drop out before earning a high-school diploma, and with it, the all-important ticket to the bevy of higher-education institutions often located in and around urban areas.

In this Southern California city, part of an arc of low-income neighborhoods on Los Angeles' southern tier, only one-third of residents 25 years or older are high-school graduates; fewer than seven in 100 have a bachelor's degree. Nationwide, 84 percent of Americans hold a high-school diploma, and 27 percent are four-year-college graduates.

Faced with that deteriorating pipeline, urban colleges, both two-year and four-year, have struggled to serve large swaths of their local neighborhoods. Just 382 Compton students attend the nearest California State University campus, at Dominguez Hills, making up about 4 percent of the undergraduate population

there, while 134 go to the campus in Long Beach, accounting for less than 1 percent of its student body. As for UCLA, Ms. Negrete's top choice, just seven of the university's nearly 25,000 undergraduates are from Compton.

Even as a college degree becomes an ever more indispensable vehicle out of poverty, the share of English-language learners, members of racial and ethnic minorities, and other groups historically underrepresented in higher education is growing in inner-city schools. The small number of students who enroll in college often struggle to succeed, battling poor preparation and juggling work and family responsibilities. And factors outside the classroom can also depress scholastic achievement. This fall alone, Compton's public-school district was notified of 460 new foster-care placements among its students.

"Increasingly, there is a gulf between the haves and the have-nots," says Houston D. Davis, project director for the national Educational Needs Index, which paints a county-by-county portrait based on educational, economic, and population data. "In cities . . . there are pockets, there are populations, that have very real needs, and those needs are getting greater."

Changing Expectations

The Compton Unified School District's slogan is "excellence in progress," and, by many measures, the city schools have far to go. The district's graduation rate lags behind the statewide average. Twenty-five percent of students drop out before graduation day. Fewer than a quarter of high-school seniors complete requirements for admission to either of California's two public-university systems, and just 27 percent of students who graduated last spring went on to a four-year college.

Despite those daunting numbers, Jesse L. Gonzales, the district's superintendent, says he wants to send the message that a college degree can open doors beyond Compton, where the unemployment rate is 11 percent, well above the national average. Partnerships have been established with local colleges, and liaisons have been appointed at each of the district's three high schools to help parents, most of whom never attended college, understand the college application process. When Mr. Gonzales visits Compton elementary schools, he says, his question to students is, "Where are you going to college?"

"It is better to set standards too high and miss them," he says, "than to set them too low and hit them."

On the face of it, Compton graduates have a multitude of postsecondary options—after all, Los Angeles County is home to more than 50 two- and four-year colleges.

But the factors holding inner-city students back can be both practical and parochial. Many Compton students are illegal residents and are not eligible for state or federal financial aid. For others, earning an immediate paycheck is more important than an eventual degree, while some struggle to balance work schedules, child care, and a three-bus commute.

For first-generation students, the "nuts and bolts" of applying for college admission and financial aid can also be a deterrent, says Robert L. Caret, president of the Coalition of Urban and Metropolitan Universities, a group of colleges that are located in, and primarily draw from, metropolitan areas.

"No one in their family or their peer group has done it, and they don't know how to begin," says Mr. Caret, who is president of Towson University, near Baltimore.

Beating the Odds

At Compton High School, every morning before classes begin, the principal, Jesse Jones, stands outside its gates, greeting each student with a booming "Good morning." He says he never misses a day.

"Many of these kids have no stability in their lives," says Mr. Jones, who came out of retirement three years ago to run the school. "It's about the image you are sending. They have to start believing in you."

The students streaming onto the campus look very much like the population of Compton as a whole. Nearly 69 percent are Hispanic, and 29 percent are black. One-third speak English as a second language.

Originally a predominantly white, middle-class community, which counts the former president George H.W. Bush among its past residents, the complexion of the area has changed significantly in recent decades. By the 1970s, the city's population was largely African-American. Today an influx of immigrants, mainly from Mexico, and the migration of Latino families from elsewhere in the Los Angeles metropolitan region have led to rapid growth of the Hispanic population, especially among school-age children.

Compton's changing demographics have brought special challenges. Although the student body is now predominantly Latino, much of the district's staff is black. In some cases, that has meant retraining teachers to adjust to students' new learning styles.

Under the now five-year watch of Mr. Gonzales, the superintendent, more Advanced Placement and college-preparatory classes have been added to the curricula of the high schools, while the most academically at-risk ninth-grade students have been singled out for extra instruction in reading and mathematics.

Students in kindergarten through the third grade have two hours of "protected" reading time each day.

There is some evidence that Mr. Gonzales's efforts are working: Since 2002, Compton students have shown improvement on California's two statewide accountability assessments.

Second Chances

Ms. Negrete says she didn't get that kind of encouragement when she went to public school here. Now she is trying to give her son the kind of support she never received. Joshua, she says proudly, is at the top of his class and wants to be an archaeologist. Occasionally, when her aunt cannot watch him, Joshua comes with her to classes at El Camino College Compton Center.

"Sometimes he complains," she says, "but I tell him that if you want to succeed, you have to have a degree."

With busy schedules and sometimes unreliable child care, Ms. Negrete is not alone in bringing a child with her to classes on the campus. On a recent sunny day, students' children darted across the college's sunny courtyard as a live band played a rollicking beat. The occasion was Fiesta Latina, part study break, part celebration of the college's continued existence after its predecessor, Compton Community College, lost its accreditation last July. Faculty and staff members joined the queue for homemade tostadas and pupusas, gathering in small clusters to scoop the food off paper plates.

"It would have been a disaster if the college had closed," says Hilda Gaytan, president of the student government, which sponsored the event. Ms. Gaytan, 50 and a Mexican immigrant, came to Compton Community College after she lost her job in the garment industry three years ago. "We all came here for a second chance."

The community college has been providing second chances to students in Compton and the surrounding towns for nearly 80 years. The community's pride in the college is palpable. Everyone, it seems, knows a young person who appeared destined to go down the wrong path but was turned around by Compton Community College professors. At night, residents stroll the parklike campus, a safety zone in a city that last year ranked as one of the nation's deadliest, with 72 murders for 97,833 residents.

In 2002, voters in Compton, where the per capita income is just $12,617, voted overwhelmingly for a $100-million bond, essentially taxing themselves for the next two decades to pay for new classroom buildings and a tutoring facility on the campus. But the amount of revenue from all sources that Compton is able to spend is about 10 percent below that of other California community colleges.

A Community's College

Community colleges in urban areas often face a struggle to make ends meet, says Alicia C. Dowd, an assistant professor of education at the University of Southern California. Ms. Dowd has found that community colleges in large cities have per-student revenues 13 percent to 18 percent lower than two-year colleges elsewhere.

Part of the reason for that, she says, is that urban colleges often lack the political clout to fight for larger state appropriations. They also might not have skilled administrators who can compete for grants from private foundations or federal and state governments.

Federal student-aid policy can also work against some types of urban postsecondary institutions, says John B. Lee, an education consultant. He notes that for-profit colleges have been pulling out of central cities since a change in financial-aid rules in the 1990s made serving at-risk students with high student-loan default rates too costly. The percentage of full-time students enrolled in proprietary schools in cities declined by 11 percent between 1996 and 2000. Meanwhile, enrollments at for-profit institutions in suburban areas increased 18 percent during the same period.

Mr. Lee says he is concerned that the loss of these institutions, which frequently offered training programs that lasted just a few months, leaves inner-city students with fewer educational options. "I worry these students are being abandoned," he says.

In Compton, an agreement to combine Compton Community College with El Camino College ensured a continued local higher-education presence in the city. The accreditation fight ended in July when Compton officials decided to drop their appeal of the decision a year earlier by the Western Association of Schools and Colleges' Accrediting Commission for Community and Junior Colleges. But that battle the subsequent merger have left a bitter taste with some city residents. They question whether El Camino, with its largely middle-class, transfer-oriented student body, can be sensitive to the needs and to the challenges of the Compton community, where students are far more likely to be pursuing a vocational degree or certification.

Because only courses approved for El Camino can be offered at the Compton center, this fall's session began without a number of basic-skills and English-language courses or its popular licensed vocational nurse-training program. (The center has since entered into an agreement with another area college, Los Angeles Trade-Technical College, to offer the practical-nursing program, and El Camino is fast-tracking approval of about 20 courses before the next semester.)

"This is our community's college," says Bruce A. Boyden, a graduate of the college and a member of the Committee to Save the Compton Community College District, a group that pushed for the college to remain independent. "Compton took disenfranchised young people and empowered them to become employable in the community in which they live. At El Camino, they are preparing doctors, lawyers, and Indian chiefs."

A Basic-Skills Gantlet

But if Compton is the community's college, it is also a reflection of the community's struggles.

One out of every five courses taken at the college is a basic-skills course. In all of California, by contrast, remedial math and writing courses account for only about 7 percent of community-college enrollment. What's more, many students appear to become mired in these remedial courses without ever making it to for-credit course work. Only about one-quarter of Compton College students who took a basic-skills class in their first year took and passed a college-level course in the same subject area within three years.

The last three years for Ms. Negrete, for instance, have largely been catching up. She is also pursuing her general-equivalency diploma and estimates it will take her another two years before she has earned the credits to transfer to a four-year college.

Becoming bogged down in remedial courses can discourage students from earning a community-college degree or going on to a four-year university, says Estela Mara Bensimon, director of the Center for Urban Education at the University of Southern California.

"The biggest barrier to success for black and Latino community-college students is basic skills," says Ms. Bensimon. "Basic skills is a gantlet."

At Compton Community College, that problem was exacerbated because writing was not integrated throughout the curriculum, says Toni Wasserberger, a professor of English at the college. Instead, many faculty members would rely on other measures of assessment, such as multiple-choice exams or short-answer responses.

As a solution, college officials decided to pair a number of courses in the English department, including some at the basic-skills level, with some in other disciplines, including history, psychology, and even math. Students take the paired courses, which have complementary syllabi and writing assignments that reinforce each other, during the same semester. The two professors leading each course review students' papers and general progress together.

With the upheaval at the college over the last two years, it is difficult to accurately measure the success of the linked courses, says Ms. Wasserberger, a tiny woman with hip eyeglasses and energy to spare. Some students, she notes, had to drop out of the linked program because of the difficulty of taking two classes while working full time.

Still, for Ms. Wasserberger, who has been at the college since 1970, helping at-risk community-college students succeed seems to be as much of an art as a science.

A student wanders into the English department's outer office, interrupting Ms. Wasserberger midthought. "Just a minute," she says, "I've got to go give this student a hug."

The student, a slender woman who appears to be in her late 20s, is equally effusive. "You're my mentor," she says, before seeking some advice on English course offerings. After she leaves, Ms. Wasserberger returns to her seat.

"She was in my class," Ms. Wasserberger says of the student. "She literally could not write a sentence."

"You don't make up for what they didn't have," she says. "You make progress."

UNIT 5

Expanding Learning with Language and Literacy

Unit Selections

Key Points to Consider

- What are effective ways to assess language literacy development?

- What is unique about second language literacy development in urban classrooms?

- Explain the difference between language input and language output.

- Why is it important to introduce controversial literature to middle school students?

- How can teachers incorporate controversial literature comfortably into their classrooms and curriculum?

- How does reading Arab children's literature help today's students?

- How is Chica Lit the same as other forms of literature? Why are the similarities useful to readers?

- How is Chica Lit different from other forms of literature? How do the differences stretch the learning?

Student Website
www.mhcls.com

Internet Reference

United States Department of Education, Office of English Language Acquisition
http://www.ed.gov/about/offices/list/oela/index.html

Language development and communication proficiency entail one's ability to think, view, listen, speak, read, and write. Learning requires a great amount of vocabulary and articulation as we acquire new knowledge, skills, and dispositions in multiple contexts; apply the newness to our individual lives at school, at home, at work, at play, to solve immediate problems, and for future reference; and we appreciate the fresh information, access, and opportunities that open doors for us cognitively, physically, affectively, and socially. We expand our language development and communication proficiency every day through the ideas and insights gained from formal and informal interactions along with various forms of text and text connections to express and exchange our discoveries. Through language and communication individuals find strengths, success, and satisfaction.

Every person is engaged in language development throughout his or her life. Not only is the wealth of words in the English language overflowing, new words are added to our vocabularies every day. Given the sundry registers of language allowing us to communicate effectively and efficiently at formal functions, during informal interactions, with job-specific jargon, and so forth, everyone is constantly discovering new words to learn, use, and enjoy.

In the United States, the English language incorporates words from many other languages. As we enrich our abilities to speak English, we realize that we have acquired vocabulary from around the world. Some words commonly used in the English language have no translation from their original languages, so English speakers incorporate those words comfortably and competently. The same outcomes occur as we expand our language and communications through the cell telephone and Internet.

Likewise, we have developed an abundance of words, phrases, accents, and dialects that are unique to specific groups of people, careers, and geographic areas found across the United States. For example, we readily detect someone from Massachusetts, Georgia, or Texas. Although we are attempting to communicate with one another and frequently share the same message, the phrases used on the east coast, mid south, deep south, the southwest, and the west coast may differ from one another. It can be both fun and frustrating to glean the meaning.

The United States is filled with people from many countries; the country began as a refuge for immigrants. Thus, there are many people who speak many different languages. When young people who do not speak English proficiently go to school, the teachers must employ their expertise in providing specific instruction. Many teacher education programs are expanding to include/require courses in English language learning so teachers can help all learners. Young people who have immigrated to the United States are challenged in their abilities to communicate with people in their new communities. Like everyone else in the United States, English language learners are attempting to balance maintenance of their own cultures and family structures while learning new customs and community structures. The challenges for the learners, their

© Blend Images/Getty Images

families, the schools, and the teachers are intense; the conversations have escalated to involve educators, communities, and politicians and will continue into the future.

The conversations related to ELL is not limited to immigrants. Sadly, although native English speakers, many people in the United States are weak in their abilities to use the English language well and communicate effectively. Again, through the power of the "generational perpetuation of practice," young people tend to acquire their primary abilities to develop language and communicate proficiently from their parents and families rather from their teachers and other educated role models. Young people echo the dialects, vocabulary, and communication skills found in their immediate circles and cultures. Teachers may attempt to introduce new vocabulary and expand upon young people's abilities to express themselves effectively, but familial influences tend to dominate.

To experience language development and communication proficiency first hand, people should read a wide variety of text. The sources are endless. By reading both nonfiction and fiction, we explore spaces from the past, present, and future, delving into the lives of many different people, real and imaginary. Through literature, we experience the descriptions and adventures first hand, as if we were there. We see exactly what the characters see or what the author wants us to see; we hear their conversations and language or what the author wants us to hear. When the literature is accompanied by a reader or a recording, we get to hear the dialogue, vocabulary, and accents exactly as the author meant for the story to be understood. The same discoveries apply to the photographs, drawings, and illustrations found in the literature. We are provided more clues to better comprehending the communication.

Literature of all kinds should be used in all classrooms to inform, instruct, and inspire students. Textbooks are read primarily to inform students about content knowledge. Assignments usually include instructions for students read as they practice specific skills. And literature, in all its various forms, is used to inspire students. Most students find it much easier to read a fictional story or book to contextualize and comprehend all of the details associated with people, places, things, and events, especially people, places, things, and events with which we are not familiar or do not understand from reading a textbook.

For example, the social studies textbook may include a page about World War II and the dropping of the bombs on Japan. However, reading the books *Hiroshima* (1954) by John Hersey or *Sadako* (1993) written by Eleanor Coerr and illustrated by Ed Young gives the reader more insight, satisfying all the senses to another place and times that most social studies textbooks and teachers cannot convey.

Integrating literature with social studies, teachers can incorporate literacy by asking students to write one of many different kinds of assignments. Math, science, technology, the fine arts, and multicultural education all fit with this unit too. The learning becomes much more inviting, exciting, and igniting as students connect with the various forms of text and one another to express and exchange their new learning.

The articles in Unit 5 probe topics and issues related to English language learning at multiple levels, dual language programs in early childhood programs, and children's and young people's literature that honor and respect students' intellect and culture.

Examining Second Language Literacy Development in an Urban Multi-Age Classroom

Sharon H. Ulanoff et al.

This paper describes a multi-year ethnographic study of literacy instruction for English language learners (ELLs) in a multi-age classroom in Los Angeles. This study was undertaken by three university professors and one of the two teachers of the multi-age classroom. Data collection began in July 2003 and initially focused on exploring the nature of literacy instruction in this classroom. Second-year data collection explored teacher and student discourse during classroom activities, focusing on teacher-student discourse and student-student discourse. This study is guided by the following question: *How does the multiage experience impact second language literacy learning for urban elementary school students in Los Angeles?*

This work is situated in a growing body of research that describes benefits and challenges for multi-age education (Anderson and Pavan, 1993; Chase and Doan, 1996; Guitierrez and Slavin, 1992; 1994; Lauer, 2000; Lloyd, 1999) and explores the implications for English literacy instruction for ELLs. Given the recent incarnation of the reading wars nationwide (Allington, 2002; Allington and Woodside-Jiron, 1999; Coles, 2000; Foorman, Fletcher, Francis, and Schatschneider, 2000; Garan, 2002) and a political move toward an English only ideology in the United States (see Crawford, 2000; García and Curry-Rodriguez, 2000; Ulanoff and Vega-Castaneda, 2003), it is important to look at ways to provide opportunities for social interaction that embed literacy instruction in context for those students learning to read and write in their second language L2.

It is also influenced by the literature that explores the ways in which teachers' and students' discourse patterns in classroom lessons and other interactions influence student learning (Cazden, 1988; Gutierrez, Rymes, and Larson, 1995). Within the framework of sociolinguistics and sociocognitive theory, it is argued that student learning is positively related to students' ". . . appropriation of social discourses" (Hicks, 1996, p. 105), which occurs as they participate in classroom interactions. Hicks (1996) suggests that "discourse is a central means through which new understandings are negotiated among participants" (p. 105). Gee (1996) further argues that students use language as a social tool to help them accomplish interactional tasks in order to internalize learning (p. 274). As students are scaffolded through the learning process by either teachers or more capable peers (Vygotsky, 1962) they are able to make meaning out of the interactions.

In addition to providing a variety of opportunities for teacher and student interactions, multi-age classrooms may have positive implications for English literacy learning and instruction for ELLs. Peer teaching and cross-age tutoring have been shown to be highly effective approaches for ELLs because they allow them to utilize language in a social and academic context thereby enhancing their overall language skills while maintaining a high degree of age-appropriate content area instruction (Johnson, 1988). They further allow for students to interact in multiple ways related to classroom discourse, specifically student and teacher talk.

Methodology

Data were collected at La Nieta School, an urban elementary school on a multi-track year-round calendar. La Nieta School has a student population of 96% Latinos, 3% African American and the rest a mix of other ethnicities. Seventy-nine percent of the students are labeled English language learners (ELLs) and 98% of the students at La Nieta receive free and reduced lunch. The neighborhood consists of both single-family homes and multiple family dwellings that were built decades ago. La Nieta School has an active relationship with a local university. There is also a Parent Center on campus. Many of the teachers at La Nieta are bilingual and others hold certification that allows them to teach ELLs.

Data were collected by three researchers from a local university who served as non-participant observers in the classroom as well as by the two classroom teachers who acted as complete participants (Gold, 1958; Junker, 1960) for a period of three years beginning in July 2003 and ending in April 2006. Instruction was provided in English at all times, although Spanish was used as needed to clarify concepts or explain unknown vocabulary. Students generally enter the class in kindergarten and exit at the end of second grade. The classroom teachers had worked together in the multi-age classroom for nine years at the time the research study began.

At the beginning of the first year of study there were thirty-six students (29 English language learners and 7 English only learners) in the classroom community, 22 boys and 14 girls. There were twelve five-years olds, eight six-years olds and sixteen seven-years olds. Although the students were technically divided between the two teachers into separate class rosters, they functioned as one classroom with students moving fluidly between two connecting rooms to form the multi-age classroom. While the demographics of the class at the beginning of the second and third years of study were similar, there was a dramatic shift in the classroom population throughout the second and third years.

Beginning in July 2003, the classroom was observed once weekly by one or more of the researchers for a minimum of two hours to a maximum of the full day. Second year data collection included twice-monthly observations. Third year data collection consisted of sporadic observations to collect data to support data gathered during the first two years. Multiple data sources were collected to develop an in-depth understanding of the culture of the multi-age classroom. Ethnographic field notes, audio and video recordings, and student artifacts were collected (Emerson, Fretz, and Shaw, 1995) during each observation. Students were interviewed periodically as deemed necessary. The researchers met with the teachers formally and informally throughout the project, as a means of conducting member checks during the data collection and analysis phase of the study, allowing the researchers to clarify and/or modify any interpretations and conclusions they had drawn. The interview data served to enrich and triangulate the findings (Merriam, 1995).

The data were analyzed, categorized, compared, and contrasted using a methodology that seeks to "elicit meaning from the data" (LeCompte & Preissle, 1993, p. 235), rather than codifying and computing it, as well as the construction of categories or domains (Spradley, 1980). A domain analysis was used to sort the data into multiple categories, allowing a portrait to emerge that is reflective of the "big picture" of the literacy practices being utilized in the classroom (Frank, 1999).

Initial data collection focused on examining the construction of practice in the classroom. The second year of the study focused on the collection and analysis of the discourse taking place within the classroom between the student/s and teacher/s, the teacher and teacher and the student/s and other student/s. Using a meaning-based definition of discourse "as

a socially and culturally organized way of speaking through which particular functions are realized" (Schriffen, 1994, p. 32), allowed the researchers to move from a strict analysis of conversation to a view of discourse as socially-situated within a particular time, place and context adding richness to the data. While sociocultural theory (Jennings and Di, 1996; Rommetveit, 1974; Vygotsky, 1962; Wertsch, 1984) formed the foundation for the study, activity theory (Engestrom and Middleton, 1996; Leont'ev, 1978; Rogoff, 1990) provided a lens through which to view and understand the interactions and activities taking place within the learning situation.

Findings

Several overarching themes serve as the context for instruction in this multi-age classroom. First, Susan and Richard focus on allowing students to make meaning of school activities, learn and use literacy in meaningful ways, while connecting new learning to prior knowledge. By design they create spaces for L2 literacy development by creating a safe classroom environment where students are free to take risks with their learning and become valuable members of the classroom community. The following themes emerged that describe the structures in place that impact the creation of that community.

Community and Respect

Students in this multi-age classroom develop a sense of community and belonging from the first day they enter the classroom. There is an instructional focus on community and respect. Returning students are expected to be role models for newcomers. There is an equal level of respect for all community members, whether they are newcomers, teachers or returning students; everyone is important rather than no one is important. For example, during one lesson, Susan was listening to a student talk when Richard walked over to ask her a question. Susan looked at Richard and said, "Excuse me, but I am listening to Viviana (a pseudonym for one of the multiage students) now so I can't talk to you at this moment," indicating to students their equal status. This incident is only one example. Similar events take place throughout the school day. Furthermore, the class members consistently demonstrate respect and value for the diversity of languages, ethnicities and cultures in the classroom.

Communication

There is a high degree of communication between the two teachers; it is almost as if they function as one person. There are differences, for example, Susan is referred to by her first name and Richard is called Mr. Rogers, acknowledging each individual teacher's preferences and culture. Throughout the day, decisions are made by both teachers as to the direction they will take both procedurally and instructionally, with continual efforts to take both perspectives into account. It is always a discussion rather than a mandate. Moreover, parents are kept in the information loop. Not only do notes go home related to class activities, parents, teachers and students consistently communicate with one another.

Print-Rich Environment

The classroom provides the students with a print-rich environment in which all of the objects are labeled with English vocabulary. This environment emerges during the first few weeks of every school year school as the classroom community works to construct a literate environment. Student work is prominently displayed and changed throughout the school year. There is a library with several bookshelves and other book containers filled with both fiction and non-fiction texts in English at a variety of reading levels. There are charts and lists with important classroom information displayed throughout the room. All classroom print is in English, but as noted above, notes go home to parents in Spanish. . . .

High Expectations in a Safe Environment

Both teachers and students have high expectations for the quality of work students are expected to complete in class. These expectations include behaviors that students exhibit in class and on the playground. Everyone looks out for one another and there is no hesitation to step in and refocus a student as needed. It seems as if the students feel responsible for the group rather than just for themselves. These expectations are consistently communicated to students and parents. As part of these high expectations Susan and Richard create an atmosphere where students are called upon to actively engage in all classroom activities. Support is provided through the use of modeling, questioning and prompting as needed, and students are free to use their native language when they do not have the English skills to participate.

Integrated Curriculum

Music, literature, writing, and science are often integrated into weekly lessons. Both teachers spend time activating the students' background knowledge when introducing a new concept, unit or book. Beginning in kindergarten, reading and writing are presented across the curriculum with a focus on strategy instruction. This is interesting in light of the fact that teachers in this public school are required to follow the district's adopted scripted reading program that is heavily based on phonics and phonemic awareness instruction. Both teachers have adapted their use of the basal materials in order to present a thematic approach that embeds their instruction in context and supports the students. Rather than engage the students in decontexualized tasks throughout the day, the teachers emphasize metacognitive awareness and students are asked to verbalize the strategies they have or will use when reading, writing or approaching a specific task.

The Role of Teacher Talk

The teachers use language in ways that not only communicate, but also teach language and usage. Susan and Richard use targeted procedural and instructional talk aimed at both classroom management and instruction. They further work to "teach" students to use both procedural and instructional talk during classroom activities, through "self-talk," aimed at helping students internalize instructional and behavioral procedures. Teachers use a "questioning mode" to impel students to search for answers to instructional and procedural questions.

Throughout the day, both teachers use "teacher talk" in ways that both describe classroom procedures and also model those very procedures. Lessons consist of direct instruction but also allowed for independent activities on a daily basis. In addition to the direct instruction students engage in inquiry activities. The first few days of the school year are spent on group building and teaching appropriate classroom behaviors to the new students in class. Newcomers are paired with returning students in newcomer/role model pairs and returning students are expected to take on expert roles in acclimating the new students to the classroom culture.

Both teachers teach and use what they call self-talk with the students. This consists of specific phrases that help students know how to behave in the classroom. The teachers model the specific behaviors that they expect of students and then students create "posters" of these statements, which are then posted throughout the room. . . . Furthermore, teachers and students engage in choral self-talk chants at the beginning of the year to help the students learn the classroom procedures. At first they chant with prompting, but after a while students are asked to repeat the self-talk without prompts.

Susan and Richard are active participants in instruction, modeling behavior and "thinking aloud" as they engage in classroom activities. They both use questioning to get students to think about classroom activities and model vocabulary usage throughout instruction, posing critical questions and often responding with questions that hold students accountable for learning. It is through the use of questions that both Susan and Richard guide the students to take ownership for their learning as well as developing a sense of collaboration within the classroom community. This is evident during reading instruction when Susan reads aloud to the class. She consistently checks for understanding and then models the use of new vocabulary, embedding it in the context of the story being read. During lessons, Susan models the expectations she has for student behavior, including turn taking behavior during lessons and discussions. While students are expected to raise their hands when guest teachers and other visitors work with the whole class during lessons, Susan focuses on holding conversations with the class where students are free to participate without waiting for recognition. She often provides wait time allowing students to chime in when they have something to say. "Show me, don't tell me." is one of the mantras frequently heard in class by both students and teachers. The expert role models are quite adept at appropriately scaffolding the procedural information for the newcomers so that they are relatively indistinguishable by the end of the first month of school.

The Role of Student Talk

Despite the fact that all instruction in this class takes place in English, the second language of most of the students in this class, students use Spanish when they are working together, especially when they are giving instructions to other students, telling them what to do. While at first glance this appeared to be little more than translating to support one another and clarify instructions, upon further examination it appears that the students are operating within their comfort zone, using their first language for communication. It may also be used as a means of forming more personal relationships with other students in the class.

However, students consistently appropriated the self-talk used by Susan and Richard in the classroom and this self-talk was in English. What is interesting is that while this type of discourse was similar to that used by Susan and Richard, there were differences, demonstrating the students' ability to internalize and modify the self-talk to meet their communication needs. For example, one student, exasperated at another student who appeared to be critiquing his work, yelled, "I did it to the best of my ability, ok, huh?" This seems to mirror a question that Susan might have asked (Did you do it to the best of your ability?) but is slightly different. Students also appropriated teacher talk when they took on leadership roles in the classroom. It was not uncommon to hear [Ivonne as she leads the calendar] say, "We have about one minute left. . . ." or "Hey, raise your hand if you know" much as Susan or Richard might say to the class.

Conclusions

The present ethnographic research study documents the use of a multi-age K-1-2 classroom situation for educating and supporting ELLs within the public school system of California. The goal of the three-year study was to make visible those processes that allow ELLs to not only acquire English, but to excel within the educational system thus allowing them access to the same occupational and educational opportunities of their English only peers. During year one of the study, researchers collected data pertaining to the instructional practices in place within the classroom.

The findings indicated that the teachers spent time developing a classroom learning community that promoted respect for one another based on a high degree of communication between teachers and students, students and students, parents and teachers, and parents and students. At all times teachers and students maintained high academic and behavioral expectations for one another, generally holding each other accountable for fulfilling these standards. Additionally,

instruction was provided in a safe, well-maintained print-rich environment through the use of a high interest, literature-rich integrated curriculum. Students were encouraged to take ownership of their learning, beginning within the first few weeks of entering kindergarten and increasing as they progressed into higher grade levels.

Over the course of the study Susan and Richard consistently engaged the students in the learning process through the use of higher-level questions, student-led lessons and activities, group-building strategies and genuine dialogue. In year two, the researchers explored the notion that students were appropriating and modifying "teacher self-talk" into conversations with their peers. It became apparent that the students had internalized much of the teacher self talk modeled and reinforced over time because they were able to alter the language and use it within different academic situations. Through this process, the students were able to create their own self-talk. This is an important finding as it shows that ELLs in the early stages of English language acquisition are able to understand and appropriate complex English language concepts through the use of scaffolded instruction by skilled teachers when it is reinforced across a period of 3 years.

These findings support the notion that students of diverse linguistic, economic and cultural backgrounds have opportunities to engage in "a continuum of teaching strategies that involves them in motivating, meaningful reading (and learning) experiences" (Au, 2002, p. 409). These experiences should take place within a safe learning environment with high academic expectations and a high degree of support from parents, teachers and students. The current study adds to the research literature by providing further support for the use of relevant instruction that promotes the active engagement of ELLs in academic dialogue within the classroom. Because students need time to acquire and internalize this language, the use of a multi-age classroom experience in the early stages of English language acquisition is suggested.

Implications

The debate over appropriate initial literacy instruction for ELLs in California is ongoing despite demonstrated success for properly implemented primary language programs (Krashen and Biber, 1988; Willig, 1985). Further arguments describe challenges to effective literacy instruction as a result of restrictions based on how and what is taught in reading (Moustafa and Land, 2002). Presently ELLs in California are being taught to read in English, most often through the use of scripted programs that do not always focus on the construction of meaning.

This study attempts to examine the impact of one multi-age experience on ELLs' literacy acquisition during their initial years of schooling in the hopes of describing ways to imbed literacy instruction within the classroom context. This study specifically explores the impact of student and teacher discourse on second language literacy learning. Advocates of multi-age education believe that the presence of older and younger children allows them to engage in meaningful literacy activities by encouraging collaboration and promoting a climate of "expected cooperation" (Katz, Evangelou, and Hartman, 1991, p. 10). It is during these exchanges that children learn to problem solve and negotiate alternative responses to the problems they encounter thereby scaffolding each other's learning experiences (Pontecorvo and Zuccharmaglio, 1990). It is during these interactions that literacy learning takes place. Multi-age classrooms encourage and promote collaborative learning experiences, and provide the context-rich environment needed to support ELLs as they acquire English.

References

Allington, R. L. (2002). *Big brother and the national reading curriculum: How ideology trumped evidence. Portsmouth,* NH: Heinemann.

Allington, D. and Woodside-Jiron, H. (1999). The politics of literacy teaching: How "research" shaped educational policy. *Educational researcher,* Vol. 28, No. 8, pp. 4–13.

Anderson, R. H. and Pavan, B. N. (1993). *Nongradedness: Helping it to happen.* Lancaster, PA: Technomic Publishing.

Au, K. (2002). Multicultural factors and the effective instruction of students of diverse backgrounds. In A.E. Farstrup & S.J. Samuels (Eds.), *What research has to say about reading instruction* (pp. 392–413). Newark, DE: International Reading Association.

Cazden. C. B. (1988). *Classroom discourse: The language of teaching and learning.* Portsmouth, NH: Heinemann.

Chase, P. (1994). Valuing. In P. Chase and J. Doan (Eds.). *Full circle: A new look at MULTI-AGE education.* Portsmouth, NH: Heinemann.

Chase, P. and Doan, J. (1994). *Full circle: A new look at MULTI-AGE education.* Portsmouth, NH: Heinemann.

Chase, P. and Doan, J. (1996). *Choosing to learn: Ownership and responsibility in a primary multi-age classroom.* Portsmouth, NH: Heinemann.

Coles, G. (2000). *Misreading reading: The bad science that hurts children.* Portsmouth, NH: Heinemann.

Crawford, J. (2000). *At war with diversity: US language policy in an age of anxiety.* Clevedon, UK: Multilingual Matters.

Doan, B. (1996). The option of choice. In P. Chase and J. Doan, (Eds.). *Choosing to learn: Ownership and responsibility in a primary multi-age classroom.* Portsmouth, NH: Heinemann.

Emerson, R., Fretz, R., and Shaw, L. (1995). *Writing ethnographic fieldnotes.* Chicago, IL: University of Chicago Press.

Engestrom, Y. and Middleton, D. (1996). *Cognition and communication at work.* New York, NY: Cambridge University Press.

Fitzgerald, J. (1995). English-as-a-second language instruction in the United States: A research review. *Journal of Reading Behavior, 27,* 115–132.

Foorman, B. R., Fletcher, J.M., Francis, D. J., and Schatschneider, C. S. (2000). Response Misrepresentation of research by other researchers. *Educational researcher,* Vol. 29, No. 6, pp. 27–37.

Frank, C. (1999). *Ethnographic eyes: A teacher's guide to classroom observation.* Portsmouth, NH: Heinemann.

Garan, E. M. (2002). *Resisting reading mandates: How to triumph with the truth.* Portsmouth, NH; Heinemann.

García, E. E. and Curry-Rodriguez, J. E. (2000). The education of limited English proficient students in California Schools: An assessment of the influence of Proposition 227 on selected districts and schools. *Bilingual Research Journal,* Vol. 24, Nos. 1 & 2., pp. 1–21.

Gee, J. P. (1996). Vygotsky and current debates in education: Some dilemmas as afterthoughts to *Discourse, learning and schooling.* In D. Hicks (Ed.). *Discourse, learning and schooling.* New York: Cambridge University Press.

Gold, R. (1958). Roles in sociological field observation. *Social Forces,* Vol. 36, pp. 217–223.

Guiterrez, R. and Slavin, R. E. (1992). Achievement effects of non-graded elementary schools: A best evidence synthesis. *Review of educational research,* Vol. 62, No. 4, pp. 333–376.

Hicks, D. (1996). Contextual inquiries: A discourse-oriented study of classroom learning. In D. Hicks (Ed.). *Discourse, learning and schooling.* New York: Cambridge University Press.

Jennings, C. and Di, X. (1996). Collaborative learning and thinking: The Vygotskian approach. In L. Dixon Krause (Ed.), *Vygotsky in the classroom: Mediated literacy instruction and assessment* (pp. 77–92). White Plains, NY: Longman.

Johnson, D. M. (1988). ESL children as teachers: A social view of second language. *Language arts,* February, 1988.

Junker, B. (1960). *Field work.* Chicago, IL: University of Chicago Press.

Katz, L., Evangelou, D., and Hartman, J. (1991). *The case for mixed-age grouping in early education.* Washington, D.C. : National Association for the Education of Young Children.

Krashen, S. and Biber, D. (1988). *On course: Bilingual education's success in California.* Sacramento, CA: CABE.

Lauer, P. A. (2000). *Instructional practices and implementation issues in multi-age classrooms.* Aurora, CO: Mid-continent research for education and learning.

LeCompte, M. and Preissle, J. (1993). *Ethnography and qualitative design in educational research.* San Diego, CA: Academic Press.

Leont'ev, A.N. (1978). *Activity, consciousness, personality.* Englewood Cliffs, NJ: Prentice Hall.

Lloyd, L. (1999). Multi-age classes and high ability students. *Review of educational research,* Vol. 69, No. 2, pp. 187–212.

Lodish, R. (1992). The pros and cons of mixed-age grouping. *Principal,* Vol. 7, No. 5, pp. 20–22.

Merriam, S. (1995). *Qualitative research and case study applications in education.* San Fransisco, CA: Jossey-Bass.

Miller, B. A. (1996). A basic understanding of multi-age grouping: Teacher readiness, planning, and parent involvement required for successful practice. *The school administrator,* Vol. 53, No. 1, pp. 12–17.

Moustafa, M. and Land, R. (2002). The reading achievement of economically-disadvantaged children in urban schools using Open Court vs. comparably disadvantaged children in urban schools using non-scripted programs. *2002 Yearbook of the Urban Learning, Teaching and Research Special Interest Group.* Los Angeles, CA: CSULA.

Ogbu, J.U. (1981). School ethnography: A multilevel approach. *Anthropology & Education Quarterly,* 12, 3–29.

Pontecorvo, C. and Zuccharmaglio, C. (1990). A passage to literacy: Learning in a social context. In Y. Goodman (Ed.), *How children construct literacy: Piagetian perspectives* (pp. 59–98). Newark, DE: International Reading Association.

Rogoff, B. (1990). *Apprenticeship in thinking-cognitive development in social context.* San Francisco, CA: Jossey-Bass.

Rommetveit, R. (1974). *On message structure: A framework for the study of language and communication.* New York, NY: Wiley.

Schriffin, D. (1994). *Approaches to discourse.* Malden, MA: Blackwell Press.

Spradley, J. (1980). *Participant observation.* Orlando, FL: Harcourt, Brace and Jovanovich.

Ulanoff, S. H. and Vega-Castaneda, L. (2003). The sociopolitical context of bilingual instruction in 21st century California. *Proceedings of the annual meeting of the Hawaii International Conference on Education,* Honolulu, HI.

Valdes, G. (1998). The world outside and inside schools: Language and immigrant children. *Educational Researcher, 27,* 4–18.

Vygotsky, L. (1962). *Theory and language.* Cambridge, MA: MIT University Press.

Wertsch, J.V. (1984). *Culture, communication and cognition.* New York, NY: Cambridge University Press.

Willig, A.C. (1985). A meta-analysis of selected studies on the effectiveness of bilingual education. *Review of educational research,* Vol. 55, No. 3, pp. 269–317.

SHARON H. ULANOFF, (California State University, Los Angeles). AMBIKA GOPALAKRISHNAN, (California State University, Los Angeles). DIANE BRANTLEY, (California State University, San Bernardino). SUSAN COURTNEY, (Los Angeles Unified School District). With RICHARD ROGERS, (Los Angeles Unified School District)

Output Strategies for English-Language Learners: Theory to Practice

Teachers need to recognize the importance of intentionally targeting the language output of children who are learning English as a second language.

ANGELA R. BECKMAN ANTHONY

With growing numbers of English-language learners (ELLs) in American classrooms (National Center for Educational Statistics [NCES], 2004, 2006), language and literacy education for ELLs is a current "hot topic" among researchers and practitioners (Cassidy & Cassidy, 2003, 2004, 2005, 2007). Topics of discussion include the challenges facing both researchers and practitioners to describe and understand the many direct and indirect factors that influence English-language learning as well as choosing appropriate, evidence-based teaching strategies (Hinkel, 2005). This article explores classroom-based teaching strategies for ELLs that target output (i.e., expressive language) and reviews the role of expression in the process of learning English as a second language. First, a theoretical basis for expanding on traditional teaching input to require output from the learner is presented. Second, teaching strategies emphasizing language production (i.e., output) are presented in four categories: collaborative conversations, vocabulary, writing, and reading.

Language Input and Output in Second-Language Learning

Input

Input has long been deemed important for all children learning language. There is evidence that both the quality and the amount of language input children experience influences native language acquisition as well as second-language acquisition. Evidence from the work of Hart and Risley (1995) showed that characteristics of parent language input (e.g., linguistic diversity, feedback) were better predictors of vocabulary scores at 9–10 years of age than were child accomplishments. Hart and Risley also found that children who received less input had lower language skills than children who received more input. This gap lasted over time and, without intervention, children deprived of large amounts of quality language input at an early

age never caught up to their language-advantaged peers who were exposed to more quality input. Work by Huttenlocher, Vasilyeva, Cymerman, and Levine (2002) showed that input is also important in classrooms and demonstrated that when teachers use more syntactically complex speech, children achieve greater syntactic growth.

In an instructional setting, input has been characterized as having communicative intent (VanPatten, 2003), and it has been identified as an important instructional factor specifically for ELLs. In a study of ELLs, students who "reached performance levels similar to native English-speaking children received instruction (i.e., input) that was rated higher quality than that in classrooms with poorer student outcomes" (Gersten, Baker, Haager, & Graves, 2005, p. 204). In this study, quality classrooms were characterized by higher ratings on the English-Language Learner Classroom Observation Instrument in the areas of explicit teaching; differentiating instruction for low performers; and greater amount and quality of instruction in vocabulary, phonemic awareness, and phonics.

All current models of second-language acquisition incorporate input (VanPatten, 2003). This theoretical framework, called the "input hypothesis," underlies what we "give" to students. The input hypothesis is rooted in the work of Krashen (1985) in which he proposed that second-language acquisition is a result of "comprehensible input" that is received by the learner.

Previous articles in *The Reading Teacher* focus on what teachers and parents can do to provide comprehensible input for children learning to speak and read in a second language. Strategies addressed include developing oral vocabulary prior to using texts for instructional purposes, developing comprehension skills, and providing first-language support (Lenters, 2004); using early literacy assessments such as the Phonological Awareness Literacy Screening to guide instruction for ELLs (Helman, 2005); and encouraging parent involvement in literacy learning (Ortiz & Ordonez-Jasis, 2005). Although these articles focus on what teachers and parents can do to help ELLs learn second-language vocabulary and transfer these skills to reading, little is said about what we should expect in turn from the children who are learning English as a second language and learning to apply that language to the reading of text.

For years, second-language learning models held the position that comprehensible input (i.e., input that is understood by the learner) was a necessary and sufficient condition for second-language acquisition (Krashen, 1985; Swain, 2005) and that second-language learning is a largely implicit process (Pica, 2005). However, recent theoretical models include output as another important part of the second-language learning process.

Output as Product and Process

Output has been traditionally defined as the *product* of learning— or how children demonstrate what they have learned (Swain, 2005; VanPatten, 2003). Teachers use output to determine what students "know" or have learned about a topic. When a teacher asks a question, the students' responses (whether spoken or written) are output. When students take a test, the answers they provide are examples of output. Thus, the term *output* has traditionally been used to describe what ELL students can produce in the spoken or written modalities.

Recently, however, output has been explored as a learning *process* as well—one in which the ELL student tests second-language understanding and learns from the feedback received. VanPatten (2003) described two processes involved in output: access and production strategies. Access involves searching the vocabulary store, or lexicon, in the brain to find appropriate words and forms of words necessary to express a particular meaning. For example, to talk about a dog, the child would need to search through his or her lexicon to find the word *dog*. Access in a first language occurs almost automatically and without much effort. However, access in a second language requires conscious attention as it is being acquired; automaticity occurs much later. Production strategies are used in putting together strings of words accessed from the lexicon to form a sentence or utterance. This requires several words to be accessed and put together in the appropriate order to express the desired idea. For example, after accessing the words *dog* and *barked* the child would use production strategies to formulate the sentence "the dog barked" to tell a peer about what he observed the dog doing. The expression of this idea using the accessed vocabulary is the output.

The importance of output in the process of learning has been relatively unexplored until recently (e.g., Izumi, 2002; Izumi, Bigelow, Fujiwara, & Fearnow, 1999; Swain, 2005; Swain & Lapkin, 1998). Swain (2005; Swain & Lapkin, 1998) presented evidence that producing the target language (i.e., output) is important for ELLs. In reviewing studies of French immersion programs in Canada, Swain (2005) noted that despite "an abundance of comprehensible input," speaking and writing abilities of second-language learners remain different than those of peers who are native speakers of the language. Additional evidence suggested that input alone was not sufficient for learning a second language (Swain, 2005), particularly when learning to use correct word order (syntax) and word forms (morphology) of the new language (Izumi, 2003; Nunan, 2005).

These findings led researchers and practitioners to explore beyond the boundaries of input and look more closely at the process of output.

Three Functions of Output

Swain (2005) discussed three possible functions of output in the learning process: noticing/triggering, hypothesis testing, and metalinguistic/reflective functions. When learners attempt to produce the target language, they may notice that they do not know how to say or write the desired message effectively. Thus, the production of output might trigger attention and direct the learner to notice something he or she needs to explore further in the new language. For example, a student might use an incorrect verb tense, recognize it as incorrect, and seek input to identify the correct production. Recognizing an error and seeking new information to fill in previous gaps in knowledge are hypothesized to require cognitive processes involved in learning a second language. These cognitive processes include generating new linguistic knowledge or consolidating existing knowledge.

The second function of output is hypothesis testing (i.e., creating a "trial run" of how to communicate a message). In this case, the student begins with a hypothesis about what the message should sound or look like, tests this hypothesis by producing it, and then receives feedback from another person regarding its correctness. The feedback should lead the student to modify the production to fit the correct form. It is suggested that this modified output prepares the student for subsequent uses of the correct form.

A third function of output, the metalinguistic (reflective) function, occurs when language is used to reflect on the language that a learner produces or is produced by others. One source of this function is collaborative dialogue in which groups of students or students with a teacher share ideas and are free to reflect on what is said and how it is said. The key element of this function is that through the process of speaking and reflecting the student must realize that he or she does not understand the use of a particular language form and then talk about that process. There is some type of externalized thinking that provides output as an object of reflection. For example, if a child says, "I walks the dog" and then recognizes the incorrect verb form, the child might then say or think, "Walks is not right." Reflection can lead to modifying output and, in a manner similar, to noticing and hypothesis testing, which can trigger cognitive processes that lead to learning (Izumi, 2003; Swain, 2005).

Implications of the Output Hypothesis

Language input is important for ELLs. At a most basic level, input is necessary to spark language production (output). As noted above, input is undoubtedly important for a child who is learning either a first or a second language. The desired outcome for ELLs has long been the ability to speak accurately and fluently; however, the focus on production of language and actively reflecting on that language as a part of the learning process has been frequently overlooked. In the current literature, emphasis is often placed on the program used and what teachers do (e.g., Carlo et al., 2004) rather than on how children learn or what encourages children to participate in activities that encourage learning. Application of the output theory is evident in some recent research (Izumi, 2002; Izumi et al., 1999; Swain, 2005; Swain & Lapkin, 1998); however, implications of the output hypothesis are only beginning to surface in current instructional recommendations. Emphasis on output (in addition to input) remains largely neglected in practitioner literature; specifically, the emphasis on intentional planning to create opportunities for student output is lacking. Thus, the goal of this article is to provide specific applications of the output theory to classroom practices.

Language- and Literacy-Based Strategies That Encourage Output

Research identifying specific strategies for ELLs "has been slow in coming and scattered in perspective" (Cohen & Horowitz, 2002, p. 33). However, many researchers suggest that strategies for teaching reading to ELLs may be quite similar to strategies that are used with native readers. As Eskey (2005) stated, "reading is reading in any context, just as language acquisition is language acquisition" (p. 564). Eskey did not deny that there may be differences between native language learners and ELLs but argued that the similarities far outweigh the differences. One primary similarity is that second-language readers cannot read texts beyond their level of proficiency; readers and texts should be matched for language and interest level. It is also suggested that reading is not only a means to an end but also a way of acquiring language.

Creating a Supportive Learning Environment

Creating a "literate environment" that is rich in input provides a safe setting in which to produce and explore a new language. Teachers can encourage the process of learning by creating "classroom conditions that enable English learners to cross over the instructional divide from confusion into meaningful learning" (Meyer, 2000, p. 228). Teachers identified as "outstanding" in promoting literacy achievements conduct reading and writing activities daily, explicitly model literacy skills and strategies, and integrate literacy instruction with the rest of the curriculum, creating naturalistic opportunities for addressing literacy skills (Pressley, 2002). To create these conditions, teachers can lower the barriers of cognitive load (i.e., the number of new concepts embedded in a lesson or text), culture load (i.e., the amount of cultural knowledge required but never explicitly explained), language load (i.e., frequency and complexity of unfamiliar English words), and learning load (i.e., what activities and tasks teachers are asking students to do with English). Teachers may also encourage the process of learning by pushing students beyond just getting their message across and by expecting a message "that is conveyed precisely, coherently, and appropriately" (Swain, 2005, p. 473).

Strategies for first-language reading intervention may also be applied to working with the ELL population. Intervention strategies should be designed to anticipate specific struggles that readers have at various ages and stages of development. To do this, five specific characteristics may be applied to instructional programs. First, explicit, repetitive procedures for problem solving or completing a task should be taught and reinforced. Second, task completion should be scaffolded with teacher assistance progressing from more to less support and tasks moving from easier to more complex. Third, integration of literacy activities into other domains should be strategic, recognizing and using children's strengths in one area to help them apply literacy strategies in another area. Fourth, background knowledge should be used to lay the groundwork for newer, higher-level tasks. Finally, review of materials and concepts should be targeted to the individual learner and the demands of the specific task (Coyne, Kame'enui, & Simmons, 2001).

Creating a supportive classroom environment is not enough to create sufficient output opportunities. In the following section, I discuss commonly recommended instructional strategies for literacy learning and explicitly identify how the output hypothesis applies. I also provide hypothetical dialogues to illustrate how activities may be intentionally designed to encourage student output and provide examples specifically related to the three functions of output: noticing, hypothesis testing, and reflecting. Strategies for creating environments that encourage output are described in four areas: collaborative conversations, vocabulary, writing, and reading.

Collaborative Conversations

Collaborative dialogues occur when students work together to discuss and solve problems. Psychological theorists believe that learning takes place in these types of dialogues—after participating in group-learning experiences children internalize knowledge. Thus, group problem solving builds skills that can later be transferred to problem solving by individuals (Swain, 2005). Cooperative learning such as this has been identified as a motivating strategy used in high-quality classrooms (Pressley, 2002).

Teachers should be aware that true collaborative dialogues consist of balanced turns between the teacher and children in the group. A common occurrence in classrooms is the routine of the teacher asking a question and children providing responses. Although this may appear to be turn taking between teacher and student, it often results in an unnatural conversation with length of turns being unbalanced (i.e., the teacher dominates talk and children provide responses limited in length). When a teacher uses too many closed questions (i.e., questions that have a "right" answer and that often can be answered with a single word or phrase), the purpose of the exchange is no longer to communicate but to test knowledge (see Figure 1). To maximize opportunities for output, interactions should have a communicative goal, and students should be expected to contribute to the conversation (VanPatten, 2003). The use of open questions (i.e., questions that the teacher does not "know" the answer to or questions that do not have one "right" answer) encourages students to contribute and to provide longer, more complex responses (Nunan, 2005). The interaction may be structured, however, to provide tasks appropriate to the student's ability

Speaker	Dialogue	Analysis
Teacher	Now it is story time. This is the book we are reading today. What is the title of the story?	Initiation of topic Closed question
Jessica	Color.	One-word answer
Teacher	*The Story of Colors* [Marcos, 1996]. What is the story about?	Teacher model Closed question
Luis	Making colors.	Two-word answer
Teacher	OK, making colors. Let's read it. [begins to read]	Close of conversation

Figure 1 Hypothetical unbalanced dialogue resulting from the use of closed questions.

Speaker	Dialogue	Analysis
Teacher	Look at the story we have for today. What do you think the title might be?	Directive Open quension
Jessica	Man makes color story.	Simple-sentence answer
Luis	*Historia de los Colores.* [reading words in Spanish on the book cover]	Reference to title in Spanish
Teacher	Luis read the title in Spanish. Jessica used some English words that are in the title. Can we figure out what the whole title is in English?	Review of known information; pushing students to think about English translation
Luis	Colores story.	Mixed Spanish and English response
Teacher	In English *colores* is *colors*, Luis. So this book is called *The Story of Colors* [Marcos, 1996].	Drawing attention to an English-Spanish cognate
Luis	*Story of Colors.*	Child repeats title in English
Teacher	Let's read to find out what the story is about. [begins to read]	Close of conversation

Figure 2 Hypothetical balanced dialogue with examples of an open question and drawing attention to cognates by the teacher and noticing and reflection by a child.

level. For example, a student with a limited English vocabulary may participate in the interaction by repeating an answer modeled by the teacher or by saying a single word; a student with more advanced skills would be expected to contribute new ideas in complete sentences (see Figure 2). In sum, the point here is that more interaction is better (VanPatten, 2003).

Vocabulary

Vocabulary provides the basis for spoken and written communication; thus, it is unfortunate that many school curricula place little emphasis on vocabulary acquisition. Beck, McKeown, and Kucan (2002) recommended "robust" vocabulary instruction; that is, instruction that is "vigorous, strong, and powerful in effect" (p. 2). This type of instruction begins with a contextualized, repetitive, meaningful introduction to an unfamiliar word

(see Figure 3). For example, when a new word is encountered in a storybook, the teacher might refer back to the text in which the word appeared, reread the sentence(s) that exemplifies its meaning, and ask the children to repeat the target word. Next, an explanation of the meaning would be provided, and examples of how the word might be used in contexts other than the one in which it was discovered could be offered. Children could be involved in this by following the teacher's example with some of their own examples of applying the word in context. Finally, children would be asked to repeat the word again to reinforce the target word.

Simply introducing vocabulary one time is not sufficient. Extended and repeated opportunities to engage in activities that offer interactions with new words are needed (Stahl & Nagy, 2006). Robust instruction involves engaging students with word

Speaker	Dialogue	Analysis
Teacher	Look at the story we have for today. What do you think the title might be? [reading text from *The Story of Colors* (Marcos, 1996)] "Old Antonio points at a macaw crossing the afternoon sky." Everyone say *macaw* with me.	Directive Open quenstion Reading sentence with a new word, *macaw*
Children and Teacher	Macaw.	Children produce the word
Teacher	A macaw is a large bird with colorful feathers. Some macaws live in the rainforests of Mexico. Have you ever seen a macaw?	Explanation of meaning Example of another context
Jessica	I saw birds in the zoo with lots of colors.	Child applying the word in context
Teacher	Jessica saw birds with lots of colors at the zoo. Maybe she saw a macaw. Let's say the word together one more time to help us remember it.	Teacher repeating the example
Children and Teacher	Macaw.	Children repeat the word again

Figure 3 Hypothetical example of a contextualized, repetitive, and meaningful introduction to an unfamiliar vocabulary word.

meanings and providing opportunities for children to actively deal with meanings of new vocabulary after they have been introduced. Students might be asked to create associations between new words and known words or phrases. After making their associations, students should also explain why the words are associated and how they made the connection (Beck et al., 2002). For example, after students have been exposed to the word *brilliant* and presented with an explanation of its meaning, this word may be associated with a *rainbow* as it is in the conversation in Figure 4. Asking students to make associations requires hypothesis testing on the student's part to determine which ideas fit together. Explaining the reasoning for associations leads students to reflect on the decisions made as well as to reflect on the meaning of the word as it is used in a particular context.

Another strategy for robust vocabulary instruction is to ask students to connect new vocabulary to personal experiences. Again, after exposure to and explanation of a new word, students might describe an experience they have had to which the word applies. Application to personal experiences may help students notice a new word or word form that they have previously used incorrectly or not used at all. For example, if students are introduced to the word *macaw,* they might make the connection to a visit to the zoo as Jessica did in the dialogue in Figure 3. This strategy also creates a meaningful experience for learning by showing students that the new word applies to their lives (Beck et al., 2002). Meaningful connections to the child's first language can also be made through the use of cognates (Bear, Helman, Templeton, Invernizzi, & Johnston, 2007). When an English word is similar to a word in the first language, students can use this background knowledge to improve their English skills. We see the teacher draw Luis's attention to the Spanish–English cognates *colores* and *colors* in Figure 2. It

should be noted that the Spanish and English languages share a large number of cognates. Thus, drawing attention to cognates is particularly useful for ELLs whose first language is Spanish (August, Carlo, Dressler, & Snow, 2005). For children with other first languages that share fewer cognates with English, this strategy may be less beneficial.

Writing

Although they did not refer to the output hypothesis in their work, Rubin and Carlan (2005) provided some recommendations related to writing that support the output process. Writing in and of itself is an exercise in output. Thus, encouraging writing and valuing it as a tool to express ideas are important. When writing, children should also be encouraged to talk about the writing process, including how they know what to write. This provides exposure to input from peers, encourages reflection by requiring children to think about the writing process, and pushes them to use language to describe the writing process. It also gives the teacher insight on what strategies children are using and opportunities to provide feedback to correct errors or clarify misconceptions about the language.

As with conversations, collaborative learning is important in the writing process. The monitoring and feedback that is initially provided by the teacher should become a part of the students' responsibility (Harris, Schmidt, & Graham, 1998). After the teacher has modeled and taught strategies for providing feedback, peers can be given this responsibility and provided with opportunities to "collaborate to generate ideas, exchange texts, and construct feedback on the content and form of written drafts" (Hedgcock, 2005, p. 605). This feedback should come from other ELLs as well as from peers whose first language is English.

Speaker	Dialogue	Analysis
Teacher	[reads text from *The Story of Colors* (Marcos, 1996)] "I see the *brilliant* streak of colors in the gray mist of a gathering rain." *Brilliant* means that the colors are very bright and beautiful. In the story, the macaw has brilliant colors.	Reading of new word and explanation of the word
	Do you think a zebra is brilliant?	Question to encourage hypothesis testing
Luis	No.	Child response to hypothesis testing question
Teacher	No. A zebra is black and white, not colorful. Can you think of something that might be bright and colorful?	Encouraging children to make an association or test a hypothesis
Jessica	A rainbow has lots of color.	Child association
Teacher	Do you think a rainbow is brilliant?	Hypothesis testing
Jessica	Yes.	Confirmation
Teacher	Yes, it is. Why is it brilliant?	Encouraging association
Luis	It has bright colors.	
Teacher	Yes, something that has lots of bright colors, like a rainbow, can be described as brilliant.	

Figure 4 Hypothetical example of dialogue that encourages hypothesis testing and making associations.

Children should be given opportunities to read aloud what they have written and, if possible, to do so in both their native and second language. By encouraging reviewing of written work, children will have opportunities to notice errors or areas in which they need support to improve the expression of their ideas. Sharing in a group provides opportunities for input from peers, as well as opportunities to receive feedback and improve their writing. This strategy also gives a sense of importance to what children write and gives them opportunities to produce language that is personally meaningful (Rubin & Carlan, 2005).

Pressley (2002) identified frequent opportunities for story and journal writing as a feature of classrooms with "expert" teachers. Daily opportunities for writing should be provided. Teachers may need to provide ELLs with focused support to help them get started with writing. For example, students might be encouraged to first make a list of things they know a lot about. This list can then serve as a starting point for identifying a topic to write about. Conversations between a student and teacher can lead to a more focused topic (Strickland, Ganske, & Monroe, 2002). For example, if a student knows a lot about basketball because he plays with his friends after school, a guided conversation with the teacher might remind him of the time he made the winning shot for his team. The story of this winning game could then become the topic for writing.

Ideas for writing may also be found in books that are read and discussed aloud. If a student makes a personal connection to a part of the story, he or she can use this as a starting point. For example, if the teacher recalls a student's connection, such as Jessica's connection of the macaw to the zoo in Figure 3,

she can be encouraged to write about this experience. These conversations also provide opportunities for children to explore and reflect on what they know and how they might convey that knowledge in writing. Strickland et al. (2002) also suggested that brief writings are sufficient, particularly for struggling writers. The emphasis does not have to be on how long the product is or the length of time spent writing—at least not all the time.

Finally, just as similarities in oral language (e.g., cognates) can be used as a way to make connections for ELLs in vocabulary, a comparison of written language can also be beneficial. The teacher should be aware of any differences between the first language and English in the written form and help the child to recognize these differences. When children are aware of these differences, they can use their first language to support writing in English (Bear et al., 2007). In order to build on their first language and their knowledge of differences between languages, children may be encouraged to write in their first language and then translate the text into English. Rubin and Carlan (2005) reviewed stages of writing development as it occurs in two languages and provided guidelines for assessing and understanding children's progress.

Reading

The reading teacher's job is thus not so much to teach a specific skill or content as to get students reading and to keep them reading—that is, to find a way to motivate them to read, and to facilitate their reading of whatever texts they have chosen to read or been asked to read. (Eskey, 2005, p. 574)

Speaker	Dialogue
Teacher	[reads text from *The Story of Colors* (Marcos, 1996)] "The macaw didn't used to be like this. It hardly had any color at all. It was just gray."
	[thinking aloud] I wonder how the macaw got all its colors. The last picture showed lots of colors.
	[reads] "It was just gray. Its feathers were stunted, like a wet chicken—just one more bird among all the others who didn't know how he arrived in the world. The gods themselves didn't know who made the birds. Or why."
	[thinking aloud] This page didn't tell me about the macaw getting its colors. I wonder if the gods decided to color the birds. I'll have to keep reading to find out.

Figure 5 Hypothetical example of a think-aloud model by the teacher.

It is well understood that an extensive reading vocabulary in a new language is best acquired through the act of reading. Books provide access to new vocabulary that can then be targeted in language production. Once ELLs have been enticed by text, the world of vocabulary and language is opened to them—if they receive appropriate support for learning. Lessons designed around books serve as a resource to generate discussion and writing opportunities. Examples of specific targets from a book have been presented in Figures 2, 3, and 4. Additional strategies for encouraging output that improves reading skills of ELLs are described in the following paragraphs.

In terms of output, several opportunities exist within the reading of text to "push" students in their language use. Choral reading of text gives students the opportunity to hear fluent reading and at the same time participate in production of language. This provides an opportunity for students to notice when they are reading something incorrectly as well as a chance to receive feedback about the correct way to read it. Students should join in reading the text to the extent that they feel comfortable and should be given multiple opportunities to do so. This strategy is particularly helpful for children who are not yet fluent in English because the indirect feedback is less embarrassing than when the child is overtly corrected in front of peers, and it allows the student to remain confident in participating (Strickland et al., 2002).

Books can also be a source of text for Readers Theatre—an activity laden with opportunities for noticing and reflecting on language. This strategy turns a text into a script to be acted out. Students must read and interpret not only meaning but also the emotions and characteristics of the speakers they are representing. Several opportunities to practice the script should be provided before students "perform" for classmates. Practice readings could also be tape recorded and played back for students. Listening to the recording would provide an opportunity for students to hear themselves talking, reflect on their productions, and notice areas that could be improved (Strickland et al., 2002).

Open role-plays may be used in a similar manner with students who are capable of participating in a less structured activity. Rather than creating a script directly from the text, students may create their own script based on interpretations of characters in a story. This type of activity encourages varied discourse and allows for several turns in a conversational exchange; however, teachers should be aware that a loosely structured role-play places more demand on the student's language ability. A more structured, scripted role-play may be used, but it does not allow for the same level of discourse as open role-play (Kasper & Roever, 2005).

Think-alouds can also be an effective strategy for ELLs. Strickland et al. (2002) suggested introducing think-alouds to students through explicit modeling and demonstration before asking students to carry out the strategy on their own. For example, while showing a passage on an overhead projector, the teacher can read aloud, stop at points of confusion, and write notes in the margins (see Figure 5). The teacher and students together can go back to these problem points and talk about strategies for understanding. After students have become familiar with the process, they may be asked to conduct think-alouds in small groups or pairs. Discussions can occur between peers with help from the teacher as needed. Again, these discussions around a shared text provide opportunities for hypothesis testing (e.g., discussing what they think the story will be about), noticing (e.g., becoming aware that their interpretation of an event is different from a peer's), and reflecting (e.g., making a personal connection to an event in the story).

Strategies for interacting with text should be employed before, during, and after reading. Eskey (2005) provided a summary of commonly used cognitive strategies used when teaching reading. Before reading, the teacher can prepare students for what they will encounter in the text. Important vocabulary can be introduced and background knowledge can be activated. Students might also be encouraged to skim the text to get an idea of what the story might be about. These activities prepare the student for interacting with the text during reading—when the student can apply his or her vocabulary knowledge and determine whether the background knowledge brought to the reading fits with the text. After reading, more critical thinking can be applied in group discussions of the text. Follow-up activities might involve reading other texts on the same topic, extending the topic into additional discussions, or writing about the text. As described earlier, these conversations or writing experiences lead students to notice, hypothesize, and reflect on the language—all of which are part of the learning process and all of which produce output.

Intentionally Targeting Language Output

The strategies suggested in this article are likely not new to reading teachers. It is no surprise that strategies for teaching reading to native language users and struggling readers can be applied to instruction for ELLs. What is potentially a new concept here is the importance of intentionally targeting language output from children who are learning English as a second language. It is no longer enough to expose children to quality language and expect that this input alone will be enough to learn a new language. Current research has debunked the input hypothesis in its pure form—input is necessary but not sufficient. The good news is that output can be intentionally targeted during common practices in teaching reading. Several of these strategies and classroom-based activities have been explored here, but this is by no means an exhaustive description. As reading teachers work with ELLs, they must expect children to not only attend to input but also to produce output as well. Teachers have the responsibility to offer opportunities for output and to respond to output by scaffolding students to produce precise, coherent, and appropriate language. Provided with these opportunities, students learning English as a second language will have a better chance to become proficient.

References

August, D., Carlo, M., Dressler, C., & Snow, C. (2005). The critical role of vocabulary development for English language learners. *Learning Disabilities Research & Practice, 20,* 50–57.

Bear, D.R., Helman, L., Templeton, S., Invernizzi, M., & Johnston, F. (2007). *Words their way with English learners: Word study for phonics, vocabulary, and spelling instruction.* Upper Saddle River, NJ: Pearson Education.

Beck, I.L., McKeown, M.G., & Kucan, L. (2002). *Bringing words to life: Robust vocabulary instruction.* New York: Guilford.

Carlo, M.S., August, D., McLaughlin, B., Snow, C.E., Dressler, C., Lippman, D.N., et al. (2004). Closing the gap: Addressing the vocabulary needs of English-language learners in bilingual and mainstream classrooms. *Reading Research Quarterly, 39,* 188–215.

Cassidy, J., & Cassidy, D. (2003, December/January). What's hot, what's not for 2004. *Reading Today, 21,* 1, 18.

Cassidy, J., & Cassidy, D. (2004, December/January). What's hot, what's not for 2005. *Reading Today, 22,* 1.

Cassidy, J., & Cassidy, D. (2005, December/January). What's hot, what's not for 2006. *Reading Today, 23,* 1, 8–9.

Cassidy, J., & Cassidy, D. (2007, February/March). What's hot, what's not for 2007. *Reading Today, 24,* 1.

Cohen, A.D., & Horowitz, R. (2002). What should teachers know about bilingual learners and the reading process? In J.H. Sullivan (Ed.), *Literacy and the second language learner* (pp. 29–54). Greenwich, CT: Information Age Publishing.

Coyne, M.D., Kame'enui, E.J., & Simmons, D.C. (2001). Prevention and intervention in beginning reading: Two complex systems. *Learning Disabilities: Research and Practice, 16,* 62–73.

Eskey, D.E. (2005). Reading in a second language. In E. Hinkel (Ed.), *Handbook of research in second language teaching and learning* (pp. 563–579). Mahwah, NJ: Erlbaum.

Gersten, R., Baker, S.K., Haager, D., & Graves, A.W. (2005). Exploring the role of teacher quality in predicting reading outcomes for first-grade English learners: An observational study. *Remedial and Special Education, 26,* 197–206.

Harris, K.R., Schmidt, T., & Graham, S. (1998). Every child can write: Strategies for composition and self-regulation in the writing process. In K.R. Harris, S. Graham, & D. Deshler (Eds.), *Teaching every child every day: Learning in diverse schools and classrooms* (pp. 131–167). Cambridge, MA: Brookline Books.

Hart, B., & Risley, T.R. (1995). *Meaningful differences in the everyday experience of young American children.* Baltimore, MD: Brookes.

Hedgcock, J.S. (2005). Taking stock of research and pedagogy in L2 writing. In E. Hinkel (Ed.), *Handbook of research in second language teaching and learning* (pp. 597–613). Mahwah, NJ: Erlbaum.

Helman, L.A. (2005). Using literacy assessment results to improve teaching for English-language learners. *The Reading Teacher, 58,* 668–677.

Hinkel, E. (2005). Introduction. In E. Hinkel (Ed.), *Handbook of research in second language teaching and learning* (pp. xvii–xxii). Mahwah, NJ: Erlbaum.

Huttenlocher, J., Vasilyeva, M., Cymerman, E., & Levine, S. (2002). Language input and child syntax. *Cognitive Psychology, 45,* 337–374.

Izumi, S. (2002). Output, input enhancement, and the noticing hypothesis: An experimental study on ESL relativization. *Studies in Second Language Acquisition, 24,* 541–577.

Izumi, S. (2003). Comprehension and production processes in second language learning: In search of the psycholinguistic rationale of the output hypothesis. *Applied Linguistics, 24,* 168–196.

Izumi, S., Bigelow, M., Fujiwara, M., & Fearnow, S. (1999). Testing the output hypothesis: Effects of output on noticing and second language acquisition. *Studies in Second Language Acquisition, 21,* 421–452.

Kasper, G., & Roever, C. (2005). Pragmatics in second language learning. In E. Hinkel (Ed.), *Handbook of research in second language teaching and learning* (pp. 317–334). Mahwah, NJ: Erlbaum.

Krashen, S.D. (1985). *The input hypothesis: Issues and implications.* White Plains, NY: Longman.

Lenters, K. (2004). No half measures: Reading instruction for young second-language learners. *The Reading Teacher, 58,* 328–336.

Meyer, L.M. (2000). Barriers to meaningful instruction for English learners. *Theory Into Practice, 39,* 228–236.

National Center for Education Statistics. (2004). *English language learner students in U.S. public schools: 1994 and 2000.* Washington, DC: U.S. Department of Education Institute for Education Sciences.

National Center for Education Statistics. (2006). *Characteristics of schools, districts, teachers, principals and school libraries in the United States: 2003–04 schools and staffing survey.* Washington, DC: U.S. Department of Education Institute of Education Sciences.

Nunan, D. (2005). Classroom research. In E. Hinkel (Ed.), *Handbook of research in second language teaching and learning* (pp. 225–240). Mahwah, NJ: Erlbaum.

Ortiz, R.W., & Ordonez-Jasis, R. (2005). Leyendo juntos (Reading together): New directions for Latino parents' early literacy involvement. *The Reading Teacher, 59,* 110–121.

Pica, T. (2005). Second language acquisition research and applied linguistics. In E. Hinkel (Ed.), *Handbook of research in second language teaching and learning* (pp. 263–280). Mahwah, NJ: Erlbaum.

Pressley, M. (2002). *Reading instruction that works: The case for balanced teaching* (2nd ed.). New York: Guilford.

Rubin, R., & Carlan, V.G. (2005). Using writing to understand bilingual children's literacy development. *The Reading Teacher, 58,* 728–739.

Stahl, S.A., & Nagy, W.E. (2006). *Teaching word meanings.* Mahwah, NJ: Erlbaum.

Strickland, D.S., Ganske, K., & Monroe, J.K. (2002). *Supporting struggling readers and writers: Strategies for classroom intervention 3–6.* Portland, ME: Stenhouse.

Swain, M. (2005). The output hypothesis: Theory and research. In E. Hinkel (Ed.), *Handbook of research in second language teaching and learning* (pp. 471–483). Mahwah, NJ: Erlbaum.

Swain, M., & Lapkin, S. (1998). Interaction and second language learning: Two adolescent French immersion students working together. *Modern Language Journal, 82,* 320–337.

VanPatten, B. (2003). *From input to output: A teacher's guide to second language acquisition.* Boston: McGraw-Hill.

Literature Cited

Marcos, S. (1999). *The story of colors.* El Paso, TX: Cinco Puntos Press.

ANGELA R. BECKMAN ANTHONY teaches at Eastern Illinois University in Charleston; e-mail arbeckman@eiu.edu.

Controversial Books in the Middle School: Can They Make a Difference?

This We Believe *Characteristics*

- An inviting, supportive, and safe environment
- Students and teachers engaged in active learning
- Curriculum that is relevant, challenging, integrative, and exploratory
- Multiple learning and teaching approaches that respond to their diversity

JEFF WHITTINGHAM AND WENDY RICKMAN

"Many of us, particularly in the dark days before the Stonewall riots, remember going into libraries to check for references that would give some validity to the vague stirrings inside us we knew marked us out as different" (Curry, 2005, p. 65).

This quote describes the search for identity through books containing gay and lesbian characters and themes prior to 1969. At that time, the search would have revealed few resources, but today there is a growing body of literature with gay and lesbian themes aimed at the middle school market. Whether the growth in popularity of such texts is driven by the views of publishing house editors or is a response to the market demands of juveniles or young adults, the fact remains that these books are now much more available in bookstores and middle school libraries across the nation.

The Dilemma for Middle Schools

The Stonewall riots, a series of violent conflicts between homosexuals and New York City police in 1969, marked the advent of the gay rights movement and led to a dramatic increase in gay and lesbian visibility. Efforts to acknowledge this movement were made by a number of groups including the American Library Association's Gay, Lesbian, Bisexual, Transgender Round Table (American Library Association, 2006). This group, since 1971, has given an annual Stonewall Book Award honoring both fiction and nonfiction literature for exceptional merit relating to the gay/lesbian/bisexual/transgendered experience.

Academia has formed departments or programs dedicated to lesbian and gay studies, and the general public has achieved a better understanding of sexual differences. Public schools, however, have continued to resist such acknowledgement, leaving homosexual students in middle and secondary schools unrecognized and often the targets of discrimination. Galley (1999) reported the results of a national survey that found 91% of homosexual students had encountered antigay comments, 69% had been verbally abused, with 34% verbally abused daily[1]. This type of discrimination is found not only in interactions between students, but in classrooms as well. While it would be rare for social studies teachers to ignore feminist leaders and authors in a unit on social movements or for literature teachers to ignore the Civil Rights Movement or the contributions of African American authors, it is often still acceptable to ignore literature written by homosexual authors or containing homosexual themes (Reese, 2000)[2]. Gallo (2004) posited that, while few people object to schools using books written about different cultures, many people devalue books addressing the interests and needs of gay teens. The diminished status of such books could be viewed as a covert form of discrimination.

Often associated with ethnicity, discrimination can assume many forms including sexual orientation. Several organizations including Human Rights Watch, have documented violence and discrimination as problems affecting gay, lesbian, and heterosexual populations in American schools. Louis Harris and Associates (1999) reported in a national survey that 25% of students responded in the affirmative when asked if there was some sort of violence-related problem in their school, 8% did not feel safe at school, 15% were very worried about being attacked at school, and 53% believed a particular group of students was more likely to be victims of violence. In addition, student concerns about safety and violence were greatest in middle school. Responding to current attitudes about discrimination, the National Council of Teachers of English Committee on Teaching about Genocide and Intolerance includes homophobia as an appropriate topic for young adults (Rabinsky & Danks, 1999).

One of the basic principles of middle school education is trying to meet the needs of *all* young adolescents (National Middle School Association, 1995, 2003). Meeting those needs includes protection from and education about discrimination. Using juvenile and young adult literature containing homosexual themes and characters appears to be one viable option to address the issue of discrimination. The dilemma for middle schools centers on whether or not these books should be introduced in the middle school and, if so, how, when, and where.

A Historical Perspective on Books with Homosexual Themes and Characters

In the collected letters of children's book editor Ursula Nordstrom, Marcus (1998) characterized Donovan's 1969 young adult novel *I'll Get There: It Better be Worth the Trip* as the "first novel for young adult readers to contain a scene sympathetically describing a homoerotic encounter between boys and the complex feelings surrounding the experience" (p. 251). An excerpt from one of Ms. Nordstrom's letters to Donovan predicts that "the book will meet with considerable resistance with certain influential persons in the children's book field" (p. 262). However, despite the publisher's anxiety, the book received almost universal praise. Both the *New York Times* and *School Library Journal* named it to their annual best books lists (Cart, 2004). This seminal piece of literature was followed by more books on the subject.

Throughout the 1970s, homosexual characters and themes emerged in literature for young adolescents. Most of these characters, however, seemed inevitably doomed to an untimely death. Cart (2004) reported that in the, "eight young adult novels that would appear in the next decade, death figures in three (*The Man Without a Face, Trying Hard to Hear You,* and *Sticks and Stones*)" (p. 2). Norton and Vare (2004) believe the death of these characters in young adult novels brought many readers to the conclusion that homosexuality, in the end, led to a horrible outcome.

The speed of homosexual themed book publishing increased in the 1980s, when a total of 41 titles was published (Cart, 2004). The decade brought books in which gay and lesbian teens found more positive depictions of homosexuality (*Annie on My Mind, Weetzie Bat*). The 1990s marked another increase in publishing, with 68 titles published (Cart, 2004). This trend in publishing continues, with current children's books offering positive examples of gay and lesbian parents and teens. These books, however, are still not common in most classrooms (Bargiel, Beck, Koblitz, O'Connor, Pierce, & Wolf, 1997).

A sampling of current titles indicates recently published novels present a balance of male and female characters in portrayals of gay and lesbian teens facing adolescent dilemmas similar to their straight peers (*Geography Club, Rainbow Boys, Boy Meets Boy*). Strides have been made in creating realistic and poignant novels for gay and lesbian pre-teens and teens. Glasgow (2001) explained that "young adult literature provides a context for students to become conscious of their operating world view and to critically examine

alternative ways of understanding the world and social relations" (p. 54). Cart (2004) added that there are increasing opportunities for teens of every sexual identity to see their faces in the pages of good fiction and to find the comfort and reassurance of knowing they are not alone, regardless of their circumstances. While literature with homosexual themes may not eliminate homophobia, well written books may help to dispel prejudices and fears and expand the views of homosexual teens' peers.

Books with Gay and Lesbian Characters and Themes in the Middle School Classroom

Carroll (1997) suggested that the process of eliminating homophobia may begin in middle school. Since the 1960s, middle school educators have begun to realize the classical canon might not meet the personal and social needs of their students and have begun to include young adult literature in the curriculum (see Figure 1). As Appleton (1996) stated, "American literature courses have [spent] too much time on works that have had little interest for students and [need] a living tradition of conversation into which students might enter" (p. 45). In contemporary middle schools, attention to students' personal, emotional, and social growth is seen as a complement to academic concerns. Young adult books can demonstrate to young teens that they are not the only ones who experience problems and confusion when dealing with their bodies and sexuality (Carroll, 1997).

Hamilton (1998) described the teaching of *Jack* (Homes, 1990) whose main character's father is gay. From his teaching experience, Hamilton learned that teachers need to "recognize our responsibility to prepare middle schoolers for their own futures by allowing them to share their diverse backgrounds, experiences, and beliefs" (p. 39).

The young adult books used in middle grades, however, need not directly address homosexuality to be effective in addressing discrimination. *The Misfits* (Howe, 2003), for example, depicts a student who is harassed for being effeminate. This situation provides an example of bullying, but it could lead to a discussion of an underlying homosexual theme.

Gallo (2004) believes books with gay characters are still forbidden in many schools and wonders if the religious beliefs and social fears of some people are preventing gay teens from coming into contact with books to which they can relate. She further asks what teachers can do to acknowledge and support gay students in the classroom. Glaeser (2003) responded that teachers should choose literature in which authors and characters are struggling with issues of identity. Further, he believes teachers must operate as a "conduit between the stories we teach and the stories of our students' experiences" (p. 10). Students sometimes view teachers as experts on human experiences simply because they are classroom authority figures (Petersen, 1999). Bailey (2005), responding to Gallo, stressed that, although school personnel, due to their own beliefs, may be uncomfortable addressing the issues surrounding homosexuality, it is nonetheless the professional responsibility of educators to provide a physically and psychologically safe learning environment for all middle school students.

The following articles, all published in the *Middle School Journal,* discuss the use of multicultural, multiethnic young adult literature in middle grades classrooms. Most contain annotated bibliographies of recommended pieces of literature.

Adams, J. & Bushman, J. H. (2006). Thematic solutions using young adult literature to increase reading comprehension. *Middle School Journal, 37*(4), 25–29.

Bacharach, N., & Miller, T. (1996). Integrating African American fiction into the middle school curriculum. *Middle School Journal, 27*(4), 36–40.

Bessant, D. (1997). Collaborating to connect good literature to middle school readers. *Middle School Journal, 29*(2), 8–12.

Jones, M. G., & Brader-Araje, L. (1999). Middle schools are communities of many voices. *Middle School Journal, 31*(2), 42–48.

Broaddus, K. & Ivey, G. (2002). Taking away the struggle to read in the middle grades. *Middle School Journal, 34*(2), 5–11.

Fleming, L. C., & Billman, L.W. (2005). "Are you sure we're supposed to be reading these books for our project?" *Middle School Journal, 36*(4), 33–39.

Perez-Stable, M. A., & Cordier, M. H. (1997). Add salsa to your classroom with young adult books about Latinos. *Middle School Journal, 28*(4), 23–27.

Vosler, J. M. (1997). No longer strangers: Books about refugees for middle school readers. *Middle School Journal, 29*(1), 52–56.

Vosler, J. M. (1997). Beyond stereotypes: Books about other cultures for middle school readers. *Middle School Journal, 28*(3), 54–57.

Figure 1 Literature that gives voice to diverse students and expands the literary experience of all learners.

Stover (1996) expanded on the issue of sexual identity. He challenged teachers to introduce young students to a variety of books that will help them question the reality derived from their limited life experiences to break down barriers based on cultural differences. George (2002) called on middle school teachers to take up the cause of social justice and use adolescent literature as a starting point for initiating crucial conversations that can inspire schools to be places where students feel safe and able to celebrate their differences and individuality. Glasgow (2001) followed this example and structured her classroom with a focus on social justice. She had students read novels that caused them to question the ways intolerance, discrimination, and homophobia were addressed in specific situations. Swartz (2003) also made a case for using young adult literature to address discrimination and insisted these books must include works that discuss racism, classism, sexism, and homophobia. Otherwise, she predicts, discriminatory attitudes will never change.

Teachers, however, need to use due diligence when selecting and presenting material with homosexual characters and themes. Suhor (1997) recounted a situation in which a teacher was challenged for distributing a reading list acquired from a local gay/lesbian group that was not intended as a resource for students. It is important to act judiciously with regard to presenting any material that might be considered controversial. The use of appropriate resources in making selection decisions is key to any successful effort and should include professionals

(e.g., school library media specialists, teachers, and counselors), organizations, and print resources. School library media specialists, in particular, are taught to apply a variety of criteria such as examining reviews and recommendations by professional sources and peers and assessment of reader-level suitability of content in making book selections.

Even well-intentioned teachers, however, may find themselves in the center of controversy. Broz (2001) described an attempt by a parent to remove *Am I Blue?* by Marion Dane Bauer from a middle school library. The book is an anthology of stories meant to help students seek to better understand themselves and contains at least one homoerotic scene. In the end, the book was allowed to remain part of the library collection. Teachers should realize that an effective reconsideration of challenged materials policy, recommended for all School libraries by the American Association of school Libraries and the American Library Association, is important in addressing such situations. The lack of such a policy should be cause for caution when selecting classroom curricula.

Allan (1999) suggested that the most logical way to teach works containing gay characters and themes is to be inclusive by integrating those books into the curriculum. She explains students need to understand they can learn about love, relationships, community, and family by working with gay texts written both by their peers and by contemporary authors of young adult fiction. She provided a list of actions teachers may take to create an inclusive environment that is conducive to the teaching of

Bauer, M. D. (Ed.). (1995). *Am I blue?* New York: Harper Collins.

Block, F. L. (1999). *Weetzie bat* (10th anniversary edition). New York: Harper Trophy.

Donovan, J. (1969). *I'll get there: It better be worth the trip.* New York: Harper Collins Publishing.

Garden N. (1982). *Annie on my mind.* New York: Farrar Straus & Giroux.

Hall, L. (1977). *Sticks and stones.* New York: Follett

Hartinger, B. (2003). *Geography club.* New York: Harper Tempest.

Holland, I. (1972). *The man without a face.* New York: Lippincott Williams & Wilkins.

Homes, A. M. (1990). *Jack.* Minneapolis, MN: Sagebrush Education Resources.

Howe, J. (2003). *The misfits.* New York: Simon & Schuster.

Levithan, D. (2003). *Boy meets boy.* New York: Knopf.

Sanchez, A. (2001). *Rainbow boys.* New York: Simon and Schuster.

Scoppettone, S. (1974). *Trying hard to hear you.* New York: Harper Collins Juvenile.

Figure 2 Young adult literature cited.

literature containing homosexual characters and themes. Some of these actions include:

- Increasing personal knowledge of gay and lesbian issues and history through self-study.
- Working to create explicit statements against hate violence in school policies and codes.
- Displaying classroom materials that include gay authors and historical figures.
- Establishing a classroom atmosphere of trust and openness, in which sexuality can be discussed in a respectful way.
- Choosing literature for in-class reading workshops that avoid gay stereotyping and promote discussion of gay-related issues.
- Including at least one required text that provides a complex look at gay characters or some aspect of gay culture and history.

Teachers are also encouraged to examine the school curriculum and incorporate gay and lesbian history, literature, and role models, just as has been done with diverse cultures, women, and people with disabilities (Bailey, 2005) (Figure 1 & 2).

Broz (2001), a university professor, lamented that he was not committed to making books about sexual orientation available to students and was not informed about the issues himself during his 25-year tenure as a public school English teacher. He challenged teachers to build a classroom library and be prepared to offer these books to students. This simple act seems to be the most obvious way for teachers to proceed when it comes to introducing books containing homosexual characters

and themes. As the person often most involved in the lives of some students, the classroom teacher is in a position to make a difference for many homosexual pre-teens and teens by building an open and honest classroom environment where students are not afraid to think and question and where they feel free to explore personal feelings without shame or fear. After all, "The purpose of literature in our classrooms should not be to create junior literary scholars but rather to help students make sense of the world" (Petersen, 1999, p. 46).

The dilemma over whether or not books with homosexual themes and characters should be used in the middle school is one that will continue to be debated and addressed in classrooms and libraries across the nation. In the past, American middle schools have actively and apppropriately addressed cultural issues related to ethnic and gender discrimination. One can expect these same schools to face the dilemma of discrimination based on sexual orientation to do what is ultimately best for students.

Notes

1. A concrete example of the consequences of not dealing with this type of harassment was experienced by the Tonganoxie, Kansas, School District in 2005. That year the United States District Court for the District of Kansas awarded a $250,000 settlement to a student who beginning in seventh grade was harassed repeatedly by "being called such names as 'faggot' and 'masturbator boy,' and being subjected to sexual-based rumors and other sexual innuendo" (Trowbridge, 2005; *Theno v. Tonganoxie Unified School District* No. 04-2195-JWL, 18 October 2005).

2. During spring semester 2006, a high school student teacher from DePauw University was forbidden to teach a Walt Whitman poem and an Alan Ginsberg poem in a junior level English class in Putnam County, Indiana, because mentioning the sexual orientation of these two authors would violate "community standards."

References

Allan, C. (1999). Poets of comrades: Addressing sexual orientation in the English classroom. *English Journal, 88*(6), 97–101.

American Library Association. (2006). *Evaluating the treatment of gay themes in books for children and younger adults: What to do until Utopia arrives. The Gay, Lesbian, Bisexual, and Transgendered Round Table of the American Library Association.* Retrieved March 5, 2006, from http://www.niulib.niu.edu/lgbt/evaluating.html

Appleton, A. N. (1996). *Curriculum as conversation: Transforming traditions of teaching and learning.* Chicago: University of Chicago Press.

Bailey, N. J. (2005). Let us not forget to support LGBT youth in the middle school years. *Middle School Journal, 37*(2), 31–36.

Bargiel, S., Beck, C., Koblitz, D., O'Connor, A., Pierce, K.M., & Wolf, S. (1997). Bringing life's issues into classrooms. *Language Arts, 74*(6), 482–490.

Broz, W. J. (2001). Hope and irony: Annie on my mind. *English Journal, 90*(6), 47–53.

Carroll, P. S. (1997). Today's teens, their problems, and their literature: Revisiting G. Robert Carlsen's books and teenage reader thirty years later. *English Journal 86*(3), 25–34.

Cart, M. (2004). What a wonderful world: Notes on the evolution of GLBTQ literature for young adults. *ALAN Review,* 1–4. Retrieved March 10, 2006, from http://www.findarticles.com/p/articles/mi_qa4063/is_200401/ai_n9385166/pg_2

Curry, A. (2005). If I ask, will they answer? Evaluating public library reference service to gay/lesbian youth. *Reference & User Services Quarterly 45*(1), 65–75.

Galley, M. (1999). New school curriculum seeks to combat anti-gay bias. *Education Week, 19*(10), 6.

Gallo, C. J. (2004). The boldest books. *English Journal, 94*(1), 126–130.

George, M. A. (2002). Living on the edge: Confronting social injustices. *Voices from the Middle, 9*(4), 39–44.

Glaeser, C. (2003). Why be normal? The search for identity and acceptance in the gifted adolescent. *English Journal, 92*(4), 33–41.

Glasgow, J. N. (2001). Teaching social justice through young adult literature. *English Journal, 90*(6), 54–61.

Hamilton, G. (1998). Reading jack. *English Education, 30*(1), 24–39.

Louis Harris & Associates. (1999) *The Metropolitan Life survey of the American teacher, 1999: Violence in America's public schools—five years later.* New York: Metropolitan Life Insurance Company. Retrieved November 10, 2006, from http://www.metlife.com/Applications/Corporate/WPS/CDA/PageGenerator/0,4132,P2323,00.html

Marcus, L. S. (Ed.). (1998). *Dear genius: The letters of Ursula Nordstrom.* New York: HarperCollins Publishing.

National Middle School Association. (1995). *This we believe: Developmentally responsive middle level schools.* Columbus, OH: Author.

National Middle School Association. (2003). *This we believe: Successful schools for young adolescents.* Westerville, OH: Author.

Norton, T. L., & Vare, J. W. (2004). Literature for today's gay and lesbian teens: Subverting the culture of silence. *English Journal, 94*(2), 65–69.

Petersen, S. A. (1999). A love affair with American literature. *English Journal, 89*(2), 40–48.

Rabinsky, L. B., & Danks, C. (Eds.). (1999). *Teaching for a tolerant world: Essays and resources.* Urbana, IL: National Council of Teachers of English.

Reese, J. (2000). Creating a place for lesbian and gay readings in secondary English classrooms. In W. J. Spurlin (Ed.), *Lesbian and gay studies and the teaching of English* (pp. 131–146). Urbana, IL: National Council of Teachers of English.

Stover, L. (1996). A new year's resolution: Breaking boundaries. *English Journal, 85*(1), 86–87.

Suhor, C. (1997). Censorship: When things get hazy. *English Journal, 86*(2), 26–28.

Swartz, P. C. (2003) Bridging multicultural education: Bringing sexual orientation into the children's and young adult literature classrooms. *Radical Teacher, 66,* 11–16.

Theno v. Tongonoxie Unified School District. U.S. District Ct. for Kansas (10th Cir.), Case No. 04-2195-JWL, October 18, 2005. Retrieved March 4, 2007, from http://www.ksd.uscourts.gov/opinions/042195-162.pdf

Trowbridge, C. (2005, August 11), Federal jury awards $250,000 to former Tongonoxie student. *The Tongonoxie Mirror.* Retrieved March 4, 2007, from http://www.tongonoxiemirror.com/section/breaking_news/storypr/8135

JEFF WHITTINGHAM, middle level program coordinator, is an assistant professor of middle level education at the University of Central Arkansas, Conway. E-mail: jeffw@uca.edu. **WENDY RICKMAN,** a clinical instructor, is director of the Technology Learning Center at the University of Central Arkansas, Conway. E-mail: wrickman@uca.edu.

Celebrating Diversity through Explorations of Arab Children's Literature

Tami Al-Hazza and Bob Lucking

Incidents of terrorism and other forms of heinous violence around the world are so dramatic and painfully wrenching that they often dictate change: in politics, in social convention, in battle, and in the classroom. The five years since the 9/11 attacks, in particular, have brought about huge shifts in the collective global view of Arabs, and it is certainly timely to examine how educators treat the literature of the people in that part of the world. While language arts teachers may feel like throwing up their arms in frustration at being asked to learn about yet another body of children's literature, it has never been more important to represent a clear-headed and balanced view of a people, their culture, and their literature. In the United States, Arabs and Arab Americans have become a minority of suspicion (Al-Hazza & Lucking, 2005), and enormous misconceptions and biases exist about these people and their culture. Mindful of all teachers' efforts to establish cultural pluralism in their classrooms (Banks, 1991), we hope to offer some guidance in defining these issues relative to children's literature that accurately reflects some of the cultural norms of the Arab world.

To begin, many educated Americans do not even know what the term *Arab* means, and many confuse the terms "Arabs" and "Muslims." People who describe themselves as Arab speak Arabic or claim the Arabic language as their ancestors' mother tongue, possess Semitic roots, and trace their lineage to the descendants of Abraham and Hagar (Goldschmidt, 1989). The majority of Arabs are from Africa and the Middle East, in a region that stretches from Mauritania, positioned on the Atlantic coast of Africa, to Oman, which is situated on the Indian Ocean coast of the Arabian Peninsula. This territory encompasses 22 countries, located in three regions: countries in northern Africa, countries situated on the Mediterranean but not in Africa, and countries located in the heart of Arabia, on the Arabian Peninsula. All Arab countries combined constitute an Arab world population of approximately 300 million people (Elmandjra, 2004). The geographic area of the Middle East is also home to Pakistani, Kurds, Turks, Iranians, Afghans, and Armenians, who are not considered Arabs. They each have their own distinct language, traditions, and cultures.

One of the most persistent points of misunderstanding is that all Muslims are Arabs and that all Arabs are Muslim. The two terms are not interchangeable. The majority of Muslims are from Indonesia; only 20 percent of the world's Muslim population is Arab (Suleiman, 2000). Arab communities also contain significant populations of Copts, Melokites, Christians, Jews, Druze, and Maronites; this diversity of faith is due, in part, to the fact that the majority of Arab countries place no restrictions on freedom of worship.

All of these nuances are lost in popular culture as there is a constant search for formulaic villains. Movies and television have prominently featured Arab villains in recent years; not since the days of "cowboys and Indians" has such a dichotomous portrayal of good and evil been more apparent. Arab extremists or Muslim fundamentalists bent on destroying the world populate contemporary films. This formulaic portrayal of villainy also can be found in comic books and action computer games (Khan, 2004).

Therefore, Arab Americans are sometimes viewed through the scrim of misconception. They often are assumed to be impoverished and lacking in education, when this is quite untrue. Whereas 24 percent of all Americans hold college degrees, 41 percent of Arab Americans are college graduates. Furthermore, the median annual income of an Arab American family living in the United States in 1999 is $47,000, compared with $42,000 for all U.S. households. More than half of such families own their own home. Seventy-three percent of people of Arab descent in the United States work as managers or professionals, while the overall U.S. average is 34 percent (Arab American Institute, 2005).

One of the reasons that Americans have a distorted view of Arabs is the dramatic and often negative image that popular culture frequently projects of the Middle East. What is missing in the images that Americans receive from, and about, the Middle East is a realistic and humanistic portrayal of a people and their culture as told from an indigenous perspective. To promote an acceptance of diverse individuals, teachers can introduce good-quality Arab children's literature that accurately depicts Arab culture, creates positive images, and credibly represents Arabs in the plots, descriptions, and illustrations (Bishop, 1997). It is essential that children are exposed to stories that describe everyday events and the thoughts and feelings of Arab children.

Traditional Literature

While teachers can select from many genres of Arab children's literature, fairy tales from the Arab world are a wonderful place to begin since these stories, as is the case of many stories from traditional cultures, are designed to transmit cultural values and mores as well as entertain readers and listeners. *Sitti and the Cats: A Tale of Friendship* (Bahous, 1999) is an excellent example of a children's fairy tale that exemplifies traditional Arab values. This fairy tale relates behavior and values that are socially acceptable for survival in a small village in Palestine. The main character, an elderly widow called Sitti who has outlived her family, is rewarded for her benevolent nature, good heart, and kind deeds to others by a gift from a family of magical cats.

Sitti's experiences offer insight into the traditional beliefs and values inherent in the Arab culture, such as generosity, fulfilling one's role in society, caring for others before oneself, and hard work. The predominant theme throughout this story is thinking of one's responsibility to the group before considering individual wants. This theme is explored as the neighbors share their crops, firewood, and other necessities with Sitti and with each other, thus caring for each other to ensure the survival of the entire village.

The importance of generosity is emphasized when Sitti is given a magical gift of gold and silver, and her immediate response is to purchase items for others. Only after she has bestowed gifts on significant individuals does she consider her own needs. Generosity is a common theme throughout Arab children's stories and is predominant in Arabs' everyday lives.

Another bedrock value in Arab societies is respect and concern for the elderly. In *Sitti and the Cats,* these traits are manifested by the neighbors who care for Sitti in a respectful fashion. They do not just give her the supplies she needs; they allow her to perform small but important services, such as babysitting or mending clothes, in exchange for her daily staples. This type of exchange allows Sitti to maintain her dignity and save face, while ensuring that she is able to sustain her standard of living and her place in society. Saving face, or preserving one's personal dignity within the social order, is a motivation common throughout the Middle East and the Far East. Losing face would involve being embarrassed or being viewed as capable of committing acts considered unacceptable by the larger society. These social strictures are deeply rooted in traditional and modern Middle Eastern culture, and it is imperative that individuals maintain a level of decorum in public in order to maintain face.

Numerous other fairy tales are available to classroom teachers that can open new doors and broaden children's cultural horizons. These tales can be found in such books as *The Golden Sandal* (Hickox, 1998), *Aladdin* (Johnson-Davies, 1995), *The Animals of Paradise* (Durkee, 1996), *Goha the Wise*

Fool (Johnson-Davies, 1993), *Sindbad: From the Tales of the Thousand and One Nights* (Zeman, 1999), and *The Storytellers* (Lewin, 1998). *The Golden Sandal* is an Iraqi version of the Cinderella story, dating back thousands of years. Elementary-age children will enjoy comparing and contrasting the American and Arab versions of this story. And while most American children will be familiar with the story of *Aladdin,* Arab versions differ somewhat from Americanized versions (especially the Disney movie by that name). Children will delight in discussing the differences and how the Disney version was made to fit an Americanized image of Arabs.

Contemporary Realistic Fiction

Rich teaching opportunities about Arab cultures are not limited to fairy tales, of course. Children's books that offer unique insight into realistic, contemporary Arab life are also available and are invaluable resources. An example of this category of children's literature is *The Day of Ahmed's Secret* (Heide & Gilliland, 1990). This story is set in the bustling Egyptian city of Cairo. The colorful narrative offers a glimpse into unique aspects of Arab life with which most American children will be unfamiliar, such as the typical clothing worn by Egyptians, the exotic image of vendors selling their wares in the streets, and buildings designed in ancient Arab Islamic architecture. The plot of *Ahmed's Secret* revolves around a young boy who is brimming with glee in anticipation of telling his family that he has learned to write his name. American children will be able to relate to Ahmed's excitement as they learn about a new world, full of a rich diversity of uniquely Arab characters engaging in traditions and occupations typical of the early 20th century and no longer seen in more modern Arab cities.

Fulfilling one's role in society is a common theme throughout Arab stories. Although Ahmed is young, he is expected to work and help support his family. While the concept of child labor is quite alien to most American youngsters, Ahmed is proud that he is old enough and physically strong enough to perform the traditional work of his father and grandfather. This pride in carrying on the family trade is an excellent point of discussion for American teachers and can be related to historical fiction from many cultures.

Another key value emphasized in this book is the centrality of the family. The recurring theme of putting the needs of others (in this case, the family) above the needs of the individual is clear as Ahmed spends his days working, instead of playing like most American children. Yet, this book also allows young readers to see the commonality between cultures and to reach across borders to share the excitement of Ahmed's day.

The strong emphasis that Arab cultures place on the cohesiveness of the family is found in this story, as Ahmed honors his family by saving his special secret to reveal first to his parents, not to the other people he meets during the day. This tradition of telling important news to the most honored members of the family first is often found in Arab society. The importance of family time together also is evident as the family waits for all members to gather at the conclusion of the day to discuss significant events of the day. This tradition can be found throughout Arab literature and among Arab families of today. Other realistic contemporary fiction books that portray the same themes are *Sami and the Time of the Troubles* (Heide & Gilliland, 1992), *Samir and Yonatan* (Carmi, 2000), *A Stone in My Hand* (Clinton, 2002), and *Habibi* (Nye, 1999).

Historical Fiction

Another genre of Arab children's literature is historical fiction. *A Peddler's Dream* (Shefelman, 1992), one such example, focuses on Arab immigration to America. This book enables teachers to introduce to students a segment of the population that historically has been distorted or excluded from the elementary school curriculum. *A Peddler's Dream* relates how Mediterranean Arabs came to America in the early 1900s to pursue an economic livelihood. Because of widespread prejudice and subsequent limited opportunities, many could only find work as peddlers, traveling from farmhouse to farmhouse selling their wares.

This book presents a realistic portrayal of an immigrant from Lebanon, through the experiences of Solomon Azar. Students will be able to explore the similarities of Solomon's perspectives and experiences to those of other immigrants. The underlying theme of Arab life found throughout this book is the value of hard work and thrift. Solomon leaves his country and the woman to whom he is betrothed to come to the United States to establish a better future. He arrives with only the dream of owning a store, his ambition to succeed, and very little money. However, Solomon is a good man whose kindness and honesty help him to prosper in his endeavors, reaping the rewards of virtue.

Other books that offer a broader understanding of Arab culture and introduce young readers to historical people and events are: *Traveling Man: The Journey of Ibn Battuta* (Rumford, 2001), *Saladin: Noble Prince of Islam* (Stanley, 2002), *The House of Wisdom* (Heide & Gilliland, 1999), and *The Shadows of Ghadames* (Stolz, 2004).

Choosing Arab Children's Literature

Folktales, contemporary realistic fiction, and historical fiction are invaluable sources for teaching children about the Arab culture and traditions. Aside from the list presented here, many other wonderful works of Arab children's literature are available (refer to Al-Hazza, 2006, for a more comprehensive list), yet it can be difficult for the educator who does not have direct experience with the culture to choose stories that accurately represent the Arab culture. Guidelines that educators utilize when selecting Arab children's books for inclusion into the elementary language arts curriculum should be based on clear criteria.

In selecting multicultural children's literature, both the author's and the illustrator's credentials must be examined (Bishop, 1997; Temple, Martinez, Yokota, & Naylor, 1998).

While being a native of the Arab culture is one of the best qualifications to write about that culture (Sleeter & Grant, 2003), others may derive their legitimacy from traveling or residing in the area. If the storyline is written from the perspective of an insider or a native viewpoint, it rings with authenticity (McMahon, Saunders, & Bardwell, 1996/1997) and thus will be more likely to capture the hearts of young readers. Additionally, Sleeter and Grant contend that the books should authentically depict well-rounded characters, rather than portraying them as terrorists, religious fanatics, or polygamists. Educators also should pay attention to the relationships between characters in the story (Manning & Baruth, 2004). Ideally, the Arab characters would exert personal power in the story and not merely serve subservient roles in the work.

Careful examination should not be limited to thematic elements alone; the images included in the book should be brought under scrutiny as well. For example, the illustrations or art in the book should reflect details of dress, setting, and physical environment in ways that do not reinforce stereotypes. The issue of Arab women covering their heads with *hijabs* (head coverings) and *burqas* (veils) and Arab men wearing long flowing robes is potentially contentious and incendiary. The majority of Arab men from the Persian Gulf region still dress in the traditional robes called *dishdashas;* however, Arabs from the Mediterranean and North Africa wear a different type of attire. Many women throughout the Arab world choose to wear a veil over their face, but significant numbers of women do not (Al-Hazza, 2004). An open discussion with youngsters is likely the best path to true acceptance.

Photos or illustrations should accurately portray Arab people, their lifestyles, and the living circumstances of these diverse people. An immediate point of examination should be the physical representations of the people themselves. While the stereotypes shown in B-grade movies would have viewers believing that all Arabs have dark complexions, black hair, and black eyes, significant numbers of Arabs who have light skin, freckles, and brown or blond hair reside throughout the world. A modern storyline depicting Arabs living in tents in the desert and riding camels would likely be inappropriate. In a historical novel this depiction would be accurate; today, however, only a small percentage of Arabs reside in the desert and live a nomadic lifestyle.

Finally, the date of publication bears examination. Books published in the mid-1960s were often written from an Anglo-American perspective (Manning & Baruth, 2004). Books with a more recent publication date are more likely to be accurate.

Carefully choosing Arab children's literature, using such clear criteria as outlined here, will yield selections that provide avenues into the hearts and culture of Arabs and the various nationalities that constitute this ethnic group. Through exploration of the above-mentioned works of literature, and similar ones, students can reach beyond the mainstream culture. Young readers may come to appreciate the diversity represented by Arabs, which is especially important in these times of suspicion and misinformation. These literary experiences hold the power to free children from the damaging effects of premature, inaccurate, and prejudiced interpretations of a different culture (Spindler, 1987). Literature about Arab peoples reflects both the universal qualities of human experience and the unique dimensions of another part of the world, where social mores and cultural norms differ from those of mainstream American life. Teachers who show respect for ethnic and cultural pluralism are more likely to have students who are similarly inclined. Such instruction integrates an examination of attitudes, accurate information, and literary exploration, involving both teacher and students in developing a broader appreciation of the potential of all cultural groups. And it is only when people of all cultures believe that they have a place in the world order that we are likely to see an end to senseless acts of violence.

Children's Books Cited

Bahous, S. (1997). *Sitti and the cats: A tale of friendship.* Boulder, CO: Roberts Rinehart Publishers.

Carmi, D. (2000). *Samir and Yonatan.* New York: Arthur A. Levin Books.

Clinton, C. (2002). *A stone in my hand.* Cambridge, MA: Candlewick Press.

Durkee, N. (1996). *The animals of paradise.* London: Hood Hood Books.

Heide, F. P., & Gilliland, J. (1999). *The house of wisdom.* New York: DK Publishing.

Heide, F. P., & Gilliland, J. (1992). *Sami and the time of the troubles.* New York: Clarion Books.

Heide, F. P., & Gilliland, J. (1990). *The day of Ahmed's secret.* New York: Lothrop, Lee & Shepard Books.

Hickox, R. (1998). *The golden sandal.* New York: Holiday House.

Johnson-Davies, D. (1993). *Goha the wise fool.* Dokki, Cairo: Hoopoe Books.

Johnson-Davies, D. (1995). *Aladdin.* Dokki, Cairo: Hoopoe Books.

Lewin, T. (1998). *The storytellers.* New York: Lothrop, Lee & Shepard.

Nye, N. S. (1999). *Habibi.* New York: Simon Pulse.

Rumford, J. (2001). *Traveling man: The journey of Ibn Battuta.* Boston: Houghton Mifflin.

Shefelman, J. (1992). *A peddler's dream.* Austin, TX: Houghton Mifflin.

Stanley, D. (2002). *Saladin: Noble prince of Islam.* New York: HarperCollins.

Stolz, J. (2004). *The shadows of Ghadames.* New York. Delacorte Press.

Zeman, L. (1999). *Sindbad: From the Tales of the Thousand and One Nights.* Toronto, Ontario: Tundra Books.

References

Al-Hazza, T. C. (2004). Women in the Gulf Arab region: A historical perspective and present day comparison. In A. Gupta & S. Sinha (Eds.), *Empowering Asian women: Language and other facets* (pp. 76-94). Jaipur, India: Mangal Deep Publications.

Al-Hazza, T. C. (2006). Arab children's literature: An update. *Book Links, 15*(3), 11-17.

Al-Hazza, T., & Lucking, R. (2005). The minority of suspicion: Arab Americans. *Multicultural Review, 14*(3), 32-38.

Arab American Institute. (2007). *Arab Americans.* Retrieved January 2007, from www.aaiusa.org/arab-americans/22/ demographics.

Banks, J. A. (1991). A curriculum for empowerment, action, and change. In C. E. Sleeter (Ed.), *Empowerment through multicultural education* (pp. 125-142). Albany, NY: SUNY Press.

Bishop, R. S. (1997). Selecting literature for a multicultural curriculum. In V. J. Harris (Ed.), *Using multiethnic literature in the K-8 classroom* (pp. 1-19). Norwood, MA: Christopher-Gordon.

Elmandjra, M. (2004). *How will the Arab world be able to master its own independent developments?* Retrieved November 12, 2005, from www.transnational.org/forum/meet/2004/El-mandjra_ArabWorld.html

Goldschmidt, A., Jr. (1989). *Concise history of the Middle East.* Cambridge, MA: Westview Press.

Khan, A. (2004). Teens slam "racist" game, but still love it. *Reuters News Agency.* April 22, 2004. Retrieved January 2, 2006, from www.mafhoum.com/press7/191T44.htm

Manning, M. L., & Baruth, L. G. (2004). *Multicultural education of children and adolescents.* Boston: Pearson.

McMahon, R., Saunders, D., & Bardwell, T. (1996–1997). Increasing young children's cultural awareness with American Indians. *Childhood Education, 73,* 105–108.

Sleeter, C. E., & Grant, C. A. (2003). *Making choices for multicultural education: Five approaches to race, class and gender.* New York: John Wiley & Sons.

Spindler, G. D. (1987). *Education and cultural process: Anthropological approaches* (2nd ed.). Prospect Heights, IL: Waveland Press.

Suleiman, M. (2000). *Teaching about Arab Americans: What social studies teachers should know.* (ERIC Document Reproduction Service No. ED442 714)

Temple, C., Martinez, M., Yokota, J., & Naylor, A. (1998). *Criteria for evaluating multicultural materials.* Retrieved February 1, 2006, from the North Central Regional Educational Laboratory Web site: www.ncrel

TAMI AL-HAZZA is Assistant Professor and **BOB LUCKING** is Professor, Darden College of Education, Old Dominion University, Norfolk, Virginia.

Chica Lit: Multicultural Literature Blurs Borders

Marie Loggia-Kee

With chick lit, it's all about the attitude: Think of the original *Diary of Bridget Jones,* a tell-all of the dating life of a singleton. Chica lit takes that sass and combines it with culture.

Alisa Valdes-Rodriguez, author of the genre-setting bestseller *The Dirty Girls Social Club,* quickly dismisses the term "Latina lit." That's not what her novels are. They're *Chica lit.* "There has been a rich tradition of Latina literature out there, most of it quite literary and heavy. Chica lit, by contrast, is bubbly, fun, irreverent, modern, and fashionable," Valdes-Rodriguez says. "I think of Chica lit as being like the *Seinfeld* show, whereas traditional Latina literature is more like *ER.*"

> **There has been a rich tradition of Latina literature out there, most of it quite literary and heavy. Chica lit, by contrast, is bubbly, fun, irreverent, modern, and fashionable.**

In May 2006 Valdes-Rodriguez joined Mary Castillo, author of *Hot Tamara: What's Life Without a Little Spice,* among others, in Miami Beach at the first Chica Lit Club. While Valdes-Rodriguez usually sets her novels on the East Coast, Castillo captures the essence of Los Angeles. Together the two authors are helping to define a new genre of writing.

When Castillo submitted her manuscript for publication, editors told her the same thing over and over again: "It's not Latina enough." Often Chica literature breaks the traditional roles and forges a new identity; the protagonist of the new fiction is not just a woman of Latina heritage, she's a strong, and strongly identified, Latina-American woman.

In *Hot Tamara's* closing notes, Castillo said that she learned more about herself and her heritage while working on the book:

> Writing *Hot Tamara* was a journey for me to realize how much of a Latina I really am. In my family we didn't speak Spanish or even identify ourselves as Mexican. I was a fourth-generation American on my dad's side, who happened to be Mexican. ("Avon's Little Black Book on Mary Castillo," cited in *Hot Tamara*)

Castillo and other writers reach a segment of the population eager for role models that reflect some of the realities and obstacles they face in real life. Authors such as Valdes-Rodriguez and Castillo touch a growing mainstream population that often relates to more than one culture.

Industry Trends

One way to distinguish the direction of the publishing industry is to look at what the major houses solicit. Chica lit is showing up on the request list. Selina McLemore, a former editor at Harper-Collins Publishers who now acquires for Harlequin, credits not only literary writers such as Isabel Allende and Sandra Cisneros for changing the voice of the literature, but contemporary writers such as Valdes-Rodriguez and Castillo as well.

"We're seeing fiction that is truly intended for the commercial market," McLemore explains. "These writers and books are a reflection of the way Latino culture has become, in the last ten years, a much more accepted part of mainstream pop culture, as has been proven in music, movies, and TV."

Rather than assimilating her characters into mainstream culture, Valdes-Rodriguez notes that they and their stories reflect the lives of her readers. "I had no idea my work would resonate with so many people—more than half a million books sold to date," Valdes-Rodriguez says. "Again and again I hear that my work has affirmed the life choices many Latinas have made, like college and a professional career, choices that none of us have yet seen reflected in the mainstream media very well."

Cultural Identity

The recently published anthology *Border-Line Personalities: A New Generation of Latinas Dish on Sex, Sass and Cultural Shifting* explores the concept of self-defining that surfaces in many of the Chica lit novels. Michelle Herrera Mulligan, one of the anthology's editors, said that her mother accused her of not staying true to the culture. "Even though I'm half white," she said, "I thought I'd bridged the gap between my mother and me. If I didn't fit into her world, where did I belong?" (xxvi). Through the process of putting together the anthology, Herrera

Mulligan said that the contributors developed a "pathology of being Latina" (xxxi):

> We realized that ultimately, it is up to us to decide if we are Latina, to individually determine what the term means. We grappled with the implications of this on our greater cultures, and argued about the word's ability to entirely define us. At the end of this process, we realized that no matter how loaded, conflicted, and difficult the term may be, we are Latinas. Through heritage and by choice. (xxxi)

Hot Latinas

Rather than falling victim to the traditions of its readers' heritage, Chica lit forges new ground. The female characters in the literature follow their dreams and take on new roles: Women can be strong, and they don't have to be dependent on or subservient to a man. McLemore says that current stories are "more reflective of real Latina women."

The female characters in the literature follow their dreams and take on new roles.

"We're not just maids anymore, nor the salacious vixens of telenovelas," McLemore explains. "These stories often reflect the lives of first- and second-generation Latinas who have grown up in the United States, who may or may not even speak Spanish. They are about blending cultures, living in what can sometimes seem to be two very different worlds."

In the opening of Castillo's debut novel, *Hot Tamara*, the protagonist forgoes the traditional values of settling down with the "right" guy—by her family's standards—in order to pursue her dream of working for an art gallery. Like Tamara, the characters of Chica lit are not necessarily disrespectful, but that doesn't mean that their elders see them as respectful. In *Hot Tamara*, Tamara's mother expresses her feelings about modern girls:

> "You're so self-centered that you can't see how your idiotic decisions hurt everyone around you." Her mom's voice cracked. "We do these things for you because you can't. You're making a mistake, and as far as I'm concerned, I want nothing to do with it. You want to move to L.A.? Fine. Go. There's nothing for you here, and when you fall on your face, don't bother to come running to us." (72)

But Tamara is willing to go against the wishes of her mother and pursue her interests. Rather than taking the safe choice, this Latina embraces the diversity within her own heritage and the wider culture that enables her freedom.

Described by *New York* magazine as "the Hispanic version of *Waiting to Exhale*" (on the back cover of the book), *The Dirty Girls Social Club* also breaks through the multicultural barrier to address stereotypes about identity and gender roles. *The Dirty Girls* follows six Latina women who come from different cultural backgrounds. Lauren, the opening narrator, is a Cuban woman who learned Spanish for a reporting job; Amber

is Californian Mexican; Usnavys is Puerto Rican; Rebecca aligns herself as "Spanish," not "Mexican"; Sara is Cuban; and Elizabeth is a black Colombian. Valdes-Rodriguez shows the cultural diversity of the characters' milieu in her descriptions, but although all of these women hail from a different heritage, they are still considered "Latina" women.

While Valdes-Rodriguez says she's very much in touch with her own heritage, she admits that she learned much while writing her novel. "I'm not Colombian, but for Elizabeth's character, [I] had to learn about Colombia. In that sense, writing has broken down a lot of barriers for me," she explains. "I think all writers should stretch to include people whose backgrounds are different from their own. Just because I'm Latina doesn't mean I speak for all Latinas. We are a diverse group. The books that succeed will be those that reflect this diversity."

Fiction also touches on some of the same language and terminology issues addressed in the nonfiction anthologies; even though the women are "Latinas," they don't truly know what the word encompasses. In *The Dirty Girls Social Club*, Valdes-Rodriguez writes, "Nobody knew that we had no idea what a Latina was supposed to be, that we just let the moniker fall over us and fit in the best we could" (34).

In a recent interview, Castillo said that the new Chica fiction doesn't necessarily get pigeonholed into the "often hard-to-find Latino" section at Barnes & Noble. Instead, her readers vary from those who happen to be Mexican Americans to those who are not. At its heart, Chica fiction touches on a reality shared by many cultures. While the market has seen changes with the acceptance of a more "mainstream" Latina lit, Castillo implied that there is still a ways to go.

"I think they need to be honest portrayals of Latinas in all their cultural, racial, and economic diversity. Readers aren't dumb and they can sniff out a faker and stereotypes," Castillo said. "This is where authors and publishing houses can experience some tension. A friend of mine was asked to make the title of her new book 'more ethnic.' That is not only confusing to us authors, but also a bit demeaning. How much do you want to bet that Janet Evanovich isn't asked to make her titles 'more white' or 'more New Jersey'?"

Chica lit shows the main characters not only embracing their culture, but also accepting the diversity that comes along with it. Rather than following the traditional roles imposed within the Hispanic culture, writers such as Castillo show that sometimes a woman's got to stay true to herself.

"Chica lit is filling a void in commercial women's fiction in the United States and elsewhere by portraying Latinas as diverse, modern, funny, smart, educated, independent, and professional," Valdes-Rodriguez offers. "Many of my Latina readers also enjoy Sophie Kinsella and Jennifer Weiner, so in a sense it's not imperative that a reader identify with the ethnicity of a character. Many of my readers, too, are not Latina at all. The most important thing a writer can offer readers is believable characters who are fundamentally human, flawed like the rest of us.

"It is the universal appeal of character that hooks readers," she continues, "regardless of the racial, cultural, or ethnic

background of the reader, writer or characters. That said, it is of course important for people to feel like their own life is somehow validated and accepted in popular culture."

References

Castillo, Mary. "Re: Answers to your questions." E-mail to the author. May 23, 2005.

Castillo, Mary. *Hot Tamara.* New York: HarperCollins, 2005.

McLemore, Selina. "Re: Latina Lit Trends." E-mail to the author. May 18, 2005.

Moreno, Robyn and Michelle Herrera Mulligan, eds. *Border-Line Personalities: A New Generation of Latinas Dish on Sex, Sass and Cultural Shifting.* New York: HarperCollins, 2004.

Valdes-Rodriguez, Alisa. *The Dirty Girls Social Club.* New York: HarperCollins, 2003.

Valdes-Rodriguez, Alisa. E-mail to the author. October 26, 2005.

With a mother who was adopted from Mexico at the age of 12 and an Italian-American father, **MARIE LOGGIA-KEE** understands growing up between cultures. In addition to writing, she teaches English and popular culture and the University of Phoenix and National University.

From *Multicultural Review,* Spring 2007, pp. 46–48. Copyright © 2007 by Multicultural Review. Reprinted by permission of The Goldman Group, Inc.

UNIT 6

Motivating Involvement and Social Action

Unit Selections

Key Points to Consider

- How can popular music be used to teach social issues that are contemporary and from the past?

- How did the three historically black universities in New Orleans find opportunities from the devastation?

- Describe examples of educational inequity.

- Why is it vital for classroom teachers to overcome education inequities for their students and themselves?

Student Website
www.mhcls.com

Internet References

Association for Moral Education
  http://www.amenetwork.org/
National Association of Social Workers
  http://www.socialworkers.org/pressroom/features/issue/peace.asp
National Economics and Social Rights Initiative
  http://www.nesri.org/?gclid=CIPVtYyWxJoCFRufnAodY1Q8sg
New Horizons for Learning
  http://www.newhorizons.org/strategies/multicultural/front_multicultural.htm

A phrase commonly used in multicultural education circles references "talking the talk and walking the walk." It is one endeavor to become knowledgeable about the multitude of topics and issues related to multicultural education and cultural competency; it is an entirely different endeavor to take steps and get involved to do something positive and productive for multicultural education. For many teacher candidates, classroom teachers, school administrators, and teacher educators, merely becoming acquainted with the vocabulary, concepts, resources, and practices informing and supporting multicultural education so they can talk the talk presents an overwhelming challenge. Walking the walk requires a different focus.

Far too many educators do not know what multicultural education is, how it is practiced, and why it is vital for every student and educator. Unfortunately, far too many educators of all ages and in all stages continue to resist multicultural education and cultural competence. Thoughts, words, actions, and interactions that are biased, stereotypical, and prejudicial are displayed in schools and classrooms across the United States. Some educators continue to demonstrate acts of power and control in order to promote selected individuals and groups of people while demoting other individuals and groups of people. Public displays of disenfranchisement and discrimination are far too common in educational settings. By chance and by choice, these disingenuous displays communicate harsh messages to both the victims and the witnesses that resonate across the community.

The actions can be both overt and covert. When actions are overt, they are not only visible and acknowledged, they are substantiated by false statements and extremely difficult to overturn due to popular support. The actions have long become ingrained into the school's traditions and local customs. For example, the names of athletic teams or schools' mascots. When the actions are covert, the actions are less visible and conducted in private; they tend to be denied as existing. The individuals responsible for the covert actions may or may not even be fully aware of their offenses. For example, schools that refer to the men's sports and the girl's sports are not using gender equal terminology. Examples of both overt and covert acts of discrimination are endless. Taking action against social injustice requires intelligence, courage, energy, determination, and support. As the famous quote stated by Margaret Mead (1901–1978), "Never doubt that a small group of thoughtful, committed citizens can change the world."

The questions of taking the best steps to overcome social injustice especially as an educator and with young people present serious challenges for everyone. Most educators can recognize inequality and are prepared in their teacher education programs to ensure that all students are treated fairly, and most educators comply with this expectation. As these educators work hard to ensure cultural competence throughout their curricular development, instructional strategies, assessment techniques, community building, and classroom management, frequently they discover that they place their students or themselves in jeopardy.

For example, a teacher may supplement the content with additional resources, engage the students in nontraditional learning experiences, administer alternative classroom assessments, rearrange the classroom seating, or practice innovative reward systems. These actions may be viewed as too extreme and threatening to other educators and some families. Classroom teachers

© Stockbyte/PunchStock

are strongly encouraged to discuss endeavors that may be considered extreme with their school administrators, share them with colleagues, and send them in writing to the students' families so everyone is informed well in advance.

Some teachers are more attuned to social injustice found in schools and society; their goal is to get their students involved in becoming part of the change. These teachers definitely should visit with their school administrators, colleagues, and community. When they are based on academic standards, grounded in learning theory, exemplifying student-centered activities and assignments, and assessed through a multitude of instruments, most activities will be approved wholeheartedly and supported profusely. Many school administrators seek mechanisms to increase attendance, achievement, and completion so the reported data are strong for their schools. School administrators also recognize that constructivist classrooms tend to produce more responsible and respectful students who serve as positive and productive role models for their peers.

Initiating activities related to educational inequities and social injustice range from classroom simulations followed by self-reflection to historical examinations accompanied with community involvement. Every aspect of the curriculum can contribute to learning the concepts of multicultural education and engaging in the practices applicable both inside and outside the classroom. The articles in Unit 6 provide guidelines and support for educators at all levels.

Popular Music Helps Students Focus on Important Social Issues

This We Believe *Characteristics*

- Students and teachers engaged in active learning
- Curriculum that is relevant, challenging, integrative, and exploratory
- Multiple learning and teaching approaches that respond to their diversity

JAMES R. MOORE

One of the biggest challenges facing middle school social studies educators is creating powerful lessons that engage young adolescents in acquiring knowledge, stimulate critical thinking skills, inspire passionate interest in social studies and social issues, encourage active participation in civic life, and provide them with opportunities to express their thoughts, values, and emotions (Bintz & Williams, 2005; Chapin, 2003; Slavin, Daniels, & Madden, 2005; Zevin, 2000). Middle school social studies educators must create lessons that are academically serious, yet provide students with varied activities that are enjoyable, intellectually challenging, developmentally appropriate, require active involvement, and incorporate other disciplines (Maxim, 2006).

Dewey (1933), when confronted with the task of balancing academic rigor with enjoyable activities, asserted, "Play degenerates into fooling and work into drudgery" (p. 286). By creating lessons that have a proper balance between hard work and pleasure, teachers can avoid Dewey's two extremes and enhance student achievement and motivation by meeting their cognitive, emotional, and developmental needs (Chapin, 2003; Davis & Thompson, 2004; Maxim, 2006).

This educational challenge is exasperated by the fact that many students, having grown up in a high-tech world characterized by rapid-fire audio and visual images, consider social studies to be the least important of the four core subjects, with little relevance to their everyday lives and future interests and goals (Chapin, 2003; Maxim, 2006). Traditional teaching methods—lectures, worksheets, reading from the textbook and answering questions—are viewed as boring, irrelevant, and mind-numbing and a primary reason why middle school students do not like social studies (Bower, Lobdell, & Owens, 2005; Chapin, 2003; Martorella, Beal, & Bolick, 2005; VanSickle, 1996). Negative

student attitudes are a logical consequence of reducing social studies to rote memorization and ignoring the controversy, passions, competing values, attitudes, and beliefs in human affairs. This is unfortunate, especially in light of the importance of social studies in producing American citizens capable of meaningful participation in a dynamic and pluralistic democracy. Therefore, it is important that teachers create activities that generate critical thought and passion in students and allow them to be actively involved in all of their educational experiences.

One of the most effective, enjoyable, and interesting ways to teach social studies to young adolescents is to integrate lessons with music, art, and other disciplines in ways that engage students cognitively and emotionally (Ference & McDowell, 2005; Mertens & Flowers, 2003; Zevin, 2000). For example, using a musical video, such as Billy Joel's *We Didn't Start the Fire,* which chronicles major events and people in American history from 1949 until 1989, to teach controversial social and historical issues provides students with a rich learning experience that combines sensory, cognitive, and emotional experiences that can be mesmerizing and thought-provoking (see Figure 1 for complete lyrics). Given that established middle school practice includes team teaching, small learning communities, active student participation, and an integrated curriculum, teaching social studies through the arts is a viable way to counter the negative attitudes formed by traditional teaching methods and show students that their personal lives—individual experiences, problems, attitudes, and goals—are intimately connected to social studies. Since middle schools were designed to foster an interdisciplinary approach to education, integrating music, new technologies, student-centered activities, and the other disciplines into social studies is a suitable way to counter the apathy and boredom spawned by traditional teaching methods.

Harry Truman, Doris Day
Red China, Johnny Ray

South Pacific, Walter Winchell,
Joe DiMaggio

Joe McCarthy, Richard Nixon
Studebaker, Television

North Korea, South Korea,
Marilyn Monroe

Rosenbergs, H-bomb
Sugar Ray, Panmunjom

Brando, The King and I
And The Catcher In The Rye

Eisenhower, Vaccine
England's got a new queen

Marciano, Liberace,
Santayana goodbye

We didn't start the fire
It was always burning since the
world's been turning
We didn't start the fire
No, we didn't light it
But we tried to fight it

Joseph Stalin, Melenkov
Nasser and Prokofiev

Rockefeller, Campanella,
Communist Bloc

Roy Cohn
Juan Peron
Toscanini, Dacron

Dien Bien Phu Falls,
Rock Around the Clock

Einstein, James Dean,
Brooklyn's got a winning team

Davy Crockett, Peter Pan
Elvis Presley, Disneyland

Bardot, Budapest
Alabama, Khrushchev

Princess Grace
Peyton Place
Trouble in the Suez

We didn't start the fire
It was always burning, since the
world's been turning
We didn't start the fire

No, we didn't light it
But we tried to fight it

Little Rock, Pasternak,
Mickey Mantle, Kerouac

Sputnik, Chou En-Lai,
Bridge On The River Kwai

Lebanon, Charles de Gaulle,
California baseball

Starkweather homicides,
Children of Thalidomide

Buddy Holly, Ben Hur
Space Monkey, Mafia

Hula Hoops, Castro
Edsel is a no-go

U2, Syngman Rhee
Payola and Kennedy

Chubby Checker, Psycho,
Belgians in the Congo

*Complete lyrics and links to many of
the topics mentioned are available at*
www.teacheroz.com/fire.htm

Figure 1 We didn't start the fire by Billy Joel.

Creative Teaching Methods Stimulate Student Interest and Achievement

Research demonstrates that innovative social studies instructional methods—a social issues approach (one that examines values, attitudes, beliefs, and both sides of controversial issues); small-group discussions; role-playing; mock trials; structured debates; simulations; cooperative learning; games; Internet applications (virtual field trips, telecollaboration, multimedia software, and access to all kinds of data); and the incorporation of art, literature, and music into the social studies curriculum—can enhance middle school student interest and academic performance (Bower, Lobdell, & Owens, 2005; Chapin, 2003; Martorella, Beal, & Bolick, 2005; Slavin, Daniels, & Madden, 2005; Sunal & Haas, 2005; Zevin, 2000). There is a wide variety of resources, such as videos, CD-ROMs, PowerPoint presentations, and DVDs that provide social studies teachers more opportunities to engage young students in exciting learning activities that incorporate multiple learning styles, new technologies, and their interests (Bower, Lobdell, & Owens, 2005; Chapin, 2003; Zevin, 2000).

These student-centered activities require active participation that allows the students to become personally involved in their learning; when students can express their knowledge, feelings, emotions, and values, they reap a host of educational and social benefits—increased motivation to succeed academically, the development of critical thinking skills, an appreciation for the connections between school and society, and the acquisition of citizenship skills—that prepare them to live in a multicultural society where free expression, dissent, persuasion, and compromise are central to the democratic process (Bower, Lobdell, & Owens, 2005; Chapin, 2003; Maxim, 2006; Zevin, 2000).

Furthermore, middle school students are capable of abstract reasoning and problem-solving if they are presented with creative instructional activities. Designing social studies lessons that revolve around controversial social issues will sharpen these reasoning skills and provide them with the intellectual tools to make informed moral decisions that are critical in a democratic society where debate, discussion, dissent, and compromise are crucial to success and political stability (Chapin, 2003; Zevin, 2000). For example, two powerful and controversial 1960s Vietnam War songs illustrated the sharp divisions in American society over the war; an examination of both songs would introduce students to multiple perspectives regarding this highly controversial event in American history. *The Ballad of the Green Berets,* by Vietnam veteran Barry Saddler, was a patriotic song that asserted that the war was a morally justified attempt to liberate Vietnam from communism. Conversely, Joe McDonald's *I-Feel-Like-I'm-Fixin'-to-Die-Rag* was a strongly anti-war song (but not anti-soldier) that asserted Americans were dying for an unjust war spawned by elite desires for profits and hegemony (see Figures 2 & 3 for lyrics of both songs).

Fighting soldiers from the sky
Fearless men who jump and die
Men who mean just what they say
The brave men of the Green Beret

Silver wings upon their chest
These are men, America's best
One hundred men we'll test today
But only three win the Green Beret

Silver wings upon their chest
These are men, America's best
One hundred men we'll test today
But only three win the Green Beret

Back at home a young wife waits
Her Green Beret has met his fate
He has died for those oppressed
Leaving her this last request

Trained to live, off nature's land
Trained in combat, hand to hand
Men who fight by night and day
Courage deep, from the Green Beret

Put silver wings on my son's chest
Make him one of America's best
He'll be a man they'll test one day
Have him win the Green Beret

Music and lyrics available at wmw.nih.niehs.gov/kids/lyrics/greenberets.htm

Figure 2 Ballad of the green berets by Barry Sadler and Robin Moore.

Yeah, come on all of you, big strong men,
Uncle Sam needs your help again.
He's got himself in a terrible jam
Way down yonder in Vietnam
So put down your books and pick up a gun,
We're gonna have a whole lotta fun.

And it's one, two, three,
What are we fighting for?
Don't ask me, I don't give a damn,
Next stop is Vietnam;
And it's five, six, seven,
Open up the pearly gates,
Well there ain't no time to wonder why,
Whoopee! we're all gonna die.

Well, come on generals, let's move fast;
Your big chance has come at last.
Gotta go out and get those reds —
The only good commie is the one who's dead
And you know that peace can only be won
When we've blown 'em all to kingdom come.

And it's one, two, three,
What are we fighting for?
Don't ask me, I don't give a damn,
Next stop is Vietnam;
And it's five, six, seven,
Open up the pearly gates,
Well there ain't no time to wonder why
Whoopee! we're all gonna die.

Huh!

Well, come on Wall Street, don't move slow,
Why man, this is war au-go-go.
There's plenty good money to be made
By supplying the Army with the tools of the trade,
Just hope and pray that if they drop the bomb,
They drop it on the Viet Cong.

And it's one, two, three,
What are we fighting for?
Don't ask me,
I don't give a damn,
Next stop is Vietnam.

And it's five, six, seven,
Open up the pearly gates,
Well there ain't no time to wonder why
Whoopee! we're all gonna die.

Well, come on mothers throughout the land,
Pack your boys off to Vietnam.
Come on fathers, don't hesitate,
Send 'em off before it's too late.
Be the first one on your block
To have your boy come home in a box.

And it's one, two, three
What are we fighting for?
Don't ask me, I don't give a damn,
Next stop is Vietnam.
And it's five, six, seven,
Open up the pearly gates,
Well there ain't no time to wonder why,
Whoopee! we're all gonna die.

Available from
www.sfheart.com/protest/Index1.html

Figure 3 I-feel-like-i'm-fixin-to-die-rag by Joe McDonald.

Obviously, these songs, while written in the 1960s, speak to contemporary American opinions concerning our war in Iraq and provide educators with opportunities to demonstrate the relevance of social studies to current events; help students draw connections between the past and the present; analyze opposing values, beliefs, and attitudes; view diversity and conflict as a part of life; and provide opportunities for students to create and evaluate solutions to these problems. It is quite possible that middle school students have family or friendship connections to people serving in Iraq; thus, studying history and current events are not merely academic exercises but learning opportunities that directly affect personal understanding of events.

The Power of Music to Enhance Motivation and Achievement

The teaching of social issues via popular music provides numerous opportunities for students to achieve multiple social studies goals: increased motivation and interest in social studies, accumulating knowledge, making links between the past and present, examining the nature of controversial issues from multiple perspectives, expressing—in socially acceptable ways—powerful emotions so evident during young adolescence, and developing defensible moral positions regarding important social issues (White, 2005). Music is a powerful teaching tool because it appeals to the mind, the

```
You don't own me                          I don't tell you what to say
I'm not just one of your little toys      I don't tell you what to do
You don't own me                          So just let me be myself
Don't say I can't go with other boys      That's all I ask of you

And don't tell me what to do              I'm young, (I'm young) and I love
And don't tell me what to say               to be young
And when I go out with you                I'm free, (so free) and I love to be free
Don't put me on display                   To live my life the way that I want
                                          To say and do whatever I please
You don't own me
Don't try to change me in anyway          Music and lyrics available at
You don't own me                          www.niehs.nih.gov/kids/lyrics/youdont.htm
Don't tie me down, cause I'll never stay
```

Figure 4   You don't own me by John Madara and David White.

body, and the emotions; music, like art and literature, is a primary means by which people express their innermost feelings, hopes, values, and experiences. Furthermore, music provides insights about different cultures and historical eras and allows students to analyze the historical or contemporary social forces that have shaped human history (Zevin, 2000). For example, students could examine the development of national anthems to foster national unity and support for military campaigns; this demonstrates the connections between the arts, propaganda, and patriotism and shows the interdisciplinary nature of social studies education.

Popular music has wide appeal to adolescents because it taps into the raw energies and issues that are so important during this difficult age. Songs that discuss individual identity; love; friendship; the frustrations and risk-taking associated with youth; the generation gap; and social issues such as war, racism, sexism, poverty, and the abuse of power are bound to strike a powerful chord in students as they navigate their way in a highly complex, and often hostile, world. For example, Lesley Gore's 1963 hit *You Don't Own Me* (Figure 4) examines a young woman's attempts to fight sexism and choose her own path in life; when Gore sings about freedom and gender equality she strikes a chord that young women and girls can identify with as they develop their own identities and freely pursue their goals. This song provides an excellent introduction into the study of feminism (it was released in 1963, the same year as Betty Freidan's classic *The Feminine Mystique*), challenges students to examine their attitudes and beliefs regarding gender, allows for cross-cultural comparisons (such as Latin American or Middle Eastern cultures), and can stimulate class discussions.

The power of music is universal; all age groups can identify with particular musical genres that reflect the social and political conditions in society at that time. Most of these musical genres offer examples of social commentary and can be used to teach history and the social sciences. The wide variety of musical genres— jazz, opera, folk, rhythm and blues, country, rock and roll, and hip-hop—reflect different origins and the unique experiences of their founders and practitioners; yet they deal with universal themes, such as love, loss, emotional pain, injustice, war, and the harshness of life, that are relevant to all people (White, 2005).

Music, like art, philosophy, and literature, must be understood within the confines of the national culture or microculture that produced it; this fact supports the assertion that social studies

education must incorporate multiple perspectives into its curriculum (Koza, 1996). The humanities have long been in the service of reflecting and challenging the status quo; it is important that students understand that many factors—race, age, religion, social class, gender, nationality, geography, and personal experiences— play pivotal roles in creating popular music that expresses strong opinions regarding social issues.

Indeed, an examination of songs from the 1950s through the present would demonstrate popular music's devotion to social issues—war, race, gender, and social class—and its commitment to challenging the status quo. There have been many songs that have dealt with issues directly related to the lives of young adolescents; songs about sex, gender equality, drugs, war, violence, peer pressure, family problems, poverty, and discrimination. By listening to these songs and analyzing the lyrics in light of current or historical social conditions, students can engage in a number of intellectual pursuits. They can (a) learn to critically examine important social issues, (b) establish cause and effect relationships, (c) appreciate the contradictions and complexities inherent in all social issues, (d) apply social studies concepts to analyze and propose solutions to these issues, and (e) develop defensible, if not debatable, moral positions that will allow them to effectively participate as informed and thoughtful citizens. An example of teaching social issues through music will demonstrate the numerous educational possibilities.

Classroom Applications: Teaching about Racism via Popular Music

While America is characterized by a host of social issues, it is educationally sound to choose issues that are directly related to the lives of many middle school students and that correspond with national or state standards in social studies education. In fact, teaching social studies and current events using popular music directly addresses the 10 major themes articulated in the *Curriculum Standards for the Social Studies: Expectations of Excellence* (National Council for the Social Studies, 1994). These standards are based on the traditional social sciences, history, and because social studies is an interdisciplinary field, are linked to the humanities and natural sciences (see Figure 5 for a partial list of these standards).

I. Culture (anthropology and sociology).
C. Explain and give examples of how language, literature, the arts, architecture, other artifacts, traditions, beliefs, values, and behaviors contribute to the development and transmission of culture.

II. Time, Continuity, and Change (history).
D. Identify and use processes important to reconstructing and reinterpreting the past, such as using a variety of sources, providing, validating, and weighing evidence for claims, checking credibility of sources, and searching for causality.

IV. Individual Development and Identity (psychology and social psychology).
C. Describe the ways family, gender, ethnicity, nationality, and institutional affiliations contribute to personal identity.

V. Individuals, Groups, and Institutions (sociology and political science).
A. Demonstrate an understanding of concepts such as role, status, and social class in describing the interactions of individuals and social groups.
D. Identify and analyze examples of tensions between expressions of individuality and group or institutional efforts to promote social conformity.

VI. Power, Authority, and Governance (political science/law).
A. Examine the issues involving the rights, roles, and status of the individual in relation to the general welfare.
H. Explain and apply concepts such as power, role, status, justice, and influence to the examination of persistent issues and social problems.

VIII. Science, Technology, and Society (interdisciplinary).
C. Describe examples in which values, beliefs, and attitudes have been influenced by new scientific and technological knowledge, such as the invention of the printing press, conceptions of the universe, applications of atomic energy, and genetic discoveries.

Figure 5 National council for the social studies, expectations of excellence: selected middle school curriculum standards.
Source: National Council for the Social Studies (1994).

For example, there are many songs that illustrate the plight of oppressed groups and their persistent demand that America fulfill its constitutional mandate to eliminate racial discrimination and provide equality and liberty for all individuals. The gospel song *We Shall Overcome*, a powerful song depicting the valiant struggles of African Americans to achieve equal rights in a segregated and racially hostile America, was the definitive anthem during the 1950s and 1960s civil rights movement because it reflected the indomitable will of human beings to fight against all forms of oppression and discrimination (see Figure 6 for the lyrics). This song directly addresses performance expectations for the following NCSS themes: Culture; Time, Continuity, and Change; Individual Development and Identity; Individuals, Groups, and Institutions; and Power, Authority, and Governance.

Racism, long the "Achilles' heel" in America's experiment with democracy, remains one of the most important social issues in the 21st century (Banks, 2006; Gollnick & Chinn, 2006).

In fact, racism is closely associated with imperialism, religious discrimination, and ethnic hostilities. This explains why so many songs, as well as other artistic forms, deal with racial issues; songs such as Three Dog Night's *Black and White*, Eminem's *White America*, B. B. King's *Why I Sing the Blues*, and Paul Revere and the Raiders' *Indian Reservation* all examine various aspects of racism, violence, segregation, and imperialism. These issues, while controversial, are a part of history and educators should expose students to the negative and positive aspects of the events that have shaped American and world history.

Teaching middle school students about prejudice, discrimination, and the treatment of minority groups throughout American history is very important and provides educators opportunities to change attitudes and beliefs about racial, ethnic, and religious groups—a prerequisite for changing behaviors. Middle school is the time when many young adolescents—struggling to develop an identity and their place in the world—fully encounter racism and discrimination in their environments. It is educationally sound to help students develop positive attitudes and beliefs—ones that are compatible with American laws and ideals regarding liberty, equality, and social justice—about all cultural groups before stereotypes become ingrained in their thought processes (Walker, 2005). The arts—particularly music that appeals to human passions—are powerful teaching tools because they are material expressions of the human spirit that is central to the cognitive and affective development of middle school students.

There are many songs about racism and discrimination that educators could use in the middle school. Of course, caution must be used to ensure that the songs are appropriate for middle school students regarding language and content. One very powerful song about racial prejudice and discrimination—a song that includes important implications regarding the role families, peer groups, and institutions play in perpetuating racial intolerance—is *Society's Child* (1967, available from www.sfheart.com/protest/index1.html) by Janis Ian. The lyrics reveal the intense pain a white student experiences because she is not allowed to date an African American male:

Come to my door, baby
Face is clean and shining black as the night
My mother went to answer you know
That you looked so fine
Now, I could understand
Your tears and your shame
She called you "boy" instead of your name
When she wouldn't let you inside
When she turned and said
But honey, he's not our kind

She says, I can't see you any more, baby
Can't see you anymore

Walk me down to school, baby
Everybody's acting deaf and blind
Until they turn and say
Why don't you stick to your own kind
My teachers all laugh
Their smirking stares
Cutting deep down in our affairs

We shall overcome, we shall overcome,
We shall overcome someday;
Oh, deep in my heart, I do believe,
We shall overcome someday.

The lord will see us through,
The lord will see us through,
The lord will see us through someday;
Oh, deep in my heart, I do believe,
We shall overcome someday.

We're on to victory,
we're on to victory,
We're on to victory someday;
Oh, deep in my heart, I do believe,
We're on to victory someday.

We'll walk hand in hand,
We'll walk hand in hand,
We'll walk hand in hand someday,
Oh, deep in my heart, I do believe,
We'll walk hand in hand someday.

We are not afraid,
We are not afraid,
We are not afraid today;
Oh, deep in my heart, I do believe,
We are not afraid today.

The truth shall make us free,
The truth shall make us free,
The truth shall make us free someday;
Oh, deep in my heart, I do believe,
The truth shall make us free someday.

We shall live in peace,
We shall live in peace,
We shall live in peace someday;
Oh, deep in my heart, I do believe,
We shall live in peace someday.

Available from www.kstate.edu/
english/help/american.studies.s98/we.
shall.overcome.html

Figure 6 We shall overcome adapted from gospel songs by Guy and Candy Carwan.

Preachers of equality
Think they believe it
Then why won't they just let us be

They say, I can't see you anymore, baby
Can't see you anymore

One of these days I'm gonna stop my listening
Gonna raise my head up high
One of these days
I'm gonna raise up my glistening wings and fly
But that day will have to wait for a while
Baby I'm only society's child
When we're older things may change
But for now this is the way they must remain

I say, I can't see you anymore, baby
Can't see you anymore
No, I don't want to see you anymore, baby

Suggested teaching procedures for this song might include using it as an "advanced organizer" to generate interest in racism and discrimination. It could also be incorporated into a larger unit plan on civil rights, slavery, segregation, or contemporary race relations in the United States. Using *Society's Child* to teach students about racism, social norms, and conflicts between individuals and society directly addresses several of the National Council for the Social Studies' curriculum standards. For example, one of the performance expectations under "Individuals, Groups, and Institutions" is to "identify and analyze examples of tensions between expressions of individuality and group or institutional efforts to promote social conformity." This song—about a white girl's love for an African American boy in a racist society—provides an excellent example of the tensions between individual desires and the pressure from families and society to conform to accepted social norms and laws (see Figure 5 for the NCSS curriculum standards). Additional ideas for using this song include these:

1. Lay a foundation for discussing discrimination in history and how the arts are often used to reflect social, economic, and political conditions. A handout with appropriate vocabulary terms—prejudice, discrimination,

ethnocentrism, racism, segregation, and stereotypes—will help facilitate an interesting discussion and provide students with background information.

2. Distribute the lyrics to the students and have them orally read the lyrics. Ask them to analyze the meaning of the lyrics, helping them understand the use of metaphors and symbols by the artist. This is a critically important skill for young adolescents; the ability to decode the messages in music can be transferred to poetry, literature, and other forms of writing. This activity can be done in small groups, and then a whole-class discussion could follow focusing on the group findings.

3. Play the song (e.g., via computer, CD player, iPod) and ask students to listen for the main idea(s) of the song. Also, ask them to identify the messages and emotions the artist is attempting to convey to the listeners.

4. Have the students reread the lyrics and conduct a class discussion with the questions in Figure 7. You could prepare a music analysis sheet with the questions, place them on an overhead projector, or display them in a PowerPoint presentation.

5. Bring closure to the activity by highlighting the key points and ask students if they have any questions or comments. It is quite possible some students (or their family members or friends) have had a similar experience. This may be true with any social issue—drug use, divorce, poverty, and child abuse. Discussion of these topics must be handled with professionalism and sensitivity.

Alternative Teaching Suggestions with Music

There are many other possible teaching suggestions integrating music into social studies and other academic disciplines. For example, if you are teaching a science or social studies class, you could select the 1969 hit *In The Year 2525* to demonstrate how changes in science and technology have profound effects on human thought, morality, politics, social institutions, the economy, and the environment. Indeed, the song asserts that our conception

a. Can you explain the most important message in the song? Do you agree or disagree with the artist? Why or why not?

b. What is the artist's point of view regarding racial discrimination?
(good listeners will note the sadness and regret in the artist's voice)

c. How does the song reflect social conditions in 1967? (you may have to provide some background information, i.e., handouts, pictures, or a short video are effective ways to impart this information)

d. Can you identify two important social studies concepts or generalizations? (this answer could include prejudice, stereotypes, the hypocrisy between American ideals and actual behaviors, judging events within their historical context, individuals are a product of their environment, and many other possibilities)

e. Why are attitudes about race difficult to change?

f. How did the laws reflect these racist attitudes? (Jim Crow laws that mandated segregation, miscegenation laws forbidding interracial marriages until 1967)

g. How has racial discrimination hurt the United States? (morally, economically, politically, and culturally)

h. How have things changed since 1967? What accounts for those changes?

All of these questions—designed to stimulate thought—offer many possibilities for creating new lesson plans, creative homework, class and group assignments, and explorations of related themes, such as the civil rights movement, slavery, anti-Semitism, and gender discrimination.

Figure 7 Questions to provoke student thinking about the lyrics of society's child.

of what it means to be human will be drastically altered by genetic engineering, medical advances, and the development of new technologies. This song, with its powerful and disturbing lyrics, could generate an excellent class discussion centered on the relationships between science, religion, and human civilizations. Moreover, teachers could assign essay papers, class debates, and research projects based on the song's major themes; the interdisciplinary nature of the song would allow team teaching (science and social studies) and cooperative learning.

You could assign students to choose their own songs related to social issues. This can be very effective because they have control and take responsibility for their learning. The ability to choose their own social issue and song will be a powerful motivator. Inevitably, they will choose something they are passionate about, and this could generate a love for social studies and active civic involvement with an eye toward making a difference in society. Many students may decide to select a song by someone who is a member of their ethnic, racial, or religious group; this will help validate the cultural experiences of all students and expose students to music from other cultures (Koza, 1996). In the latter case, if students played and analyzed their songs for the entire class, they would learn that multiculturalism is an important

theme in all disciplines, and music reflects social realities, such as class, race, ideology, and gender. This activity could be part of a larger assignment that would involve gathering and analyzing data, reading numerous sources, and writing a reflective essay. Students could create an audiovisual presentation in accordance with specific guidelines from the teacher. They would learn to ask important questions, research the origins of social issues, recognize injustices in society, develop a moral position, and propose viable solutions to the problem; all of these activities involve higher order thinking skills such as analysis, synthesis, and evaluation.

Surfing the Internet will offer a wide variety of songs from different genres and eras that would be appropriate for history, government, economics, religion, and sociology. However, music, like all forms of expression, can advocate many different, and highly controversial, positions. There are songs that advocate drug use, violence, sexual promiscuity, and contempt for all forms of authority. While many students may listen to these songs at home, they may not be appropriate for middle school educational activities. The issues and songs listed in Figure 8 are some examples that teachers could use in their classes to impart knowledge, stimulate critical thought, propose viable solutions, and promote democratic ideals. This list reflects the diversity of the United States and includes Native American, Latino, African American, and female artists along with the work of Anglo males.

Conclusions

Many important social issues are directly related to the lives of middle school students. These young adolescents are at a very important developmental stage in their lives; they are developing a personal identity replete with attitudes, beliefs, and values that will affect their academic performance in high school and beyond. Therefore, middle school educators must find creative ways to teach social studies to maximize student achievement, stimulate critical thought, engage their passions and interests, and produce competent citizens capable of participation in a democratic society. Teaching social studies through the arts—music, art, and literature—is a highly effective method with students. Music provides students with important insights into the specific political, economic, and social conditions in a given historical era. By playing music or showing a music video, teachers can provide students with a vast array of images, sounds, symbols, and actions to analyze and discuss in ways that appeal to the intellectual, social, and emotional needs of young adolescents. Furthermore, there are numerous resources and materials, including the rapidly increasing number of educational Web sites, which offer teachers exciting ideas to teach social studies. By combining serious academic work with pleasurable and intellectually challenging activities, teachers can improve student achievement and motivation, create involved citizens who demonstrate a passion for social studies, and make a positive difference in students' lives; music can be an excellent antidote to adolescent apathy regarding social studies and other subjects.

Social Issue	Song	Artist
Native-Americans/genocide	*American Holocaust*	Georgie Jessup
Child sex abuse	*Luka*	Suzanne Vega
Race and colonialism	*War*	Bob Marley
Racism	*Black and White*	Three Dog Night
Patriotism/disillusion	*America*	Santana
Injustice/violence	*Where Is the Love*	Black Eyed Peas
Violence/war	*What's Going On*	Marvin Gaye
Drug abuse	*Kicks*	Paul Revere/Raiders
Gender inequality	*You Don't Own Me*	Lesley Gore
Political assassinations	*Abraham, Martin, and John*	Dion
Technology and society	*2525*	Zager and Evans
Major historical events	*We Didn't Start the Fire*	Billy Joel
War and politics	*Sky Pilot*	The Animals

Figure 8   Social issues and songs useful for creating stimulating social studies lessons.

References

Banks, J. A. (2006). *Cultural diversity and education.* New York: Allyn & Bacon.

Bintz, W. P., & Williams, L. (2005). Questioning techniques of 5th and 6th grade reading teachers. *Middle School Journal, 37*(1), 45–52.

Bower, B., Lobdell, J., & Owens, S. (2005). *Bring learning alive: The TCI approach for middle and high school social studies.* Palo Alto, CA: Teachers Curriculum Institute.

Chapin, J. (2003). *A practical guide to middle and secondary social studies.* Boston: Allyn & Bacon.

Davis, D. M., & Thompson, S. C. (2004). Creating high-performing middle schools in segregated settings: Fifty years after Brown. *Middle School Journal, 36*(2), 4–12.

Dewey, J. (1933). *How we think.* Boston: D. C. Heath.

Ference, R., & McDowell, J. (2005). Essential elements of specialized middle level teacher preparation programs. *Middle School Journal, 36*(3), 4–10.

Freidan, B. (1963). *The feminine mystique.* New York: W. W. Norton.

Gollnick, D. M., & Chinn, P. C. (2006). *Multicultural education in a pluralistic society.* (7th ed.). Upper Saddle River, NJ: Merrill Prentice Hall.

Koza, J. E. (1996). Multicultural approaches to music education. In C. A. Grant & M. L. Gomez (Eds.), *Making schooling multicultural: Campus and classroom.* (pp. 263–287). Englewood Cliffs, NJ: Merrill Prentice Hall.

Martorella, P. H., Beal, C. M., & Bolick, C. M. (2005). *Teaching social studies in middle and secondary schools* (4th ed.). Upper Saddle River, NJ: Merrill Prentice Hall.

Maxim, G. W. (2006). *Dynamic social studies for constructionist classrooms: Inspiring tomorrow's social scientists* (8th ed.). Upper Saddle River, NJ: Merrill Prentice Hall.

Mertens, S. B., & Flowers, N. (2003). Middle school practices improve student achievement in high poverty schools. *Middle School Journal, 35*(1), 33–43.

National Council for the Social Studies. (1994). *Curriculum standards for social studies: Expectations of excellence* (Bulletin 89). Washington, DC: Author.

Slavin, R. E., Daniels, C., & Madden, N. A. (2005). "Success for All" middle schools add content to middle grades reform. *Middle School Journal, 36*(5), 4–8.

Sunal, C. S., & Haas, M. E. (2005). *Social studies for the elementary and middle grades: A constructionist approach* (2nd ed.). Boston: Allyn & Bacon.

VanSickle, R. L. (1996). Questions of motivation for achievement in social studies. In B. G. Massialas & R. F. Allen (Eds.), *Critical issues in teaching social studies: K–12.* (pp. 81–110). New York: Wadsworth.

Walker, M. (2005). Critical thinking: Challenging developmental myths, stigmas, and stereotypes. In D. Comstock (Ed.), *Diversity and development* (pp. 47–66). Belmont, CA: Thomson Brooks/Cole.

White, C. (2005). Integrating music in history education. *Academic Exchange Quarterly, 9*(2), 94–98.

Zevin, J. (2000). *Social studies for the twenty-first century: Methods and materials for teaching in middle and secondary schools* (2nd ed.). Mahwah, NJ: Lawrence Erlbaum.

JAMES R. MOORE is an assistant professor of social studies education at Cleveland State University in Ohio. E-mail: j.moore2@csuohio.edu.

Framing the Effect of Multiculturalism on Diversity Outcomes among Students at Historically Black Colleges and Universities

BRIGHID DWYER

Historically Black colleges and universities [HBCUs] have been a tremendous asset for African Americans seeking higher education over the past 150 years (Anderson, 1988). Before 1950, traditionally Black institutions educated more than 75 percent of African American college students (Anderson, 1984). Although the percentage of African Americans educated at HBCUs has decreased to 20% since that time (U.S. Department of Education, 2005), retention rates among Black students at HBCUs are significantly higher than at traditionally White institutions (TWIs) (Redd, 1998). In addition, HBCUs reported better outcomes in student learning and self-confidence (Allen, 1992; 1996; Fleming, 1984). For example, compared to Black students at TWIs, Black students at HBCUs are more likely to report higher grade point-averages, better psychological development, greater satisfaction with campus activities and cultural support, and academic growth and maturity (Allen, 1987, 1992, 1996; Fleming, 1984). Moreover, students have better relationships with faculty and staff and are more likely to aspire to an advanced degree (Allen, 1996; Harvey & Williams, 1996). Furthermore, because of racially hostile campus climates at TWIs (Hurtado, 1996), HBCUs provide students with an alternative to predominantly White campuses wherein African American students may spend much of their time feeling alienated, frustrated, and unsupported (Oliver, Rodriguez, & Mickelson, 1985; Smith, 1989; Watson & Kuh; 1996).

However, greater numbers of African American students are choosing to attend TWIs over HBCUs (Allen & Jewell, 2002; Harvey & Williams, 1996; Redd, 1998). Harvey and Williams (1996) suggest that this shift has occurred because African American students now have a large array of institutions to choose from. As a result of the school desegregation acts of the 1950s (i.e., *Brown v. Board,* etc.) and the desegregation of higher education in the 1970s through the 1990s,[1]

HBCUs must now contend not only with being one of several institutions, historically Black or otherwise, from which African American students choose to attend, but must also consider admitting greater numbers of non-Black students into their institutions (Allen & Jewell, 2002; Blake, 1991; Brown, 2002). As a result of the greater numbers of White, Hispanic, Asian American, and Native American students attending HBCUs (Brown, 2002), the already existing international student population, and the diverse faculty that teach at these institutions (Anderson, 1988), HBCUs are becoming more racially diverse institutions.

The diversification of HBCUs has emerged as a result of factors specific to these institutions, yet despite the contributing factors, their bent towards diversity aligns with the recent push in higher education towards greater diversity, inclusion, and multiculturalism. Although diversity outcomes and multicultural curricula have been a part of an important discourse within mainstream higher education, these conversations have in large part neglected discussing multiculturalism and diversity outcomes at HBCUs. This investigation addresses this gap by examining the multiculturalism literature, as well as the literature specific to HBCUs, in an attempt to answer the question: *What is the effect of multiculturalism on diversity outcomes of HBCU students?*

Defining Diversity Outcomes

Before progressing with the discussion, it is important to define the way in which the term *diversity outcomes* will be employed. In a 2002 research investigation conducted by Gurin, Dey, Hurtado, and Gurin, the concept "diversity experiences" was used to describe both the classroom and informal interaction with college students from diverse experiences. This term describes most closely the phenomenon that is investigated in this study. However, I use *diversity outcomes* as a way of capturing the experiences students have as they interact with diverse others within their college environment; as well as the ways in which these experiences shape the interactions students will have with the world once they graduate from college. This term has been chosen in order to shift the focus away from the broad term "learning outcomes," and a more specific term, "democracy outcomes." *Diversity outcomes* describes more specifically the learning that occurs from exposure to diversity. Furthermore, it is an attempt to intentionally highlight students' facility with diversity and draw closer connections between diversity experiences and multiculturalism.

Contextualizing Multiculturalism and Multicultural Education

Multiculturalism within education is defined and contextualized in different ways depending on the specific educational field. The literature within higher education discusses multiculturalism in terms of democratic outcomes and the ways in which exposure to diverse others in college provides individual and societal benefits (e.g., Bowen & Bok, 1998; Gurin et al., 2002; Hurtado, 2003; Milem, 1994). In comparison, the literature in educational studies on multiculturalism is described as, "a nonhierarchical approach that respects and celebrates a variety of cultural perspectives on world phenomena" (Asante, 1991b, p.172). Furthermore, most often in educational studies, the topic of multiculturalism is discussed by using the term multicultural education (Banks, 1993). I have included literature from K-12 research in order to provide an additional perspective on multiculturalism in education and to discuss how these approaches may inform work in higher education, particularly the ways in which they contribute to a conceptual framework for understanding multiculturalism in HBCUs.

Multiculturalism

The higher education literature contextualizes multiculturalism in two main ways, as democratic outcomes—the ways in which exposure to multiculturalism in college provides benefits to the greater U.S. society (Bowen & Bok, 1998; Gurin et al., 2002; Hurtado, 2003; Hurtado, Engberg, Ponjuan, & Landreman, 2002); and through curricular means (Clayton-Pedersen & Musil, 2003). Democratic outcomes are discussed first within the context of learning outcomes students acquire in college, and secondly in terms of the benefits to society attained as students are exposed to diverse others (Antonio, 2001; Greene & Kamimura, 2003; Gurin, Dey, Gurin, & Hurtado, 2004; Gurin et al., 2002; Hurtado, 2003; Hurtado et al., 2002; Hurtado, Bowman, Dwyer, & Greene, 2004; Milem, 1994). These different discussions of multiculturalism, most often occur concurrently within studies and cumulatively demonstrate that diversity experiences influence students' learning in college, their sense of civic responsibility once they graduate, and better equip them to work in this increasingly diverse

society (AAC&U, 2002; Carnevale & Fry, 2000; Gurin et al., 2004; Gurin et al., 2002; Hurtado, 2003).

Some of the educational outcomes associated with interactions between students with diverse backgrounds include: cognitive skills (e.g., cognitive flexibility, sociohistorical thinking, and critical thinking); socio-cognitive outcomes (e.g., leadership skills, social, and cultural awareness); democratic outcomes (e.g., propensity to vote in elections, a belief that conflict enhances democracy, and a concern for the public good), prejudice reduction, cultural awareness and cultural acceptance (Antonio, 2001; Astin, 1993a, 1993b; Cheng, 2003; Hurtado, 2003, Milem, 1994).[2]

Although all of the previously mentioned learning outcomes occur on college campuses, they each occur in different ways, and as a result of various campus circumstances. Research shows that structural diversity, or a critical mass of students from underrepresented groups, impacts students' interaction with diverse others on campus (Gurin et al., 2002; Hurtado, Carter, & Kardia, 1998). Additionally, the literature is rich with quantitative studies that analyze the curricular, co-curricular, and informal experiences students have interacting with diverse peer groups (Antonio, 2001; Hurtado, 2003; Hurtado et al., 2002; Hurtado et al., 2004; Greene & Kamimura, 2003; Pascarella, Edison, Nora, Hagedorn, & Terenzini, 1996).

Moreover, further literature on multiculturalism within higher education indicates that multiculturalism is found, practiced and implemented through the curriculum—either through required courses that meet what has been termed a "diversity requirement" (AAC&U, 1995a, 1995b; Levine & Cureton, 1992), or through departmental infusion of multiple perspectives into the curriculum (Levine & Cureton, 1992). While the departmental infusion is haphazard, the more common method of implementing multiculturalism into the curriculum has been through university-wide diversity requirements that expose students to experiences different from their own. These curricular experiences include courses on gender studies, ethnic studies, institutional or societal racism, religion, ethnicity, intolerance, and social class (Butler & Walter, 1991; Humphreys, 1997; Hurtado, Milem, Clayton-Pedersen, & Allen, 1999). In addition, diversity requirements may also take a more social justice orientation and analyze systems of inequality and discrimination (Humphreys, 1997).

Multicultural Education

The K-12 literature uses the term multicultural education and addresses it in a multifaceted way. Banks' (1993) model of multicultural education considers several dimensions including: content integration, knowledge construction, prejudice reduction, equity pedagogy, and empowering school culture. Banks' (1993) *content integration* explains the extent to which teachers use "examples, data, and information from a variety of cultures and groups to illustrate key concepts, principles, generalization and theories" (p. 5). Furthermore, it pertains to Gay's (1997) discussion about multicultural infusion through the curriculum. *Knowledge construction* refers to the frames of reference and the cultural experiences that inform thinking and produce knowledge. Loewen (1995) and hooks (1990) purport that the knowledge constructed is dependent upon the frame of reference from which it is taught. *Prejudice reduction* describes strategies that can be used to enhance democratic values among students (Lynch, 1987). Furthermore, prejudice reduction occurs not only through exposure to diversity within the curriculum, but is also affected by the racial awareness of children and occurs when youth have greater interaction with others of different racial and cultural backgrounds (Milner, 1983).

Equity pedagogy occurs when teachers utilize instructional techniques that are beneficial to students of various racial, ethnic, and socio-economic backgrounds. Banks' concept of *empowering school culture* builds off the previously discussed dimensions of multicultural education. Banks (1993) suggested that while content integration, knowledge construction, and equity pedagogy occur within the school, "the school itself can also be conceptualized as one social system that is larger than its interrelated parts (e.g., its formal and informal curriculum, teaching materials, counseling programs, and teaching strategies)," (p. 33) and schools are cultural systems with specific values, traditions, customs, and shared meanings (Willis, 1977).

The literature within higher education, as well as with educational studies, offer specific notions about what multiculturalism and multicultural education are and how they apply to specific settings. However, they do not address the way in which multiculturalism exists at HBCUs, nor the way multicultural education in K-12 settings relates to or prepares students for HBCUs. As a result, there is only a small collection of works that discuss aspects of multiculturalism at HBCUs.

Multiculturalism at HBCUs

Sims (1994) posited that multiculturalism should accessible to all students regardless of the institutional type they attend. Furthermore, she stated that experiences with diversity are just as important to foster at HBCUs as in other institutions of higher education. She echoed the majority of literature on diversity in higher education, stating that diversity promotes awareness, respect for difference, and a variety of cultures. In addition, Bey (2004) indicated the importance of multiculturalism at HBCUs by highlighting the 71% increase in White student enrollment at HBCUs between 1976 and 1994. Willie, Grady and Hope (1991) imparted that exposure to non–African American students is beneficial for African Americans as this helps disconfirm stereotypes. This exposure is particularly important due to highly segregated high school environments from which both African American and White college students come (Orfield, Frankenberg, & Lee, 2003).

With this in mind, multiculturalism at HBCUs is an important topic that warrants attention. The limited literature that is present on multiculturalism at HBCUs does not define itself as such, nor is it comprehensive. Rather, separate and unrelated pieces have been published covering various aspects of HBCUs including: curricular multiculturalism at HBCUs,

White students at HBCUs, diverse faculty at HBCUs, identity development of students at HBCUs, and a single study on diversity outcomes at HBCUs. Within this article I will attempt to bring this literature together, forming a portrait of multiculturalism at HBCUs and identify areas for future research. Although these disparate studies relate to multiculturalism at HBCUs, they do so indirectly and some perhaps address it unintentionally. However, they are useful in this discussion because, as I will argue, they inform a conceptual framework for research that can directly address diversity outcomes and multiculturalism at HBCUs.

Curricular Multiculturalism at HBCUs

In a mixed methods study conducted by Bey (2004), multicultural education at two HBCUs in Virginia was investigated. In her study, Bey sought to understand the ways in which multiculturalism is situated within the general education curriculum of HBCUs, how faculty and administrators defined it, and the extent to which there was an institutional responsibility to promote multicultural education. In this examination she found that in all of the general education courses with titles that suggest inclusion of underrepresented persons, only two of them included multiple perspectives, and according to her index, provided a moderate amount of multicultural education. Furthermore, both courses concentrated on people of African descent. However, in 45% of her interviews with faculty, respondents indicated that diversity was promoted not by the structure of the general education curriculum, but by the faculty within the classroom.

The chief academic officer at one of the institutions studied by Bey (2004) indicated that multiculturalism was at the core of their institution because of their diverse faculty and student population, as well as the "large number of multicultural and diversity courses taught throughout the curriculum" (p. 178). However, additional findings indicated that definitions of multicultural education included: appreciation of cultural differences, integration of cultural material, expanding knowledge, and valuing difference. Within these definitions, more than 50% of respondents at both institutions defined multiculturalism in terms of African American or Black experiences; thus indicating a very narrow definition of multiculturalism. Bey (2004) suggested that these definitions may indicate that respondents did not understand the multidimensional aspects of multiculturalism, or that the HBCU setting influenced the definition of the term.

Bey's (2004) research also found that faculty and administrators were split approximately 50-50 as to whether or not a multicultural education perspective should be included in discipline specific requirements, or be made a part of the general education requirements. Yet faculty suggested that they employ multicultural teaching tactics by encouraging students to insert their own experiences into educational contexts, allowing sources other than the instructor to serve as information centers, and encouraging students to challenge conventional notions of knowledge. They also believed that multicultural education was an important empowerment tool for the well being of students. However, respondents indicated that issues pertaining to multiculturalism and the curriculum were not the most pressing ones at these institutions.

Bey's research finds that multicultural education does exist within the core curriculum at HBCUs, but not in the traditional sense. She suggests that HBCUs affinity towards African American centered multiculturalism is rooted in the history and mission of HBCUs to serve and prepare the African American community.

White Students at HBCUs

Brown (2002) indicates that in 1994 White students comprised 16.5% of the HBCU enrollment and that there have been significant demographic shifts within the HBCU student population since 1976. During this 18-year period there was a 19% decrease in African American enrollment, a 70% increase in White student enrollment, a 45% increase in Hispanic enrollment, a 274% increase in Asian student enrollment, and a 139% increase in the Native American student enrollment at HBCUs. Despite this growing diversity among the student body at HBCUs, research has focused almost exclusively on the experiences of White students on these campuses. This dearth in scholarship on other non–African American students at HBCUs is problematic and needs to be addressed; however, because of the nature of this review, I am limited to discussing existing research.

The growing number of White and other minority students at HBCUs has added an aspect of multiculturalism to HBCUs. By virtue of diverse students being present on campus, they are creating greater structural diversity (as defined in Hurtado et al., 1999) at HBCUs which helps inform Banks' (1993) dimensions of knowledge construction and prejudice reduction. However, as Hurtado et al. (1999) and Gurin et al. (2002) insisted, structural diversity is not enough. Simply because student bodies are more diverse on HBCU campuses it does not mean that a multicultural climate is being fostered. In fact, according to Conrad et al. (1997), many White students choose to attend HBCUs not with the intension of diversifying HBCU campuses or interacting with African American students, but rather for specific reasons such as to enroll in particular majors or due to scholarships and financial aid. Conversely, Conrad and associates (1997) also found that some White students do attend HBCUs because of the welcoming environment they perceive on theses campuses and because they view them as multiracial institutions that are supportive and inclusive.

However, while the above mentioned examples may speak to the reasons White students choose to attend HBCUs, the experiences they have on campus can be quite different than anticipated. One White student on Howard's campus explained that he "experienced pressure to remember that [he] was a guest and not challenge the campus culture" (Ruffins, 1999, p. 22). Furthermore, Sims (1994) found that African American students do not see White students as peers due to the historical experiences of slavery that Whites have not endured.

Although the experiences White students have at HBCUs may be uncomfortable and challenging for them, studies have shown that the experiences they have interacting with diverse peers develops their sense of understanding and learning. Brown (2002) and Willie (1983) both stated that White students who attend HBCUs have greater ease communicating with people of different backgrounds. Furthermore, in her quantitative dissertation White (2000) highlighted this learning that White students obtain as she states:

> It is important that White students possess an opportunity to enhance their learning experience by developing an awareness and sensitivity to the Black student's experience, as well. Efforts in this direction may serve to counteract the pervasiveness of racial and ethnic stereotypes within the college environment. (p.13)

Although White students seem to benefit from attending HBCUs, there is some concern about the ways in which greater numbers of White students at HBCUs will lead to changes in campus climate at HBCUs and specifically to a decrease in service to African American students. Bluefield State University (BSU) is often presented as a case in point of such shifts. Once an institution with a large majority of African American students, in 1994 the student enrollment of BSU was 92 percent White as was the percentage of White faculty (Brown, 2002). Today, many argue that BSU bears very little resemblance to a traditional HBCU because its Black Greek organizations are absent, as is its marching band, and the president of this institution is White (Brown, 2002).[3] Because climate and culture are the primary contributors to African American student success at these institutions (Allen, 1992, 1996; Brown, 2002) there is great concern over the possibility of a changing climate at HBCUs.

Furthermore, although Brown (2002), White (2000), and Willie (1983) indicated the benefits White students experience from their attendance at HBCUs, direct connections are not drawn between the benefits White students obtain, the benefits Black students gain, and the campus contributions that can occur as a result of White student attendance at HBCUs. Overall the research was primarily concerned with the experiences of White students at HBCUs. However, the focus of this area of literature is either on the individual benefits White students experience from attending HBCUs, or the fear associated with White students' HBCU attendance. Thus, because of their growing and diversifying campuses, HBCUs do not appear to be promoting multiculturalism through interactions between their students from diverse backgrounds.

Diverse Faculty at HBCUs

Although the literature on democracy outcomes has focused almost exclusively on the peer to peer interactions of students, literature on structural diversity (see Gurin et al., 2002; Hurtado, et al., 1998, 1999) and learning outcomes states the important role faculty play in student learning and persistence (Tinto, 1997). Additionally, Bey (2004) indicated that a chief financial officer she interviewed stated that presence of a diverse faculty contributed to their institution being multicultural in nature. Furthermore, Allen (1992) noted that at HBCUs students have more positive relationships with faculty. More-over, Harvey and Williams (1996) explained the importance of students interacting with diverse faculty by stating:

> Black colleges have always served as welcoming forums for visiting scholars, political statesmen, and business leaders, irrespective of their race, creed, or religion . . . Black colleges' students receive wide exposure to a variety of racial and ethnic groups, and they benefit from the exchange of diverse opinions and views. (p. 236)

In addition to being historically welcoming, HBCUs have attracted a diverse group of Latino, Asian American, and inter-national scholars in more recent years. Yet, despite these shifts in population, the literature on non–African American HBCU faculty focuses on White faculty (Anderson, 1988; Jewell, 2002). Due to their White missionary founding, HBCUs have a history of having White as well as African American faculty members. Bey (2004) found that the presence of such faculty on HBCU campuses created a multicultural setting by which African American students took classes from White profes-sors and interacted with White faculty outside of class. How-ever, Drewry, and Doermann (2001) offered that during the 1980s as African American students began to choose to attend TWIs, African American faculty were heavily recruited to these institutions to help them become more diverse and sup-portive for African American students. In some cases HBCU faculty were recruited to TWIs and wooed by larger salaries. Although there has been a resurgence of African American students to HBCUs, acquiring African American faculty and retaining them still remains a struggle for HBCUs.

Despite this challenge some argue that HBCUs must retain an African American faculty and that having a multiracial faculty composition on campus can be detrimental to the Afrocentric perspectives some HBCUs teach to their students (Johnson, 1971, as cited by Foster & Guyden, 2004). Johnson (1971) suggested that some White faculty teach at HBCUs out of convenience and never fully understand the culture of Afri-can Americans and HBCUs. However, as illustrated below, this is not the case for all White faculty members at HBCUs.

Foster and Guyden (2004) present a case study of a White male faculty member who worked at two HBCUs. Although this individual did not seek out employment at an HBCU, he found that the experiences he had at these institutions were some from which he benefited tremendously. He was aware of the racial difference between himself and his students and took advantage of situations in which racial identity was broached to create teaching moments for his students. Furthermore, he learned a great deal about himself, race, and the way in which he could teach history from multiple perspectives. Moreover, a study conducted by Willie, Grady, and Hope (1991) found that White faculty who left HBCUs to teach at TWIs were not satisfied because of the lack of faculty diversity and negative race relations on campus.

The few findings on faculty at HBCUs suggest that the environment is welcoming for African American and White faculty alike, and students at HBCUs benefit tremendously from the close interactions they have with these faculty mem-bers. However, other opportunities, including higher salaries at TWIs, draw instructors away from HBCUs.

Identity Development at HBCUs

The present social and psychological conditions of African Americans are distinct from those of other racial and ethnic backgrounds, specifically due to the impact of slavery upon them (Merelman, 1993; White, 2000). Arnold (1997, as cited by White, 2000) found that environment plays a significant role in the adjustment of students to college. He stated that "students enter college with their own personalities, attributes, values, skills, and needs based on their prior experience in their homes, families, communities, and peer groups" (White, 2000, p. 23). Similar findings have been noted by many edu-cation scholars including Dey and Hurtado (1994) who found that "students bring values and attitudes associated with larger social forces into academe, thereby creating change within the higher education system" (p. 249).

In White's (2000) quantitative study of racial identity development at HBCUs and TWIs she coupled the research of Arnold (1997) with the historical experiences of African Americans. In doing so she indicated that African American students come to college not only with their family experi-ences, but embedded within these are historical experiences of being a descendent of enslaved people. In her study, White (2000) measured the racial identity brought to college by African American students who attended HBCUs and Afri-can American students who attended TWIs. Her findings sug-gested that this identity related to historical oppression brought to college by students is salient. Furthermore, White (2000) found that African American students at HBCUs reported greater gains in internal racial identity and cultural awareness than African American students at TWIs. Although her find-ings indicated positive racial identity outcomes for African American students at HBCUs, she also found that students at HBCUs reported that there was less of an emphasis on racial diversity.

Additionally, Sleeter (1991) believed it is imperative that African American students develop a sense of group identity because it helps them navigate the racialized educational and societal hardships they will face in school settings. Further-more, Merelman (1993) stated that African American students come to school with "the makings of a strong sense of group identity on which the teaching of black history can build" (p. 336). He further suggested that African American students' excellence in African American history is a demonstration of group loyalty. Together these studies suggest the importance of identity and identity development among African Ameri-cans at HBCUs.

Diversity Outcomes at HBCUs

Through investigating literature on diversity outcomes at HBCUs only one study was found which dealt specifically with interracial interaction among students at HBCUs. This single study was Wathington's (2004) dissertation in which she examined the "relationship between pre-collegiate experiences, attitudes, and behaviors and the amount of interracial interaction students engage in before entering college" in four public research institutions, one of which was an HBCU (p. 11). The HBCU in Wathington's study was homogenous with 95% of students identifying racially as African American. Her research focused on specific pre-college characteristics of students including background characteristics, values, beliefs, and prior interracial interaction.

Wathington's findings indicated that of the entering HBCU students, the only background characteristic that predicted interracial interaction was race. Moreover, African American students beginning at this HBCU were more likely to interact with other African American students and less likely to interact with students of different racial backgrounds. Finally, Wathington determined that the values students perceive other groups to have are strong deterrents for cross-racial interaction.

Wathington's study established the pre-college effects of cross-racial interaction among students attending one public HBCU. Her introduction to this literature is valuable, yet it alone does not tell the story of cross-racial interaction or multiculturalism at HBCUs. However, together with Bey's (2004) research on multiculturalism in the HBCU curriculum, White's (2000) study on identity development at HBCUs, the research studies on White students and diverse faculty at HBCUs, a portrait of multiculturalism at HBCUs begins to emerge. It is the collective of these studies that informs my conceptualization of multiculturalism and diversity outcomes at HBCUs presented below.

Conceptual Framework

As discussed, the literature related to multicultural issues at HBCUs is rather scare, disparate, and largely unconnected. However, after reviewing this research, I believe that synthesizing the various areas of study can inform the construction of a conceptual framework that examines diversity outcomes and multiculturalism at HBCUs. Through this effort five components of multiculturalism at HBCUs have emerged which create diversity outcomes: (1) classroom multiculturalism, (2) structural diversity, (3) pre-college experiences, (4) internal development, and (5) empowerment. They can be grouped more specifically into two sub-categories—HBCU institutional factors and the individual factors brought to the HBCU by students. In the following sections, I will discuss each of the five components of the framework in greater detail.

Institutional Factors

Classroom multiculturalism. This dimension is informed by the contributions of Bey's (2004) research on the core curriculum at HBCUs, Banks' (1993) study that addresses equity pedagogy, and a concept I have labeled "cultural relevance" which combines the work of both Bey (2004) and Banks (1993). Bey's (2004) research on multiculturalism at

HBCUs is an introduction to literature in this area. Bey's findings indicated the presence of multiculturalism within the core curriculum of the two institutions in her study. Furthermore, she found that the teaching methods employed in classrooms are considered to be inclusive of diverse perspectives, and finally that the most frequently used "diverse perspective" at the HBCUs in her study is an African American one.

Banks' (1993) presents equity pedagogy as one of the dimensions of multicultural education that is transformative for students' education. He describes this dimension as one which takes into consideration the cultural or ethnic background of the students in order to better assist their learning. This dimension can be applied to HBCUs as Bey's (2004) research indicated that HBCU instructors invoke the African American perspective within their classrooms.

The use of equity pedagogy by HBCUs to employ an African American perspective that is taught in the HBCU curriculum is what I have chosen to call cultural relevance in the curriculum. Within the study conducted by Bey (2004) the HBCUs she examined were institutions with a large majority of African American students. As a result, the employment of education that utilized an African American perspective takes into account the cultural background of the majority of students in the classroom. Collectively, the findings of Bey (2004), Banks (1993) and classroom cultural relevance, form a component of multiculturalism at HBCU—*classroom multiculturalism.*

Structural diversity. The other HBCU institutional dimension that comprises multiculturalism at Black colleges is *structural diversity.* In addition to the developmental benefits accrued by African Americans in the above-mentioned studies, African American students may also receive benefits from the increasing structural diversity at many HBCUs. As a result of the desegregation legislation (i.e., *Adams v. Richardson, Ayers v. Mabus, United States v. Fordice*) that brought more White students to public HBCUs (Blake, 1991; Brown, 1999; Williams, 1988), the history of inclusion at HBCUs (Anderson, 1988; Jewell, 2002), and the greater numbers of White faculty to HBCUs (Anderson, 1988; Bey, 2004; Foster & Guyden, 2004; Jewell, 2002), many of these campuses are more structurally diverse.

Due to this additional diversity, students have greater opportunities to interact across racial groups. However, Wathington's (2004) research found that upon entering an HBCU, African American students have a very low likelihood of interacting cross-racially. Furthermore, Gurin et al.,'s (2002) study found structural diversity in and of itself is not enough to promote cross-racial interaction; rather, institutions must take an active role to create opportunities for diverse interactions. Yet there is not existing research that investigates the extent to which HBCUs promote cross-racial interactions between students let alone research that measures the benefits of these interactions. Additionally, it should be noted that many HBCUs are already structurally diverse; therefore, many institutation may already promote cross-racial interaction. However, without further exploration we cannot know the extent of institutional initiatives and programs.

Individual Factors

Pre-college experiences. The *pre-college experiences* dimension is grounded in the research studies conducted by Hurtado (2003), Hurtado et al., (2004), and Wathington (2004). This dimension consists of four components—prior diversity experiences, interactions with diverse others, Black students being less likely to interact cross-racially, and perceptions of different racial group values.

The research conducted by Hurtado (2003), Hurtado et al. (2004), and Wathington (2004) all found that students have predispositions to diversity prior to college attendance. Although the research conducted by Hurtado et al. (2004) did not explicitly focus on African American students, nor on HBCUs, it found that a student's racial background, their gender, SAT score, mother's education, experience with discrimination, previous participation in diversity related activities, and social identity awareness are determinants of "whether or not students developed cultural awareness during their first two years of college" (p. 24). Furthermore, the portion of Wathington's (2004) study that focused on HBCUs found that incoming Black HBCU students were less likely to interact across racial lines. Moreover, she determined that the lack of interaction across racial lines was the result of Black students' perceptions that non-Black students had different values from them.

This last finding of Wathington's indicates that Black HBCU students are predisposed not to cross-racially interact. Although not explicitly stated, nor a part of Wathington's research, this finding, coupled with Hurtado and her colleagues' research, suggests that African American HBCU students could also be positively predisposed to interact cross-racially depending on their pre-college experiences. Furthermore, depending on their pre-college experiences, African American HBCU students may also be positively or negatively predisposed to other pre-college dimensions of multiculturalism in addition to cross-racial interaction. However, other pre-college dimensions of multiculturalism among HBCU students have not been researched and therefore were unable to be included in this model.

Internal development. *Internal development* includes four main concepts that have emerged from the research of White (2000), Allen (1992, 1996), and Gurin and Epps (1975). White's (2000) research on the identity development of African American students at HBCUs and TWIs found that more positive racial identity outcomes are obtained for African American students at HBCUs than at TWIs. White's findings align with results from other studies on students learning and internal development outcomes at HBCUs, such as Allen (1992, 1996) and Gurin and Epps (1975). The studies conducted by Allen found that African American students on Black campuses fare better in terms of psychological development. Furthermore, Gurin and Epps (1975) determined that African American students at HBCUs had a strong positive self-image, racial pride, and high aspirations. Collectively these studies present a comprehensive picture of the dimensions of the internal development of HBCU students. Finally, the addition of the internal development dimension contributes to the individual factors that make up multiculturalism at HBCUs.

Empowerment. In her study Sleeter (1991) indicated that when multicultural education and empowerment are combined they make for a very effective education for African American students. The literature on empowerment that relates to HBCUs and multiculturalism has led me to determine that there are five aspects that comprise this dimension: (1) African American history and culture, (2) an accepting environment, (3) the enforcement of a positive sense of self, (4) race negotiation, and (5) networks of support. These aspects have emerged as the result of the literature from Asante (1988, 1991a, 1991b), Banks (1993), Freeman and Cohen (2001), Ginwright (2004), and Merelman (1993). Additionally, as a collective they create a diverse view of empowerment. However, more than any of the other dimensions of multiculturalism at HBCUs previously discussed, empowerment is the most complex. Not only is its literature diverse, but the concepts overlap. Furthermore, this dimension as a whole, acts on another dimension of multiculturalism—internal development—creating dynamic interactions within the conceptual model.

Banks (1993) suggested that creating an empowering school culture centered on multicultural education does not come solely from the curriculum, but rather from the formal and informal curriculum, teaching materials, counseling programs, and teaching strategies. However, Ginwright (2004) took a different approach to empowerment and suggested that an Afrocentric curriculum is the way to empower African American students. Although all of the concepts from Banks' research do not explicitly appear in the visual depiction of my conceptual model, his research along with Ginwright's set the stage for empowerment as a dimension of multiculturalism at HBCUs.

Freeman and Cohen (2001) align with Ginwright (2004) in their determination that empowered African American students are created by providing them with African American history and culture. However, where Ginwright's research focuses on Black high school students and Afrocentric education, Freeman and Cohen specifically address issues at HBCUs. In addition, Freeman and Cohen found that HBCUs create empowered students through the existence of a welcoming atmosphere, a reinforced sense of self, providing students with the tools necessary to confront race in academic and work environments, and assisting with the development of personal as well as professional relationships and networks.

Finally, in his study of empowerment in predominantly African American schools that have a multicultural curriculum, Merelman (1993) found that students were not empowered to create change, but rather acted as followers as change occurred. Based on this finding he suggested that students needed more encouragement in order to be empowered and create change without simply following others.

Cross-Dimensional Connections

In addition to the connections made between the researchers within the dimension of empowerment, Asante's (1988, 1991a, 1991b) research creates links between the empowerment dimension and the internal development dimension. Furthermore, his work highlights the reciprocal relationship between the institutional and individual factors of multiculturalism at HBCUs.

Asante (1991a, 1991b) believes that for African Americans to have higher achievement levels they must be empowered and centered in their classrooms. Furthermore, he deemed that "by 'centering' their students of color, teachers can reduce feelings of dislocation engendered by our society's predominantly 'White self-esteem curriculums'" (Asante, 1991a, p. 28). To Asante, centering allows African Americans to see themselves in their education and it makes learning more intimate as well as interesting for students. This concept relates to Banks' (1993) notion of equity pedagogy. Thus, these researchers draw connections between individual and institutional factors of multiculturalism at HBCUs.

In addition to connecting internal and institutional dimensions, Asante's research also illustrates the connections between two internal factors—internal development and empowerment. In one of his 1991 articles Asante (1991b) indicated that seeing themselves within the curriculum created a "renewed sense of purpose and vision" in the lives of African American students (p. 177). Moreover, in his 1988 book on Afrocentricity, Asante described that the way in which one becomes more Afrocentric has much to do with focusing on personal identity. Therefore, this focus on personal identity as a component of empowerment can promote self reflection among students, thereby allowing them to delve into another dimension of multiculturalism at HBCUs presented in this framework—internal development. Asante's research leads me to believe that while empowerment is in and of itself a dimension of multiculturalism at HBCUs, it also informs this second dimension—internal development.

Additions to the Conceptual Model

Up to this point, the discussion of the conceptual framework has focused on the aspects that have been included within the model and substantiated by existing research. However, there are additional components that may in fact be relevant to this framework, but have yet to be researched. One such component is college experiences with diversity, specifically, interactions with diverse peers in co-curricular and informal settings. As was noted in the discussion of pre-college experiences, African American HBCU students in Wathington's (2004) study did not interact cross racially. Although this may be the case for students entering HBCUs, it is possible that students interact with diverse others in their later college years. Despite the possibility that these interactions may occur, there is no existing research that covers the experiences of racial interactions among HBCU students in their later years of college.

Thus, the insertion of a sixth dimension of multiculturalism at HBCUs, *college experiences,* has been included as possibility, but its specific components have not been detailed as it should be examined in future studies.

Similarly, the inclusion of *co-curricular and informal experiences* with diversity have been added in this model. The historical literature on HBCUs indicates that co-curricular learning opportunities have been incorporated into Black colleges and universities (Drewry & Doerman, 2001). Additionally, higher education literature found that co-curricular learning and informal interactions are ways in which students can obtain benefits from interactions with diverse others (Antonio, 2001; Hurtado et al., 2004; Milem, 1994). However, there is no empirical research that specifically focuses on the outcomes associated with exposure to the HBCU co-curriculum or informal settings. Therefore, like college experiences, these dimensions are included in this model as components that should be tested in future studies.

This review and framing of the literature has utilized the term *diversity outcomes* as a way to highlight the learning students obtain as a result of their experiences in college with diversity. However, undergoing this investigation has revealed that at HBCUs, little research reports on the interactions students have with diverse others. Without information on the college experiences HBCU students have in relation to diversity, the outcomes they will obtain are unable to be determined. Thus, in order to gain an understanding of this concept, additional research must be conducted on the college diversity experiences of HBCU students. Additionally, because limited research exists on this topic, the conceptualization of the term *diversity outcomes* is in its infancy and its definition deserves further consideration in future studies.

Furthermore, structural diversity along with the presence of curricular multiculturalism at HBCUs, the history of inclusion of diverse faculty and students, the sense of empowerment cultivated at HBCUs, and the internal development of African American HBCU students (including: racial identity development, positive psychological development, positive self image, and racial pride), suggests that despite HBCU students' predisposition not to interact cross-racially, I suggest that HBCUs have the potential to promote diversity outcomes among their students. Finally, credence should be given to the possibility that HBCUs may already be promoting diversity outcomes among their students; however, the lack of research in this area does not allow for this conclusion to be definitively drawn.

Expanding current conceptual models. Through the organization of this literature on multiculturalism at HBCUs I have found that the ways in which the pieces fit together differs from the organization employed by previous studies that address multiculturalism and exposure to diversity within higher education. Specifically, Hurtado (2003) discussed that context, pre-college experiences, college experiences, and some internal characteristics contribute to students' formation of democratic outcomes related to diversity. Similarly, Gurin et al., (2002) examined students interactions with diverse others, classroom diversity, and informal interaction in college environments. However, due to a lack of literature on diversity outcomes and because Hurtado's (2003) research along with Gurin et al.'s (2002) research was not designed to specifically consider the diversity experiences of HBCU students, the framework presented in this review expands previous conceptualizations in order to create one that more adequately reflects the needs of HBCUs. Unique factors in this framework that do not appear in Hurtado's (2003) research, nor Gurin et al.'s (2002) research, but contribute to diversity outcomes at HBCUs include the presence of empowerment and the prominence of structural diversity.

Future Research on Multiculturalism and HBCUs

The work of Bey (2004), Wathington (2004), and White (2000) is valuable to the research on multiculturalism and diversity outcomes at HBCUs. They provide new information about the HBCU curriculum, predispositions to diversity, and identity development, all of which are previously undocumented. However, three studies cannot adequately comprise an entire area of research. Their work provides an important foundation and suggests areas that need to be studied further. Furthermore, future research on HBCU curricular multiculturalism should address the HBCU curriculum from the vantage point of students to determine their perceptions about multicultural education, as well as to determine the types of diversity outcomes these students obtain from their attendance at HBCUs. Additionally, there are aspects of campus in addition to the curriculum life that contribute to multiculturalism and diversity outcomes that warrant examination. Thus, future research should investigate the multiple dimensions of multicultural education on HBCU campuses.

Further investigation of students' experiences is greatly needed. For example, Wathington (2004) looked at students' pre-college experiences at a single public research institution. Future research should examine the types of cross-racial interactions students have at various types HBCUs. It is also important to expand upon White's (2000) comparison of identity development among African American students at HBCUs and TWIs. White's findings indicate that the greater gains in identity development of HBCU students is largely due to the environment, however, the specific environmental effects that contribute to this development are not specified. Additional studies in this area should tease out the specific environmental forces that contribute to positive gains in identity development of HBCU students.

Furthermore, Sims' (1994) model of diversification at HBCUs could be expanded. Her depiction of diversity at HBCUs confronted only the experiences of African Americans and White students which omits out the experiences of other ethnic and racial groups. Although Sims indicates that she has omitted other groups from this study due to the history of Black-White relations in this nation, the experiences of Latinos, Native Americans, and Asian American students are necessary components to this country's racial composition which need to be explored.

Moreover, future research on multiculturalism at HBCUs should look beyond the Black-White paradigm to better understand the experiences of students, faculty, and staff on HBCU campuses that are neither African American, nor White. Statistical projections indicate that by 2015, 8% of college students will be Asian American, and 13% will be Hispanic in addition to the 15% of African American students, and the 63% that will be White (Carnevale & Fry, 2000). With these changing college student demographics it is increasingly likely that more non-African American students will be attending HBCUs in years to come (Allen & Jewell, 2002; Brown, 2002; Sims, 1994). Additional benefits can be achieved from surveying and interviewing students of various racial and ethnic backgrounds in order to determine the experiences of various students on HBCU campuses. Moreover, Bey (2004) suggests, further research on multiculturalism should be conducted at other minority-serving institutions to investigate the ways in which diversity and multicultural education exists within these contexts. Specifically, she suggested that research should investigate the definitions other HBCUs have for multicultural education and the pedagogy of instructors at these institutions.

Through employing the conceptual framework presented in this piece and embarking on the future research suggested above, a more cohesive picture of multiculturalism at HBCUs should be able to be developed. By further developing literature we should then be able to better understand the role multiculturalism plays in relation to diversity outcomes. Furthermore, it is from these developments that the question posed at the beginning of this article should be able to be answered. That is, we should be able to better understand *what the effects are of multiculturalism on diversity outcomes among HBCU students*.

Conclusion

Although there is limited research that explicitly addresses multiculturalism or diversity outcomes at HBCUs, there is existing research relating to HBCUs that embodies multiculturalism. HBCUs have a clearly established mission of serving African American students, and providing opportunities for students that they may not have at TWIs. Because of increasing diversity at HBCUs and the continuing debates about desegregation and equality in education, HBCUs continue to occupy an interesting yet contentious role in the U.S. In a nation that simultaneously values colorblindness and multiculturalism, these institutions must answer to a mainstream society that views them as primarily single race institutions, and so called relics of the past that have outlived their purpose and mission (Jewell, 2002).

Further research is necessary to inform these conversations about the changing roles and social contributions of HBCUs. Bey's (2004) dissertation should not remain as the sole research study that directly examines multiculturalism at HBCUs, rather as she states, "the limited amount of multicultural research generated by HBCUs needs explanation in light of a 71% increase in white enrollment at such institutions between 1976 and 1994" (p. 3). Additionally, HBCUs must individually decide the ways in which their institutions will promote diversity and multiculturalism on their campuses. However, in order to be colleges and universities that fully embrace multiculturalism HBCUs must ensure that:

> their institutions' diversity efforts help all members learn to see phenomena through others' eyes as well as their own and that each institutional member has the opportunities to find his or her place within the institution and create more tolerance and understanding of those who are different. (Sims, 1994, p.17)

The literature examined within this paper reveals that HBCUs are clearly still needed within the higher education context. Over the course of their existence HBCU's have maintained their mission to serve African American students by creating social mobility for those who have been left out of higher education. Not only do HBCUs diversify the college choice pool, they still provide educational opportunities for students that may not otherwise be able to afford college (Sims, 1994), and provide learning environments which benefit African American students more than White schooling environments (Allen, 1992, 1996; Fleming, 1984; Gurin & Epps, 1975). Furthermore, HBCUs have shown themselves to be institutions committed to creating and maintaining supportive learning atmospheres and valuing difference while educating the disenfranchised (Jewell, 2002).

Notes

1. Higher education desegregation cases include, but are not limited to: *Adams v. Richardson*, 1972, *Ayers v. Mabus I*, 1987, *Ayers v. Mabus III* 1990, and *United States v. Fordice* 1992.

2. A majority of the literature on diversity outcomes originates from Hurtado and her associate's work on the Diverse Democracy Project at the University of Michigan. This project was a two-year longitudinal study of students from 10 Research I institutions located throughout the United States.

3. Greek organizations and marching bands are traditional markers of HBCUs and are often integral components to the culture of these institutions (see Taylor et al., 2005).

References

Allen, W. R. (1992). The color of success: African American college student outcomes at predominantly white and historically Black public colleges and universities. *Harvard Educational Review, 62*(1) 26–44.

Allen, W. R. (1996). Improving Black student access and achievement in higher education. In C. Turner, M. Garcia, A. Nora, L. I. Rendon (Eds.), *Racial & ethnic diversity in higher education. ASHE Reader Series.* Needham Heights, MA: Simon & Schuster.

Allen, W. R., & Jewell, J. O. (2002). A backward glance forward: Past, present, and future, perspectives on historically Black colleges and universities. *The Review of Higher Education, 25*(3), 241–261.

Anderson, J. D. (1984). The schooling and achievement of Black children: Before and after Brown. Topeka, 1900–1980. *Advances in Motivation and Achievement, 1,* 103–122.

Anderson, J. D. (1988). *The education of blacks in the south, 1860–1935.* Chapel Hill, NC: University of North Carolina Press.

Antonio, A. (2001). The role of interracial interaction in the development of leadership skills and cultural knowledge and understanding. *Research in Higher Education, 42*(5), 593–617.

Arnold, M. (1997). *The environmental factor.* Unpublished manuscript. Graduate Student and Faculty Forum, University of Florida.

Asante, M. K. (1988). *Afrocentricity.* Trenton, NJ: Africa World Press.

Asante, M. K. (1991a). Afrocentric curriculum. *Educational Leadership,49*(4), 28–31.

Asante, M. K. (1991b). The Afrocentric idea in education. *Journal of Negro Education, 60*(2), 170–180.

Association of American Colleges and Universities (AAC&U). (1995a). *American pluralism and the college curriculum: Higher education in a diverse democracy.* Washington, DC: Association of American Colleges and Universities.

Association of American Colleges and Universities (AAC&U). (1995b). *Integrity in the college curriculum: A report to the academic community.* Washington, DC: Association of American Colleges and Universities.

Association of American Colleges and Universities (AAC&U). (2002). *Greater expectations: A new vision for learning as a nation goes to college.* Washington, DC: Association of American Colleges and Universities. Retrieved on October 20, 2002 from: http://www.greaterexpectations.org/

Banks, J. A. (1993). Multicultural education: Historical development, dimensions, and practice. *Review of Research in Education, 19,* 3–49.

Banks, J. A., & Ambrosio, J. (2003). Multicultural education. In J. W. Guthrie (Ed.), *Encyclopedia of education, Second edition.* New York: Thomson Gale.

Bey, F. J. (2004). *A study of multicultural education in the general education programs at two historically Black colleges in Virginia.* Unpublished doctoral dissertation. George Mason University.

Blake, E. (1991). Is higher education desegregation a remedy for segregation but not educational inequality?: A study of the Ayers v. Mabus desegregation case. *The Journal of Negro Education, 60*(4), 538–565.

Bowen, W. G., & Bok, D. C. (1998). *The shape of the river: Long term consequences of considering race in college and university admissions.* Princeton, NJ: Princeton University Press.

Brown, M. C. (1999) *The quest to define collegiate desegregation Black colleges, title VI compliance, and post-*Adams *litigation.* Westport, CT: Bergin & Garvey.

Brown, M. C. (2002). Good intentions: Collegiate desegregation and transdemographic enrollments. *The Review of Higher Education, 25*(3), 263–280.

Butler, J. E., & Walter, J. C. (1991). *Transforming the curriculum: Ethnic studies and women's studies.* Albany: State University of New York Press.

Carnevale, A. P., & Fry, R. A. (2000). *Crossing the great divide: Can we achieve equality when generation Y goes to college?* Princeton, NJ: Educational Testing Service.

Chang M. J. (2001). Is it more than about getting along? The broader educational relevance of reducing students' racial biases. *Journal of College Student Development, 42*(2), 93–105.

Clayton-Pedersen, A. R., & Musil, C. M. (2003). Multiculturalism in higher education. In J. W. Guthrie (Ed.), *Encyclopedia of education,* (2nd ed.). New York: Thomson Gale.

Conrad, C. F., Brier, E. M., & Braxton, J. M. (1997). Factors contributing to the matriculation of White students in public HBCUs. *Journal for a Just and Caring Education, 3*(1), 37–62.

Drewry, H. N., & Doermann, H. (2001). *Stand and prosper: Private Black colleges and their students.* Princeton, NJ: Princeton University Press.

Fleming, J. (1984). *Blacks in college.* San Francisco: Jossey-Bass.

Freeman, K., & Cohen, R. T. (2001). Bridging the gap between economic development and cultural empowerment: HBCU's challenges for the future. *Urban Review, 36*(5), 585–596.

Foster, L., & Guyden, J. A. (2004). Colleges in Black and White: White faculty at Black colleges. In C. M. Brown & K. Freeman (Eds.), *Black colleges: New perspectives on policy and practice.* Westport, CT: Praeger Publishers.

Gay, G. (1997). The relationship between multicultural and democratic education. *The Social Studies.*

Ginwright, S. A. (2004). *Black in school: Afrocentric reform, urban youth, and the promise of hip-hop culture.* New York: Teachers College Press.

Greene, S. R., & Kamimura, M. (2003). Ties that bind: Enhanced social awareness development through interactions with diverse peers. Presented at the annual meeting of the Association for the Study of Higher Education. Portland, OR, November.

Gurin, P. Dey, E. L., Gurin, G. & Hurtado, S. (2004). The educational value of diversity. In P. Gurin, J. S. Lehman, E. Lewis (Eds.) *Defending Diversity: Affirmative action at the University of Michigan.* Ann Arbor, MI: University of Michigan Press.

Gurin, P., Dey, E. L., Hurtado, S., & Gurin G. (2002). Diversity and higher education: theory and impact on educational outcomes. *Harvard Educational Review, 72*(3), 330–66.

Gurin, P., & Epps, (1975). *Black consciousness, identity, and achievement: A study of students in historically Black colleges.* New York: Wiley.

Harvey, W. B. & Williams, L. E. (1996). Historically Black colleges. Models for increasing minority representation. In C. Turner, M. Garcia, A. Nora, L. I. Rendon (Eds.), *Racial & ethnic diversity in higher education. ASHE Reader Series.* Needham Heights, MA: Simon & Schuster.

hooks, b. (1990). *Yearning: Race, gender, and cultural politics.* Boston: South End Press.

Humphreys, D. (1997). *General education and American commitments: A national report on diversity courses and requirements.* Washington, DC: Association of American Colleges and Universities.

Hurtado, H., Milem, J., Clayton-Pedersen, A., & Allen, W. (1999). *Enacting diverse learning environments: Improving the climate for racial/ethnic diversity in higher education.* ASHE-ERIC Higher Education Report 26, Number 8. Washington, DC: George Washington University, Graduate School of Education and Human Development.

Hurtado, S. (1996). The campus racial climate. Contexts of conflict. In C. Turner, M. Garcia, A. Nora, & L. I. Rendon (Eds.), *Racial & ethnic diversity in higher education. ASHE Reader Series.* Needham Heights, MA: Simon & Schuster.

Hurtado, S. (2003). *Preparing college students for a diverse democracy: Final report to the U.S. Department of Education, OERI, Field Initiated Studies Program.* Ann Arbor, MI: Center for the Study of Higher and Postsecondary Education.

Hurtado, S. Bowman, J. Dwyer, B., & Greene, S. (2004). *Undergraduate students and cultural awareness: Examining the relationship between interaction with diverse peers and cultural awareness development.* Presented at the annual meeting of the Association for Institutional Research. Boston, MA, June.

Hurtado, S., Carter, D. F., & Kardia, D. (1998). The climate for diversity: Key issues for institutional self-study. *New Directions for Institutional Research.* San Francisco: Jossey-Bass.

Hurtado, S., Engberg, M. E., Ponjuan, L., & Landreman, L. (2002). Students' precollege preparation for participation in a diverse democracy. *Research in Higher Education, 43*(2), 163–86.

Jewell, J. O. (2002). To set an example. The tradition of diversity at historically Black colleges and universities. *Urban Education, 37*(1), 7–21.

Johnson, T. (1971). The Black colleges as system. *Daedalus, 100*(3), 798–812

Levine, R., & Cureton, J. (1992). The quiet revolution: Eleven facts about multiculturalism and the curriculum. *Change, 24*(1), 24–29.

Loewen, J. (1995). *Lies my teacher told me: Everything your American history textbook got wrong.* New York: Simon & Schuster.

Lynch, J. (1987). *Prejudice reduction and the schools.* New York: Nichols.

Merelman, R. M. (1993). Black History and cultural empowerment: A case study. *American Journal of Education, 101*(4), 331–58.

Milem, J. F. (1994). College, students, and racial understanding. *The NEA Education Journal.*

Milner, D. (1983). *Children and race. Ten years on.* London, UK: Ward Lock Educational.

Oliver, M. L., Rodriguez, C. J., & Mickelson, R. A. (1985). Brown and Black in White: The social adjustment and academic performance of Chicano and Black students in a predominantly White university. *The Urban Review: Issues and Ideas in Public Education, 17,* 3–24.

Orfield, G., Frankenberg, E. D., & Lee, C. (2003). The resurgence of school segregation. *Educational Leadership, 60*(4), 16–20.

Pascarella, E., Edison, M., Nora, A, Hagedorn, L. S., & Terenzini, P. T. (1996). Influence on students' openness to diversity and challenge in the first year of college. *The Journal of Higher Education, 67*(2), 174–195.

Redd, K. E. (1998). Historically Black college and universities: Making a comeback. In J. P. Merisotis & C. T. O'Brien (Eds.), *Minority-serving institutions: Distinct purposes, common goals.* San Francisco: Jossey-Bass.

Ruffins, P. (1999). In a society that is increasingly diverse, what's an HBCU to do? *Black Issues in Higher Education, 15*(23), 22.

Sims, S. J. (1994) *Diversifying historically Black colleges and universities: A new higher education paradigm.* Westport, CT: Greenwood Press.

Sleeter, C. (1991). *Empowerment through multicultural education.* Albany, NY: State University of New York Press.

Smith, D. G. (1989). The challenge of diversity: Involvement or Alienation in the academy? *ASHE-ERIC Higher Education Report 5.* Washington, DC: George Washington University.

Tinto, V. (1997). Classrooms as communities: Exploring the educational character of student persistence. *The Journal of Higher Education, 68*(6), 599–623.

U.S. Department of Education, Office for Civil Rights (2005). Retrieved on November 8, 2005 from: http://www.ed.gov/about/offices/list/ocr/docs/hq9511.html

Wathington, H. D. (2004). *In search of the beloved community: Understanding the dynamics of student interaction across racial and ethnic communities.* Unpublished doctoral dissertation. University of Michigan.

Watson, L. W., & Kuh, G. D. (1996). The influence of dominant race environments on student involvement, perceptions, and educational gains: A look at historically Black and predominantly White liberal arts institutions. *Journal of College Student Development, 37*(4), 415–24.

Williams, L. E. (1988). Public policies and financial exigencies: Black colleges twenty years later, 1965–1985. *Journal of Black Studies, 19*(2), 135–149.

Willie, C. V. (1983). *Race, ethnicity and socioeconomic status.* Dix Hills, NY: General Hall.

Willie, C. V., Grady, M. K., & Hope, R. O. (1991). *African Americans and the doctoral experience: Implications for policy.* New York: Teachers College Press.

White, V. Y. (2000). Racial identity development among Black students at a historically Black and a predominantly White university in Florida. Unpublished doctoral dissertation. University of Florida.

Brighid Dwyer is a doctoral candidate in the Center for the Study of Higher and Post Secondary Education at the University of Michigan, Ann Arbor, Michigan.

Building the Movement to End Educational Inequity

Teach for America is working, Ms. Kopp argues. And studies show that TFA teachers do as well as or better than teachers with traditional certification.

WENDY KOPP

Teach for America exists to address educational inequity—the stunning reality that in our nation, which aspires so admirably to be a land of equal opportunity, where one is born still largely determines one's educational outcomes. Despite plenty of evidence that children growing up in poverty can do well academically—when given the opportunities they deserve—the stark reality in our nation today is that the 13 million children growing up below the poverty line are already three grade levels behind children in high-income communities by the time they are 9 years old. Moreover, even the half of low-income children who do manage to graduate from high school are performing, on average, at the level of eighth-graders who live in affluent communities.

Why do we have this problem? We believe that the foremost reason is that children in low-income communities face extra challenges of poverty that other children don't face, including lack of adequate health care and housing and lack of access to high-quality preschool programs. The situation is compounded by the fact that the schools they attend were not designed to put children facing extra disadvantages on a level playing field with students in other areas. These circumstances persist because our national policies and practices, driven by our national priorities, have not been sufficient to tackle either the socioeconomic challenges or the inadequacies in our school systems.

At Teach for America, we know we can solve this problem because we see evidence in classrooms across the country that, when students growing up in poverty are given the opportunities they deserve, they excel. Knowing that we cannot expect every teacher to go above and beyond traditional expectations to the extent necessary to compensate for all the weaknesses of the system, however, we believe our best hope for a lasting solution is to build a massive force of leaders working from inside and outside education who have the conviction and insight that come from teaching successfully in low-income communities. We need such leadership working at every level of our school systems, working outside the system to address

the socioeconomic factors that contribute so significantly to the problem, and working in policy and the sectors, such as journalism and business, that influence policy. In order to provide more students growing up in poverty today with excellent teachers and also to build this force of leaders, Teach for America recruits our nation's most promising future leaders, invests in the training and professional development necessary to ensure their success as teachers in our highest-poverty communities, and fosters their ongoing leadership as alumni.

The evidence indicates that our approach is working. Last year, more than 35,000 graduates of top universities competed for the opportunity to teach in urban and rural communities. Our incoming corps of 4,100 members achieved an average GPA of 3.6; 89% of them held at least one leadership position in a campus activity. Thirty percent of the corps members identify as people of color, and 32% are male. They come to this effort with a desire to reach the nation's most disadvantaged students, and based on the results of the most rigorous evaluation conducted to date, they are in fact teaching students who begin the year, on average, at the 14th percentile against the national norm.

The research actually does not show that our teachers have less impact than fully certified teachers, as Megan Hopkins seems to suggest. Multiple rigorous studies, such as the one she cites by Thomas Kane, Jonah Rockoff, and Douglas Staiger, have actually found that certification is a weak predictor of effectiveness and that Teach for America teachers do as well as or better than those from traditional preparation routes.

Moreover, the "small study" to which she refers was conducted by Mathematica Policy Research; the random-assignment methodology used in that study is widely considered the "gold standard" in research. This rigorous study found that students taught by Teach for America corps members made more progress in both reading and math than would typically be expected in a single year. In math, the impact of hiring a Teach for America teacher over another new teacher was the equivalent of reducing class size by eight students (as in the Tennessee class-size reduction experiment). The study found that Teach for America teachers produced gains in math that were not only larger than those of other beginning teachers but also larger than those of veteran and certified teachers.

The preponderance of evidence shows that corps members effect greater academic gains than other teachers in their schools. And while fewer than 10% of corps members report that they might have taught even if Teach for America hadn't been an option, more than 60% of our 17,000 alumni are working full-time in education. While they are still in their twenties and thirties, they are pioneering vital reforms, modeling excellence as teachers, serving as school principals and district administrators, and even getting appointed to superintendencies. They are making a tangible difference in communities across the country where we have been placing corps members for a decade or more. In our nation's capital, for example, Teach for America alumni serve as the schools' chancellor, deputy chancellor, 10% of school principals, one of two newly elected state board members, a policy advisor to the mayor, and the only national teacher of the year in the city's history. Other Teach for America alumni work from the social services and the legal profession to mitigate the pressures on schools in the first place, and still others work from corporations to marshal additional resources toward the effort.

In our program's 19-year history, we have engaged in ongoing research to continuously improve our program. In the process, we have given extensive thought to the suggestions made by Ms. Hopkins and have made decisions based on evidence of what is likely to maximize the impact of our model. For example, we have not moved to a three-year commitment because of evidence that doing so would significantly decrease the size, diversity, and quality of our corps, particularly in such key areas as math and science. We weigh this information against the reality that most of our corps members do, in fact, remain in education over the long term, despite the two-year commitment. We have also remained committed to enabling corps members to make first-year teacher salaries, knowing that asking them to work for a stipend or reduced salary would reduce the socioeconomic—and in turn racial and ethnic—diversity of the corps.

While we do remain committed to placing corps members in schools where they can reach our country's most underserved children, we have also made an unprecedented investment in their professional development. This is hard work, but by investing in measuring corps members' academic impact and in the continuous improvement of the training and professional development we provide, we aim to produce a corps of first- and second-year teachers who move their students forward significantly more than would typically be expected in a year.

It is also worth noting that principals in our partner schools give consistently high ratings to the preparation of our corps members. In a recent nationwide survey of principals with corps members in their schools, nearly all reported that corps members' training is at least as good as the training of other beginning teachers, and nearly two-thirds rate the training of corps members as better than that of other new teachers.

In very recent years, to increase the impact of our alumni, we have launched initiatives to support those who aim to pursue educational leadership through continued teaching, principalships, launching new social enterprises, policy and advocacy, and securing elected office. In some ways this development is responsive to Ms. Hopkins' suggestion that we offer incentives to entice members to remain in teaching, though, as outlined above, we continue to believe that it is important to foster the efforts of Teach for America alumni to effect change from other professions as well.

We laud the efforts of the local programs that Ms. Hopkins highlights. These programs show much promise for meeting the national need for qualified teachers. As we see evidence of their success, we look to such programs to help us identify good practices, and we incorporate those practices into our approach when applicable. Still, Teach for America is not beginning to meet the demand from districts and education reformers for our corps members and alumni, and this continuing demand fuels our commitment to grow even as we strengthen our program model and even as others experiment with new approaches to meeting the need for talent.

Finally, we are grateful to the university partners who work with us in pursuit of our mission. You can read about some of these partnerships elsewhere in this special section. We hope this conversation will open more opportunities for collaboration with others in the higher education community, and we appreciate Ms. Hopkins' willingness to bring this discussion to a broader audience.

WENDY KOPP is founder and chief executive officer of Teach for America, New York, NY.

UNIT 7

Providing Professional Development for Teachers

Unit Selections

Key Points to Consider

- What causes the stress for multicultural educators?

- How can multicultural educators reduce their stress?

- What is the promise of Black teachers' success working with Black students?

- How can this promise be fulfilled?

- Why is it essential to diversify the teaching force?

- Describe various ways of diversifying the teaching force.

- How can professional development transform teachers from the sense of surviving to the reward of thriving?

- How can multicultural educators inform and support other educators?

Student Website
www.mhcls.com

Internet References

International Project: Multicultural Pavilion
   http://curry.edschool.virginia.edu/curry/centers/multicultural/papers.html
Library of Congress
   http://www.loc.gov/index.html?gclid=CLTW28rd2JkCFRINDQodpgGqVA
Social Statistics Briefing Room
   http://www.whitehouse.gov/fsbr/ssbr.html
State of the World's Children
   http://www.unicef.org/apublic/
Statistical Abstract of the United States
   http://www.census.gov/prod/www/statistical-abstract-us.hmtl

Becoming an accomplished multicultural educator is never easy or achieved. Like all parts of education and life, multicultural education entails a process, a never-ending journey. For most educators, pursuing cultural competence encompasses the most exciting aspect of being an educator. During our teacher preparation programs, we learned what is required for us to become teachers to fulfill the state and university expectations. Our minds were opened as we completed series of courses in our academic content areas such as math and science, then we launched into a series of courses about pedagogy, the science of teaching and learning, as we embarked on the path in learning how to teach.

We put it altogether once we arrived in a classroom during practica and internships. At last we could connect theory, research, and practice to focus on when and where to teach. We began to align the curriculum, instruction, and assessment while we struggled to manage our new classrooms. For most of us, we were amazed at the amount of responsibilities and number of decisions for which classroom teachers are accountable. And we zipped through each day hoping to keep one breath ahead of the students' interests and energies.

As we reflected upon our classrooms, we suddenly became much more aware of the learners both as individuals and as members of various groups. We became attuned to each class and the group's ability to function as a community of learners. As we became acquainted with individual students, we realized that each student is unique and special; each student is the manifestation of nature and nurture connected with family, friends, community, school, and life. During our reflections and connections, many of us discovered that truly getting to know our students is indeed the multicultural education journey.

Helping each student to find strengths, success, and satisfaction requires the teacher to know the individual student. Teachers must explore every avenue possible to understand how each student processes the cognitive, physical, social, and affective domains of learning. Teachers must talk with prior teachers; read cumulative folders; visit with parents and family members; assess prior knowledge, skills, and dispositions through speaking and writing; hold conversations and listen as each student shares formally and informally before, during, and after class. Getting to know the students takes time, energy, and patience. Yet, each student is entitled to and deserves an education that is equitable and excellent.

Professional development equips teachers with opportunities to provide the most efficient and effective learning experiences for every student in honor of and respect for each student's heritage, needs, and interests. Novice teachers tend to be concerned with classroom management techniques and the teacher's abilities to keep students on task. Few novice teachers recognize that by getting to know their students both as members of the learning community and, more important, as individuals, classroom management will no longer pose such great challenges. All teachers, novice and veteran, who are stymied by their classroom management techniques would benefit

© amana images inc./Alamy

from redirecting their expectations on changing the students to changing the teacher.

This type of transformation is difficult for teachers to comprehend and to trust. Teachers have come to believe that they need to be the commanders of their classrooms. However, teachers will soon discover that they get more power by giving power away. By collaborating with their students, constructing a sense of shared governance in the classroom, getting to know one another personally, and connecting the academic expectations with the local and global environments, teachers soon realize that classroom management is no longer a major issue and greater attention can be placed on learning and achievement.

Staff developments should recognize that professional development must be powerful and worth teachers' time and energies. Teachers readily express that school administrators may not honor their responsibilities or provide them with the tools and techniques that will help them become more efficient and effective. Most efforts to promote multicultural education as professional development are avoided or resisted; frequently the professional development has not been prepared or facilitated appropriately.

School administrators, especially staff developers, are strongly encouraged to find professional developers who can quickly connect with and engage teachers in identifying the specific challenge(s), accessing resources, and implementing change based on theory, research, and practice. Many accomplished teacher educators are available to provide effective professional development.

Unit 7 offers a range of research and practices to support educators in their personal growth, professional development, and pedagogical expertise in pursuing cultural competence. All multicultural educators accept that the journey inside and outside the classroom is stressful and challenging; that each of us must seek us new avenues to make information, access, and opportunities readily available for all educators, students, and their families; and that each of us doing the best possible to ensure equity and excellence.

Sustaining Ourselves under Stressful Times: Strategies to Assist Multicultural Educators

PENELOPE WONG AND ANITA E. FERNÁNDEZ

Resistance that educators face in teaching multicultural education courses, particularly from preservice teachers, is well documented (Carpenter, 2000; Cochran-Smith 2004; Cruz-Janzen & Taylor, 2004; Horton & Scott, 2004; McGowan, 2000, O'Donnell, 1998; Valerio, 2001). Much of the literature around resistance tends to focus on strategies that multicultural educators can employ in overcoming preservice teacher resistance (Young & Tran, 2001).

However, preservice teacher resistance is not the only kind of resistance to multicultural education. Less well documented is the resistance to multicultural education from fellow educators who sometimes exhibit the same kinds of resistance as preservice teachers (Ahlkvist, Spitzform, Jones, & Reynolds, 2005; Ghosh & Tarrow, 1993). While there is little literature concerning teacher/faculty resistance to multicultural education, even more sparse is any literature concerned with *the effects* of such resistance on multicultural educators.

The small body of literature in this area, more often than not, has focused on multicultural educators of color and the resistance they face in teaching such topics and the strategies they used to counter such resistance (Boutte, 1999; McGowan, 1996, 2000; Valverde, 2003). Rarely has there been any discussion on how multicultural educators cope and sustain themselves in the face of continual resistance. In fact, there is virtually no literature on *how* multicultural educators address these effects and the *strategies* they employ to sustain themselves on a daily basis.

The purpose of this article to address this void in the field by providing a theoretical framework of the ways in which multicultural educators might address such resistance so as to preserve themselves and keep from suffering some of the negative effects of continual resistance, such as despair, hopelessness, and burnout.

Rationale/Motivation behind the Creation of the Framework

The development of this framework occurred over a period of three years when the authors, two women of color teaching in a predominantly White rural northern California teacher preparation program, were hired to address multiculturalism and diversity, which was lacking in the program. We soon came to the realization that a number of stakeholders, not only students but also fellow faculty and administrators, thought that the *idea* of multiculturalism and multicultural education was more appealing than the actual practice of it.

This discomfort from various stakeholders manifested itself in the forms of passive resistance on one hand (e.g., not wanting to address or engage on multicultural education topics at all) to outright hostility on the other (e.g., denouncing various multicultural education concepts). As a result of these reactions, we were forced to develop strategies to help us continue to be effective and healthy educators.

As we struggled to figure out strategies and any means to handle the effects of such resistance (i.e., frustration, anger, sadness, etc.) we began to systematically identify dimensions of our personal and professional lives that were impacted by the resistance we encountered. Specifically, we identified five aspects of our lives that we felt were most directly impacted by resistance to our work. They were the intellectual, emotional, physical, ethical, and spiritual dimensions of ourselves.

Methodology and Overview of the Framework of Sustainment

The development of the framework evolved as we encountered various incidents of resistance and collected data in the form of personal journal entries, notes from conversations and meetings, minutes from meetings, and other documents. It was only after months of reflection that the framework assumed its present form. During the first year, there was no framework because we realized that we were individually addressing each instance of resistance as a unique event seemingly unrelated to any other events of resistance. It was only over time were we able to detect patterns.

For example, fairly early on (in the first year) it was clear that one of the most pervasive and immediate types of resistance we encountered was in the intellectual realm when the credibility of the content we were teaching was questioned. Once we recognized this pattern, we came up with systematic ways to address this intellectual challenge.

Another area in which the resistance was extremely challenging was the emotional arena. While we could intellectually rationalize the resistance we encountered toward the various multicultural issues, such as sexual orientation, it was much more difficult to deal with the *feelings* of anger, hurt, and frustration associated with addressing these issues. The emotional energy expended on handling conflicts in the classroom, hostility, and passive resistance was at times almost overwhelming, and we had to come up with concrete psychological strategies to ensure we did not lose hope and simply give up in despair.

Another area of our lives that was showing signs of stress during this time was our physical health. We both realized early on that being constantly challenged intellectually and emotionally did take a physical toll on our health. In short, we were more vulnerable to being sick, suffering from fatigue and lacking vitality precisely because our positive energy was being diverted to addressing the intellectual and emotional resistance we encountered. When we realized what was happening, we came up with some very specific and personal strategies to make sure that we maintained our physical health, so we could continue working.

While it was incredibly helpful to specifically identify the kinds of resistance (i.e., intellectual, emotional, and physical) we encountered so we could address each type of resistance with specific strategies, sometimes we still felt we needed something more. It was at these moments we turned to the spiritual dimension of our lives. This dimension provided a rather unique lens through which to examine our experiences. For one of the authors, the spiritual dimension was the most significant and critical one in enabling her to affirm *why* she continued to be engaged in such demanding work.

Finally, we considered the ethical dimensions of our work. Unlike the other above-mentioned dimensions, we found the ethical dimensions of who we are as educators raised more questions than provided answers. However, it was the process of deliberating the ethical aspects of the various incidents of resistance we experienced that helped reaffirm our work and purpose.

In providing this brief overview of the framework we want to stress a few points. First, these dimensions are perhaps best visually seen as interconnected rings, much like the symbolic Olympic rings. Or, as some people recommended, as slices of a pie. Others saw the dimensions as separate boxes all leading to one bigger box of overall health. The point is that the framework can take any form, but what matters is that it works for the individual who is using it.

Second, these dimensions are not necessarily equal in significance or presence to one another. In other words, for one of the authors, the spiritual dimension was the most prominent dimension in her overall health for awhile, and for the other author it was the physical dimension. The point is that these dimensions are somewhat fluid. At different times, different dimensions will offer the answers sought at just the right time and will be prominent in one's exploration of how to address and overcome resistance. At other times, other dimensions will

be foregrounded. To this end, even though the dimensions will be individually discussed in a linear fashion, we are in no way implying that there is a hierarchy of importance.

Finally, by using ourselves as models, we provide a case example to concretely illustrate how a particular incidence of resistance seemed to speak to a specific dimension of our health; then we discuss how we addressed the resistance using strategies and resources that enabled us to directly draw on this dimension and work through the resistance. This framework is based on the unique experiences of two multicultural educators and is offered as a strategy to current educators and future educators alike to help them proactively think about how they will handle resistance they potentially or are currently encountering.

Expressions of Resistance

While the purpose of this article is not to discuss resistance per se, it is necessary to briefly identify the common types of resistance that have been discussed among multicultural educators because sometimes one type of resistance falls in the province of one of the dimensions we discuss and thus requires a specific set of strategies to be addressed.

Dittmar (1999) and Tatum (1994) have documented facing resistance and outright hostility when addressing multicultural issues in teacher education. Griffin (1997) divides resistance into four types: anger, immobilization, distancing, and conversion. While anger tends to be the kind of resistance that is most uncomfortable for educators, all four of these types of resistance contribute to the overall feelings of stress and disequilibrium which we attempt to provide strategies for preventing.

The Intellectual Dimension

The situation: Having completed her doctoral work in anti-racist, multicultural education, one of the authors accepted a position at an institution seeking a faculty member with expertise in the area of multicultural education. She accepted the position expecting to continue the work she had been doing over the last several years. Once her new role of teacher educator began, it became quite clear that not only were many of the students she worked with completely skeptical of and resistant to multicultural education, but also most faculty and administers as well. This assistant professor was faced with the reality that her new colleagues were much more prone to "talking the talk" than "walking the talk" and she found herself constantly having to explain, defend, and justify multicultural teacher education to a variety of stakeholders.

This scenario was not all that unusual as multicultural educators around the country face similar challenges when trying to teach about issues that challenge students' preconceived notions of diversity. The surprising element was the resistance on the part of faculty and administration to understanding the need for students to engage in addressing difficult and challenging multicultural topics. As students complained, some faculty members started to question the need for such a course. In essence the very existence of multicultural education was being questioned.

Naturally, in an attempt to defend the validity of multicultural education as a body of knowledge and justify the need for future teachers to study it, she employed an intellectual response. She realized it was important to speak the language of the context—in this case the academy. Students, faculty, and administration would only ever be convinced of the legitimacy of multicultural education if it could be presented in terms they knew: theory, statistics, current literature, and research results.

With regard to the above mentioned scenario, the author realized that the intellectual dimension was the most tangible way to sustain herself as a multicultural educator. Thus, the strategies she employed in this realm were to strengthen her theoretical framework by remaining current in the literature and learning ways to use this intellectual information in such a form that was not threatening or radical to her colleagues or students.

More specifically, when confronted with resistance, she would reach into her intellectual side to ask the question *what does the literature say about this?* By doing so, she found that her ideas were affirmed because she could use state law, current research, and testimonies as intellectual rationalizations for the topics being addressed.

A second intellectual response to the situation above was to find allies who shared the same intellectual philosophy concerning multicultural education and diversity. In this case, it was the authors of this article supporting one another. Without the support of a colleague to discuss multicultural issues, and the resistance that comes with those issues, there is a danger of being worn down and overwhelmed by the resistance.

Intellectual allies were another source of critical information that could be used in countering the resistance. They can play the role of "devil's advocate," or in this case "resister to multicultural education," and provide sound counsel on how to handle various situations. Just as importantly, intellectual allies were those individuals who were willing to publicly support multicultural education and faculty who taught such courses.

All of these elements of the intellectual dimension of sustaining ourselves were deeply interconnected with the emotional dimensions as well. As our intellect supported us in *what* kind of work we did (i.e., the content), our emotions often determined *how* we did the work (i.e., the teaching approaches and strategies).

The Emotional Dimension

The situation: After viewing the film Color of Fear *a class of preservice teachers were asked to write down their immediate reactions on an index card. As the instructor read through the cards she came across one that said, "If White culture is the dominant culture, then it is meant to be that way, for it has been for centuries. If non-White people have a problem with that get off your butts and do something about it. Change the system, SHOW ME YOU ARE BETTER THAN ME!" Although not completely surprised by this comment, this incident, combined with recent local hate crimes and a lack of support for multicultural education in her college, put this instructor in an emotionally drained state.*

We defined the emotional dimension of the framework as the feelings or the affective responses we had to the work we did as multicultural educators. The emotional output that one engaged in during the course of teaching a multicultural education course was unlike that of many other disciplines. As we heard about the

daily injustices that not only occured in larger society but also in schools, it is easy to feel emotionally taxed.

However, this situation, combined with the resistance from our students and colleagues to either not acknowledge and/or not be willing to address such issues made a difficult situation even more challenging and we often feel "burned out" or completely emotionally exhausted.

One of the ways we have attempted to sustain ourselves emotionally was to recognize when we were reacting emotionally versus when we were reacting intellectually. We noticed that when students made comments, such as the one above, our immediate reactions were emotional ones (i.e., anger, frustration, etc.). The author in this scenario engaged in a strategy that focused on reacting with empathy rather than anger or disgust at such beliefs. bell hooks referred to this as engaged Buddhism. In other words, the work of multicultural educators is built on loving kindness and it is this loving kindness that can prevail in times of deep emotional crisis.

A second strategy was to train oneself to never react immediately to something that triggered a negative reaction. We found that participating in a cool-down period enabled us to respond to faculty and student comments in a purposeful and controlled manner and prevented further escalation of an already emotionally trying situation. By spending some time thinking about why the resistance occurred, we could be more rational and less emotional when actually responding to an individual.

Finally, it was crucial for our emotional well-being to celebrate the small victories rather than becoming overwhelmed by the big picture or the constant state of inequity around the world and in many schools. When a student reached an epiphany about diverse perspectives or an administrator seemed to better understand why it is we feel so strongly about the work we do, such was a small victory to be applauded and it raised our spirits immeasurably.

The Physical Dimension

The situation: Four young males of large stature were becoming increasingly volatile during a conversation about gay and lesbian issues in education. As the discussion proceeded, they became physically agitated: They were red in the face, postured defensively, raised their voices, and gestured aggressively. At the height of the outburst, one of the males yells, "What do those fags expect parading around the Castro [the location of an annual gay pride parade in San Francisco]?" The instructor immediately addressed the language that was used but was cut off and interrupted by the other three males. At this point she noticed that her heart was racing, she was breathing heavily, perspiring, and physically distancing herself from them.

We define the physical dimension as the "bodily" realm of the work we do as multicultural educators. For the the purposes of this article, we define "bodily" as literally our physicality. In this situation, the author was caught off guard by the violent reactions of the students, precisely because they were expressions of physical resistance rather than the more traditional emotional and intellectual forms of resistance we were accustomed to experiencing. This was not a situation one would expect in a classroom setting, particularly in a university. An immediate strategy the author employed in this "fight or flight" situation was to defuse the tension by switching topics.

While changing the topic achieved the immediate effect of defusing a potentially volatile physically violent reaction, it was clear the issue could not end on this note. In the days before the next class meeting the instructor agonized over her next course of action and felt physically ill (i.e., stomach cramps) at the thought of having to face the same students in class. She had trouble sleeping and suffered physical signs of stress.

In reflecting on the class, the instructor wondered if any of the students themselves were also suffering physical signs of stress due to disruptive nature of the previous class meeting. So the instructor began the subsequent class by asking students to respond in writing to the situation that had taken place the week before. In reading the responses, it became clear that many of the students, mostly the females, felt physically intimidated to come to class.

To handle such situations, we developed a set of strategies to address the physical nature of this aspect of our work. When facilitating tense classroom situations, we made a point of explicitly monitoring and being aware of our own and our students' physical reactions to the situation.

For example, we monitored our breathing (i.e., took a few deep breaths), monitored our facial expressions, and spoke in a calm and quiet voice. However, we also held on to the role of teacher-leader by staying on our feet and moving about the room when necessary. With respect to our students, we became much more adept at reading body language and taking short breaks if students exhibited signs of physical stress.

Finally, at the beginning of new classes, we discussed with students this scenario and how it was (1) inappropriate behavior, (2) what they should do if they feel themselves being physically stressed out, and (3) that to some degree such physical stress will likely happen in reaction to some topics discussed over the course of the semester.

Along with these in-class strategies, we also recognized the importance of stress-reducing practices to maintain our own physical health in order to avoid illness. For example, both of us began practicing yoga, which conferred a number of benefits, such as stress-reduction, breathing techniques, and an overall sense of well being. Additionally, one of the authors engaged in more physically active and intensive activities, such as horseback riding.

Multicultural educators must engage in some physical activity that provides an outlet for the intensity and stress they experience. Although the physical dimension of teaching was not commonly considered, we found that it had a great impact on our overall well-being as well as our teaching both in and out of the classroom.

The Spiritual Dimension

The situation: After several years of teaching the department's multicultural education course, one of the authors noticed a gradual but definite change in attitude among preservice teachers. There was clearly less tolerance for diversity, let alone acceptance, and more and more students were emboldened to immediately denounce the concept of multicultural education from the beginning, whereas several years earlier, students were just questioning its legitimacy. Perhaps most disturbing, the usual responses to such challenges were failing. Intellectual responses grounded in statistical, empirical, and other data were ignored by unwilling intellects. Affective approaches highlighting personal stories of individuals who had experienced a life different from the status quo fell on deaf ears. Even ethical explorations that asked students to examine for themselves current injustices (let alone past injustices) could not penetrate their hearts. It was at this point that one of the authors realized she was on the brink of despair and turned to the spiritual dimension of her life to look for answers that could address this professional crisis.

The spiritual dimension was perhaps the most elusive and difficult to articulate of all the dimensions of the framework we have discussed so far. To begin with, the "spiritual" aspect of education is a topic infrequently discussed (Noddings, 1992). While a universal definition of the spiritual dimension of teaching would be impossible to articulate, Parker Palmer, who has written extensively on this subject, offers a definition of spirituality in the context of teaching which is helpful. He defines spirituality as "the eternal human yearning to be connected with something larger than our own egos" (Palmer, 2003, p. 377). It is this definition that we use as a departure point for exploration of the spiritual dimension of teaching.

In addition to being difficult to define, it is also difficult to articulate exactly how the spiritual dimension of education functioned in the lives of educators because this was often a very personal endeavor. Some strategies that worked for one of the authors in exploring this aspect of her professional life included three main activities: (1) meditation, (2) journaling, and (3) identifying role models and mentors (not necessarily in education) who drew on their spirituality to sustain them.

In terms of meditation, the author explored this activity by learning as much as possible about it (i.e., reading and instruction) and incorporating it into her daily life. In terms of journaling, the author wrote daily to engage in consistent and deeper self-reflection about her experiences. It provided a safe place to explore any ideas. Finally, the author sought role models and mentors who engaged their spiritual side as a source of inspiration and instruction for the work they did. For example, she read about ordinary individuals who engaged in activist causes, such as antiracist work, and learned how spirituality sustained them (Thompson, 2001).

For one of the authors, the above mentioned strategies were extremely beneficial precisely because strategies in the other dimensions were failing her. By utilizing non-educational sources of guidance, such as spiritual texts (Tolle, 2005), Buddhist and Taoist works, and other alternative information sources, she was able to view her work as a multicultural educator in unique, non-traditional, non-academic ways that helped her reaffirm her commitment to multicultural education.

The Ethical Dimension

The situation: A student was seeking admission into a teacher preparation program. The candidate was not atypical from many of her peers: She was from a small town and had little experience working and interacting with individuals culturally different from herself (i.e., racially, religiously, linguistically, politically, etc.). She was not a particularly strong student academically but expressed a sincere desire to be a teacher. Over the course of the semester in a multicultural education course, the student's comments during class discussions, in various papers, and in journal reflections revealed some disturbing features: racism and homophobia. When the candidate was asked to examine the beliefs and values that undergirded these apparent tendencies, she became a bit withdrawn and shut down in class. In effect, she refused to examine her belief system and its possible impact on the children she would be teaching. The faculty denied her admission to the program, using the same criteria used for all other candidates. However, due to parental pressure, the denial of admission reached the highest administrative levels of the University, who overturned the faculty's decision despite protests from some of the faculty.

Of all the scenarios discussed thus far, the above-mentioned one was perhaps the most challenging to us as multicultural educators because the action that should have been taken seemed so clearly unequivocal—the student should not have been admitted. However, as the vignette clearly illustrated, not all the parties who had the power to take action were in agreement.

In this very complex situation there are two salient ethical dilemmas. When, if at all, is it ethical to deny a candidate admission to a teacher preparation program based on his/her dispositions? How do multicultural educators maintain their ethical integrity (i.e., commitment to social equity and justice) in the face of institutional pressure asking them to do otherwise? We will not discuss the first dilemma (though it is extremely significant) because it is beyond the scope of this article and because it does not directly pertain to the issue of sustainment of multicultural educators.

So, what strategies might multicultural educators/faculty who find themselves in a similar situation do to maintain their own sense of ethical integrity under seemingly impossible circumstances? Our first strategy was to garner all the professional and institutional codes of ethics we could find that demonstrated that there are credible professional bodies that do consider the ethical dispositions of future teachers to be a critical criterion for admission.

In our case, we had the National Education Association and American Federation of Teachers' "Codes of Ethics." We also had the California Standards of Teacher Practice and our own Department's mission statement concerning democratic education. In short, there was no lack of ethical codes of conduct to support our decision not to admit the candidate in this regard.

We quickly learned that ethical codes or frameworks were just that. They were not binding documents; they were not legal mandates. In essence, they held no weight. They were regarded as "helpful guides" but if necessary could be ignored when they interfered with a desired administrative decision.

What we realized in hindsight was that ethical codes, and even our own Department's mission, meant nothing if the faculty as a group was not clear about the values they held regarding critical multicultural issues. The faculty initially voted to not admit the candidate; it only took some external pressure for

individual faculty members to cave and submit to the administration's overturning of the decision. While some faculty stuck to their original vote, others were willing to compromise and/or abandon ethical principles under duress.

It was in hindsight that we realized there should have been ongoing and sustained discussion about cases such as this one, where faculty were given the time and space as a group to converse and clarify the multicultural and social justice values they believed future teachers should possess. Additionally, use of a systematic ethical framework to shape discussions (Strike & Soltis, 1998) would have also helped individual faculty members clarify their positions on various issues and allow the faculty as a group to reach consensus, not mere agreement of the majority, on key issues.

It was unlikely in this particular case that even if the faculty had been unequivocal, clear, and strong in their reasons for non-admission, that the outcome would have been different. The administrative pressure at the highest institutional levels was just too strong. At the very least, however, the case would have generated much needed discussion and possible future action to prevent another similar event from occurring.

So, what are multicultural educators to do when they want to "walk the talk" and maintain their ethical commitment to social justice and equity but in the end are forced to compromise such principles due to political and legal power? There seemed to be only two viable choices: Accept the decision and continue to do the work we were doing, or resign. We both chose to resign from the institution. One of us resigned immediately and the second one a year later.

Many may have viewed this situation as "giving up." Others pointed out that if change agents keep leaving then change will never occur. But as we have hopefully and convincingly demonstrated throughout this article, multicultural educators must also be very protective about sustaining themselves. In this particular context, sustainment meant knowing that we had done all that was professionally possible to maintain our ethical integrity in terms of multicultural issues. Our ethical response as multicultural educators was to recognize the point at which we had effected as much change as possible at that particular institution at that particular time.

Most important, when we realized it would be impossible to maintain any sort of individual ethical integrity concerning our beliefs about multicultural education and social justice, we realized we had to separate ourselves from that particular institution. In hindsight we both felt we made the correct decision because it reinforced our commitment and beliefs in multicultural education and allowed us to sustain ourselves not only ethically but also in the other dimensions we have described in this article, and thereby continue our work elsewhere.

Conclusion

As stated earlier, this framework can take many forms and include different dimensions, depending on the individual. In presenting this framework at a recent National Association for Multicultural Education annual conference, one participant recommended that we consider the "political" dimension in future research. The framework suggested here is the one that fit our individual needs at the time and should be altered as necessary.

While some of the dimensions for either of us might have taken on different levels of significance at different times, we both felt that these five dimensions were at work at some level for both of us and strategies of how to take care of each of these dimensions of our teaching lives were necessary to achieving balance and thus overall "good health" in dealing with the resistance we encountered.

References

Ahlkvist, J., Spitzform, P. Jones, E., & Reynolds, M. (2005). Making race matter on campus. In N. Peters-Davis & J. Shultz (Eds.), *Challenges of multicultural education: Teaching and taking diversity courses.* Boulder, CO: Paradigm Publishers.

Boutte, G. (1999). Higher education. In G. Boutte (Ed.), *Multicultural education raising consciousness* (pp. 199–227). Menlo Park, CA: Wadsworth.

Carpenter, A. (April 2000). An ethnographic study of preservice teacher resistance to multiculturalism: Implications for teaching. Paper presented at the annual meeting of the American Educational Research Association, New Orleans, LA.

Cochran-Smith, M. (2004). *Walking the road: Race, diversity, and social justice in teacher education.* New York: Teachers College Press.

Cruz-Janzen, M., & Taylor, M., (2004). Hitting the ground running: Why introductory teacher education courses should deal with multiculturalism. *Multicultural Education, 12*(1), 16–23.

Dittmar, L. (1999). Conflict and resistance in the multicultural classroom. In J.Q. Adams & J.R. Welsch (Eds.), *Cultural diversity: Curriculum, classroom, & climate.* Macomb, IL: Western Illinois University.

Ghosh, R., & Tarrow, N. (1993). Multiculturalism and teacher educators: Views from Canada and the USA. *Comparative Education, 29*(1), 81–92.

Griffin, P. (1997). Facilitating social justice education courses. In M. Adams, L. A Bell, & P. Griffin (Eds.), *Teaching for diversity and social justice. A sourcebook.* New York: Routledge.

Horton, J., & Scott, D. (2004). White students' voices in multicultural teacher education preparation. *Multicultural Education 11*(4).

McGowan, J. (1996). African American faculty challenges in the classroom at predominately White colleges and universities. Paper presented at Kansas Regents Diversity Conference, October, University of Kansas, Lawrence, KS.

McGowan, J. (2000). Multicultural teaching: African-American faculty classroom teaching experiences in predominantly White colleges and universities. *Multicultural Education, 8*(2), 19–22.

Noddings, N. (1992). *The challenge to care in schools: An alternative approach to education.* Teachers College Press: New York.

O'Donnell, J. (1998). Engaging students' recognition of racial identity. In R.C. Chavez, & J. O'Donnell, (Eds.), *Speaking the unpleasant: The politics of (non) engagement in the multicultural education terrain* (pp. 56–68). Albany: State University of New York Press.

Palmer, P. (2003). Teaching with heart and soul: Reflections on spirituality in teacher education. *Journal of Teacher Education, 54*(5), 376–385.

Strike, K., & Soltis, J. (1998). *The ethics of teaching.* New York: Teachers College Press.

Tatum, B. D. (1994). Teaching White students about racism: The search for White allies and the restoration of hope. *Teachers College Record, 95*(4), 462–476.

Thompson, B. (2001). *A promise and a way of life: White anti-racist activism.* Minneapolis, MN: University of Minnesota Press.

Tolle, E. (2005). *A new earth: Awakening to your life's purpose.* New York: Penguin.

Valerio, N.L. (2001). Creating safety to address controversial issues: Strategies for the classroom. *Multicultural Education, 8*(3), 24–28.

Valverde, L. (2003). *Leaders of color in higher education: Unrecognized triumphs in harsh institutions.* Walnut Creek, CA: Rowman & Littlefield.

Young, & Tran, (2001). What do you do when your students say "I don't believe in multicultural education"? *Multicultural Perspectives 3*(3), 9–14.

Penelope Wong is a professor in the Department of Education at Centre College, Danville, Kentucky, and **Anita E. Fernández** is a professor in the Department of Education at Prescott College, Prescott, Arizona.

The Promise of Black Teachers' Success with Black Students

H. RICHARD MILNER, IV

In this article, I discuss African American[1] researchers' perspectives on the experiences, impact, and success of Black teachers with Black students in public schools. This study builds on an earlier study that focused specifically on these researchers' insights about the impact of the *Brown versus the Topeka Board of Education* decision on Black teachers, Black students, and Black communities (see Milner & Howard, 2004). In that work, the interviewed researchers focused on the experiences and impact of Black teachers in improving the learning opportunities of Black students, both past and present. In short, based on that study with a focus on *Brown,* the researchers who participated in the study pointed to a need for the recruitment and retention of Black teachers in public schools to improve the academic, cultural, and social experiences of all students but particularly African American students. In this study, I attempt to focus on what we know about successful Black teachers of Black students to (a) contribute to the ever-growing literature about successful teachers of Black students for the benefit of teachers from various ethnic backgrounds; and (b) outline several salient suppositions that may help us in advancing the research and theory about successful teachers of Black students. Clearly, outlining some of the practices of Black teachers and their success with Black students can be insightful for all teachers interested in teaching Black students.

For the purposes of this study, I focus specifically on the following questions:

- From what features of successful Black teachers and their teaching might others learn and benefit? and
- What types of questions should we investigate and address in order to improve the learning opportunities for Black students?

It is critical to note that it is not my intent to engage in a form of what Gay (2000) called "professional racism"—

by underscoring the need for more teachers of color. The need for more Latino, Asian, Native, and African American teachers in U.S. schools is unquestionable. But to make improving the achievement of students of color contingent upon fulfilling this need is based on a very fallacious and dangerous assumption. It presumes that

membership in an ethnic group is necessary or sufficient to enable teachers to do culturally competent pedagogy. This is as ludicrous as assuming that one automatically knows how to teach English to others simply because one is a native speaker . . . (p. 205)

Engaging in this professional racism is not my goal or mission in this article. I agree with Gay and believe her perspectives here around the danger in assuming that Black teachers, for instance, carry all the knowledge, skills, and commitments necessary to successfully teach African American students. To the contrary, there is a huge range of diversity even within groups, and we cannot oversimplify the characteristics of any group of teachers. I have observed some less than successful and knowledgeable teachers from various ethnic backgrounds, including Black teachers. Moreover, as Gay explained,

. . . knowledge and use of the cultural heritages, experiences, and perspectives of ethnic groups [of students] in teaching are far more important to improving student achievement than shared group membership. Similar ethnicity between students and teachers may be potentially beneficial, but it is not a guarantee of pedagogical effectiveness. (p. 205)

Still, based on the findings of my study, I want to focus on Black teachers' experiences and success both pre and post desegregation for insights about how all teachers can deepen and broaden their knowledge and understanding to better meet the needs and situations of students at present, particularly among Black students. In addition, I hope to encourage and inspire other researchers to continue investigating what we know about successful teachers of Black students. By outlining several central suppositions that emerged from this study and from the literature, more research is needed to build on what we know (theoretically) and how we know it (empirically).

Black teachers and their multiple roles, identities, and contributions have been the focus of many research articles, commentaries, and conceptual analyses (Foster, 1997; Milner, 2003; Mitchell, 1998). The seminal work of Michele Foster, Jackie Irvine, and Vanessa Siddle-Walker, for instance, has helped shape the field for the study of and implications for Black teachers and their teaching. The literature on Black teachers and their teaching is conceptualized in several important ways: It spans the pre-desegregation era to the present and focuses on P-12 schools as well as higher education. The research is clear that having more Black teachers in the teaching force could potentially improve a wide range of situations and needs of Black students. However, we must not focus exclusively on the recruitment and retention of Black teachers in P-12 classrooms. Rather, I argue that understanding Black teachers and Black students' situations and needs are also important to equip teachers from various ethnic backgrounds with the knowledge and skills necessary to become successful teachers of Black students. In other words, what teacher education programs and teachers do until more Black teachers are recruited is perhaps just as important as recruiting teachers of color for public school classrooms. Thus, what can we learn about Black teachers and their teaching of Black students to benefit all teachers, regardless of their ethnic, cultural, and racial background?

Black Teachers and Their Teaching

Much has been written about Black teachers, their experiences, their curriculum development, and their teaching in public school classrooms (Dixson, 2002; Foster, 1990, 1997; Holmes, 1990; Hudson & Holmes, 1994; Irvine & Irvine, 1983; King, 1993; Milner, 2003; Milner & Howard, 2004; Monroe & Obidah, 2004), and this literature is not limited to public schools but also highlights Black teachers' experiences in higher education, namely in teacher education programs (Baszile, 2003; Ladson-Billings, 1996; McGowan, 2000; Milner & Smithey, 2003). Agee (2004) explained that a Black teacher "brings a desire to construct a unique identity as a teacher . . . she [or he] negotiates and renegotiates that identity" (p. 749) to meet their objectives and to meet the needs and expectations of their students.

hooks (1994) makes it explicit that Black female teachers carry with them gendered experiences and perspectives that have been (historically) silenced and marginalized in the discourses about teaching and learning. Although teaching has often been viewed as "women's work," Black women teachers and their worldviews have often been left out of the discussions—even when race was the topic of discussion (hooks, 1994). Similarly, in colleges of education and particularly preservice and inservice programs, the programs are largely tailored to meet the needs of White female teachers (Gay, 2000), and Black teachers along with other teachers of color (male and female) are left out of the discussion. Where curricular materials were concerned in her study, Agee (2004) explained that "the teacher education texts used in the course made recommendations for using diverse texts or teaching diverse students based on the assumption that preservice teachers are White" (p. 749). Still, Black teachers often have distinctive goals, missions, decision making, and pedagogical styles that are important to understand.

In her analyses of valuable African American teachers during segregation, Siddle-Walker (2000) explained,

consistently remembered for their high expectations for student success, for their dedication, and for their demanding teaching style, these [Black] teachers appear to have worked with the assumption that their job was to be certain that children learned the material presented. (pp. 265–266)

Clearly, these teachers worked overtime to help their African American students learn; although these teachers were teaching their students during segregation, they were also preparing their students for a world of integration (Siddle-Walker, 1996). Moreover, as Tillman (2004) suggested, "these teachers saw potential in their Black students, considered them to be intelligent, and were committed to their success" (p. 282). There was something authentic about these Black teachers. Indeed, they saw their jobs and roles to extend far beyond the hallways of the school or their classroom. They had a mission to teach their students because they realized the risks and consequences in store for their students if they did not teach them and if the students did not learn. An undereducated and underprepared Black student, during a time when society did not want nor expect these students to succeed, could likely lead to destruction (drug abuse, prison, or even death).

Pang and Gibson (2001) maintained "Black educators are far more than physical role models, and they bring diverse family histories, value orientations, and experiences to students in the classroom, attributes often not found in textbooks or viewpoints often omitted" (pp. 260–261). *Thus, Black teachers, similar to all teachers, are texts themselves, but these teachers' text pages are inundated with life experiences and histories of racism, sexism, and oppression, along with those of strength, perseverance, and success.* Consequently, these teachers' texts are rich and empowering—they have the potential to help students understand the world (Freire, 1998; Wink, 2000) and to change it.

However, as evident from the literature, these African American teachers still often felt irrelevant and voiceless in urban, rural, and suburban contexts—even when the topic of conversation was multicultural education (see, Buendia, Gitlin, & Doumbia, 2003; Ladson-Billings, 1996; Milner & Woolfolk Hoy, 2003; Pang & Gibson, 2001). These experiences are unfortunate given the attrition rate of Black teachers in the teaching force. Black teachers are leaving the teaching profession and quickly (Howard, 2003; Hudson & Holmes, 1994).

Pre and post desegregation, Black teachers have been able to develop and implement optimal learning opportunities for students—yet in the larger school context, they were often ridiculed for being too radical or for not being "team players." As evident in my own research (Milner, 2003) and this study, Black teachers can feel isolated and ostracized because they often offered a counter-story or counternarrative (Ladson-Billings, 2004; Ladson-Billings & Tate, 1995; Parker, 1998; Solorzano & Yosso, 2001; Tate, 1997) to the pervasive views of their mostly White colleagues. Black teachers' ways of connecting with their students were successful—yet often inconsistent with their non-Black colleagues. In short, different does not necessarily mean deficient, wrong, or deficit.

Black teachers can have a meaningful impact on Black students' academic and social success because they often deeply understand Black students' situations and their needs. For instance, Mitchell (1998), in her qualitative study of eight recently retired African American teachers, reminded us of the insight Black teachers can have in helping us understand the important connections between the affective domain and student behavior. Building on lessons learned from Black teachers, Mitchell explained that in order for teachers to establish and to maintain student motivation and engagement, they should be aware of the students' feelings and their social needs. Students' feelings and emotions matter in how they experience education; Black students often bring a set of situations that have been grounded in racism, inequity, and misunderstanding (Milner, 2002). Racism and inequity can emerge not only through their daily interactions but also through institutional and structural circumstances.

The teachers in Mitchell's study "were critically aware of the experiences of the students, both in and out of school, and of the contexts shaping these experiences" (p. 105). The teachers in the study were able to connect with the students in the urban environments because they understood that the students' behaviors (whether good or bad) were often a result of their out of school experiences. There were reasons behind the students' behavioral choices. In Mitchell's words,

> . . . [The teachers] recalled situations in which factors outside of the school adversely affected students' behavior. They described students listless because of hunger and sleepy because they worked at night and on weekends to help support younger siblings. They described students easily distracted and sometimes belligerent because of unstable living environments. (p. 109)

Thus, these retired teachers understood the important connections between the students' home situations and school, and they were able to build on and learn from those out of school experiences and situations in their teaching. The Black teachers understood that many of their students were doing drugs, living in poverty, and were acting as adults in their homes in terms of bringing in money to support their families. However, the teachers did not use these realities as an escape. The teachers still put forth the effort necessary teach and to teach well.

It is easy for teachers to grant students "permission to fail" (Ladson-Billings, 2002) when they consider the complex and challenging lives of their students outside of the classroom. However, successful teachers of Black students maintain high expectations for their students (Siddle-Walker, 1996) and do not pity them but empathize with the students (McAllister & Irvine, 2002) so that students have the best possible chance of mobilizing themselves and empowering their families and communities. To explain, teachers who are committed to improving the lives of their students do not accept mediocrity, and they encourage and insist that their students reach their full capacity, mainly because these teachers understand that allowing students to "just get by" can surely leave them in their current situation or even worse. Thus, teachers cannot adopt approaches that do not push their students—high expectations, as Siddle-Walker

(1996) explained, are necessary to help the students emancipate themselves and to move beyond their current situations. Irvine (1998) described an interaction between a student and teacher below by borrowing James Vasquez' notion, "warm demanders," a description of teachers of color "who provide a tough-minded, no-nonsense, structured, and disciplined classroom environment for kids whom society has psychologically and physically abandoned" (p. 56):

> "That's enough of your nonsense, Darius. Your story does not make sense. I told you time and time again that you must stick to the theme I gave you. Now sit down." Darius, a first grader trying desperately to tell his story, proceeds slowly to his seat with his head hanging low. (Irene Washington, an African American teacher of 23 years; from Jacqueline Irvine's (1998) *Warm Demanders*)

An outsider listening and observing the Black teacher's tone and expectations for Darius may frown upon the teacher's approach. However, this teacher's approach is grounded in a history and a reality that is steeped in care for the student's best interest. In short, the teacher understood quite deeply the necessity to help Darius learn. She understood the necessity to "talk the talk." There is a sense of urgency not only for Irene to "teach her children well but to save and protect them from the perils of urban street life" (p. 56). Indeed, Black teachers often have a commitment to and a deep understanding of Black students and their situations and needs because both historically and presently these teachers experience and understand the world in ways similar to their students. In addition, the teachers have a commitment to the students because they have a stake in the African American community. Students often do not want to let their teachers down because the teachers are concerned for the students (Foster, 1997), and this concern has been described as other mothering (Collins, 1991), and I would add other fathering. The students sense this care of the teachers, and this care pushes them to do their best in the teachers' classroom.

Method

In an attempt to understand some of the impact of *Brown* for Black teachers, for Black students, and for Black communities, I invited six experts (educational researchers) to participate in an interview. For the purposes of this study, I focus specifically on these researchers' perspectives of the experiences and impact of Black teachers[2] to provide information for other teachers, teachers from various ethnic backgrounds, on successful teaching of Black students and to think about a research agenda that points to some central suppositions for future study. The six experts that I selected and invited to participate in the interview met several criteria: (a) They had engaged in research and writing about *Brown* (and in some cases taught courses that highlighted *Brown* from various perspectives); (b) they were experts and researchers who had been in their respective fields of study for longer than five years; and (c) they were willing to participate in the interview and follow-up interviews if necessary. I found it necessary to have conversations with experts around the country who had studied these and similar issues to get their viewpoints at the 50-year anniversary of *Brown* in order to assess where we have been, to think about where we are presently, and to chart a research agenda about where we are going.

From the six invitations extended, three experts agreed to participate in the study. I conducted the phone interviews, which lasted approximately 45 minutes to an hour. Participants in the study were asked several questions. As themes and issues emerged throughout the interviews, follow up questions were posed. Thus, these interview questions (listed below) are not exhaustive. Rather, they represent the thrust of questions posed: (a) what happened to Black teachers after the *Brown* decision (e.g., morale, dedication, self-concept, and retention)? (b) What impact might the *Brown* decision have on Black teachers leaving the profession? (c) How might *Brown* have influenced the education of Black students? (d) Why is it important to have Black teachers educating Black students? (e) How might we think about increasing the number of Black teachers in the teaching profession? (f) What types of questions should we be researching and addressing regarding the *Brown* decision around Black teachers, Black students, and Black communities? (g) In other words, where should we (researchers, teachers, and policy makers) go from here in order to reverse (Ford, 1996) the underachievement of Black students? Finally, the experts were given the opportunity to add additional comments at the end of the interview. Interestingly, consistent features and characteristics of successful teaching and teachers emerged in the interviews, which spoke to the question: What can we (teacher educators, other Black teachers, and teachers in general) learn about the teaching of successful Black teachers and their practice that can benefit others in the profession?

Analysis of Interviews

An interpretive perspective (Guba & Lincoln, 1994) was used to guide the interview analyses in this study. Interviews were tape-recorded and transcribed. Upon reviewing the interview transcripts, themes emerged from all three transcripts. In several instances, the themes overlapped, and I used them to guide much of the discussion in subsequent sections of this article. As themes emerged throughout the interviews, I developed coding categories to better understand the issues and to organize the data. These categories were named conceptually but were, in essence, themes that were stressed and pointed out by the participants to guide further inquiry. The posing of interview questions followed an inductive cycle, where a broad and general question was posed and experts were given the opportunity to expand upon those issues based on their perspectives and knowledge base.

The Participants

Participant one[3] (hereafter referred to as Barbara) is an endowed professor at a research university. She has been in the field of education for longer than 20 years. Participant two (hereafter referred to as Vince) is a lead researcher in a research institute. Vince has been in the field of education for seven years. Participant three (hereafter referred to as Peggy) is a professor at a research university who has been in the field of education for longer than 20 years. All three participants have written scholarly articles and/or book chapters about the *Brown* decision, Black teachers, and/or Black students. Moreover, in two cases, the researchers

have written books that focus (in some form and to some extent) on these important matters. The discussion shifts now to reveal the researchers' perspectives, offered in the interviews.

Researchers' Perspectives

In this section, I discuss several themes that emerged from the interviews with the researchers: Black teachers' importance and refocusing teacher education; roadblocks, barriers, and rolemodels; and culturally informed relationships.

Black Teachers' Importance and Refocusing Teacher Education

Among other issues, one theme that consistently emerged among the interviewed researchers when asked about the educational experiences of Black students as related to *Brown* was that of the need for more Black teachers. The participants all stressed the importance of having Black teachers in the teaching profession. In addition, the participants also stressed the importance of refocusing how teachers are educated. To illuminate, the researchers stressed the impact of, the relevance of, and the possibilities of having Black teachers teaching in public schools for the benefit of all students and especially Black students. All three experts reported the great need for an increase in the Black teaching force. For instance, Barbara and Vince stressed the importance of recruiting Black teachers, particularly for the benefit of Black students.

It is also important to note that Barbara stressed that White teachers [or teachers of any ethnic background] can be successful teachers of Black students. Barbara's perspective is consistent with that of other research that shows how teachers from any ethnic background can be successful teachers of Black students (Cooper, 2003; Ladson-Billings, 1994). However, Barbara also made it clear that in order for more meaningful learning to occur with Black students, "we're going to have to change dramatically the way we train teachers." Barbara's attention to the ways in which we educate Black teachers suggests that teacher educators, policy makers, principals, and teachers need to focus on more innovative ways to educate teachers as these teachers work to provide learning opportunities for students in P-12 classrooms; that is, we cannot focus all our attention on recruiting Black teachers but must (re)focus our attention on how teachers are educated such as building on successful features and characteristics of successful teachers from any background, including Black teachers.

While the interviewed researchers pointed out that many Black teachers serve as role models for their students, Barbara explained that there are too many barriers and roadblocks present that prevent Black teachers from entering the teaching profession.

Roadblocks, Barriers, and Role-Models

On one level, Vince explained that Black students need "to see other Black teachers" in order to have role models. He stated that, "What people experience day-to-day effectuates how they view and vision the possibility of their lives." Pre-*Brown,* Black students went from schools where all of their teachers and principals were Black to schools (post-*Brown*) where most, if not all, of their teachers were White. The magnitude of Black students "now being taught by White teachers" cannot be stressed enough, according to Vince. One can only imagine the quality of instruction that Black students received from White teachers, some of whom were opposed to the very notion of desegregation and teaching Black students from the very outset of the *Brown* decision. New Black teachers as well as Black students seemed to lose their Black teacher role models. Consequently, Black teachers, in large measure, started to select alternative fields. Whereas, historically, teaching, in the Black community was perceived as one of the most prestigious professions for Blacks (Foster, 1997), the perception of the teaching profession changes when this "equilibrium" is imbalanced according to Vince. Black students and new Black teachers need to see experienced, successful Black teachers. To illuminate, in Vince's words:

> . . . If students are growing up in schools that they don't see Black teachers, that they don't see Black principals or Black superintendents, how the hell are they going to imagine themselves being one?

Role models are critical in helping students decide on a profession and in helping students visualize the possibilities of their life.

On another level, Barbara stressed that

> teacher education programs and states are going to have to eliminate or re-envision some of the barriers and road blocks that keep Black teachers out of the profession. And most of them [barriers and road blocks] come from the standardized tests of assessment that summarily declare that these Black candidates, in teacher education, aren't worthy or capable enough to become teachers.

Importantly, the push to recruit and to retain talented Black teachers is framed by these teachers' abilities to relate to and to connect to other Black students, socially, academically, pedagogically, and culturally. Barbara explained:

> And so Black teachers are important to have not because we want them [only] as role models, but that's important. But that's not the only reason we want [and need Black teachers]. We want them because they have a way of teaching [Black] kids that leads to achievement. They know how to come up with examples in the kids' lives that make the lessons come alive, and they [Black students] retain the material.

In essence, both Barbara and Vince stressed the importance of Black teachers' contributions as role modes for Black students. Further, Barbara pointed to some central reasons she believed many capable Black teachers are not making it into the classroom: roadblocks and barriers (primarily standardized tests). Still, if the researchers have found that teachers from various ethnic backgrounds can be successful teachers of Black students, we need to further investigate the extent to which teachers can become role models and how they develop and provide vivid examples to help Black students learn. Thus, successful teachers of Black students act as role-models and develop pedagogical strategies that bring lessons to life through examples provided.

Barbara and Vince consistently referenced the importance of cultural connections between Black teachers and their Black students as a fundamental reason to increase the Black teaching force. At the same time, how do other teachers (Black) and teachers from various—different—ethnic backgrounds develop those connections with their Black students?

Culturally Informed Relationships

In many instances, there are cultural informed relationships that exist between Black teachers and Black students. In addition to Black teachers' having the ability to construct meaningful instructional examples with Black students, Peggy pointed to the connections between the hidden curriculum (or what students learn through the implicit nature of teaching and learning) and Black teachers. In other words, Peggy stressed the importance and benefits of Black teachers teaching Black students because there are inherent, unstated, lessons that emerge in classroom interactions that show up between teachers and students. For instance, she stressed that "cultural connections" are often prevalent in relationships with Black teachers and Black students. These culturally informed relationships allow Black teachers to develop meaningful, relevant (Ladson-Billings, 1994) and responsive (Gay & Kirkland, 2003) curricula and pedagogy in classrooms with Black students. To elaborate, Peggy stated,

> It comes in subtly [or through the hidden curriculum]; it comes in the talks that they [Black teachers] had with the students. It comes up in club activities . . . so the hidden curriculum was to explain what it means to be Black in American, to [be] role models . . . And I would add this deep understanding of culture. It's not just that I have high expectations of you and . . . believe in your capacity to achieve, and they're [Black teachers] willing to push you [Black students]. The teachers also had an intuitive understanding of the culture because they lived it . . . I [the teacher] live in the community. I go to church in the community. You know, in this segregated world . . .

Peggy discussed how Black teachers often expressed and demonstrated "high expectations, deep care for Black children, [and] beliefs in their [Black students'] capacity to succeed." These issues were inherent in the implicit curriculum as Peggy explained. Peggy goes on to explain what she refers to as the "bottom line":

> But the bottom line is that . . . teachers had the advantage of understanding the culture and being apart of it [during segregation]. They didn't have to be taught it. We [Black teachers] understood it. They understood you don't talk down to parents, okay?—That you don't treat people negatively. I mean they understood these things, wherein after desegregation, we're still trying to figure out how to understand it.

Thus, the idea is that Black teachers, by virtue of their out of school interactions and their deep cultural understanding of what it meant and means to be Black in America, often brought a level of knowledge and connectedness into the classroom that showed up in their teaching. Because Black teachers often interacted with Black students and parents outside of school (in the grocery stores, and at church, for instance) they had an insider's perspective on how Black students lived and experienced life outside of the classroom, and they were able to use this knowledge and understanding in the classroom with their students—to provide optimal learning opportunities for students. Black teachers were equipped to bring cultural understanding and connections into the classroom, partly because of how they lived their lives outside of the classroom. In essence, there were culturally informed relationships that existed in the classrooms between Black teachers and Black students that enabled success for all involved. We need to know more about how teachers can build cultural knowledge and how they can use that knowledge in the classroom.

Teaching and learning extended beyond the walls of the school as teachers found themselves sitting next to the parents of their students in church, for example. In Barbara's words,

> Many of the Black teachers were also Sunday school teachers at church. They lived in the community. And so they lived in the community and went to church with these [Black] kids; these things all connected in some interesting kinds of ways . . . it's not the building, necessarily. It's not the supplies, but it's the relationship between a teacher and a student that is the critical piece for Black kids. When you take that out of the equation, everything else fails. It doesn't matter how fine of a building, or how nice the books are, you've got to have a confident teacher who your kids all trust and care for. And if the teacher doesn't like the kids, it all falls apart.

The relationships that existed in the classroom enabled success for teachers and students alike. The researchers that I interviewed stressed the importance of teachers' ability to establish relationships with their students, and they believed that teachers from various backgrounds can develop these relationships to benefit Black students.

The discussion shifts to discuss, in more depth, some of the findings in this study. In particular, I discuss and conclude with features of successful teachers of African American students as I believe these features and characteristics can serve as data to assist all teachers in teaching Black students well. Moreover, what issues and perspectives as outlined in the previous section need additional attention through careful inquiry?

Discussion and Conclusions

Clearly, teachers from any ethnic background can be effective and successful teachers of Black students (Cooper, 2003; Gay, 2000; Ladson-Billings, 1994). As Gay (2000) stressed "the ability of teachers to make their instruction personally meaningful and culturally congruent for students account for their success, not their [ethnic] identity *per se*" (p. 205). However, much can

be learned from the ways in which Black teachers have engaged and empowered Black students (both pre and post desegregation). Again, one of my goals in this article is to discuss some of the pervasive strategies, philosophies and characteristics of Black teachers that can help teachers, any teacher, become more effective and successful pedagogues of Black students. As evident in this article, teachers can provide learning environments that foster student learning, and many Black teachers, historically, have succeeded in fostering optimal learning opportunities for students, especially for Black students.

In Figure 1, I attempt to outline some important features of successful Black teachers of Black students. The figure could prove useful in at least two interrelated ways: (1) the chart outlines a set of suppositions around practice that appear central to successful teachers of Black students, and other teachers—teachers from any ethnic background could benefit from the list; and (2) the chart provides a list of suppositions that surely need to be (re)visited, (re)searched, and (re)investigated. That is, replicate studies and studies that investigate the suppositions can possibly assist researchers, teachers, policy-makers, and teacher educators as they work collectively to improve the learning opportunities for Black students. It is important to note that the features in Figure 1 emerged from past and current research as well as other scholars' research (as outlined in previous sections of this article). It is my desire that teachers of any ethnic background would learn from what Black teachers often bring into the classroom as all teachers work to improve their practices with students.

In conclusion, the loss of African American teachers and the interactions Black students had with these teachers has been detrimental to the overall success of African American students. Hudson and Holmes (1994) explained that: ". . . the loss of African American teachers in public school settings has had a lasting negative impact on all students, particularly African American students and the communities in which they reside . . ."(p. 389). More than anything, Siddle-Walker (2000) concluded that because of the hard work and dedication of Black teachers "students did not want to let them down" (p. 265). The students put forth effort and achieved academically and socially because

> teachers held extracurricular tutoring sessions, visited homes and churches in the community where they taught, even when they did not live in the community, and provided guidance about "life" responsibilities. They talked with students before and after class, carried a student home if it meant that the child would be able to participate in some extracurricular activity he or she would not otherwise participate in, purchased school supplies for their classroom, and helped to supply clothing for students whose parents had fewer financial resources and scholarship money for those who needed help to go to college. (Siddle-Walker, 2000, p. 265)

In short, much can be learned from the success of Black teachers with Black students. While the increase in the Black teaching force could potentially be advantageous for Black students and all students, learning about how and what these teachers

Culturally Responsive (Gay, 2000) Classroom Management (Weinstein, Thomlinson-Clarke & Curran, 2004) Approaches: Teachers may be less likely to refer their Black student to the office for suspension and expulsion because they implement firm, no-nonsense management styles in their abilities to create optimal learning opportunities and spaces where learning can occur. They understand how to get students involved in lessons, and they have strict and successful classroom management approaches.

Culturally Informed Relationships: Teachers understand Black students and their experiences both inside and outside of school. They use cultural knowledge about the students' (home) community to build and sustain relationships with them.

Mentoring and Role-Models. Students often see the possibilities of their futures by the mentoring and role-modeling from their teachers. Black students often think: "If they (as Black teachers, principals, and superintendents) can be successful, I can too."

Parental Connections: They learn and deepen their knowledge, understanding, and awareness about Black parents and their concerns in many out of school contexts such as church or the beauty shop. They respect parents of their students; they do not insult or talk down to parents, and the parents respect the teachers. They work *together* for the benefit of the students.

Culturally Congruent (Gay, 2000) Instructional Practices: Teachers refuse to allow their students to fail (Ladson-Billings, 2002). They develop appropriate, relevant, responsive, and meaningful learning opportunities for students. Teachers have high expectations for students and push students to do their best work. Teachers often see expertise, talents, and creativity in their students, and they insist that students reach their full capacity to learn.

Counter-Narratives on Behalf of Black Students; Teachers offer a counter-story or counter-perspective on the situations that Black students find themselves dealing with in school. Because of their deep cultural knowledge about Black students, these teachers often advocate for Black students in spaces where others misunderstand their life experiences, worldviews, and realities.

Figure 1 Suppositions of successful teachers and teaching.

have done to be successful with Black students has the potential to assist us in thinking about the education of teachers (any teacher—from any ethnic background) at the present time. That is, what are some characteristics, philosophies, and insights about Black teachers that other teachers, from any ethnic background, can use to improve their experiences and impact with Black students? In addition, it is important for researchers to continue this line of inquiry to build on, substantiate, and redirect what we know and how we know it as we work to provide the very best learning opportunities for all students—and especially Black students.

Notes

1. Throughout this article, the terms "Black" and "African American" are used interchangeably.

2. It is important to note that these "experts" had studied *Brown* in some dimension of their research. In some cases, the experts may form speculative arguments about the nature of questions posed because they had not studied (with any depth) that particular issue. In such cases, I was sure to frame these speculative claims as such. That is, I trust the level of expertise that the experts shared but understood that in some cases the researchers were relying on a data set that *related to* an issue rather than focus *specifically on* that issue. Finally, the terms "experts" and "participants" will be used interchangeably throughout this article.

3. Pseudonyms are used to mask the identity of the participants and their institutional affiliations.

References

Agee, J. (2004). Negotiating a teaching identity: An African American teacher's struggle to teach in test-driven contexts. *Teachers College Record, 106*(4), 747–774.

Baszile, D.T. (2003). Who does she think she is? Growing up nationalist and ending up teaching race in white space. *Journal of Curriculum Theorizing, 19*(3), 25–37.

Buendia, E., Gitlin, A. & Doumbia, F. (2003). Working the pedagogical borderlands: An African critical pedagogue teaching within an ESL context. *Curriculum Inquiry 33*(3), 291–320.

Collins, P.H. (1991). *Black feminist thought: Knowledge, conscious, and the politics of empowerment: Perspectives on gender, Volume 2.* New York: Routledge.

Cooper, P.M. (2003). Effective white teachers of Black children: Teaching within a community. *Journal of Teacher Education 54*(5), 413–427.

Delpit, L. (1995). *Other people's children: Cultural conflict in the classroom.* New York: The New Press.

Dixson, A.D. (2002). "Let's do this!": Black women teachers' politics and pedagogy. *Urban Education, 37*(5) 670–674.

Ford, D.Y. (1996). *Reversing underachievement among gifted Black students: Promising practices and programs.* New York: Teachers College Press.

Foster, M. (1990). The politics of race: Through the eyes of African-American teachers. *Journal of Education, 172,* 123–141.

Foster, M. (1997). *Black teachers on teaching.* New York: The New Press.

Freire, P. (1998). *Pedagogy of the oppressed.* New York: Continuum.

Gay, G. (2000). *Culturally, responsive teaching: Theory, research, & practice.* New York: Teachers College Press.

Gay, G., & Kirkland, K. (2003). Developing cultural critical consciousness and self-reflection in preservice teacher education. *Theory into Practice 42*(3), 181–187.

Guba, E., & Lincoln, Y. (1994). Competing paradigms in qualitative research. In N. Denzin & Y. Lincoln (Eds.), *Handbook of qualitative research* (pp. 105–117). Thousand Oaks, CA: Sage.

Holmes, B. J. (1990). New strategies are needed to produce minority teachers. In A. Dorman (Ed.), *Recruiting and retaining minority teachers.* (Guest Commentary). Policy Brief No. 8. Oak Brook, IL: North Central Regional Educational Laboratory.

hooks, b. (1994). *Teaching to transgress: Education as the practice of freedom.* New York: Routledge.

Howard, T.C. (2003). Who receives the short end of the shortage?: America's teacher shortage and implications for urban schools. *Journal of Curriculum and Supervision, 18*(2), 142–160.

Hudson, M. J., & Holmes, B. J. (1994). Missing teachers, impaired communities: The unanticipated consequences of Brown v. Board of Education on the African American teaching force at the precollegiate level. *The Journal of Negro Education, 63,* 388–393.

Irvine, J. J. (1998, May 13). Warm demanders. *Education Week, 17*(35), 56+.

Irvine, R.W., & Irvine, J.J. (1983). The impact of the desegregation process on the education of black students: Key variables. *The Journal of Negro Education, 52,* 410–422.

King, S. (1993). The limited presence of African-American teachers. *Review of Educational Research, 63*(2), 115–149.

Ladson-Billings, G. (1994). *The dreamkeepers: Successful teachers of African American children.* San Francisco: Jossey-Bass Publishers.

Ladson-Billings, G. (1996). Silences as weapons: Challenges of a Black professor teaching White students. *Theory into Practice, 35,* 79–85.

Ladson-Billings, G. (2002). Permission to fail. In L.Delpit & J.K. Dowdy (Eds.), *The skin that we speak: Thoughts on language and culture in the classroom.* (pp. 107–120). New York: The New Press.

Ladson-Billings, G. (2004). Landing on the wrong note: The price we paid for *Brown. Educational Researcher, 33*(7), 3–13.

Ladson-Billings, G., & Tate, B. (1995). Toward a critical race theory of education. *Teachers College Record, 97,* 47–67.

McAllister, G., & Irvine, J. J. (2002). The role of empathy in teaching culturally diverse students: A qualitative study of teachers' beliefs. *Journal of Teacher Education, 53*(5), 433–443.

McGowan, J.M. (2000). Multicultural teaching: African-American faculty classroom teaching experiences in predominantly White colleges and universities. *Multicultural Education, 8*(2), 19–22.

Milner, H.R. (2002). Affective and social issues among high-achieving African American students: Recommendations for teachers and teacher education. *Action in Teacher Education, 24*(1), 81–89.

Milner, H.R. (2003). A case study of an African American English teacher's cultural comprehensive knowledge and (self) reflective planning. *Journal of Curriculum and Supervision 18*(2), 175–196.

Milner, H.R., & Howard, T.C. (2004). Black teachers, Black students, Black communities and *Brown:* Perspectives and insights from experts. *Journal of Negro Education 73*(3) 285–297.

Milner, H.R., & Smithey, M. (2003). How teacher educators created a course curriculum to challenge and enhance preservice teachers' thinking and experience with diversity. *Teaching Education 14*(3), 293–305.

Milner, H. R., & Woolfolk Hoy, A. (2003). A case study of an African American teacher's self-efficacy, stereo-type threat, and persistence. *Teaching and Teacher Education 19,* 263–276.

Mitchell, A. (1998). African-American teachers: Unique roles and universal lessons. *Education and Urban Society, 31*(1), 104–122.

Monroe, C. R., & Obidah, J. E. (2004). The influence of cultural synchronization on a teacher's perceptions of disruption: A case study of an African-American middle-school classroom. *Journal of Teacher Education, 55*(3), 256–268.

Pang, V.O., & Gibson, R. (2001). Concepts of democracy and citizenship: Views of African American teachers. *The Social Studies, 92*(6), 260–266.

Parker, L. (1998). Race is . . . race ain't": An exploration of the utility of critical race theory in qualitative research in education. *Qualitative Studies in Education 11*(1), 45–55.

Siddle-Walker, V. (1996). Their highest potential: An African American school community in the segregated south. Chapel Hill: University of North Carolina Press.

Siddle-Walker, V. (2000). Valued segregated schools for African American children in the South, 1935–1969: A review of common themes and characteristics. *Review of Educational Research, 70*(3), 253–285.

Solorzano, D.G. & Yosso, T.J. (2001). From racial stereotyping and deficit discourse toward a critical race theory in teacher education. *Multicultural Education 9*(1), 2–8.

Tate, W. F. (1997). Critical race theory and education: History, theory, and implications. In M. Apple (Ed.), *Review of research in education* (Vol. 22, pp. 195–247). Washington, DC: American Educational Research Association.

Tillman, L.C. (2004). (Un)Intended consequences? The impact of Brown v. Board of Education decision on the employment status of Black educators. *Education and Urban Society, 36*(3), 280–303.

Weinstein, C. S., Thomlinson-Clarke, S., & Curran, M. (2004). Toward a conception of culturally responsive classroom management. *Journal of Teacher Education, 55*(1), 25–38.

Wink, J. (2000). Critical pedagogy: Notes from the real world. (2nd Ed.). New York: Longman.

H. Richard Milner, IV, is Betts Assistant Professor of Education and Human Development, Peabody College, Vanderbilt University, Nashville, Tennessee.

Approaches to Diversifying the Teaching Force

Attending to Issues of Recruitment, Preparation, and Retention

Ana María Villegas and Danné E. Davis

The widening cultural chasm between teachers and students in elementary and secondary schools is a serious problem in American education demanding concerted action. As the works in this special issue of *Teacher Education Quarterly* make clear, the shortage of teachers of color has real consequences for all students, but especially for students of color. Despite the urgency, programs of teacher education are not giving this matter the attention it deserves. In this context of relative inattentiveness to the need for teachers of color, it is encouraging to read a collection of articles that feature a variety of carefully designed and well documented approaches to diversify the teaching force. Our goal in this commentary is to place the approaches described in this issue within the broader discussion of recruiting, preparing, and retaining prospective teachers of color.

Bringing People of Color into Teaching

Programs of teacher education have historically played a passive role in student recruitment. It has generally been assumed that the market need for teachers will automatically draw students into teacher education. The passage of the Civil Rights Act of 1964 inadvertently challenged this approach to recruitment, however. Prior to the enactment of this legislation, teaching was one of the few careers available to women and people of color. As a result, programs of teacher education—whether at Predominantly White Institutions (PWIs) or Historically Black Colleges and Universities (HBCUs)—had a captive pool of talented people from which to draw students. As professional opportunities opened up in this country for women and racial/ethnic minorities, undergraduates from these groups began to defect in large numbers from education to other fields such as business, engineering, and the health professions (Carter & Wilson, 1992; Urban, 2000). The declining popularity of teaching, coupled with increased demand for teachers over the past fifteen years, has pushed programs of teacher education to take on a more active and thoughtful role in recruiting students. Below we discuss the major approaches used during this time to bring candidates of color into teaching, weaving throughout our discussion the approaches described in this issue. Such approaches are distinguished primarily by the population targeted for recruitment, as we explain below.

Enrolled Undergraduates with Undeclared Majors

Teacher education programs seeking to diversify their enrollments often recruit undergraduates of color at their institutions with undeclared majors. An advantage of this approach is that potential recruits are on campus already and generally eager to give direction to their professional futures. Unfortunately, because the number of students of color who matriculate directly at four-year colleges is limited, programs of teacher education must compete aggressively with other fields on campus for this small population. To promote interest in teaching, recruitment efforts are crafted to help identified students understand the valuable contributions that educators make to society, the many opportunities available to someone with a teaching credential, and the type of preparation and support the teacher education program is ready to provide.

This recruitment approach is exemplified by the teacher preparation program Wong, Murai, Avila, White, Baker, Arellano, and Echandia describe in this issue. Although the Multilingual/Multicultural Teacher Preparation Center (M/M Center) at California State University, Sacramento, was designed as a fifth-year credential program, the recruitment of potential students begins as early as their freshman year in college. The Freshman Seminar, sections of which are taught by M/M Center faculty, exposes students to the merit of a teaching career. Faculty from the M/M Center also offer an undergraduate minor in Multicultural Education (into which the pre-requisites to the teacher credential program are built) and teach capstone courses for Social Science majors with an interest in teaching. These contacts enable program faculty to effectively nurture the young people's interest in a teaching career and to help them begin to envision themselves as the type of social justice teacher the program aims to prepare.

Once admitted to the program, participants receive support services designed to help them navigate the intricacies of the higher education bureaucracy, such as connecting student to sources of financial aid, providing assistance with their application to the teacher education program, tracking their progress through the program to ensure the timely completion of requirements, and creating a built-in network of peer support through the use of cohort groups. Beyond recruitment and support services, students benefit from exposure to a coherent, race- and language-conscious curriculum that is thoughtfully designed to prepare teachers to create learning opportunities for poor students from diverse racial and ethnic backgrounds and to advocate on their behalf. In fact, one of the more important contributions of this article to the literature is the attention it gives to the content of the preparation participants receive in the program to enable them to act as agents of change in schools. In so doing, the authors move the discussion about the diversification of the teaching force beyond the customary focus on issues of recruitment and support services needed.

Targeting students of color already admitted into four-year colleges/universities for recruitment is an approach best suited for institutions that serve large numbers of racially and ethnically diverse students, such as HBCUs and Hispanic Serving Institutions (HSIs). Because the overwhelming majority of teacher education programs in this country are housed in PWIs, settings with consistently low enrollments of students of color, this recruitment approach alone—while helpful—is not likely to alter the overall racial/ethnic composition of the U.S. teaching force in any appreciable way. To significantly increase the representation of people of color in teaching, the pool of potential candidates must be expanded beyond those who are already enrolled in four-year colleges/universities. It is not surprising, then, that most efforts to diversify the ranks of teachers recruit non-traditional candidates—pre-college students who might not otherwise go to college, community college students, paraprofessionals in elementary and secondary schools, and people of color who already hold a bachelor's degree and are open to making a career switch. The literature shows that such recruitment approaches are tailored to the targeted population and provide recruits with the necessary support to experience success, as we describe below.

Pre-College Students

One way of expanding the pool of potential teachers of color is to identify likely candidates prior to their senior year in high school, even as early as the middle grades, and involving them in intervention programs that aim both to cultivate the students' interest in teaching and to facilitate their admission to college. Project FUTURE, described in this issue by Stevens, Agnello, Ramirez, Marbley, and Hamman, is illustrative of the early recruitment approach. This Texas Tech University initiative targets students enrolled in sixth grade through senior year in high school and involves them in an array of activities over the years to strengthen their resolve to go on to college

and to promote their teaching self-efficacy. As Stevens et al. detail, Project FUTURE advances these two goals by bringing students on campus frequently to give them a window into college life, involving them in exercises that allow them to better understand the relationship between having a college degree and earning potential, providing information about financial aid for college as well as the college application process, offering workshops that focus on the development of test-taking strategies, engaging students in teaching simulations to give them practice with instructional strategies, and exposing them to different teaching styles and having them reflect on those experiences. As described by the authors, this initiative builds on the collaboration of members from the university community, the school districts in which the participants are enrolled, and the broader communities in which those schools are located. Other types of activities used in early recruitment efforts, as reported in the literature, include Future Educators Clubs, introductory teacher education courses that offer college credit to high school juniors and seniors, inspirational speakers who give students information about the teaching profession and encourage them to become part of it, summer programs that provide students intensive teaching experiences in addition to academic support, and work study programs in which upper high school students of color tutor younger children in community programs (Zapata, 1998).

While teacher cadet programs, such as Project FUTURE, have the potential to bolster the pool of racial/ethnic minorities for teaching, they are long-term efforts that take minimally five to eight years to produce results, and typically much longer. Equally important, while such programs have been shown to increase the number of racially and ethnically diverse college entrants, they do not necessarily guarantee that college recruits will actually seek admission into teacher education or that those who are admitted continue in this field through graduation (Clewell et al., 2000).

Community College Students

Community college students represent another important, yet largely untapped pool of prospective teachers of color (Hudson, Foster, Irvine, Holmes, & Villegas, 2002). After all, the overwhelming majority of people of color who pursue a postsecondary education first enroll in community colleges. Since teachers must earn a bachelor's degree before they can be certified, students who start at community colleges must transfer to four-year colleges or universities to become teachers. Sadly, the transfer rate from two- to four-year institutions is disappointingly low (Nettles & Millet, 2004). As discussed in the literature, part of the problem is the lack of clear articulation agreements between the partnering institutions that establish which community college credits will be accepted at the four-year institution. As a result, community college students often lose credits upon transfer. The difficulty of the transfer process is confounded further by a general lack of support services to facilitate the students' successful integration into the teacher education program at the four-year institution once the transfer occurs.

The Teacher Academy Learning Community at the University of Texas, San Antonio—featured in the Busto Flores,

Riojas Clark, Claeys, and Villarreal article—typifies initiatives that focus recruitment efforts on the community college student population. This program was designed primarily to meet the needs of students transferring into teacher education from San Antonio College, the largest two-year college in the geographic area serving a largely Latino population. (The University of Texas component of the program is also open to incoming freshmen and students with undeclared majors at the institution.) The article focuses on the support structures put in place to facilitate the integration into the university system of transfer students pursuing teacher education. A key element of the support structure is a collaborative network of student service offices at the partner institutions through which transfer students are identified for program participation. Support begins with careful advisement of students at the community college to ensure they take the appropriate courses prior to their transfer into teacher education at the University of Texas. Upon transfer, students are involved in a Summer Bridge Institute that gives them an orientation to university life and exposes them to other activities intended to strengthen the academic and problem-solving skills they will need to succeed at the university.

Once on campus, participants receive a variety of supports including monitoring of their progress through the teacher education program; referrals for assistance with time management, study skills, and tutoring when such needs are identified; counseling with personal issues that present a threat to their persistence in college; activities that guide them through an exploration of their professional dispositions; and mentoring and coaching on professional matters both throughout the teacher education program and during their initial year of teaching. These support services not only smooth the transfer process to the university, but also enhance the capacity of the teacher education program at the University of Texas, San Antonio, to produce teachers of color who will persist in the profession. Particularly noteworthy in this initiative is the mentoring and coaching support graduates of the teacher education program receive during their initial year of teaching, a time in which teachers are most vulnerable to attrition. There is little in the literature about the mentoring of new teachers of color.

Residents of Communities of Color

Partnerships between teacher education programs at colleges and universities and various types of organizations/agencies in communities of color have been established with the goal of increasing the supply of certified teachers of color for schools in those communities. This "grow your own" recruitment approach builds on the belief that people of color who live in the community are particularly well suited to teach children from that community. These individuals are said to bring to teaching personal insight into the lives of the students and a commitment to improving the young people's academic performance. Indeed, there is much evidence in the literature to support these claims (Villegas & Davis, in press). Most of this work has focused on paraprofessionals in schools. Programs of teacher education that recruit paraprofessionals work closely with the school districts that employ them. As part of these "career ladder" initiatives, paraprofessionals continue their

salaried positions while enrolling in courses each semester toward the completion of requirements for teaching certification, and usually a bachelor's degree as well. Such programs, which typically take a minimum of three years to produce teachers, offer a variety of support services to enable participants to make it through graduation and obtain their certification (Villegas & Clewell, 1998).

The Pathways Program at Armstrong Atlantic State University (AASU), described by Lau, Dandy, and Hoffman, is a good example of a career ladder program for paraprofessionals. In this initiative, AASU collaborates with the Savannah-Chatham County Public School District (SCCPS) to select participants for the program. The selection process gives attention to a variety of indicators of ability and future success as teachers, including exemplary track records as paraprofessionals in schools and commitment to teaching in high need school environments. Because one of the goals of the program is for completers to be hired as teachers in the partner district, recommendations from SCCPS teachers and administrators carry special weight in selection decisions. To address the needs of paraprofessionals—many of whom bring academic lags resulting from inequitable schooling, have children to support, and shoulder major financial responsibilities for their households—the program offers various services. These include tight monitoring of participants' academic progress, tutorials and other academic supports for those experiencing difficulties in courses, a system of peer support promoted by the use of cohort groups, test-taking preparation for certification exams, and financial assistance in the form of tuition scholarships and textbook vouchers. Among the many salient features of this nationally recognized program, two stand out. One is the creative arrangement that the partnering school district and institution of higher education have worked out to secure release time with pay for paraprofessionals to attend classes at the university, thereby shortening the time they would otherwise need to complete the required coursework. The second is the successful restructuring of the student teaching experience so that participants can complete this certification requirement without having to lose salary and benefits during this time.

Two other initiatives featured in this issue—the Hopi Teacher for Hopi Schools (HTHS) program described by White, Bedonie, De Groat, Lockhard, and Honanie, and Project TEACH described by Irizarry—also use the grow your own recruitment approach. But instead of limiting recruitment efforts to paraprofessionals, these two programs targeted adults in the community with an interest in teaching, including paraprofessionals. This broader reach was possible because the partnership involved formal relationships with the community beyond the local schools. A community-based organization committed to creating pathways into higher education for community residents was a key collaborator in Project TEACH, helping to identify potential participants and securing funding to cover the cost of tuition for some of them. Similarly, the HTHS program was planned and implemented with direct input from representatives of the Hopi Nation. Given the sense of program ownership on the part of the communities involved, the strong critique of the university curriculum evident in both articles is not surprising. In the university/ tribal collaboration, for example, the program was pushed to make the coursework for participants more inclusive by adding elements of "red pedagogy" to the curriculum. In Project TEACH, participants were offered "supplemental" professional development activities to compensate for the relative lack of attention given to issues of diversity and social justice in the teacher education courses they took.

Readers of the Irizarry article, in particular, walk away with a clearer understanding of the difficulties involved in respectfully integrating into existing programs of teacher education people from historically oppressed groups who are committed to returning to their communities to work toward changing the many inequities built into the everyday fabric of schools. For this to happen, programs of teacher education need to attend to issues of recruitment and provide support services to see the recruits through graduation. But equally important, if not more so, programs must be willing to rethink the curriculum in fundamental ways. As Irizarry astutely explains, recruiting people of color into teacher education, while "failing to prepare them to promote educational equity does little to alter a system of education characterized by significant disparities in opportunity and achievement. Solely focusing on the representation of teachers of color in university or K-12 classrooms is tokenism and not transformative. Representation, while important, is not enough." Unfortunately, most of the literature on diversifying the teaching force continues to focus on representation, without giving sufficient attention to the type of preparation new recruits of color need to serve as agents of change in schools. We were pleased to see that the Wong et al. article in this issue dealt squarely with this topic.

Holders of Bachelor's Degrees

People of color who already hold bachelor's degrees in fields other than education comprise another important pool from which to draw new teachers. In fact, schools with severe teacher shortages, overwhelmingly urban schools, routinely fill vacant positions with candidates from this pool, either by issuing them provisional certificates or bringing them into teaching through an alternative route program. The latter option generally allows recruits to take on instructional positions in subject areas with teacher shortages, contingent on their successful completion of a program that provides some preparation in pedagogy and an internship experience in classrooms. The provisional certificate approach allows individuals without preparation in pedagogy to work as teachers for a period of time, usually three to six years, during which they are expected to complete the requirements for certification. While these two pathways into teaching receive a fair amount of criticism in the literature, they are nevertheless used widely to fill vacancies in urban schools. In fact, without them, teacher shortages in those settings would be even more severe than they currently are. Clearly, traditional programs of teacher education must work harder to produce more teachers for urban schools, regardless of their race/ ethnicity. In addition, they need to assume some responsibility for ensuring that those who enter teaching in urban schools with provisional certification or through alternative routes have the preparation they need to teach students successfully. Project

29, highlighted in the Sakash and Chou article, is an example of such an effort.

The goal of Project 29, a collaborative initiative involving the University of Illinois at Chicago and the Chicago Public Schools (CPS), was to enable provisionally certified bilingual (Latino) teachers in the partner district to secure their standard teaching credentials while receiving in-class support to speed their development of pedagogical skills for teaching English language learners (ELLs). Several elements of the program contribute to its documented success over the past 13 years. To begin with, participants are carefully selected based on attributes that program staff have found predictive of future success as teachers, such as parenting experience, involvement in activism and leadership activities, and perseverance in overcoming problems, in addition to having an acceptable grade point average. Participants receive an individualized plan of study after a careful review of their transcripts. They meet regularly throughout the program in small "advisory" groups for peer support on academic, professional, and personal issues of concern to them. The curriculum focuses on assisting the Scholars, as participants are called, to see connections between what they learn at the university and what they experience daily as teachers of ELLs in urban schools.

Ongoing observations of the Scholars' performance in their classrooms by university field instructors serve two critically important functions in the program. They provide participants support and guidance for improving their pedagogical skills and enable the faculty to continuously modify the content of the education courses to address the specific difficulties Scholars are experiencing in their teaching. The redesigned "student teaching" experience—which calls for participants to complete inquiry projects in their own classrooms and to conduct a project on issues related to the education of ELLs jointly with a general education monolingual teacher from the school—provides a more authentic learning experience for this population of teacher candidates than the traditional student teaching. This curricular modification also allows participants to complete the "student teaching" requirement without experiencing an interruption in salary and benefits. In brief, the article by Sakash and Chou shows how a teacher education program committed to improving the conditions of urban schools can do so.

It is interesting to note that the majority of people of color entering teaching over the past 15 years did so either as provisionally certified teachers or through some form of alternate route (Allen, 2003). This is explained, at least in part, by the challenges involved in getting candidates of color from nontraditional teacher pools into and through traditional teacher education programs. We suspect, however, that another explanation is the blasé attitude toward diversifying the ranks of teachers that prevails in many programs of teacher education. Even when publicly claiming to be committed to that goal, little energy is actually devoted to making this happen.

Looking across the Approaches

From reading this collection of articles, several conclusions can be drawn about how best to diversify the teaching force, all of which are consistent with the existing literature on this topic.

Collectively, these works suggest that to increase the proportions of teachers of color will require more than luring college-bound students of color away from financially profitable fields into teacher education. A true expansion will necessitate developing the potential of others who might not otherwise go on to four-year colleges. A comprehensive recruitment approach, one that targets different pools of potential talent—pre-college students, community college students, and others who serve children and families within the community in addition to college students with undeclared majors—is needed. The article by Landis and colleagues, in this issue, underscores this conclusion.

Another lesson learned is that programs of teacher education seeking to diversify the teaching force must collaborate with different organizations/agencies to successfully recruit candidates from diverse racial and ethic backgrounds. To recruit from the pre-college student population calls for the involvement of the school districts in which those students are enrolled. Partnerships with school districts are also needed to recruit employed paraprofessionals. Clear articulation agreements that spell out which community college courses will be accepted by the partnering four-year college are essential to tap the large pool of students of color in two-year colleges. Collaborations with organizations based in communities of color—including churches, civic organizations, and various types of service agencies—are also helpful in identifying potential recruits with an interest in teaching and a commitment to return to their communities as teachers. (For a detailed explanation of the central features of such partnerships, see Clewell & Villegas, 2001.)

To successfully recruit teacher candidates of color from non-traditional pools, tuition assistance is essential. Several articles in this collection emphasize this point. Without financial incentives, few candidates from non-traditional teacher pools can afford to complete an undergraduate program of study. To address this need, teacher education programs could secure scholarships through grants from private foundations and/or government agencies. Forgiveness loans that are erased after graduates have taught in schools for a specified period of time are similarly helpful. The recent difficulty finding funding sources for this purpose presents a major obstacle to diversifying the teaching force, as the authors of several articles in this issue rightly point out.

From the works published in this issue of *Teacher Education Quarterly* we also learn that teacher education programs must work diligently to retain students of color from non-traditional pools through graduation and certification. As the authors explain, this involves offering a comprehensive network of academic and social support services, including orientation to the college/university, a strong advisement and monitoring system, prompt referrals to academic support services for students experiencing difficulties with their coursework, workshops designed to help participants develop test-taking skills, and the use of structured groups or cohorts to promote peer-support.

Looking Ahead

Upon reflecting on the literature, it is clear to us that we already know much about how to recruit people of color into teacher education and how to support them through graduation and certification. We know relatively little, however, about how to adequately prepare prospective teachers of color and how to facilitate their successful transition into the profession. Part of the rationale for increasing the diversity of the teaching force is that people of color bring to teaching knowledge about the lives of students of color and insider experiences that enable them to relate well to students of color and to build the necessary bridges to learning for them. However, unless teacher candidates of color are appropriately prepared to draw on this unique knowledge and insight to shape their pedagogy, the yield of those resources will be limited at best. Similarly, unless teacher candidates of color are appropriately prepared to act as change agents, their commitment to making schools more equitable and just for students of color is not likely to produce the desired results. Unfortunately, there is little in the literature that speaks directly to these two important topics.

We have argued elsewhere that the addition of large numbers of teachers of color represents our best chance to make schools in this country more democratic and just (Villegas & Davis, in press). But to maximize the benefits that could be derived from having a diverse teaching force, programs of teacher education must go beyond issues of recruitment and retention and attend to the preparation candidates of color need for the task. That is the immediate challenge ahead for those who are truly committed to diversifying the ranks of teachers.

References

Allen, M. B. (April 2003). *Eight questions on teacher preparation: What does the research say?* Denver, CO: Education Commisison of the States.

Carter, D. J., & Wilson, R. (1992). *Minorities in higher education: Tenth annual report.* Washington, DC: American Council on Education.

Clewell, B. C., Darke, K., Davis-Googe, T., Forcier, L., & Manes, S. (2000). *Literature review on teacher recruitment programs.* Washington, DC: The Urban Institute.

Clewell, B. C., & Villegas, A. M. (2001). *Ahead of the class: A handbook for preparing new teachers from new sources: Design lessons from the DeWitt-Reader's Digest Fund's Pathways to Teaching Career Initiative.* Washington, DC: Urban Institute. http://www.urban.org/url.cfm?ID=310041.

Hudson, M., Foster, E., Irvine, J.J., Holmes, B., & Villegas, A.M. (2002). *Tapping potential: Community college students and America's teacher recruitment challenge.* Belmont, MA: Recruiting New Teachers.

Nettles, M., & Millett, C.M. (2004). *Student access in community college* (Issue Paper). Washington, DC: American Association of Community Colleges.

Urban, W. J. (2000). *Gender, race, and the National Education Association: Professionalism and its limitations.* New York: Routledge-Falmer.

Villegas, A. M., & Clewell, B. C. (1998). Increasing teacher diversity by tapping the paraprofessional pool. *Theory Into Practice, 37*(2), 121–130.

Villegas, A. M., & Davis, D. (In press). Preparing teachers of color to confront racial/ethnic disparities in educational outcomes. In M. Cochran-Smith, S. Feiman-Nemser, & J. McIntyre (Eds.), *Handbook of research on teacher education: Enduring issues in changing contexts* (3rd ed.). Mahwah, NJ: Lawrence Erlbaum.

Zapata, J. (1998). Early identification and recruitment of Hispanic teacher candidates. *Journal of Teacher Education, 39,* 19–23.

ANA MARÍA VILLEGAS is a professor of curriculum and teaching and **DANNÉ E. DAVIS** is an assistant professor of early childhood, elementary education, and literacy education, both with the College of Education at Montclair State University, Montclair, New Jersey.

Collaborative Recruitment of Diverse Teachers for the Long Haul—TEAMS

Teacher Education for the Advancement of a Multicultural Society

MARCI NUÑEZ AND MARY ROSE FERNANDEZ

The recruitment of qualified teachers is an immense and demanding job, particularly for high-poverty urban schools. Urban schools often turn to the common practice of recruiting teachers who are underqualified, most of them with no teaching experience and limited training. Because of their lack of preparation, coupled with the difficult working conditions they face and the inadequate support within their schools, these beginning teachers are likely to leave the profession soon after they enter. The attrition data is challenging: 33% of beginning teachers leave within the first three years of teaching, and almost 50% leave within five years. This attrition in turn produces yet more recruitment, again of a new group of under-prepared teachers, creating a "revolving door" phenomenon that has come to characterize the teaching profession. Thus, students in high-poverty schools often see new, under-prepared teachers year after year, despite the fact that these very students are in most need of quality, experienced teachers. These students are denied the opportunity to learn from well-prepared, committed teachers who are in the profession for the long haul.

The TEAMS (Teacher Education for the Advancement of a Multicultural Society) Teaching Fellowship Program is a collaborative model of positive recruitment that prepares diverse teachers, paraprofessionals, and counselors for service in urban, public school with the goal of increasing the academic success of all students. The TEAMS Program has evolved a unique model that provides a winning situation for all who are involved by using creative partnering to recruit, prepare, and support a confident, critical, and diverse teaching force prepared to tackle the challenges of inner-city teaching for the long haul.

Background

TEAMS has provided a network of teachers, like-minded educators, and resources for a diverse group of professionals who are attempting to create change in today's school system. TEAMS not only provides critical financial support for honorable work going on in the classroom, but helps teachers reach out to each other to receive the learning that they need to become better equipped to serve their students. Without the commitment of programs such as TEAMS, educators such as me would not be able to network and develop as effectively as leaders of social change and diversity.

—Angela Devencenzi

For over eight years, TEAMS has implemented a model of teacher development that attempts to defy these disheartening recruitment and attrition rates by annually enrolling more than 400 teachers along the West Coast in the program. The program model rests on the assumption that by providing financial support to acquire a teaching credential, focusing training activities on diversity, multiculturalism, and effective teaching strategies for urban schools, developing a network of like-minded educators, and intentionally targeting communities of color for recruitment, a diverse group of capable teachers committed to a career in public school teaching will emerge.

Our unique collaboration of higher education institutions, K–12 public school districts, and community-based organizations is led by the University of San Francisco (USF). We seek to develop a highly qualified teaching force that is reflective of the racial and ethnic diversity of students in urban K–12 schools up and down the West Coast, with a particular focus in the San Francisco Bay Area, Los Angeles, San Diego, and Seattle-Tacoma metropolitan areas.

Established in 1998 by the USF School of Education, the Multicultural Alliance, and several K–12 schools, TEAMS was created to address the critical shortage of teachers of color in San Francisco Bay Area urban schools. After the closure of the Multicultural Alliance in 2000, USF assumed a leadership role in TEAMS by becoming its fiscal agent and host institution. Creatively leveraging the resources that each of our partners brings to the collaborative, the program has been able to provide this unique combination of financial, educational, career, and professional development support to over 3000 aspiring and new teachers during its existence.

We are primarily funded by AmeriCorps, a program of the Corporation for National and Community Service. This AmeriCorps funding is the most significant way we are able to provide financial support for new teachers. Each year we receive an operating grant along with 400 AmeriCorps Education Award slots for Fellows. Fellows earn an education award of $4,725 each year for two years to use towards their teacher education by serving in an urban public school as a teacher of record, paraprofessional educator, or counselor.

Seeking Diversity in Teacher Recruitment

It is apparent that the increasingly diverse student population in urban public schools requires not only teachers who are credentialed, but also those who reflect the racial and ethnic diversity. Currently, students of color make up one third of our nation's schools while people of color comprise only 13% of the teaching force. In urban schools, students of color make up 75% of the student body while people of color represent only 36% of the teaching force. Furthermore, the increase in students of color is expected to continue at a significant rate. Nationally, predictions put the numbers of students of color at half of the student population by 2020[1] while the percentage of teachers of color is not expected to increase.[2]

We in TEAMS have always believed and insisted that any discussion on teacher quality must necessarily include a focus on teacher diversity if the racial achievement gap and growing student diversity is to be addressed in a meaningful way. In the "Assessment of Diversity in America's Teaching Force: A Call to Action," the National Collaborative on Diversity in the Teaching Force points out that "although teacher quality has been accepted and internalized as a mantra for school reform, the imperative for diversity is often marginalized rather than accepted as central to the quality equation in teaching." One of the key findings of the study is that "students of color tend to have higher academic, personal, and social performance when taught by teachers from their own ethnic groups" Furthermore, the study found that the academic achievement of students of color increased significantly when taught by teachers using culturally responsive strategies.

Breaking Down Financial Barriers

TEAMS was developed to intentionally and systematically address diversity in its recruitment process by targeting communities of color and reducing the financial and access barriers that commonly face candidates of color. The AmeriCorps Education Award provides an incentive for each stakeholder in the recruitment process. For potential teachers, it provides financial support for the educational costs of pursuing and attaining their teaching credentials as well as an incentive to work in urban schools and serve the community.

TEAMS Partners in Education—both teacher education programs and urban school districts—also have an incentive to recruit members to the program, thereby providing the individual advisement and referrals needed to attract TEAMS applicants. The Education Award provides teacher education programs with the means to offer an alternative source of financial aid to prospective candidates, which helps recruitment efforts, particularly among people of color. For urban school districts, which are already employing non-credentialed teachers to meet their immediate needs, both the program components and its education award are a means to improve the quality and preparation of their non-credentialed teachers and to support career-ladder programs for paraprofessional educators.

We have also been fortunate in using the Education Awards as leverage to get some of our higher education partners to provide matching funds in the form of scholarships to Fellows enrolled in their teacher education programs. Other forms of financial support we have been able to provide for Fellows include a housing subsidy, funded by the Teachers' Housing Cooperative of San Francisco, and in past years, mini-grants for service-learning projects. In a recent survey of Fellows completing the program, a majority (63%) responded that the financial support offered by the Program was the top reason why they joined and over 70% pointed to it as a very important factor in their development as a teacher. As voiced by one participant, TEAMS "was the only way for me to pay for my continuing educational goals."

Outreach and Credentialing

Outreach is critical to recruit the diverse population we support, including those who might not necessarily see themselves reflected in the teaching profession or might not think they have the means to do it. Many of the candidates we recruit are people of color, first generation college students, people from lower socio-economic backgrounds, and/or people moving into teaching from other careers (including para-educators who seek to advance their career). We rely heavily on personal connections and relationships for this recruitment. It is surprising how successful Fellows are in recruiting other teachers by simply sharing with them their experience in TEAMS. Other recruitment methods include referrals from partner institutions, holding of informational sessions, and participation in career and graduate school fairs.

For candidates who have considered teaching as a profession, but have not pursued it because of a lack of understanding about the process or lack of financial capacity to afford teacher credentialing, our recruitment information focuses more on the different teacher education institutions that TEAMS partners with, thereby offering a variety of locations for potential Fellows to pursue their credential, the financial incentives available, and information on the steps to become licensed.

Each year, about 70% of the Fellows who participate are people of color. One higher education partner not only tripled the diversity in its program, but also doubled its teacher education enrollment in the first year of partnership with TEAMS. It is important to note that we do not see recruitment and development efforts as separate from one another. Candidates must be enrolled in one of our partner credential programs and must be placed in an urban public school before being officially accepted into the program. Thus, academic coursework, practical experience, and the additional training and support are what we offer to prepare teachers for a long-term career in the teaching field.

Teacher Preparation and Culturally Responsive Pedagogy

Our primary pedagogy encourages Fellows to be educational leaders by helping them to understand the impact that teachers have in the classroom, in the school, and in the community. Also, by understanding the impact of policies and other external factors on the ability of teachers to be effective, Fellows are motivated to act as change agents in educational reform. Overall, the purpose is not just to develop the teacher, but also to help the teacher become more effective in developing diverse students in urban schools.

Methodology: Providing the Missing Link

TEAMS utilizes four specific methods to prepare teachers: (1) Enrollment in a credential program; (2) Service as a teacher or school counselor; (3) Attendance at pedagogical seminars; and (4) Completion of a service-learning project. We recognize that teaching service provides important practical training for new teachers, particularly when that service occurs while teachers are also gaining academic preparation. Thus, Fellows receive both the preparation offered by the teacher education program and the experience of working in an urban public school.

Below, we describe the professional development training opportunities provided by TEAMS, in particular, the pedagogical seminars, the family network, the service-learning projects, and the Cesar Chavez Service and Leadership Initiative. Through pedagogical seminars and service-learning projects, key components are offered that are often "missing links" for new teachers in urban schools.

Pedagogical Seminars

The TEAMS pedagogical seminars are designed to help Fellows build teaching skills, address critical issues in urban education, and network with peers and experts in the field. Topics addressed in the pedagogical seminars vary from year to year, but always retain a focus on multiculturalism, social justice, and youth empowerment while exploring teaching strategies that have been effective in diverse, urban classrooms.

Examples of previous seminar themes include: "Critical Curriculum Planning," "Moral Commitment and Ethical Action in the Classroom," "Building Diversity in Public Education," "Teachers as Visionaries and Change Agents," "Culturally Responsive Pedagogy," and "Transforming Hearts, Minds, and Society in a Standards-Based, High Stakes Climate," among others. At each seminar, a practitioner, researcher/scholar, teaching veteran, or educational leader is invited to address the group and the theme.

Each seminar incorporates an aspect of four areas: network, theory, practice, and motivation. The seminars provide opportunities for Fellows to interact with other new teachers and with experienced teachers. Presentations, discussions, and small group work provide opportunities to exchange ideas and develop relationships.

Service-Learning

The TEAMS program in a large sense kept me in the teaching profession. The service-learning project has enabled me to work with students in a building a community. It has been essential in keeping me more focused on real teaching. It has enhanced my teaching of Pre-Algebra and Science because I can link it to the community.

—Dante Ruiz

In addition to attending the seminars, each Fellow is required to complete at least one service-learning project per year with his or her students. Through the pedagogical seminars, Fellows learn about the *Youth Empowerment Model* of service-learning. Examples of actual projects implemented by Fellows in the past are presented so Fellows can see how the project impacted the classroom, school, community, and student learning. Service learning projects help Fellows develop practical skills in building community in the classroom, collaboration with other community members, and creative approaches to curriculum development.

The service-learning projects often become the highlight of the Fellows' experience, many of them receiving local and even national recognition. It is not surprising that a majority of Fellows have reported that the service-learning training they received and the project they undertook were a positive transformative process for them as teachers and also for their students. As echoed by one Fellow,

TEAMS gave me real world experience with service-learning projects that I otherwise would not have had. Me and another Fellow took the students out of the classroom and into their community to try and teach them about community responsibility and pride. I believe that this out-of-class curriculum was more beneficial than anything that could have been accomplished with a book in a classroom.

The following are two examples of community action projects that took place in the San Francisco Bay Area:

A Public Health Campaign: Wendy Ginsburg, a Fellow from 2004–2006, worked with her students to educate families in the Mission District of San Francisco about the dangers of a popular candy that contained lead. This candy was widely sold in stores around the neighborhood. Wendy decided to do her service-learning project in her 5th grade math class, where she wanted students to be able to compare, analyze, and interpret different data sets (math standard 1.0). The students did candy consumption surveys, tallied the data, created charts, and formulated conclusions based on their data. In addition, Wendy arranged a partnership with the local Department of Public

Health (DPH) to help students learn more about the effects of lead, and also to gain access to educational materials that the DPH had on the topic.

Armed with their new knowledge, the students decided to do an educational campaign, which included presentations to the school, talking to merchants in the neighborhood to urge them to stop selling the lead-tainted candy, and making fliers and posters warning about the dangers of the candy. Wendy was able to get through her academic content by this very creative process, one that engaged the students in a "real-world" situation and in service to others. Their project gained them a spot on the local news and in the newspaper.

A Youth-Friendly Resource Guide: Another Fellow described how her service-learning project in publishing a youth-friendly resource guide to San Francisco enabled her students to impact their community through research, reflection and creative expression:

> Impact High students were engaged in a community building research project that brought them together as a group of teenagers in the juvenile justice system to look at the issues that contributed to their contact with the system. My students came to the conclusion in their research that one of the main issues that drives students into the system is a lack of resources. Out of this came the idea to create a youth-friendly resource guide for San Francisco youth.

> In this way students were able to strengthen their own sense of community, develop their resourcefulness while researching what services exist for youth in San Francisco, publish their writing as a way to get their voices and perspectives that have been historically marginalized heard, and learn about what it takes to publish a magazine. The service activity was based in writing and research so it furthered my curricular goals for my writing workshop class. Writing for an authentic audience and knowing that their writing would be published pushed otherwise unmotivated students to draft and be thoughtful about their poetry and prose.

> The students completed the magazine, which was a compilation of student poetry and other writing and a guide to resources and services available to youth in the San Francisco area ranging from employment to health. A community publishing event was held where students provided a poetry performance and food to the community as a way to distribute their resource guide. The magazine was impressive and the students came away with a great sense of accomplishment knowing that their work truly made a significant impact on their peers and community.

Both of these projects illustrate the youth empowerment approach (YEA) to service-learning that we adopted and implemented which evolved from a partnership with REAL (Revitalizing Education and Learning), a community-based organization involved in youth development. The YEA model involves students in a problem posing, creative planning, action, reflection cycle that encourages intelligent engagement with social problems and mirrors Paulo Freire's concept of praxis. Through service-learning projects, students are engaged in their own learning process while contributing to their schools, the families their schools serve, and the broader community beyond their schools. Fellows are encouraged and provided with resources to work with other Fellows, other teachers in their schools, parents, and community agencies to plan and implement the service projects.

The Cesar Chavez Leadership and Service Initiative

The Cesar Chavez Leadership and Service Initiative is an optional program for TEAMS Fellows in California to implement a project specific to the United Farm Workers labor leader Cesar Chavez, in addition to or to meet their service-learning requirement. Fellows receive resources and training that highlights his life and work. It is another example of the youth empowerment model of service-learning.

Service-learning projects based on this initiative begin with a study on the life and work of Chavez, the social struggles he was engaged in, and a consideration of how those struggles manifest in the communities students live in today. TEAMS Fellows and curriculum consultants share lesson plans on Chavez that meet content standards for various grade levels.

The process engages students by having them identify community needs and how they will address problems through their service. It works to build community in the classroom as students dialogue, brainstorm, and work as a team to reach consensus. Fellows utilize interdisciplinary approaches to experiential learning, such as social studies and history for the Chavez lesson, math and science for students to study the chosen problem and assess results, and writing for the after-service reflection.

In years past, the initiative culminated in the Cesar Chavez Conference on Service and Leadership for middle and high school students in the San Francisco Bay Area who have been involved in service learning. Held at USF, 100 middle and high school students participated in an all-day conference of workshops and mural-making that depicted the ten values of Cesar Chavez. The murals that were created went beyond our expectations. The students not only conceptualized the content and design, they also created the actual murals, which turned out to be stunning pieces of art. The murals were mobile, designed to travel to different schools to raise awareness about Chavez, the impact of the labor movement he led, and to serve as an example of student work.

There were other significant outcomes from the Conference, most notably, the high school students, many of whom had not been to a college campus before, had their interest piqued because of their experience with their college student hosts that day, and asked numerous questions about how to get in to college (USF specifically, but also college in general). Of equal significance, the USF college students (students of color from a multicultural on-campus group called FACES) who had volunteered as hosts to the high school students reported that the experience inspired them to work with young people in the future.

Teacher Support

Teachers need programs like this to continue motivating themselves while receiving financial support. So many things prevent people from entering and staying in the education field, I feel TEAMS bridges this gap and gives so many people the opportunity to become and stay an educator.

—Renata Elmore

Support for teacher development is tied to recruitment, preparation and development, and long-term retention. Newly hired, inexperienced teachers who do not receive induction and mentoring are more than twice as likely to leave their position after the first year, and a higher percentage leave the teaching field entirely as opposed to moving to another position. Among the key reasons teachers leave the profession, lack of support and a poor working environment are factors that are often cited.

Not surprisingly, the support that we generate through seminars and a support network are important factors in TEAMS Fellows' decisions to stay in teaching:

This program was a tremendously helpful teacher education and teacher support program. I had the support of the TEAMS staff, fellow teachers, and all the leaders and presenters. This program helps teachers who teach in urban schools. We felt respected and we all realized that we were all struggling with the same things. The program helps us learn how to be more effective with our schools, students, and families. My teaching has been greatly affected and I am a better teacher for it.

Families

Fellows are grouped into "families" that meet consistently throughout the program year. Families are organized by grade level, subject area, or teaching specialty (Special Education, Bilingual Education). Within families, Fellows develop deeper relationships with a smaller group of teachers who share a similar teaching context. A family leader who is a veteran teacher, current practitioner, and/or teacher educator facilitates each family group. The program has engaged TEAMS alumni in the role of family leader as well.

Within their families, Fellows build community, discuss issues brought up in the seminars, share best practices and resources, and troubleshoot problems. Families are encouraged to communicate with and support each other outside of the seminars. Some families use their network to visit each other's classroom, exchange lesson plans and teaching strategies, or meet socially for support outside of the seminars.

The theoretical aspect introduces new knowledge and intellectual engagement, while practice helps Fellows to build skills in applying that knowledge. Presenters share best practices on effective teaching strategies and facilitate hands-on approaches to content development. Lastly, it is an important way for Fellows to have the opportunity to reflect upon their learning, be inspired and challenged, and strengthen their commitment to the field of teaching.

Developing Professionals

Furthermore, we strive to emphasize professionalism among our Fellows and encourage them to continue their development through research and collaborative projects. For example, through a grant acquired by the program, a group of Fellows, alumni and TEAMS Staff co-presented a service-learning workshop at the National Service Learning Conference in 2004, focusing on the outcomes of their Cesar Chavez-focused service-learning projects.

Alumni are also encouraged to stay connected to the program, to share their expertise, and mentor new Fellows. They are regularly invited to present workshops to current Fellows at pedagogical seminars, thus keeping them active participants in TEAMS and vital resources of support for Fellows as our network grows.

Teacher Network

We consistently work to foster and strengthen connections among Fellows in their cohort community that extend into the TEAMS network to include past Fellows, mentor teachers, other teachers at schools where Fellows are placed, and other educators, administrators, politicians, parents, and community members who support TEAMS. We nurture this network through public forums, social events, invitations to participate in Fellows' service-learning projects, an online community (including an area for sharing of curriculum and lesson plans, a job board, and chat room), and leadership development for network members by sharing their expertise at seminars.

Kate Shoemaker, an alumnus of the program, described the importance of the network in this way:

TEAMS provided me with professional support during my first two years of teaching. I was overwhelmed when I entered my own classroom. Knowing I had TEAMS seminars to look forward to and compatriots with whom to consult made the tough times manageable. Now, I have a fantastic life-long network of professional resources.

Hanging in for the Long Haul

Through innovative collaboration, an intentional focus on diversity and culturally responsive pedagogy, and a training design focused on providing teachers with the tools to be successful in urban public schools, we have created in TEAMS an innovative model of teacher development and a strong network of dedicated teachers. However, the work does not stop there. We receive many more requests for support from Fellows than we have the capacity to provide. Many Fellows want the opportunity to observe other's classrooms, be mentored by a master teacher, and be able to see examples of great teaching in a high-stakes, highly scripted curriculum. Furthermore, as testing continues to be a focus of teacher credentialing, we will need to provide opportunities for our Fellows to be well prepared to pass those tests, as well as be able to afford them, while helping them not lose sight of the reason why they are in the profession: their students.

Everyone interested in the future of public schools must pay equal attention to the problems of teacher recruitment and retention. Vigorous efforts on teacher recruitment and development must continue if we are to produce enough qualified teachers to meet current and future needs. At the same time, teacher retention must also be addressed if the "revolving door" of recruitment and attrition is to be stopped and well-prepared, critically-minded, and professionally-supported teachers will hang in for the long haul.

Notes

1. Borman, G. D., Stringfield, S., & Rachuba, L. (2000). *Advancing minority high achievement: National trends and promising practices.* New York: College Board.

2. National Collaborative on Diversity in the Teaching Force. (2004). *Assessment of Diversity in America's Teaching Force: A Call to Action.* Washington, DC: Author.

MARCI NUÑEZ is assistant director of student activities and **MARY ROSE FERNANDEZ** is director of the TEAMS Program, both at the University of San Francisco, San Francisco, California.

Ain't Nothin' Like the Real Thing
Preparing Teachers in an Urban Environment

NANCY ARMSTRONG MELSER

In her first journal reflection, Stephanie, a preservice teacher, described her initial impression of the urban school in which she was working. She wrote, "To be totally honest, my first impression was that I have never seen so many black people in my entire life!" While this comment may be surprising and jarring, Stephanie was being upfront about what many of my students were feeling in their first days of the Urban Semester Program at Ball State University.

According to the National Center for Education Statistics (2000), almost 40 percent of the total U.S. public school population is made up of students of color; in many metropolitan school districts, that number exceeds 80 percent. However, as the demographics of schools in the United States are changing, the population of preservice teachers remains much the same. As Roman (1999b) states:

> The student body in the United States is becoming more diverse than ever, while the teaching population is becoming less so. Teachers of European American background have had very little experience with bicultural students, and they may in fact harbor negative or stereotypical ideas about them. Further, many teacher education programs have a poor record of educating teachers for diversity. (p. 97)

With a growing number of African American students as well as those from other cultures, who will teach the children in large urban schools? Most likely, it will be young, white, females who are fresh out of college, with little experience and with little knowledge about those children's cultures.

The student body in the United States is becoming more diverse than ever, while the teaching population is becoming less so.

Colleges and universities are presented with the problem of preparing teachers for diverse classrooms on a daily basis. As educators, we realize the importance of teaching preservice teachers about diversity. We offer courses in multicultural training, we teach about black history, and we even teach students about using appropriate classroom materials that are not biased or prejudiced. However, the majority of this education is offered in small parts and isolated courses. According to Abdal-Haqq (1998):

> Isolated courses in multicultural education are unlikely to equip teachers for such work [work with diverse populations]. Many such courses appear to take the "music appreciation" approach to diversity. They promote acceptance, tolerance, and even respect for diversity, but they do not necessarily affirm it. (p. 68)

The lack of preparation for teaching in urban settings is one problem. In addition, research indicates that many new teachers in urban schools will leave within their first years of teaching. Since "as many as 50% of beginning teachers [are] leaving urban schools within the first five years" (Allen, 2003, p. vii), colleges and universities must prepare preservice teachers to work with students of various races and cultures. Teaching future educators to survive in a variety of settings is a key factor in their success or failure as urban educators. According to Watzke (2003):

> "Survival" has been characterized by many researchers as an initial stage in teacher development, marked by stress and issues of classroom management, an obstacle that must be overcome in order to advance in teaching practice. Veenman (1984) described this stage as one of reality shock-new teachers must adapt to the realities of classroom teaching from which they have been sheltered through traditional teacher education programs. (p. 223)

At Ball State University, we wanted to make this "reality shock" less severe for our preservice teachers, and better prepare them for the children they would someday teach. We knew that something had to be done to place preservice teachers in an alternate environment where diversity training occurred on a daily basis. Thus, the Urban Semester Program at Ball State University began.

The Urban Semester Program

The Urban Semester Program is an immersion program for junior level students. In this immersion experience, participants take a semester of classes while spending all day, five days a week, working in one of two elementary schools in the Indianapolis

Public Schools System. The populations of the two elementary schools are largely poor (96 percent and 94 percent free and reduced meal eligibility) and largely African American (89 percent and 88 percent), in sharp contrast to the university population of preservice teachers, who are mostly European American (95 percent). The Indianapolis school system was chosen for this collaborative project because it represented a true urban setting, had a diverse population of students, and was located only an hour from the Ball State campus. The goals of this partnership were to debunk the myths about teaching in an urban location while also promoting positive attitudes about teaching in such a setting. The ultimate goal was to recruit students for job openings in the urban environment by preparing them through field placements in diverse surroundings.

> **The student teachers learn about children in urban settings and how to become more empowered in reaching and teaching them on a daily basis.**

By working side by side with experienced urban teachers, the college students learn about real-life issues teachers face while completing methods classes. The students are able to apply what they have learned with the children in the classrooms while obtaining immediate feedback about their lesson plans. The classes the preservice teachers complete in the Urban Semester include Math Methods, Science Methods, Social Studies Methods, Introduction to Special Education, and Classroom Management. College students attend all of these classes in their elementary buildings, and the professors travel from campus to teach and supervise field experiences. When they are not in college classes, the students participate in every aspect of teaching while assigned to one elementary classroom. They teach lessons, create teaching materials, attend teacher inservice sessions, and learn to manage the classroom on their own. Most important, they learn about children in urban settings and how to become more empowered in reaching and teaching them on a daily basis. Opportunities to develop relationships with families are another focus of the semester. Preservice teachers participate in parent-teacher conferences and extracurricular and community events where, for the first time, they have the opportunity to dialogue with children's families and members of the urban community.

The students in this program tell us that they learn more in a semester of urban experience than they do from years of on-campus classes. The following pages describe lessons they have learned.

Attitude Is Everything

As in the journal entry previously mentioned, many of the preservice teachers come to this program with existing stereotypes and preconceived notions. One of the best ways to change these ideas is to immerse the students into every

aspect of the school and community through such practices as Back to School Night and parent-teacher conferences. All Urban Semester students participate in these events and in the discussions that are held afterwards. The day after parent-teacher conferences, for example, several students reported that few parents had attended, therefore concluding that the parents "just didn't care!" Many preservice educators hold such beliefs, according to Ann Scott (1999). In her essay titled "Reaction to Ethnic Notions," she states:

> Because of their cultural uniformity, and unless there are conscious strategies to the contrary, pre-service programs often serve as a mechanism for reproducing negative and racist attitudes and beliefs that later get translated into teaching approaches that continue to create unequitable education, (p. 31)

Scott goes on to state that "the general assumption among preservice teachers was that the parents did not really care about their children or their children's education" (p. 31). To debunk this notion, we held a brainstorming session in the Urban Semester Program about *why* the parents did not attend, and the students eventually realized that the parents may have been working at a second or third job, may not have been able to secure transportation to the school, or may not have had child care for their children at home. Over time, the preservice teachers understood that the urban parents, in most cases, were truly doing the best they could to provide for their children, even though they did not attend all school events.

Materials Do Matter

Another area that is strongly addressed in the Urban Semester Program is that of using culturally responsive materials in lessons and bulletin boards. Since the majority of the preservice teachers in this program are white, a major focus of our classes is to expose them to multicultural literature, diverse learners, and the contributions of all people, regardless of color, gender, or race. In the elementary education course, for example, students create a multicultural literature pack, which must include a book that appropriately represents a culture other than their own. In class, we discuss examining materials for bias and stereotypes and making appropriate curriculum decisions for the learners in their classrooms. In science class, the students create lessons about famous inventors who are not the stereotypical "dead white males" whom they often learn about in school. The students draw on material about people from other cultures, in the process learning a great deal about other cultures so they can transfer this information to the children they teach. By participating in the Urban Semester, the preservice teachers learn about developmentally and culturally appropriate teaching in ways that are not possible on campus.

Kids Are Key

The immersion in the urban setting also shows the preservice teachers that it is hard to teach students with whom you have not yet connected. According to Delpit (1995), culturally diverse students find themselves at a disadvantage for many reasons, including the fact that:

> Nowhere do we foster inquiry into who our students really are or encourage teachers to develop links to the often rich home lives of our students; yet teachers cannot hope to begin to understand who sits before them unless they can connect with families and communities from which their students come. (p. 179)

By getting to know the communities in which the children live, taking part in home visits, and initiating family events, our preservice teachers are learning about the students they teach and making connections to the lives of the children in their classrooms.

One event, called Family Fun Night, was created by the students in our program to bring parents, families, and community members into the schools to participate in hands-on science activities that can be easily duplicated at home. This event allows preservice teachers to interact with families and learn more about the children they are teaching, and it provides a rewarding teaching experience. This event also provides an opportunity for rich professional growth in the area of community building among our students, and creates parent and family involvement experiences that are often lacking in traditional college courses.

Management Is Major

A fourth lesson learned by participants in the Urban Semester Program is that of managing a classroom of diverse learners. At the beginning of the semester, many of the students in this program are unsure of their discipline approaches, are shy about correcting students, and are hesitant to reprimand children for misbehavior because they do not want the students to dislike them. While this attitude is typical among all beginning teachers, the students in the Urban Semester Program soon learn to put aside their fears.

During their placements, the preservice teachers learned that their disciplinary methods were often different than those of the teachers in their classrooms. For example, the preservice teachers often worry about "being mean" when telling a student to do something, while the veteran urban teachers are more direct in their approaches and don't worry about winning popularity contests with their students. Also, the preservice teachers are often quiet and timid when correcting students, while the practicing teachers use a firmer and often louder voice. Finally, the veteran teachers are often more culturally responsive to the children and know more about the discipline techniques that work with children in an urban environment.

According to Lisa Delpit, the author of *Other People's Children: Cultural Conflict in the Classroom* (1995), this is indeed a normal reaction of teachers who are placed in a different culture than their own (p. 121). However, by learning about the discipline strategies that are used in urban settings, the preservice teachers soon learned that the behaviors of children are often reflective of their culture and are best dealt with directly. This

approach also validates the research of Weinstein, Tomlinson-Clarke, and Curran (2004), who state that:

> A lack of multicultural competence can exacerbate the difficulties that novice (and even more experienced teachers) have with classroom management. Definitions and expectations of appropriate behavior are culturally influenced, and conflicts are likely to occur when teachers and students come from different cultural backgrounds. (p. 26)

The authors also point out that very little is written in management texts about how to deal with cultural diversity and cultural conflict in classrooms. Our Urban Semester students learn about what works with a variety of children, and can practice these techniques on a daily basis. The professors also learn to teach more current methodology and processes that are culturally appropriate to the learners in this environment. By working daily with students and teachers of diverse backgrounds and cultures, our students learn a great deal about management that will assist them in their future teaching careers.

Conclusion

Overall, the immersion of preservice teachers into an urban setting has many benefits. The most important one, however, is learning the culture and pedagogy of the students whom one teaches. By working hand in hand with urban students, the preservice teachers learn lessons that cannot be taught in a book, and cannot be learned in a lecture hall. As Roman (1999a) states:

> To have knowledge of another culture does not mean to be able to repeat one or two words in a student's language, nor is it to celebrate an activity or sing a song related to their culture. To acknowledge and respect is to be able to understand and apply this knowledge to everyday classroom activities. It is to be able to make changes in one's curriculum or pedagogy when the needs of the students have not been served. It is to be patient, tolerant, curious, creative, eager to learn, and most important, non-authoritarian with students. In order for a teacher to promote excellence in education, there has to be a real and honest connection between the needs of cultural values of teachers and students. (p. 144)

In brief, the Urban Semester Program helps preservice teachers make these connections to students, staff, and self. We know it is working when several students each year take jobs in urban settings and when the final journal entries appear different than the first. In Stephanie's case, the unease reflected in her initial journal entry changed to the following sentiment:

> Now I know why I took these classes. Sure, I still see colors and differences, but now I know to celebrate them and assist the children in learning to the best of my abilities. I *know* that an urban school is where I belong and I am sure that I can make a difference!

References

Abdal-Haqq, I. (1998). *Professional development schools: Weighing the evidence.* Thousand Oaks, CA: Corwin Press.

Allen, E. (2003). *Surviving and thriving in the beginning years as an urban educator.* Bloomington, IN: 1st Books Library Publishers.

Delpit, L. (1995). *Other people's children: Cultural conflict in the classroom.* New York: The New Press.

National Center for Education Statistics. (2000). *Fast facts* (available at www.nces.ed.gov). Washington, DC: U.S. Department of Education.

Roman, L. (1999a). Cultural knowledge and culturally responsive pedagogy. In S. Nieto (Ed.), *The light in their eyes: Creating multicultural learning communities* (pp. 144–146). New York: Teachers College Press.

Roman, L. (1999b). Social class, language, and learning. In S. Nieto (Ed.), *The light in their eyes: Creating multicultural learning communities* (pp. 90–97). New York: Teachers College Press.

Scott, A. (1999). Reaction to ethnic notions. In S. Nieto (Ed.), *The light in their eyes: Creating multicultural learning communities* (pp. 22–32). New York: Teachers College Press.

Watzke, J. L. (2003). Longitudinal study of stages of beginning teacher development in a field-based teacher education program. *The Teacher Educator, 38*(3), 223–229.

Weinstein, C. S., Tomlinson-Clarke, S., & Curran, M. (2004). Toward a conception of culturally responsive classroom management. *Journal of Teacher Education, 55*(1), 25–38.

Nancy Armstrong Melser is Assistant Professor of Elementary Education, Ball State University, Muncie, Indiana.

Test-Your-Knowledge Form

We encourage you to photocopy and use this page as a tool to assess how the articles in *Annual Editions* expand on the information in your textbook. By reflecting on the articles you will gain enhanced text information. You can also access this useful form on a product's book support website at *http://www.mhcls.com*.

NAME: DATE:

_____

TITLE AND NUMBER OF ARTICLE:

_____

BRIEFLY STATE THE MAIN IDEA OF THIS ARTICLE:

_____

LIST THREE IMPORTANT FACTS THAT THE AUTHOR USES TO SUPPORT THE MAIN IDEA:

_____

WHAT INFORMATION OR IDEAS DISCUSSED IN THIS ARTICLE ARE ALSO DISCUSSED IN YOUR TEXTBOOK OR OTHER READINGS THAT YOU HAVE DONE? LIST THE TEXTBOOK CHAPTERS AND PAGE NUMBERS:

_____

LIST ANY EXAMPLES OF BIAS OR FAULTY REASONING THAT YOU FOUND IN THE ARTICLE:

_____

LIST ANY NEW TERMS/CONCEPTS THAT WERE DISCUSSED IN THE ARTICLE, AND WRITE A SHORT DEFINITION:

We Want Your Advice

ANNUAL EDITIONS revisions depend on two major opinion sources: one is our Advisory Board, listed in the front of this volume, which works with us in scanning the thousands of articles published in the public press each year; the other is you—the person actually using the book. Please help us and the users of the next edition by completing the prepaid article rating form on this page and returning it to us. Thank you for your help!

ANNUAL EDITIONS: Multicultural Education 10/11

ARTICLE RATING FORM

Here is an opportunity for you to have direct input into the next revision of this volume.
We would like you to rate each of the articles listed below, using the following scale:

1. **Excellent: should definitely be retained**
2. **Above average: should probably be retained**
3. **Below average: should probably be deleted**
4. **Poor: should definitely be deleted**

Your ratings will play a vital part in the next revision.
Please mail this prepaid form to us as soon as possible.
Thanks for your help!

RATING	ARTICLE	RATING	ARTICLE
	1. Becoming Citizens of the World		21. Educating Vietnamese American Students
	2. As Diversity Grows, So Must We		22. The Need to Reestablish Schools as Dynamic Positive Human Energy Systems That Are Non-Linear and Self-Organizing: The Learning Partnership Tree
	3. Colorblind to the Reality of Race in America		
	4. Beyond "Culture Clash;" Understandings of Immigrant Experiences		
	5. One Nation, Many Gods		23. Moment of Truth
	6. "Because I Had a Turban"		24. In Urban America, Many Students Fail to Finish High School
	7. Metaphors of Hope		
	8. "What Are You?" Biracial Children in the Classroom		25. Examining Second Language Literacy Development in an Urban Multi-Age Classroom
	9. Dare to Be Different		
	10. Teaching for Social Justice in Multicultural Urban Schools: Conceptualization and Classroom Implications		26. Output Strategies for English-Language Learners: Theory to Practice
			27. Controversial Books in the Middle School: Can They Make a Difference?
	11. The Human Right to Education: Freedom and Empowerment		28. Celebrating Diversity through Explorations of Arab Children's Literature
	12. Asian American Teachers		
	13. Mother Goose Teaches on the Wild Side: Motivating At-Risk Mexican and Chicano Youngsters via a Multicultural Curriculum		29. Chica Lit: Multicultural Literature Blurs Borders
			30. Popular Music Helps Students Focus on Important Social Issues
	14. Promoting School Achievement among American Indian Students throughout the School Years		31. Framing the Effect of Multiculturalism on Diversity Outcomes among Students at Historically Black Colleges and Universities
	15. Family and Consumer Sciences Delivers Middle School Multicultural Education		
			32. Building the Movement to End Educational Inequity
	16. Discarding the Deficit Model		33. Sustaining Ourselves under Stressful Times: Strategies to Assist Multicultural Educators
	17. Arts in the Classroom: "La Llave" (The Key) to Awareness, Community Relations, and Parental Involvement		
			34. The Promise of Black Teachers' Success with Black Students
	18. The Trail to Progress		35. Approaches to Diversifying the Teaching Force: Attending to Issues of Recruitment, Preparation, and Retention
	19. An Investigation of How Culture Shapes Curriculum in Early Care and Education Programs on a Native American Indian Reservation		
			36. Collaborative Recruitment of Diverse Teachers for the Long Haul—TEAMS: Teacher Education for the Advancement of a Multicultural Society
	20. A Critically Compassionate Intellectualism for Latina/o Students: Raising Voices above the Silencing in Our Schools		
			37. Ain't Nothin' Like the Real Thing: Preparing Teachers in an Urban Environment

||||

BUSINESS REPLY MAIL
FIRST CLASS MAIL PERMIT NO. 551 DUBUQUE IA

POSTAGE WILL BE PAID BY ADDRESSEE

McGraw-Hill Contemporary Learning Series
501 BELL STREET
DUBUQUE, IA 52001

ABOUT YOU

Name   Date

Are you a teacher? ❑ A student? ❑
Your school's name

Department

Address   City   State   Zip

School telephone #

YOUR COMMENTS ARE IMPORTANT TO US!

Please fill in the following information:
For which course did you use this book?

Did you use a text with this ANNUAL EDITION? ❑ yes ❑ no
What was the title of the text?

What are your general reactions to the Annual Editions concept?

Have you read any pertinent articles recently that you think should be included in the next edition? Explain.

Are there any articles that you feel should be replaced in the next edition? Why?

Are there any World Wide Websites that you feel should be included in the next edition? Please annotate.

May we contact you for editorial input? ❑ yes ❑ no
May we quote your comments? ❑ yes ❑ no